MAKING AND UNMAKING LITERATURE IN THE WARSAW, LODZ, AND VILNA GHETTOS

THE TAUBER INSTITUTE SERIES FOR THE STUDY OF EUROPEAN JEWRY

The Tauber Institute Series is dedicated to publishing compelling and innovative approaches to the study of modern European Jewish history, thought, culture, and society. The series features scholarly works related to the Enlightenment, modern Judaism and the struggle for emancipation, the rise of nationalism and the spread of antisemitism, and the Holocaust and its aftermath, as well as the contemporary Jewish experience. The series is published under the auspices of the Tauber Institute for the Study of European Jewry—established by a gift to Brandeis University from Dr. Laszlo N. Tauber—and is supported, in part, by the Tauber Foundation and the Valya and Robert Shapiro Endowment.

For the complete list of books that are available in this series, please see https://brandeisuniversitypress.com/series/tauber.

Sven-Erik Rose
Making and Unmaking Literature in the Warsaw, Lodz, and Vilna Ghettos

Amit Levy
A New Orient: From Jewish Scholarship to Middle Eastern Studies in Israel

*Juliet Carey and Abigail Green, editors
Jewish Country Houses

Noa Shashar
The Marital Knot: Agunot in the Ashkenazi Realm, 1648–1850

Jehuda Reinharz and Motti Golani
Chaim Weizmann: A Biography

Blanche Bendahan
Yaëlle Azagury and Frances Malino, eds.,
Mazaltob: A Novel

*Scott Ury and Guy Miron, editors
Antisemitism and the Politics of History

Jeremy Fogel
Jewish Universalisms: Mendelssohn, Cohen, and Humanity's Highest Good

Stefan Vogt, Derek Penslar, and Arieh Saposnik, editors
Unacknowledged Kinships: Postcolonial Studies and the Historiography of Zionism

Joseph A. Skloot
First Impressions: Sefer Hasidim and Early Modern Hebrew Printing

*Marat Grinberg
The Soviet Jewish Bookshelf: Jewish Culture and Identity Between the Lines

*A Sarnat Library Book

MAKING AND UNMAKING LITERATURE IN THE WARSAW, LODZ, AND VILNA GHETTOS

SVEN-ERIK ROSE

BRANDEIS UNIVERSITY PRESS

in association with the

UNITED STATES HOLOCAUST MEMORIAL MUSEUM

Waltham, Massachusetts

Brandeis University Press

Manufactured in the United States of America
Designed by Richard Hendel
Typeset in Huronia and Meta Serif by Passumpsic Publishing

This book is published in association with the United States Holocaust Memorial Museum's Jack, Joseph and Morton Mandel Center for Advanced Holocaust Studies, whose mission is to ensure the long-term growth and vitality of Holocaust Studies. The opinions expressed in this publication represent those of the author and are not endorsed by the Museum or the Mandel Center.

Library of Congress Cataloging-in-Publication Data
NAMES: Rose, Sven-Erik, author.
TITLE: Making and unmaking literature in the Warsaw, Lodz, and Vilna ghettos / Sven-Erik Rose.
DESCRIPTION: Waltham, Massachusetts : Brandeis University Press in association with the United States Holocaust Memorial Museum [2025] | SERIES: The Tauber Institute series for the Study of European Jewry | Includes bibliographical references and index. | SUMMARY: "This book is a study of literary texts written by Jewish authors while interned in Nazi ghettos. Poetry and other literary genres were centrally concerned with the question of what it meant to narrate the catastrophic realities of ghetto life into received literary forms"—Provided by publisher.
IDENTIFIERS: LCCN 2025006573 (print) | LCCN 2025006574 (ebook) | ISBN 9781684582730 (cloth) | ISBN 9781684582754 (paperback) | ISBN 9781684582747 (ebook)
SUBJECTS: LCSH: Polish literature—Jewish authors—History and criticism. | Polish literature—20th century—History and criticism. | Jewish literature—Poland—20th century—History and criticism. | Jewish ghettos—Poland—History—20th century. | Jews—Poland—Intellectual life. | Poland—Intellectual life—1918–1945. | Poland—History—Occupation, 1939–1945.
CLASSIFICATION: LCC PG7035.J48 R67 2025 (print) | LCC PG7035.J48 (ebook) | DDC 891.8/5098924—dc23/eng/20250401
LC record available at https://lccn.loc.gov/2025006573
LC ebook record available at https://lccn.loc.gov/2025006574

5 4 3 2 1

To the memory of

those who perished before they could write,

those who wrote but whose writings were destroyed,

those whose writings were rescued,

and those who rescued them.

And to past and future readers of their words.

This publication is made possible in
part through the generous support of the
Martin A. Coleman & Ruth Benjamin Coleman '57
Endowment for Holocaust Studies

CONTENTS

ACKNOWLEDGMENTS

I am grateful to friends and colleagues who commented on portions of the book manuscript or of article manuscripts that preceded it: Jeremy Braddock, Amos Goldberg, Sonia Gollance, Rachelle Grossman, Dan Magilow, Margaret Rhonda, David Roskies, and Sam Spinner. Enormous thanks go to Naomi Seidman and Na'ama Rokem, the two no-longer-anonymous peer readers of my manuscript for Brandeis University Press, for their incisive comments which have made this book significantly better.

Anna Klosowska translated portions of the apparatus of the Zydowski Instytut Historyczny volume of literary works from the Oyneg Shabes archive, and shared insights into the original Polish text of Juliusz Słowacki's poem "Księżyc" (Moon) and Gustawa Jarecka's "The Last Stage of Resettlement Is Death" ("Ostatnim etapem przesiedlenia jest smierc"). Cecile Kuznitz and Sam Spinner analyzed passages with me in poems by Yoysef Kirman and Itzkhak Katzenelson, respectively. Yael Teff-Seker helped me on several occasions with Hebrew-language scholarship, in particular Yechiel Szeintuch's introduction and Szeintuch and Vera Solomon's apparatus to their edition of Shaye Shpigl's Lodz ghetto manuscripts. Michael Griffith suggested several novels grappling with near-contemporary crises that helped me more clearly see the singularity of Zelman Skalov's novel of the Jewish experience in Warsaw 1939–1941. Aaron Saint John provided excellent assistance formatting notes and bibliography. Sam Kassow retrieved his copy of the typescript of Herman Kruk's literary reportage "Zeks tlies" (Six gallows) from his personal archives in a storage facility and sent it my way. Abraham Ariel Rubin's comments on early drafts of portions of this manuscript helped me realize that my focus in this project should be on specifically literary writing from the ghettos. I owe a debt of gratitude to the students in my undergraduate and graduate courses on literature of the Holocaust over the last decade for the perspectives and ideas they shared in discussions and papers. Sylvia Fuks Fried supported this project with sage advice—and patience—over the long period of its gestation.

The seed that grew into this book was planted at the 2007 Jack and Anita Hess Faculty Seminar on "Literature and the Holocaust" at the US Holocaust Memorial Museum's Mandel Center for Advanced Holocaust Studies, co-led by Sara Horowitz and David Roskies. I thank Sarah and David for their teaching, and the Hess family and Mandel Center for their support. David's portion of the seminar introduced me to the corpus of wartime writing in Yiddish, which I have been thinking about ever since. I am honored that this book is being published in association with the USHMM.

This project benefited from support from several other entities, which I gratefully acknowledge: The Simon-Dubnow-Institut für jüdische Geschichte und Kultur, in Leipzig, Germany, granted me a residential fellowship for the month of August 2014, where I conducted early research on this project; the Deutsche Akademische Austauschdienst (DAAD) supported my participation in a 2016 Faculty Summer Seminar led by Jonathan Boyarin at Cornell University, where I presented early versions of parts of this book. I thank Jonathan and all the participants in that vibrant seminar for their collegiality and dialogue. My selection as a University of California Davis Chancellor's Fellow (2017–2022) provided much appreciated research funds, as did a UC Davis Academic Senate Small Grant for Research and publication support from the Dean of Letters and Science and the Office of Research. I am also grateful to UC Davis for granting me two quarters of sabbatical in winter and spring 2021.

Thank you to the UC Davis Shields Library ILL staff and research librarian extraordinaire Adam Siegel for help finding myriad materials. And thank you to Maurice Samuels and the librarians at Yale that he put me in touch with, for aiding and abetting my quest for Max Spitzkopf stories.

I thank the following institutions for invitations to present parts of this book as it was evolving, and to the colleagues who organized my visits: the Richard S. Dinner Center for Jewish Studies at the Graduate Theological Union, Berkeley (Deena Aranoff and Sam Shonkoff); California State University, Fresno (Amila Becirbegovic); Princeton University (Tom Trezise); Johns Hopkins University (Sam Spinner); the University of Pennsylvania (Simon Richter); the Tauber Institute for the Study of European Jewry at Brandeis University (Sylvia Fuks Fried and Eugene Sheppard); Lunds universitet, Sweden (Matt Johnson); Temple B'nai Israel, Sacramento (Terri and Jon Cristy); and the Mondavi Center for the Performing Arts, UC Davis (Ruth Rosenberg). I thank Ruth von Bernuth, Eric Downing, and the Carolina Center for Jewish Studies for the honor of being able to present work in progress from this project at the Jonathan M. Hess Memorial Symposium in April 2019 at the University of North Carolina, Chapel Hill. I am grateful to the Nir family and Jeff Grossman for inviting me to present the 2020 Nir Family Lecture at the University of Virginia, Charlottesville. I thank the audiences of all these talks for their questions and comments, and I also thank the audiences at the following conferences for their engagement with my work on this book over the last decade: the Association for Jewish Studies Conference; the Duke German Jewish Studies Workshop; the German Studies Association Conference; the Lessons & Legacies Conference; and the West Coast Germanists' Workshop.

I am grateful to the publishers of the journal articles and book chapters in which portions of this book were previously published: "Writing Hunger in a Modernist Key in the Warsaw Ghetto: Leyb Goldin's 'Chronicle of a Single Day,'" *Jewish Social Studies: History, Culture, Society* 23, no. 1 (Fall 2017): 29–63; "Oskar Rosenfeld, the Lodz Ghetto, and the Chronotope of Hunger," in *The Aesthetics and Politics of Global Hunger*, edited by Manisha Basu and Anastasia Ulanowicz (New York: Palgrave Macmillan, 2017), 27–56; "A poetik fun skhite: yitskhok katzenelson un yoysef kirman in varshever geto" (A poetics of genocide: Itzhak Katzenelson and Yoysef Kirman in the Warsaw ghetto), *Afn shvel*, no. 380–81 (Summer–Fall 2018): 16–22; "A Poetics of Genocide: The Jewish Dead Confront their German Murderers in Itzhak Katzenelson's Warsaw Ghetto Poem 'Vey dir,'" in *Nexus: Essays in German-Jewish Studies*, Vol. 5, *Moments of Enlightenment: In Memory of Jonathan M. Hess*, edited by Eric Downing and Ruth von Bernuth (Rochester, NY: Camden House, 2021), 135–63.

My father Jim Rose has always been a model of integrity and hard work; he and my stepmother Anne Bower have been a source of unfailing support. My dearest *shviger* Athene Goldstein has been generous with her enthusiasm for this book, and at some point generously stopped asking when it would be published. To Claire Goldstein's and my sons, Asher and Noam, we could not be prouder of the thoughtful and engaged young men you have become. How did I get so lucky as to be your father? Claire, thank you for being my constant interlocutor and my first, last, and best reader, even on planes to treatment centers and in hospital rooms. I am eternally grateful for your love, enveloping and undoubtable, like music.

Sven-Erik Rose
Davis, California, August 2024

AUTHOR'S NOTE ON TRANSLATION AND TRANSLITERATION

Unless otherwise indicated, translations in this book are my own. My translations generally aim to be more literal and less poetic, though truly literal translation is of course impossible. I generally transliterate Yiddish according to the YIVO transliteration system, except when citing published work or in the case of names in widespread use in English.

MAKING AND UNMAKING LITERATURE IN THE WARSAW, LODZ, AND VILNA GHETTOS

INTRODUCTION

After surviving three weeks in Auschwitz and approximately half a year in a labor camp in Saxony, Shaye Shpigl made his way after liberation back to his native Lodz, where he had lived his entire life from 1906–1944, the last four years confined with the rest of the Jewish population to the ghetto. One of the first things he did was return to the apartment where his parents had lived before they were deported with Shpigl in August 1944 as part of the Nazis' final liquidation of the Lodz ghetto. Shpigl's parents and three of his sisters were murdered in Auschwitz. His wife survived Auschwitz but perished in Stutthof. Shpigl returned to his parents' apartment in the hopes of recovering the manuscripts he had written in the Lodz ghetto and that he and his father had buried in the cellar shortly before they were deported.[1] When Shpigl reached the apartment he learned that his manuscripts had been thrown out. Shpigl and a brother who had also survived spent several days combing through trash heaps in the courtyard. They managed to find some three hundred pages.[2] Shpigl would refer to these salvaged works of secular literature as his *sheymes*, the term for papers containing God's name (*sheymes* literally means "names") such as pages torn from holy books, which must be preserved or buried.[3] All of the stories I discuss in the final chapter of this book were among those buried and recovered pages.[4]

I begin this study of literary texts written by Jewish authors while they were interned in Nazi ghettos in three cities that had belonged to interwar Poland—Warsaw, Lodz, and Vilna—with this story because it powerfully conveys the importance that the literature written in Nazi ghettos held for its authors. It equally illustrates the extent to which we cannot take for granted the fact that the literary works studied in this book survived and have come down to us. Shpigl was able to recover some of his buried pages through a combination of planning, determined effort, and incredible luck. He took numerous other manuscripts with him to Auschwitz, where they were taken from him and destroyed. The fate of so much Holocaust-era writing (of all types) was to be destroyed, and for the most part we have no way of knowing what was lost along with the very lives of authors. The story of Shpigl's recovery of his manuscripts is dramatic, but so, in fact, is the story of nearly every text written by victims of the Holocaust that we now have. The majority of the texts I discuss in this book were buried in biscuit tins or milk cans in the Warsaw ghetto in the massive, multilingual archival project led by the historian Emmanuel Ringelblum under the code name "Oyneg Shabes" ("enjoyment of the Sabbath," because the clandestine group met on Saturdays). Ringelblum and his handpicked staff aimed to document Jewish life in Poland under German occupation, especially in the Warsaw ghetto, as thoroughly and from as many different perspectives as possible. The archive was eventually buried in three tranches, two of which were unearthed after the war (in 1946 and 1950), giving us approximately thirty-five thousand pages of texts and artifacts.[5] Only three people with knowledge of where the archive was buried survived the genocide: Hersh Wasser, his wife Bluma, and Rokhl (Rachel) Auerbach. Auerbach survived after the destruction of the Warsaw ghetto by passing as non-Jewish on Warsaw's "Aryan side."[6] Hersh Wasser survived by leaping from a train bound for the death camp Treblinka. Without them and their tireless efforts to unearth the archive we likely would not have it. The story of the survival of Oskar Rosenfeld's Lodz ghetto notebooks is also captivating, and that of Herman Kruk's extensive Vilna ghetto diary is truly astounding. I recount them in the chapters devoted to works by these authors (chapter 7 for Kruk and chapter 8 for Rosenfeld).

It may seem slightly odd, or even jarring, to think of Nazi ghettos as sites of literary and broader culture production, but this, I would argue, has more to do with the ways that the cultural life of Holocaust victims has tended to figure as no more than (and frequently less than) a peripheral concern within mainstream historiographical approaches to the Holocaust. The pronounced tendency among the most widely read Holocaust historians at least until Saul Friedländer's 2007 *Nazi Germany and the Jews: The Years of Extermination* was to ignore victims' perspectives as extraneous to the central question of detailing how the Nazis perpetrated the genocide. The texts authored by victims that have received the most attention have, moreover, tended to be testimonial works, generally regarded as more crucial than fiction or poetry for understanding victims' experience. Scholars of Holocaust literature, for their part, have focused overwhelmingly on texts written after, not during, the Holocaust.[7] Although scholars including Samuel Kassow, Alan Mintz, David Roskies, and Yechiel Szeintuch have underscored the importance of distinguishing between texts written during—as opposed to after—the war years, this distinction is seldom insisted on as forcefully as it deserves to be.[8]

I hope in this book to show that it is misguided to argue, as many Holocaust historians do implicitly by their example and as some scholars, such as the philosopher Berl Lang, do expressly, that we should privilege the least literary modes of discourse as somehow closer to the brute reality of the catastrophic events. Such approaches presuppose a neat distinction between reality, on the one hand, and the vagaries of literature, on the other, that is simply not tenable. The sheer prevalence of literary writing—and, to be sure, of reading literature—among those persecuted in the Holocaust powerfully testifies to how intricately literature was woven into the traumatic fabric of their experience of the Shoah. This was as true for an assimilated Parisian university student like Hélène Berr, whose published diary includes a page-and-a-half-long list of the literary titles she referred to and reflected on at length throughout the years prior to her death in Auschwitz, as it was for the working-class Lodz teenager Dawid Sierakowiak, who regularly recorded what he was reading and writing about in the Lodz ghetto, and not infrequently registered his abjection by his inability to read or write due to hunger-induced lethargy. The teenaged Yitskhok Rudashevski likewise documented his and his cohort's literary and cultural activity in the Vilna ghetto—to mention but one further example of wartime diaries that richly attest to the importance of literature to victims of the Holocaust during the very years the catastrophic events were unfolding.[9] Even in the camps, literature, above all poetry, was prominent in the minds of prisoners, as we know from numerous accounts, including Primo Levi's famous description of trying to affirm his and a fellow Auschwitz inmate's humanity by translating the "Ulysses Canto" from Dante's Inferno (Canto 26) from memory into imperfect French while performing forced labor under the scrutiny of Nazi guards;[10] Ruth Klüger's account of reciting canonical German poems from memory in Nazi concentration camps and composing poems of her own about Auschwitz while in Christianstadt, a satellite camp of Gross-Rosen, where she was interned after Auschwitz;[11] and Chava Rosenfarb's account of inscribing with a pencil stub on the ceiling above her bunk in a forced labor camp in Sasel, near Hamburg, the poems that she could remember from among the many she had composed in the Lodz ghetto.[12] Whether we look to canonical works of Holocaust literature or to writings by little-known authors, we find that literature was not extraneous or even secondary to how victims experienced the Holocaust but was one of the key frameworks through which they grappled with their terrible and ever-changing realities.

As I will go into in more detail in a moment, this study is not a history or sociology of literary activity in the ghettos but rather an attempt to engage in depth with a diverse—but by no means exhaustive—array of literary texts. Some attention to the place of literature in the social and cultural context of Jewish interwar Poland is, however, crucial at the outset, as the explosion of literary culture prior to World War II goes far in explaining why people confined to ghettos continued to read, write, and think with literature, even as they had to contend with their awful circumstances and the constant threats to their very existence.

LITERARY CULTURE IN JEWISH INTERWAR POLAND

In a classic study of the British literary reckoning with the experience of the Great War, Paul Fussel argues that British soldiers experienced and remembered the war in unprecedentedly literary terms. He attributes this to "two 'liberal' forces" then at their peak in England: the "belief in the educative powers of classical and English literature" and "the appeal of popular education and 'self-improvement' . . . , still conceived largely in humanistic terms" (Fussel, *The Great War and Modern Memory*, 157).[13] Fussel notes the "unparalleled literariness of all [British] ranks who fought the Great War" (156). He sees this distinctly British literary dimension of the Great War as intimately tied to what he calls "a consciousness of an indispensable national literature" (mediated not least through Sir Arthur Quiller-Couch's *Oxford Book of English Verse*) and the virtually universal sense that English held the greatest modern literature (158). Moreover, he describes British soldiers having "no feeling that literature is not very near the center of normal experience" (157–58).

While the literary coordinates were more diverse and cosmopolitan, and less tied to an established national canon, European Jewish society in the early twentieth century and, especially, in the Second Polish Republic was likewise vibrantly and pervasively literary. Among the most significant developments in Polish Jewish society between the world wars was the emergence of Jewish youth movements, in whose mission of education and self-improvement literature and literary culture, in the form of literary recitations, reading groups, theatrical groups, and lectures, played a pivotal role.[14] Even as the total number of Jewish students attending high school represented some 20 percent of all high school students in Poland, secondary education remained out of reach for the vast majority of Jewish youth. Polish state or communal *gymnasiums*, while free, sometimes limited Jewish enrollment with quotas, and publicly-run or private Jewish secondary schools charged fees that were often prohibitive for impoverished Jewish families.[15] Jewish youths tended to end their formal schooling at a young age to join the workforce, but dedication to self-education beyond and in lieu of formal education became widespread among young men and women alike.[16] Each club headquarters (*lokal*) was likely to have a library where members could access books, which were too expensive for the vast majority of Jewish families to purchase. Indeed, the popularity of a given organization frequently hinged on the size of its library.[17] Usually affiliated with a particular political party (Zionist of all varieties, Bundist, or clandestinely communist), each youth movement had its own ideological orientation that inflected the reading its members undertook; yet they all equally stressed the importance of self-education through wide-ranging reading, very much including high-, middle-, and lowbrow *belles lettres* whether by authors writing in Yiddish and Hebrew, Jewish authors writing in European languages, or by a wide array of non-Jewish authors from across Europe.[18] David Shavit estimates that of the 450,000 Jewish youths in Poland between the wars, at least two-thirds of them read on average one book a week. Drawing on the work of Moyshe Kligsberg, Shavit concludes that young Jews in Poland read some fifteen million books annually, or that "the collection of each library was read 15 times over."[19] Kligsberg notes that "reading, endless reading [*leyenen, on a shir leyenen*] was one of the most striking features of young Polish Jews. Among them it was a passion [*laydnshaft*] that sometimes grew into an obsession [*banumenkeyt*]" (Kligsberg, "Di yidishe yugent-bavegung," 161).

Extensive networks of Jewish libraries also developed independently of the youth movements (although they, too, were often used primarily by young readers).[20] Labor unions, professional societies, and even sport associations provided libraries. For example, Tarbut, the cultural and educational organization of the General Zionists, operated 425 libraries with 290,000 volumes on the eve of World War II. A far-reaching network of workers' libraries was also gathered under the auspices of the Kultur-lige, the cultural organization of the Bund, the largest, best organized, and most popular being the Grosser Library in Warsaw, energetically led by Herman Kruk, under whose directorship it grew to an impressive 30,000 volumes by 1936.[21] Yet while the Grosser was the most significant of the Kultur-lige libraries, it was only one among 264 Kultur-lige libraries throughout Poland, and but one of more than 50 Jewish libraries in Warsaw.[22] On the eve of World War II, there were roughly seven hundred towns and cities in Poland with five hundred or more Jews, and each had at least one and usually several libraries.[23] Jewish readers also made avid use of municipal libraries throughout Poland. The reading that these various political and cultural organizations and libraries facilitated was by no means exclusively literary; however, Shavit calculates that "the majority of readers read fiction."[24]

Based on analysis of hundreds of autobiographies submitted by Polish Jewish youths in response to a series of three YIVO prize contests in the 1930s, Ido Bassok concludes that the various youth movements in interwar Poland, in particular the Zionist movements, strove to fulfill, in a more secular register, the totality of needs that had traditionally been met by the *kehillah*.[25] It is important to situate the explosion in literary reading in this context of secularization, for literature was one of the chief means through which a new generation of Polish Jews negotiated the transition out of an older traditional Jewish social, cultural, and religious framework into secular European society and what they conceived of as something like human citizenship.[26] Bassok argues that especially for the younger generations of interwar Polish Jewry, reading came to define one's status as a "human being" over against "lesser" beings, and that, consciously or not, this distinction echoed in a secular key the traditional one between those who could engage in Torah study, and those who could not.[27] The encounter and identification with secular literature, in particular with Abraham Mapu's 1853 Hebrew novel *The Love of Zion* (*Ahavat Tsiyon*), as a catalyst for a partial break with traditional Jewish cultural values and practices in favor of modernization and Europeanization is a prevalent leitmotif in nineteenth-century Haskalah autobiographies and novels, as Naomi Seidman has shown. While European literary models and codes, at various times adopted enthusiastically or regarded with ambivalence and skepticism, figured prominently in East European Jewish writers' and readers' trajectories of modernization, secularization, and Europeanization from the mid-nineteenth century through the fin-de-siècle, the explosion of secular literary culture in interwar Poland was a truly generational phenomenon.[28]

READING LITERATURE IN NAZI GHETTOS

Jews imprisoned in ghettos remained committed to reading books, and above all literature, as a facet and measure of their very humanity. As late as June 1942, and thus at most weeks before the Great Deportation of the Warsaw ghetto began on June 22, Emanuel Ringelblum considered the reading habits of ghetto inmates to be a matter of great human and historical importance.

> What are people reading? This is a subject of general interest; after the war, it will intrigue the world. What, the world will ask, did people think

> of on Musa Dagh or in the Warsaw Ghetto—people who knew for a certainty that death would no more skip over them than it had over the other large Jewish settlements and the small towns. *Let it be said that though we have been sentenced to death and know it, we have not lost our human features; our minds are as active as they were before the war.* The serious Jewish reader is fascinated by war writings. Lloyd George's memoirs are much read, novels from different countries dealing with the First World War, and the like. People particularly enjoy descriptions of the year 1918 and the downfall of the Germans. (Ringelblum, *Notes from the Warsaw Ghetto*, 298–99; emphasis added)

Ringelblum saw as significant the particular topics people were reading about in the Warsaw ghetto, after they had been "sentenced to death" and knew it, namely topics about the previous world war that had resulted in the Germans' ultimate defeat. Such books as well as works about Napoleon (in particular, parts of Tolstoy's *War and Peace*), Ringelblum remarked further, reminded the doomed ghetto inhabitants of how invincible-seeming tyrants can fall. "In a word, being unable to take revenge on the enemy in reality, we are seeking it in fantasy, in literature" (300). Yet beyond the particular topics that most resonated with the ghetto's population, Ringelblum sees the fact that they were reading literature at all as evidence that Jews maintained their humanity, or "human features."

In the above quote Ringelblum draws our attention to what people were reading in the Warsaw ghetto at most weeks before the vast majority of them were murdered. Reading was a constant dimension of ghetto life for the full duration of the existence of the ghettos.[29] In *Hunger for the Printed Word: Books and Libraries in the Jewish Ghettos of Nazi-Occupied Europe*, Shavit details the remarkable efforts that Jews interned in the ghettos of Warsaw, Lodz, Vilna, Kovno, and Terezin expended to preserve books—a manifestation of Jewish cultural life systematically targeted by the Nazis, as Philip Friedman noted in an essay published in 1958—and to (re)assembling libraries large and small and getting books into the hands of readers, whether in large reading rooms tolerated by the Nazis, in private homes, through courier librarians of clandestine small mobile libraries, or through diverse other types of libraries organized privately and under the auspices of ghetto institutions from the Judenräte (administrative Jewish Councils mandated by the Nazis) to grassroots organizations such as, in Warsaw, the house committees, the extensive Aleynhilf (self-aid) network, and YIKOR (Yidishe Kultur Organizatsye / Jewish Cultural Organization), one of the larger cultural organizations of the political underground, and CENTOS (Centrala Opieki nad Sierotami / Organization for the Care of Orphans).[30] Although political parties and their associated youth groups were proscribed in the ghettos, most of them formed cells and continued their work, including their cultural and educational work.[31] As a measure of the importance that the Oyneg Shabes team saw in the reading culture of the ghetto's population, it bears noting that the Oyneg Shabes's "Two-and-a-Half Year Plan," embarked on in spring 1942 and intended to synthesize the archive's findings and provide an overview of "various problems and important phenomena in Jewish life" in the Warsaw ghetto, was to have included a section devoted to "Jewish libraries and librarianship under the conditions of the ghetto, the state of the book trade, book collections, and the structure of the reading public and its interests in [the] Warsaw Ghetto during the period of the war."[32]

The largest ghetto library and the one about which we have the most detailed information is the Vilna Ghetto Library headed up by Herman Kruk, who prior to the war, as already noted, had been the chief librarian of the Grosser Library in Warsaw. The sizable collection was assembled out of the remains of Vilna's ransacked Mefitze Haskalah Library, augmented by the many books orphaned by the murder of their owners in the Ponar woods near Vilna, both prior to and after the formation of the ghetto (originally two ghettos) in fall 1941. It was opened on September 10, 1941, only days after Jews were forced into the ghetto, and it was part of the official cultural department of the Jewish Council.[33] Kruk was himself surprised at the amount people read even in fall 1941 while the Germans and their Lithuanian auxiliaries were systematically murdering tens of thousands of Vilna Jews. As he wrote in a diary entry of May 7, 1942, under the rubric "Books and Readers":

> A unique page of ghetto history is the Jewish reader.
>
> Even in November, during the great Aktions, when the population systematically declined by about 30 or 40 percent, the number of books borrowed increased by almost a third.
>
> How people read, and what they read, we have already written about in greater detail.[34]

Indeed, Kruk and his staff composed a report on the ghetto library and reading habits over the course of the first year of the ghetto's existence.[35] In the "Vilna Ghetto Library Annual Report, 1941–1942," he expanded on people's reading habits during periods of horrific violence.

> On 1 October [1941], Yom Kippur, about 3,000 people were extracted from various hiding places and taken out of the Vilna ghetto, and already on 2 October there were gigantic queues of readers waiting for a book. That same day, 390 books were circulated by the library. On the third and fourth, masses of people were removed from Ghetto No. 2. The tension in Ghetto No. 1 was beyond description, but already on the fifth no fewer than 421 books were circulated. On the twenty-fourth the Action of the "Yellow Certificates" took place; on the twenty-sixth people returned from Ghetto No. 2 to Ghetto No. 1, where aside from the general destruction they encountered doors torn from their hinges and pillaged household goods. And already on the ninth the library circulated 381 books. Thus, from Action to Action, purge to purge.[36]

If Kruk was somewhat amazed at how much people continued to read in the Vilna ghetto, even in the face of the direst phases of the genocidal killings, he was disappointed by *what* the vast majority of people were reading. Just as in the reading culture of the interwar period, in the Vilna ghetto, fiction was most popular, accounting for 78 percent of books circulated by the Vilna Ghetto Library.[37] A Bundist cultural activist, Kruk was committed to promoting serious literature in Yiddish. To his dismay, the greatest appetite among ghetto readers was for lowbrow genre fiction in Polish.[38] While, driven by a search for analogies to their present predicament, a minority of readers were drawn to substantial works of Jewish history, or historical novels by Sholem Asch, or to renowned war novels, including Tolstoy's *War and Peace* and Franz Werfel's *The Forty Days of Musa Dagh* (about the Armenian genocide during World War I) or others by the likes of Jaroslav Hašek, Erich Maria Remarque, R. C. Sheriff, and Emile Zola, "the broad mass of readers does not seek analogies" but rather "reading matter that removes them from reality, carries them off to distant regions, whether via detective stories, suspense, romance, and so forth" (Kruk, "Library and Reading Room," 195). If people in the Vilna ghetto were reading merely to escape, who could fault them? Yet the fact that Kruk himself, in a text I explore in chapter 7, drew in rather complex ways on detective fiction to grapple with the distinction between appearance and reality in the Vilna ghetto might suggest that some of these readers were also thinking with literature, even with lowbrow genre literature, in creative ways that Kruk, within his particular cultural project, may not have been well equipped to notice.

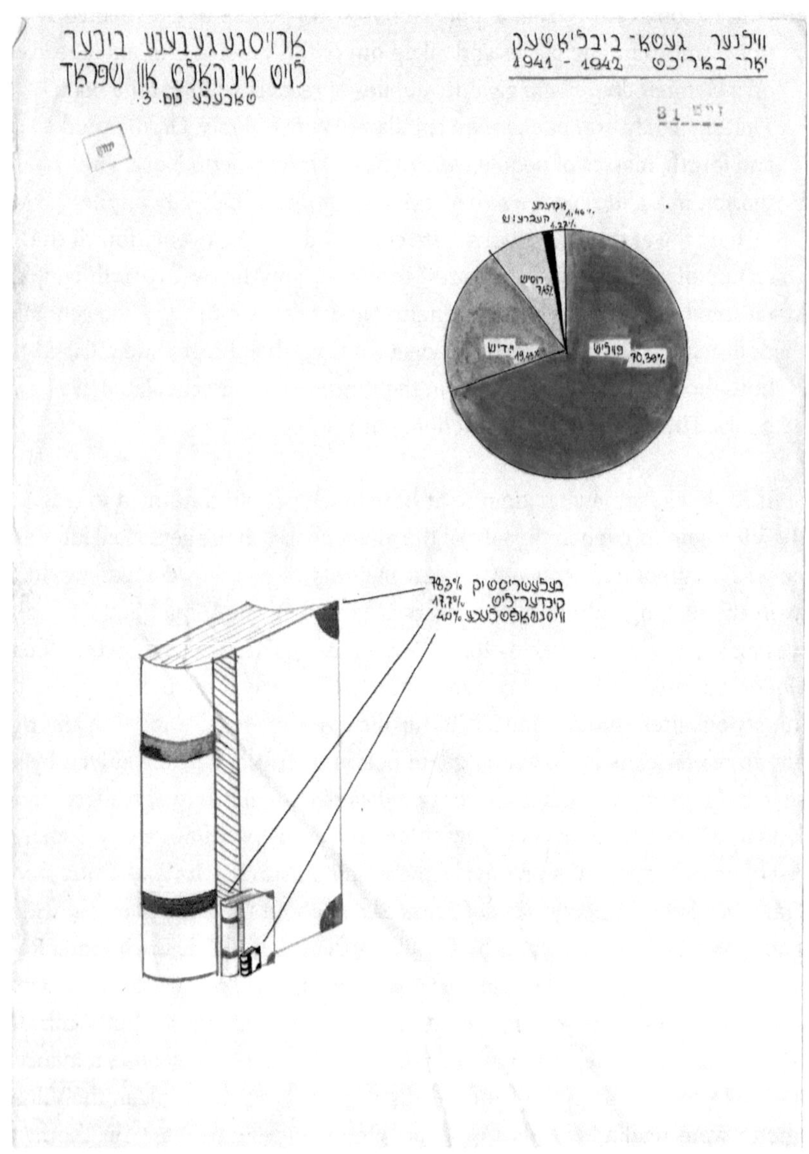

FIGURE 1: *Chart from the Vilna Ghetto Library Annual Report, 1941–1942: "Borrowed books according to content and language." The pie chart indicates that 70.39% of the books borrowed were in Polish, 19.43% in Yiddish, 7.45% in Russian, 1.27% in Hebrew, and 1.46% other languages. The drawn books indicate that 78.3% of the books borrowed were literary works (*beletristik*), 17.7% children's literature, and 4% scientific literature. Courtesy of the Archives of the YIVO Institute for Jewish Research, New York.*

WRITING LITERATURE IN NAZI GHETTOS

If the avid reading of the prewar period continued in the ghettos, the impulse to write in fact markedly increased. The prevalence of writing among Jews during the Holocaust is remarkable—and was noted at the time. As Ringelblum observes in an essay he wrote in late January 1943 providing an overview of the Oyneg Shabes archive and its aims: "The Germans did not care what the Jews did in their own homes. So the Jews began to write. Everyone wrote: journalists, writers, teachers, community activists, young people, even children. The majority wrote diaries, in which daily events were illumined through the prism of personal experiences. A great deal was written, but the largest part by far was destroyed along with the end of Warsaw Jewry in the Deportation. All that remained was the material preserved in O.S. [Oyneg Shabes]."[39]

Writing was widespread in other ghettos as well. As the prominent postwar Yiddish writer and survivor of the Lodz ghetto Chava Rosenfarb relates: "Even children and old people were infected with the literary bug. In the ghetto, along with tuberculosis, typhus, and dysentery, there raged the epidemic of writing. The drive to write was as strong as the hunger for food. It subdued the hunger for food. Each writer nurtured the hope that his or her voice would be heard. It was a drive to raise oneself above fear through the magical power of the written word, and so to demonstrate one's enduring capacity for love, for singing praise to life."[40] As was the case in Warsaw, so in Lodz (and every other ghetto) the vast majority of these texts perished with their authors. In Rosenfarb's case, none of the "hundreds upon hundreds of poems" she wrote survived—but *she* did. Nonetheless, a substantial body of texts in a wide array of forms and genres have come down to us from Jews confined to ghettos and hiding places. In the estimation of Yechiel Szeintuch, who has worked throughout his career to recover, edit, publish, and call attention to the importance of texts written during the Holocaust, "It seems that in no other period [of Jewish history] was so much written in a limited number of years by so many authors" (Szeintuch, "The Corpus," 1986).

READING VICTIMS' PERSPECTIVES IN YIDDISH LITERATURE

While as I have mentioned the dominant strains in Holocaust studies long eschewed serious engagement with victims' perspectives, the field has more recently seen what we could call a cultural turn. By this I mean victim-centered cultural-historical studies of Jews' specific experience of the catastrophe as it unfolded, elaborated by scholars across diverse disciplines including (but not limited to) Svenja Bethke, Nicholas Chare, Barbara Engelking, Alexandra Garbarini, Amos Goldberg, Samuel Kassow, Hannah Pollin-Galay, Jacek Leociak, David Roskies, Jan Schwarz, Amy Simon, and Dominic Williams. While the body of wartime literary writing by Holocaust victims remains underexplored, the fact that it is discernible as a crucial corpus at all is largely the achievement of Roskies's pioneering scholarship. Like Szeintuch, he has written widely over decades on writings produced during the catastrophe. Indeed, when Alan Mintz over two decades ago contrasted the then-dominant "exceptionalist" model to a relatively neglected "constructivist" approach to Holocaust representation, his constructivist model was essentially a theoretical distillation of Roskies's scholarly approach.[41] As the hold of the exceptionalist paradigm emphasizing the limits of representation and unspeakability has waned, a growing body of scholarship has turned to the work of reconstructing the cultural resources, strategies of articulation, and hermeneutic frameworks that the Holocaust's first interpreters, the victims themselves, availed themselves of as they grappled with their situation and the collapse of social and cultural structures, institutions, and meanings.[42] Scholars engaging in cultural reconstruction have tended to shift their focus from the camps, the quintessential site of the exceptionalist model, to victims in hiding and, especially, in ghettos. If one is interested in the experiences, thoughts, and perspectives of the victims of the Holocaust, the ghettos were places where they still had cultural resources, however strained and imperiled, to think, and where they were far more likely than in the camps to have basic material resources like a writing instrument and paper with which to record their thoughts. With this book I aspire to contribute to and further stimulate this dynamic and inspiring scholarship that listens to, learns from, and thinks with the victims.

One of the most salient aspects of literary writing by victims during the Holocaust that Roskies has illuminated is their tendency to turn to archetypes from the Bible and Jewish textual tradition in a desperate search for analogies with purchase on the unfolding horrors. Garbarini's groundbreaking work on diaries (which we might call a literary border genre) written by victims during the Holocaust emphasizes, in contrast, how Jews were engaging in a wider European cultural practice. The corpus of texts written by Jews during the Holocaust is so vast and heterogeneous that both of these scholarly perspectives—and many more—are helpful and necessary. How we locate Holocaust writing by Jewish authors within Jewish or wider European frames of reference, or both simultaneously, must vary from author to author and text to text, and of course according to the questions we bring to these texts. I explore certain allusions to Jewish liturgy or the Bible, for example Yoysef Kirman's evocation of the medieval *piyut* (Jewish liturgical poem) "Unetanneh Tokef," one of the most memorable texts of the Rosh Hashanah and Yom Kippur liturgy, and Psalm 22 in his poem "Di oygn blaybn ofn." However, my focus in this book falls predominantly on how writers attempted to place aspects of ghetto life within or against or at the limits of literary models and the humanistic values they understood literature to embody, through diverse strategies including pastiche, satire, and intertextual citation of modern European literary works.

My project in this book is not to provide a systematic or encyclopedic overview of the large corpus of literary works written in the ghettos, as worthwhile as such a project would be.[43] I aspire, instead, to give a limited number of remarkable texts some of the prolonged attention they deserve. Literary writings demand to be read as such and not exclusively as historical documents (which they of course also are). I would indeed argue that their greatest documentary value often inheres in their literary component, for they document precisely the importance that literature and thinking with literature held for many people even during their confinement in Nazi ghettos. These texts bear witness to their authors' active and creative reflections on their dire and always perilous situations, and call on us to engage with the intricacies of the thinking in literary keys that they embody and perform. In a word, these writings demand readings.

While literature in general can be understood as a complex mode of thought, I mean something more specific when I characterize the work that these texts perform as a form of literary thinking or thinking with literature. One of the central arguments of this book is that imprisonment in ghettos engendered in many writers a self-consciousness about their strained relationships to literary traditions and conventions as they surveyed them from their positions of radical exclusion and destitution. Reading and writing provided a resilient means for victims of the Holocaust to grapple, in real time, with what they were going through. At the same time, the extreme condition of being confined to a ghetto imposed a perspective from which they had to look with self-awareness and skepticism at a whole array of social and symbolic structures, ideologies, and cultural models and traditions that in the course of the war and the Holocaust lost their self-evidence, and sometimes collapsed.[44] While a place of extreme destitution, hunger, epidemic, and mass death, the ghettos were also—almost ineluctably—places from which it was possible and necessary to question the self-evidence of received social and cultural frameworks, including those of literary conventions and genres.

In my selection of texts language has been a (painfully) limiting factor. My focus is on Yiddish works. This book's penultimate chapter, chapter 8, focuses on a short story written in the Lodz ghetto by the German-language Viennese writer Oskar Rosenfeld. The only Polish-language text I analyze (in translation) is Gustawa Jarecka's essay "The Last Stage of Resettlement Is Death," written in the drastically reduced Warsaw ghetto after September 1942 (that is, after the Great Deportation), and my central concern with her text is how she invokes the literary hero Sherlock Holmes as a figure capable of restoring justice as part of her reflection on what it meant to write in the face of death. All the other works I explore were written in Yiddish.

Although the limits of my linguistic competence—and certainly not a sense that the works written in ghettos in Poland in Polish or Hebrew are inherently less rich or significant—have largely dictated my focus on Yiddish texts, the attention to Yiddish in particular is important for at least two less contingent reasons.[45] First, Yiddish was the historical vernacular of Ashkenaz, the language of the folk. Although Yiddish was rapidly losing ground to Polish in interwar Poland, especially among the youth, only Yiddish could, both literally and symbolically, be seen as the language of the Jewish people (naturally as East European Jews conceived of the Jewish people). If Yiddish as a language and a culture was struggling in the Second Polish Republic, in the Holocaust it was being murdered along with its speakers. It was itself a victim of the catastrophe that Yiddish writers used it to reflect on. Second, modern Yiddish literature evolved in energetic but also frequently ambivalent dialogue with European literary traditions, and that ambivalent and self-conscious vantage point vis-à-vis literary models necessarily became more pronounced in the literature written in ghettos, from positions of radical exclusion from European society.

The fact that modern Yiddish literature was a late arrival to many currents of European literature only heightened Yiddish cultural self-consciousness: the developments in major European literary traditions over a century or more, from the Romantics through modernism, crashed into Yiddish in the span of a few decades. One effect of such telescoping was that Yiddish writers' projects of self-invention often involved self-consciously adapting, refracting, ironizing, and subverting the myriad models that modern European literature proffered. Naomi Seidman traces the Jewish literary negotiation of European bourgeois culture, in particular its ideology of romantic heterosexual love and companionate marriage, and argues that "Jews fell in love with love, and with literature" ambivalently.[46] Even as Yiddish writers frequently criticized Jewish culture and social practices, they equally parodied the bourgeois models to which Jewish society failed to conform. That is, Jewish artists and intellectuals critiqued, undermined, deflated, carnivalized, parodied, and otherwise looked askance at the very European standards by which they sometimes measured Jewish shortcomings. Conceptions of Ashkenazic culture as a minority culture, Seidman suggests, may be wont to miss the way that East European Jews not only experienced Jewish distinctiveness in terms of stigmatization from without but also "wielded" Jewish distinctiveness to critique hegemonic European culture.[47]

As unsettling as it may be to think of the Nazi ghettos as culturally rich Jewish contexts, they emphatically were. Contending with starvation, disease, desperate housing conditions, and the (at times dimly, at times lucidly, perceived) threat of being murdered, the inhabitants of ghettos in Poland nonetheless made them sites of Jewish cultural production. My readings of works of ghetto literature in this book reveal how their authors both took refuge in the humanistic resources of literature and also wielded their Jewish distinctiveness to put the codes and conventions of various literary genres as it were on trial. They leveraged the radical destitution of ghetto existence to probe the limits of what literature can and cannot encompass. In the extreme circumstances of a ghetto, typical literary scenarios, tropes, plot lines, and generic conventions, including those of nature lyric, modernist interior monologue, the realist social novel, the detective story, and the gothic horror tale offered writers crucial resources for thinking through their individual and collective plight. At the same time, these literary resources frequently proved to be inadequate to the particular experience of Jews imprisoned in ghettos.

Literary writing maintained its humanizing thrust, and to write not only documentary prose but *literature* was indeed an act of asserting one's humanity. Writers, however, also took stock of the peril they were facing—the way that human status is a fragile thing and the way theirs was being systematically denied and eradicated—by variously highlighting the ironic incommensurability between the worlds presupposed by established literary genres and the world of the ghetto. Sometimes such incommensurability infiltrated literary projects implicitly and ineluctably; sometimes authors highlighted it self-consciously. Thus, the bleakest possible iteration of the Ashkenazic ambivalence vis-à-vis European literary models played out in the ghettos. On the one hand, writers longed to embrace literature and, indeed, to assert their human status by writing literature. On the other hand, they wrote with the bitterly ironic awareness that the horrors Jews were facing in the ghettos could not easily be squared with generic conventions and ideals; that imperiled, destitute, starving, and humiliated people could not, for example, play the roles of typical protagonists in conventional literary scenarios. These writers both looked at ghetto existence via literature and looked at literature, in literature, from the critical vantage point that the ghettos imposed. In other words, writers in ghettos, with varying degrees of self-consciousness, both made literature and denatured it by making it confront something it was ill-equipped to absorb—the systematic assault on the human status of Jews.

This book's title—*Making and Unmaking Literature in the Warsaw, Lodz, and Vilna Ghettos*—signals my concern with both how authors in ghettos availed themselves of literary models to depict and interpret their circumstances and with how their recourse to literary genres, characters, and conventions highlighted disjunctions between literary traditions and this particular reality. I am keenly interested in how authors thought in extremis with literature and at the limits of literature. Given the radical figurative and literal alienation from European society that confinement to ghettos entailed, reaching for established European literary genres was not something that authors in ghettos, generally speaking, did naively. On the contrary, they constantly had to question the aptness, the serviceability, and indeed the very possibility of various literary models and conventions within their radically changed circumstances. Literature and its very possibility was, in myriad ways, in question for these authors as they were writing it. In this book I thus attend to questions that inform—whether implicitly or, at times, quite self-consciously—literary writing in the ghettos, such as: Will or can what we are experiencing add up to a literary narrative? A novel? Is a lyric poem about frozen and dismembered corpses on the ghetto streets even possible? How do the realities of ghetto life mock the presuppositions of an array of literary genres and models? How are they incompatible with typical plot lines? How do temporalities of ghetto life, imposed above all by gnawing hunger, compare with literary treatments of time, including in modernist prose? How are inhabitants of ghettos able or unable to embody the roles of stock literary protagonists? Authors used literature as a touchstone with and against which to think through and take stock of their volatile and often unfathomable realities. While places of great suffering and misery, the ghettos were also places of profound literary thinking.

Beyond privileging texts that I see as in some way thinking with, against, or at the limits of literature, I also wanted to treat a wide (albeit by no means exhaustive) array of genres of literary writing in ghettos. These genres include a novel (Zelman Skalov), poems (Shmuel Marvil, Itzhak [Yitzkhok] Katzenelson, Yoysef Kirman), short stories (Oskar Rosenfeld, Shaye Shpigl), literary reportage (Herman Kruk), experimental autofiction (Leyb Goldin), and autobiography (Yehoshue Perle). While my selection of texts is generically diverse, the authors, regrettably, are nearly all male. Just as Gustawa Jarecka is the only Polish-language author that I discuss in this book, she is also the only woman writer. Relatively few ghetto texts by women have survived. Even though their circumstances remained quite dire, writers in ghettos tended to receive a modicum of support in the form of relatively protected jobs under the auspices of the Judenrat, or additional nourishment or stipends, whether from the Judenrat or from grassroots initiatives like the Warsaw ghetto Aleynhilf, the network of non-Judenrat social welfare organizations supported chiefly by Joint Distribution Committee funds.[48] Such support generally went to men. While some known and undoubtedly many unknown women authors wrote literature in the ghettos, their texts were presumably even more likely than those of their male counterparts to be destroyed. My commitment in this book to exploring only texts written in ghettos (and not any that were remembered, rewritten, or reconstructed after the war) steered me away from dealing with Chava Rosenfarb's poems of the Lodz ghetto, except as a point of comparison. Rokhl Auerbach wrote her stunning eulogy for the murdered Polish Jews, "Yizkor 1943," in Polish (although she would later translate it for publication in Yiddish). Strictly speaking it is also a commemorative, post-ghetto (though still wartime) text, as she composed it in hiding in Warsaw after the ghetto had been destroyed.[49] I do not deem works written or reconstructed after the war to be any less significant or worthy of study than wartime writings. Wartime writing and postwar writing and re-writing, however, are distinct phenomena and warrant being studied in their historical specificity.

OVERVIEW OF THE ORGANIZATION OF THE BOOK AND THE CONTENT OF THE CHAPTERS

Three (to some extent competing) organizational principles inform the order of the chapters: chronology, place, and genre. Location is the most straightforward of these criteria. The book's first six chapters all treat works composed in the Warsaw ghetto, and the last two chapters (8 and 9) explore short stories written in the Lodz ghetto by Oskar Rosenfeld and Shaye Shpigl, respectively. Chapter 7 discusses an essay composed in the Warsaw ghetto by Gustawa Jarecka but focuses primarily on a work of literary journalism from the Vilna ghetto by Herman Kruk.

Local context, both place and chronology, is crucial for interpreting texts written in ghettos. Ringelblum remarked in an often-quoted passage on the dramatic shifts that even short spans of time measured by the clock could bring to life in the ghettos: "The war changed Jewish life in the Polish cities very quickly. No day was like the preceding. Images succeeded one another with cinematic speed. For the Jews of Warsaw . . . every month brought profound changes that radically altered Jewish life. . . . Each day was like decades in an earlier time" (Ringelblum, "Oyneg Shabes," 391). In light of the importance of what Roskies has called "reading in time" when approaching Holocaust-era works, I have generally organized the chapters exploring Warsaw ghetto writings according to the chronological order in which they were written.[50] I depart from strict chronology, however, in order to preserve the generic coherence of the sections of this book dealing with Warsaw ghetto poetry (part 2, chapters 2–4) and Warsaw ghetto short prose life writing (part 3, chapters 5 and 6). While chronology and micro-context are paramount for my interpretation of Kruk in chapter 7, this is the sole chapter focused on the Vilna ghetto. Similarly, while micro-context is critical for my discussion of Lodz ghetto short stories by Rosenfeld and Shpigl in this book's final two chapters, chronology is less determinative of the order of these chapters, not least because the texts by Shpigl that I explore were written over the course of years in the ghetto and their precise date of composition is usually unclear.

The book begins with an exploration of Zelman Skalov's unfinished, and I will argue unfinishable, novel "Di hak on krayts" (literally, the "axe without a cross," but a homonym for the Yiddish word for *swastika*). Skalov's project is a fascinating attempt to absorb the unfolding events of the first two years of the German occupation of Poland (from Germany's initial invasion of Poland in September 1939 until Germany's invasion of the Soviet Union in June 1941) into the temporality and generic conventions of a realist social novel centered on the predominantly but not exclusively Jewish residents of a Warsaw tenement. It is significant that Skalov chose the genre of the novel roughly a year before the establishment of the Warsaw ghetto and abandoned it less than a year into the ghetto's existence. The novel was not a prominent genre of ghetto literature. Not only did authors generally lack the security of space, health, and nutrition required for sustained labor on a longer work, but the rapidly and radically changing realities of ghetto life also mocked the stability of a novelistic world. Not for nothing did Ringelblum evoke the cinematic speed rather than the novelistic sweep of ghetto time. In this sense, Skalov's novel takes us both chronologically and generically into the Warsaw ghetto. Grappling in its opening scenes with the German invasion of Poland, neither "Di hak" nor its author could know that the ghetto, much less the genocide, was in the offing. Skalov's recourse to the novel was something between a presumption and a leap of faith that things would not get so bad that they would explode the very coherence of the world of a conventional social novel. Thus while the work must be judged as a generic failure, as a failed novel, this failure is not primarily due to lack of talent on the part of its author but rather to the ultimately unnovelizable nature of the events in which he found himself caught. It is less a failed novel in any conventional sense than the promise of a novel orphaned by the extreme violence and social disruption of ghettoization. In its final pages before breaking off, Skalov's novel tellingly evokes two non-novelistic genres, lyric poetry and reportage. While novels would not figure prominently in the literary corpus produced in the ghettos, poetry and reportage, as well as short fiction and autofiction, would, and it is to these genres that the rest of the book turns.

The truth of Ringelblum's remark about the cinematic speed of change in ghetto life is powerfully illustrated in the poems on which the three chapters of part 2, devoted to poetry from the Warsaw ghetto, focus: Shmuel Marvil's "Di gas" ("The Street"; chapter 2); Itzhak Katzenelson's "Vey dir" ("Woe to you"; chapter 3); and Yoysef Kirman's "Di oygn blaybn ofn" ("The Eyes Remain Open"; chapter 4). Written in the Warsaw ghetto within a span of approximately six months from spring to fall 1942, the contexts of these three poems is each radically distinct. Marvil's poem grapples with the unfathomable phenomenon of ambient death by starvation, epidemic, and freezing in the frigid winter of 1941–1942. The speaker of Marvil's searing poem repeatedly apostrophizes the poem ("my song") itself, taking the measure of the scenes of dehumanization that the poem depicts by asking—desperately, aggressively, and imploringly by turns—to what extent they are even compatible with the tradition of lyric poetry. Katzenelson wrote his ferocious poem "Vey dir" in reaction to the news of the destruction of the Jewish community of Lublin in spring 1942, an enormous tragedy in its own right and a sign that the Nazis would not stop at ridding of Jews, by murder or displacement, the portions of Poland they had annexed to the Third Reich but would murder the millions of Jews in the occupied Generalgouvernement. Katzenelson brilliantly exploits temporal dynamics of lyric apostrophe to allow the Jewish collective, which the poem envisions will soon have been murdered and reduced to ghosts, to speak beyond its collective death in an unsettling *now* that is not superseded or silenced by the unfolding of the anticipated genocidal murder that did indeed come to pass. While relentlessly cursing the German perpetrators, the poem also implies a collective readership not of Germans but of Yiddish-speaking Jews whose collective murder is imminent and who know this. As we read the poem today, I argue, we are haunted by the way it speaks to us but also past us, in search of its annihilated audience. Kirman depicts and meditates on scenes from the Great Deportation of the Warsaw ghetto in the summer and early autumn of 1942, when the mass murder of the Jews of Warsaw no longer looms as a threat on the horizon, as in Katzenelson's poem, but is by and large an accomplished fact. His poem "Di oygn blaybn ofn" eschews esthetic refuge from the events and instead confronts readers with the phenomenological temporality of their unfolding, their terrible duration.

The pair of chapters that make up part 3 are each devoted to a work of short autobiographical prose: Leyb Goldin's autobiographical short story "Khronik fun a mes-les" ("Chronicle of a Single Day"; chapter 5) and "4580" by the Yiddish novelist Yehoshue Perle (chapter 6). The epigraph of Goldin's brilliant "Chronicle of a Single Day" quotes I. L. Peretz's epochal 1888 poem "Monish," hailed as a milestone in modern secular Yiddish literature, as a way of evoking the dialogue with European culture that "Monish" stages. Goldin updates this conversation by engaging in sustained dialogue with modernist texts by Knut Hamsun, Thomas Mann, and Arthur Schnitzler from the particular vantage point of a man starving in the Warsaw ghetto in the summer of 1941. Perle recurrently cites Sholem Aleichem's beloved novel *Motl, Peysi the Cantor's Son* in "4580" as a way of measuring the distance of his situation from the guiding coordinates of that famous work, a further example of this ramified practice of intertextual citation. As the most famous orphan in Yiddish literary history, Motl also serves as one of the key ways that Perle explores his own unprecedented status as an orphan in the Warsaw ghetto after the Great Deportation of summer 1942. He finds himself in the situation not of having survived a parent but of having (temporarily) survived the annihilated Ashkenazic community that lent his name and identity significance before they were taken from him and replaced by the work permit number, signified by his text's title, that Perle was assigned as a slave laborer in a ghetto factory. Only by this stroke of dubious "luck" was Perle able to survive long enough to write this final text of his life, a personal and collective autobiography written from the impossible position of a man orphaned by genocide and reduced to a number, a text full of rage, grief, guilt, and despair—and infinite love for the language, people, and culture that gave his name meaning.

All of the works discussed so far were written in the Warsaw ghetto. The final part of this book engages with short prose written in the ghettos of Vilna and Lodz. Chapter 7 takes up two texts that each invoke the figure of Sherlock Holmes and the detective paradigm—"The Last Stage of Resettlement Is Death" ("Ostatnim etapem przesiedlenia jest smierc"), written by Jarecka in the Warsaw ghetto in fall 1942, and "Six Gallows in the Vilna Ghetto: A Criminal Literary Chronicle of the Vilna Ghetto" ("Zeks tlies"), written by Kruk in August 1942.[51] Jarecka's text is the introduction to a planned report for the Oyneg Shabes on the Great Deportation of the Warsaw ghetto that she was ultimately unable to complete. Kruk's narrative is a literary reportage, a "true crime" story of murder-robbery followed, eventually, by a guilty verdict pronounced by a Vilna ghetto court, and the execution of the criminals carried out by the Vilna ghetto police. In different ways Jarecka and Kruk each approach questions of epistemology, the distinction between surface appearance and underlying truth, and the status of ethical agency and the prospects for rendering justice in Nazi ghettos, via references to Arthur Conan Doyle's master detective. In doing so, these authors anticipated what would become a widespread recourse to the detective paradigm in postwar reckonings with the Holocaust and its legacy.

The final two chapters examine works written in the Lodz ghetto. Like Jarecka and Kruk, Oskar Rosenfeld and Shaye Shpigl draw on popular genre fiction. In his German language short story "Meine zwei Nachbarn" ("My Two Neighbors"), the focus of chapter 8, Oskar Rosenfeld rifles through a vast reserve of stock characters and scenarios from detective novels, thrillers, and romance, none of which prove commensurate with his protagonist's mostly dreamed actions. Hauntingly, the story stages the intrigue that unfolds between the protagonist and his two neighbors—and the many genre fiction roles and scenarios in which it involves them—as taking place in the virtually empty space of an apartment house whose erstwhile residents have recently been deported.

In the final chapter (chapter 9), I analyze ways that one of the most prolific prose writers in any ghetto, Shaye Shpigl, drew on motifs from gothic horror fiction in several short stories. Perhaps due to the gothic genre's taint of trashiness, Shpigl's creative and abiding deployment of gothic tropes has gone unremarked. I show how Shpigl draws on gothic literature's central concern with boundaries, (failed) projects of containment, and uncanny proximities between different realms. Gothic works dramatize the mutual interpenetration of the everyday and the extreme, the familiar and the irrational and unfathomable. All these gothic ingredients readily served Shpigl in his literary treatment of the Lodz ghetto. I trace in particular how the Yiddish term *umheymlekh* resonates like no other word throughout Shpigl's ghetto texts. Like its German equivalent *unheimlich*, which Sigmund Freud famously theorized in his 1919 essay "Das Unheimliche" ("The Uncanny"), it figuratively means "uncanny" but is literally composed of the negating prefix *um* (in English and German, *un*) and *heymlekh*, an adjectival form of the word *heym* (home) meaning *secret*. Shpigl always tethers the term *umheymlekh*, which is so often used in highly abstract ways, to a literal loss of home. The condition of homelessness suddenly and violently imposed on Jews in the Holocaust is the terrifying existential reality that undergirds other, less tangible forms of unfathomable strangeness in Shpigl's wartime stories. I end the chapter with a reading of Shpigl's story "Shtroy" (Straw) as a meta-literary reflection on relationships between gothic literary devices and conventions, on the one hand, and the very real conditions of destitution, disease, and death in the Lodz ghetto, on the other.

In this book's coda I recall early postwar efforts by survivors to collect all possible documents pertaining to the Jewish experience under Nazi occupation, very much including the literature that victims wrote during the Holocaust. I consider how early survivor historians of the Holocaust, who were concerned with all aspects of Jews' lives and daily struggles in the ghettos were unable to set parameters for Holocaust historiography or for the dynamics of Holocaust memory and how, instead, the history of the perpetrators, based on German sources and assiduously eschewing Jewish sources, became the dominant historiographical strain. I argue that the recent calls for incorporating the study of the Holocaust into a comparative genocide studies framework as well as related calls for moving beyond well-worn paradigms of Holocaust memory and representation such as the model of "multi-directional memory" proposed by Michael Rothberg, despite their many intellectual and ethical virtues, run the risk of continuing to frame the woefully underread archive of East European sources out of consideration. This book begins to explore the profound thought these neglected texts embody. We still have much to gain by thinking with them.

I. NOVEL

CHAPTER 1

NOVELISTIC TIME, HISTORICAL TIME, AND THE END OF OMNISCIENCE

ZELMAN SKALOV

Due to the precarious living conditions and the volatile events that defined life in Nazi ghettos, the most prevalent forms of literature written in them were short: poems, reportages, short stories. The sole novel that has come down to us from the Warsaw (or any other) ghetto is "Di hak on krayts" by Zelman Skalov (pen name of Lejb Pluskałowski). Skalov's title is a somewhat awkward pun: literally meaning "ax without a cross," "hak on krayts" is a homophone in Yiddish for *swastika*.[1] The novel depicts far-flung experiences of a group of characters initially residing in the same Warsaw tenement, from the German invasion of Poland in September 1939 until the German invasion of the Soviet Union in June 1941. It treats events and dynamics including the German bombing of Warsaw; relations between Jews, Poles, and Polish ethnic Germans; sexual and sexualized abuse of Jewish and Polish women by Germans; massacres of Jewish civilians and Jewish POWs; Jews' attempts to adapt to increasingly bleak possibilities of earning livelihoods; the experience of labor camps; the establishment of the ghetto; smuggling, mass hunger, and epidemics; and the destitution of refugees deported into the ghetto from provincial towns.

Skalov did not survive the war. His novel and some other writings did, in the Oyneg Shabes archive headed by Emanuel Ringelblum. Skalov's novel is in two parts, comprising 67 and 104 typescript pages, respectively, and two typescript copies of each part were preserved (with varying degrees of damage). The original title of part 1, "Ratevet!" (Help!), has been stricken on both copies and replaced by hand with "Di hak on krayts," (copy 1) and "1ster teyl Hak on krayts" (copy 2).[2] The typescript of part 2 is subtitled "Kvo vadis?" (Quo vadis?).[3] No accurate and complete edition of Skalov's novel has yet been published in the original Yiddish. In 1954, Ber Mark, then director of the Jewish Historical Institute (Zydowski Instytut Historyczny or ZIH) in Warsaw, home of the recovered Oyneg Shabes archive, published an edition of *Di hak on krayts* with the Polish state-sponsored Yidish-bukh publishing house that was significantly corrupted, frequently but not only for obviously ideological reasons.[4] A German "adaptation" (*literarische Bearbeitung*) of this corrupted edition, which strays markedly from its already dubious "original," was included in the 1966 East German anthology of prose from the Warsaw ghetto, *Ghetto: Berichte aus dem Warschauer Ghetto 1939–1945*.[5] The Warsaw Jewish Historical Institute edition of literary works from the Oyneg Shabes archive (original versions of Polish-language works and Polish translations of works written in Yiddish and other languages) includes a translation of the complete manuscript of "Di hak on krayts."[6] The work has not yet been translated into English and to this day has received slight critical attention.

Skalov had published two collections of stories in Yiddish before the war, *Vayse hent* (White hands, 1936), a literary critique of exploitative labor relations in Palestine, based on his own sojourn there, and *Tsaytn baytn zikh* (Times are changing, 1938), published by the prestigious (and in the 1930s, increasingly leftist) Literarishe bleter, the press of the Association of Jewish Authors and Journalists in Poland.[7] In the Warsaw ghetto, Skalov was a close collaborator of Ringelblum's in the Oyneg Shabes project, for which he (usually under the pseudonym H. Groyl, meaning "horror") also wrote reportages on expulsions of Jews from Polish *shtetlekh* (market towns), on street life in the ghetto, and on the so-called *punktn*, the overcrowded and disease-ravaged centers for starving and homeless refugees.[8] Skalov's novel and a substantial reportage on the punktn were preserved in the first cache of the Oyneg Shabes, which was buried on August 3, 1942, and recovered in September 1946.[9] In his notebooks Ringelblum recorded admiring lines about Skalov's tireless and fearless work, especially in the times of greatest danger during the deportations to the death camp Treblinka. He also noted his belief that Skalov was arrested in 1942 in the brush factory where Ringelblum had helped secure him employment, and then deported to his death.[10]

As I will elaborate on in a moment, the preserved typescript leaves little doubt that Skalov was attempting to novelize the events of the first two years of the German occupation of Poland virtually concurrently with those events themselves; his perspective on unfolding events was more sidelong than retrospective. The question I explore in this chapter is how Skalov's manuscript embodies tensions between novelistic form and the radical contingencies of catastrophic history unfolding in the present. How and why does Skalov endeavor to accommodate the events he reckons with in something approaching real time within the formal constraints of a novel, and how and why does the attempt break down? The novel, to state the obvious, is among the most significant ways that we tell humanly meaningful stories about ourselves. How Skalov's project tries, partially succeeds, and largely fails to add up to a novel is a matter not merely of narrow literary interest, but rather it offers a window onto an attempt to sustain structures of human meaning in the ghettos, and the vulnerability in extremis of such structures to collapse.

A striking feature of Skalov's literary experiment is its eschewal of formal literary experimentation. While modernist novelists had for decades been deploying an array of innovations to try to do justice to the shocks, speed, and disruptions of modern life, Skalov, writing in what was undeniably one of the most shocking, fast-paced, and disruptive periods in the history of Polish, and even more so of Polish Jewish, society, opted to pursue an utterly conventional mode of literary realism. It is plausible that Skalov, as a fellow-traveler of the Left, may have been influenced in his commitment to the realist social novel by Soviet writers and Left intellectuals more broadly. The question of socialist realism was a burning one among Soviet (including Soviet Yiddish) writers in the 1930s. The First All-Union Congress of Soviet writers of August 1934 officially sanctioned socialist realism as the sole appropriate literary mode for Soviet writers.[11] Beyond the stormy Soviet discussions about socialist realism, György Lukács championed realism—from nineteenth century realists including Balzac, Stendhal, and Tolstoy to twentieth-century inheritors of this tradition like Gorky and Heinrich and Thomas Mann—in debates about realism and the avant-garde ("expressionism") in the late 1930s.[12] Whether animated by political commitments or simply by an esthetic affinity for conventional novelistic realism, however, Skalov, by attempting to remain within models established by the nineteenth-century European social novel (*Gesellschaftsroman, roman social*), arguably destabilizes the form and its underlying assumptions about epistemology and social ontology more radically than he would have had he pursued more experimental formal means to grapple with the increasingly extreme and unmasterable circumstances.[13] Indeed, among the most poignant aspects of Skalov's project is that when he embarked on it in fall 1939 he was ostensibly confident that he would be able to render the events in the offing in the form of a symbolically coherent and humanly meaningful story about Polish—especially but not exclusively Polish Jewish—society in crisis under the German occupation; that these events, in a word, would ultimately harmonize with the generic demands of a *novel*.

The exposition of "Di hak" promises a social novel in the mold of Honoré Balzac's *Père Goriot* (1834–1835) and Émile Zola's *Pot-Bouille* (Stew pot, 1882–1883). Skalov initially sought to organize his novel around the social microcosm of the inhabitants of an urban tenement on Graniczna Street in Warsaw. Were we to read the opening pages of Skalov's novel knowing nothing of how the events of World War II and the Holocaust played out, these pages would seem to set the stage for a broad portrait of how different classes and generations of Polish Jews (and some of their non-Jewish neighbors) negotiated the crises of the German occupation. In attempting to remain within the conventions of the social novel while accommodating the increasingly dire context, Skalov ultimately pushes these conventions to their breaking point. The apartment-building novel presumes structural homologies between building, city, and society that could not hold as Polish society became radically disaggregated and Jews were imprisoned in ghettos. Indeed, not even the most basic constitutive assumption of the genre of the social novel—that the representatives of different social strata will, however bitter their fates, remain part of "society" itself—was borne out by the history Skalov was trying to novelize. The social milieu initially presented as a microcosm of the wider society would not remain even remotely intact, nor would other key elements of conventional novels remain stable, including basic presumptions that characters will retain sufficient integrity to remain legible as characters in a novel rather than slip into inscrutable states of abjection, or that the would-be omniscient narrator will be able to maintain authoritative knowledge regarding the shape of the far-flung events.

Whether Skalov followed Lukács's politico-esthetic interventions on realism in the 1930s or not, the central terms of Lukács's critique illuminate key tensions in Skalov's project. Lukács centrally opposes what he deems pseudo-realist works, which merely register surface phenomena of fragmented capitalist modernity (and, as it were, miss the forest for the trees), with what he regards as authentically realist works, which convey a clear sense of the social totality on the basis of the underlying objective forces shaping a given historical moment. While pseudo-realism (exemplified for Lukács by the "photographic" realism of Zola) succumbs to subjective bewilderment, authentically realist works situate events and subjective experiences within the wider context of the social and economic forces that engender them and render them meaningful. But what constitutes social totality in the context of the radical removal of Jews from society by means of mass shootings, ghettoization, and rampant death from abject poverty, hunger, and disease? The historical events that Skalov set out to novelize starting in 1939 would see Jews systematically excised from the society that "Di hak on krayts" endeavors to situate them within. The lack of a social totality that could serve to order the chaos of events contributes to the limited (strained and contrived) nature of the omniscience at work in Skalov's text. Whereas in Lukácsian "authentic realism" the omniscient narrator grasps the underlying social totality subtending the various events and subjective experiences within the novel, Skalov's attempt to write a realist social novel amidst the violent disaggregation of Polish society results in a breakdown in omniscience. Skalov imagined that he was in possession of a generic framework—and a vision of social totality, in Lukács's sense—within which he would be able to accommodate whatever events might be coming (i.e., what his novel would specifically be about). He could not know, when he began trying to novelize from within the midst of events, that these events would simply exceed the universe of the realist novel.

Rapid and fundamental paradigm shifts were what Ringelblum was getting at with his comment, quoted in this book's introduction, about the "cinematic speed" with which the war transformed Jewish life in Poland:

> The War changed Jewish life in the Polish cities very quickly. No day was like the preceding. Images succeeded one another with cinematic speed. For the Jews of Warsaw, now [after the Great Deportation of the ghetto, July–September 1942] closed in within the narrow confines of a shop, the ghetto period seems like a paradise and the pre-ghetto period an unreal dream. Every month brought profound changes that radically altered Jewish life. It was therefore important to capture at once every event in Jewish life in its pristine freshness. What a quantum leap from the pre-Deportation shop to that which came after! The same is true of smuggling, and of social and cultural life; even the clothes Jews wore were different in the different periods. O[yneg] S[habes] therefore tried to grasp an event at the moment it happened, since each day was like decades in an earlier time. We succeeded in doing this with many of the events. What greatly aided us in this task was that some of our own coworkers kept diaries. (Ringelblum, "Oyneg Shabbes," 391)

Surely few things could have been further from Ringelblum's mind when he wrote these lines than the esthetico-political debates of the 1930s about which representational modes and strategies were most apt for comprehending and rendering the fragmentation, disruption, and disorientation of modern life, yet we can productively read Ringelblum as grappling with questions closely related to those at the heart of these debates. Although he is not concerned with the speed and shocks of urban modernity writ large, but specifically with Jewish life in extremis in wartime Polish cities, Ringelblum nonetheless addresses problems of representing the Jewish experience of the war years via a model of novelistic realism *à la* Lukács. While for Lukács, modernist literary modes from naturalism to impressionism, expressionism, and surrealism fall short by remaining on the surface of things and abstracting from immediate subjective experience without grasping the all-important underlying social totality, Ringelblum here argues that in view of the pace and degree of disruption of Jewish social, economic, and cultural life, it was in fact imperative to attend vigilantly precisely to surface phenomena; paradigms of understanding based on deeper wholes would only misunderstand —or indeed simply miss—what was happening. As Jewish life changed with cinematic speed, something like cinematic representation became necessary to capture "every event in Jewish life in its pristine freshness" as opposed to looking for abiding social structures underlying merely epiphenomenal events. Ringelblum does not evoke "cinematic" speed merely to highlight the rapidity with which "images" of Jewish life moved in these years but also and especially to highlight the discontinuous manner, akin to cinematic jump cuts, in which this movement proceeded by "quantum leaps." The various contextual wholes in which events might be situated were in a state of perpetual transformation and collapse and provided little epistemological purchase; the surest way to grasp something of the essence of the experience of these years was to fasten one's gaze to phenomenological surfaces. As I argue later in this chapter, Skalov's project is torn by incommensurable commitments—to bearing witness to the chaotic events, circumstances, and experiences of Jewish Warsaw during the first two years of World War II, on the one hand, and to ordering them into a novelistic totality, on the other.

Writing virtually concurrently with the events he endeavored to novelize, Skalov constantly had to project a plot—and a total horizon, a social totality —within which the action would remain. But the totality that Skalov envisioned at the outset—the whole that delineated the contours of the novel he was setting out to write—ultimately could not hold as his writing traced history from the first phase of the German invasion of Poland, when Jews fought valiantly if unsuccessfully alongside their Christian fellow citizens to repel the German aggressors, to Jews starving and dying abjectly en masse in the streets and in the squalid refugee centers (punktn) in the Warsaw ghetto. The book's initially conceived novelistic structure proved incapable of ordering the increasingly catastrophic events and so unraveled. While Skalov would rifle through much of the inventory of conventional ways to construct novels —from novels anchored in social microcosms inflected by class relations to love plots to narratives of emerging authors—none of these attempts to re-establish novelistic order succeeded. As I argue in the latter half of this chapter, however, while Skalov's writing of this work may have been "processual" as Saul Gary Morson theorizes that term, he was a processual novelist not out of esthetic or ethical conviction but rather *malgré lui* due to his implacable circumstances.

CONCURRENT NOVELIZATION

The events of the first twenty-one months of World War II that Skalov endeavored to organize into a novelistic narrative rarely lay more than a few months in the past at any point that he was writing about them and were frequently more proximate than that to the time of writing. With the knowledge of the proximity between the contingent historical events and Skalov's attempts to accommodate them in a novelistic composition, we can better understand what this project can tell us about the relationship between the lived experience of Jewish ghetto inmates and the generic presuppositions of the social novel.[14] The typescript of part 1 of Skalov's attempted historical novel of the unfolding present is dated "Warsaw, New Year's, 1940."[15] If this dating is accurate, then Skalov was indeed writing his text virtually concurrently with the events he treats.[16] The Warsaw ghetto per se is not mentioned until relatively late in Skalov's manuscript—roughly midway through the second and final part.[17] It seems reasonable to infer that most of Skalov's treatment of events prior to the sealing of the ghetto in November 1940 was likewise written before that date. In fact, this hypothesis may find support in an earlier mention in part 1 of the coming ghetto. Two-thirds of the way through the typescript of part 1 (page 46 of 67), Skalov begins a section with an ellipsis followed by the word "ghetto" in a large font followed in turn by three exclamation points: ". . . GETO!!! // This morning this note spread throughout Warsaw" (part 1, 46). An authorial footnote off of this sentence explains, however, that "after an intervention by the Jewish Community [*fun der yidisher gemeynde*] the date [*termin*] was postponed" (part 1, 46), whereafter the text abruptly moves in a different direction. It first draws our attention to a story that catches Bernard's eye in a Lodz newspaper (Skalov reproduces an entire page of this—real or invented—story, a melodramatic romance), then recounts the traumatizing humiliation and rape of Jewish women by Nazi officers in Lodz.[18] Skalov's allusion to the establishment of a ghetto here is clearly to the Germans' first plan to set up a ghetto in Warsaw, revealed to the Jewish Council on November 4, 1939. Word of this plan spread quickly among Warsaw Jews.[19]

We can likely infer from Skalov's narrative that he initially thought that the November 1939 order to set up a ghetto would be something he would be writing about at length; but when the order was soon abandoned he continued in a different direction. His footnote is written with the knowledge of a certain degree of hindsight—he knows that the plan has been postponed —but still with no firm knowledge of when the ghetto would eventually be established (a year later, in November 1940). Presumably this had not yet occurred.[20]

Early on in part 2 of "Di hak," subtitled "Quo Vadis," the middle-class Wolf family decides to rent a bigger apartment near Iron Gate Square (Plac Zelaznej Bramy).[21] The guests at the housewarming talk about forced labor and the news that Jews must leave certain city neighborhoods (part 2, 19). While we now know that in forcing Jews to leave certain areas for others over the course of 1940 the Germans were preparing to establish the ghetto, throughout much of 1940 exactly where, or even if, a ghetto would be created in Warsaw remained a subject of debate among German authorities and of rumor and speculation among Warsaw Jews. Skalov's narrative perspective betrays no knowledge that the forced removal of Jews from their homes was part of the process of establishing the ghetto because, we can again infer, this outcome remained far from clear to Skalov as he was writing this portion of the work. Everything suggests that Skalov is essentially looking sidelong rather than back at the events he is novelizing.

We cannot be certain how soon after the German invasion of the Soviet Union in June 1941—the last historical event alluded to in the novel—Skalov broke off work on his manuscript, but it seems unlikely to have been more than a few months—at most—thereafter. The only hard date we have is that the first cache of the Oyneg Shabes documents, including Skalov's novel, was buried on August 3, 1942, in the context of the Great Deportation. Skalov's reportage on the punktn, however, is dated November 1941, and since the last part of his novel ventures into the milieu of the punktn, it seems likely that he moved from the novel to that reportage, a point I will return to at the end of this chapter. Such a progression would suggest that he stopped writing the novel in the summer or fall of 1941.

OVERVIEW OF THE EXPOSITION AND ACTION OF SKALOV'S NOVEL

Skalov's novel presents a particularly thorny example of a problem familiar to scholars who work on little-known texts, that of how much to summarize. Skalov's novel reads like a breathless summary of itself—and this dense summary is not easily summarized. There are no neat through-lines or other ordering principles that structure the whole. Indeed, as I argue, the text exhibits a series of failed attempts to achieve such global coherence. Furthermore, because Skalov's novel is virtually unknown (and Ber Mark's 1954 edition is corrupt), a substantial summary is both more necessary than usual and inherently more awkward. While my account of (much) of the novel's main characters, events, concerns, and subplots (in a real sense, there are only subplots) is tidier than the text itself, at the risk of trying readers' patience, I want it to convey a sense of the sheer density of the action and of how Skalov's serial attempts to organize the work around socially rich topographical sites and to deploy typical novelistic plots only ever manage to gain limited structural purchase on the shifting traumatic events. I hope this overview of the only extant novel written (in part) in a Nazi ghetto will thus go some way in illuminating why the novel genre was so rare in ghettos. I hope it will furthermore illuminate how closely tied ghetto writing is to the micro-chronology of the moment of its composition and also provide some minimal familiarity with the specific moments in Skalov's text that I analyze later in the chapter.

To judge from the exposition, the differentiated social space of an apartment building, or *hoyf,* on Graniczna Street in Warsaw was to serve as the novel's center of gravity. With so many of the tenement's residents displaced or dead within a few short months, however, the Graniczna hoyf could no longer serve this purpose. Skalov thus has the remaining residents abruptly be evacuated, and he reorganizes the work around a second building, this time on Zamenhof Street (which unlike Graniczna would eventually be incorporated into the ghetto). The Zamenhof building, however, likewise cannot bear the novelistic strain put on it of having to organize the growing chaos and desperation of ghetto existence, and eventually Skalov lets it literally collapse. The miserable Warsaw ghetto refugee centers, the punktn, provide the novel's last social space and novelistic ordering principle before Skalov abandons the project altogether.

Prominent among the Graniczna hoyf's residents are two branches of a family, the Bermans and the Shapiros. We get backstory about the family's history and economic background. The venerable patriarch of the family, Gedalye Berman, lives with his daughter-in-law Hodes (her husband, Gedalye's son, died before the novel begins) and her children, Bernard, Aron, and Ede. Gedalye's daughter Mine and her husband Yoysef Shapiro, an accountant, and their only child, Rafael, a humanities student at the University of Warsaw, occupy a different flat in the same building. Bernard Berman, in Polish military uniform, boards a train to the front in the novel's opening scene. Yoysef and Rafael are in Vishkov (Wyszków) on their annual father-son summer getaway, delayed this year by Rafael's months-long hospitalization in the wake of being stabbed in an attack on Jewish university students.

The Berman-Shapiro clan's hoyf neighbors represent different class strata. The resourceful but economically precarious Srolke lives in a cellar apartment with his wife Beyle and their five children: Salek (eighteen years old), who is in love with Sabine, the daughter of Shifra the butcher's wife; Zsheni (fourteen years old); and three younger daughters. Also living in the cellar apartment are Beyle's sister Blimtshe and her husband Sender, whose family connections in Lodz provide the most significant window in "Di hak" onto events unfolding there. Several other occupants gather in this cellar apartment during the German air raids, notably Mr. and Mrs. Wolf, representatives of the Jewish bourgeoisie; their daughter, Lolo; and their Jewish nanny, Lize. We also meet the very decent Polish building superintendent Walenti, his wife, and their son Wacław. All the ingredients for a social portrait of the wartime experiences of different classes and generations of Warsaw Jews (and some non-Jews) seem to have been assembled.

Even by the end of part 1, however, dated New Year's 1940, few of the apartment building's residents are still residing in it, and many are dead. We can be fairly confident that Skalov planned from the outset to have Yoysef and Rafael die as victims of a massacre of Jewish civilians near Vishkov and that news of this historical atrocity that occurred in September 1939, in the course of the German invasion of Poland, was what inspired Skalov to "send" father and son there in the text's opening pages.[22] But it is hard to imagine Skalov anticipating that so little of the social microcosm his exposition introduces would remain only a few historical and novelistic months later. By the end of 1939, the grandfather Gedalye, a traditional Jew, has been harassed and humiliated by Germans and has suffered a fatal heart attack while performing forced labor. The teenaged lovers Salek and Sabine die shortly after being rescued from their weeks-long entrapment beneath the rubble of a bombed building. Beyle's husband and Salek and Zsheni's father, Srolke, is also dead. He has been resourceful in providing for his family, for example working as a glazer replacing bombed-out windows as winter approaches. Eventually, however, he is reduced to earning money by substituting himself for others selected by the Germans for forced labor details. After being made to stand all day in the rain, he becomes ill and loses first his wits and then his life.

Several characters have left for the Soviet Union, including Mr. and Mrs. Wolf (although Skalov will bring them back in part 2) and two of Hodes's three children, Ede and Aron, the latter of whom has left with Lize, the Wolfs' nanny. Before leaving for the Soviet Union, Ede travels to Lodz in the hope of obtaining thread (*fodem*) in order to secure income by putting her grandfather Gedalye's knitting (*trikotaszh*) machine to use. While there, as I have already alluded to, she is nabbed on the street by German soldiers, and made with other Jewish women to scrub the floors and windows of a large apartment. Instead of being released in the evening, the exhausted women are ordered to go into the bathroom and wash their "dirty bodies." Then they are raped until morning. "The torture lasted the entire night. There was no shortage of men. They couldn't get enough of their prey. When day broke, the women were thrown out onto the street like mangy bitches [*kretsike tsoygn*]" (part 1, 48).

Skalov's wanton destruction of the novelistic microcosm of the Graniczna hoyf reflects the pervasive and indiscriminate violence experienced by Polish citizens and especially Polish Jews in these months. Even with his broad panorama of characters ostensibly meant to show diverse social and character types, Skalov simply did not have enough characters to depict the full range of violence and death visited on his community. It may be an index of a realization that there was precious little of his original novelistic conception left to work with that in the final pages of part 1 Skalov proceeds to kill off three further characters in rather arbitrary ways. Hodes and Bernard, the only two characters left living in the Bermans' apartment, are robbed and shot to death by Polish bandits. Wacław Walenti, the son of the building's superintendent, is executed one day after reprimanding fellow Poles for attacking and robbing Jews. Thus by the end of part 1, of the Berman-Shapiro clan only Mine (Yoysef's wife and Rafael's mother) is left in the building on Graniczna. More characters from the basement apartment remain: Beyle (Srolke's widow) and their daughter Zsheni and her three younger sisters, as well as Blimtshe, Sender, and their infant son. Shifra the butcher's wife is alive and will appear in part 2; Walenti the superintendent remains alive, but he all but drops out of the novel.

Skalov populates part 2 of his novel, subtitled "Quo Vadis," by and large with a new cast of characters. The hoyf on Graniczna plays a far less central role and functions less as a social microcosm and more as a centripetal contrivance, a shared reference point tenuously linking far-flung events and characters.[23] The first event that Skalov treats at length in part 2 is a novelized version of a historical massacre of Jewish POWs. Seven hundred Jewish POWs are being forcibly marched by German soldiers north from Lublin in the direction of Biała Podlaska, between the shtetlekh of Lubartov (Lubartów) and Partshev (Parczew). The vast majority are murdered, particularly in the course of one night when they are forced into barns and then removed, twenty at a time, and machine-gunned to death. Not all the POWs are shot, but of those who are, only two survive, Moyshe and Dovid. Dovid turns out to be the younger brother and brother-in-law of Sender and Blimtshe of the crowded Graniczna cellar apartment.

In a related, similarly contrived plot line, a boy named Shiye escapes a concentration camp near Königsberg after his grandfather and twin brother have been shot to death. Shiye makes his way to Warsaw, where Dovid and Moyshe recognize him. We learn in a flashback that their POW camp had been next to Shiye's concentration camp and that they had seen him when he was forced to bury his own kin. Through Dovid and Moyshe, Shiye gets a room with Mine Shapiro, now the chair of the house committee of the hoyf on Graniczna. Although Skalov tenuously connects these far-flung episodes back to the Graniczna hoyf, there is only one major scene in part 2 still set there, a charity evening to help its most needy residents (I will return to this scene below). Roughly one-third into part 2 (on page 31 of the 104-page typescript), the few remaining residents of the building are evacuated, and the Graniczna hoyf plays no further role (although several of its former residents certainly do).

Albeit representative of similar evacuations in the summer of 1940, Skalov's novelistic evacuation of the building on Graniczna may have been driven more by the crumbling of his originally envisioned novelistic architecture than by any particular historical event. It is possible that the text presumes readers will understand the evacuation of the Graniczna hoyf as part of the preparations for the coming ghetto, but this is far from clear. Whereas characters in a scene some ten pages prior to this one (and set ostensibly in August 1940) discuss the news that Jews must leave certain city neighborhoods, the evacuation of the building on Graniczna is presented more as an arbitrary than a systematic action by the SS: "From time to time on the order of the SS an apartment here or a building there was emptied of all its residents. The evacuation usually happened in a matter of minutes. The house on Graniczna was subject to such an order" (part 2, 31).[24] On August 23, 1940, the *Gazeta Zydowska* reported on the division of Warsaw into three districts (Jewish, Polish, and German) and on August 31 published a list of boundary streets of the Jewish district, with Marszałkowska as the border along the district's southeastern edge.[25] This plan would have left Graniczna within the topography of the Jewish district, suggesting that Skalov was not motivated by the anticipation that the hoyf on Graniczna would soon fall outside the Jewish district (whether sealed as a ghetto or not). It is also instructive to consider the example of Aleksander Ford's feature film from the early post-war era, *Ulica Graniczna* (Border street, 1948), which, consistent with Skalov's ostensible initial plan, traces the fates of different residents (Jews, Jewish converts to Catholicism, Poles, and Polish ethnic Germans) in an apartment building on the very same street, Graniczna. The Jewish Libermann family is not made to leave their home until they are forced into the ghetto. Had Skalov seen a rationale for continuing to anchor his novel in the Graniczna hoyf, he could have done so longer than he did. Presumably he chose not to because he could already see that this initially envisioned social microcosm was no longer capable of accommodating the violence and social disruption with which Warsaw Jews were contending.

Skalov significantly expands the circle of bourgeois Jews, which the Wolfs had represented in part 1, introducing several new characters. The Wolfs had left for the USSR in part 1, but in part 2, Skalov brings them back as part of a population exchange in March 1940.[26] Having forfeited their spacious apartment when they left, they find the room they are able to sublet upon their return too cramped. The housewarming for the Wolf's new apartment near Iron Gate Square introduces us to this middle-class milieu, which includes Fayfer, "the insouciant Christian convert [*meshumed*] of the family" (part 2, 19), a dentist in the vicinity of Zshuravye (Zurawia) Street, whose pious Catholic and thoroughly Polish-identified children are distraught to learn that they are now considered Jews. Also in attendance is Mrs. Wolf's (or Estusia's; only after being brought back in part 2 does she receive a first name) sister Perle, Perle's husband, Khemye Fusnagl, and their twelve-year-old son Leybush.

Khemye owns an apartment building on Zamenhof Street, which will effectively if only temporarily replace the Graniczna hoyf as the residence of most of the significant characters in part 2, including Khemye's sister Gute and her husband, Albert, after they are evicted from their home on Marshalkovske (Marszałkowska) Street, as well as of several of the characters evacuated from the Graniczna tenement—Mine; Beyle and her infant son and daughter Zsheni; Blimtshe and her infant son; and Blimtshe's brother-in-law Dovid. The sisters Beyle and Blimtshe (and their children) plus Dovid move into the cellar apartment of the married couple Yankl and Fanye, who have a malnourished infant daughter. This basement apartment is also frequented by Moyshe (the co-survivor with Dovid of the POW massacre in part 1) and an attractive young woman named Reyzl. There are few opportunities for securing income; Yankl is reduced to going to work "for the Germans" each day for a meager wage (part 2, 74–75). Moyshe has the idea of converting the kitchen into a laundry (*vesheray*), which they do, temporarily providing everyone with work. The fate of these poor characters is played off that of the (erstwhile) Jewish bourgeoisie inhabiting the upper floors and in this way reproduces the upstairs-downstairs social dynamics of the building on Graniczna.

Skalov continues to work with representative types and has them experience key fates. Such characters include the "good German" in the guise of the Wehrmacht officer Herr Nickel, a friend of Albert's from Albert's extended sojourn studying metallurgy in Berlin. A Goethe- and Schiller-quoting humanist who admires the Jews, Herr Nickel disdains the Nazis and deems socialism the only viable way to end hatred between peoples. Adding to the examples of good Poles from part 1 such as superintendent Walenti, his son Wacław, and a peasant couple who discover and try to aid the dying Rafael after he has been shot in the massacre near Vishkov, we meet an unpretentious young woman from the country, Wanda, who has worked as domestic help for some of the novel's bourgeois Jewish characters. Wanda and Dovid fall in love, but she is taken away to Germany, allegedly to perform agricultural labor, but, as she writes in secret messages hidden beneath stamps on the postcards she is made to send with falsely rosy accounts of her well-being, she has in fact been forced into a brothel, where she eventually dies. We also see morally dishonorable Jews: the Christian convert Fayfer, for example, puts himself "in the service of the enemies and [becomes] an informant" (part 2, 42). Eventually, Moyshe becomes a Jewish policeman, although, at this early stage, the characters around him do not seem to resent his decision, which is presented as, on Moyshe's part, pursuit of income after his other attempts to secure a livelihood have ceased to be viable.[27]

Smuggling figures among the major ghetto phenomena Skalov treats. Late in the novel, the narrator informs us that the hoyf in which Moyshe's fiancée, Reyzl, and her mother live on Swietojerska Street had previously also had an entrance on Długe. Internally divided with the Długe side Aryan and the Shvientoyerska side Jewish, this hoyf has now become a site of smuggling activity by both Christians and Jews (part 2, 81). After Moyshe moves in with Reyzl, he decides to start smuggling as well. Smuggling is lucrative but risky. While Moyshe and Dovid are selling haberdashery out of a suitcase on the Eyzer-Nestoyer Square on New Year's Eve (1940–1941), a man in civilian dress leads a uniformed German soldier to them to check their permits. With images of the executions at Lubartov and Partshev flashing before their eyes, Moyshe and Dovid make a run for it. Dovid escapes but Moyshe succumbs to a bullet fired by the soldier.

Skalov also sutures into his text the harrowing experiences of Jewish men sent to labor camps. Both Albert and Khemye are nabbed on the street. But whereas Khemye is able to produce documentation from the Judenrat falsely vouching that he worked there, the impractical Albert, not having secured any such papers, comes to share the bitter fate of the poor. Even after being thrown out of his apartment on Marshalkovske (Marszałkowska), life had still had a meaning for Albert.[28] Now, however, the poorest shack was a palace compared to the conditions he and his fellow workers have to endure (part 2, 59). There is no straw; the workers sleep on dried dung. Albert is ill and receives beatings daily. He anticipates being shot by someone in uniform and joining the ever-increasing number of corpses in the field (60). A tall, twenty-year-old youth named Wotek distinguishes himself among the labor camp guards in his boorish sadism. The camp where Albert and Wotek encounter each other as prisoner and guard is Belzec—in its first incarnation as a labor camp before it later became a killing center.[29]

In another of the novel's contrived coincidences, Wotek turns out to be the only son of Mazur, a brute and opportunistic ethnically German Pole who plays a central role in the main novelistic subplot that occurs between the bombings of Warsaw and immediate occupation of Poland, and the establishment of the ghetto. It is a tragic story of infidelity, a sort of lowbrow, miniature *Madame Bovary* or *Effi Briest* set against the changing social and power dynamics of Jews and Poles under the German occupation in 1940. Before the war Mazur was the owner of a modest tearoom, but under the occupation he seizes the opportunity to profit from his (distant and possibly specious) Swabian ancestry. As a Volksdeutscher Mazur manages to become the commissar for the apartment buildings—including Khemye's—on Zamenhof Street.

More importantly, Mazur and Estusia enter into an affair. Skalov depicts several instances where the changing circumstances under the German occupation, and eventually the ghetto, dramatically affect people's romantic and sexual lives. The heretofore always docile Gute, for example, erupts at her husband Albert, whom she perceives to be an ineffectual intellectual incapable of managing under the trying new circumstances (part 2, 53–54). Indeed, when not novelizing key events and typical experiences of ghetto life, Skalov continues to rely heavily on conventional novelistic triangulations of desire, albeit desire transformed by the unprecedented circumstances. As she is falling for Mazur, Estusia comes to see her husband as the embodiment of the weak, emasculated *goles-yid* (Jew wearied by exile; part 2, 28). Further, as part of a complex set of relationships of desire, jealousy, and traumatization among mostly poorer characters late in the novel, Reyzl finally stops resisting the significantly older Moyshe's advances—despite having earlier signaled her romantic indifference to him and her sense of him as an older brother—after she is publicly humiliated and abused. Uniformed German soldiers seize Reyzl on the street and force her to dance at length with an elderly Jew, to the shock and disgust of passersby. Shortly thereafter, she gets caught up in a *reynigungsaktsye* (from the German *Reinigungsaktion*, literally a cleaning "action," or round-up). As described in Skalov's novel these notorious actions involved putting Jewish buildings under quarantine, ostensibly due to typhus. The residents were sent to steam baths, and the Polish disinfectors would come in and plunder at will. Reyzl is sent to such a bath, where her hair is cut off.[30] Only after this double dose of abuse and humiliation does a broken Reyzl welcome the devoted Moyshe as her fiancé (part 2, 79–80). Upon Moyshe's announcement that he and Reyzl are getting married, Beyle comments to Moyshe that if not for the war he'd never have gotten her, and Blimtshe wisecracks, "You've won the war and are laughing at the world" (part 2, 80).

Mazur's brutish character reveals itself fully as his and Estusia's affair advances. Claiming he is taking her to a movie theater (forbidden for Jews), he takes her to a hotel room. Mazur succeeds in breaking down the thoroughly disgusted Estusia's resistance only by threatening to destroy her family. He has sex with her in degrading ways while she remains in a frozen, lifeless state. Eventually police knock on the door and take Estusia into custody (hotels were also forbidden to Jews), and it takes a hefty bribe from Khemye to get her out (part 2, 41). In the aftermath of this affair, whose tawdry reality gave the lie to the fantasies Estusia had lost herself in, Estusia becomes depressed and attempts to kill herself and her daughter Lolo by opening the gas valve in their kitchen. Wolf discovers his wife and daughter in time to save Estusia, but Lolo is dead (part 2, 46).[31] While the text does refer to Estusia's moral "fall" (part 2, 42), there is little overt moralizing, and the narration as well as certain characters, especially Mine, show considerable empathy for Estusia. This tragedy obviously complicates the Wolfs' marriage, but it does not end it, and they relocate to Khemye's building. Eventually, however, Wolf disappears and later writes to Estusia from a provincial town about how his life with her had become a hell that he needed to flee (part 2, 68). The Wolfs seem to reconcile at Lolo's grave near the very end of the text (part 2, 97). As a pendant to her earlier tragedy, Estusia is swindled late in the text out of her last diamond, which she was planning to sell in the hopes of getting an apartment and starting anew with Wolf. Wolf suspects that Fayfer set her up (part 2, 99).

The extent to which Skalov invests in this melodramatic romance plot is remarkable (it dominates pages 36–48 of part 2). The scene that follows this novelistic miniature is set in fall (1940), so we can infer that the Estusia-Mazur interlude occurred in spring and summer 1940. While as Agnieszka Żółkiewska and Marek Tuszewicki note, the ill-fated fictional romance points up "a real social problem connected to the behavioral changes among Jewish women in the ghetto, for whom maintaining sexual contacts with the non-Jews was one of the ways to survive," Skalov does not really present Estusia's affair with Mazur as responding to such a predicament (it also predates the establishment of the ghetto).[32] Estusia and Wolf are still living relatively comfortably, and we are not given the sense that Estusia acts out of a desperate need to survive. Skalov's romantic plot seems more banal than this: not unlike Emma Bovary, Estusia seems bored with her husband and loses herself in romantic fantasies powerful enough to temporarily bestow erotic enticement upon even the brutish Mazur. One way to understand Skalov's recourse to such a novelistic set piece is as an attempt to revert to a standard novelistic scenario after the trauma of the German invasion and occupation of Poland—including specific forms of violence directed at Polish Jews—had exploded his original novelistic architecture. That there was just enough time to squeeze in a miniature *Madame Bovary*, so to speak, between the initial violence and shock of the German attack, on the one hand, and the establishment of the ghetto, on the other, may be an index of both the fact that in the first half of 1940 the historical circumstances of formerly better-off Jews, who still had some savings to live on, were not yet entirely abject, and of Skalov's ongoing wish to see the hopes, desires, agency, and fate of the Jews of Warsaw as compatible with the individualized and class-inscribed experiences, however tragic they might be, of characters in the novelistic tradition.

The fate of Jews in the Warsaw ghetto in the winter of 1940–1941 would make continued adherence to standard novelistic characters and plots increasingly difficult. While compared to later periods in the history of the Warsaw ghetto and, obviously, the period of the Great Deportation of summer 1942, the initial period of the ghetto treated in Skalov's novel from November 1940 to June 1941 could only seem relatively less awful, that period was catastrophic and unprecedented in its own right. The early period of the ghetto was plagued by extreme overcrowding, rampant poverty and starvation, and epidemics of typhus and other diseases. Even before the ghetto was sealed, 90,000 Jewish refugees arrived in Warsaw—refugees from areas annexed to the Third Reich, refugees from Krakow, and Jewish POWs.[33] A second wave of about 50,000 deportees from the western area of the District of Warsaw into the since-sealed ghetto between January and the end of March 1941 swelled the ghetto's population to its peak of 460,000 people. Due above all to the high mortality rate, the ghetto population would shrink, despite a constant influx of transportees, to 415,000 in autumn 1941.

Having few possessions and usually few connections, the refugees and deportees into the ghetto, numbering some 130,000 in April 1941, experienced extreme difficulties securing dwellings. They were commonly assigned to refugee centers, the punktn. April 1941 saw the largest number of people in such centers: 17,000. The number of such centers peaked at 165 in May 1941 and then fell systematically.[34] This most vulnerable population experienced the highest mortality rates in the ghetto.[35] In April 1941 the number of new typhus cases began to spike dramatically, with the epidemic reaching its height in summer and autumn of 1941. Even more catastrophic than the typhus epidemic were deaths due to malnutrition. The chronic shortage of food in the ghetto during its first six months caused death rates from starvation to soar to above 1,000 for the month of February 1941, over 2,000 in March, and 3,800 in May. As a report by the German *Oberfeldkommandant* in Warsaw of May 20, 1941, described, "The situation in the Jewish quarter is catastrophic. The corpses of those who have died of starvation lie in the streets. The death rate, 80 percent from malnutrition, has tripled since February."[36]

This period of refugee crisis, extreme overcrowding, starvation, epidemic, and soaring death rates is the historical context that Skalov tries to integrate into the final part of his evolving novelistic project. Even as he turns to the fate of poorer and abjectly destitute characters, Skalov continues in part to deploy constellations of desire as a sort of novelistic glue; but while the romantic plot he limns involving Fanye, Yankl, Reyzl, and Moyshe permits him to infuse their relationships with drama and to introduce backstory, the romantic plot is unable to sustain itself in the face of the ambient mass suffering and death.

The final chapters of Skalov's novel—chapters 10–13, or pages 74–104 of the typescript—by and large turn away from the wealthier people in Khemye's orbit to focus on the fates of the poor. With Mine's help, Beyle moves into Fanye and Yankl's cellar apartment in Khemye's building. Beyle's sister

Blimtshe and Blimtshe's brother-in-law Dovid likewise move in. Yankl and Fanye have a young daughter, and Beyle and Blimtshe each have young sons. As previously noted, on the suggestion of Dovid's friend Moyshe, the inhabitants of this crowded apartment, all struggling to feed their children and themselves, convert the kitchen into a laundry. The warm apartment becomes a popular place for people to gather. In addition to Moyshe, Reyzl is among those who frequently drop in. The following romantic plot emerges: Yankl and Reyzl were each other's first love, and they still have strong feelings for each other. Reyzl's father, a wealthy carpenter, however, would not accept Yankl, a poor orphan, as a match for his daughter.[37] As also noted above, Moyshe pursues Reyzl—unsuccessfully until she is broken by a series of humiliations at the hands of the Nazis and accepts his marriage proposal, to Fanye's great relief.

This characteristically novelistic romantic plot, however, is overwhelmed by the abject misery against which it is set. Skalov devotes much of his text to depicting the collective misery. The scale of suffering becomes difficult to channel through individual characters.

> "I'm hungry . . ."
>
> This cry was screamed from basement rooms, from attic apartments, from movie theaters, elementary schools and houses of study and prayer, from all the "punktn" where the destitute from the provinces and Warsaw were concentrated. Enfeebled people lay on the street, and it seemed as if the slabs of the sidewalk emitted the desperate cry:
>
> Bread, bread, bread . . .
>
> The alarming shout hovered over courtyards, over streets and squares, was screamed from hundreds, from thousands of mouths like a lonely voice in the vastness of the desert:
>
> "I'm hungry . . ."

When Skalov does use familiar characters to convey the abject suffering, they tend to become engulfed by it and at times slip below the threshold of subjective integrity generally required of novelistic personas.

Skalov's shift from the crowded cellar apartment—and from the upstairs-downstairs logic in which it participates—to an exploration of far more dire mass poverty, misery, and death involves the abandonment of Khemye's building on Zamenhof, the site that had chiefly served to organize the novel since the residents of the hoyf on Graniczna had died, left for the Soviet Union, or been evicted. As I argued was the case when Skalov abandoned the Graniczna hoyf, here again he seems motivated less by ineluctable topographical realities than by a realization that the (in this case literal) architecture of his novel was not equipped to do justice to the new circumstances. We can see Skalov's lack of anticipation of his novel's shift of focus away from Khemye's building in the abruptness with which it occurs and the weak rationale he invents for it. We learn only on page 90 (of 104) of part 2 that the German bombardments of Warsaw had left a crack in Khemye's building, which neither Khemye nor Commissar Mazur had adequately heeded. As a result, amidst a thunderous noise, the roof suddenly falls to the floor. Mine, Khemye, and Estusia had all moved out slightly earlier; Albert and Perle are injured but survive; and their son Leybush was not in the building at the time. The basement apartment where Fanye and Yankl and their subletters live remains intact but is too dangerous to remain in. The laundry there had at any rate ceased to be lucrative due to the rising price of coal and soap. Thus Beyle, Blimtshe, and their children, as well as Yankl, Fanye, and their daughter, all take a room in one of the punktn, together with the "hundred thousand other homeless who were hoping for support from the Judenrat and the American Joint" (part 2, 90). The final pages of the text are dominated by the milieus of the punktn and the streets, each filled with the desperate and dying.

We see the undoing of human subjectivity (and novelistic character) in the figure of Beyle's daughter Zsheni, who has been a character in the novel from the outset and has featured in important scenes intermittently throughout. She was injured, disfigured, and temporarily blinded in the bombings of Warsaw, went missing, and was ultimately found. She becomes close with the Wolfs' nanny, Lize, to whom she confides her desire to write a story after she recovers her health, a story not of someone's life but of how they want their life to be (part 1, 30). This sort of novelistic signaling early in Skalov's text leads readers to expect Zsheni to emerge eventually as a writer, but Skalov's text never makes good on this novelistic promise. Instead we ultimately witness Zsheni slipping beneath the threshold of personhood due to starvation.

Her and her siblings' final descent begins on a day when coupons for bread are distributed. A boy on the street snatches the bread Zsheni has in her basket, and it is soon devoured by several boys, who even lick up the crumbs along with manure from the dirty pavement. On that day Beyle's children become street beggars, whose cries fall on deaf ears (part 2, 92). Weakened from time in a work camp, Yankl is also reduced to singing on the street. Zsheni helps him as he sings his own songs and songs from the orphanage where he grew up. They occasionally receive a couple of groschen, but a whole day's income will not buy even a bowl of *borsht*. Soon they are reduced to sticking their hand out in silence and develop weakness of the heart, swollen feet (or legs; *fis*), darkness under the eyes, and foam on their lips.

We last glimpse Zsheni sitting apathetically on the stairs of the courthouse (*gerikhts-palats*) on Lesh (Leszno) Street. She is as if turned to stone, with pale, vacuous eyes and dry lips. Only her chest moves, almost imperceptibly. Passersby notice the girl's translucent body. Someone puts a piece of candy in her mouth, someone rubs her temples. From somewhere a glass of lemonade appears, a spoon of soup. Finally, her teeth move, and her eyes pop out. The Jewish police stop in front of the courthouse to collect the people lying on the sidewalk, their bodies like desiccated straw. These "living skeletons" will be put into quarantine because the Power (the Germans) have demanded *Ordnung* at all costs (part 2, 93). Skalov's text does not state but certainly implies that Zsheni is taken by the Jewish police at this time.

While Zsheni sinks into the anonymous collectivity of living skeletons facing imminent death, the promise of writing that she had earlier held devolves to Yankl, who comes to embody the question of the possibility of writing in the face of mass starvation and death—questions that carry self-reflexive urgency for Skalov's project. Though poor and uneducated, even as a child Yankl felt a connection to poetry (part 2, 102). He tries to earn money for bread by singing his songs in the streets but as already mentioned falls ineluctably into silent begging.

Skalov's novelistic drama appears increasingly labile as its protagonists experience the ravages of ghetto existence. After Moyshe's death Dovid and Reyzl have become partners in smuggling, and the two of them occasionally visit the ailing Yankl at the punkt on 3 Dzshike Street. They bring Yankl a meal, but this only depresses him. Fanye also feels oppressed by Reyzl's attractive appearance. She hides her swollen legs as if they are a mark of shame and forces her lips into a smile. Yankl looks over a little sheet of paper. He bites his lips and does not move a limb. "Does he possess real talent? Is he capable of depicting the deep sorrow of the good Fanye? How she hides from him her powerlessness and is expiring quietly like a candle. Can he depict his own powerlessness, pain, grief, grievances?" (part 2, 102). Unlike another resident at the Dzshike 3 punkt, who is holding out hope of receiving aid from a rich relative in America, Yankl, an orphan, is not waiting for any miracles. Instead, he seeks recourse in poetry to express himself and the weight he has always felt of his class and his people. Yet he recognizes the cruel paradox that marks his quest to capture hunger in verse: doing so requires a full stomach:

"You can only depict hunger in its full horror when you are full [*zaterheyt*]" (part 2, 102).

Remembering being seventeen and falling in love with the daughter of his employer, Yankl apostrophizes his first love: "Reyzl, whose finger will set back the hand of time?" (part 2, 102). This moment both continues a melodramatic novelistic strategy and acknowledges its inadequacy. Just as Yankl is nostalgic for Reyzl and an earlier romantic innocence, Skalov's novel is nostalgic for an earlier time when it could be a conventional novel; it is now a dying novel nostalgic for itself as a novel. The answer to Yankl's question comes in the allegoric figure Fanye resembles in her emaciated state: she has become the figure of Death with his sickle, the figure of Hunger (103). Yankl looks out the window, seeking answers and succor in the night sky. The scale of hunger has indeed taken on cosmic proportions: "As if, from a howl somewhere, a gnashing of stars and skies were buzzing in his ears amid the silence of endless space—that is how the awful lament of the spirit [*vey-lid fun gemit*] wailed for which Yankl was supposed to find the glowing word, the expression in verse" (103). Yankl dies, pen in hand, with an uneaten piece of bread that Fanye had given him in his mouth, over his unwritten poem, "Dos lid fun hunger" (The song of hunger). In his quest to find the glowing word, the expression in verse—the lament—of hunger, Yankl gets no further than the title.

Skalov's self-reflexively resonant decision to have Yankl pursue verse adequate to hunger is anticipated by a slightly earlier, equally self-reflexive moment involving the humanist intellectual Albert. Albert walks the ghetto streets in the early morning. Skalov depicts the people of the ghetto as a dehumanized throng, an abject, collective, gangrenous ooze. The normally individual category of a "has-been" now becomes collective. Skalov depicts a mass of *gevezene* (former or erstwhile people), against which rare individuals who have managed to benefit from the ghetto's black-market economy conspicuously stand out.

> Ghetto, early morning. Every open gate pressed out poor people with tarry clothing [*farsmalyetn onton*]. Each door was blackened like a gangrenous wound from which, from early morning on, there flowed a constant sticky ooze [*klepike rope*]. The street filled up with a stream of rubbed-out human figures. Here and there the red lips of a made-up female smuggler, or the tan neck of a wealthy merchant, would flash out from among the mass of 'erstwhilers' [*gevezene*].

> Albert sought a powerful word that would express the meaning of the present time. (part 2, 99)

As he grapples for adequate expression for the increasingly abject reality of the ghetto, Albert attempts to relate to the suffering people on a human and individual level by distributing alms on the street. "He looks at those lying on the street. The shadow of Belzec had not stopped pursuing him. Albert dug in his pockets like someone who wants to give away his whole worth [*farmegn*], to buy himself out and be free of a great torment" (99). The early hour notwithstanding, Albert is immediately swarmed by starving street children who press him, pull his sleeves and hands and ask, "'Us, us too, why not us, good gentleman.' . . . Albert felt caught in a sticky web from which it was impossible to extricate himself" (100).[38] The need of the destitute street children is too great for Albert to meaningfully address by distributing the limited money he possesses. Even as he seeks to protect his own individual integrity by distributing the resources at his command to individuals, these individuals quickly become a throng that threatens to engulf him and overwhelm his integrity as an individual altogether. Albert manages to extricate himself, barely, from the swarming children by jumping into a rickshaw. He recalls his brother-in-law Khemye's warning: "You're insane if you think you can feed the whole world." Khemye's word *insane* leads to Albert's negative epiphany: voilà the expression he had been seeking: "oysnzinikeyt, psikhos" (insanity, psychosis). "Insane is what the people are who caused the war, whose system is a method of destruction but never of construction [*boyung*]. Insane is also what the animalistic ego is that allows death by starvation in the middle of the street" (100). Seeking to express the sense of the ghetto, Albert finds only senselessness, insanity.

To say that toward the end of his novel project Skalov was grappling with questions of the viability of literature, esthetic form, and, surely, of the genre of the novel to capture the tale of Polish Jewish society in crisis would be an understatement. As the novel shifts its attention increasingly toward mass abjection in the streets and refugee centers, not only does it seem impossible to salvage an overarching narrative arc that could hold the novel together, but the status of human subjectivity itself becomes so threatened that characters begin to fall below the threshold required of novelistic individuals; they enter the anonymous—and oozing—mass of suffering. As I will return to in the conclusion of this chapter, it is thus highly significant that the final pages of Skalov's novel manuscript gesture toward two non-novelistic genres—the lyric poem (Yankl's unwritten "Song of Hunger") and the reportage—insofar as Skalov's treatment of those dirty, lice-filled centers for desperate and dying refugees in "Di hak" resembles, and presumably led into, his next major undertaking as a writer, a reportage about conditions in the punktn and the experience of their inhabitants. Poetry and reportage would prove far more viable genres than the novel for depicting the unprecedented, catastrophic, and fast-changing circumstances in the Warsaw (and other) ghettos. Had Skalov not already started his novel in fall 1939 and wished to continue it, one can wonder whether he would have attempted a novel at all from within the ghetto. At any rate, he broke his novel off and shifted to reportage after approximately the first seven or eight months of the ghetto's existence.

A HISTORICAL NOVEL OF THE EVER-SHIFTING PRESENT

Even though I have alluded to many of the novel's episodes and subplots, there are many more that I have not touched on. The text's various threads are indeed quite difficult to keep track of, especially because no central plot drives the narrative. As we have seen, to hold the would-be novel's far-flung episodes minimally together, Skalov had to resort to the sort of narrative contrivances that are familiar from popular postwar fictionalizations of the Holocaust like NBC's 1978 miniseries, *Holocaust*, in which members of the representative German Dorf and the Jewish Weiss families are victims of, or participants in, an implausible number of key sites and events of the Holocaust, including Kristallnacht, the Wannsee Conference, the Babi Yar Massacre, the Sobibor Revolt, the Warsaw Ghetto Uprising, Buchenwald, and Auschwitz. But the NBC miniseries—as well as less contrived attempts to represent the experience of the Warsaw ghetto in novel form such as John Hersey's 1950 *The Wall* or Bogdan Wojdowski's 1971 *Bread for the Departed*—sorts the "key" events it will depict by definition in retrospect.[39] Post-Holocaust works plot significant and representative events with the knowledge of hindsight, precisely what Skalov, writing in something approaching real time, lacked. In a 1973 essay, Chava Rosenfarb, who survived the Lodz ghetto, Auschwitz, and other camps, and went on to become a major postwar author of Yiddish poetry and prose, including the three-volume novel about the Lodz ghetto, *Der boym fun lebn* (*Tree of Life*; 1972), recalled her misgivings while contemplating writing a novel about the Holocaust: "Was not the novel too elegant and too polished a literary form for such a story, was it not too detached from any lived reality, too much a game of cleverly concocted plots? In writing a novel about the Holocaust would I not end by sinning against a reality that was impossible to encompass?" (Rosenfarb, *Confessions*, 17). Rosenfarb's reservations about the novel, as "too polished a literary form" inevitably straying from lived reality, certainly point up a tension evident in Skalov's project, which repeatedly signals plot arcs that the lived realities of the ghetto ultimately cancel. We can also see Skalov struggling with the sort of contrivances of plot that gave Rosenfarb pause, and also, in a quite self-reflexive manner, with how to represent an overwhelming reality that was becoming impossible to encompass. The crucial difference, again, however, is that Rosenfarb grapples with these concerns from the perspective of a survivor wondering if it is possible to write "a novel about the Holocaust" from the postwar vantage point of knowing what the Holocaust is. Skalov, in contrast, began writing his novel not knowing that what we call the Holocaust was taking shape. Whereas Rosenfarb's knowledge of the Holocaust gives rise to her doubts about the adequacy of the form of the novel, Skalov starts with faith in the viability of the genre to accommodate all possible coming events. The repeated literal and figurative collapses of the novelistic architecture he tries to erect, and his shift into reportage and the evocation of lyric poetry in the last pages of his project, are all measures of the extent to which the unprecedented events he was trying to novelize implacably diverged from novelistic conventions.

Reviewers of the 1954 edition of Skalov's novel (who were unaware that this version was bowdlerized and manipulated) underscored its shortcomings as a novel, in particular its lack of a central plot. Melech Ravitch wrote in a review in the Montreal Yiddish newspaper *Der keneder odler* (The Canadian eagle), "It would be irrelevant to rehearse the contents. It is the welter of a sinking ship, of a train wreck."[40] And Sholem Shtern wrote in the New-York based *Yidishe kultur* that the novel "lacks a narrative backbone" and "is not a unified work, not because [Skalov] wanted to incorporate too much (that too, perhaps) but because the events were so sudden, tragic, and convulsive that it was impossible to tie them together in one complete work. It is sooner a bundle of tragic events involving Jewish people who wrestle with death and ultimately succumb." (Sholem Shtern, "An interesante khronik fun khurbn yidishn-poyln," 45).

Shtern also aptly notes that Skalov's book is more of a chronicle than a novel.[41] Tension between the open-ended epistemology and temporality of a chronicle and the demands of novelistic coherence placed a massive strain on Skalov's attempt to novelize the chaotically unfolding events. This tension distinguishes Skalov's singular project as bold and important, even as it eventually rendered the project impossible to sustain.

For all the sheer conventionality of the novelistic devices "Di hak"—ultimately unsuccessfully—trades in, including melodramatic plot lines and stereotypical characters, Skalov's attempt to novelize the present in extreme crisis is virtually unprecedented. There are many genres that writers reach for to capture the present—including poem, diary, memoir, letter, and reportage—but the novel is rarely among them. Even novelistic approaches to (near-) contemporary crises such as World War I or, more recently, the AIDS crisis, 9/11, and the COVID-19 pandemic tend to adopt far less open-ended strategies than Skalov did in trying to accommodate unfolding events into a novelistic framework. While many soldier-poets famously wrote poems in the trenches of the Great War, novels appeared only years later. Erich Maria Remarque wrote *Im Westen nichts neues* (*All Quiet on the Western Front*), for example, in 1927–1928, a decade after the war ended. Rebecca Makkai's AIDS novel, *The Great Believers* (2018) similarly looks back—from an even greater remove—at the crisis of the 1980s. Topical novels frequently displace a contemporary crisis into an earlier historical moment. Emma Donoghue's *The Pull of the Stars* (2021), for example, is a COVID novel set in a Dublin hospital ward during the 1918 flu pandemic; similarly, Colum McCann's *Let the Great World Spin* is a 9/11 novel set mainly in the World Trade Center in 1975.

Of course, had Skalov survived, he may well have used his text, which often reads like a series of breathless sketches, as notes for a retrospective novel. One could thus argue that a better comparison between Skalov and novels that look back on crises or catastrophes might be the notes that authors have taken during ongoing catastrophes that they later drew on to write novels. Yet such a comparison would elide an absolutely crucial aspect of Skalov's undertaking. For however compressed and jagged Skalov's text may be, it strains to be a novel and not simply notes for a novel. Skalov really was attempting to novelize the shifting present of fall 1939 through summer 1941.

Israel Joshua Singer's novel *Di mishpokhe karnovski* (The family Carnovski, 1943) provides an illuminating contrast to the contingent temporality of Skalov's project. Anita Norich underscores how "the action of The Family Karnovski ends almost at the moment of publication in 1940–41." Norich continues: "Time . . . thus appears . . . cramped and even frenetic. Toward the novel's end, all sense of historical distance ends and, given the events it depicts, the present becomes disturbingly immediate. With no possibility of knowing exactly where current horror would lead, but with an almost paralyzing hopelessness, Singer tried to come to terms with the early moments of what we now call khurbn, or Holocaust."[42] Singer's strategies for dealing with the increasing convergence of historical and novelistic time ultimately differ markedly from Skalov's, however. As Norich notes, "Horror is controlled" in Singer's novel "when it is figured in the person of Yegor, a disturbed adolescent who confronts public tragedy in the form of personal trauma." By figuring the terrifying and uncontrollable events threatening Jewish life in Europe "metonymically" in Yegor, Norich argues, they become symbolically manageable: "Since history is too overwhelming in this novel, there is a shift to the individual whose progress and fate may, at least theoretically, be encompassed by the novel" (Norich, *Homeless*, 54). This sort of resort to allegory in which the multigenerational history of a Jewish family culminates in—and the history and collective fate of the Jews by extension is displaced onto—a traumatized individual struggling for his psychological health and identity was simply not available to Skalov given the circumstances that he sought to novelize in Warsaw and Poland more broadly. As Norich argues, Singer's novel acknowledges but also displaces attention away from the urgent and unresolved dangers facing European Jews. It was a strategy he could pursue from New York, a locus from which the fate of Jews in Europe loomed oppressive but also remained distant and relatively vague.

Irène Némirovsky's two-part novel *Suite française* is the perhaps most comparable project undertaken during the war years, yet it, too, contrasts markedly with Skalov's text. Némirovsky wrote the two loosely connected short novels that would become *Suite française* in the town of Issy-l'Evêque, where she and her family moved after the Germans occupied Paris in June 1940. She began her novelistic project, which she envisioned would comprise several additional parts, in 1941 and continued to work on it into June 1942, when she was arrested by the French police and deported to Auschwitz, where she died on August 17, 1942. (Although she and her husband had converted to Catholicism before the war, they were Jews according to the law defining Jewishness in terms of race passed in France on October 3, 1940.) The first part, *Storm in June,* depicts a range of different characters' experiences fleeing in the exodus from Paris as the German army was swiftly advancing in June 1940. We follow their material and psychological upheaval as they are forced to abruptly abandon their homes and routines and face an unknown and frightening future; and we see many of them return to Paris some weeks and months later when the initial shock and chaos of the German invasion have subsided. Part 2, *Dolce,* is set in the fictional village of Bussy, where we again follow a range of French characters as they negotiate their ethical and emotional relationships to each other under the Vichy regime and, especially, to a garrison of Wehrmacht soldiers billeted there for a three-month period between April 13 (Easter Sunday) and June 1, 1941, when the unit is deployed to Germany's new Russian front.

Like Skalov, Némirovsky novelizes events in the quite recent past, and both novels end at the same historical juncture, the German invasion of the Soviet Union. Yet the relationships between novel and current history in each work contrast starkly. Whereas Skalov takes a maximal approach to the events he tries to incorporate into his novel, Némirovsky decided to privilege esthetic coherence, which in her extant notes on her unfolding project she repeatedly conceives of by analogy to musical models, over historical substance.[43] While the events depicted in *Storm in June* are chaotic, they are also relatively uncomplicated and, from the vantage point from which Némirovsky was writing, already largely resolved: Parisians flee en masse, undergo shocking and traumatic upheaval, then (mostly) return to some sort of at least provisional stability. In *Dolce* relatively few major events occur, and the focus is squarely on the emotional and moral journey of the village inhabitants —and the occupying German soldiers—as they negotiate the terms of their fraught proximity amid the looming absence of the local young French men, most of whom have been removed to Germany as prisoners of war. While Némirovsky's own ultimately tragic situation was decidedly not resolved as she wrote *Dolce,* almost exactly one year after the fictionalized period of April–June 1941 in which *Dolce* is set, the danger she found herself in as a Jew finds no explicit treatment in her text. The depicted interlude thus appears remarkably settled.

Beyond the relatively settled nature of the episodes Némirovsky depicts in each of the two completed parts of *Suite française* and her (compared to Skalov) greater temporal remove from them as she wrote, the relative coherence of French society compared to the radical social disaggregation in Poland culminating in the ghettoization and annihilation of Polish Jews was a condition of possibility of Némirovsky's remarkable achievement of esthetic unity. Although French society as Némirovsky depicts it appears to be held together by nothing so much as the mutual suspicions and resentments of its constituent groups, such animosities indeed serve as agonistic bonds. Némirovsky enhances this (fraught) social unity significantly by foreshortening her social panorama and focusing overwhelmingly on French society's upper financial echelons. Other than the Michauds, a middle-aged couple who are both lower middle-class employees at a bank co-directed by another character, Maurice Corbin, non-wealthy people appear chiefly as servants, or mistresses, to the more central characters. The novel features no proletarian characters and, importantly, no Jews (and scarcely any foreigners).[44] Thus while Némirovsky's novel contrasts the perspectives and experiences of various mildly antagonistic groups—including Bussy inhabitants and farmers living outside the village; wealthy farmers and landed aristocrats; cultured esthetes and those they deem vulgar and uncouth—the novel maintains the sense of French society as a coherent if strained entity throughout.[45] While Némirovsky's novel betrays considerable sympathy for common people by way of its biting satire of the hypocrisy of privileged bourgeois and aristocratic characters, its depiction of common people, and certainly of working class people, remains fugitive.

Ultimately social categories serve as the backdrop for the novel's central questions regarding the (im)possibilities for individual freedom and for would-be universal human fulfillment and connection across externally-imposed barriers. Thus the central (melo)drama of *Dolce* revolves around the intricacies and difficulties of the genuine love that develops between the German officer Bruno von Falk and Lucille Angellier, who is unhappily married to a philandering and oafish French soldier currently in a German POW camp. Némirovsky is chiefly—and to be sure, exquisitely—concerned with "universal" human emotions and moral dilemmas. The near-contemporary historical setting serves as the stage for this human drama. Némirovsky could not be more explicit in her privileging of trans-historical themes over historical specificity. In a journal entry of June 2, 1942, she writes, "Never forget that the war will be over and that the entire historical side will fade away. Try to create as much as possible: things, debates . . . that will interest people in 1952 or 2052. Reread Tolstoy. Inimitable descriptions but not historical. Insist on that."[46] Whereas in his commitment to tracing a specifically Jewish experience of rapidly occurring catastrophic historical events, Skalov ultimately overwhelms novelistic unity, Némirovsky manages to achieve esthetic harmony precisely by abstracting from historical events and highlighting would-be "universal" human experiences against a cataclysmic background.[47]

RADICAL CONTINGENCY

Gary Saul Morson's theorization of what he calls "processual novels" in his 2013 *Prosaics and Other Provocations: Empathy, Open Time, and the Novel* can help illuminate Skalov's project at the same time as the processual novels

Morson highlights diverge from what Skalov was attempting. For Morson, the key distinction between conventional novels governed by structure (or esthetic necessity) and open-ended processual novels comes down to the different relationships they exhibit between authorial knowledge and narration, on the one hand, and temporality, on the other. When all of a work's parts are ordered within a coherent whole, the appearance of present-tense contingency is only that—an illusory appearance. In processual works, by contrast, contingent presentness is a constitutive element of the work's composition: "At each moment we sense that whatever happens is not inevitable. The work seems to be perpetually in process. The author tries out a possibility leading he is not sure where. He adjusts his writing in response to what he has written or, perhaps, to the judgment of readers. He may double back, leaving untouched the record of false starts. The work resembles a published notebook for itself. The entire process of forming it—moment by incomplete moment—defines the work" (108–9).

Morson points to several aspects of processual writing with and against which we can better understand Skalov's situation and project. First, he draws our attention to how authors like Tolstoy and Dostoevsky respond to current events, something we can best observe in works published in installments. Part 8 of Tolstoy's *Anna Karenina* is about the Eastern War, which occurred years after the publication of part 1, proving "beyond the possibility of doubt that the author responds to events outside his control" (121). Similarly, Dostoevsky treats a contemporary legal case, the Gorski Case, in part 2 of *The Idiot*, a report on which Dostoevsky read on March 10, 1868, after *The Idiot* had already begun to be published. The case could not have figured in the work's initial design, and as Morson notes, "The news could not have been more current and readers could hardly have missed that the author was adjusting his novel as he went along" (121). Second, Morson underscores the impossibility of foreshadowing in processual works because foreshadowing "presumes a pregiven future sending signs backward," which is impossible in works written out of the present in which the future remains open-ended and unknown.[48] And third, he notes how in processual works seemingly significant plot elements are sometimes simply abandoned. Alluding to such instances in Dostoevsky and Tolstoy, Morson writes, "In neither *The Idiot* nor *War and Peace* can one presume that the narration of an event guarantees its future significance. That could be true only if the future were already given, but these works genuinely develop in open time, as their themes demand. Some plot nuggets lead somewhere and some do not" (114).

Analyzing Skalov's "Di hak" with these three characteristics of processual prose narrative in mind—the incorporation into the work of current events that occur after the work has already been partially composed or even published; the absence of foreshadowing; and the "dropping" of seemingly significant plot elements—will throw light on both the overlap and the stark difference between Skalov's project and the sort of processual novels Morson theorizes.

The standard narratological opposition between story (essentially: what happens) and narrative discourse (when and how what happens is revealed, the myriad ways a story can be told) construes *story* as the stable, settled component and *narrative discourse* as the infinitely variable one. But in Skalov's novel of unfolding events, it is the story itself that is dynamic—perilously and intractably so—whereas the plot and narration strain to order the contingent events of the unstable story. The temporal proximity of the narration to the narrated explains a number of elements in the novel's construction and why the type of novel the exposition seems to promise is not ultimately delivered. Indeed, the strain between the closed narrated time of Skalov's third-person omniscient narrator, who narrates in the conventional past tense throughout, and the chaotic, open-ended time of both its unsettled story and its writing, throws into greatest relief that what Skalov was attempting with his novelistic project was anti-processual in its ambitions and processual only by necessity.

Perhaps the most obvious difference between the sorts of processual novels Morson analyzes and Skalov's "Di hak" is a matter of scale. While novels like *Anna Karenina* or *The Idiot* incorporated contingent events that occurred in the midst of their own composition, the number of such events remained limited and never threatened to overwhelm the novels' diegetic worlds. By contrast, Skalov was not merely allowing a handful of current events to enter his novelistic world but rather trying to build a plausible novelistic world to encompass what he endeavored to identify in real time as the most significant and representative experiences and events in the lives of Warsaw's Jews. The events that Skalov was trying to novelize in close to real time were so numerous, intractable, and ultimately catastrophic, however, that they eventually overwhelmed the author's best laid novelistic plans.

Whereas Morson theorizes processual writers' omniscience as never total because always limited by the contingency of present events and the unforeseeable directions they may take, I would describe Skalov as trying to impose formal omniscience and an ordered novelistic temporality on a threatening and ever-changing set of events. He deploys conventional third-person omniscient narration, which consigns the events depicted to the past. As horrible as so many of these events are, they are related to us by a narrator who has outlived them. The narrator indeed resides beyond the events he relates in an inviolable narrational temporality. No matter what terrible things happen, and no matter how many characters in the novel are killed, the extradiegetic narrator, at a structural remove from the catastrophe, not only knows what has happened but lives on (has always already lived on) to tell the tale. I am suggesting that we approach Skalov's recourse to conventional novelistic narration as essentially prophylactic: in narrating the enormously threatening events of the first two years of World War II in Poland, he constructs a buffer against them, an unbreachable narrative remove. Unlike Tolstoy and Dostoevsky, Skalov does not start by inventing a diegetic world into which he allows a limited number of current events to enter. Rather, he starts from the contemporary German invasion of Poland and tries to accommodate, or contain, this and subsequent crises within conventional novelistic structures and narrational strategies.

When events overwhelm the narrative (and literal architectural) structures that Skalov erects, we are not dealing with the sort of contingency whereby "some plot nuggets lead somewhere and some do not," to re-quote Morson. Many of the instances in "Di hak" that point to plans that the novel never makes good on—its signaling that Zsheni might one day become a writer mentioned above is but one example—could arguably be accounted for within the terms of novelistic processual open-endedness. The rapid death of the majority of the characters Skalov ostensibly thought would serve as a novelistic microcosm for Polish-Jewish society under the German occupation, however, is of another order of contingency and magnitude of catastrophe. A whole register of characters, moreover, contend with the fate of sinking, through mass starvation and epidemics, from the struggles of the working class into an abject, anonymous ooze. What we see is not a willing relinquishing of novelistic omniscience but (ineluctably unsuccessful) attempts to impose order on events from a position of would-be omniscience. Whereas processual novelists to varying degrees embrace the open-endedness of the present, Skalov works valiantly to mitigate that radical and radically dangerous contingency. The inherent incompleteness of his novel does not harmonize with broader philosophical and esthetic commitments as in the case of, say, Tolstoy and Dostoevsky, but rather strains against and undoes the conspicuously conventional narrative gambits and techniques with which he endeavors to make his subject matter conform.

Throughout Skalov's text there are moments where we as readers are in the eerie position of knowing more about what is to come than the ostensibly omniscient narrator. For example, the narrator remarks early on that among the group of Polish soldiers, including Bernard, heading to the front, "scarcely anyone believed that the threatening fire would actually flare up" (part 1, 2). Even as the narrator intimates that characters in the novel fail to foresee how bad things are about to get, we know that he himself does not begin to suspect how bad things are in fact about to get. The dissonance that our historical knowledge introduces into our reading notwithstanding, however, the narrative posture of authority and omniscience is pronounced, altogether in keeping with Skalov's default use of conventional omniscient narration. The (omniscient) narrator's rhetorical questions about Sender's fate after Sender, having returned from Warsaw to his native Lodz, is forced into punitive labor around the time of Lodz's incorporation into the Third Reich, are exemplary in this regard. Sender is part of a Jewish work detail forced to pull stones out of the muck of pig pits outside the city. Jewish forced laborers are then ordered to put Sender in the muck and to throw at him the stones they have piled up. Sender must then break the stones with a heavy hammer and pave the mud around him. Left there overnight, he sinks ever further. At this moment of conventional novelistic suspense, the narrator poses the following questions: "Did he possess enough strength to pull himself out of the pit, to flee from the city? And where to? Blimtshe didn't see him again" (part 1, 58). Sender's wife, Blimtshe, does not see him again, but readers of "Di hak" do, if only briefly, as he is making his way to the Soviet border. We eventually learn of Sender's death, but the salient point is not his exact fate but that the narrator's rhetorical questions signal knowledge—not ignorance—of this fate and that the narrator ultimately makes good on this promised omniscience. This example is typical of how Skalov strives to circumscribe the events and myriad subplots of his novel within a conventionally omniscient narrator's purview.

We also encounter moments, however, where the text itself or its narrator seem to wonder what the future might hold. Questions recur, whether rhetorical questions posed by the narrator or questions posed by a character, that point up the narrator's epistemological limitations. As mentioned above, "Di hak" depicts a charity evening held on August 16, 1940, with the aim of alleviating the suffering of the Graniczna hoyf's most destitute residents. Mine, now the director of the hoyf's house committee, supports the idea, and the building's wealthiest members agree to donate food, cigarettes, and schnapps to be sold off. Srolke and Beyle's daughter Zsheni, whom we encounter earlier in the novel as a sensitive, sophisticated, and musically talented but also frail and, due to an injury sustained in a German bombing, slightly disfigured girl, has by now, her facial scar notwithstanding, blossomed. "Each one of the boys asked her to dance. They all felt comfortable and at home [*heymish*]. For a minute the shadow of the war, of the nightmare, lifted. The youth sparkled with quiet joy. Wasn't this a presentiment of an imminent end [of the war]? Was this a deep belief in the victory of justice? A hope that the bad dream would be resolved for the better [*az der beyzer kholem vet zikh oyslozn tsum gutn*]?" (part 2, 17–18).

On one level the text here certainly performs narrative omniscience. The first question ("Wasn't this a presentiment of an imminent end [of the war]?") can be interpreted variously—as a question running through the minds of the youth in a rare happy moment and conveyed in free indirect discourse, as a question posed by the narrator to the text's narratee, or both. In any case, the narrator clearly knows that the war's end is not imminent and that such an interpretation of the youth's fleeting happiness would be naïve. Yet with the following two questions ("Was this a deep belief in the victory of justice? A hope that the bad dream would be resolved for the better?") the narrator seems to step part way out of his position of sovereign knowledge vis-à-vis the characters whose hopes he is describing. In asking if we should not see in their capacity for joy a deep belief in the ultimate victory of justice, the narrator touches on a belief he may share, and at any rate one that he cannot ironize from an omniscient perch without signaling a cynicism wholly foreign to Skalov's project.[49] Thus in the slippage between the sovereign ironizing of the first question and the more ambiguous enunciative valence of the second, I suggest that we can observe an abrupt attenuation of the narrator's omniscience.

As is generally the case in Skalov's text, such moments do not mark an embrace of open-ended presentness or a processual esthetic but rather the inevitable erosion of the bulwark of the highly conventional, anti-processual novel Skalov was attempting to write. The context and novelistic devices around the above example throw this into relief. Skalov frames the charity evening against a bleak backdrop: two months prior, in June 1940, Italy had joined the war effort against England, Paris had fallen, and the French army had capitulated. More immediately, during the charity evening itself, some people (*ver-nisht-ver*) are pouring over General-Governor Hans Frank's appeal to the Polish people just published in the newspaper that day, August 16. Frank tells the Poles that an independent Poland would be their misfortune but tells the Jews that they will be removed from the face of Europe. Despite this deeply troubling context, however, most people (*di merheyt*) at the evening have fun. The general merriment and hopefulness the characters experience are thus presented as a temporary reprieve from so much bad news and the compelling signs that the war will likely not be ending any time soon. The bleak context underscores the naïve wishful thinking and willed ignorance, and the fleeting nature of the joy the youth feel.

The effervescent bubble, which has the youths and even their elders wanting to believe that all that is happening might be like "a passing hurricane, whose winds [*hoykh*] would disappear as does a plague" (part 2, 18), is burst, moreover, with a conventional novelistic gesture when the boy Shiye suffers a heart attack and "suddenly it became clear to him that his dance was done [*az zayn tants iz shoyn oysgetantst*]" (part 2, 18). Clearly, the scene is drenched in conventional novelistic tropes, from the objective bad news about the course of the war to Shiye's heart attack, which signal the narrator's omniscience vis-à-vis the characters' deluded yearnings. Unlike these momentarily optimistic characters, the sovereign narrator knows, and signals that they know, that the war is not about to end and that this joyful moment is fugitive. And yet, even amidst so much performance of conventional novelistic omniscience, questions arise that the narrator cannot know the answer to, as do hopes that the narrator ostensibly shares in and thus cannot dismiss as simply naïve. At moments such as this, the narrator becomes invested in real, open questions about the ultimate victory or defeat of justice and in hopes about the ultimately favorable resolution of the current crisis that no available knowledge can substantiate.

Several other instances occur where the narrator or characters in the narrative pose questions that exceed the narrator's would-be omniscience. For example, Skalov's narrator relates how, in the face of soaring food prices that only the wealthy in the ghetto can afford, Jews ask each other about the future and their chances of survival: "Jews ask each other [*a yid hot gefregt dem tsveytn*]: are we going to survive this? When will all these cruelties end?" (part 2, 77). Even if we bracket what we know as a function of hindsight, Skalov's narrator can hardly muster the authority to make us believe they know the answer to these questions.

Yet what is remarkable about Skalov's novelistic project is not that at certain moments it must inevitably confront the limits of its own would-be omniscience but rather the degree to which it tries to mitigate the radical contingency of the circumstances in which it was written by absorbing the unfolding events into ostensibly omniscient, novelistic narrative in the first place. Moments that betray the narrator's epistemological limits are the exception, not the rule. Even as Skalov relates myriad forms of suffering and death, he deploys conventional omniscient narration to stabilize the horror and to evoke, both implicitly and explicitly, a safe afterward when the storm will have been weathered.

I would argue that Skalov's strategy of stabilizing the dangerous present by novelizing it is an inherent feature of his entire project, but it becomes more conspicuous in the various ways that "Di hak" anticipates the future via forms of prolepsis or foreshadowing. Skalov's deployment of prolepsis also very neatly lays bare the different relationship Skalov's book maintains to open-ended time compared to processual novels, which Morson theorizes as wholly incompatible with foreshadowing and the omniscience or foreknowledge it requires. Prolepsis is closely tied to omniscience: novels frequently render the future past by alluding to events to come in a way that signals the narrator's foreknowledge of them. Readers may or may not correctly interpret the narrator's clues about what is to come, but whatever will ultimately happen, readers can presume that it will have a place within the novel that the narrator is narrating—for the novel has already been written, and the narrator knows how the story plays out. Morson's category of processual novels complicates this picture considerably, as the narrators of such works may indeed not know how the story ends. Articulated from within a historical presentness, "processual works," as Morson pointedly writes, "are inherently incomplete, not accidentally incomplete in the way *The Mystery of Edwin Drood* remained when Dickens died" (116). Skalov's novel is likewise inherently incomplete, but not due to its embrace of a processual esthetic but rather due to the radically contingent forces of history that it could neither control nor transcend.

PROLEPTIC MEMORY

Rather than reconciling the narration of his novel to the open-ended presentness of events, Skalov repeatedly endeavors to approximate a retrospective vantage point while still very much in the midst of a perilous historical present. He resorts to proleptic memory, by which I mean the anticipation of how events will come to be remembered in history. By figuring a future moment beyond the threatening flux of current events, Skalov proffers, in Frank

Kermode's classic phrase, the "sense of an ending."[50] Three key instances signaling future memory will illustrate his strategy of mitigating historical contingency and danger through novelistic means.

The first example occurs when Skalov's narrator describes the mass killing of Jewish POWs, depicted at length in the novel's first part, as one of the "historic" moments of the "Jewish war": "Precisely there, on the way from Lublin to Biale, between the shtetls Lubartov and Partshev, one of the historic episodes of the 'Jewish' war took place" (part 2, 2). Skalov strains to transcend the flux of catastrophic history and to assess the importance of this near-contemporary event retrospectively from a projected future. Although not yet in a stable position to assess the significance of this atrocity vis-à-vis still-unfolding events, the narrator can transport himself into a novelistic future in which this event, barely remembered today, is recalled as one of the key atrocities of the Jewish experience of the war. Historical events would of course not follow this proleptic script.

A conversation involving Khemye, Albert, and Albert's old friend from his days in Berlin, Herr Nickel, the novel's representative "good German," more complexly exemplifies Skalov's strategy of stabilizing crisis through prolepsis. Nickel shows up one day at Khemye's building in search of Albert. Albert and his wife Gute, Khemye's sister, have recently moved in after being forced out of their apartment on Marszałkowska Street. A socialist and antifascist, Nickel is dismayed with the direction Germany has taken, and he is moved by the poverty of the Jews in the streets. The conversation is dominated by Nickel's pronouncements about the future, which are grounded in his socialist philosophy of history, beginning with: "'Tyranny alone has no power to rule,' the guest predicted, as if by way of offering solace. 'History tolerates no wrongs against humanity [*avles legabe der mentshlekhkeyt*]. Time crushes all who offend against the laws of basic morality [*Di tsayt tsetret yedn eynem, ver es iz oyver af di gezetsn fun der elementarer moral*]'" (part 2, 33–34). While Nickel is vocal—indeed long-winded—about the ultimately unstoppable march of progress and justice, he is more reticent about the Germans' more immediate plans for the Jews. When Khemye asks Nickel, "What will become of us? What do they (the Germans) want from us?" (part 2, 34), Nickel "evaded giving an answer. It was apparent that he knew something but did not want to spoil the mood still further" (part 2, 34). Nickel's evasion raises interesting questions about the status of the narrator's knowledge. In a conventional omniscient novel, we could be confident that the narrator is in possession of the knowledge they describe Herr Nickel as showing visible signs of having but not revealing. That may well be the case here too: historically, Jews were forced to leave Marszałkowska Street in September 1940, so it is quite possible that the narrator is alluding to knowledge Nickel has of the coming ghetto (established in November 1940). But not necessarily. It also seems plausible that Herr Nickel here serves as a cipher for the Germans' plans, which the Germans presumably have but which have not yet been revealed to the Jews of Warsaw —or, as it were, to the narrator of this scene. In other words, the character Herr Nickel may here in fact know more than the narrator. The narrator sees that Nickel is withholding knowledge, but what he knows remains inscrutable.

What Herr Nickel does go on to say continues to limn the ultimate triumph of socialism and justice as inevitable. Many of his pronouncements ring hollow from our historical vantage point, but they may have sounded far less so to Skalov, himself politically left, writing in 1941, although it should be noted that Skalov renders Nickel's optimistic historical forecast complex and ambiguous by intermixing it with comments that reveal a casual antisemitism on the part of even this "good" German. In this way, Skalov points up ways that Nickel's confidence in the ultimate triumph of justice glibly abstracts from the immediate and specific plight of Jews. However one interprets this subtly slippery issue, the way that Nickel and also, more briefly, Albert project a postwar (Jewish) future bear reading in full. The conversation unfolds as follows:

> "The Jews, yes . . . I got to know the Jews of Poland back in the time of the world war. Have no doubt that your brothers, aside from their virtues like energy and stamina, also possess great faults. We Germans don't like soaked [*tseveykte*] faces, slovenly [*gekholyete*] hands, or translucent bodies. But what people doesn't have faults . . .
>
> "I can tell you one thing," he rounded off these thoughts [*hot er geentfert af dem alem*], "the Jewish question [*yudn-frage*][51] in general is an issue of oppressed national minorities. The only thing that will resolve that issue is true socialism, which will once and for all—whether you want it to or not—abolish the barrier between rich and poor—and maybe you don't want this—also between one people and another . . . Well, maybe it won't happen right away, it doesn't matter; the way of world progress [*velt-progres*][52] is limned by technical achievements. Every interruption can only delay the course of history but not prevent it. Time is patient . . .
>
> "I have no doubt, whoever wins the war in the end, that the productivity of the Jewish people and especially of its most threatened,

ruined part, will rise with tremendous strength. I observed this after the previous war. . . .

"Yes, it wouldn't be as dire with you if it weren't for your own pretentious asses [*voyl-eyzlekh*] . . . I mean the mixed ones who by their ancestry are half horse and half donkey—the so-called *Volksdeutschen* —your erstwhile Poles. Those characters [*bruim*] have the ambition of mimicking all the evil of our Adolfs and Hanses.[53] Instead of emulating their industriousness and diligence, they redouble their efforts [*bamien zikh drayfakhik*] to exceed their criminal atrocities."

Albert, who for the moment had forgotten all his ills, took lively interest in this conversation.

"I think that after the war the great virtues of the average Jew will become clear to the world," he said in impeccable German. "His perseverance and his adaptability to the direst of circumstances. The times will change, but it will be considered a particular privilege [*a bazundern skhus*] to have experienced all these atrocities firsthand [*afn eygenem leyb*]."

Nickel was bathed in smoke from his own cigar. "Atrocities? Yes. . . . the atrocities of our cultivated persons surpass the atrocities of the most primitive barbarians, among other reasons because they are part of a system which has created a moral justification for them . . . However that may be, that path is a false one and sooner or later doomed to perish. Because manifestations of tyranny have always been symptoms of death, not of birth."

They spoke about racism, the social order after the war, systems.

"The greatest enemy of culture is bestial egoism, which lurks in each of us, irrespective of nationality or race. The most apt system will be the one that is capable of curbing or mitigating precisely that harmful characteristic. Racism, which creates barriers between one person and another, as well as the entire system of fascism, is based upon bestial egoism, upon the harmful division between different masses and different nations, which sooner or later must collapse or be scattered like abominable dust [*nevolesher shtoyb*].

"Systems will change. And the better part of humanity will always strive to fill in the abyss between people, not deepen it." (part 2, 34–35)

Unlike the previous (or the next and final) example of prognostications of the postwar future, these remarks are voiced by characters in a dialogue rather than by the narrator. Thus they less obviously exemplify an attempt to stabilize the dangerous present via recourse to a projected future (which is not to say that they do not also serve this function). Herr Nickel's and Albert's comments at any rate reveal a great deal about the outer limits of what was imaginable to Skalov, writing in 1941, right around the time of the establishment of the ghetto. Both the Jewish Albert and the German Herr Nickel anticipate a trying wartime experience for the Jews of Poland, but one they will be able to ride out and from which they will be able to bounce back stronger. Even as it is poignant to read these novelistic anticipations of possible futures in possession of the knowledge of the catastrophic future that came, we must always bear in mind that the immediate future whose dangers Skalov's characters are trying proleptically to mitigate is not the Holocaust. That catastrophe is something we can see, after the fact, as the future soon awaiting the Jews of Poland of 1941; but it was not among the possible novelistic futures any character in "Di hak" could imagine, nor—and this largely amounts to the same thing—was it imaginable to Skalov writing at that time. Even as we read Herr Nickel's insistence that only a true and just socialism will ultimately provide a solution, once and for all, to the *Judenfrage*, we must not backshadow his vision with our knowledge of the "Final Solution" to the Jewish Question that the Nazis and their local collaborators carried out.[54] Similarly, when we read Albert's hopeful sentiment that it will be "a particular privilege" to Jews to have experienced the atrocities (*akhzoyres*) they are suffering firsthand (or literally, "on their own body," *afn eygenem leyb*) because it will demonstrate to the world the Jews' perseverance and adaptability, it is crucial if also impossible not to contrast the atrocities Albert evokes with those of the Holocaust. And yet, the dangers Polish Jews were experiencing in autumn 1940, when this particular scene is set, and more broadly in the open-ended period Skalov's novel treats—fall 1939 to summer 1941—were palpable, terrifying, and ever-growing. There was every reason, even as what we call the Holocaust remained simply unimaginable, for Skalov and his characters to attempt to ward off present dangers with novelistically projected futures.

My final example of proleptic dynamics in "Di hak" comes in the form of a reckoning with the year 1940. Writing with only minimal distance from the events of 1940, Skalov both underscores characters' anxious lack of knowledge about what is to come and deploys novelistic omniscience to project moments in the future from which recent events will be safely remembered. His narration, that is, both acknowledges peril and contingency, and tries to mitigate them. The narrator presents tormented questions that "constantly hang in the air," questions that people ask about the future, the chances of surviving, and when the war will end. People, the narrator informs us further, like to daydream of a peaceful elsewhere and of a safe future when only "crosses and memorials" will bear witness to the millions of victims. Meanwhile, however, the war remains in full force, and no one can foresee how it will play out. Even as the passage signals the unreliability of the realm of dream and fantasy in which terrified people are wont to seek refuge, the narrator eventually proffers their own vision of how the events of the year 1940 will be remembered a decade later. This vision does not seem to be part of the world of dreams into which people flee, but rather a proleptic pronouncement, an attempt on the narrator's part, rather than on the part of possibly deluded characters, to assert a reliable locus outside the current suffering, a safe afterward beyond the reach of current suffering, from which it will later be recalled. The oscillation between underscoring characters' merely escapist flights to imagined elsewheres and the narrative's own assertion of an ostensibly sober vision of postwar recollection is remarkable.

> Will I [or *one* or *we*: men] survive this? When will the brutal war end?
>
> These questions constantly hung in the air. And many were those who rode the wings of their imagination into a realm of dreams, into a kingdom of a peaceful elsewhere . . . one wanted to believe:
>
> In ten years' time, a mother will put her child to bed with a lullaby, a stream will roll gently through a valley. And its waves will tell wondrous stories of yore. Only crosses and memorials [*tslomim un denkmeler*] will bear witness to a past storm which devoured millions of victims
>
> 1940 . . . In just ten years Jewish parents will tell their young [*minderyerike*] children all that happened in this year. The young ones will listen eagerly with wide-open eyes and that number will sound strange in their ears—1940.
>
> Meanwhile the war is in full swing. No one can yet predict its end. But one thing is clear for those who have suffered the fate of a Jew [*adurkhgemakht dem goyrl fun a yid*]:
>
> Famous names of today will be transformed into shameful ones. Stories of the recent past will sound like legends from time immemorial, when pure animal instincts ruled over reason and sentiment.
>
> 1940! You sprouted in the blood of your predecessor and in blood you grew. Will your start and end also be the way of your successor?

> Poland of 1940. How much gloom hangs on the branches of your trees, how much senselessness [*umzin*] hovers in the air above you!
>
> Once more a new year stands bound upon the threshold. Like one condemned to death, it kneels before the executioner, filled with dread. But a hope blossoms in his heart. He awaits aid in the last minute—tidings of mercy and liberation. (part 2, 84–85)

The image of a mother rocking her child to sleep in a bucolic setting is clearly a comforting fantasy in the minds of beleaguered (and not necessarily Jewish, as the memorial crosses suggest) citizens of Warsaw. The status of the next paragraph, envisioning Jewish parents circa 1950 telling their young children, who had not experienced 1940 firsthand, about its incredible events, however, is ambiguous. The narrator seems to return from depicting the comforting daydreams of citizens of Warsaw to projecting, on their own authority as narrator, a scene of intergenerational transmission of memory in Jewish families. Having no knowledge of what would transpire in 1942, the would-be omniscient narrator can even evoke a future in which intact Jewish families in Poland relate to their children, ostensibly in Yiddish, the events of 1940 as the traumatic nadir of the war.

This alternation between acknowledgment of radical uncertainty about the future, and narratorial assertion of near certainty about it, continues as the passage points up the fact that "meanwhile the war is in full swing" and that "no one can yet predict its end" before immediately asserting that Jews experiencing current events can be certain of a form of ultimate justice, namely that many whose power and prestige have been augmented during the war will be reduced to a shameful status and that, in the near future, the events of 1940 will be remembered incredulously as belonging to a quasi-mythic time when animal instincts ruled over human values.

The final portion of the above-quoted passage encompasses two apostrophes, one to the year 1940 and one to Poland of 1940, and it is rounded off by the analogy between what the coming year may have in store and the fate of a person condemned to death but hoping to be reprieved. The apostrophes emphatically reassert the narrator's voice—it is the narrator and not any character who speaks—but the would-be omniscient narrator's authority remains necessarily limited. While they hint at a possible foreknowledge of ultimate mercy, they possess precious little ability to transcend the uncertainty of the contingent present in which questions like "Will we survive?" and "When will the brutal war end?" hang in the air. Despite the projection to a safer and more just postwar Poland in which Jewish life has remained intact, the narrator remains in a position of non-omniscience. Like all those who pose such questions, the narrator does not know which of these possibilities—execution or reprieve—will come to pass and can only share in the fears of the former and the hopes for the latter. In this way, the narrational dynamics of the passage as a whole exemplify both the way Skalov draws on the resources of the novel to try to assert a certain knowledge of, and power to shape and contain, events—especially via projected scenes of retrospection—and the way in which the radical contingency of historical time constantly erodes novelistic authority, omniscience, and narrative design. Precisely this central tension makes Skalov's ineluctably failed novel a profound literary-historical text.

FROM NOVEL TO REPORTAGE

The ghettos were not amenable to the writing of novels, not only because the dire conditions were hardly auspicious for undertaking such long-term projects but also because of a basic tension between novelistic structure and the radical instability of life in the ghettos. This tension is everywhere visible in Skalov's novelistic project, which strains serially and unsuccessfully to achieve sustainable narrative arcs and to make later parts of the story harmonize with what has been foreshadowed earlier on. Skalov first set—and first began to write—his novel before the ghetto was established. As the novel moves into the ghetto, Skalov's project falters and breaks off relatively quickly. We see an increased density and urgency of the present accompanied by an attenuation of narrative omniscience. With the advent of mass destitution, disease, starvation, and death, the experience of the ghetto overwhelms the novelistic form as the scale of suffering tends to exceed the focus on representative individuals that is the social novel's purview. In its later pages Skalov's text aptly and self-reflexively evokes the non-novelistic genres of the lyric poem and reportage, genres which proved more viable than the novel for reckoning with ghetto existence and which for this reason, and in contrast to Skalov's rare, valiant attempt at a novel, are richly represented among the corpus of literary works that have come down to us from the ghettos, including the works I explore in the remaining chapters of this book.

As I have already mentioned, Skalov would turn away from his novel project and devote himself to an important work of reportage on the refugee centers. Although the punktn serve as the last social milieu in Skalov's novel, he presumably found the novel genre ill-equipped for treating them. Had he been reporting on an earlier period in the wartime experience of Warsaw Jewry, perhaps Skalov would have availed himself of reportage's capacious generic eclecticism and authored highly novelistic reportages, as Peretz Opoczynski so vividly did in his third-person depiction of the personalities living in the apartment building at 21 Wołynska Street and their struggles, intrigues, tensions, and rivalries during the early period of the German occupation, prior to the enclosing of the ghetto.[55] But given the time and subject that he was confronting, I conjecture that reportage offered Skalov a framework for confronting conditions in the ghetto less constrained by novelistic structure and plot arcs. Skalov's reportage indeed evinces an emphatic break with novelistic discourse. Skalov eschews any pretense of omniscience in "A shpatsir iber di punktn" (A stroll through the refugee centers) and narrates in the first rather than the third person. The text is structured as a series of monologues by inhabitants of various punktn, to which Skalov as narrator listens: he has no privileged knowledge about the stories that the various refugees tell him. Far removed from the would-be omniscience of the novelistic narrator of "Di hak," the narrator of "A shpatsir iber di punktn" receives the many stories of diverse refugees from a position of epistemological deficit.

It is not surprising that Skalov ultimately abandoned his novel project in the Warsaw ghetto. What is altogether remarkable is that he set out to write a novel at all, and that he remained dedicated to the task for as long as he did—nearly two years. To be sure, Skalov's jagged novel points up profound tensions between novelistic conventions, including the genre's most basic constituent components and narrative structures, and the radical contingency of the present that he was attempting to novelize. Yet it also shows the deep resources that the novel made available to Skalov for grappling with the experience of the first two years of the German occupation of Poland, as well as, perhaps more importantly, the humanistic values that the novel embodied for Skalov—values diametrically opposed to those that culminated in the catastrophe. For Skalov's project of novelizing the present was not only a startling literary experiment (paradoxically at its most experimental in its investment in conventional novelistic strategies) but also a leap of faith that the events of the war years would finally be able to be lent coherent, symbolic form and shaped into a humanly meaningful story; that they would be able to be rendered, precisely, as a novel.

Even as he attempted to novelize the present of September 1939 through June 1941, Skalov was not reconciled to a processual temporality but rather endeavored to tame temporal contingency with narrative structure, omniscience, and prolepsis. The aspirationally omniscient yet ineluctably threatened and unstable novelistic perspective from which Skalov looked (back) at, ordered, and managed historical events remains as a poignant and eerie virtual site of memory in a projected fictional world adjacent to our own. Skalov's novelistic temporality affords nearly forgotten suffering the dignity of being remembered in a novelistic future not so overwhelmed by tragedies as the historical future that came.

II. POETRY

THREE POEMS FROM THE WARSAW GHETTO, 1942

PREFACE TO CHAPTERS 2–4: THEODOR ADORNO AND "POETRY AFTER AUSCHWITZ"

Most theoretical treatments of relationships between poetry and the Holocaust disregard the poetry that victims wrote during the time of the genocide.[1] I discuss some of the political, institutional, and discursive factors that have militated against engagement with the cultural production from the ghettos in general in the epilogue to this book. The neglect of poetry from the ghettos in particular has in part been an unintended consequence of the debate that Theodor W. Adorno initiated with his intentionally provocative and lapidary dictum from "Kulturkritik und Gesellschaft" ("Cultural Criticism and Society," written 1949 and published 1951) that "nach Auschwitz ein Gedicht zu schreiben, ist barbarisch" (Writing a poem, after Auschwitz, is barbaric).[2] While frequently misquoted, taken out of its intricate context, and reduced to an empty soundbite, Adorno's pronouncement set the terms for the most prominent critical conversation about poetry and the Holocaust, the effects of which are still evident today.[3] Other scholars have explored various aspects of the Adorno-inspired poetry-after-Auschwitz discourse.[4] Here it will suffice to note how the very terms that structured the poetry-after-Auschwitz cultural discourse in its differentiated entirety have had the regrettable and abiding consequence of helping to place and keep poems written by victims *during* the Holocaust, above all in Yiddish, in a blind spot. A far-ranging discussion about poetry (or art tout court), barbarity, and ethics in the wake of the Nazi genocide of European Jewry emerged, became widely ramified, and, arguably, exhausted itself without ever looking seriously at the poetry produced by the victims of that genocide. The question of "poetry after Auschwitz" indeed tends to position the Holocaust at an absolute remove from poetry. There was poetry before Auschwitz, and now, after Auschwitz, "we" must grapple with the terms on which "we" may or may not continue to write and read it. Indeed, by reducing the temporal ("after") and geographic ("Auschwitz") reach of the Holocaust, the phrase "after Auschwitz" and the cultural perspective it both reflects and perpetuates tend to frame the literature written during the Holocaust out of consideration, relegating it to cultural, historical, and theoretical oblivion. The discourse of poetry-after-Auschwitz thus seldom considers Holocaust victims as poets and intellectuals who have something to contribute to the conversation. Instead, victims remain perfectly silent, or even serve as figures of a perfect silence, to which poets and intellectuals writing after Auschwitz must strive to do some sort of justice. Consequently, still in the third decade of the twenty-first century many of the most important poetic engagements with what we now call the Holocaust remain unknown even to the vast majority of scholars who regularly teach and write on Holocaust literature.[5]

However, as Nachman Blumental, the member of the postwar Jewish Historical Commission in Poland with arguably the most abiding interest in literature, noted already in 1945, poetry was a privileged genre in the ghettos, written in highbrow literary circles and prominent in street culture as well, as *gasn-zingers* (street singers) informed, warned, and entertained in verse.[6] To begin to read victim-authored wartime poetry in its historical, phenomenological, esthetic, and ethical complexity thus requires that we step outside the paradigm that has governed the far-ranging conversation between Adorno and his many interlocutors and critics about poetry "after Auschwitz." It requires reading the texts that have for far too long been framed out of discussion.

CHAPTER 2

SHMUEL MARVIL'S TORN WORDS

"Di gas" ("The Street") is one of two poems by the little-known Warsaw Yiddish poet and playwright Shmuel Marvil (1906–1943) preserved in the second cache of the Oyneg Shabes archive, recovered in December 1950.[1]

A self-described "rabbi's son . . . steeped in the good pages of Gemara," Marvil was born in a *shtetl* (market town) outside Warsaw (Letter to Giterman). After a traditional education—*kheyder, beysmedresh,* and *yeshiva*—he had an office job with a Warsaw business and later moved into trade. He began publishing quite young, debuting in 1927 at age twenty-one with a four-act play, *Di libe* (Love), published in installments in the journal *Inzere* [*sic*] *hofenung* (Our hope), edited by the prominent Yiddish author and mentor to younger Yiddish writers Itse Meyer Vaysenberg (Isaac Meir Weissenberg). In addition to publishing reportages and sketches in the Warsaw Yiddish newspaper *Express* and the provincial periodical press, Marvil went on to publish five books in Warsaw between 1930 and 1937: four further dramatic works —*Di makhsheyfe* (The witch), a dramatic poem (1930); *Ver arop un ver aruf* (Some rise and some fall), a four-act play (1934); *Der vanderer* (The wanderer), a dramatic poem in three scenes (1935); and *Shaul hameylekh* (King Saul, 1935)—and a volume of poems, *Trern in der nakht* (Tears in the night, 1937).[2]

From his letter of April 13, 1942, to Yitzhak Giterman, preserved in the Oyneg Shabes archive, we know that Marvil continued to write prolifically in the Warsaw ghetto.[3] He wrote the letter to thank Giterman for arranging a modest stipend of one hundred zlotys a month to support him after he had fallen ill (Marvil wrote the letter from his sickbed, recuperating from his third bout with pneumonia). He expresses his "joy" in receiving this support "not as an ordinary person but as a writer." He states further that the one hundred zlotys give him "strength to do something for our people and our literature," and he assures Giterman that he has written "a lot" lately and has finished "several books." Marvil's letter provides a window onto a number of important aspects of writing and writers in the ghettos: they were often supported, with small sums of money or an extra bowl of soup, by grassroots organizations such as the Warsaw ghetto Aleynhilf, the Judenrat, or a combination thereof.[4]

We can also see how meaningful it was to people like Marvil to see himself and to be recognized as a *writer,* and this beyond the desperately needed material support that came with such recognition. Being a writer still meant a great deal, even—and perhaps especially—in such dire circumstances: literature retained its status as a venerable humanistic enterprise worthy of being supported and worthy of devoting oneself to. Writing literature in Yiddish was also, Marvil felt, a way of doing something for the Jewish people. Marvil's grave illness equally attests to the fact that the modest support writers often received was hardly able to lift them out of the danger of dying from disease or starvation.

All of Marvil's many writings were lost save for the two poems he sent to Giterman with his letter (presumably Giterman, who had strong ties to Ringelblum and supported the Oyneg Shabes project, passed them on to the archive)—"Tsu di hern" (To the gentlemen), a political poem in eleven quatrains imploring the "gentlemen" responsible for the war to stop the senseless slaughter; and the longer and more complex and unsettling "Di gas" ("The Street"). Although "Di gas" is not dated, Marvil mentions it in this letter as belonging to the poems he had written "lately."[5] As always when thinking about life and cultural production in the ghettos, chronology is crucial. Marvil's letter places the poem's creation in late winter or early spring 1942. This timing tells us that the poem was completed at the latest approximately four months before the Great Deportation of the Warsaw ghetto (late July through early September 1942). The exact circumstances of Marvil's own death in 1943 at age thirty-seven are unknown.[6]

Marvil's poem is so titled because it describes horrors that the autobiographical poet persona sees in his ghetto street during the frigid winter of 1941–1942, including starving orphaned children, people fighting dogs for rotten food from garbage cans, and frozen and dismembered corpses eaten by dogs and crows. Yet these awful scenes are only one of the poem's two main themes: the question of the very possibility of writing a poem in and about such suffering, destitution, and loss of human status is also something that the poem self-reflexively ponders at length. Marvil meditates on the status of poetry in relation to such horrors as a way of gauging their nature, extent, and ramifications, and also the potential for literature—poetry specifically—to vouch for the humanity of the victims.

THEMES AND DYNAMICS OF ADDRESS IN "DI GAS"

Since Marvil's poem is not widely known, in this section I provide an overview of its main themes and its different iterations of address, in other words what it speaks about and to whom or to what it speaks. In subsequent sections of this chapter I contextualize and analyze moments in which the poem confronts three threats to the human status that likewise threaten its own status as a poem: the inability to meet death on such a massive scale with rituals of purification and burial, the disintegration of the human body into anonymous body parts, and the collapse of the human/animal distinction.

Consisting of thirty-seven quatrains, "The Street" is written in pentameter using various feet but a consistent ABCB rhyme scheme. Intermittently throughout the poem, the authorial speaker addresses "my poem."[7] The horrors of the ghetto have changed the relationship between author and poem, and the speaker beseeches his poem, in his poem, to release him from the obligation it is imposing on him to write the poem. A paradoxical constellation of relationships emerges between the lyric persona, apostrophized poem, and the terrible scenes and images that fill the poem. Only while intermittently begging his poem to free him from the awful task of giving a poetic account of the ghetto does the poet give this account, the poem "Di gas."

The tension out of which "Di gas" is born between tormenting poem and resisting poet comes to the fore already in the poem's first two stanzas:[8]

Nisht mon bay mir lid mayns, nisht paynik ikh ken nisht
Dikh shafn un shlayfn, vi amol in dem haynt.
Far mir bistu itst a shtik roye materye
Vos flist fun dir umet, tsar un gevayn.

Amol bistu lid mayns gevezn mayn zinger,
dayn klang hot farzist mayne troymen un tsayt,
haynt bistu fremd mir, ikh muz es dir zogn,
ven trogst in dir veyton fun toyznte layt.

Don't demand of me, my poem, don't torment me, I can't
craft and hone you today as I once did.
Before me now you are a piece of raw substance
emanating sorrow, grief, and tears.

Once, my poem, you were my singer,
your sound sweetened my dreams and time;

today, I must tell you, you're strange to me,
when you carry within you the pain [*veyton*] of thousands of people.

The stanzas dramatize the poem's changing voice: it used to be a personal singer for the poet's pleasure and self-expression ("your sound sweetened my dreams and time"), but the poetic sound (*klang*) has metamorphosed into a degree of pain that exceeds the bounds of the lyric subject: "When you carry within you the pain [*veyton*] of thousands of people." *Veyton* contains a pun, as it means both hurt or pain (*VEYton*) and sound or tone of woe (*veyTON*). The fact that these two verses rhyme further emphasizes the poem's transformation: "Mayne troymen un *tsayt*" have yielded to "veyton fun toyznte *layt*" (emphasis added). The pain of thousands overwhelms the lyric voice; it is radically incommensurate with the inner experience—joyful or painful—of which a traditional lyric subject is equipped to sing. The poet also highlights the active work of poetic craft by doubling the verbs *shafn un shlayfn*, which play off each other phonically. In contrast to his poetic virtuosity in the past (once, *amol*), the content of his poem confronts him today (*haynt*) as raw substance: unmasterable and overflowing with pain.

The poet persona's opening and intermittent subsequent apostrophes to the poem color how readers encounter the narrative portions that make up the bulk of the text. Even when the speaker is narrating horrific scenes from the Warsaw ghetto street, the poem remains a crucial—though not the only —narratee. The terrible scenes from his ghetto street that the speaker narrates (as it were, under protest, when he is not directly imploring the poem to release him from the task) are always (also) narrated to the poem itself. The speaker indeed seems to place these scenes before the poem—often despondently, sometimes aggressively and defiantly—to take measure of whether or not they can be reconciled with poetry. At every stage, the poem poses implicit and explicit questions about its own uses or uselessness in the face of the current circumstances and, more broadly, about the viability of poetry as a cultural institution when the most basic human values that poetry both affirms and presupposes are collapsing. Are these raw scenes of awful suffering and degradation really reconcilable with lyric subjectivity and poetry? And what is at stake in this question, or, to put it differently, in the poem's act of putting itself and poetry writ large on trial?

Although as we will see, "Di gas" addresses various and often overlapping addressees, including readers (implicitly) and God (explicitly), and although the speaker's voice at times also merges with those of the hapless depicted figures, the poem itself remains the speaker's most abiding narratee, even when the poem is not being apostrophized expressly. While the speaker at times presents the horrors of the ghetto for readers to see and for God to see, throughout the text they are most insistently presented for the poem, or poetry, to see and grapple with. Just as for Adorno writing after the war, for Marvil, writing in early 1942, the cultural institution of lyric poetry does shorthand for broader questions, albeit different questions, about subjectivity and human status in the face of systematic dehumanization. With its dynamics of address, "Di gas" puts itself on trial and effectively presents its subject matter as a challenge to its status as a poem.

The poem's position as its own primary narratee becomes evident early on. In stanzas 1 through 3, as we have seen, the speaker apostrophizes his poem directly: "Don't demand of me, my poem, don't torment me, I can't" or "Before me now you are a piece of raw substance" (stanza 1); "Once, my poem, you were my singer . . . today, I must tell you, you're strange to me" (stanza 2); "Don't ask me my poem, to recount the horrors" (stanza 3). The next five stanzas (4 through 8) narrate a scene of starving children accompanying their mother, who has just died on the street, until her corpse will be taken away and thrown into a mass grave. The smoothness of the transition back to directly addressing the poem in stanza nine—"Don't beg of me, poem, I beg you, don't ask, / the horror of these times permeates every task"—makes clear that the horrific ghetto street scene narrated between these direct apostrophes has been narrated to the poem; the poem is always speaking to itself, whether directly or indirectly.

The function of the poem as its own primary narratee can also be seen in the seamless way the apostrophe to the poem in stanzas 9 and 10 yields to further description. In stanza 10, the poet persona twice apostrophizes his poem, the second time in an imperative demanding that the poem witness the heartbreaking sight of an elderly man with swollen, disfigured legs slowly expiring in the street:

> Tsi filstu nisht lid mayns, dem vey in mayn hartsn,
> vi s'tsitert der zokn in gas, dort far kelt?
> Ze di fis zayne grobe, geshvolene belkes.
> un ingantsn, ingantsn a farloshene velt.
>
> Do you not feel, my poem, the woe in my heart
> at how the old man in the street shivers with cold?

See his legs, heavy, swollen timbers,
utterly and completely an extinguished world.
(trans. modified)

The speaker narrates the harrowing scenes of collapse and death to his poem, challenging the poem to confront its non- (or anti-) lyric content. Three instances of apostrophe in stanzas 11, 12, and 14 lend greater complexity to the poem's dynamics of address. The poem has already established a pattern of moving between self-apostrophe and descriptive scenes narrated to the poem. The introduction in stanza 11 of an aside appealing to God—"My God, see this! (*got mayner ze dos!*)"—proliferates the number and kinds of entities to which the poet appeals:

Di oygn fargleyzlt, farshtelt shoyn dos lebn,
S'tunklt dos umkum fun im azoy shvarts
azoy zitst er teg op—got mayner ze dos!
Vi er geyt oys a shtiler nokhn takt fun zayn harts.

With eyes glazed over, life hidden from view,
His end darkens all before him so black,
he sits so for days—My God, see this!
How he dies in silence with the beat of his heart.
(trans. modified)

Does God now supplant the poem as primary addressee? Or does the appeal to God to "see this" remain contained within the broader structure of scenes narrated to the poem?

Marvil seems to prolong and build on this ambiguity with the open-ended apostrophes in stanzas 12 and 14, which could plausibly be understood as directed to the poem, God, the reader, or any combination of these: "Oh see how he stretches out down on the rubble, / does he want to die so all will be over?" (stanza 12); "Oh see how the woman there picks at the garbage, / and keeps on eating the rot that she finds" (stanza 14). The addressee of these exhortations to witness these horrors is not specified as either the poem or God, but contextually they seem to be directed to both, as well as to the poem's implied reader. This sort of expansive apostrophizing of various addressees recurs later in the poem, even as the poem itself remains a constant addressee/narratee and the only one expressly invoked at multiple junctures. Thus, after the speaker in stanzas 14 through 16 depicts the scenes of people foraging in foul garbage bins and fighting dogs for rotten cabbage, in stanzas 17 and 18 he once again apostrophizes the poem, now in the form of an aggressive challenge, effectively asking his poem if it really wants to hear more of the horrors he has been detailing, implying that it might not be able to and still remain a poem. The speaker then goes on to depict how he accidentally steps on a frozen corpse only to realize that he is surrounded by numerous frozen corpses who collectively seem so unreconcilable with individual human beings that (a moment I return to below) he does not know whom he can even ask forgiveness of.

The poem's layers of apostrophe may translate the poet's very real fear that no one is truly seeing the dire plight of the Jews in the ghetto. In stanza 21 we see his pain transform into anger, his pleas to curses.

> Un ikh hob gesholtn, gloyb mir gesholtn,
> mikh, un di mentshn, un di gasn afile,
> un s'harts hot geveytont, leybish gebrumt,
> tsum himl, tsum himl, a gebrokhene tfile.
>
> And I did curse, believe me I cursed,
> myself and the people and even the streets,
> and my heart ached and, like a lion, growled
> to the sky, the sky, a broken prayer.
>
> (trans. modified)

The speaker asks his poem and its readers to believe him that he cursed other addressees: himself, the streets, and the sky (his curse a broken prayer to an ostensibly absent God).

Stanzas 22 and 24 each pose, again to a vague and capacious addressee or set of addressees, the rhetorical question regarding a crow that is eating human flesh: "Who can disturb her in this, oh who?!" Such questions recur in the following stanzas, as when the narrator wonders in stanza 28 who it was who mumbled the words, upon seeing a dead child in the street, "Not the first, not the last." At times, questions voiced by various figures on the street coincide with rhetorical questions posed by the narrator, as for example when, in the next stanza (29), the questions, "Who knows whose this is there? Who gave birth to it? / For whom too soon sacrificed from this world?" can be read as questions voiced by people gathered around the dead child and as rhetorical questions posed by the narrator of "Di gas." The speaker poses a further rhetorical question in stanza 31 apropos of a man who has run out in the snow stark naked: "And how can you help him?"

In the poem's final four stanzas the speaker returns to direct apostrophe to his poem. As I will explore below, although the damage to the manuscript makes it impossible to know for certain what these closing stanzas say, they clearly pose the question of the (im)possibility of returning to a more conventional, gentler, and individual-affirming genre of nature lyric after the harrowing scenes that have filled the poem to that point. Marvil chooses to invest the question of whether lyric poetry as conventionally understood is still possible with all the weight of the unfathomable crisis in which he is caught in the Warsaw ghetto. As I will discuss, the poetry that Marvil struggles with and (literally) interrogates belongs to a specifically lyric tradition. This is significant and by no means self-evident. One could easily imagine Marvil's staging of lyric poetry interrupted—the poem/song (*lid*) that had heretofore served his individual voice but has now become overwhelmed by the pain and death of thousands—yielding to a collective lament. Yet it does not. Even as "Di gas" depicts a community facing inhumane conditions and mass death, unlike Rokhl Auerbach's stunning prose poem of November 1943 commemorating the destroyed Jewish community of Warsaw, "Yizkor 1943," Marvil's poem tends not to draw on communal mourning rituals. Instead, the central drama continues to play out between poet and poem, and, as we will see, the sole instance when the narrating poet persona speaks in the first-person plural, the *we* he utters consists of him and his poem. The speaker presents the inhumane suffering of the ghetto inhabitants before a certain conception and cultural institution of lyric poetry. Marvil's poem takes stock of the profundity of the crisis largely through questions of how and why poetry can or cannot accommodate such suffering and such collapse.

SELF-APOSTROPHE IN "DI GAS"

While it would be hazardous to claim that the self-apostrophe of Marvil's poem, its particular way of addressing (and challenging) itself as a poem, is unprecedented, self-apostrophe in "Di gas" is decidedly more radical than in many other poems that deploy it. Marvil uses it to question the very possibility of lyric poetry in the face of the dehumanization taking place in the Warsaw ghetto streets. Several poems' speakers call on the poems they are speaking to fulfill subjective needs, to venture into and perform tasks in the world, or to have effects on or deliver messages to readers. By contrast Marvil uses self-apostrophe to ask whether the conditions of the Warsaw ghetto are compatible with the conditions of possibility of poetry. Unlike other self-apostrophizing poems, "Di gas" does not assume that it is in fact a poem in the lyric tradition and thus capable of being called on to do the sorts of things such poems usually do. Voiced in response to a radical threat to human existence, Marvil's poem confronts poetry as such from a place of extreme precarity. Unlike in my analysis in chapter 5 of how Leyb Goldin engages with a very specific set of European, modernist prose intertexts, my following analysis of the dynamics of poetic (auto-)address extends into poems that likely were not—or that chronologically could not have been—part of Marvil's frame of reference. My aim in placing Marvil's poem in this far-flung constellation of poems is to throw into relief the specificity and poignancy of Marvil's poetic self-apostrophe.

Before we take up the question of the distinctness of self-apostrophe in "Di gas" vis-à-vis other self-apostrophizing poems, it will be helpful to distinguish poetic self-apostrophe from the considerably more widespread phenomenon of self-reference. Poems and songs that refer to themselves are common, from T. S. Eliot's high modernist "The Waste Land" ("These fragments I have shored against my ruins") to John Ashbery's postmodern "Paradoxes and Oxymorons" (from his 1980 collection *Shadow Train*), which opens with the line, "This poem is concerned with language on a very plain level"[9] to contemporary American poet Karen Glenn's "The Poem Wants a Drink" ("In the workshop, students analyze / what each poem wants, what each one / strives to be. Well, this poem is / a layabout with limited ambitions. It wants / a drink") —and many, many poems in between. Equally prominent in popular songs, this sort of self-reference occurs, to point to but a few examples, in Bob Dylan's early "Song to Woody" ("Hey, hey Woody Guthrie, I wrote you a song / 'Bout a funny ol' world that's a-comin' along"), Elton John's "Your Song" ("Oh, I know it's not much, but it's the best I can do / My gift is my song and this one's for you"), and James Taylor's "Fire and Rain" ("I walked out this morning and I wrote down this song / I just can't remember who to send it to").

The self-apostrophe of Marvil's poem likewise differs from a more common apostrophic trope whereby poems address the abstract entities of poetry or poesy or related concepts such as intellectual beauty. (Again, such poems apostrophizing poetry or poesy writ large should not be conflated with the many poems that merely refer to poetry, such as Marianne Moore's famous "Poetry.") If William Wordsworth effectively replaced the muse with Nature, other poets cut out the middle woman altogether and address poetry or related entities directly. Percy Bysshe Shelley, for example, apostrophizes intellectual beauty in his 1816 "Hymn to Intellectual Beauty" ("I vow'd that I would dedicate my powers / To thee and thine: have I not kept the vow?"; lines 61–62). John Keats apostrophizes poesy in his 1816 "Sleep and Poetry" ("Oh Poesy! For thee I grasp my pen / That am not yet a glorious denizen / Of thy wide heaven"; lines 53–55). Such examples could be multiplied.

Marvil's poet-persona's apostrophe of his poem is of course related to such appeals to the broader and often muse-like categories of poetry, beauty, and so forth, yet it belongs to a more restricted set of poems that address not poetry writ large but themselves as specific works. Even this narrower category of self-apostrophizing poems is internally varied and has a long history. In the fifth book of *Troilus and Criseyde,* for example, Geoffrey Chaucer addresses his epic poem, "Go litel bok, go, litel myn tragedye." The poetic voice instructs his "litel bok" how to behave in the world (or in the world of poetry): it should not be envious but rather humbly respect the tradition of poesy (Chaucer's poem is instructed to kiss the steps where Virgil, Ovid, Homer, Lucan, and Stace pace). The poem's narrator furthermore tells his poem that he has asked God to see to it that it not be misread or miscopied and that it be understood widely notwithstanding the great prevailing diversity in spoken and written English.

Variations on such instructions and wishes regarding what a poem or book of poems should do and how it should fare—what tasks it should accomplish and how it should be read and received—are at the heart of probably most instances of self-apostrophizing poems. The poet speaker of Joachim du Bellay's sixteenth-century sonnet "À son livre" (from his 1558 collection *Les Regrets*) instructs his book, as it is heading off to the prince's court without its author, to wish a happy life to anyone who receives the book graciously. Comically piling up curses for anyone who would slight the book, however, he instructs it to wish any such clever critic the tears their slight has caused it, the author's annoying pains, and also that they should take a long journey and the whole time pine away for home, and that they should grow old in servitude, experiencing nothing but ingratitude to the bitter end, while their fortune gets spent ("qu'on mange son bien") while they are gone! Robert Louis Stevenson in "Envoy," the first poem proper after a four-line dedication of his 1887 book of poems *Underwoods,* echoes Chaucer, albeit in an insipidly convivial mode, by instructing his "little book" regarding the blessings it should give readers:

Go, little book, and wish to all
Flowers in the garden, meat in the hall,

A bin of wine, a spice of wit,
A house with lawns enclosing it,
A living river by the door,
A nightingale in the sycamore!

The opening lines of "Mandheela" (1980) by the Somali poet Gaarriye (Maxamed Zaashi Dhamac) provide a further, albeit a far more political, example of this same broad function of poetic self-apostrophe. I quote here from the rough and more literal bridge translation (which preserves the poem's apostrophe to itself) rather than the final translation (which removes it):

Oh poem! Hear me.
Oh head! Pregnant. [with creativity]
Praise the *jiifto*. [i.e., in writing an excellent *jiifto* you are praising the form; the *jiifto* is a type of poem of which the meter is the same as that used in this *hees* poem]
Oh masafo! Be ready to fight. (?) [*masafo* is another type of poem with a line metrically equivalent more or less to two *jiifto* lines]
Oh water in a well! Do not come to an end. . . . [water here is representative of the creative poetic impulse]

Oh gun! Do not stop.
Oh criminal! Do not sleep.
Oh lactating brain [a reference to the way the brain is full of poetry which is sustenance]
do not leave the poem alone. [i.e., do not give it up][10]

As we can discern from this admittedly unsystematic sample, self-apostrophe in poems has at least two (often overlapping) functions: (1) the poem is summoned much like a muse and beseeched not to abandon the poet and to bestow upon them the creative powers necessary to write the poem, and (2) the poem is given instructions or blessings indicating the effects it should have in the world. In the above examples, Chaucer's, du Bellay's, and Stevenson's apostrophes to their books fall into the second category (go out in the world and do such and such, have such and such a fate, or have such and such effects on readers), and Gaarriye's "Mandheela" constitutes a hybrid. In Gaarriye's poem, the poetic voice both beseeches the poem to supply him with creative powers, and prays that his poem, as his political weapon, his "gun," will have real effects in the world.

The apostrophes of Marvil's poet to his poem in "Di gas" do not follow either of these models of poetic self-apostrophe. Marvil's poet apostrophizes his poem in ways that recall the invocation of the poem itself as a sort of muse, yet "Di gas" turns this trope inside out. The poet does not beg his poem to remain with him and lend him the necessary powers to bring it to fruition. On the contrary, he repeatedly beseeches his poem to release him from the unbearable process of its composition; he would ostensibly like nothing better than for his poem to abandon him, the sooner the better! As for the tradition of bestowing wishes and instructions on the poem and its effects and fate in the world, "Di gas" again ventures into different territory. While the poem can be said to imply its readers (as any text does), Marvil notably does not take up the issue of his poem's possible audience or legacy in any explicit way. Any concern with the poem's effects or fate in the world or with who might read it (and when and how) remains muted and implicit. In addressing their books, Chaucer, du Bellay, and Stevenson refer to them as completed texts ready to go find readers and carry out various tasks in the world. The status of possible readers of "Di gas," of its own stability and transmissibility to such readers, and indeed of "the world," are all radically in question in ways that the work of apostrophe in Marvil's poem reflects.

The contingency of all possible addressees of "The Street"—very much including itself—is one of several fundamental ways it differs from the poem "Mimaamakim" ("From the Depths"), which Chava Rosenfarb wrote in Brussels in September 1946, after she was liberated from Bergen-Belson the previous year. Looking back at the Lodz ghetto, Rosenfarb's poem, like Marvil's "Di gas," unfolds as an extended apostrophe primarily to itself.[11] The structural similarity of these poems in the use they make of auto-apostrophe—the extended way they each address themselves as poems—highlights key differences in the dynamics of address of a poem written during the volatile and radically uncertain circumstances of a ghetto, and one written after—if only shortly after—the end of the war to commemorate the perished inhabitants of a ghetto. The authorial lyric voice in Rosenfarb's poem of nearly fifty quatrains apostrophizes her "song" itself throughout, from the opening lines "Fun di tifenishn ruf ikh dikh, / Lid fun farshnitener heym . . ." ("From the depths I call you, / Song of home interrupted . . .") to the final stanzas:

To ruf ikh dikh fun tifenishn, du mayn lid
Gey uf fun zeyer ash un zeyere beyner;
Kum arayn in mayn yungn, tsefibertn guf

Mit zeyere nisht derkholemte benkshaftn
Un nisht deryomerte geveynen.

Un eybik zey in mayn yedn tog,
Un heylik in mayn yeder shure,
Gey uf in mayn yontefdikn blut
Mit griner hofenung un mit gvure.

So, I call to you from the depths, you my song,
Rise up from their [the murdered generations'] ash and bones
Come into my young, feverish body
Bring their undreamt yearning and unwailed moans.

And make them rise in my joyous blood
With the green of hope, with pride.
Make them live forever in my every day,
Make them holy in my lines.

(trans. Hannah Pollin-Galay)

Along the way, Rosenfarb's lyric voice revisits sites and scenes of Lodz ghetto life in which she sees "you," her "holy song of ruined home." She sees her song, that is, as already there in the ghetto, already emerging in the ghetto scenes and flowing, as it were, into the song that she now sings (shortly) after the fact. This merging of songs and voices, ghetto scenes and their commemoration, becomes most explicit when the apostrophized song visits the home of Rosenfarb's friend, mentor, and, according to Hannah Polin-Galay, possibly lover, the Lodz ghetto poet Simkhe-Bunim Shayevitsh.[12] In the pocket of Shayevitsh's shirt, strewn over his daughter Blimele's doll cradle, Rosenfarb's song discovers the rotted and tear-stained paper on which the murdered poet had written and rubbed out lines. (The reference is to Shayevitsh's 1942 Lodz ghetto poem "Lekh-lekho," which, as Rosenfarb explains in a note, had not yet been recovered at the time she wrote "Mimaamakim.") Rosenfarb's song is a kind of resurrection of Shayevitsh's poem, born (in Blimele's cradle) of the eroticized union between her and Shayevitsh's voices.

After the war, Rosenfarb retroactively invests scenes of Lodz ghetto life with significance that allows them to merge seamlessly with her commemorative vantage point as a survivor. At the time they were lived, the moments of ghetto life recalled in "From the Depths" could scarcely have been experienced as the apotheosis of nearness to God, or sweetness of food, or brightness of the home ("Nowhere else had life held such purpose / And no one had ever felt so close to God"; "Never was a bite so sweet / As there around that ghetto table / Where a mother served hot water-stew"; "And never did walls gleam so bright / As they did at home, by windows in the dark / As at that last meal, that last time / During those final family talks"). It is only after having lived beyond the radically contingent temporality of the ghetto years, paradoxically, that Rosenfarb can absorb scenes of ghetto life into a sentimentalizing and sacralizing narrative of continuity with her poem, as though the essence of ghetto life were always already moving toward its distillation in her commemorative song. This poetic *mise-en-scène* of continuity allows Rosenfarb to "see" her song roaming through scenes from the Lodz ghetto and to describe it as merging with the voices of the murdered in general and with Shayevitsh's in particular, and to call on her song to make the sacred dead live on eternally in her song's lines. The confidence of Rosenfarb's lyric persona in the power of her song to reach back to the Lodz ghetto, embody and sacralize the dead, and lend them eternal poetic life contrasts markedly with the tormented ways that Marvil, in light of the dehumanizing thrust of the scenes recounted in his song, insistently questions its very status as a song and whether or not it can ever be reconciled with his own subjectivity and aims as its not-quite-willing singer.

Jonathan Culler's reassessment of apostrophe and its relationship to poetic tradition and lyric transcendence is highly suggestive for an appreciation of the ramifications of the speaker's appeal in "Di gas" for pity and release from his poetic calling. Culler's work also helps us more fully understand what is at stake in the tension in Marvil's poem between, on the one hand, narrative vignettes describing the horrors of the Warsaw ghetto streets and, on the other, lyric transcendence.

In the early 1980s Culler challenged the tendency among scholars of poetry to neglect or suppress the role of apostrophe in the lyric tradition or to discount its singularity by assimilating it to other functions such as description. Culler provocatively identified precisely this "embarrassing" device as the poetic trope par excellence, for at least two reasons.[13] First, he sees in the deployment of apostrophe a prime way of signaling that one is engaging in poetic speech, speaking as a poet: "The vocative of apostrophe is a device which the poetic voice uses to establish with an object a relationship which helps to constitute him. The object is treated as a subject, an *I* which implies a certain type of *you* in its turn. One who successfully invokes nature is one to whom nature might, in its turn, speak. He makes himself poet, visionary. Thus, invocation is a figure of vocation. This is obvious when one thinks *how often invocations seek pity or assistance for projects and situations specifically related to the poetic vocation*" (Culler, *The Pursuit of Signs*, 142; emphasis added).

Second, Culler theorizes how in deploying apostrophe the lyric subject situates (or attempts to situate) itself within a long tradition of sublime poetry: "It [apostrophe] is the pure embodiment of poetic pretension: of the subject's claim that in his verse he is not merely an empirical poet, a writer of verse, but the embodiment of poetic tradition and of the spirit of poesy. Apostrophe is perhaps always an indirect invocation of the muse. Devoid of semantic reference, the O of apostrophe refers to other apostrophes and thus to the lineage and conventions of sublime poetry" (143). The vocative performance of apostrophe can carry such weight for Culler because he sees such performance as intimately tied to lyric temporality and lyric transcendence. Apostrophe's vocative is an essentially timeless *now* of poetic enunciation, and is thus always in tension with the sequential time of narrative.[14] Lyric for Culler is the triumph of the apostrophic over the narrative (149). That this is so can be seen, Culler submits, in the great Romantic odes, in which, on the level of narrative, precious little happens: "Nothing need happen because the poem itself is to be the happening" (149). The time of apostrophe, in other words, is the time of the happening of poetry itself as an event, as opposed to the time of narrative, which describes and recounts fictional or historical occurrences.

For Culler, apostrophe serves as something like the on-ramp by which poets enter the poetic tradition. The sustaining of apostrophe is, at its core, the production of the event of the poem itself. In apostrophizing natural objects, poets constitute themselves as embodiments of poetic speech and the legatees of earlier poets. Marvil, however, takes up the quintessentially lyric device of apostrophe to starkly different ends. He deploys apostrophe not so much to inscribe his lyric voice in a poetic tradition as, rather, to confront the limits of that tradition. This crucial difference is legible in the fact that Marvil's poet does not apostrophize objects but rather his poem itself. Were the poet figure to apostrophize the awful things he encounters—dying people, abandoned children, rubbish, crows, dogs, frozen human corpses, and dismembered body parts—he would remain, albeit excruciatingly, within traditional lyric models. He would speak poetically even of these things, and any claim regarding the impossibility of speaking poetically in or of such circumstances would be forcefully contradicted by the fact of the apostrophic vocative performance. A similar contradiction may, strictly speaking, arise when the poet figure in "Di gas" announces that he cannot write a poem "as before" about the horrors of the ghetto streets—any poem articulating its own impossibility must deny this claim by its very existence—but the fact that in Marvil's poem the claim is made to his poem itself complicates the picture in significant ways. Marvil does not apostrophize objects in order to inscribe himself in the tradition of lyric but rather apostrophizes his poem to question whether the poetic tradition is compatible with the degradation of human status so wantonly evident in the ghetto streets. Marvil, that is, short-circuits apostrophe, the device that provides the way into the poetic tradition, in order to confront it from its outer edge.

The fact that the poem itself is the primary narratee of both the descriptive or narrative segments and the intermittent apostrophes heightens the challenge Marvil's poem presents to poetry per se. As Culler argues, the inherent conflict that lyric stages between apostrophe and narrative is typically resolved with poems as events triumphing in apostrophe and apostrophic temporality over narrative events and temporality. In Marvil's poem, however, apostrophe and narrative are more inextricably entangled, and whether the former can in fact transcend the latter remains profoundly in doubt. As we have seen, the narration of horrific events to the poem and the apostrophes to the poem about its status as a poem in the face of such events flow in and out of each other almost seamlessly. The apostrophes do not allow for winged poetic speech to soar over the narrated events because both the narration and the apostrophes arrive at the same address, the poem. Instead, the events described pile up before the poem as narratee, and the apostrophes to the poem question whether a lyric poem as such can remain possible in view of them. The poem's striking apostrophes do not permit the event of the poem straightforwardly to occur but fundamentally and repeatedly question the possibility of such a poetic event. If in the great Romantic odes that make such free use of apostrophe, little happens or needs to happen because the event of the poem is happening, in Marvel's tormented poem of and from the Warsaw ghetto, far too many horrible things are happening in the street for the horror to be transcended in the event and lyrical temporality of a poem. In this way, too, Marvil deploys the mechanism of lyric transcendence—apostrophe—to derail transcendence.

LYRIC IN THE STREETS?

While Marvil's "Di gas" is markedly self-referential in its central structures of address—its narrator's apostrophe to the poem itself—it is not hermetic. On the contrary, as its title signals, what the poem brings to bear on the question of the possibility of writing a lyric poem is precisely life—and death—in the Warsaw ghetto streets. The poem's recursive apostrophes to itself as a poem do not serve to seal it off from the conditions of the street but rather highlight, as a condition of possibility for lyric poetry, a certain social and cultural—or we might say, more broadly, human—infrastructure that the depicted street scenes reveal to be in ruins. The poet persona's struggle to produce, and to evade, his poem reveals his subjective lyric voice to be both situated over against the objective conditions of the street, and to be inextricably bound to those horrific conditions. In other words, the poem lays bare how the lyric subject is not hermetically protected from the street and why they thus cannot achieve poetic transcendence. In fact, as I will argue, the ostensible turn inward that Marvil's poem takes, its self-reflexive preoccupation with itself qua poem, reflects the radical precarity of all the most basic elements of the cultural infrastructure that are required to sustain (even) would-be transcendent lyrics.

Marvil's poem takes us through three main, interrelated aspects of the state of collapse with which it deems itself as a poem to be incompatible yet that it cannot escape: the collapse of ritual containment of death, the collapse or disintegration of the human form into dismembered body parts, and the collapse of the distinction between human and animal. Looking more closely at the poem's treatment of each of these forms of collapse will help us better comprehend the poem's striking structure of self-apostrophe as a response to the collapsing human infrastructure that is lyric poetry's—usually invisible—condition of possibility.

Marvil's poem, especially in its first extended vignette (stanzas 4–8), highlights how the magnitude and nature of death in the Warsaw ghetto in the winter of 1941–1942 was overwhelming the resources the ghetto's inhabitants could muster to bury and mourn the dead. Children sit by their mother's corpse and bewail that they will not be able to find her grave, as she will be buried anonymously in a mass pit:[15]

Nisht kenen gefinen ir keyver, O vey undz!
Di grub vert farfult mit ir gebeyn
vi zi vert gevorfn, tsuzamen mit tsendlik
un keyn mes hot di skhie—tsu ruen aleyn.

Not being able to find her grave, woe to us!
The pit will be filled with her bones

as she's thrown in with scores of others,
and no corpse has the privilege of resting alone.
(stanza 8; trans. modified)

The ubiquity of death and the radical collapse of the cultural norms that normally surround it manifest a loss of human status that makes the poet question whether the horrors of the ghetto are compatible with a lyric poem or lyric subjectivity.

Nisht mon bay mir lid mayns, ikh bet dikh nisht mon,
dem groyl fun di tsaytn, vos geyt uf yedn-tog,
far di oygn di tribe, vos faykhtn in trern
un s'harts vos s'tsapelt azoy in a klog.

Don't exhort me, my poem, I beg you don't demand of me
the horrors of these times, which rise each day
before my sad eyes wet with tears
and my heart trembling in lament.
(stanza 9; trans. modified)

The speaker beseeches his poem not to compel him to convey the horrors of the street because bearing witness to such horrors is irreconcilable with what lyric has heretofore meant for him. If the poem demands to be about the horrors of the street, it can no longer be his song, and the sine qua non of lyric poetry, the poet's subjectivity, is threatened; the poem no longer obeys its author (or sings his song) but rather assaults him. While writing a poem formerly distilled and articulated his subjectivity, writing a poem about the ghetto streets threatens to annihilate it.

The suffering and destitution of the ghetto's population have become so dire that humans can barely remain distinct from animals. People rummage in the garbage for putrid remains of food such as rotten bones of non-kosher animals like horses (stanzas 14–15). Not infrequently, people must fight with dogs for rotten cabbage:

Shteyn mentshn un hint un klaybn tsuzamen
viln eyner dem tsveytn, dem bisn aroysraysn,
treft oft, az iber a kroyt a farfoyltn
muz mentsh un hunt in hefker zikh raysn!

Dogs and people stand foraging together,
want to tear pieces from each other's mouths,

so it happens often over cabbage that's rotten,
man and dog will stand fighting it out!
(stanza 16)

Human being and dog square off as equals in this macabre scene, each trying to tear foul food from the other's jaws.

The speaker literally steps on corpses, and sees how dead human bodies, and body parts, are eaten by crows and dogs. The stanzas directly preceding the turn to depictions of the anonymous and dismembered dead in the streets, left to be fed upon by animals, mark a turning point in the speaker's relationship to his poem. Whereas heretofore, he has pleaded with his poem to release him from the task of depicting the horrors of the street, in stanzas 17 and 18, at the midpoint of the thirty-seven-stanza poem, he becomes more confrontational vis-à-vis his unrelenting *lid*:

Tsi vilstu, nokh lid mayns hern un hern,
dem groyl fun di gasn, in toyznter farbn,
vi s'geyen oys mentshn, un zinkn fun hunger.
Un vi andere vider faln un shtarbn?!

To her vos af gasn kh'hob haynt bagegnt:
Untern shney ligt a toyter, fardekt un bahaltn.
Ikh hob nisht gezen un af im kh'bin getretn
Nisht derkent kh'hob dem mes, fun a yungn tsi an altn.

Do you, my poem, still want to hear more,
the horror in the streets in thousands of hues,
how people are expiring, sinking from hunger,
and others just drop dead?

So listen to what I encountered today:
under the snow a hidden corpse lay
I did not see him, and on him I stepped,
and I couldn't tell if he was young or old.
(trans. modified)

Instead of begging for release, the speaker now aggressively challenges his poem to bear witness to the full extent of the horror. We could paraphrase the speaker as saying: "My poem, if you still insist on me writing you, after all I've shown you that is incompatible with poetry, then listen to *this* and tell me if you still think that you can remain a poem!" Tormented by the unrelenting demands of his poem, the speaker seems to suggest that he will now push the poem to its breaking point.

The anti-poetic evidence the poet now presents to the poem delves further into the loss of human status: he accidentally steps on a frozen corpse, which he cannot recognize as young or old (stanza 18). Wishing to beg forgiveness of the man on whom he had tread, he quickly realizes that he is in fact surrounded by the corpses of numerous people who "all had died like dogs" in the freezing night (stanza 20).[16] Amid so many dead bodies the speaker does not know of whom to ask forgiveness, and so asks these frozen "friends": "To vemen bet men mekhile?!—zogt mir fraynd!" (So of whom does one ask forgiveness?!—Tell me, friends! [stanza 20]). The speaker's rhetorical question poignantly evokes comparison between the catastrophic magnitude of anonymous death and the traditional Jewish practice of *taharah*, an elaborate set of cleansing and purification rituals performed by the *khevre-kedishe* (burial society) to prepare the deceased for burial.[17] Throughout the course of these ritual preparations, the deceased is treated with utmost respect, and members of the *khevre-kedishe* twice address them by name and ask forgiveness for any indignity they may inadvertently cause them despite their best intentions (the prayer for *mekhile* before the washing is undertaken) or may have caused them (the prayer after the *taharah*). It is worth noting that traditionally any body part or even any cloth or bandage containing the deceased's bodily fluid is buried in the coffin in order to respect the integrity of their body. By contrast the speaker in Marvil's poem is surrounded by frozen corpses and anonymous body parts. None of these dead bodies will be properly buried, and their namelessness and disintegration leave the speaker unable even to beg them for forgiveness.[18]

As the speaker is unleashing curses, a crow wanders by and treads on and begins to devour the corpses, a scene that greatly intensifies the collapse of the human/animal distinction:

A kro hot farblondzshet shvarts vi di tsayt,
un geyt mit a trit, fun a tayvl, nisht mer,
tret iber meysim un kukt iber zey,
un ver ken ir in dem shtern, o ver?!

Amol flegt zi ophitn katsovishe shteln,
mitn royb in shrek farshvindn af dekher.

Haynt geyt zi um fray tsvishn toyte
un pikt in di meysim oys—shtiker leber

Frest zi di fleyshn fun mentshlekhe gufim,
un geyt mit a trit, fun a tayvl, nisht mer
trit iber meysim un shendet zey.
Un ver ken ir in dem shtern o ver?!

A crow has wandered this way, black as the times,
and walks with the step of a devil, no less,
steps over corpses, inspecting them,
and who can stop her in this, o who?

Once she trained her sights on butchers' stalls,
escaped in fright to the roofs with her spoils.
Today she walks freely among the dead
and pecks out of the corpses—pieces of liver.

She devours the flesh of human bodies
and walks with the step of a devil no less,
steps over corpses and defiles them.
And who can stop her in this, o who?
(stanzas 22–24; trans. modified)

Whereas the devilish crow who embodies the darkness of the times formerly swooped down to steal scraps from the stalls of non-kosher butchers (*katsovishe shteln*), she now treads unencumbered on the corpses of Jews and pecks out pieces of their livers. Human beings have become carrion, and no one in the ghetto can muster the resources to prevent this ("And who can stop her in this, o who?").

In stanzas 25 and 26, we get a glimpse of what becomes of the human corpses that cannot be placed beyond the reach of hungry animals and properly buried:

Oft trefst in gas a shtik fleysh a gefroyrns,
mit ayz un shney fartulyet, fardekt.
Dernebn a hunt, a dershrokn-oysgeshnirter,
rayst fun dem fleysh azoy girik un lekt.

Derkenstu a hant, a fus, fun a mentshn,
vos ligt shoyn avade lang un fargesn,

un s'iz shoyn nishto vos tsu bagrobn,
ken im der hunt fray do ufraysn!

In the street you often come upon a frozen piece of flesh,
wrapped, covered in snow and ice.
Nearby a dog, frightened and emaciated,
greedily licks and tears at the flesh.

You recognize a hand, a foot of a person
that without doubt has long lain there forgotten,
and there is no longer enough to bury,
so the dog can tear at it freely!
(trans. modified)

The assault on the integrity of the human form initiated by the demonic crow in stanzas 22 through 24, we learn, continues until only dismembered and largely devoured human remains are left. The persona "often" comes upon pieces of frozen human flesh that only sometimes can be recognized as distinct body parts (a hand, a foot). If no one could impede the crow who began pecking out the livers of the dead, certainly there is nothing to stop the hungry dogs from eating the remaining disarticulated body parts.

Throughout the poem, Marvil draws on the rhetorical device of hypotyposis (vivid description) of a death or a dead body. Hypotyposis of someone's death or of a dead person typically serves to individualize and memorialize a particular figure. This is sometimes the case in Marvil's poem, as for example when he describes a dead boy in the street who has lain himself down "like a holy offering" that no mother or father, and no one else, comes to claim (stanza 28). Frequently, however, one corpse merely displaces the next. The speaker attempts to memorialize the anonymous dead, but the dead are so numerous that they exceed the limits of poetic memorialization. Death in the street becomes unmemorializable: ultimately, not even intact anonymous bodies remain but only body parts, ravaged by animals.

In the face of the unrelenting assault on the human status evident everywhere in the Warsaw ghetto streets, the poet figure's would-be song no longer sings his human subjectivity, it threatens to cancel it. The poet would like his poem to offer him refuge from the pain and death of the ghetto, but he finds that the ghetto streets inexorably invade the space of what is no longer "his" poem but rather his shattering torment. The question poses itself: what is the speaker's new relationship to his poem if it is no longer that of singer to his song? This question requires us to return to the poem's seeming absorption of scenes from the ghetto streets into a dialogue between poet and poem. In this way we can take fuller measure of the crisis that the poem's ostensible self-absorption dramatizes.

The precarity, disease, starvation, and death that permeate the streets in which the speaker moves not only threaten the integrity of his own subjectivity but also throw into doubt whether any audience will receive his words. Even lyric poetry, the most subjective of verbal arts, requires some minimal external supports. So basic that they are usually taken for granted, these include the transmissibility of the poem in a safe recorded form to a culturally intact readership that can receive it. But in this case, the physical survival of the text and the physical and cultural survival of a Yiddish readership could hardly be taken for granted. Were Marvil to instruct his poem to go out in the world and do certain things, or about how to be received by readers, he would presume a number of things that underlie the more typical types of self-apostrophe in Chaucer and Stevens—or indeed in Rosenfarb, trying to write again after the catastrophe—discussed above: a more or less stable physical and cultural world, a readership, and a transmittable text. Marvil cannot depend on any of these fundamental entities. The entire inward-spiraling structure of lyric self-apostrophe at the heart of the poem reflects a crisis in cultural infrastructure: the poem addresses itself, I would argue, not least because all the other candidates to receive it are in dire peril. Marvil's poem remains inextricably caught in the contingency and horror of the present of its writing and cannot confidently envision its own survival, transmission, and ultimate reception by readers. Marvil's small circle of readers (or auditors), friends in the Warsaw ghetto including Sh. Stefinski, Hillel Zeitlin, and Itzhak Katzenelson, provided an immediate supportive audience but could not resolve the broader crisis of the ultimate fate and readership of works written in the ghettos.[19]

To whom can this poem be addressed if not to itself? Who else is in a position to receive it? Other candidates to be the poem's addressee—a "dear reader," posterity, fellow ghetto inmates, God—all seem variously vulnerable. Poetic transcendence's usually invisible material preconditions become visible in their disintegration. No longer a vehicle for subjective expression or a refuge for the lyric subject to retreat into, the poem provides, in lieu of stable cultural institutions guaranteeing transmission and communication, a minimal structure of vocalization. The poem no longer voices the plenitudinous lyric subject but does function as perhaps the only remaining addressee that allows the tormented and imperiled subject to speak at all. What remains is a poetic self-apostrophe meditating on how a poem is incommensurable with such inhuman circumstances. And yet, "The Street" is of course a poem. It is a poem, however, that confronts poetry at the limits of poetry's own conditions of possibility. The speaker's foothold in the Yiddish cultural world and in the world tout court is fast eroding as the ghetto is reduced to destitution and death.

THE MOON AND THE STARS, SEEN FROM THE GHETTO

The poem's closing stanzas crucially dramatize the changed meanings and functions of poetry in the face of the unfolding catastrophe. Towards the poem's end the lyric persona manages to return part way to a more conventional poetic mode—nature lyric. It is difficult to parse what is at stake in this attempted return to traditional themes of nature because the manuscript itself poignantly embodies the breakdown of cultural infrastructure that the poem has been contending with throughout: the final page of Marvil's poem was badly damaged during its time underground. The manuscript is missing the last words of the last two verses of stanza 34, and we also have only the beginnings, and progressively less, of each verse in the final three stanzas (35–37; see figure 2).[20] If, as I have argued, Marvil's poem speaks to itself in large part because there is no obvious other stable addressee who could receive it, the damaged manuscript aptly manifests this crisis in transmissibility. The text's very survival was always radically uncertain, and who might ever receive it is a question that haunts Marvil's poem and animates its particular use of apostrophe and self-apostrophe. The fate of the poem since being unearthed in December 1950 demonstrates that the crisis of address it implicitly dramatizes would not be resolved by a postwar readership. To this day, Marvil's "Di gas" has never been properly published in Yiddish. To my knowledge it has never been printed in any journal or anthology. The only form in which Marvil's poem is readily available to readers in the original remains the handwritten manuscript that survived in the Oyneg Shabes archive, electronic copies of which are available online. Sarah Traister Moskovitz's translation published on her website is, to my knowledge, the only available English rendering of Marvil's poem.[21]

The damaged final stanzas of Marvil's poem (33–37) read:

Azoy geyn uf di bilder, di bilder far di oygn.
Groylik un brudik in hefker fun vey.

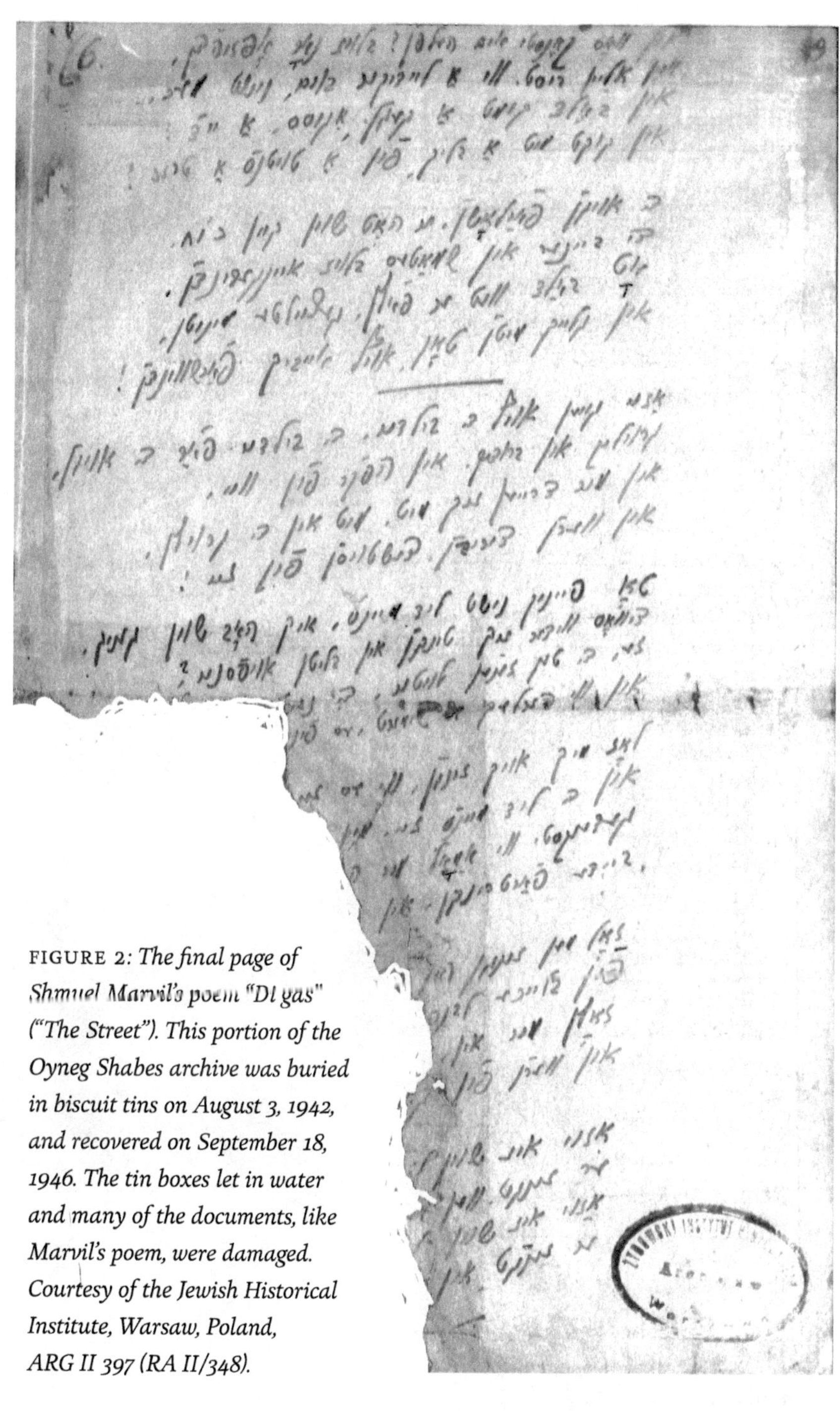

FIGURE 2: *The final page of Shmuel Marvil's poem "Di gas" ("The Street"). This portion of the Oyneg Shabes archive was buried in biscuit tins on August 3, 1942, and recovered on September 18, 1946. The tin boxes let in water and many of the documents, like Marvil's poem, were damaged. Courtesy of the Jewish Historical Institute, Warsaw, Poland, ARG II 397 (RA II/348).*

Un mir dreyen zikh mit, mit in di groyln,
un vern tseribn, tseshtoysn fun zey!

To paynik nisht lid mayns, ikh hob shoyn genug.
Tsuvos vider mikh tunkn in blutn afsnay?
Ze, di teg zenen loyter, di nekh[t . . .]
Un vi herlekh [gl?]limert es fun . . .

Loz mikh oykh zingen, vi es zin[. . .]
Un du lid mayns zay mayn [. . .]
Gedenkst vi amol mir h[obn . . .]
Beyde fartrunkn in [. . .]

Zol mayn zingen fun [. . .]
Fun bleykher levone [. . .]
Zoln mir in [. . .]
Un vern fun [. . .]

Azoy iz shoyn l[. . .][22]
Er zingt ven er [. . .]
Azoy iz shoyn l[. . .]
Er zingt un [. . .]

So rise these pictures before my eyes,
Gruesome and filthy in a chaos of pain,
And we too swirl along in the horrors,
and get shredded and crushed by them!

So don't torture me poem, I've had enough.
Why dip me in blood yet again?
See how clear the days are, the nights [. . .]
And how lovely [it glimmers from?]

Let me, too, sing like [missing] sing[s]
And you, my song, be my [. . .]
Remember how we once [. . .]
Both drowning in [. . .]

Let my singing [be?] of [. . .]
of pale moon [. . .]
May we in [. . .]
and become of/from [. . .]

So there is already/So it is already [. . .]
He/It sings when he/it [. . .]
So already is [. . .]
He/It sings and [. . .]
(trans. modified)

A possibility for the first two lines of stanza 36 is that "Zol mayn zingen fun . . ." might end with: "[missing noun] un" or "[missing noun] zayn un." Alternatively or additionally, the following line, "Fun blaykhe levone," could also end in "zayn."[23] Either possibility (or the combination of both) would yield the meaning: "Let my singing [be about . . . and] about the pale moon" or, less awkwardly but less literally, "Let me sing about . . . and/about the pale moon."

While the damaged manuscript renders it impossible to know precisely what Marvil was attempting with this return to nature lyric, one can certainly appreciate the ironic structure of the poem's extensive "detour" through the Warsaw ghetto streets en route to its ultimate arrival at lines extolling the beauty of the pale moon and (it seems likely) the shimmering stars. I do not mean to suggest that the poem's irony vis-à-vis the traditional paean to natural beauty with which it concludes is a gesture of glib or derisive dismissal. The fragmentary extant text of Marvil's closing stanzas seems tonally ambiguous. It is thus possible that he may have been presenting his return to the long tradition of lyric poetry about the moon or stars only as a despairing gesture meant to emphasize its own impossibility. Given the sincere pathos throughout Marvil's harrowing text, however, I am inclined to read the speaker's attempt to seek this poetic refuge from the horrors his poem has been detailing as a sincere, if obviously strained, search for solace in a lyric relation to nature and the cosmos.

The moon and the stars evoke a rich vein of European poetry about, and indeed often addressed to, these celestial bodies—a representative strain in precisely the tradition of lyric poetry that Marvil's poem has been putting on trial through its self-reflexivity in extremis. Romantic poems about and to the moon and stars written in English, French, German, Polish, Russian, and Yiddish establish an intimate connection between these celestial bodies and the most personally meaningful and intensive forms of subjective interiority. Whether this subjective intensity manifests itself in the form of erotic desire or, more in keeping with the situation of Marvil's poet figure, involves a troubled individual seeking celestial succor, this strain of Romantic nature lyric is where the lyric subject is fully affirmed, is quintessentially at home, whether in joy, amazement, sadness, mystical or erotic longing, or, for that matter, in homesickness.[24] This is the lyric tradition for which Marvil's appeal to the moon (and possibly stars) does shorthand and to which the speaker, a lyric subject in ruins, would like to be able to return.

In the European Romantic lyric tradition, the moon and stars tend to illuminate or bear witness to lovers or to solitary figures welling with emotions, and they frequently hear their words. These celestial bodies serve as the objective correlatives of heightened subjective intensities, as Percy Bysshe Shelley's apostrophe of the moon aptly demonstrates: "Thou chosen sister of the Spirit, / That gazes on thee."[25] The apostrophized titular "bright star" of John Keats's sonnet "Bright star, would that I were stedfast as thou art" embodies the steadiness with which the speaker would like to be able to devote himself to his lover.[26] In Alexander Pushkin's early poem "The Moon," moonlight stirs up the lyric speaker's troubled memories of the trials of desire, his agony over the transitory nature of sensual love.[27] Moonlight and stars figure prominently in several poems by Heinrich Heine, for example in an untitled poem first published in his *Heimkehr* (Homecoming) cycle in 1826, in which the lyric subject dreams that, as the moon looks on and the stars shine, both sorrowfully (*traurig*), he is transported the several hundred miles separating him from his beloved, and sees her pale figure, illuminated by the moonlight, peering out of her window.[28] Baudelaire's moon in "Tristesses de la lune" appears like a beautiful, languid seductress, caressing her breasts on the cusp of sleep. She sheds a furtive, iridescent tear, which an insomniac poet takes in the hollow of his hand, and into his heart. The moon provides balm for the speaker's soul in Goethe's "An den Mond" (To the moon), the speaker having withdrawn from the world, reeling from the joys and sorrows of a past love.[29] During Joseph von Eichendorff's titular "Mondnacht" (Moonlit night) of 1837, the lyrical speaker's soul, witnessing the scenes of calm natural beauty, "spread / Her wings out wide, / Flew across the silent land, / As though flying home."[30] The speaker in sixteen-year-old Polish Romantic poet Juliusz Słowacki's poem "Księżyc" (Moon, 1825) apostrophizes an imaginative and empathetic woman who, alone at her rural retreat, looks with awe at the moon and confides her sorrows to it (part 4); and in part 5 of this long poem, he tells the moon that he will spend the night composing songs of remembrance "of the moments when you, looking from the heights of the skies / could see me in joy, sadness, or delight"—the scenes that unfold in parts 6 through 9 and are broken off by the advent of the dawn in part 10.[31] In Dovid Eynhorn's 1910 poem "In a levone-nakht" (In a moonlit night), a forlorn, solitary figure softly plays harp strings and is filled with longing.[32]

Marvil was not alone among ghetto poets in playing against the rich tradition of moon and star poems, or against the broader lyric tradition that they exemplified. Both Katzenelson and Avrom Sutzkever did so in poems they wrote in 1942 as well. The speaker in Katzenelson's second of two "Songs of the Cold," dated February 10, 1942, very close to the time Marvil wrote "The Street," adamantly rejects as false the promise of joy that the moon and stars extend:[33]

It's cold indoors and dark.
Quietly one night I pulled the black paper shades
down from my windows
and the high moon looked in
and poured her cold and misty light on me.
Just as happened long ago,
When innumerable stars
Glittered through a crack and said:
"Joy and gladness, joy and gladness."
—Will you stop it!—It's just a trick. You're cheating,
Making eyes at me,
As in those nights of long ago.
Stop it!

But the stars pretended not to understand,
And did not tear away from me
Their threads of trembling gold.
They did not stop winking at me.
—Go to hell!
Ardently I stretched out cold hands
To my old friends the stars:
—Oh, go to hell!

(Trans. Elinor Robinson, in Roskies,
Voices of the Warsaw Ghetto, 179–80)[34]

Katzenelson's poem reckons with the moon and stars and how they seem to hearken to happier times for the speaker as a person and as a poet. The way the moon and stars figure beauty and a sense of (lyrical) possibility is altogether comparable to their function in Marvil's "Di gas." Instead, however, of longing to be able to return to the lyric tradition for which these celestial bodies do shorthand, as Marvil's speaker does, Katzenelson's speaker adamantly rejects—assaults, even—this false offer of refuge in celestial and lyrical beauty, telling the moon and stars on high to "go to hell," the anti-transcendent thrust of which is if anything more direct in the Yiddish "vert ayngezunken!" and "o, ayngezunken zolt ir vern!" Katzenelson's speaker bids the celestial bodies literally to "get sunk!" imaginatively inviting the figure of heavenly heights to remove itself to the lowest of places.

Sutzkever's Vilna ghetto poem "Glust zikh mir tsu ton a tfile . . ." (I feel like saying a prayer), dated January 17, 1942, stages a crisis of poetic address.[35] The speaker feels urgently that he would like to say a prayer, but there is no obvious addressee to whom he might direct it: "I feel like saying a prayer—but I don't know to whom." God ("the one who once comforted" the speaker) will no longer hear it, so the speaker considers sending his prayer to a star:

> Efsher zol ikh betn bay a shtern: "Fraynt mayn vayter,
> Kh'hob mayn vort farloyrn, kum un zay im a farbayter!"
> Oykh der guter shtern
> Vet es nit derhern . . .
>
> Maybe I should ask a star: "My distant friend,
> I've lost my word; come and be a substitute for it!"
> Also the good star
> Will not hear it . . .

It can strike one as peculiar that the speaker ponders asking the star to substitute for his lost word, for while a star can substitute for words' addressee, one must strain to imagine how a star might offer a substitute for the lost words themselves. Two (not necessarily mutually exclusive) possibilities suggest themselves. One is that the star, precisely as a figure of lyric poetry, might be able to stand in for the words the speaker is unable to find. It seems more plausible, however, that the speaker has lost his word precisely because words require addressees. Without anyone at all to say a poem or a prayer to, one's words become lost, and by offering the speaker an address for his words, it would be returning his words to him. However, Sutzkever's speaker can muster as little faith in his distant friend the star as he could for God. Since he nonetheless feels inwardly compelled to say a prayer ("nor a tfile zogn muz ikh, emets gor a noenter / paynikt zikh in mayn neshome un di tfile mont er" [but I must say a prayer; someone within me / is tormenting me and he demands the prayer]), the speaker babbles (*plaplen*) incoherently (*on a zinen*) until dawn. Having lost faith in God and in the star, traditionally the lyric subject's "distant friend," Sutzkever's speaker can only mutter his prayer become poem or poem become prayer in the darkness, to no one in particular.

Yet while there are clear family resemblances among Marvil's, Katzenelson's, and Sutzkever's evocations via the moon and stars of the ruined state of a tradition of lyric poetry and lyric subjectivity when viewed from the ghettos, each of these three poets perform this gesture in distinct ways, each with different implications. Even in his rejection of the star as a possible addressee for his poem-prayer, Sutzkever's mystical faith in the power of poetry itself shines through.[36] While Sutzkever's speaker has lost his conventional addressees, he has not lost his creative powers; he continues to "babble." And while the speaker has lost his faith in God, his mumbled prayer bears witness to his faith in poetry and, indeed, the power of poetry to push beyond the limitations of a now problematic lyric tradition. Sutzkever's speaker feels compelled to speak because of an inner need that refuses to be quashed even in January 1942, after half of Vilna's Jewry had recently been murdered in the woods of Ponar. Marvil's speaker, by contrast, wishes not to have to speak yet is forced to by his unrelenting poem. The tormenting poem no longer serves his wishes, wishes that align quite well with the conventions of lyric poetry that the unfathomable brutality of the ghetto has so overwhelmed.

Although also obviously related to Katzenelson's rejection of the moon and stars as figures of lyric transcendence, the predicament of Marvil's speaker is, again, distinct. Marvil's speaker is less confident and more ambivalent in his defiance of lyric conventions than Katzenelson's. He does not tell the moon and stars to go to hell. Rather, he longs to be released from the tortures his poem inflicts on him so that he might return to the lyric self-affirmation that poems about such celestial bodies traditionally afford. While Sutzkever and Katznelson variously reject the moon and stars and the lyric tradition they evoke, Marvil's speaker yearns for (but is painfully exiled from) them. Such a lyrical refuge, if it can be achieved at all, remains fugitive and haunted by the ambient horror of the streets from which it would retreat or that it would transcend. The poem's irony is thus that it profoundly knows that the crisis it has so agonizingly underscored regarding the (im)possibility of writing a lyric poem from the locus of the dehumanizing Warsaw ghetto streets is not one that can be resolved with a mere change of subject matter.

Three instances near the poem's end where the speaker uses the first person plural—the only three instances in which he does so throughout its thirty-seven stanzas—highlight the altered nature of lyric and lyric subjectivity in view of the unfolding horrors. While early in the poem the children mourning their dead mother speak in a collective *we*, the poet persona never does until near the end of the text. The poem conspicuously opts out of speaking on behalf of the imperiled Warsaw ghetto community. Equally conspicuously, as we saw in the scene in which the speaker curses himself, the streets, the people, and the sky, the poem declines to identify agents responsible for the suffering it details. The poet does not curse, say, the Nazis or the Germans (as the speaker of Katzenelson's poem "Vey dir," which I explore in the next chapter, does relentlessly), or the Judenrat or Jewish police. The poem does not invoke a we-versus-them structure, even where one might expect it to. (Marvil's other extant Warsaw ghetto poem, "To the gentlemen," does indict the agents, albeit vaguely conceived agents, behind the war, e.g., "Oh you gentlemen so fine! / from London, Washington, Peking, / leave the world alone in joy.")[37] Instead, the only *we* the narrator of "The Street" invokes is that of poet and poem.

> Azoy geyn uf di bilder, di bilder far di oygn.
> Groylik un brudik in hefker fun vey.
> Un mir dreyn zikh mit, mit in di groyln,
> un vern tseribn, tseshtoysn fun zey!
>
> So rise these pictures before my eyes,
> Gruesome and filthy in a chaos of pain,
> And we too swirl along in the horrors,
> and get shredded and crushed by them.
>
> (stanza 33)

The status of the *we* here, by itself, could seem ambiguous; it seems clear in context, however, that this collective consists of poet and poem. In the very next line the speaker apostrophizes the poem: "So don't torture me, poem, I've had enough" (stanza 34). In stanza 35, moreover, the poet seems clearly to be apostrophizing his poem when he prods the poem's memory, as it were, regarding the good old lyric days: "Gedensk vi amol mir hobn . . ." (Do you remember how once we . . .). Similarly, when using the Yiddish first person plural *mir* in stanza 36, the narrator seems to be wishing for him and his poem to be able to turn to more comforting, less harrowing images of natural beauty: "Zoln mir in . . . / Un vern fun . . ."

Let my singing [be about] . . .
And about the pale moon . . .
May we in [*Zoln mir in*] . . .
And be [or become; *Un vern fun*] . . . by . . .

The context—and the complete absence anywhere else in the poem of any invocation of a *we* comprising the collective of Warsaw ghetto inhabitants—bolsters the interpretation of the *mir* in stanza 33 as likewise consisting of poet and his poem. This is the *we* that gets sucked into the vortex of horrible images: "And we too swirl along in the horrors / and get shredded and crushed by them." The poem provides the authorial persona with the only communion he invokes over the course of the poem, but it is a communion of the doomed. The longing look to the moon and stars is predicated upon the knowledge shared between poet and poem of how radically damaged and precarious their poetic enterprise has become.

POETRY MUTILATED, NOT NEGATED

In probing the limits of poetry in the face of the collapse of human status and human infrastructure he was witnessing, Marvil draws on the trope of preterition (passing over or omission) or, more specifically, on a subcategory of preterition known as paralipsis, a technique by which an author or speaker draws attention to something in the rhetorical act of declining to speak about it. Preterition frequently comes in the form of an authorial voice claiming to possess insufficient powers of description (e.g., "It is so horrible it cannot be described"). Marvil, however, inverts the trope of indescribability. He does not claim that the horrors of the street are so awful as to defy representation. On the contrary, his poem is not only possible, it is tormentingly ineluctable. Much as he would rather be released from the obligation, the poet must render the images and voices that are assaulting him. Marvil insists not that poetry can or should be deemed obsolete or henceforth impossible but rather that it must take stock of how it has been overwhelmed and brutalized by untranscendable mass violence, how lyric and lyric subjectivity, poems and poets, become engulfed by the dehumanizing vortex. Adorno's much discussed statements that after Auschwitz poetry had become barbaric and impossible are part and parcel of his broader appreciation of art that resists a dystopian modernity of reification and instrumentalized reason through esthetic negation, by saying no to the barbarity of reality as configured in late capitalist society. In negating the reigning reality, art must paradoxically also negate its own esthetic means, and Adorno thus champions precisely what he sees as the self-negating art of writers like Samuel Becket, James Joyce, Franz Kafka, Robert Musil, and others. In Adorno's rather Manichean worldview in which modernity is totally dominated by dehumanizing instrumentality, art marks out, negatively, the possibility of a space beyond the dehumanized hell.[38] In contrast, Marvil does not deploy strategies of (self-)negation to try to protect art from the genocidal forces he witnessed everywhere around him. For Marvil, the horrors that are incommensurable with a certain conception of poetry, that cannot be esthetically domesticated, and that threaten to overwhelm lyric subjectivity, are terrifyingly renderable; this is the awful thrust of his unwanted and relentless poem. "The Street" is a poem written in extremis. The speaker is unsure of the compatibility of the ghetto street he is writing from and about with the poetic tradition in which he is inscribing it, not because to write a poem in the face of such horror is barbarous but because this barbarity can and must be written; the poet cannot *not* describe the horrors that he deems incompatible with poetry. Marvil articulates the impossibility of writing a poem about the horrors of the Warsaw ghetto streets in a poem about the Warsaw ghetto streets: he shows that poetry has the capacity and the responsibility to exceed its own limits rather than to maintain them negatively. He makes poetry witness scene after dehumanizing scene from the ghetto streets, and poetry becomes mutilated, not negated, in the process. It becomes as torn as Marvil's manuscript.

CHAPTER 3
THE JEWISH DEAD CONFRONT THEIR GERMAN MURDERERS
ITZHAK KATZENELSON

The most significant, most prolific, and best-known poet and dramatist who wrote in the Warsaw ghetto, Itzhak Katzenelson, was in fact not from Warsaw. Katzenelson came to Warsaw as a refugee from Lodz, where he directed (until 1939) three interlinked, private Hebrew schools—a kindergarten, an elementary school, and a secondary school—that he and his family had founded. He published prolifically as a Hebrew pedagogue, including a large number of works of children's literature in Hebrew, while also writing in Hebrew as both a dramatist and a poet.[1]

While Katzenelson's inclination as a Zionist and Hebrew educator was to publish in Hebrew, in the Warsaw ghetto he wrote predominantly in Yiddish in order to be able to reach a wider Jewish audience. (After this wider East European Jewish collective had mostly been murdered, Katzenelson would revert to Hebrew in his diary from the Vittel detention camp in France, where he was a prisoner between May 1943 and April 1944.)[2] A great deal, though far from all, of Katzenelson's Warsaw ghetto writings—more than thirty of the over forty works he wrote in the Warsaw ghetto—were preserved, in part in the Oyneg Shabes archive but predominantly along with the archives of the Zionist youth movement Dror Hechalutz, with which Katzenelson was closely aligned. The Dror Hechalutz archive was buried just days before the Great Deportation of the Warsaw ghetto began on July 22, 1942, and was recovered after the war. Katzenelson's ghetto writings include biblical dramas, plays for children, poems, and chronicles; and several of his works had a public resonance. Some of his plays were performed in different venues, and he frequently read his work to friends and sometimes to larger audiences.[3] Some were also published underground in the ghetto by Dror Hechalutz. An excellent critical edition of Katzenelson's extant Yiddish ghetto writings was published in 1984 by the Israeli scholar of Yiddish literature Yechiel Szeintuch.[4]

"Vey dir" ("Woe to You"), the remarkable poem I will explore in this chapter, was written in spring 1942, and Katzenelson dated it May 31, 1942.[5] In an extended set of curses articulated over thirty-seven rhymed quatrains, the poem vehemently condemns—indeed curses—the Germans Katzenelson judges to be actively and passively responsible for the genocide of European Jews. Despite having been published in Yiddish as early as 1950 in *Di goldene keyt* (The golden chain, the preeminent postwar Yiddish literary journal, published in Tel Aviv by the poet Avrom Sutzkever) and in English translation in the *Jerusalem Quarterly* in 1982, it has met with little scholarly interest. In my reading of Katzenelson's poem, I try to draw out how it theorizes its own terrible predicament as an intervention in the form of a Yiddish poem in the ongoing genocide of Yiddish-speaking Jewry. "Vey dir" deserves to be read for the devastatingly brilliant way that it poetically explores some of the experience, including the rage and the search for voice and agency, of people facing their own individual and collective destruction. Katzenelson's poem draws on traditional Ashkenazic liturgy as well as intricate lyric enunciative dynamics to make East European Jews speak even beyond the death that was overtaking them.

TOPOGRAPHIES OF GENOCIDE

Although "Vey dir" was published in prominent postwar journals in Yiddish and in English translation, Katzenelson's most widely read poem written during and about the Holocaust—and one that has had considerable resonance in Germany, largely due to Wolf Biermann's 1994 German translation accompanied by his two lengthy essays about Katzenelson—is "Dos lid funem oysgehargetn yidishn folk" ("The Song of the Murdered Jewish People"). This text richly deserves all the readers it can find, yet, having become established as Katzenelson's signature poem of the Holocaust, it has overshadowed the texts he wrote in the Warsaw ghetto, including "Vey dir." One of the reasons, I would propose, that Katzenelson's "Song" has found a place, although still not a central place, in the Holocaust literary cannon, while "Vey dir" has not, is the latter poem's retrospective vantage point. Although Katzenelson's "Song" was composed between October 1943 and January 1944, while the events of the Holocaust were still ongoing, it was written after the destruction of the entire Warsaw ghetto. Katzenelson writes, to use David Roskies's term, "as a survivor" (although he would not survive for long).[6] Deported and murdered on August 14, 1942, Katzenelson's wife Hannah and their youngest two sons, Benjamin and Benzion, were among the nearly 300,000 ghetto inhabitants taken in cattle cars to Treblinka and murdered in the Great Deportation of the Warsaw ghetto (late July–September 1942). The poet and his oldest son Zvi evaded deportation at that time and were eventually smuggled out of the ghetto to the so-called Aryan side. They were caught up in the Hotel Polski trap, hoping to be able to leave Europe with forged Honduran passports.[7] From Warsaw, they were sent to the detention camp in Vittel, France, where Katzenelson penned his *Vittel Diary* and "Song," before being sent to the internment and transit camp in the Parisian suburb of Drancy. From there on April 29, 1944, they were sent on a convoy to Auschwitz, where father and son were murdered upon arrival.[8]

The retrospective, commemorative orientation of "The Song of the Murdered Jewish People" allows it to be more readily harmonized with postwar Holocaust memory than is the case with the complex, chronologically specific, and unresolved temporal dynamics of "Vey dir." Katzenelson's "Song" is enunciated from a vantage point after the end, as it were, by a solitary mourner, the "last of the last Jews," as Katzenelson puts it, in full knowledge of the entire tragic narrative arc of events.[9] It opens by evoking Psalm 137 and King David, the archetypical Jewish poet, even as the speaker struggles with the call, as the last Jewish poet, to "sing the last song," to "sing of the last Jews on Europe's soil" ("Song," canto 1, stanza 1).[10] A further crucial element of Katzenelson's "Song" that has made it serviceable to postwar memory is its dramatic account of the Warsaw Ghetto Uprising of April–May 1943 (cantos 13 and 14), which Katzenelson participated in and thus knew firsthand. The heroism of the Warsaw ghetto fighters and the way the uprising refutes the charge that Jews went to their deaths in the Holocaust without resistance, "like lambs to the slaughter," figures large in Biermann's appreciation of Katzenelson's poem.[11] Armed Jewish resistance in the Warsaw ghetto provided a psychologically and politically usable Holocaust *lieu de mémoire*, and the uprising remained the centerpiece of Holocaust commemoration throughout the first postwar decades.[12]

Notwithstanding the emphasis that Katzenelson places in his "Song" on the heroism of the Warsaw ghetto fighters, the poem ends by lovingly recalling and bewailing the removal of so many forms of Jewish life and culture from the Lithuanian and Polish soil where they had so long been at home: Jewish boys and girls will never again inhabit these places; gone are the "radiant" old Jew in the window reciting psalms and the masters and students of the Talmud in the yeshivas. Bundists, communists, and Zionists will no more wrangle with each other. While the markets will remain, and will be crowded, they will seem dead and empty because devoid of Jews. Gone, too, are the Jewish poets, theaters, musicians, and painters.[13] As Katzenelson writes: "Listen, listen: Apartments will not stay vacant and empty homes will not remain empty. / Another people is moving in, another language and a different way of life" ("Song," canto 15, stanza 6). Katzenelson mourns a people, a cultural nation—a way of life and a language—that was rooted in specific geographies and public and private spaces, rituals, and institutions.

The attention to cultural genocide in "Song"—the eradication of specific cultural practices and ways of inhabiting specific spaces and geographies; in a word, of an Ashkenazic world—recalls the equally topographical concerns of "Vey dir." Yet whereas "Song" tends to separate Jewish heroism and violent resistance (the Warsaw Ghetto Uprising) from the elegiacally remembered Jews and Jewish way of life now forever removed from East Europe, "Vey dir" is an angry poem that imagines the radical victimization of the Jewish people as, paradoxically, a vehement force that will pursue the Germans everywhere, destroy every aspect of their being, and leave them no peace. The poem imagines that the murdered Jews will wield their very defenselessness—their lack of weapons—as their most forceful weapon:

> Vey dir, du host a folk farnikht an umbavofnts
> Un nit farteydikte fun keynem hostu farnikht!
> Veys, nit farteydikte fun keynem veln harb dikh shtrofn,
> Du vest far umbavofnte zikh shteln tsum gerikht.
>
> Woe to you, who have destroyed an unarmed people,
> Who have destroyed a people unprotected by anyone.
> I tell you, those who were unprotected will punish you severely:
> You will be judged by the people without weapons!
>
> (stanza 3)

> Ir vet farblutikte un umreyne antloyfn
> In a bafalener aykh, vilder shrek,
> Mir veln, toyte, ale shlyakhn aykh farloyfn,
> mir veln aykh farshteln yedn veg.
>
> Bloody, unclean, you'll run away
> And a savage terror will seize you:
> We, the dead, will head you off on every road,
> we'll block you on every path.
>
> (stanza 9)[14]

"Vey dir" was written not only before the Warsaw Ghetto Uprising but indeed before the Great Deportation of the Warsaw ghetto. Whether or not any sort of armed resistance seemed imaginable to Katzenelson in spring 1942, what he dramatized in "Vey dir" is the unrelenting power and violence not of armed fighters but of the murdered Jews themselves or, to do better justice to the poem's future-perfect vision, of the Jewish collective who will have been murdered. These are not dead Jews who can be remembered in ceremonial reverence but Jews whose fingernails have grown, as Katzenelson writes, "sharper after death" (stanza 17). The poem's relentless curses refuse to allow the silence of these murdered Jews to remain silent.

In the phantasmatic reversal at the heart of "Vey dir" it is the destruction of the Jewish people in East Europe, their removal from the topographies that they inhabited, that will, in turn, deprive the Germans of any foothold in this world, pursue them everywhere, infiltrate all possible spaces of refuge and cut them loose from all possible ontological moorings:

> Zukht, merder, ayer heym un r'zolt zi nit gefinen . . .
> Blondzhet um vi mir, vi mir af dr'erd un zukht—
> Un zukhndik af khurves—geyt arop fun zinen
> Un zayt in meshugas in ayern farflukht!
>
> Search, murderers, for your home and may you not find it . . .
> Wander, as we do, over the earth, and search—
> And searching through the ruins, may you lose your mind
> And in your madness be cursed!
>
> (stanza 14)

The Jewish places and spaces that have been destroyed include houses of prayer (*shtiblekh*), synagogues, homes, towns, and cities. In the poem's genocidal version of Georg Wilhelm Friedrich Hegel's master-slave dialectic, the "nation of murderers," "the lowest murderers on God's earth," in wreaking such destruction, will have foreclosed on all possible places to dwell (stanza 1, line 3; stanza 12, line 4). Katzenelson's enumeration of the topographies that will become antagonistic to German life is unrelenting: the silent Jewish dead will pursue Germans on every road, every path; the Germans' homes will be destroyed, and even every cave or hole in which they might seek refuge, even the rubble of the ruins—others' and their own—will remain alien (*fremd*) to them (stanzas 12–13). Nature, too, will reject them: the Germans will be cursed by the trees along the roads that they will be cursed to wander and by the blades of grass and by "every frog on the bank of every river" (stanza 15, line 4). Indeed the very earth will ultimately vomit out the dead Germans so that they, like the Jews, will have to lie dead in the streets (stanza 31).[15]

In short, "Vey dir" articulates a fantasy of the Germans coming to know the destruction of every possible ontological anchor: family, home, soil, their own bodies. The poem's important play on *woe* and *know*—*vey* and *veys*—invokes epistemological pain or a painful epistemology. "Vey dir" attempts to curse the Germans with knowledge: the undoing of a people's existence must not remain unknown to them. In being confronted by the Jewish people and culture that the poem anticipates they will have removed from the face of the earth, the German people, the "nation of murderers," should come in turn to know radical ontological undoing. And this process of negative enlightenment should hurt.

FURY: KATZENELSON'S CURSES

"Vey dir" richly confirms and amplifies the argument that Naomi Seidman and others have made that much Jewish rage has been suppressed in the politics of translation and the formation of the canon of Holocaust literature.[16] The poem's anger is white hot. It does not strive to be conciliatory, nor does it for the most part make distinctions between the German perpetrators of the genocide and the German people as a whole.[17] Katzenelson wrote the poem in response to the liquidation of the Lublin Jewish community, carried out between March 17 and mid-April 1942.[18] News of the murder of this major Jewish community reached the Warsaw ghetto toward the end of April 1942, and Katzenelson was among the few to grasp the significance of this first such "action" within the Generalgouvernement, the central region (including Warsaw) of the interwar Polish Republic that Nazi Germany occupied but did not annex to the Third Reich, as it did Poland's westernmost regions.[19] Yet the poem has a longer genesis that situates it in a liturgical tradition and an Ashkenazic messianic ideology in which curses of the Gentiles play a key role. The poem was inspired by an incident in spring 1940, when Katzenelson heard his friend and roommate at the time, the important journalist and author (and, unlike Katzenelson, observant Jew) Hillel Zeitlin, cursing the Germans in Yiddish while reciting morning prayers.

Katzenelson intended to publish "Vey dir" for a wider Warsaw ghetto audience before the Great Deportation disrupted his plan, and decimated this audience.[20] The poem was to be published underground by the labor Zionist youth movement Dror Hechalutz in an edition of Katzenelson's "tsorn-lider" (poems of wrath) (Dror Hechalutz had in June 1941 published Katzenelson's play *Iev: biblishe tragedye in dray aktn* [Job: A biblical tragedy in three acts]).

The manuscript was completed, but instead of being published it was buried in the basement of the Dror Hechalutz compound on June 20, 1942, just two days before the Great Deportation began, and recovered after the war by surviving members.[21] Katzenelson recounts in his *Vittel Diary* that he carried a copy of "Vey dir" with him at all times in the months prior to, and during, the Great Deportation, and that he read it to Zeitlin before the deportation began and to other friends on the eve of the Great Deportation's final days, the so-called Cauldron on Mila Street, when between September 6 and 12, 1942, some fifty thousand of the remaining Jews in the Warsaw ghetto were assembled in streets near the Umschlagplatz and deported to Treblinka.[22] While the poem is titled "Vey dir" in the recovered copies, it was referred to by both Katzenelson and other diarists and memoirists who heard it in the Warsaw ghetto as "di klole" (the curse).[23]

Zeitlin's curses on the Germans overheard by Katzenelson were almost certainly an ad lib on the *birkat haminim* (or *birkas haminim* in the Ashkenazic pronunciation), the twelfth benediction in the weekday version of the *amidah*, Judaism's central prayer.[24] To call the birkat haminim a benediction is misleading, however, because it is indeed a malediction, a curse: the prayer asks God to eliminate the *minim*—literally, kinds or sorts—which in this context refers to sectarians deemed by the rabbis to be heretical. Although the prayer has received a great deal of attention as evidence of tensions between Jews and early Christians, the most thorough recent scholarship, particularly Ruth Langer's 2012 study of the history of the birkat haminim, shows that the record is simply too sparse to allow us to identify the vexing minim as Jewish Christians or any other specific group. Whether or not the birkat haminim was anti-Christian in its origins, it certainly became so by the high Middle Ages at the latest, and it remained a flashpoint for Jewish-Christian relations for centuries, with the prayer often being censored by Christian authorities. Such censorship and repression of the prayer destabilized the original text. Finding the poem, long deployed as a curse of Christians, offensive to modern sensibilities, nineteenth-century practitioners of *Wissenschaft des Judentums* such as Leopold Zunz, as well as various figures within liberal Jewish movements, devised various strategies of reinterpreting, emending, eliminating, or euphemistically translating the fraught text.

Katzenelson's "Vey dir" has its origins in his friend's ad lib on the birkat haminim, and it both recapitulates and revises the messianic ideology that lent meaning to the prayer's curses of the Christians. As Langer notes, the birkat haminim is part of the section of the *amidah* asking God "to ensure that the justice inherent in the messianic world will manifest itself first in the punishment of people who seek to harm the Jewish community, and then in the reward of those who act correctly."[25] In a study of how Jews and Christians perceived each other in late antiquity and the middle ages, Israel Jacob Yuval expounds at length upon the role of what he calls "vengeful redemption" as the dominant messianic vision among Ashkenazic Jewry (as opposed to "proselytizing redemption" central to the Sephardic tradition).[26] According to Yuval, "The dominant view in Ashkenaz saw the annihilation of the Gentiles as a principal component of the messianic vision. This is a notion that wishes to correct history retroactively, assigning to vengeance the role of correcting the past before a new world order can be established."[27] Alluding specifically to the birkat haminim, Yuval remarks further: "The central place occupied by vengeance in the messianic process serves to explain a unique ritual widespread in Ashkenaz during the Middle Ages: that of cursing non-Jews."[28] In its final three verses, Katzenelson's poem offers a vision of a chorus of nations singing out together in "love and faith" after the Germans have been destroyed. Among those singing in this chorus of nations is "the eternal Jew" (*der eybiker der yid*).

The status of "the eternal Jew" who sings a marvelous or glorious (*a herlekhe*) song in the chorus of nations remains ambiguous: does it represent an actual Jewish presence in an envisioned postwar world, or does the eternal Jew, a symbolic figure, embody a Jewish "spirit" of a postwar chorus of nations in which there are no actual Jews left to sing? "Dos [lid] zingt in felker-kor der eybiker der yid!" (stanza 36) could be read both ways—the eternal Jew could signal a surviving Jewish community raising its voice in the chorus of nations, or the voice of the eternal Jew being raised in the chorus of nations which, however, does not include actual Jews. This ambiguity points to the predicament that "Vey dir" grapples with: how to face the likelihood of impending collective death, and yet to speak beyond it. Katzenelson carried his friend Hillel Zeitlin's improvised curses on the Germans with him in his thoughts for two years and finally formulated his own poetic iteration of them at the moment when he could and did envision the genocidal erasure of Ashkenazic Jewry by the Germans. The poem thus revisits the long history of vexed relations between Jews and Christians in Europe and the Ashkenazic vision of vengeful redemption—always a strategy for imagining the Jews' ultimate triumph over their Gentile rulers—from a vantage point of radical powerlessness. Katzenelson's "Vey dir" deploys lyric enunciation to pursue vengeance from a place not only of weakness but of collective death.

HOW THE DEAD SPEAK

One of the most arresting features of "Vey dir" is how it complicates the seemingly ineluctable fact that, unlike survivors, what Primo Levi called the "true witnesses," the murdered, cannot speak.[29] The poem imagines murdered Jews exacting vengeance on Germans after the Jewish people will have been liquidated. This anticipated futurity is absolutely crucial, yet it is the play between the future scenes that the poem projects and the enunciative *now* of its extended apostrophe of the murderers that lends "Vey dir" its awesome, unsettling force. The poem conjures future scenes of Jews confronting and punishing their murderers beyond their deaths, and, as it were, it realizes this envisioned future in the performative *now* of its lyric enunciation. The future that "Vey dir" imagines remains always anterior to the *now* when the speaker curses the murderers. The future scene has always already happened yet the speaker—not-yet-murdered and already murdered—still speaks. In the lyric *now* of its apostrophic curse of the murderers, the speaker(s) of "Vey dir" thus speak as the ghosts the poem imagines the East European Jewish community collectively becoming.

All thirty-seven stanzas of "Vey dir" apostrophize the perpetrators of the Jewish genocide in various guises. In stanzas 1 through 6, the speaker addresses the Germans, a "nation of murderers" (*merder-folk*, stanza 1, line 3), with the second-person singular pronoun *du* and the dative form *dir*, as in "vey dir," the curse that begins stanzas 1 through 4 and stanza 6. In these early stanzas, the speaker also uses first-person singular possessive pronouns when referring to victims of the Germans—Jewish children, Jewish elderly, and Jewish cities (stanzas 1–2 and 4). From stanza 7 on, the speaker addresses the Germans with the second-person plural pronouns *ir* (nominative), *aykh* (dative and accusative), and *ayer* (possessive).[30] Accordingly, from stanza 7 on, the speaker employs the first-person plural pronoun when speaking of the Jews/the Jewish people: *mir* (we) and *undz* (us). The poem generally continues to address the Germans in the second-person plural to the end, although it sometimes singularizes the address, as in stanza 20: "Tref yederer fun aykh tsu zayn tsefaln hoyz, / un nit treft di vayber ayere baym lebn, / un toyt di kinder ayere in zeyer shoys" (May each of you find his ruined house / and find not your wives alive, / and [find] your children dead in their laps; *tref* is the singular, *treft* the plural imperative form). Stanza 30 also reverts once to *du*, presumably for the sake of the rhyme with *ru*:

Zayt ale, zayt farsholtn,
fun got un mentsh farsholtn, du vilde khaye, du!
. . . un tif in dr'erd nit visn zolt ir fun keyn ru

May you, may all of you, be cursed,
Cursed by God and man, you wild beast you!
. . . and, deep in the earth, may you know no peace

The poem's final stanza expresses the wish that all memory of the Germans should be blotted out, and reverts, in its final line, to second-person singular address of the Germans, now apostrophized as "a nightmare" or "evil dream": "Es zol nit keyn gedekhtnish fun aykh farblaybn / a kholem beyz, vert opgemekt, farvey in vintn!" (May no memory of you remain, / Evil dream, be erased, be gone with the wind!)

Katzenelson's choice of second-person lyric address crucially ensures that the present tense of the enunciation of the poem's extended curse subsumes and channels its other complex verbal tenses and temporalities. Although "Vey dir" deploys the past participle (frequently, as we will see, in ways that imply a future perfect), it does so as a way of intensifying the curse being spoken in the poem's enunciative *now*. In the poem's culminating messianic vision, for example, Germans are apostrophized as follows: "Hert, vi s'hot oysgelaytert klor nokh aykh der himl" (Hear how the sky has brightened after you; stanza 35, lines 2–3). The past participle *hot oysgelaytert* implies a future perfect (hear how the skies will have cleared after you will have been dealt justice), but the temporal complexities of this vision of the future remain in a fundamental way in the service, we could say, of the enunciative present tense of the imperative *hert* (hear).[31] The point of sketching the future (or future perfect) scene is for it to be heard now, as a curse. (The point of even the scene in which the Germans could be said to be hearing in the future is for them to hear this future hearing *now*.) In this crucial sense, "Vey dir" is not primarily a mimetic poem, even as it clearly deploys mimetic elements in depicting multiple scenarios. Instead, it conjures past and future scenes and events in the service of the curses being enunciated in the lyric present; these mimetic moments lend force and weight to the series of curses that the poem enacts. One of Jonathan Culler's most fundamental interventions in *Theory of the Lyric* is to argue against the dominant critical paradigm according to which readers are encouraged to read lyric poems as dramatic scenes spoken by characters, whose inner and outer situations it is our primary task as readers to reconstruct. As discussed in chapter 2, Culler underscores instead how lyrics strive to constitute themselves as performances, as events. In the case of "Vey dir," the poem is both an enunciative performance and, by and large, a series of performatives in a more restricted linguistic sense—curses. The way the enunciative *now* of the poem's series of apostrophic curses dominates throughout is indeed what lends "Vey dir" both its coherence and its unrelenting intensity.

Working through some examples will illuminate the predominance of the lyric *now* in "Vey dir" and how the *now* of the poem's lyric performance tends to coincide with the performative *now* of the curses it addresses to the perpetrators of genocide. The poem's seventh stanza reads as follows:

Mit vayb un kind, mit zeydes un mit bobes,
di oysgeshosene fun aykh umzist,
dos folk vos ir hot lebedik bagrobn,
mir veln shteyn un onkukn aykh vist.

With wife and child, with grandpas and grandmas,
those shot by you for no reason,
the people you have buried alive,
we shall stand and stare at you emptily.

Here we have references in the past participle to atrocities already committed ("dos folk vos ir hot lebedik bagrobn") and a scenario-to-come depicted in the future tense ("mir veln shteyn un onkukn aykh vist"). But what greatly enhances the intensity of these past and future events is that the speaker mobilizes them to address the murderers (*ir/aykh*) with aggressive directness in an enunciative *now*.

In this stanza and several others the temporal status of the past participle is ambiguous. "Dos folk vos ir hot lebedik bagrobn" refers both to acts of murder already committed and to further acts that have not yet occurred but that will have come to pass by the time "mir veln shteyn un onkukn aykh vist." Crucially, the *we* (mir) who will confront the Germans in silence includes the speaker, who makes up part of the folk that will have been "lebedik bagrobn." In the preceding (sixth) stanza, the speaker says, "Mir veln fun di kvorim undzere aroys" (We'll come out of our graves), and in the following (eighth) stanza, the speaker says, "Mir veln shtume shteyn un shtume fregn: / farvos hot ir geharget undz farvos?" (We will stand silently and silently ask: /

why have you murdered us, why?). Some of the members of this people have already been murdered; others, like the speaker, have not been murdered yet. However, they, too, have already been murdered in relation to the *now* of the lyric enunciation insofar as the (silent) articulation of the accusatory future question flows into and intensifies the speaker's present-tense apostrophe of the murderers. The corpses and ghosts who will be speaking in the future are always already speaking in the curses that "Vey dir" performs. In this sense, even the poem's reference to future events that might initially seem posterior to the *now* of articulation ultimately remain anterior to it. They have yet to occur historically but, poetically, they have always occurred already in relation to the voice that curses you (*dir/aykh*) for having perpetrated this killing. The poem's speaker conjures scenes of the future and future perfect in order to punish you, the murderers, more stringently in the enunciative *now* of the series of curses of which "Vey dir" consists. The articulation of the curses in "Vey dir" in this way outlives the death of their speakers, the murderers' victims: you will have killed us, but in the *now* of our enunciation, we abide and confront you with your acts, and curse you. We the dead—the not-yet-dead yet already-dead—curse you our murderers now. No future, not even that of our genocide, can overtake the enunciative *now* in which we curse you: We curse you now, again and again, and always.

Consider the question of who is speaking in stanza 23: "Farvos hot ir undz oysgeharget?" (Why have you massacred us?). Who speaks these words? We could interpret this moment in dramatic terms as the direct speech of the dead who have refused to remain in their graves. Yet while we are certainly dealing with a dramatic scene, I would argue that here, as throughout "Vey dir," the dramatic scenario remains in the service of the curse being enunciated now, such that the question uttered by the dead essentially coincides with the lyric enunciation itself—the poem as curse. That is, this question is posed less by dramatic figures within the poem than by the lyric speaker who apostrophizes the murderers, says "vey dir," etc. throughout: it is voiced at least as much in a lyric *now* as in a dramatized future. Moreover, the question of who exactly is speaking can remain ambiguous because, no matter who is speaking, and no matter on what temporal plane, all the scenes in "Vey dir" and all its verbal tenses ultimately support and intensify the central act of cursing the perpetrators in the lyric present.

The silence with which the (soon-to-be) dead confront their murderers in Katzenelson's poem is decidedly not the ineluctable silence of those whose death has robbed them of any means to speak. On the contrary, "Vey dir" dramatizes the dead speaking across the barrier not just of individual death but indeed of genocidal, collective, and cultural death. It struggles against the Nazi project of killing the very language of Yiddish along with its speakers. The poem addresses the Germans collectively, on whom it wishes violence comparable to that which Katzenelson witnessed Germans visiting on his people. It elaborates a proleptic fantasy in which the murdered Jews, in death, will haunt and torment what Katzenelson indicts as a German nation of murderers, guiding them and forcing them to see, carry, and even viscerally to embody the Jewish dead. And the poem realizes these projected scenarios in the *now* of its enunciation.

> Mir veln shteyn derhargete un kukn,
> onkukn aykh shtum in undzer payn;
> un kukndik af aykh, aykh shtumerheyt fartsukn,
> mir esn in di beyner aykh zikh ayn.
>
> In ayer ekldikn layb, in kark in roytn,
> vi in a brudikn a zump, in shlyam un leym,
> ir hot geteyt undz lebedike, trogt undz toyte
> trogt af di pleytses undz tsu aykh aheym.
>
> We the slain will stand and look,
> Stare at you mutely in our anguish;
> And, staring at you, devour you in silence,
> We'll cling to your very bones.
>
> With your disgusting body, to your red neck,
> As though you had killed us, the living,
> In a filthy swamp, in mud and clay,
> Carry us, the dead, carry us home on your shoulders.
>
> (stanzas 10–11)

As we see in these lines, the collective dead *we* in the poem generally stares at and otherwise confronts, plagues, and literally weighs on the accursed perpetrators in silence. However, this is not an impotent silence. Rather, "Vey dir" vehemently voices and weaponizes the silence of the dead, the silence of those already killed and of the collective culturally Yiddish Jewish people, including the poem's speaker, who will have been killed by the time of this projected future confrontation. The silence to which death has reduced them only enhances the intensity with which they enunciate their curse in a haunting *now*.[32]

CAN POETRY SPEAK TO THE DEAD?

A recurrent theme running through the scholarship on second-person narration is the ambiguous sphere of overlap between the second-person narratee and potential flesh-and-blood readers: when is the *you* in a text also me, the text's actual reader?[33] Had postwar cultural history in Germany followed a different path and Katzenelson's "Vey dir" been translated and become widely read instead of, or alongside, Paul Celan's "Todesfuge," for example, such questions might have been discussed and hotly debated in German culture: identification with the apostrophized *you* of Katzenelson's poem might have been partially accepted, vehemently insisted on, resisted, rejected as unfair, and so forth, from myriad positionalities. One can at any rate speculate that Katzenelson's aggressive deployment of second-person narration to curse the Germans would have provided a site for what Brian Richardson sums up as the "heightened engagement between reader and [narratee] protagonist" that second-person narration tends to engender.[34] Now more than eighty years after it was written, the *you* of Katzenelson's poem is far removed from the empirical Germans it aimed to curse. This is not to dismiss the possibility that we, the poem's contemporary readers, could still confront and wrestle with the question of our relationships to the poem's narratee—its cursed *you* —in various ways.

What I want to explore here, however, is less the possible relationships between the narratee of "Vey dir" and contemporary readers than the relationship between contemporary readers and the poem's implied reader or authorial audience. This latter relationship challenges an assumption made in much theoretical work on Holocaust discourse, namely that, just as the dead cannot speak, they also cannot be spoken to. In her theorization of what she aptly calls "corpse poems," Diana Fuss takes as axiomatic that the dead do not speak but are only ventriloquized, and that the primary function of the ventriloquized speech of the dead is to offer solace to the living. It follows that such poems are not for (cannot be for) the dead but only for the living.[35]

Some skepticism seems warranted as to whether corpse poems must ineluctably be for us, the living, simply due to the fact that (a structural bias to end all structural biases) it is we the living who make the claim. Although Fuss makes a number of broad claims about the importance of the Holocaust for the (im)possibilities of modern elegy, she bases these claims on readings of a small number of poems, all written after the Holocaust. As arguably the most significant corpse poem about the Holocaust, "Vey dir," written from within the ongoing genocide, expands the ways we can understand virtually every aspect of how and to whom a corpse poem can speak in the face of the Nazi genocide. Is "Vey dir" indeed ineluctably for us, the living? In some sense, of course: by writing a poem, Katzenelson placed a text into the world to be read by whomever it might reach. In relation even to this most basic component of our access to this poem—that we have it and thus can read it—we should, however, proceed with caution. One must assume that Katzenelson wrote with the awareness that "Vey dir" and his other ghetto writings might be destroyed. At some level, the poem is aware of its radical contingency and does not presume that it will survive for posterity. An admittedly paradoxical ethical and hermeneutical challenge that "Vey dir" presents us with is thus to read it as though it had never reached us. "Vey dir," however, gives us other compelling reasons to question the assumption that it can only be for us.

Culler proposes a model of triangulated address in *Theory of the Lyric* that can shed light on the nature of address and audience in "Vey dir," even as Katzenelson's poem significantly complicates Culler's model. By triangulated address, Culler means the way that lyric poems speak to listeners via apostrophe of various other entities. This is certainly the case, yet Culler's triangulated model implies that there are only three key components: the lyric speaker, the apostrophized entity, and the poem's listeners or audience. Such a model presumes "the" audience to represent only a formal position in this triadic and infinitely repeatable structure. Culler locates in the *now* of lyric enunciation an iterable structure allowing for reperformance by future readers.[36] As both speakers and hearers of the poem, readers assume the position of both the lyric speaker/poet and the audience. What Culler's formalist model does not account for, however, is how lyric address can sometimes imply specific listeners for whom future readers may not be able to substitute themselves unproblematically.[37] "Vey dir," I argue, implies specific listeners or readers, of whom a haunting residue remains that partially disrupts the poem's structural iterability and calls into question our ability as readers to substitute ourselves for the specific implied readers.

There is a crucial disparity between singular and plural second-person addressees in "Vey dir," the apostrophized German perpetrators—who do not speak Yiddish—and its implied readers, who belong to the Yiddish cultural community under threat of imminent genocidal erasure and who are signaled with the first-person plural.[38] The poem allows its implied readers—and perhaps some of its actual first readers or auditors in the Warsaw ghetto—to participate in a fantasy of post-death agency, retribution, and justice. To be sure, the implied and real audience's "knowledge" of its impending death is complex and intermixed with its own denial; much of the poem's point, surely, was to cultivate the hope that its apocalyptic vision of genocide would not, in the end, come to pass. An anticipation of their own impending murder is nonetheless a constitutive quality of the poem's implied recipients. This is astounding and worth reflecting on. Katzenelson's poem elaborates what we can rightly call a poetics of genocide by implying an audience, a specifically Yiddish audience, that knows it will soon be murdered—individually, collectively, and culturally erased. I can think of no other literary work that so concertedly postulates an authorial audience that is about to be collectively murdered and know it.

The terms "implied reader" and "authorial audience," in the narratological sense in which I am using them, refer to the text's ideal recipient, the kind of reader able to receive and interpret the text's meanings.[39] It is thus a virtual construct suggested by, or inferred from, the text and not necessarily synonymous with the text's actual, empirical readers. Narrators of literary works often enough can be aware of their own impending death, as can personae depicted in literary works; and works can and do apostrophize dying persons. What is going on in "Vey dir," however, is something different. The poem evokes or summons a community of readers who know that they and their very language and cultural idiom are in the throes of genocidal destruction. And when we are dealing with genocide, the theoretical distinction between empirical and ideal readers becomes acutely problematic, for ideal readers, in the end, require the empirical persons in contradistinction to whom they are defined. In the limit case of the genocide of a people and its culture, the virtual notion of the ideal reader must confront the empirical existence of the actual collective carrying the cultural competence for which the ideal reader does shorthand. The author has died various deaths in theory, but Katzenelson's poetics of genocide does something unprecedented in confronting the death of his poem's authorial audience. The poem attempts to respond to the unfolding murder of Ashkenazic Jews in the Yiddish language and culture being murdered with its speakers.

To return to Culler's model of triangulated lyric address, "Vey dir" presents us with a situation of disrupted iterability. The lyric present does not allow us to step into the position of the poem's poet/speaker or that of its listeners because these positions are indelibly marked by a specific genocidal situation and temporality. There are thus at least two audiences in play when we read "Vey dir"—we contemporary readers and the poem's implied audience, knowingly caught in the throes of genocidal destruction. When we read and hear this poem, then, there are speakers and listeners who do not cede their formal positions to us as we reperform it. In hearing the poem's apostrophe we also hear the hearing of that apostrophe by the implied audience of not-yet-murdered/already-murdered Yiddish-speaking Jews.[40]

At a very basic level, then, "Vey dir" is indeed for the dead and not for us. Much of what is so powerful and irreducibly vexing about the poem as a verbal performance is that, however we try to read it, we find ourselves having to contend with the fact that we read it in the place of its not-yet-murdered/already-murdered ideal recipients, who embody a Yiddish culture that fell prey to the Nazi genocide. All sorts of texts can, both intentionally and unintentionally, obstruct the capacity of empirical readers to join the interpretive community they postulate as their authorial audiences. Historical and cultural distance from a text's authorial audience can introduce further such obstacles. I would argue that "Vey dir," however, stands out as a text presenting singular barriers that disrupt the ability of contemporary readers seamlessly to join what Peter Rabinowitz describes as the "particular social/interpretive community" of its authorial audience.[41] By no means do we get to settle into a self-congratulatory posture of the attentive readers who have come to recover or "redeem" this text. On the contrary, it situates us as interlopers of sorts, who assume, or usurp, the place of the readers the poem summons. Whereas a number of texts written by victims during the war years can be described as messages in bottles seeking a posterior reader witness, "Vey dir" remains unassimilable to this model of communication. It has not, in us, at long last found its rightful destination. On one very important level, it is certainly for us, the living. Yet on another equally important level, it is a poem spoken by the dead for the dead—the not-yet-dead yet already-dead—and our readings of it must try to attune themselves to this haunting modality of address.

Concepts familiar from the Adorno-inspired cultural discourse about poetry and the Holocaust seem here to be both beside the point and grotesquely apposite. Katzenelson's poem does nothing if not grapple with the dismantling of the very elements that make it possible—precisely what Adorno called on post-Holocaust literature and art to do. Yet the most basic of the conditions of possibility whose dismantling Katzenelson's poem contemplates is the very existence of the Yiddish cultural community. Katzenelson's poem tries to find a way to speak beyond the collapse of its own cultural and historical conditions of possibility. It thus situates anyone reading it today not before the question of whether poetry can continue to be written after Auschwitz (Adorno's question), but rather of what ethical and cultural position we occupy as we read a poem that seeks its annihilated audience.

CHAPTER 4

YOYSEF KIRMAN'S POETICS OF DURATION

Among the small number of texts by the Warsaw poet Yoysef Kirman preserved in the Oyneg Shabes archive were two remarkable poems, "Nokh der blokade (a khronik)" ("After the Blockade [a Chronicle]") and "Di oygn blaybn ofn" ("The Eyes Remain Open"). Kirman wrote these poems after having experienced firsthand the Umschlagplatz, the departure point from which Jews in the Warsaw ghetto were deported to their deaths at Treblinka. Kirman was seized in a courtyard by three members of the Jewish police and taken there forcibly; he resisted.[1] In desperation, he sent a note to his influential friend Yitzhak Giterman (the same person who had arranged a monthly stipend for Shmuel Marvil, as discussed in chapter 2), who was able to extricate him.[2] After the Great Deportation, Kirman obtained one of the highly sought-after factory (so-called shop) posts that temporarily shielded from deportation the slave laborers "lucky" enough to have secured them. He worked in the same Többens artificial honey and sugar factory as Rokhl Auerbach and Yehoshue Perle, whose text "4580," about having his name replaced by the work permit number he was assigned for this shop, is the focus of chapter 6. Unlike Kirman and Perle, Auerbach would ultimately survive, by securing false papers and passing as a non-Jewish Pole in Warsaw on the "Aryan side." Auerbach, Bluma Wasser, and Bluma's husband Hersh Wasser, who survived by leaping from a train bound for Treblinka, were the only people still alive after the war who knew where the Oyneg Shabes documents were buried.

Most of what we know of Kirman's life in the Warsaw ghetto comes from Auerbach's memoirs.[3] One of the most striking things she relays about Kirman is the urgency with which he turned to literature, poetry in particular. When walking together, Kirman would sometimes abruptly pull Auerbach into a doorway or courtyard and read her his latest poem. "It was always a poem about what we were seeing before our eyes," Auerbach recalls, "and we felt that the image that was now burning in our souls would probably perish along with us, like the scenes on a sinking ship" (Auerbach, "Yoysef Kirman," 146).[4] Auerbach's memories of Kirman tell us a great deal about his poetics in the Warsaw ghetto. In terms both of its content and the occasions when he

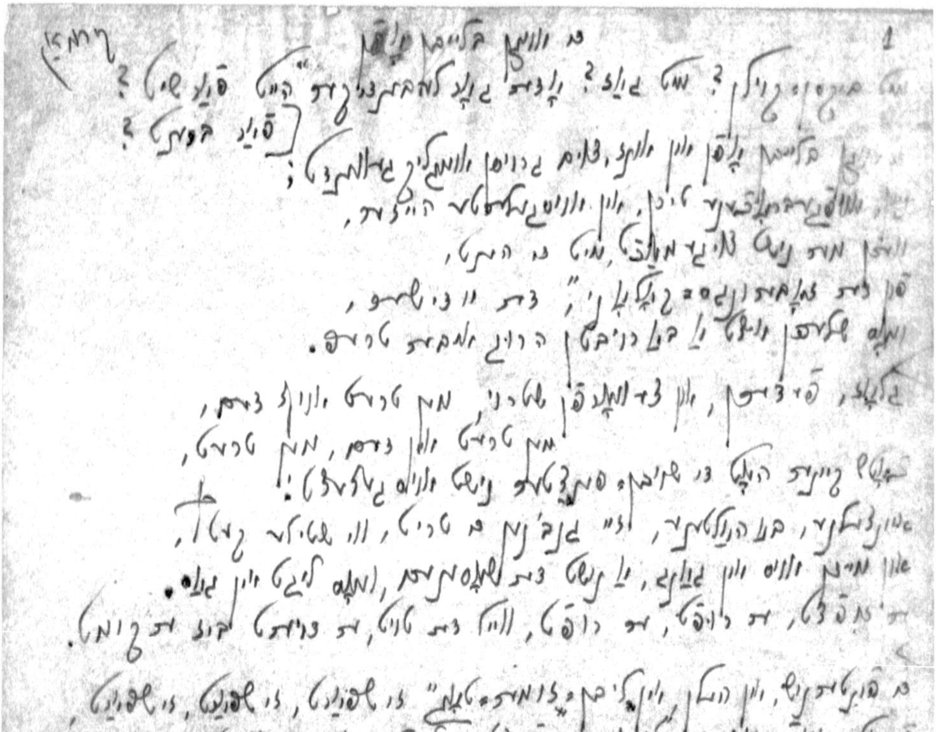

קירמאַן

די אויגן בלייבן אָפֿן 1

1942

FIGURE 3: *Handwritten manuscript of Yoysef Kirman's poem "Di oygn blaybn ofn" ("The Eyes Remain Open"). Preserved in the second cache of the Oyneg Shabes archive, buried February 1943 and recovered December 1, 1950. Courtesy of the Jewish Historical Institute, Warsaw, Poland, ARG II 396 (RA II/351).*

felt inspired to read it to Auerbach, his poetry was of the moment. His poems reflected on the immediate situation at hand, and his readings of poems also remained woven into the texture of daily ghetto life, set apart only minimally by, say, the space of a doorway.[5] As I will be arguing, the phenomenological thrust of Kirman's poetics, his commitment to writing a poetry of the events occurring in real time, is largely what lends his two poems of the Umschlagplatz their considerable force, and also something that makes Kirman's poems particularly important for this exploration of poetry written during the escalation of what we now call the Shoah. If the temporal phrase "after Auschwitz" has structured much of the discussion of relationships between poetry and the Holocaust, Kirman's poems were not only written, like all wartime writings, during the unfolding events, they, more crucially still, pointedly dramatize the experience of the catastrophe precisely in its temporal unfolding. By characterizing Kirman's poetics as phenomenological, it is his emphasis on the temporal experience of the catastrophic events that I mean to underscore. Even the subtitle of Kirman's poem "After the Blockade (a Chronicle)" announces the centrality of phenomenological temporality to his poetics, as does the title of "The Eyes Remain Open": the eyes of those experiencing the genocide remained open throughout the duration of the unfolding horror. Kirman's poetics locates poetry emphatically, vehemently even, in the temporal midst of the unfolding genocide, before, we could say, there was the "after" in the question of "poetry after Auschwitz," a question that has foreclosed discussion of so much of the most significant poetry of the Holocaust.

Most of Kirman's poems indeed went down with the ship. Auerbach relates that, when they were working in the Többens shop in the vastly reduced ghetto, she asked Kirman if he still had the poems he had written and used to recite to her on Leszno Street, and if it might not be wise to send them off for safekeeping (presumably to the Oyneg Shabes archive), but Kirman told her his poems had remained in a bundle of his things in Dzshelne Street, and he now had no way of recovering them.[6] "The Eyes Remain Open," "After the Blockade," and a handful of short pieces of literary reportage and prose poems are all that we have of Kirman's prolific ghetto writings.[7] While we only have two of the great many poems Kirman wrote in the Warsaw ghetto, his extant prose pieces offer insight into his poetics in the face of the unfolding catastrophe. In addition to two texts about or addressed to children that I will come to in a moment, Kirman composed two highly literary reportages, both dated 1941, about the harrowing refugee centers (punktn) where the ghetto's most vulnerable inhabitants, those displaced into the ghetto, often, albeit certainly not only, from provincial shtetlekh, were housed.[8] As discussed in chapter 1 (like Kirman, Zalmen Skalov also wrote a reportage on the punktn for the Oyneg Shabes), these centers were overcrowded and dirty, ridden with lice, typhus, and other diseases. Their starving inhabitants had few connections in Warsaw and correspondingly little access to employment or meaningful assistance; the death rate among this population was astounding.[9] One of Kirman's reportages about the refugee shelters, "Fun pleytim shtetl—Dzhike un Niske" (On the refugee-shtetl—Dzika and Niska [Streets]) offers a global depiction of the mass of people displaced into the ghetto from far and wide who ended up in the shelters—or who indeed were reduced to lying and dying on the streets outside them. During the day, they can only beg, to little avail. A recurring theme in this text is these people's dehumanization, as when Kirman describes them as "di nekhtike gevezene mentshn" (yesterday's former human beings), now "in khayes varvandlt" (transformed into beasts).[10] Kirman's second refugee center reportage, "Froy Krashevitshes toyt" (The Death of Mrs. Krashevitsh) is more focused on specific people, the twenty-eight-year-old titular Mrs. Krashevitsh, her young children, and her septuagenarian mother-in-law, as they face their hopeless and deadly circumstances. The minimal distance from the streets and punktn that we see in Kirman's literary reportage continues in his poetry. It too is a form of esthetic reportage chronicling and reflecting on traumatic scenes from the Warsaw ghetto. Kirman's poetics demands that literature, including poetry, remain excruciatingly proximate to the catastrophic events it depicts, even as it renders these events from complex, reflexive esthetic vantage points.

Kirman was born in Warsaw in 1896 and grew up in a poor family. He published his first poems in 1919 and published his sole volume of poetry, *Iber shtok un shteyn* (Across rough terrain) with the prestigious Kletskin press in 1930.[11] He also published poems in a wide array of Warsaw-based periodicals including the most prestigious Yiddish literary journal of the day, *Literarishe bleter*. Auerbach describes Kirman in his youth as having been a disciple of Perets Markish's (provocatively modernist) school.[12] His poems in *Iber shtok un shteyn,* written in long, unrhymed lines of blank verse, treat a rich variety of topics. His own experience growing up in a poor family informs several poems depicting Jewish poverty, hungry children, and suffering mothers. The volume also introduces motifs that were rare if not unprecedented in Yiddish verse such as the experience and psychology of prostitutes and their clients.

Kirman earned his livelihood, however, not by writing for the Yiddish press, as did so many other Yiddish poets, but rather by making walking sticks and galoshes in a Warsaw factory.[13] According to Shmuel Charney and Jacob Shatzky's *Leksikon fun der nayer yidisher literatur* (Biographical Dictionary of Modern Yiddish Literature), Kirman completed only a *kheder* education before becoming a laborer, and lived in poverty. He was arrested by the Polish police for political activity.[14] During the war, Kirman and his wife arranged for her and their two children to be hidden with Poles in his wife's hometown. As Auerbach recounts, it eventually became devastatingly clear to Kirman that this arrangement had not saved his family.[15] Kirman was eventually deported from the Warsaw ghetto to the Poniatowa concentration camp near Lublin and murdered on November 3, 1943, during the mass executions of the Jews in the Lublin camps.[16]

Auerbach vividly describes Kirman's love for children. In part transferring his love for his own children onto "children in general," Kirman would frequently distribute his last coins to street kids in the ghetto, who all knew him.[17] His concern for children is evident in two texts that Kirman published in underground Bundist journals. His prose text "Der khesed fun a shtiln toyt (dos kind der umshuldiker korbn mont zayn kheshbn)" (The blessing of a quiet death [the innocent child victim demands his due]), which Kirman published in the December 20, 1941, issue of the *Bundist Biuletin* (Bundist Bulletin), consists of harrowing vignettes describing the plight of desperate and dying children who lack all support. For them, the ghetto hospital has become a haven, which they try desperately to gain entrance to and to stay in, even though the hospital cannot restore them to life but can only offer them "a quiet death." A haunting, recurrent theme of this text is the tragic innocence with which these children often matter-of-factly, without pathos, describe their dire circumstances, as in the case of the boy who recounts how his entire family has died, summing up: "Ikh bin aleyn" (I am alone).[18] Kirman's prose poems entitled "Kh'red tsu dir ofn, mayn kind: kurtsinke poemes in geveyntlekher proze (shtimungen, bilder, troymen in geto) (I speak to you openly my child: short poems in ordinary prose [moods, images, dreams in the ghetto])" were published in the February–March 1942 issue of the underground Bundist journal *Yugnt shtime* (Voice of youth). In these works the speaker recounts to his son scenes he has witnessed (and some that they have experienced together) in the streets of the ghetto and reflects on their meanings and the lessons he would like his son to take from them.[19]

Like his reportages on the refugee centers, these works of prose and prose poetry serve as esthetic recording devices; they render scenes of ghetto life and the predicaments facing the ghetto's inhabitants. Kirman's esthetic reflection on situations unfolding before his eyes continues into his poetry. In "The Eyes Remain Open," Kirman uses the tools of lyric poetry to render the lived experience of genocidal time. He situates lyric beyond its traditional tendency to leap into timelessness or sublime eternity. "The Eyes Remain Open" enacts a phenomenological poetics of duration that insists on the extended lived experience of the process of catastrophe and death—and on poetry's place within it. By situating itself within the chaotic time of the Great Deportation of the Warsaw ghetto to Treblinka, Kirman's poetics refutes any neat opposition between poetry, on the one hand, and the genocide of European Jews, on the other.

"The Eyes Remain Open" was first published in full in Yiddish in 1958 in the Warsaw journal *Yidishe shriftn* (Yiddish writings), edited by David Sfard, and was published again in 1972 in *Di goldene keyt*, edited by Avrom Sutzkever. Sarah Traister Moskovitz published the only English translation of the poem that I am aware of on her website Poetry in Hell.[20] (To the best of my knowledge, Kirman's poem "After the Blockade" was never published even in Yiddish prior to its inclusion on Moskovitz's website.) "The Eyes Remain Open" is short enough to quote in full; my translation is adapted from Moskovitz's:

DI OYGN BLAYBN OFN

Mit biksn-koyln? Mit gaz? Oder gor lebedikerheyt farshit? Farbrent?
Di oygn blaybn ofn in undz tsum groysn umglik gevendt;
Neyn, ufgebrokhene tirn, un oysgelerte hayzer,
vern mer nisht tsugemakht, mit di hent,
fun der "zoberungs-koloni", der yidisher,
vos shlepn itst a baroybtn hoyreg iber trep.
Gloz, federn, un tsevorfn shtroy, men tret af dem,
men tret in dem, men tret.
Khotsh keyner hot di shoybn-fentster nisht oysgezetst:
Eyntselne, bahaltene, zey ganvenen di trit vi shtile kets,
Un maydn oys in gang, a nisht dershosenem, vos ligt in gas,
Er ziftst, er ruft, er ruft, vayl der toyt, er doyert biz er kumt.
Di finsternish, in heln, in libn-"zumer-tog"
zi shpart, zi shpart, zi shpart,
Fun ale oysgerisene tirn, un fentster-lekher, in der vister gas arayn,
Un eyne shteyt und shrayt:
Tsu finf zlot, di letste dray bintn meyern zise!
Got, mayn got, host dem handl, un dos lebn nokh nisht umgebrakht,

Afile afn "Umshlag Platz" baym plombirn di vagonen,
Farn optransportirn tsum toyt,
Hot men gegesn roye kartofl, un gehandelt mit broyt.

THE EYES REMAIN OPEN

By rifle bullets? By gas? Or even buried alive? Burnt?
The eyes remain open within us, turned toward the great disaster;
No, ripped-open doors and plundered houses
Do not get closed again by the hands
Of the Jewish "clearing detail,"
Who now drag a corpse, murdered and despoiled, on the stairs.
Glass, feathers, scattered straw, they step on that,
they step in that, they step.
But no one has broken the window panes!
Lone individuals, hiding, steal like silent cats,
Keeping clear of a man lying in the street, shot but not yet dead,
He groans, he cries out, cries out because death lasts until it comes.
The darkness in a bright, "lovely summer day"
presses, presses, presses
Out from all the ripped-out doors and gaping windows into the
 deserted street,
And a woman stands and cries:
"Five zlotys each, the last three bunches of sweet carrots!"
God, my God, you haven't yet killed the market and life,
Even at the "Umschlag Platz" while the trains were being sealed
For deportation to death
People ate raw potatoes and traded in bread.

(1942)

Kirman's poem opens in medias res with ambiguous questions: "By rifle bullets? By gas? Or even buried alive? Burnt?" Who voices them, and to whom are they addressed? Perhaps it is the lyric speaker's own voice or, more likely, that of anyone and everyone among the terrorized "us." Is the speaker speaking to himself? To fellow victims? To God? The opening line, to be sure, echoes the medieval *piyut* (Jewish liturgical poem) "Unetanneh Tokef" (or Unesaneh Tokef in the Ashkenazi pronunciation), one of the most memorable parts of the Rosh Hashanah and Yom Kippur liturgy. This poem describes the awe of the Day of Judgement and imagines all humankind passing before the Creator, who will apportion their destinies for the coming year. The liturgical portion of the *piyut* recited on the Jewish High Holidays reads:

> On Rosh Hashanah will be inscribed and on Yom Kippur will be sealed how many will pass from the earth and how many will be created; who will live and who will die; who will die at his predestined time and who before his time; who by water and who by fire, who by sword and who by beast, who by famine, who by thirst, who by storm, who by plague, who by strangulation, and who by stoning. Who will rest and who will wander, who will live in harmony and who will be harried, who will enjoy tranquility and who will suffer, who will be impoverished and who will be enriched, who will be degraded and who will be exalted.
>
> But repentance, prayer, and charity remove the evil of the decree! (Artscroll *Rosh Hashanah machzor*, 483)

Kirman begins his poem with allusions to this most resonant portion of the Jewish High Holiday liturgy in the form of ambiguously or multiply voiced questions directed likewise to multiple possible addressees—questions that indeed seem to be "in the air"—for good reason.[21] In their cruelty the Nazis frequently coordinated deportations of Jews and other calamities with the Jewish liturgical calendar. Thus they began the Great Deportation of the Warsaw ghetto on July 22, 1942, which was the Jewish holiday of Tisha b'Av (July 22–23, 1942). The days immediately leading up to Rosh Hashanah (September 11–12, 1942) were a vortex of death known in Yiddish as "dos kesl" (The Cauldron).[22] Between September 6 and 12, all the Jews remaining in the ghetto were forced to assemble in a small group of streets adjacent to the Umschlagplatz and not allowed to leave. Those who were not able to obtain numbered permits to work in slave labor factories—some fifty thousand people—were deported to Treblinka in cattle cars. Abraham Lewin, a popular historian and co-founder of the Oyneg Shabes archive who kept a diary of the Great Deportation, was unable to record any entries during the days of the Cauldron and only recounted the events on the eve of Rosh Hashanah, Friday, September 11, 1942. The last transport of the Great Deportation left the Umschlagplatz for Treblinka on September 24.

Kirman's evocation of the liturgy of the *yomim neroim* (Days of Awe or High Holidays) of Rosh Hashanah and Yom Kippur is thus saturated with terrible significance. During this period, Jews traditionally reflect on and try to right the wrongs they have committed during the previous year. They repent and prepare themselves for God's judgment of who, on Rosh Hashanah, will be inscribed and, on Yom Kippur, sealed in the Book of Life for the coming year.[23] The opening questions in Kirman's poem approach collective interior monologue of all those caught in the murderous storm. The question implied behind the poem's questions "By rifle bullets? By gas? Or even buried alive? Burnt?"—namely, "How will I be murdered?"—remains unstated because it is understood. The inescapability of death seems self-evident.

The phenomenological quality of the poem's opening questions, presumably running through various minds, announces the poem's concern with the temporality of the unfolding catastrophe as experienced by its victims. The verse from which the poem's title derives introduces two modes of seeing. The opening rhymed couplet (*farbrent-gevendt*) establishes that the people the poem renders in strikingly visual terms are themselves actively seeing. Their eyes remain open to everything happening around them, and their inner eyes imagine the forms that the brutal death awaiting them will take. Holocaust victims are here above all subjects of seeing ("we"), and this has the effect of doubling, or multiplying, each of the images and scenes later readers encounter as we read the poem. We see in our mind's eye people in the ghetto seeing the unfolding destruction and seeing in their mind's eye the forms that their inevitable untimely death will take.

Kirman repeatedly uses rhythm, repetition, and internal rhyme to create a lyric stutter that dramatizes the agony of duration. One of the most vexing and painful aspects of the roundups and deportations for Jews to witness, and one that elicited some of their most vehement condemnations, was the participation of other Jews in the process.[24] Kirman's disgust and rage toward the Jewish policemen who participated in rounding up fellow Jews for deportation to their deaths is on display in both of his poems about the Umschlagplatz. His ire is even more pronounced in "After the Blockade":

> Un zey, di verk-shuts-layt, di yidishe, un di ordenungs-politsey, zey haltn vakh un zenen greyt,
> Zey zenen greyt, zey zenen greyt, opgebn di noenste fun zikh, vi es vert farlangt fun zey shoyn itst.
> Di eltern, di kinder un afile di vayber oykh, abi nisht zikh.
>
> And they, the factory security people, the Jewish ones, and the Order Police,
> they stand guard and are prepared,

They are prepared, they are prepared to deliver their nearest, as even now they are being demanded to do.
Their parents, children, and even their wives, so long as not themselves.

In "The Eyes Remain Open," Kirman highlights the acts of the "clearing detail" of the Jewish ghetto police (Kirman uses the German term *Säuberungskolonne* rendered phonetically in Yiddish). The members of this detail drag the corpse of someone who has been murdered and robbed of all valuables —most likely by them—across stairs and the debris left in the wake of the violent roundup: glass, feathers, and straw. If the line quoted above from "After the Blockade"—"and are prepared, they are prepared, they are prepared"—suggests with moral incredulity the struggle of a dawning terrible realization, Kirman's use of repetition in verse 7 of "The Eyes Remain Open" to imprint this searing image approaches cinematic montage techniques: "they step on that, / they step in that, they step" (*men tret af dem, / men tret in dem, men tret*). If we were to compare Kirman's visual poems to a visual medium, it is not the photographic snapshot they most resemble but Sergei Eisenstein's experimental cinematic montage. Kirman's lines do not render the momentary suspension of time but rather time's jagged traumatic movement. This awful moment is magnified in the way it stutters, repeats, and extends. As with the questions that open the poem, we do not know precisely who sees this image (perhaps a specific person, perhaps the lyric persona, perhaps several people caught up in the chaos), but the repetition conveys the experience (or multiple experiences) of this moment unfolding in time.

The next line, verse 8, provides a further arresting example of the poem's phenomenological temporality and mode of seeing. It conveys the astonished realization that, amid the destruction, "No one has broken the window panes!" (*Khotsh keyner hot di shoybn-fentster nisht oysgezetst*). Like the poem's opening questions, the statement has the quality of a thought running through a person's (or several people's) mind, an ostensibly trivial yet somehow miraculous detail amid the chaos of the murderous roundup.

Kirman further underscores the theme of duration in his description of the figure he refers to as "a nisht dershosenem" (a man not yet dead from a gunshot), a phrase that condenses considerable temporal complexity. A *dershosener* is someone who has been shot to death. Kirman negates *dershosener* (the remaining individuals in hiding avoid *a nisht dershosenem*) to indicate that, while the man will die of his shot wound, he has not died yet. One of the poem's most striking lines describes this man's death as an agonizing process:

"He groans, he cries out, cries out because death lasts until it comes." The alliteration and internal rhyme of the Yiddish line (verse 11) poignantly continues the device of repetition to signal duration in time: "Er ziftst, er ruft, er ruft, vayl der toyt, er doyert biz er kumt." Kirman deploys a similar repetition in verse 14 ("presses, presses, presses" [*zi shpart, zi shpart, zi shpart*]) to convey the experience of time stuttering but not stopping (or, to be sure, being transcended). It is as though the gears of time momentarily slip; they fail to engage, causing time to thicken and proceed haltingly; but proceed it does.

Di finsternish, in heln, in libn-"zumer-tog"
zi shpart, zi shpart, zi shpart,
Fun ale oysgerisene tirn, un fentster-lekher, in der vister gas arayn,

The darkness in a bright, "lovely summer day"[25]
presses, presses, presses
Out from all the ripped-out doors and gaping windows into the deserted street

"The Eyes Remain Open" contemplates the coming end, situates itself near that end, and features victims contemplating their imminent end. And yet, the text does not offer any end in the form of a clean break, not even the tabula rasa of total destruction. Instead, time momentarily stalls again and again only to endure, compounding the devastation.

The end of Kirman's poem remains emphatically in the midst of the terrible catastrophe that is unfolding but has not yet reached its endpoint. As the darkness is pressing, pressing, pressing out of the wrecked doors and windows of the homes of those who have been removed for deportation, "a woman stands and cries: / 'Five zlotys each, the last three bunches of sweet carrots!'" Even at such a moment, time does not stop. The market endures, the market in sustenance that continues to sustain buyers and sellers through the duration of the ongoing end.

The perspective from within the unfolding genocidal process likewise governs "After the Blockade." The "after" of the title signals neither a locus posterior to the concluded murderous violence, nor a new beginning. Instead, its temporal vantage point is in the midst of the continuing horror:

Di shrank, zi iz umgedreyt, un der dershosener, er ligt in der ofener tir,
Dos vayb ober, un di kinder zayne, di libe, zey lebn nokh,
zey zenen itst nor vos, afn "Umschlag Platz" gebrakht,

un krign oykh, vi s'kumt, af yedn kop, tsvey kilo broyt geteylt—
Got vi lang vet doyrn bay dir dos lebn zeyers? Vi lang?
Un dos umglik fun tog af tog? Fun tog af tog?!

The armoire is turned around and the man, shot to death, lies in the open doorway.
His wife and children, those he loved, are still alive, however;
they have just been brought to the "Umschlag Platz"
and are allotted, as promised, two kilos of bread per head;
God how long will their lives continue with you? How long?
And this tragedy continues day after day? Day after day?

Much as he does in a more complex way in "The Eyes Remain Open," Kirman here takes up the issue of sustenance in the form of bread, the two-kilogram loaves with which the Nazis tried to entice Jews to come to the Umschlagplatz. Hard for starving people to resist, and intended by the German authorities as a deceptive sign that the deportees might actually be sustained for labor rather than immediately killed, bread in Kirman's poetics sustains only the long process of destruction, death's duration.

The final four verses of "The Eyes Remain Open" develops this theme further, expressing negatively sublime amazement at the fact that the destruction is not yet total. In a pronounced undertone, the lyrical *I* voices incomprehension that God—still (*nokh*)—has not completed the job.

Got, mayn got, host dem handl, un dos lebn nokh nisht umgebrakht,
Afile afn "Umshlag Platz" baym blombirn di vagonen,
Farn optransportirn tsum toyt,
Hot men gegesn roye kartofl, un gehandlt mit broyt.

God, my God, you haven't yet killed the market and life,
Even at the "Umschlag Platz" while the trains were being sealed
For deportation to death
People ate raw potatoes and traded in bread.

Just as the poem's opening line alludes to a famous Jewish liturgical poem, "Got, mayn got" (God, my God) quotes Psalm 22: in Robert Alter's translation, "My God, my God, why have You forsaken me? / Far from my rescue are the words that I roar" (*The Writings*, 66).[26] This psalm is of course most famous today because of its prominent role in the Passion narratives, an association that Kirman could well be playing off of.[27] Equally important, however, Jewish tradition attributes the psalms to King David—with his harp, the archetypal figure of the Jewish poet. By evoking King David and Psalm 22, Kirman implicitly recalls the beginning of the Jewish poetic tradition as he situates himself near (but never at) its end, anticipating Katzenelson's similar, more elaborated gesture in "Song of the Murdered Jewish People."

Psalm 22 ends by affirming faith in God's righteousness and responsiveness to the needs of those who pray for God's help in times of danger. In contrast, Kirman's poem holds out no faith in God's saving powers. Moreover, even as this sentiment is arguably intermixed with a stunned admiration for Jews' resiliency even in the face of their mass murder, "The Eyes Remain Open" conveys more than a hint of dismay at God's refusal, or inability, to make the destruction total. Just as "death lasts until it comes," the mundane abides throughout the duration of annihilation: even at the Umschlagplatz people eat raw potatoes and barter with bread. Kirman begins his otherwise unrhymed poem with the rhymed word pair *farbrent-gevendt* (burnt-turned) and ends it with the rhyme *toyt-broyt* (death-bread): even on the Umschlagplatz, as the wagons were being sealed, "Farn optransportirn tsum toyt, / Hot men gegesn roye kartofl, un gehandelt mit broyt."[28] The quintessential daily sustenance, the so-called staff of life, here sustains only the duration of death. Kirman places *toyt* (death) first, not last, in the final rhymed couplet. The opposite order would have been possible, and it would have lent the poem a compelling note of closure: death. But he rejects this option and ends the poem, conspicuously, on *broyt* (bread). There is no reprieve from this massive, unfinished violence, neither in life nor in the time-suspending esthetic transcendence of lyric poetry. "The Eyes Remain Open" dismisses the possibility of absolute breaks in time, and of esthetic refuge from the phenomenology of the devastation.

Kirman's poetics of duration signals that poetry cannot transcend the unfolding catastrophe but rather, not unlike the market in carrots, potatoes, and bread, continues within it. The temporality of Kirman's poem and the poetics of genocide that it projects are phenomenological, even provocatively and grotesquely quotidian. It is a singular poetics emphatically of during rather than after the catastrophe, one that has been eclipsed by the almost exclusive emphasis on the poetry of aftermath or, in Adorno's shorthand, of poetry "after Auschwitz." Kirman uses the literary genre most closely associated with esthetic transcendence since its privileging by the Romantics—the lyric—to insist that no lyric transcendence is possible. While Kirman makes use of a number of poetic devices, from the hovering questions that inaugurate the poem to the searing images throughout, which conventionally produce what we could call an eternity effect, a transcendence of phenomenological time, he consistently does so in ways that disrupt this very effect. Kirman's poetics insists on the duration and experience of time in its unfolding, whether it is a matter of ambiguously vocalized questions of how I or we will die, the image of "a nisht dershosenem" who "groans, . . . cries out, cries out because death lasts until it comes," or the market in carrots and bread and the eating of raw potatoes even as the cattle cars to Treblinka are being sealed. At every turn, Kirman's poem amplifies the experience of the time of catastrophe; Kirman's lyric phenomenology disrupts the temporality of lyric transcendence.

By dramatizing the experience of genocide in terms of terrible, ineluctable duration, "The Eyes Remain Open" challenges the neat before-and-after schema on which the ubiquitous iterations of the phrase "after Auschwitz" rely. The problem before which Kirman's poem situates us is not that it is, in Adorno's famous dictum, "barbaric" to keep writing poems after the Nazi genocide. Rather, it is that poetry's locus is not only before or after, but also in the midst of, this unfolding horror. Like the eating of raw potatoes and bartering with bread, poetry did not stop, even as the wagons were being sealed on the Umschlagplatz for transport to Treblinka. Much of the agony of Kirman's poem, I would argue, stems from the fact that, even in the face of violence on such a massive scale, time does not simply come to a halt. It may stutter, but it does not stop. It allows of no definitive breaks between a before and an after; it endures. Kirman's poetics of genocide likewise has no recourse to an after or a beyond.

III. SHORT PROSE: ONE

SELF-WRITING IN THE WARSAW GHETTO

CHAPTER 5

WRITING THE HUNGERING SELF IN A MODERNIST KEY

LEYB GOLDIN

HUNGER IN THE GHETTO LITERATURE CORPUS

As one of the most ubiquitous and defining experiences of the ghettos, hunger is an ineluctably obsessive motif running through the great diversity of ghetto writings. Hunger and all that it entails—helplessness, despair, and dehumanization—figures as a major concern across all the genres of ghetto literature by celebrated, obscure, and anonymous authors alike.[1] Notable authors of reportage deal centrally with hunger, for example Peretz Opoczynski (Warsaw), Oskar Singer, and Yosef Zelkovicz (both Lodz), as do diarists such as Dawid Sierakowiak (Lodz).[2] Starvation is probably the single most prevalent theme of poetry written in the ghettos as well, including by Warsaw ghetto poets "Hershele" Danielovitch, Itzhak Katzenelson, Yoysef Kirman, and Shmuel Marvil.[3] In the Vilna ghetto, Avrom Sutzkever penned a number of poems directly and indirectly treating starvation.[4] Hunger is an equally insistent focus of literary prose writers in the ghettos. As I discuss in chapter 9, Shaye Shpigl grapples with the uncanny transformations wrought by starvation in stories including "Malkhes geto," "Durkh a shpare," and "Shtivl,"[5] and Oskar Rosenfeld, who like Shpigl wrote in the Lodz ghetto, depicts a starving man drifting in and out of delirium due to hunger in "Meine zwei Nachbarn" (the focus of chapter 8).[6] As Ber Mark writes in the introduction to his 1955 anthology of Yiddish prose from the Warsaw ghetto, "The main theme of all the works [in the anthology] is: hunger" (Mark, "Forvort" to *Tsvishn lebn un toyt*, 8). The Yiddish writer and literary critic Yitskhok Bernshteyn wrote a number of remarkable texts, for example "Varshe 5701" (Warsaw 5701/Warsaw 1941), exploring the nature and status of ethics and the sacred amid the catastrophic loss of life and collapse of social structures in the midst of mass starvation and suffering.[7] Yehuda Feld also wrote a number of short stories in the Warsaw ghetto in which starvation figures prominently, for example "Hunger" and "A kholem fun a mamen" (A dream of a mother).[8]

In these and other writings the time and space of the ghetto repeatedly become synonymous with hunger; hunger permeates every aspect of individual and collective life until the ghetto simply *is* hunger. Hunger surely imposed silence on many of its victims, but it also elicited diverse forms of speech and reflection. A great many inhabitants of Nazi ghettos grappled with the multi-faceted experience of hunger in writing even as—and because—hunger marked the dividing line between freedom and internment; the retention of memory and integral personhood, and their loss; the human and the animal; life and death. They wrote, courageously and sometimes brilliantly, at the momentous threshold that hunger demarcated. Whereas significant energy has been invested in theorizing the ghostly and by definition silent threshold figure of the Muselmann, less has been directed at trying to receive the speech voiced by and about subjectivities approaching the threshold of hunger-induced physical and psychological disintegration.

Many people who wrote while starving in the ghettos consciously linked hunger to language in both private and public characterizations of reading practices. Dawid Sierakowiak frequently felt too exhausted or sick to read or think,[9] but on multiple occasions he describes reading in lieu of eating. He wrote in his diary on December 6, 1942: "Recently I've been possessed by a wish to forget myself in intensive reading" (Sierakowiak, 236). On December 30, 1942, he noted: "We have had our last potato in a water soup. As usual in the times of hunger, I have to turn to forced intensive reading to drive away the sense of deprivation with this 'opiate.' My brain seems to have become much too exhausted" (244). And with grim humor, he noted on January 2, 1943: "I go to bed earlier if possible because it's really cold at home. Everything is beginning to mold again because of the moisture. We don't cook suppers anymore, so I eat my last meal (rutabaga soup and sometimes a piece of bread with radishes) at four o'clock. However, I read more and more in bed. Every cloud has a . . ." (246). The connection between starving and reading was also acknowledged in public settings. The following notice hung in the Vilna ghetto library "in the circulation area, near the card catalogs":

> Books are our only comfort in the ghetto!
> Books help you forget your sad reality.
> Books can transport you to worlds far away from the ghetto.
> Books can still your hunger when you have nothing to eat.
> Books have remained true to you, be true to the books.
> Preserve our spiritual treasures—books!
>
> (quoted in Fishman, *Book Smugglers*, 47)

In his essay on the Vilna ghetto library and its reading room, the library director Herman Kruk noted "Analogies: It was established that a hungry person reads eagerly about hunger, while someone with a full stomach cannot abide that kind of subject matter" (Kruk, "Library and Reading Room," 194).[10]

LITERATURE OF HUNGER AND LITERATURE REGARDED FROM HUNGER: LEYB GOLDIN'S "KHRONIK FUN A MES-LES"

From the considerable body of literary treatments of the phenomenon and experience of starvation in Nazi ghettos, in this chapter I elaborate a close reading of one of the most stunning, a work of literary prose that constitutes both a writing of hunger and a critical (in every sense) reading of European literature—in particular works of literary modernism—by a hungering subject in the Warsaw ghetto. Leyb Goldin's "Khronik fun a mes-les" ("Chronicle of a Single Day," or, alternatively, "Chronicle of 24 hours") is an autobiographical text that grapples with subjectivity at the mental and physiological limits imposed by the starving body.[11] It moreover meditates, not least in the intertextual dialogue it carries on with an array of literary works, on the status of culture, the intellectual, and the self in the face of radical destitution. Goldin's "Chronicle" certainly documents experiences and events in the Warsaw ghetto, but it is also a self-consciously literary text.[12] My analysis thus pays particular attention to the intertextual relationships Goldin's text maintains with Jewish and European literature, especially modernist works preoccupied with temporality, subjectivity, and consciousness, as it attempts to render the "modernist" temporality of subjectivity brought to its breaking point by starvation.

Writing in the Warsaw ghetto in summer 1941, when starvation in the ghetto was at its most acute, Goldin adopted the modernist trope, famous from texts including James Joyce's *Ulysses* (1922) and Virginia Woolf's *Mrs. Dalloway* (1925), of measuring personal time and the vagaries of consciousness against clock time and the temporal boundedness of a single day.[13] Goldin's text provocatively writes hungering subjectivity and hunger time into the modernist matrix of temporal experience and consciousness and explores how the experience of the ghetto radicalizes, strains, and disfigures these central modernist concerns and esthetic strategies.

Goldin's text is not only modernist but also, and more importantly, metamodernist in at least two related ways. First, it self-consciously sifts the resources of European literature—and above all, of modernist prose—in search of models for rendering the experience of consciousness at its breaking point precipitated by starvation. Second, by drawing on, pushing to their limits, and denaturing available literary models and their attendant cultural coordinates, both waxing nostalgic for and acerbically mocking their guiding humanistic assumptions that appear to be at such radical variance with life in the ghetto, "Khronik fun a mes-les" dramatizes the agonizing experience of excision from the cosmopolitan cultural community that many East European intellectuals, writers, and readers thought they had meaningfully joined, not least through their embrace precisely of modern European culture.

Goldin's text rifles through available literary modes and measures them against the situation of the wasting individual severed from the wider human community and condemned to slow death by starvation in the Warsaw ghetto. His text thus constitutes a kind of intertextuality in extremis. Intertextuality is one of the key dynamics on which David Roskies has focused in his interpretations of wartime Holocaust literature, but he has illuminated above all how authors writing during the Holocaust turned to archetypes from the Bible and Jewish textual tradition in a desperate search for analogies for, and language adequate to, the unfolding catastrophe. In his reading of Goldin's "Chronicle" Roskies most certainly acknowledges the modern and modernist nature of Goldin's intertexts, yet perhaps because they fall outside Roskies' primary focus on Holocaust texts' fraught recourse to traditional archetypes, he does not fully attend to the dynamics of modernist intertextuality in Goldin's literary monologue that are my chief concern here.[14] Aside from the excellent, albeit brief, pages Roskies devotes to Goldin's text in various books, it has received scant critical attention.[15]

Goldin wrote his largely autobiographical text in the Warsaw ghetto in August 1941, and it was preserved in the in first cache of Emanuel Ringelblum's Oyneg Shabes archive, which was buried on August 3, 1942, and unearthed on September 18, 1946.[16] The date of the composition of "Chronicle of a Single Day" is highly significant. The death rate of 5,560 for August 1941 due to disease and starvation was the worst for any single month in the Warsaw ghetto. Among myriad other causes of this extreme crisis, the advent of the war between Germany and the Soviet Union in June 1941 entailed that packages were no longer permitted to enter the Warsaw ghetto from Soviet territory.[17] As Jonas Turkow recalled the situation in a postwar memoir: "After the outbreak of the war with Soviet Russia, when no more packages were arriving from there, the situation became catastrophic. People dropped like flies from hunger."[18] The text was published in 1955 in *Tsvishn lebn un toyt* (Between life and death), an anthology of prose literature from the Oyneg Shabes archive edited by Ber Mark, then the director of the Jewish Historical Institute in Warsaw, where the archive was (and is) housed. An English translation of Goldin's text by Elinor Robinson was published under the title "Chronicle of a Single Day" in Roskies' 1988 anthology *The Literature of Destruction: Jewish Responses to Catastrophe*.[19]

We know relatively little about Goldin: before the war he worked as a journalist, literary critic, and a translator of European literature into Yiddish. A secular leftist, Goldin had been a communist and served time in Polish jails for his political activities (an experience alluded to in "Chronicle," 425, 427 / "Khronik," 51, 54). He eventually left the Communist Party and in 1936 joined the Bund.[20] Goldin died in the course of the Great Deportation of the Warsaw ghetto at some point after August 3, 1942.[21]

Goldin's experimental "chronicle" is at once a bracing phenomenology of a twenty-four-hour period in the life of a Yiddish intellectual starving in the Warsaw ghetto, and a wide-ranging meta-reflection on what it means to write from that particular place of radical destitution. Goldin embarks on this reflection in "Chronicle" by revisiting—from the radically circumscribed vantage point of a single starving man's consciousness within a single day in the Warsaw ghetto—the complex dynamic of modern Yiddish literature's borrowing and innovative appropriation of European literary models.[22]

"Chronicle" signals its meta-cultural reflection from the outset, with an opening epigraph paraphrasing the symbolically inaugural work of modern Yiddish literature, the 1888 ballad "Monish" by I. L. Peretz. In *Yiddish Fiction and the Crisis of Modernity, 1905–1914*, Mikhail Krutikov underscores how early twentieth-century Yiddish writers looked beyond the "classical" triumvirate of Abramovitsh (Mendele), Sholem Aleichem, and Peretz to European literary models.[23] Of the three classical Yiddish authors, however, Peretz, both in his own use of naturalism and symbolism and in his tireless support of younger Yiddish writers, represented the pivot to European literary culture. While some facets of Peretz's multifaceted literary project, such as his neo-Hasidic Romanticism, may have offered little that younger writers, responding to crises of economics, revolution, and immigration, wanted to emulate, Peretz remained the symbolic founder of modern secular Yiddish literature and an enduring point of reference within it. In Goldin's text, Peretz's "Monish" marks an originary moment, the beginning of modern secular Yiddish literature in and through its creative appropriation of the resources of European literary culture. Roskies aptly characterizes Goldin's Peretz epigraph as "telescop[ing] the distance traveled since Peretz's debut in 1888" (*Apocalypse*, 213).

This is the paraphrased couplet from Peretz's "Monish" with which Goldin opens his text:

Andersh volt mayn lid geklungen
Ven kh'zol megn *altsding* zingen—
(Parafraze fun "Monish," 49)

My song would sound different
If I were able to sing *everything*

Or, in Elinor Robinson's more poetic, less literal, rhymed translation:

How differently my song would sound
If I could let it all resound
("Chronicle," 424)

With this paraphrase, Goldin cites lines from a portion of Peretz's poem that ironically laments, in Yiddish, the poverty of Yiddish as a vehicle for a ballad of a full-fledged European Romantic hero. The stance that Peretz's poem takes up, however, is one of complex irony vis-à-vis both the ostensible poverty of Yiddish and the ostensible richness of European culture. It is important to appreciate this complexity because, with his paraphrased epigraph of Peretz, Goldin signals that his project will be to resume Peretz's complex measuring of Yiddish and European literature against each other, now under radically altered circumstances. He will weigh the resources of European literature against the destitution of a Yiddish writing of hunger in the Warsaw ghetto, a Yiddish writing literally from hunger.

The eponymous protagonist of "Monish" is a pious yeshiva *bokher* who, because of his moral purity, awakens the interest and ire of Satan, who plots, with Lilith, to corrupt him. Temptation comes in the guise of Maria, who arrives in Monish's hometown from Germany and proceeds utterly to enchant Monish with her singing (the charms of European, and particularly German, culture). Maria eventually seduces Monish to swear—by his teacher, mother, father, *peyes, tsitsis, tfiln*, by the *paroykhes* (Torah Ark curtain), the Messiah and his *shoyfer*, and by God—that he loves her, truly and eternally. The story does not end well for Monish: Maria laughs at him; God immediately strikes

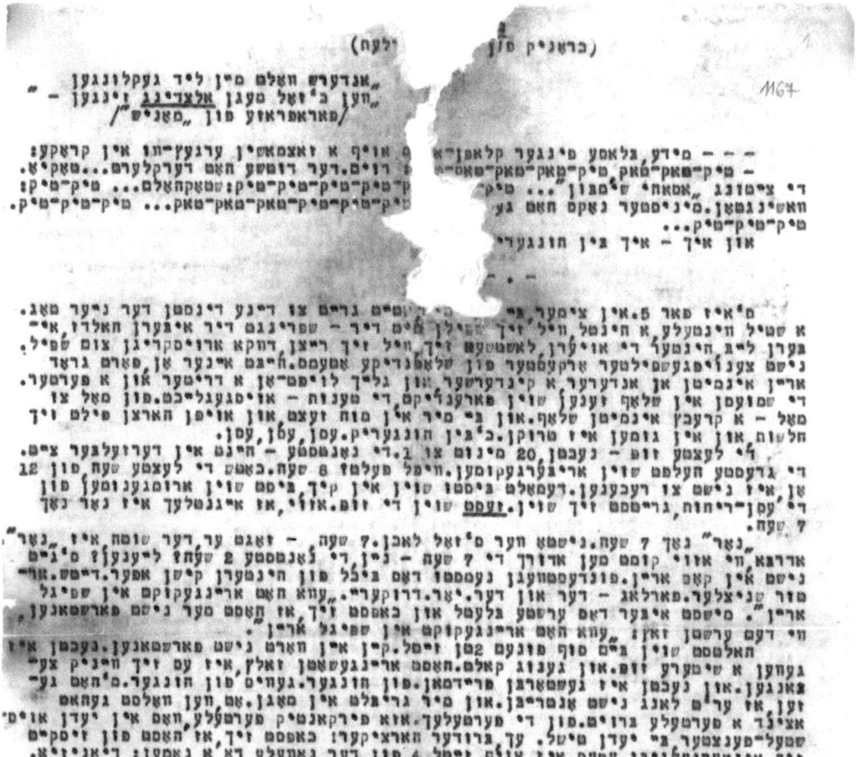

FIGURE 4: *Typescript of the first page of Leyb Goldin's story "Khronik fun a mes-les," preserved in the first cache of the Oyneg Shabes archive, unearthed on September 18, 1946. Courtesy of the Jewish Historical Institute, Warsaw, Poland, ARG I 1219 (RA I/1167).*

him dead with a lightning bolt; and he continues to be laughed at in his afterlife in Gehenna.

Peretz engages in gentle self-mockery regarding the humble literary possibilities of Yiddish language and culture as compared to the seductive charms of the European literary tradition. In the section of "Monish" that Goldin references, Peretz reflects on East European Jewry's lack of adequate vocabulary for the sort of sexual desire and romantic love that is at the heart of European love poetry. Equally, however, I would argue, "Monish" ironizes European culture from Yiddish culture's position of ostensible poverty, suggesting that the riches of European romance might perhaps best be left to non-Jews.

Andersh volt mayn lid geklungen,
Kh'zol far goyim goyish zingen
  Nisht far yidn, nisht "zshargon!"—
  Keyn rekhtn klang, keyn rekhtn ton!
S'hot far libe, far gefil
Nisht keyn pasnd vort keyn stil . . .

Undzer yidish hot nor vitsn,
Hot nor shpitsn, blanke blitsn;
  Verter vi farsamte shpizn!
  In im lakhn, vaynen, rizn!
R'iz vi gal, vi pyolun biter
Un er dresht dos layb mit riter
[. . .]
Keyn eyntsik vort iz tsart un glat,
Es iz far libe toyt un mat—
  "Hertsl," "zele," "shats," un "shetsl"—
  S'hot a tam vi lakrits-pletsl—
Es hot keyn tam, es hot keyn zalts,
Un es shmekt nokh khazer-shmalts!

(Peretz, *Ale verk,* vol. 1: 20–21)

My song would sound different
Were I singing in a non-Jewish tongue for non-Jews
  Not for Jews, not "*zhargon*!"—
  No fitting timbre, no fitting tone!
For love, for sentiment,
It has no suitable style . . .

Our Yiddish has only witticisms,
Has only barbs, lightning flashes;
        Words like poisoned dishes!
        Giants laugh and cry in it!
It's bitter as gall, as wormwood
And it lashes one's body as if with switches
[. . .]
Not one word is tender and smooth,
For love, it's dead and flat
        "Dear heart," "my soul," "darling," "treasure"—
        It tastes of licorice confection—
It has no taste, no salt,
And it smells of pig fat!
            (my translation)

I have quoted from the revised 1892 version of "Monish." In the original 1888 version, Peretz's debut work published in the first volume of Sholem Aleichem's *Folks-biblyotek*, the last couplet quoted above reads: "Es hot keyn geyst, es hot keyn zalts—/ Un shmekt nokh tsu mit genzn-shmalts!" ("It has no spirit, it has no salt / And, what's more, smells of goose fat!" Quoted in Dan Miron, *Traveler*, 61). This section of "Monish" on the challenges of Yiddish is generally read as lamenting that Yiddish is too unesthetic to express the nuances of love, the quintessentially individual experience of romantic longing and erotic pleasures.[24] This is surely true, but the 1892 text makes emphatically clear that what Naomi Seidman has aptly called "the double-edged comedy of Peretz's translation of high-German love into low Yiddish farce" cuts in two directions (Seidman, *Marriage Plot*, 56). The substitution of *khazer-shmalts* (pig fat) for *genzn-shmalts* (goose fat) is so striking that I am inclined to suspect that Peretz here is restoring rather than revising his original word choice.[25] Whereas the 1888 text can be read as saying that it is hard to write love poems in a language that smells of schmaltz, the—revised or restored—text of 1892 insists that the language of love, when translated into Yiddish, has the taste of licorice confection and the smell of pig fat—the former an insubstantial (and possibly repulsive) food, and the latter the quintessence of *treyf*. Words that smell of pig fat suggest words that would have been repellent indeed for most East European Jews in 1888 to take into their mouths. Clearly, though, Peretz is not simply faulting Yiddish for its reluctance, as it were, to ingest and incorporate the *khazer-shmalts* of the romantic conventions of

European literature; rather, he is looking askance at the (cloying) richness of this aspect of European culture from Yiddish's position of relative poverty, even as he does not deny but indeed highlights this poverty.[26] A comparable ambivalence is likewise legible on the level of the ironies of the plot of "Monish": Monish is struck down by God and laughed at by his German goddess. On the one hand, Peretz is poking fun at the belief that any departure from traditional parochialism in the direction of engagement with European culture will lead ineluctably to doom. On the other hand, an anxiety remains that the European culture you may fall in love with may not love you back.[27]

Goldin's modernist text self-consciously takes up the complex weighing of the ostensible riches of European, and especially German, literature over against the ostensible poverty of Yiddish that Peretz had begun at the symbolic inception of modern secular Yiddish literature, now with the threat of its end looming. Goldin questions the adequacy of the rich palette of European literature to render the experience of the ghetto and/as starvation.[28] His song would sound different if he were writing "literature" for a reading public that embodied the codes and values of European literary culture. But he is not; he is cut off from the world, imprisoned in the Warsaw ghetto, at the threshold of death by starvation, and writing Yiddish for an uncertain audience and possibly for none at all. This is the specific place of poverty from which Goldin will enter into dialogue with the rich resources of European literature.

The text of "Chronicle" proper (after the Peretz epigraph) begins and ends with the image of tired fingers ticking away on a typesetting machine at a news agency somewhere in Cracow.

> Tired, pale fingers are setting type somewhere in Cracow:
> Tik-tak-tak, tik-tak-tak-tak. Rome: the Duce has announced . . . Tokyo: the newspaper *Asahi Shimbun* . . . Tik-tik-tik-tak . . . Stockholm . . . Tik-tik . . . Washington: Secretary Knox has announced . . .[29] Tik-tik-tik-tak . . .
> And I am hungry. ("Chronicle," 424 / "Khronik," 49)

Goldin's framing of his text with a reference to world events as related via the *Gazeta Zydowska* (the final lines of "Chronicle" reiterate, although not verbatim, this opening passage) establishes a stark contrast between the time of hungering subjectivity in the ghetto and both the time of world events and the dynamics of prewar (public, political) newspaper culture.[30] Published twice weekly in Cracow from July 1940 to July 1942, the *Gazeta Zydowska* was the only Jewish newspaper officially permitted in the ghettos of Nazi-occupied Generalgouvernement Poland. Amos Goldberg has analyzed the role that the restriction of the press in the ghettos played in radically transforming the Jewish public sphere: a highly literate public culture, mediated largely by an avidly read periodical press, was abruptly supplanted by an information-starved public culture of rumor.[31] Widely-despised as an organ of propaganda (evident here in how it conveys what "the Duce has announced"), the *Gazeta Zydowska* fails to connect the narrating *I* of "Chronicle" to world affairs or to a public sphere devoted to discussing and debating them. Instead, it highlights his isolation.[32] The ticking of the type doubles as the ticking of clock-time. A disembodied, homogenous world-time stands in sharp contrast to the subjective hunger-time of the narrator, who is radically localized and isolated in the Warsaw ghetto, with long hours to endure until his next meal. The ticking clock that marks the time of the depressing events occurring in the wider world at war in summer 1941 narrows to the somaticized time of the hungering body as "tik" reechoes finally in "hungerik." Time's tik-tik-tiking its way into the localized, embodied hunger-time in *hungerik* reiterates the theme of time already introduced in the title, "Chronicle of Twenty-Four Hours." Significantly, rather than claim a literary genre like story, novella, or even monologue, Goldin chooses to present his project under the generic label "chronicle," a type of writing that privileges time itself in its sheer unfolding over the ways that literary texts typically shape time, namely into the patterns that literary readers recognize as themes, plots, and stories. And what will be chronicled is a temporal unit, twenty-four hours. A certain unit of a certain modality of time, hunger-time, is what Goldin will try to render.

A single temporal divide structures the day of the first-person narrator-protagonist Arke: waiting for the midday soup (his only sustenance), consuming it, and recommencing the long wait.[33] The minimal plot introduces us to important scenes and aspects of ghetto life, which Arke either remembers or encounters as he walks to and from the soup kitchen.[34] He remembers the burial in a mass grave of his friend Friedman, who had died the day before, of either starvation or suicide. We see food tantalizingly for sale but at prohibitive prices; we see second-hand dealers in the streets. On his way to the soup kitchen, Arke nearly trips over a corpse lying on the ground. We encounter the *palatzovka* workers, who went daily to work outside the ghetto, and Arke and his stomach debate whether he should have tried to get himself a spot among them (by now he is so emaciated that he could not possibly). He fantasizes about writing to the chairman of the Judenrat (Adam Czerniakow, although he is not mentioned by name) to ask for a modest daily bread ration. At the kitchen, we are introduced to the system of meal tickets.

Preoccupied with people sitting at another table, Arke does not notice when the server fills his bowl without taking his ticket. He thus has a rare opportunity—posing both an ethical dilemma and, should he be caught, a grave danger—of having his bowl filled a second time. Returning from the kitchen, Arke is plagued by self-recriminations about his own moral decline and by a bout of paranoia that everyone—in particular the director of social assistance, who passes by conveyed in a rickshaw, a means of transportation for the "privileged" of the ghetto—can see that he cheated the system to receive a second bowl of soup and that he will now have his soup-kitchen privileges revoked.[35] Arke has further luck when he finds a cucumber lying in the street. The final, highly significant, external event is a surgical operation that Arke witnesses through the window of the children's hospital in the ghetto. Arke has frequently asked himself if the Jews in the ghetto have been reduced to the status of beasts; this operation convinces him that they have not. Even though Arke characterizes the operation as possibly "pointless or even criminal" ("Chronicle," 434 / "Khronik," 65), it is unmistakably human: "Animals do not operate on their young!" ("Chronicle," 434 / "Khronik," 65).

While these events are important to "Chronicle," the narrative, an extended interior monologue (or interior dialogue, between Arke and his stomach), consists overwhelmingly of Arke's flights into thought, reverie, memory, and the world of various literary texts and topoi, which are intermittently undercut by Arke's literally-minded stomach, who mocks all such "stories." Featured prominently among the remembered and imagined "stories" of before and beyond the ghetto are classics of Western literature and, in particular, of European modernism. It is largely through the dialogue it maintains with other literary models—and in particular through assaying the limits of modernist preoccupations and esthetics—that Goldin's experimental text gives a searing account of the subjective experience of a life reduced, second after second, to hunger. Goldin's modernist psychological portrait depicts consciousness hard up against its physiological limits; it is an extended interior dialogue between a man and his stomach in which the stomach threatens to displace the narrating subjectivity altogether. Arke's interior monologue self-consciously rifles through numerous Russian and European Romantic, realist, and modernist tropes as it situates itself implicitly or expressly vis-à-vis an array of authors and texts including Goethe, Romain Rolland, Tolstoy, Balzac, and Jakob Wassermann. Arke discards the majority of these literary models as quickly as he invokes them as being wholly incommensurate with the experience of the ghetto. Yet, as we will see, in three modernist authors,

Knut Hamsun, Thomas Mann, and Arthur Schnitzler, Arke finds more adequate resources to draw on, push to their limits, and derange in an attempt to render the experience of exclusion from the wider human community and the fracturing of consciousness in hunger-time.

Goldin evokes Goethe to contrast the conflicted Romantic soul, which features prominently in so many literary works, with the starving self in the ghetto, utterly dominated by the stomach. The allusion to Goethe occurs in a rich passage in which Arke's stomach emerges as a voice that fractures the integrity of Arke's consciousness. The passage moves from Arke remembering his past commitments (as a leftist intellectual) to collective over individual concerns. Arke reproaches himself for thinking obsessively about bread:

> Maybe it isn't nice to think about oneself in this way—only about oneself, oneself. Remember once; preached a thousand times: the century of the masses, of the collective. The individual is nothing. Phrases! It's not me thinking it, it's my stomach. It doesn't think, it yells, it's enough to kill you! It demands, it provokes me. "Intellectual! Where are you, with your theories, your intellectual interests, your dreams, your goals? You educated imbecile! Answer me! Remember: every nuance, every twist of intellectual life used to enchant you, entirely possess you. And now? And now!" ("Chronicle," 425 / "Khronik," 50)[36]

The "me" of Arke's stomach provokes and indicts, as "you," Arke's "me" as an intellectual, reducing Arke's past political commitments, and intellectual pursuits more generally, to mere "phrases." The stomach's brutal undercutting of cultural pretensions and political ideologies is part and parcel of the text's broader complex reassessment of cultural forms, identities, and values from the standpoint of the starving body.

As the passage continues, the stomach becomes increasingly dominant and aggressive, and with dark irony Goldin contrasts the fractious dialogue between stomach and diminishing self with the Romantic trope of two people battling within one (whose locus classicus is Goethe's Faust).[37]

> Why are you yelling like that?
>
> "Because I want to. Because I, your stomach, am hungry. Do you realize that by now?"
>
> Who is talking to you in this way? You are two people, Arke. It's a lie. A pose. Don't be so conceited. That kind of split was all right at one time when one was full. Then one could say, "Two people are battling in me," and one could make a dramatic, martyred face.

> Yes, this kind of thing can be found quite often in literature. But today? Don't talk nonsense—it's you and your stomach. It's your stomach and you. It's 90 percent your stomach and a little bit you. A small remnant, an insignificant remnant of the Arke who once was. The one who thought, read, taught, dreamed. . . . Yes, stomach of mine, listen: such an Arke existed once. Once, once, he read a Rolland, lived side by side with a Jean-Christophe, admired an Annette, laughed with a Breugnon. Yes, and for a while he was even a Hans Castorp, by some writer . . . Thomas Mann. ("Chronicle," 425 / "Khronik," 50–51)

"Literature" has a double function in Goldin's text. It serves Goldin as a means of conveying the extra- (or the sub-) literary reality of a life of starvation in the ghetto—albeit negatively, precisely insofar as Arke's stomach rejects "literature" as a viable way of rendering this reality. Literature, however, also serves Arke as a memory anchor. It recalls his former self in a world in which the conditions to support the humanistic values for which "literature" does shorthand still obtained, a world in which it was still possible to be the contemporary of Romain Rolland's characters Jean-Christophe, Annette, and Colas Breugnon.[38] (As we will see, Goldin's relationship to Mann's *Zauberberg*, the protagonist of which is Hans Castorp, is more complex.) Goldin's text is thus both anti-literature and literature at the same time, both a reckoning with literature's now-useless illusions and an abiding attempt to continue to contribute to, to produce, literature even under the inhuman conditions of the Warsaw ghetto. Arke resists literature's collapse even as he narrates it, indeed even by narrating it.

Goldin's self-testing vis-à-vis "literature" is a prominent strategy of "Chronicle." It is in fact while Arke is gazing at other faces in the soup kitchen, lost in a reverie about how ill-equipped the conventions of realist prose would be for rendering them, that he unknowingly receives his first bowl of soup without having his ticket taken.

> Somehow the people sitting here all have such long faces, not-having-eaten faces, with swollen ghetto spots under their eyes, which give the face a Mongolian look. You think of a master of world literature, a Tolstoy, a Balzac, a Wassermann. How they made a fuss over people, they chiseled every feature, every move. "You seem to be somewhat pale today!" one of these geniuses would write, and the world was enraptured. "You seem to be somewhat pale today," and women dabbed their eyes with handkerchiefs, critics interpreted and serious, business-like

> gentlemen, owners of textile factories or partners in large, comfortable manufacturing businesses beneath white marble signs felt a quiver in their cheeks—reminiscent of the first kiss, fifty years ago. "You seem to be somewhat pale today" ha, ha! If someone today were to read or write, "You seem to be somewhat pale today," when the whole world is deathly pale, when everyone, everyone has the same white, chalky, lime-white face. Yes, yes, it was easy for them to write. They ate, and knew that the readers were going to eat and that the critics were going to eat. Let these masters now show their true colors and write! ("Chronicle," 431 / "Khronik," 59)

Arke's meditation is on how and whether the experience of the ghetto and its pervasive hunger can be depicted in literature. Whereas modern European literature is well equipped to express one person's concern for the wellbeing of another singular person, Arke questions whether it can accommodate the ubiquitous experience of hunger in the ghetto. The representational conventions of European realism function in symbolic exchanges between authors, readers, and critics only under certain social conditions, the most basic being that authors, readers, and critics all eat. Even the symbolic codes of literary representation presuppose a biological substratum that in the Warsaw ghetto simply cannot be taken for granted. In the face of the individual and collective experience of starvation, much of the usually unquestioned idiom of literary representation loses its self-evidence, becomes labile, and collapses. The self-alienation experienced in starvation is here reflected in the alienation of banal phrases from any socio-literary context in which they could sustain meaning. At the physiological limit between culture and naked biology, such literary commonplaces are no longer banal, but grotesque.[39] (A comparable literary reflection on alienation from the conventions and preconditions of literary practice occurs in Oskar Rosenfeld's story "Meine zwei Nachbarn," which I analyze in chapter 8.)

Albeit ambivalently, Goldin consistently highlights how ghetto conditions generally, and starvation in particular, mock "literature" and other narratives of extra-ghetto existence. Arke's stomach yanks Arke back from a reverie about love and lovers still existing somewhere in the world (where "they don't think about food") with the retort "Sick fantasies!" and by further characterizing Arke's wandering thoughts about love as "nonsensical stories":

> "Sick fantasies!" interrupts the scoundrel, my stomach; he's woken up, the cynic. "What a dreamer! Instead of looking for a practical solution,

> he lies there deluding himself with nonsensical stories [*Shtot tsu zukhn a takhles, ligt er un redt zikh ayn a lung-un-leber*]. There are no good or evil stomachs, no educated or simple ones, none in love and none indifferent. In the whole world if you're hungry, you want to eat. And by the way, it's all nonsense [*In agev—di gantse mayse heybt zikh nisht on*]. There are good providers for their stomachs, and there are unlucky wretches [*shlimazls*] like you. You can groan, you idiot, but as far as filling me up—damnation [*s'kadokhes*], what's the time?" ("Chronicle," 428 / "Khronik," 55)

The term Arke's cynical stomach uses to deride the "nonsensical stories" with which Arke-deludes himself is "a lung-un-leber," literally lung and liver. Even when referring to Arke's escapist chimeras, the stomach eschews ethereal, abstract terms and uses one that designates a dish which, however simple and unappealing in normal times, would have been welcome in the ghetto. The stomach's language somaticizes abstraction and, in referring to other, edible bodily organs, hints at the auto-cannibalization of the starving body. The idiom the stomach uses to dismiss Arke's fantasies as nonsense—"di gantse mayse heybt zikh nisht on" (the whole story fails to begin)—epitomizes how the stomach's hunger short-circuits the very possibility of stories, or narrative per se. Arke's stomach also disrupts an expression of defiance on Arke's part toward the better-off class of ghetto inhabitants with the derisive question, "Tell me, friend, are you starting up with your stories again?" ("Chronicle," 428 / "Khronik," 56). In a breathtaking instance of dark irony and interior perspectival shifts, Goldin has Arke reason that his friend Friedman must have died of hunger, not suicide, because suicide "is something from the good old days" when unrequited love, despair at having a serious illness, and the like, could inspire one to commit suicide after penning a "stylized note with 'It's nobody's fault' and 'I'm doing the world a big favor'" ("Chronicle," 425–26 / "Khronik," 51–52). All sickness is human, Arke reasons, but "hunger is a bestial, a wild, a rawly primitive—yes, a bestial thing. If you're hungry, you cease to be human, you become a beast. And beasts know nothing of suicide" ("Chronicle," 426 / "Khronik," 52).[40] Arke's stomach responds to this discourse: "Brilliant, my pet, an excellent theory! So how long is it, wise guy, till twelve o'clock?" ("Chronicle," 426 / "Khronik," 52). Arke reduces the convention of the suicide note to sheer banality, and suicide itself to self-indulgence on the part of a sort of psychological and emotional human self that has all but ceased to exist in the ghetto. Arke's dismissal of the bourgeois self, however, only amounts, in the brutal judgment of Arke's condescending stomach, to more idle intellectualism: "An excellent theory!" Even the evocation of reduction to bestial existence remains too figurative and literary for the stomach; the stomach mocks even the desperate irony of Arke's reflection on the human status of starving ghetto inhabitants.

Yet Goldin does not evoke literary models (and other illusions, "phrases," "fantasies," and "stories") only to reject them. In more sustained and meaningful ways, he also engages three (modernist) authors: Knut Hamsun, Thomas Mann, and Arthur Schnitzler. In these authors, Goldin finds, among other things, an anti-literary template for how to grapple with the breakdown of the human subject precipitated by hunger (Hamsun); a compelling contemplation about the relativity of temporal experience (Mann); and resources for rendering the subtleties of fragmented consciousness in interior monologue (Schnitzler). Arke meditates on Mann and Schnitzler explicitly and at length. Although never mentioned expressly, Hamsun's innovative and seminal 1890 novel *Hunger* (*Sult*) must be understood as a major intertext in Goldin's literary treatment of hunger in "Chronicle." As a well-read translator of European literature, Goldin would have been familiar with Hamsun's novel, which he could have read in any number of translations, including German (1890), Russian (1892), and two different Yiddish translations (1909, by A. Frumkin, and 1929, by Miryam Reyzin). Hamsun had a considerable impact on European modernism, including Yiddish modernism. With particular reference to *Hunger*, Isaac Bashevis Singer characterizes Hamsun as "the father of the modern school of literature in his every aspect—his subjectiveness, his fragmentariness, his use of flashbacks, his lyricism. The whole modern school of fiction in the twentieth century stems from Hamsun, just as Russian literature in the nineteenth century 'came out of Gogol's greatcoat.' They were all Hamsun's disciples: Thomas Mann and Arthur Schnitzler, Jacob Wassermann and Stefan Zweig, . . . Hamsun even had an effect on Hebrew and Yiddish literature. Agnon, Schoffmann, and Bergelson were influenced by him. This writer was enchanted with Hamsun's prose for years" (Singer, "Knut Hamsun, Artist of Skepticism," ix).[41] Goldin's Arke invokes three of the authors Bashevis Singer refers to as "Hamsun's disciples"—Mann, Schnitzler, and Wassermann—as he casts about in his mostly unsuccessful search for confrères in the increasingly foreign realm of European literature.

Hamsun's novel, moreover, circulated among Jews confined to Nazi ghettos. In his diaries from the Lodz ghetto, published under the German title *Wozu noch Welt* and in English as *In the Beginning Was the Ghetto*, Oskar

Rosenfeld refers repeatedly to Hamsun's *Hunger* (109/138, 147/170), including to a Yiddish translation (76/106).[42] Though it would be safe to assume that Hamsun's *Hunger* also circulated in the Warsaw ghetto, we do not need to assume. S. Sheynkinder's "Oyf di gasn" (On the streets), a text composed in the Warsaw ghetto in 1941 and recovered in the first cache of Oyneg Shabes documents, relates a scene of street life in the ghetto in which Hamsun's book figures memorably. Sheynkinder's text consists of a brief introduction and four vignettes. In the fourth (*daled*) vignette, entitled "Der Bukh-hendler" (The book seller), the narrator describes how a book seller offers "pearls of world literature [that] lie promiscuously in a dirty basket—all for 50 groshn" (Sheynkinder, "Oyf di gasn," 99). The clever young book seller wittily suggests a book apposite for each customer: "'Hello, Mister,' he says, turning to a customer, 'you absolutely must buy the book *Hunger*—just 50 groshn" (Sheynkinder, "Oyf di gasn," 99).[43] Whether or not Hamsun's Jewish readers in Nazi ghettos were aware of his support for Hitler and Nazism is not clear from these sources.

Both *Hunger* and "Chronicle" are interior monologues of a starving persona, literary phenomenologies of a person's consciousness fractured by hunger into discontinuous, endangered psychic fragments. In a letter to Gustaf af Geijerstam in May or June 1890, Hamsun characterized *Hunger* as "an attempt to describe the strange, peculiar life of the mind, the mysteries of the nerves in a starving body" (Sverre Lyngstad, introduction to *Hunger*, xiv). Hamsun's project offered a model of literary anti-literature that Goldin draws on in his experimental "chronicle." Hamsun insisted his book was not a novel, as it lacked plot and characters in any traditional sense, and the protagonist, like Goldin's Arke, remarks repeatedly, indeed compulsively, on the incommensurability of "literature" and starvation.

Like Goldin's later text, Hamsun's experimental novel also plays centrally on the non-synchronicity of clock-time and subjective hunger-time. After its minimal frame situating what is to come in the text as having transpired in the past, Hamsun's first-person tale of hunger begins with the strike of a clock:

> It was in those days when I wandered about hungry in Kristiania, that strange city which no one leaves before it has set its mark upon him. . . .
>
> Lying awake in my attic room, I hear a clock strike six downstairs. (Hamsun, *Hunger*, 3)

The starving protagonist is dependent upon the public clocks of the city's normative social institutions (university, church, jail). His fateful inability to synchronize his own temporal experience with generic clock-time runs as a leitmotif throughout Hamsun's novel,[44] a temporal disparity radically amplified in Arke's experience, compressed within a twenty-four-hour period. The contrast between precise temporal indications and measurements, and a temporally deranged subjective experience that belies them, is likewise a major feature of Yisroel Rabon's 1928 modernist classic *Di gas* (*The Street*), as Chone Shmeruk has observed.[45] Leonard Wolf posits that "clearly, Knut Hamsun's *Hunger* (1890) is the formal model for *The Street*" (Wolf, "Afterword," 190). Rabon's anti-novel about a socially dislocated Jewish protagonist contending with extreme destitution and hunger exemplifies how Hamsun's thematics and modernist techniques were creatively taken up by Yiddish writers of the early twentieth century.[46]

Yet as unmistakably as Hamsun provided a crucial formal model for Goldin, the distance between the experience of hunger and time that the two texts render remains unbridgeable. As the opening of Hamsun's novel, quoted above, shows, the first-person protagonist of *Hunger* narrates retroactively; he renders the subjective immediacy of hunger-time but does so from a temporal remove. Indeed, at the book's end *Hunger*'s protagonist leaves Kristiania on a ship. Goldin, by contrast, does not recall hunger-time in a literary text but rather writes literature from within the experience of starvation, a locus from which there is no escape. Whereas Hamsun's seminal text launched new possibilities for modernist writing, Goldin's sifted through the detritus of modernist works and techniques as the very possibility of sustaining modern Yiddish literature, its writers and readers, had to be measured in seconds.

Literary modernism's experimental exploration of time is one of the recurrent reference points for Goldin's text, which is less a story of events than an evocation and exploration of hunger-time. Notwithstanding the reference already quoted to Mann's Hans Castorp as a figure with whom Arke once identified but who now seems hopelessly quaint, Mann's exploration of the malleability of time in *Der Zauberberg* (*The Magic Mountain*) has profound resonances for Arke as he experiences the paradoxes of time while starving in the ghetto.

> Maybe it [the day's soup, which is not always served at the same time] will already have been poured; oh, how magnificently Thomas Mann describes it in *The Magic Mountain*.
>
> I remember his thoughts, the way he delineated them. Never has their brilliant truth appeared so clear to me as it does now. Time—and

> time. Now it stretches like rubber, and then—it's gone, like a dream, like smoke. Right now, of course, it's stretched out horribly, horribly, it's really enough to kill you. The war has been going on for a full two years, and you've eaten nothing but soup for some four months, and those few months are thousands and thousands of times longer for you than the whole of the previous twenty months—no, longer than your whole life until now. From yesterday's soup to today's is an eternity, and I can't imagine that I'll be able to survive another twenty-four hours of this overpowering hunger. But these four months are no more than a dark, empty nightmare. Try to salvage something from them, remember something in particular—it's impossible. One black, dark mass. ("Chronicle," 427 / "Khronik," 54)

Here, Arke does not, as he had with Goethe, Tolstoy, Balzac, Wasserman, and, perhaps less emphatically, with Rolland, dismiss a literary model as incompatible with the experience of the ghetto. Instead, Mann's experimentation with time captures a "brilliant truth" that, Arke says, has "never . . . appeared so clear to me as it does now." It is precisely Mann's modernist experimentation that seems capable of doing some justice to the temporal disorientation of hunger-time in the ghetto, in which the acute experience of every painful moment coincides with the non-experience of time as a dark expanse devoid of content.

And yet, Goldin is playing with Mann, ironizing the famous ironist. Given how Arke pivots from wondering if the day's soup has been poured to his meditation about Mann's treatment of temporality, Goldin seems to be alluding specifically to the first section of chapter 5 of Mann's novel, titled "Ewigkeitssuppe und plötzliche Klarheit" ("Eternal Soup and Sudden Clarity"). This subchapter indeed contains some of *Der Zauberberg*'s most memorable reflections on time, and uses daily soup to evoke a certain subjective temporal disorientation. Mann describes how even a long stretch of days spent convalescing from an illness pass quickly because the utterly uniform days form an immobile *now* (*stehende*[*s*] *Jetzt*) or eternity (*Ewigkeit*; Mann, *Der Zauberberg*, 243). One is brought midday soup at the same hour every day, and one resides in the suspended time of the eternal soup or *Ewigkeitssuppe*. Arke's experience of illness, eternity, and soup obviously differs radically from the timeless satiety of the Berghof sanitarium. As he says to himself in the above quote, "From yesterday's soup to today's is an eternity [*an eybikayt*], and I can't imagine that I'll be able to survive another twenty-four hours of this overpowering hunger." Arke's eternity is not that of the plenitudinous hour of the *Ewigkeitssuppe* but the excruciating *eybikayt* of hunger-time separating one day's *zup* from the next. Thus when Arke attests that he has never before understood the "brilliant truth" of Mann's thoughts about the malleability of time, we can discern sincere appreciation but also an undercurrent of cutting irony.

The author that Goldin engages with the greatest depth and nuance is the fin-de-siècle Viennese master of psychological subtlety and interior monologue, Arthur Schnitzler. In the case of this German-language modernist, too, Goldin's posture is far from simply dismissive. After awaking at five in the morning, Arke attempts to pass the remaining hours until the midday soup by reading a book by Schnitzler.

> How does one get through the seven hours—or the nearest two? Read? Your brain won't take it in. All the same, you pull the book out from under the pillow. German. Arthur Schnitzler. Publisher so-and-so. Year. Printer. "Eva looked into the mirror." You turn the first page and realize you've understood no more than the first sentence: "Eva looked into the mirror."
>
> You've reached the end of the second page. Didn't understand a single word. Yesterday the soup was thin and almost cold. You sprinkled in some salt, which didn't dissolve properly. And yesterday Friedman died . . . of starvation. Definitely of hunger. You could see he wouldn't last long. And there's a gnawing in my stomach. If you only had a quarter of a loaf now! One of the quarter loaves over there, a square-shaped quarter loaf, like the ones in that display window, by that table. Oh brother! You realize that you've jumped up, the idea was so delicious. There's some name or other on page four of the novella: Dionysia. Where she's from, and what she wants—you don't know. There! A quarter of a loaf. There! A bowl of soup! You would make it differently. You would warm it through until it began to boil. ("Chronicle," 424–25 / "Khronik," 50)

This diegetic "book" may correspond to an actual published volume of Schnitzler's writings, but the allusions to the Schnitzler text that Arke tries to read suggest that it does not. I know of no Schnitzler text that begins with the sentence, "Eva looked into the mirror" (or that even has a character named Eva), certainly not *Die Hirtenflöte,* the Schnitzler novella to which Goldin alludes when he mentions its protagonist "Dionysia." With the sentence "Eva looked into the mirror," Goldin may have had in mind the famous mirror scene toward the end of Schnitzler's novella *Fräulein Else,* which, like

"Chronicle," consists entirely of an extended interior monologue. But if this is the case, Dionysia could not make an appearance only pages after Else's mirror scene ("Eva" looks in the mirror on page 1, Dionysia appears on page 4), which at any rate does not begin, but comes near the end of, the novella *Fräulein Else.* Goldin's evocation of another Schnitzler scene further suggests that he is alluding to scenes—or perhaps even evoking Schnitzler-esque scenes—from memory: "I realize that I'm still holding the book. Page seven. Let's see if I can get through it. I turn the pages. Somewhere, on one of the pages, my eye spots the [German] word Wonne. Ecstasy. A piquant, magnificent erotic scene. A few pages earlier they were eating in a restaurant. Schnitzler gives you the menu. No, no, don't read it. Your mouth becomes strangely bitter inside, your head spins. Don't read about what they ate. That's right—just as old people skip descriptions of sex. What's the time? Half past six. Oh, how early it still is!" ("Chronicle," 426–27 / "Khronik," 53).

One might here think of the seduction scene involving the husband and the sweet young thing (*der Gatte und das süsse Mädel*) that transpires in a *Cabinetparticulier* of a Vienna restaurant in Schnitzler's play *Reigen*; Schnitzler's stage directions indicate remnants of a meal including fruit, cheese, pastries, and Hungarian white wine. However, the word *Wonne* does not occur in the play. Whether Goldin simply uses poetic license in staging Arke's reading of a "book" by Schnitzler, or if his rather impressionistic evocation of Schnitzler texts and characteristic scenes is due to the vagaries of (a starving man's) memory, it is significant that he chooses to stage the encounter with Schnitzler as an attempt on Arke's part to navigate an actual book, with a publisher, year, printer, and specific page numbers. Whereas Arke merely remembers Thomas Mann and his treatment of time, he tries to read a book by Schnitzler. Schnitzler, I would argue, is both a foil and a model for Goldin's writing of hunger.

Goldin's literary depiction of reading Schnitzler in the Warsaw ghetto should be understood as part of the wider phenomenon of reading by victims during the Holocaust, which was noted and theorized by Hermann Kruk already during the Holocaust. Kruk, the author of the literary reportage "Six Gallows," the central focus of chapter 7, led a successful effort to open a library in the Vilna ghetto, about which he composed a report, dated October 1942, describing the library's collections and activities between September 15, 1941, and September 15, 1942.[47] In this remarkable document, Kruk ventured beyond statistical details concerning how many books had been lent to what age groups, to which gender, and in which languages—interesting as these are in their own right—and tried to render a psychological portrait of types of readers in the ghetto, or, as he put it, to "cast the ghetto reader into biblio-psychological relief" (171). Kruk identified two main types of readers, those who pursue "reading for the purpose of intoxication—that is, in order to stop thinking—or the contrary, reading in order to ponder, to become interested in comparable fates, to make analogies and reach certain conclusions" (193). Even the "overwhelming majority" (192), for whom, in Kruk's assessment, "the book became a narcotic, a means of escape" (192), sought in reading books connections to the outside world and their former lives; in a word, confirmation of their fundamental humanity: "The new ghetto inhabitant . . . clings to the little bit of what remained from before. Books carried him away, over the ghetto walls and into the world. A reader could thus tear himself away from his oppressive isolation and in his mind be reunited with life, with his stolen freedom" (192). The more serious reader, according to Kruk, "often likes to use a book as a mirror, as a reflection of his situation and the surrounding conditions. Readers look for analogies in books" (193). Kruk points to different sorts of texts in which readers sought analogies to their own situations, from books about hunger to books about the history of the Jews during the Middle Ages and the Crusades or the Inquisition or, as in the case of Sholem Asch's *Kidush ha-Shem,* the Chmielnicki pogroms of 1648–1649. Kruk further notes that books about war were particularly in demand, including Tolstoy's *War and Peace,* Jaroslav Hasek's *The Good Soldier Svejk,* Emile Zola's *La Débâcle,*[48] British playwright R. C. Sheriff's play about World War I, *Journey's End,* Erich Maria Remarque's *All Quiet on the Western Front,* and Franz Werfel's *The Forty Days of Musa Dagh,* about the Turkish genocide of the Armenians during World War I.[49] Kruk mentions many other books that were in similar demand in the Vilna ghetto, but these suffice to demonstrate the diversity and breadth of Jewish and non-Jewish literature in which victims of the Holocaust sought points of comparison and analogies.[50] Ghetto readers held up books "as a mirror" of their situations.[51]

Goldin's dramatization of Arke's meditation on literature and his attempts to read Schnitzler from the vantage point of the ghetto strain the functions that reading had for Holocaust victims of providing analogies and a sense of connection to the world and one's prior life and self. The literary examples Goldin's text rifles through for the most part seem woefully inadequate for capturing the ghetto experience and tend to underscore just how alien Arke has become to his pre-ghetto self to whom such literature spoke. And yet, just as some aspects of ghetto experience confirm, by radicalizing them, certain insights of modernist literature, such as the malleability of temporal experience, Schnitzler's oeuvre becomes radically legible in the ghetto in ways that simultaneously illuminate and disfigure Schnitzlerian insights and narrational dynamics. To an extent, Arke rejects Schnitzler, as he does other writers. Arke is too hungry and exhausted even to process Schnitzler's sentences, and there is little in the content of Schnitzler's stories to which Arke can relate. The one tantalizing element in Schnitzler's texts is not his erotic preoccupations but his depictions of food, which must be skipped over "just as old people skip descriptions of sex"—a note of poignant humor. However, what Goldin is doing with Schnitzler is more complex and profound than a simple gesture of rejection. In Goldin's story Schnitzler is transformed from discrete texts into fleeting, scrambled impressions that juxtapose and fuse what should be kept apart. Schnitzler's texts melt into one another. Fräulein Else (?) is renamed Eva; her famous mirror scene appears to inaugurate a novella, four pages into which Dionysia appears; and by page 7, the erotic fairy tale narrative of "Die Hirtenflöte" (the only Schnitzler text featuring a Dionysia) has yielded to a realistic portrayal of a Viennese restaurant scene, followed in turn by an erotic interlude. Arke, that is, does not merely fail in his ability to concentrate on a recognizable text by Schnitzler, but quite radically deranges Schnitzler's oeuvre as he reads it from a position of extreme hunger. Arke's modernist reading in extremis is almost cubist in the way it skips back and forth to events and pages ("A piquant, magnificent erotic scene. A few pages earlier they were eating in a restaurant . . .") rather than reading sequentially, even as his own hunger-thoughts cut in and out of frame. Strikingly, Arke's inability to read Schnitzler lucidly and straightforwardly, his incapacity to remain focused on the page or to extract anything from the text but fleeting words, names, and impressions, results in an unmistakably Schnitzler-inflected form of interior monologue. The very distraction from Schnitzler as a bound book reproduces and pushes to a radical limit the chief literary innovation for which Schnitzler is rightly known—the subtle rendering of fractured subjective experience through interior monologue. Goldin appropriates Schnitzlerian interior monologue to capture part of the limit experience of the Warsaw ghetto precisely, if paradoxically, by using interior monologue to depict the limit at which Schnitzler's literary project becomes both thematically and literally, physiologically unreadable.

Goldin's double gesture vis-à-vis Schnitzler is evident already in the initial reference to the "book" by Schnitzler and Arke's inability to concentrate on it. Arke's failed attempt to keep his thoughts from straying results in an equally

Schnitzlerian and anti-Schnitzlerian stream of liminal consciousness that is unable to think about anything but food. Goldin, however, does not leave it at this but instead reiterates this double gesture of rejection and appropriation vis-à-vis Schnitzler on a grander plane when he has Arke, already well into the narrative, realize that he is still holding the Schnitzler volume and once again try to read it. Between the first and second attempts at reading Schnitzler many of the most crucial aspects of Arke's memory and current interior life are introduced. An extremely rich interior monologue unfolds —about communism, memories of confinement in jail, Friedman's death and the cultural status of suicide, about life reduced to animality and whether or not death would be preferable. All this occurs between attempts to concentrate on pages of—one could also say, in the space of the failure to read—the book by Schnitzler: these topics are where Arke's mind wanders because he is too hungry and spent to read Schnitzler. As I have suggested, however, such a non-reading of Schnitzler is also a reading in extremis. It is at the same time an ironic dismissal and an homage. Just as the famous mirror scene in Schnitzler's *Fräulein Else* dramatizes the eponymous protagonist's relationship to her distorted (self-)image, Goldin holds up Schnitzler's oeuvre as a refracting mirror. The very thoughts that make it impossible for Arke to read Schnitzler in the ghetto take the form of a—violently disfigured—Schnitzlerian text.

Arke's stomach's belittling of literature, culture, and intellectuals reveals the vanity of cultural pretensions and pursuits from the vantage point of the wasting body. Yet even as Arke's stomach threatens to crowd out Arke's self entirely, a waning sliver of Arke remains that mourns the loss of literature, the books he can no longer identify with or even read. And Arke's stomach, we should not forget, appears in Goldin's literary text. Hard up against the biological limits of any possible writing, Goldin continued to make literature, to engage, in writing, with the catastrophic complexity of his situation. He took up the fragments of European culture still at his disposal to try to sustain himself, and to sustain literature. Much as the operation on the child in the ghetto hospital, which reaffirms for Arke the ghetto population's humanity, asserts the value of human life in the face of utterly desperate and doomed circumstances, Goldin, at the threshold of physiological collapse, insists on writing literature. Goldin's literary project mirrors his wasting body: just as his body is cannibalizing itself in order to sustain itself; eating itself in order to feed itself; killing itself in order to live, Goldin's text decomposes and metabolizes a literary corpus of above all modernist works in order to sustain itself. Goldin's text is a work of literature trying to feed on literature, and starving.

It rifles through various literary modalities only to arrive at the ultimate limit to the usefulness of literature in the Warsaw ghetto, which is that one could not eat it. Goldin's text is in this sense a self-metabolizing work of literature, a writing of and from hunger.

The work of intertextuality in all its myriad forms involves writing that is at the same time a specific practice of reading, and vice versa.[52] Texts cannot be written without recourse to the intertexts they recycle, but they do not leave these texts unchanged. Nor does Goldin's "Chronicle" leave the modern and modernist European intertexts it cannibalizes unscathed. The experience of the ghetto was one of being radically excluded from broader society and culture and ultimately from existence itself. European culture, both popular culture and the high modernist literature of Mann and Schnitzler et al., went to the ghettos along with its aficionados and readers imprisoned there. Many ghetto readers sought connections to the outside world through literature, but the hungering intertextuality of Goldin's radically literary text insists on writing the ghetto into the very culture from which he had been removed. Goldin's "Chronicle" pulls the cosmopolitan world of European literary culture into the Warsaw ghetto by insisting that the experience of the assault on human subjectivity, community, and basic human status that occurred there be inscribed into the wider European cultural conversation; that modern literature engage this radical experience of modernity that threatens the very possibility of literature itself.

CHAPTER 6

THE AUTOBIOGRAPHY OF A NUMBER

YEHOSHUE PERLE

In his autobiography *Dichtung und Wahrheit* Johann Wolfgang von Goethe reflects, "A person's personal name is not like a coat that is merely draped around him and that one can tug and tear at but rather like a perfectly fitting garment, indeed like a skin that has grown over every inch of him and that one cannot scrape or flay without injuring the person himself."[1] The philosopher Ludwig Wittgenstein expands: "The prisoner has a number for a name. No one would say about such a number what Goethe says about personal names."[2] Goethe exemplifies the way Western modernity has understood names to be inextricably bound up in a person's self-identity and social identity. Wittgenstein underscores that the loss of a person's name is generally part and parcel of being removed, or abjected, from the social.

Both the personal and social aspects of the reduction of one's name to a number that Wittgenstein proposes as a limit case for Goethe's conception of the ontology of names resonate deeply in the autobiographical text "4580," written at the end of 1942 in the Warsaw ghetto by Yehoshue Perle, a prominent interwar Yiddish novelist.[3] Perle's discourse articulates itself in the space of the gulf, measured with grotesque irony, between his erstwhile relationship to his name, and the number that now marks his status as an enslaved laborer in the drastically reduced Warsaw ghetto. Writing after the murder of the vast majority of the ghetto's inhabitants in the summer of 1942, Perle struggles to write the experience of personal erasure—the substitution of a number for his name—against the backdrop of the erasure of East European Jewish life in the Nazi genocide.

Crucially, Perle resists being reduced to a generic cipher by depicting the intimate and sociocultural pathways that had lent meaning to his name, for himself and others. He gives voice to the experience of loss by vividly and idiomatically evoking what has been lost: the wider contexts in which his name circulated.

Perle's title refers to a numbered work permit that he was assigned, one of roughly thirty thousand that the Germans issued. These work permits granted Perle and other "numbers" reprieve from immediate deportation while they worked as slave laborers in ghetto factories, called "shops." Samuel Kassow sets the historical scene:

> In September 1942, as Perle was writing "Khurbn Varshe," Shmuel Winter secured him a job in the artificial honey factory on Franciszkanska 30—the same factory that would also employ Rachel Auerbach. Now only Jews with numbers—hung around their necks like dog tags—had a right to live, working up to fourteen hours a day for meager rations. The Germans handed out 30,000 numbers in all, and Perle wrote another essay about his new name, "4580." The Bible had admonished Jews to blot out the name of Amalek, the treacherous tribe that had attacked the Israelites in the desert. Now the Germans, with the consent and connivance of the Judenrat, were turning the tables on the Jews. They had already killed 300,000. And now they were blotting out the names of the few they allowed to linger on in the ghetto shops. (Kassow, *Who Will Write Our History?*, 195–96)[4]

In anything like normal social conditions, a prisoner is removed from a society that remains intact. Being reduced from having a name to having only a number is a terrible but, in principle, reversible individual fate.[5] For Perle, however, the alternative to being a numbered slave laborer is not regaining his name and returning as a full person to a functioning society, for the Polish Jewish society into which he was born in 1888 was being eradicated.

For Perle, the only alternative to a twilight existence as a number is to rejoin the wider community in death. Thus the abysmal irony—an irony born of genocide—at the heart of Perle's incendiary satire: being a mere number is in fact a privilege. The narrating bearer of the number 4580 calls himself "lucky," and in a grotesque allusion to a traditional self-understanding of the Jews, one of the "chosen people" (*ato-bakhartonikes*). All the conditions and contexts on which his name and its intimate and social meanings were predicated have now been upended. With the Great Deportation of the Warsaw ghetto in the very recent past, Perle reflects on not only the loss of his name as a personal and interior experience, but also on the collapse of the wider modes of reference including kinship networks, specific ceremonial and cultural practices, and circuits of public celebrity that served, to adapt David Lauer's apt term, as the "ontological infrastructure" that lent his name meaning.[6]

Perle's satire is desperate and highly volatile because it can find no stable social or ethical locus from which to articulate its caustic criticism. Perle shifts frequently in tone and register, for example from incendiary, white-hot anger at "Amalek" (the Germans) and the Judenrat, whom Perle faults for carrying out the Nazis' orders, to self-reproach and implicit acknowledgement that he is only alive to rage against the Judenrat because of the help he has received from the Judenrat. Perle's text likewise careens between mordant sarcasm and nostalgic lyricism and tender memories of his wife and mother. Perle's juggling of the wreckage of a murdered culture in "4580" thus challenges the (thankfully less and less prevalent) discursive reduction of Holocaust victims to mere biological existence beneath the threshold of meaningful speech.[7] Perle does not respond to the fate of having his personally and culturally significant name replaced by a number—whose function is to aid the Nazis in the administration of dehumanization, enslavement, and genocide—by falling into a culturally generic silence. On the contrary, his tour de force text uses richly idiomatic Yiddish, refers to numerous popular Ashkenazic cultural practices, and marshals a repertoire of literary allusions and biblical and modern intertexts to reflect, fiercely, on the erasure of his personal identity in the context of the genocidal erasure of the wider cultural community within and against which his personhood was positioned. Against the reductive and thus terrifyingly transparent text of the number "4580" as interpreted through a Nazi hermeneutic, Perle offers a thick—or, adopting the Yiddish idiom, a juicy—description of the circuits of signification that his name has traveled.

In this sense, "4580" is a paradigmatic example of a text that demands—and indeed works to perform—a context-rich "constructivist" (while resisting an abstracted "exceptionalist") reading, to use Alan Mintz's helpful terms.[8] The violently imposed numbers are aimed to dehumanize their bearers, who along with their names are also stripped of their erstwhile domiciles, all their possessions, and the vast majority of the people who made up their families and their society.[9] Such a number thus seems to be devoid of any human significance or cultural repertoire. It is against precisely this hermeneutic of dehumanizing transparency that Perle will evoke a cultural world.

We should fully appreciate that Perle's approach in "4580" was anything but obvious or inevitable, lest we take for granted and thereby minimize the significance of his linguistic and cultural performance. One can well imagine Perle taking a radically different tack and depicting life in a slave-labor "shop" in the remnant of the Warsaw ghetto in autumn 1942 in an intentionally depleted, generic, transparent, and wholly uprooted Yiddish that would capture the emptiness, radical alienation and exploitation, as well as the human, cultural, and biological destitution of the toiling "numbers." The title novella of the best collection of Perle's short prose, "Nayn a zeyger inderfri" (Nine o'clock in the morning)—published in 1930 by the prestigious Kletskin publishing house—was originally published in 1923 with the title "Tsifern" (Numbers, or ciphers).[10] Set in a Polish-speaking work milieu of a bank—the Kenig Brothers, Warsaw—owned by the assimilating brothers Yozef and Mikhal Kenig, the novella aims at and achieves what we could call a zero degree of style in order to convey the arid existences, devoid of hope or passion, of the accountant-protagonist Yakuv Vinkler and his colleagues, who spend their workaday lives writing, recording, and checking and re-checking numbers. The title refers to this alienated world of abstract and lifeless numbers and to the ciphers like Vinkler who devote their meaningless days, months, and years to being their custodians. Even Vinkler's family life is thoroughly dominated by his preoccupation with the empty world of his work. An accountant by profession, Perle knew this sort of soul-killing milieu intimately and deployed a wholly transparent and depleted Yiddish to capture it; "Nayn a zeyger inderfri" is written with all the juiciness of an accountant's ledger. Needless to say, the dehumanizing quality of the labor depicted in "Tsifern" is of a wholly different order than that of the numbered slave laborers in Warsaw ghetto factories, but a radical version of cultural and stylistic depletion was certainly available to Perle as a representational strategy as he contemplated writing "4580." He chose to go in an emphatically different direction and to adopt a style that David Roskies characterizes as "more idiomatic than ever" to depict not the reduced life of numbered shop workers but the rich individual and communal life that hides beneath and haunts an ostensibly meaningless cipher.[11]

In "4580" Perle never directly states the name that he has lost, although he alludes to it when he writes: "A person's name is like a living organism; it has flesh and blood. You can't feel it or see it, but you can't live without it. I wore it, this name of mine, as a lovely woman wears a still lovelier string of pearls. It was mine, entirely mine. I had, after all, inherited it from my grandfathers and great-grandfathers. I absorbed it, together with my mother's blood, together with the sweat of my overworked father."[12] The Yiddish for "a still lovelier string of pearls" is "a nokh shenere shnur perl," and in the word *perl* (pearls), one can hear Perle's surname.[13] Even as Perle here asserts that his name was entirely his, he situates this personal possession in a wider generational context: his name also carries the history of his forebears, his father's sweat, his mother's body and blood. Further on, Perle alludes to the continued generational transmission of his name to his child and grandchild. The evocation of the name's implication in wider kinship networks is more emphatic in the original of Perle's simile, "A nomen bay a mentsh iz azoy vi a lebedik eyver"[14] than in the English rendering "A person's name is like a living organism" (Roskies, *Literature of Destruction*, 450), for *eyver* signifies not a self-contained whole but a part within a wider whole, a body part, a limb or member or organ rather than a self-sustaining organism. And like the word *member*, *eyver* can also mean *penis*. Following immediately after Perle's allusion to his receiving of his name according to the Jewish custom at his circumcision ceremony eight days after his birth, it is clear that this wider body is the Jewish people. "Eight days later, as is the custom among Jews, they made a blessing over me and said, 'May his name in Israel be—so and so'" (Roskies, *Literature of Destruction*, 204; translation modified; "Mit akht teg shpeter, vi es firt zikh bay yidn, hot men gemakht iber mir a brokhe un gezogt—veyikorey shmo beyisroel—azoy un azoy," Mark, *Tsvishn lebn un toyt*, 143). Perle's need to preserve his anonymity in his rendering of the Jewish naming ceremony has the effect of highlighting the wider entity—the Jewish collective—within which (in Israel, *beyisroel*) he and his name will have a place. Eight-day-old boys receive their names upon becoming Jews by entering the covenant of circumcision. Perle becomes a member of the community of Israel when the covenant is inscribed on his *eyver*. Individual *eyvrim* participate in the ritual and biological continuity of the community. Perle's text stresses how this wider context is in many ways more important than individual names; while the name can be alluded to as "so and so," it is among the Jewish people ("in Israel") that the name—whatever the name—will have resonance.

Writing in the Warsaw ghetto could be a dangerous—and was thus often a clandestine—undertaking. Many writers resorted, as we see Perle doing here, to writing anonymously. "Secrecy," Kassow notes of the Oyneg Shabes, "was paramount. The staff constantly worried that the slightest mistake, the smallest misjudgment could destroy the entire project" (Kassow, *Who Will Write Our History?*, 218). The lengths to which the Oyneg Shabes staff went to keep the identities of contributors concealed made it difficult for those sifting through the unearthed documents after the war to distinguish originals from copies, or to identify documents' authors.[15] Perle's reticence to state his proper name directly must be understood in this context. Yet the irony cannot have been lost on Perle that his work permit number would have been, for the Nazis (and the Judenrat) a more precise identifier than even his name. Yehoshue and Perle were both common names among East European Jews, but in late 1942 the work permit numbers that allowed thirty thousand "lucky" people to continue to live "legally" in the ghetto as slave workers were presumably all unique. For this reason, I break with what seems to be a general consensus among readers of this text and deem it unlikely that "4580" was the actual number Perle was assigned. The manuscript of "4580" in Perle's hand supports this reasoning.[16] Several times throughout the opening pages Perle first writes "fifteen hundred and eighty" before crossing that number out and substituting for it "four thousand five hundred eighty" (see figure 5). It may not be possible to tell conclusively, but it also appears that Perle used "1580"—in numeral form—for his original title and later changed the "1" to a "4."[17] It is possible that one of these two numbers was the actual one that Perle was assigned, but it seems unlikely. Why would he switch between them and leave both legible on the page? To imagine that Perle could simply have had a lapse and forgotten what his work permit number was seems implausible. Given the two vying numbers, it seems more likely that Perle opted for a number that would not easily identify him (and, perhaps, would avoid reproducing anyone else's actual number as well).

Regardless of the question of the authenticity of the numbers Perle evokes in this text, the question of names—or numbers—as reliable referential markers goes to the heart of how Perle theorizes autobiographical writing from his unprecedented vantage point within the ongoing genocide. It bears recalling that in Philippe Lejeune's highly influential theorization of an "autobiographical pact" the proper name is the crucial element that distinguishes autobiography from adjacent genres like the novel.[18] For Lejeune the sine qua non of the autobiographical pact between author and reader is that the author asserts—and the reader believes—that the author, the narrator, and the principle character of the work are identical (Lejeune, "The Autobiographical Pact," 3). The referential anchor capable of securing this crucial identity is precisely the proper name:

> It is . . . in relation to the proper name that we are able to situate the problems of autobiography. In printed texts, responsibility for all enunciation is assumed by a person who is in the habit of placing his name on the cover of the book, and on the flyleaf, above or below the title of the volume. The entire existence of the person we call the author is summed up by this name: the only mark in the text of an unquestionable world-beyond-the-text, referring to a real person, which requires that we thus attribute to him . . . the responsibility for the production of the whole written text. In many cases, the presence of the

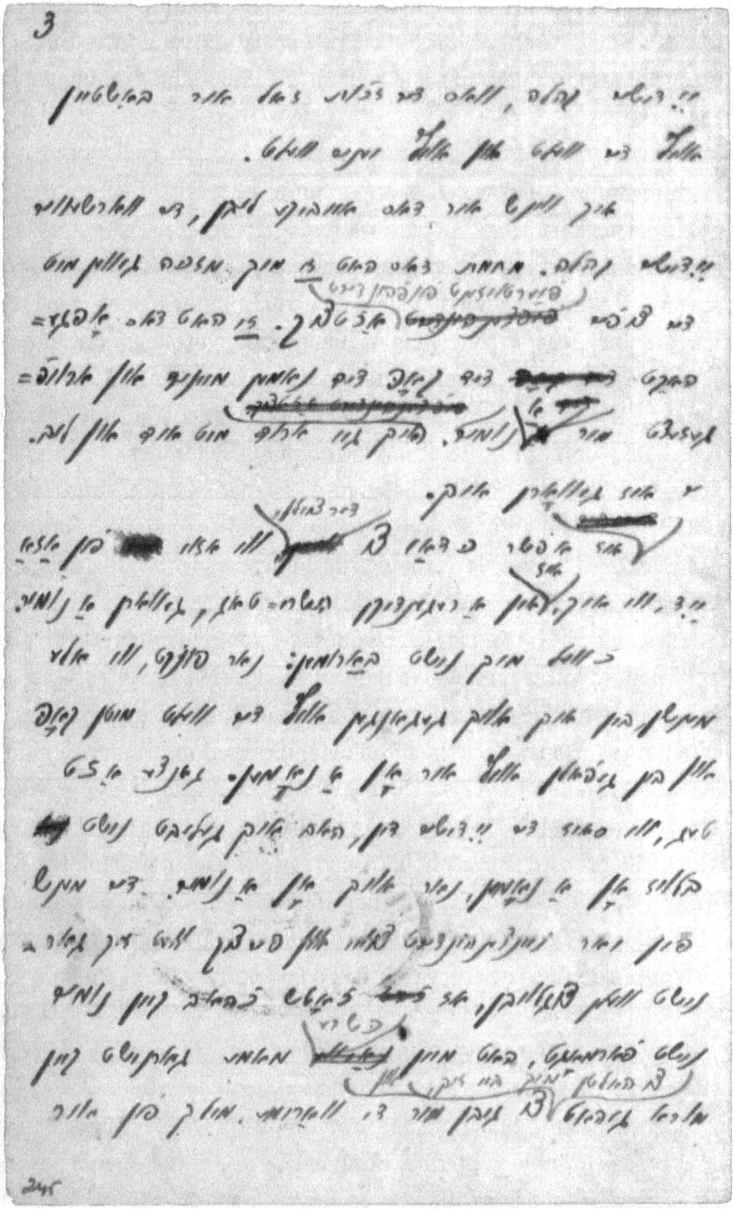

FIGURE 5: *Page in the author's hand from Yehoshue Perle's "4580." Perle first wrote out the number "1580," then crossed it out and wrote out "4580." This text was preserved in the second cache of the Oyneg Shabes archive, recovered December 1, 1950. Courtesy of the Jewish Historical Institute, Warsaw, Poland, ARG II 254 (RA II/245).*

> author in the text is reduced to this single name. But the place assigned to this name is essential: it is linked, by a social convention, to the pledge of responsibility of a real person. (Lejeune, "The Autobiographical Pact," 11)

With regard to Perle's text it is important to note that it is the referential link to a real person, the author of the autobiographical text, that is at issue for Lejeune, not the authenticity of a proper name. Lejeune views pseudonyms as, in general, functionally equivalent to actual proper names as far as the autobiographical pact is concerned. While pseudonyms may occasionally be used to deceive readers, "literary pseudonyms are in general neither mysteries nor hoaxes. The second name is as authentic as the first" (12). Indeed, the case of Yehiel De-Nur (born Yehiel Feiner), who published under the pseudonym of Ka-Tsetnik 135633—the number that was tattooed on his arm as a prisoner in Auschwitz—aptly demonstrates how even the radically dehumanizing signifier used by the Nazis for logistical purposes within their machinery of enslavement and genocide can indeed function as a viable, if unsettling, authorial signifier. The answer to the question, can one enter into an autobiographical pact with a number? is, then, in certain circumstances, yes.

However, what distinguishes Lejeune's and Perle's meditations on the function of the proper name in autobiographical writing is precisely the circumstances. Lejeune (needless to say, wholly understandably) presumes a functioning society in which books are published, circulate, and are read, and in which certain conventions hold. What Perle's locus of articulation within the continuing genocide reveals is that the proper name can perform its referential function in the autobiographical pact only in the context precisely of such a functioning society with intact conventions and insitutions. In the final analysis, the referential thrust of a proper name inheres less in the name itself and more in the conventions that allow the name to signify. Lejeune presumes (can presume) this social foundation to obtain, and thus zeros in on the proper name as the linchpin of the autobiographical pact. Perle, however, must approach autobiographical writing in the face of the ongoing genocide that has already eradicated the very society and culture according to whose conventions and practices his proper name marked him as a person and an author. The radical disparity between the principal character and the narrator in Perle's text already throws into question the identity between character, narrator, and author that Lejeune identifies as constitutive of the autobiographical genre. But insofar as this is the case, it is not due to a mere structural discrepancy between autobiographical protagonist and narrator—for this structural distinction is indeed basic to autobiographical theory, which tends to separate the experiencing *I* (protagonist) from the narrating *I* (narrator).[19] The more radical disparity between protagonist and narrator in the case of "4580" stems not from narratological structure but from catastrophic history: the protagonist had a name and a world, and the narrator, reduced to a number, has neither. It is this genocidal context that also renders the status of Perle's name radically uncertain as a cultural signifier—beyond any merely psychological disparity apparent between character and narrator—and brings to light the predicament in which he is caught. The autobiographical crisis that "4580" enacts is not born of doubts as to whether that number can functionally indicate the person who is the author Yehoshue Perle but rather of the fact that so many of the social and cultural circuits and conventions that Lejeune presupposes to be operative when a proper name (or pseudonym, even a number) performs this referential function have been destroyed. Lejeune underscores how in accordance with a social convention a proper name or its functional substitute can referentially link a real person, the author, to the narrator and principal character of an autobiographical work. Perle asks, by contrast, can a person remain a person when the society and culture in which their name signified—among other ways, as an author—have been decimated? This is the haunting question that Perle returns to implicitly in different ways throughout his autobiographical text, enunciated from within the Nazi genocide of European Jews in general and, in Perle's case, also the cultural genocide of Yiddish society in East Europe in particular. At every turn, Perle underscores the connection between his (erstwhile) name and the wider social and cultural matrices that lent it its existence and significance.

Perle opens his text by presenting his number as a hermeneutic puzzle. At first glance, it seems to have no meaning and to say nothing. Yet the thrust of Perle's discussion of this ostensibly meaningless number will be to underscore specifically Jewish ways of making meanings and the way this apparently insignificant cipher speaks of the pain and suffering of the murdered Polish Jewish community. "A round number. At first glance it looks silly and seems to have no specific meaning. A detached number such as this can be likened to those grey people who go through life alone and die without confession [*on vide*]" (Roskies, *Literature of Destruction*, 450). Isolated and detached, this number appears to be mute and devoid of meaningful context. When Perle likens it to people who die without confessing their sins, he ostensibly has in mind the social aspect, the care, that is part of this ritual: those approaching death should not be alone, and should be encouraged by those at their side to confess in a way that maximally preserves their mental health and self-respect.[20] Not making a deathbed confession thus suggests the lack of such minimal social connection or support network. "Die without confession" (*shtarbn on vide*) in the above quotation replaces Perle's first formulation, "also die unseen" (*shtarbn oykh nisht gezeenerheyt*), which he struck.[21] Perle's invocation of the practice of deathbed *vide* is thus one instance in "4580" where he chose to replace an idea that he initially conveyed in a less culturally specific formulation with a more particular reference to a Jewish cultural practice. The contrast between a more generic and a more specifically *yidish* idiom—in the double sense of Yiddish and Jewish that the word *yidish* has in Yiddish—is likewise evident in Perle's choice to rewrite a formulation in the sentence translated above as, "At first glance it looks silly and seems to have no specific meaning." Perle's original formulation for "and seems to have no specific meaning" was "zet zi oys narish un zogt keynem gornisht" (it looks foolish and says nothing to anyone). He struck this and replaced it with "zet zi oys narish un hot gornisht vos tsu zogn" (it looks foolish and has nothing to say). Whereas the first formulation suggests that the unremarkable number does not appear to anyone to have any particular meaning, the second stresses that the number appears not to have anything to say. In the first formulation, it is so many potential interpreters of the number who fail to see in it any particular significance; in the second, it is the number itself that ostensibly lacks the capacity to speak. The distinction is somewhat subtle, but Perle's preference for "un hot gornisht vos tsu zogn" better sets up a central tension in Perle's text between appearing stripped of all cultural specificity and vehemently insisting on the capacity to speak in a culturally specific idiom. The ostensibly nondescript number 4580 *does* have something to say, and *yidish* culture has the resources to say it. In view of a prevalent propensity in much theoretical discourse on the Holocaust to reduce the voices and writings of victims to nullity and silence, it is significant that in "4580" Perle is already rejecting reduction to the generic and mute status of a number, and marshalling the considerable resources of a Yiddish and wider Jewish language and frame of reference to speak. Perle writes fiercely against the implication that a number's bearer must lack the ability and the resources to be able to say anything. Perle suggests that "People will . . . not believe that great suffering and pain cry out from the number, and so does the disaster of the people from whom it is my lot to be descended" (Roskies, *Literature of Destruction*, 450). At the outset of his text, Perle insists that, despite all appearances, this number embodies great personal suffering and the communal catastrophe of his people—and that it will not be reduced to silence.

After introducing the number as an ostensibly, but only ostensibly, silent and meaningless cipher, Perle rifles through ways that it might be interpreted and misinterpreted. The hermeneutic practices that he invokes for deriving meaning from the number 4580 are significant. He first alludes to mystical numerological interpretive possibilities, then to rational ways such a number attached to a person could signify within a normally operating society. Perle's invocation of Jewish numerological hermeneutics is dismissive, even as it, one might say winkingly, invites the very "foolish" interpretation it ridicules. "But if an arithmetician or astrologer were to ponder this number at length, they might spin out some half-baked conjecture or contrive a gematria from which fools would later deduce either the end of the world or the advent of the days of the Messiah" (Roskies, *Literature of Destruction*, 450). On the one hand, Perle demonstratively dismisses the practitioners of gematria and astrology who might spin out specious conjectures as to the meanings of the numeral 4580 (or 1580), and of the "fools" who might later derive from them apocalyptic significance. On the other hand, these are culturally specific Jewish interpretive practices that differ fundamentally from the Nazi reduction of human beings to numbers. Whether hocus pocus or not, gematria is a way of seeing numbers as "living" and as part and parcel of human and divine meanings.[22] Moreover, there is much to suggest that Perle is inviting us to engage in precisely the gematria that he is rejecting as so much *narishkayt*. It may be a "foolish" hermeneutic practice, but it is a cultural practice with deep Jewish roots, and one that is living and open and generative rather than murderously reductive.

The Hebrew for 4580 would be ד"תקף. Leaving off the *daled* (4), 580 (תקף, *tekaf*) means to attack or attack violently.[23] Perle may have opted to change 1580, his first choice of number, since 1580 (אתקף) would mean "I attack" (the 4 [ד] has less obvious significance). Perle's allusion to the verb *to attack* (or attack violently) is altogether in keeping with his relentless assault on the Warsaw Judenrat for what he saw as its role in carrying out the Nazis' murderous plans. Yet another culturally resonant interpretation of 580 would be to read תקף as *tokef*, as in the *piyut* "Unetanneh [or Unesanneh] Tokef." This *piyut*, moreover, has a strong link to the specific context in which Perle wrote "4580" and to the hated Judenrat. As I discuss in chapter 4, Yoysef Kirman invokes this famous poem, one of the most memorable moments in the Rosh Hashanah and Yom Kippur liturgy, in his poem "The Eyes Remain Open."[24]

In 1942 Rosh Hashanah fell on September 11 and 12, which was also (and not coincidentally) the horrific culmination of the so-called Cauldron (*kesl*), when between September 6 and 12 some fifty thousand souls were forced into a few streets adjacent to the Umschlagplatz and not allowed to leave before finally being deported to their deaths in Treblinka. For the last day of the mass deportations from the Warsaw ghetto to Treblinka the Nazi authorities chose Yom Kippur, September 21. Perle authored "4580" sometime in late 1942, not long after the Great Deportation, and the allusion via the gematria of 580 to the "Unetanneh Tokef" evokes the genocidal violence the Nazis perpetrated leading up to and during the most recent High Holidays.

The image in the "Unetanneh Tokef" of Jews passing before God like a flock beneath a shepherd's staff as God counts and records them and decides who among them will live and who will die, is part and parcel of Perle's wider strategies in this text of savaging the Nazis and Judenrat in ways that point up the grotesque subversion of traditional Jewish understandings of God and the sacred. Whereas the former *kehile kedoyshe varshe* ([the leadership of] the holy congregation of Warsaw) engaged in sacred work, serving the community and God, the new *kehillah*, the Judenrat, participates in the destruction of the Warsaw Jewish community at the command not of God but of the Nazis. Similarly, the lucky numbered few *ato-bakhartonikes*, or Chosen Ones (more literally, "He has chosen us-niks"), have not been chosen by God but by his unholy usurpers, the Nazis and Judenrat. Perle's numerological allusion to the "Unetanneh Tokef" does similar work, placing the Nazis and Judenrat in the usurped role of God, who decides with inexhaustible compassion who will remain among the living. Upon reflection Perle's invocation of how "fools" might see in "4580" signs of the end of the world or the advent of the Messiah seems less contemptuous of the misguided, "foolish" mystics who engage in such unfounded interpretations and more poignant—for what he is marking in this text is indeed the end of a world, his world, the world of Polish Jewry.[25]

Perle's brief invocation of possible rational rather than mystical ways to interpret the hermeneutic puzzle posed by the numeral 4580 is no less significant. Perle distinguishes between people who are assigned numbers within a social context, as part of their social functions, including prisoners who, while they reside at the edge of the social totality, have not lost all social legibility, and people like himself, whose assigned numbers are part and parcel of a radical loss of social identity due to a radical loss of one's society itself. "Sober minds, if they consider it, will probably take it [the protagonist's number] to be the Identity Number of a policeman, a railroad porter, a prisoner [*katorz-*

shnik], or—pardon the proximity—a dog, or the devil knows what else. But that this foolish number should be a substitute for the name of a living person, who was never a policeman, a railroad porter, a prisoner, or even a dog—that will be difficult to believe" (Roskies, *Literature of Destruction*, 450). The unfathomable nature of the number in question as compared to the social legibility of the numbers of policemen, railway porters, and even prisoners derives from the loss of the social whole within which these numbered persons and their social functions can be identified. Such numbers have social legibility because they are part of a society. The living person whose name has been replaced by a number, by contrast, has no recourse to their former society. Such persons were first removed from the broader society of which they were a part when Jews were confined to the ghetto, and the Jewish society confined to the ghetto was then murdered. The number in question has no place within a society but marks a position outside or beyond or after the murdered collective—and this is what renders the substitution of number for name so radical, irreversible, and hard to fathom.

Perle's treatment of possible hermeneutic approaches to the ostensibly meaningless numeral 4580 hinges on the terrifying distinction between the social meanings and identities people (even people who bear numbers) possess within a social context, and the loss of identity entailed by the radical annihilation of the society that constituted one's ontological context. His autobiographical meditations are on what remains of him not in the face of social ostracism but rather of having, however temporarily, outlived his murdered society.

As "4580" continues Perle will at every turn highlight the wider Jewish cultural context that provided the very ground of his name. Much of Perle's text explores ways that his (erstwhile) name was not just a label for himself as an individual but something that sutured him into intersubjective and wider social dimensions of human experience. "But don't think that my name was a slave to me," he writes, "that it didn't have a say and a will of its own. On the contrary, when I fell into a melancholy mood and started thinking about the world to come, my name asked to have this world. And just as my mother wished that I should survive her, so my name wanted to survive me" (Roskies, *Literature of Destruction*, 451). The name's wish is to leave a mark in Perle's cultural world, this world, and not to disappear anonymously into the world to come. This and the name's wish to outlive its bearer presuppose a sociocultural and linguistic context—or world—where the name can, as it were, make a name for itself, and remain alive.

Perle recalls how his name, in dark periods (*atsves*), tied him to ethical norms. When he had wanted to "harm himself, his neighbor and his enemy," his name checked him: "My name stood up and sternly warned me not to do it" (Roskies, *Literature of Destruction*, 451). Perle's name extended beyond the reach of the self into the ethical values of the community. Thus at such times his name admonished him: "'You must not put me to shame,' it said. 'If people point their finger at you, their finger will reach me first. I am the phylactery on your forehead. Without me you may shout "I am Solomon,"[26] and nobody will believe you. And if you want to know, I'll whisper a secret to you: I no longer belong only to you. Your life wanted me to be in the public domain. And if indeed I am in the public domain, no blemish may appear on me'" (Roskies, *Literature of Destruction*, 451). Perle understands his name as a symbolic hinge that mediates between his subjective interiority and the wider social and cultural world in which selves, identities, and roles are forged and recognized.

Remarkably, Perle underscores the exteriority of his name not only when touching on his life as a public figure but even, albeit differently of course, when describing his late wife's relationship with the name she received from him. (Although Perle does not say this directly in "4580," his wife Sarah had died by suicide in 1926.)

> Just as she bore with proud pleasure her majestic head of hair, so did she bear my name with proud pleasure. To her it was the loveliest, the cleverest. She caressed and drew it out. I often didn't recognize it, so strange did it sound. But when I heard it issuing from her pure lips, with all the delight she put into it, I heard it anew, fresh, bathed in her young laughter.
>
> Cruel fortune willed that in her youth she should carry it with her to the grave. . . . The name has turned to stone in the tablet that guards her grave. And I believe with absolute faith that, just as I cannot forget her name here, so she cannot forget my name there. (Roskies, *Literature of Destruction*, 451)

We conventionally think of a wife taking the name of her husband, but Perle draws our attention to how he experienced his name from the perspective of his late wife. She delighted in and transformed the name and gave it back to him anew. Perle's name is not so much a subjective possession as a symbolic structure that mediates intersubjective exchange, both intimate and public. While Perle voices the faith that his late wife remembers his name in the afterlife, just as he cannot forget her name in this world, the memorialization of her (and his) name on her tombstone takes part in a realm of cultural ritual that is now collapsing.

In a sardonic parenthesis, Perle says he believes he could still live to the proverbial ripe old Jewish age of 120 (the age at which Moses died) and receive a proper Jewish burial. But if so, how would he report his name, as was required according to folk custom, to the Angel Dume (*malekh-doyme*) who would come to his grave? The angel "will take a trip down and knock on my tombstone: 'Mah shimkho?' 'What is your name.' . . . How will I answer him then? That my name is Four Thousand Five Hundred and Eighty? But won't he look at me as if I'm crazy?" (Roskies, *Literature of Destruction*, 452; Mark, *Tsvishn lebn un toyt*, 145; translation modified).[27] Amid ubiquitous death, Jewish ways of ritualizing death and the folk traditions around death also die. The number 4580 signals the destruction of this wider cultural world. Not even biblical archetypes can remain adequate to the scale of slaughter: "From under my fortunate number leaps out the cry of tens of thousands of poisoned, strangled Jewish children. In the dark nights I hear the great weeping of the mother of all mothers, our Mother Rachel. She walks across the desolate fields and wraps her dead children in burial sheets. With her beautiful, delicate hands she washes the blood off her sons and daughters. But can she wrap all of them in burial sheets. Can she wash them all?" (Roskies, *Literature of Destruction*, 454; "Nor kon zi den ale in laylekher viklen? Kon zi den ale opvashn?" Mark, *Tsvishn lebn un toyt*, 149). Perle's allusion to Rachel (in Jeremiah 31:15) both looks to the Bible for figures that might do justice to the present catastrophe, and acknowledges the inadequacy of biblical archetypes in the face of the already largely accomplished genocide.[28]

Perle ends his text with the image of these children, whose death has become unritualizable.

> They lie, the slaughtered creatures, naked and shamed, scattered and spread, impurified for burial, without a Kaddish, without a gravestone, violated by the murderous hands of Amalek, with the consent of the holy congregation of Warsaw.
>
> I'm alright. I'm a number. (Roskies, *Literature of Destruction*, 454)

The scale of the genocide has overwhelmed the cultural and ritual capacity to contend with it. In writing, in some of his final lines, that the cries of the murdered children—embodiments of innocence and of ethnic and cultural futurity—leap out from under his number, Perle again underscores that beneath the loss of his personal name lies the loss of the wider East European Jewish world that sustained its various and intricate meanings.

Perle's indictment of not only the Nazis but also the Judenrat in these final lines echoes similar enraged statements throughout. In a formulation in which caution regarding calling out hated groups and institutions by their name converges with sardonic contempt, he refers to the Judenrat as the "kehile kedoyshe varshe." Elsewhere I have explored Perle's eyewitness account of the Great Deportation of the Warsaw ghetto, "Khurbn varshe," and the controversies that swirled around this text in the Yiddish-speaking world after it was recovered in the second cache of the Oyneg Shabes archive in the midst of the Cold War in December 1950 and published in a Warsaw journal.[29] "Khurbn varshe" appeared shockingly at odds with the emerging sacralizing terms of the memorialization of Holocaust victims because it fiercely indicted the Judenrat for what Perle saw as its complicity in carrying out the Nazi genocide. Perle continues in the same vein in "4580," never missing an opportunity to insist that the Judenrat carried out the Nazis' orders "to the letter" or to cover in withering mock praise the "Warsaw Jewish kehillah" for its "good deeds" (Roskies, *Literature of Destruction*, 451), or its chairman Marek Lichtenbaum (who assumed that role after Adam Cherniaków's suicide on July 23, 1942) for his "learning and wisdom . . . known throughout the Jewish Diaspora" (Roskies, *Literature of Destruction*, 452).

Perle's contempt for (and overestimation of the agency of) the Judenrat notwithstanding, "4580" dramatizes its narrator's eventual realization of the analogy between his own and the Judenrat's predicaments. Even as he rails against the Judenrat for taking his name from him and replacing it with a number, and for its complicity in the Nazi killing machine, the narrator acknowledges that he cannot extricate himself from such complicity; he is only alive by virtue of this very number, and the condition for retaining the number is continued participation in the process of self-destruction. Perle and his son Lolek, a member of the illegal Polish Communist Party, had fled to Soviet-occupied Lwów/Lemberg soon after the outbreak of the war. Upon Perle's return to Warsaw after the German invasion of the Soviet Union, Shmuel Winter, who worked in the Judenrat while also maintaining close ties to both the grassroots Jewish Self-Help network (the Aleynhilf) and Ringelblum's Oyneg Shabes archive, secured Perle a job in the Judenrat's clothing department, which Winter ran.[30] It was also Winter, who worked tirelessly to support writers in the Warsaw ghetto, who secured Perle the job at the artificial honey factory that protected him from being killed in the Great Deportation.[31]

Although it will grow in intensity throughout the text, self-recrimination and an acknowledgement of complicity is evident from the outset: "May it merit eternal life, the Warsaw Jewish *kehillah*. For it was the *kehillah* that favored me with the number: four thousand five hundred and eighty. It was the *kehillah* that cut off my head—my name—and set a number in its place. I go around with it and live; it has become 'me'" (Roskies, *Literature of Destruction,* 450). Even here, the speaker's rage at the Judenrat is inseparable from the acknowledgment that he is only alive because the Judenrat granted him the number that has displaced his former self and become "me." Later in the text, Perle elaborates on the hopeless complicity of the "lucky" numbers, describing how the head of the *kehillah* (Judenrat) constantly threatens those in possession of numbers with their revocation should they refuse to "build the bleak wall that confines you as with a chain, and wants to strangle and choke you" or to hand over to Amalek (the Germans) such things as "the candlesticks that your dead mother used when she blessed the Sabbath candles" or "the pillow on which your child slept" (Roskies, *Literature of Destruction,* 453). Perle entertains the hope, while acknowledging it to be an impossible fantasy, of getting his name back by refusing the Judenrat's orders. In the idiom Perle deploys, this would constitute rising from the dead and becoming human again:

> To tell the truth, I'm delighted by these fearsome warnings that I'll stop being a number: I'll become "I" again! I'll get my name back! To put it simply—I'll rise from the dead [*kh'vel oyfshteyn tkhies-hameysim*; Mark, *Tsvishn lebn un toyt,* 147]. Since the world began, not a single Jew has risen from the dead: the Messiah hasn't arrived yet. I'll be the first resurrected Jew. So why shouldn't my heart rejoice? On the other hand, I remember that if I stop being a number there's an executioner's ax waiting for me. No longer being a number means good-bye to the clayey quarter loaf each day, good-bye to the smell of the year-old egg, good-bye to the little room they allotted me to live in, good-bye to the potato that other people steal from my plate of grits, good-bye to honor; no longer an aristocrat, no longer of the Club of the Chosen [*Oys numer iz der taytsh—oys a fertl leymik broyt a tog . . . oys koved, oys yakhsn, oys ata-bakhortonik*; Mark, *Tsvishn lebn un toyt,* 147]. (Roskies, *Literature of Destruction,* 453)

The speaker knows full well that, were his name to be returned to him, he would become completely ostracized, like "his neighbor" who "kept his name. His beautiful human name" (Roskies, *Literature of Destruction*, 453). The narrator describes this named but numberless human being as being as "clever," "learned," and "polite" as himself, yet whose "honest name" "doesn't get the quarter of a loaf, doesn't taste the flavor of a little grits, has nowhere to lay its head, hides itself in holes together with cats and stray dogs. My neighbor's name has been erased from the Communal Register" (Roskies, *Literature of Destruction*, 453). (Perle here uses the name of the traditional Ashkenazic communal register—"mayn shokhns nomen iz oysgemekt fun koolshn pinkes" [Mark, *Tsvishn lebn un toyt*, 147, emphasis added]—for the grisly bookkeeping within the Judenrat, once again grotesquely underscoring how utterly upended traditional institutions and values have become.) "The friends of yesterday, who have numbers, no longer say good morning to him, no longer sit with him at the same table, no longer pray with him at the same house of prayer. He has become a leper, this neighbor of mine, with the honest name and without the paper number" (Roskies, *Literature of Destruction*, 453).

Under the reigning circumstances, for the speaker to get his name back —through detachment from the number that has taken his name's place— would not entail becoming re-integrated into Jewish society but rather being utterly, abjectly removed from whatever vestige of a Jewish collective there still remains. The name cannot reaffirm his individuality because the name, and the individual it denotes, require the wider society and culture that sustain them. There is no recovering his name for the speaker because there is no society to return to, no outside to this prison. This society—those who would normally constitute the collective into which a prisoner would reintegrate —has been killed. There is no returning from the dead, no *oyfshteyn tkhies-hameysim*, to rejoin the world of the living, for the living are now dead. Even as this prison and this number entail the violent loss of personhood, they also become the only remaining refuge for continued existence, reduced and compromised as it is. Not, as is evident in the final lines of "4580," that this keeps Perle from impugning and continuing to assign outsized agency to the Judenrat, but he certainly, if torturously, appreciates that he, like the Judenrat, finds himself in the impossible position of having no choice but to participate in the Jews' systematic destruction. The only available pseudo choice is between dying immediately and staving off death long enough to participate in the destruction of the small remaining fragment of Jewish life. Even though Perle continues to impugn the Judenrat until the end, with this acknowledgement much of the ironic distance that his fierce sarcasm worked to establish between him and the "Warsaw kehillah" collapses, as he finally lacks any perch from which to level such criticism without becoming an object of the same criticism. Had he not received the number of a slave laborer via connections at the Judenrat, after all, Perle would not still be alive to lambast the Judenrat for assigning him precisely that number.

Written in the face of the destruction of East European Jewry, Perle's fraught autobiography both continues and is necessarily dislodged from a wider tradition of Jewish autobiography (both actual and fictional), which it implicitly and sometimes expressly evokes. As prominent scholars of Jewish autobiography including Alan Mintz, Marcus Moseley, and Michael Stanislawski have highlighted, Jewish autobiography is paradoxical in the way it virtually always involves a demurral of the autobiographical impulse.[32] This autobiographical disavowal of autobiography takes various forms but, in Moseley's words, "is so often repeated as to become almost an item in the etiquette of the production and exchange of autobiographical texts that characterized Hebrew and Yiddish literature" (Moseley, *Being for Myself Alone,* 440). Cutting very much against the Rousseauian model of revealing one's self in all its uniqueness,[33] Jewish autobiographers generally insist that they could not possibly be of interest to readers as individuals, but only as mirrors of the wider community.[34] Indeed, this disavowal of the autobiographical impulse is so thoroughgoing that Stanislawski identifies it as still at work in Stefan Zweig's 1942 *Die Welt von Gestern* and Sarah Kofman's 1994 *Rue Ordener, Rue Labat.*[35] The long tradition of this dialectic of individuality and typicality in Jewish autobiographical writing continues into Perle's text, where it confronts unprecedented circumstances: ostensibly lacking all individuality, the nondescript number 4580 in fact harbors the unique history of the individual whose name it has replaced. And the loss of individual humanity the number signals is not a merely individual but a devastatingly typical fate, shared by the entire murdered community of Polish Jewry.

Jewish autobiography in both its straight and fictionalized forms does of course deal with unique individuals. Frequently, however, these complex individuals lack agency and future-oriented confidence. The modern individual's break with the traditional Jewish community and way of life often results in paralysis and suspension rather than liberation. Mintz analyzes the *talushim* in the autobiographical fiction of the Hebrew revival as futureless splinters of a rapidly dissolving traditional Jewish society.[36] Becoming fully modern individuals was one thing; having any social space in which to thrive, another. The figures populating modern Jewish autobiography who become alienated from tradition while accruing psychologically intricate, albeit ineffectual, interiority are thus part and parcel of the widespread phenomenon (and motif) highlighted by Moseley of orphanhood in Jewish autobiography.[37] Moseley regards as something of an enigma the prominence of orphanhood as part of the impulse behind, and a theme within, Jewish autobiography.[38] Yet it makes sense that orphanhood would find such resonance among East European Jewish writers negotiating encounters with modernity: whether literally bereaved of a parent or not, they are in some sense all orphans of history, for the vanishing traditional world is the matrix of their very selves. How to construct oneself as a modern Jewish author in relation to a traditional Jewish world perceived to be moribund and disintegrating was a major task for a great many writers from the late nineteenth and early twentieth centuries.[39] Perle's own towering literary achievement, his dazzling, autobiographical 1935 novel *Yidn fun a gants yor: a bukh fun a fargangen lebn*, participates in this modern Jewish literary project. Perle's novel enjoys two English translations. Shirley Kumove renders the main title *Ordinary Jews* and the subtitle *A Book about a Life That Was*, whereas in the translation by Maier Deshell and Margaret Birstein, the full title reads *Everyday Jews: Scenes from a Vanished Life*.[40] A more literal rendering of the subtitle would be "a book of a bygone [or past] life."[41] Authors depicted a "lost" Jewish past and their relationships to it in diverse ways, including nostalgically and in the spirit of ethnographic salvage (Sholem Abramovitsh), with fiercely unsentimental criticism (I. J. Singer), and in what I would characterize as a non-tendentious effort to evoke the greatest possible psychological complexity and uniqueness of this world's "ordinary" inhabitants (Perle). Yet however variously, one of the key ways that modern East European Jewish authors constructed themselves in autobiographical texts was precisely against the backdrop of "disappearing" Jewish worlds. Inevitably, this tradition of writing against the backdrop of lost Jewish worlds follows Perle into the writing of "4580." Now, however, the forces driving the disappearance of traditional Jewish worlds, including secularization, economic modernization, urbanization, war (especially World War I and its aftermath), revolution, and the collapse of empires and emergence of new nation-states, had come to include the Nazi genocide—and the vanished Jewish worlds to include not only traditional milieux but all of East European Jewish society.

Like so many other modern Jewish autobiographical works, Perle's *Everyday Jews* evokes orphanhood as the condition of the modern Jewish author. While Mendl, the child narrator of *Everyday Jews*, does not lose either of his parents, his beloved maternal grandfather dies some thirty pages before the text's conclusion. Far more than his father, who is a hardworking and poignant figure but also silent and illiterate, Mendl's grandfather embodies this world. His death broadly coincides with Mendl's symbolic coming of age as a bar mitzvah. Cut off from the receding world of his grandfather, Mendl's relationship to it will ostensibly be primarily esthetic; Perle's novel is (among other things) a portrait of the artist as a pre-bar-mitzvah boy from the Polish provinces.

The wider context of orphanhood as a master trope in Jewish autobiographical writing, and Perle's own participation within this tradition, helps us better appreciate Perle's repeated quotation in "4580" of one of the most famous orphans in Jewish literary history: Motl, the eponymous child narrator of Sholem Aleichem's last (and unfinished) novel, *Motl, peysi dem khazns: ksovim fun a yingl a yosem* (Motl, Peysi the cantor's son: Writings of an orphan boy).[42] Perle's use of Motl as an intertextual leitmotif throughout the second half of "4580" widens his repertoire of cultural references (which as we have seen encompass biblical archetypes, folk beliefs, and Ashkenazic cultural practices) to include modern secular writing in Yiddish. It is noteworthy that in his review of Perle's *Yidn fun a gants yor*, Shmuel Charney, the most renowned Yiddish literary critic of his generation, remarked on the affinity between Sholem Aleichem's innocent and optimistic Motl and Perle's child narrator.[43] *Yidn fun a gants yor* beautifully follows the narrator's awakening consciousness over the course of a year (literally *a gants yor*) in the life of an "ordinary" Jewish family (i.e., a poor, hard-working family, lacking education and prestige). If Sholem Aleichem's Motl served as one narrative model for Perle's book of *fargangen lebn*, Motl also serves, in "4580," as a reference point for measuring the extent of a different sort of "vanished life"—not a bygone but an eradicated life.

The character Motl embodies Sholem Aleichem's literary strategy of what Roskies has called "laughing off the trauma of history."[44] The naïve Motl feels he has had a stroke of good luck in becoming an orphan because everyone is suddenly so nice to him. Sholem Aleichem's text analogously deploys humor to weather the violence and dislocation of Jews fleeing pogroms in Eastern Europe and starting life anew in New York, where Motl's Yiddish becomes increasingly Americanized, which makes for good but also poignant comedy insofar as it acknowledges that secular Yiddish culture will not be able to sustain itself in the United States. No matter: "We will laugh our way through this," Sholem Aleichem seems to assure his readers.

In "4580" Perle repeatedly redeploys Motl's most famous line "Mir iz gut —ikh bin a yosem! [I'm alright; I'm an orphan!]"[45] to measure the distance between this model of meeting crises with plucky comedic optimism, on the one hand, and the predicament of writing within the genocidal eradication of East European Jewish life, on the other. Four times in the second half of his short text—the final time indeed serving as the final words of "4580"—Perle writes "I'm alright; I'm a number!" (Mir iz gut, ikh bin a numer!).[46] While Motl's refrain naively makes something good out of dire circumstances, the darkly updated version of the line in "4580" signals that the "luck" of being among the chosen few who have been granted temporary reprieve from deportation in no way mitigates the catastrophe that has befallen Polish Jewry. Perle's laughter is fiercer than Sholem Aleichem's, more outraged, hysterical even, and finally impotent. This destruction is not something that he, or a fast diminishing, numbered "we," will be able to laugh off. "I'm alright, I'm an orphan!" works by comedic innocence. The speaker of "I'm alright, I'm a number!" knows himself to be doomed.

Reflecting on intertextual references in Warsaw ghetto (and post-ghetto) writing—such as Chaim Kaplan's quotation, in his diary, of Hayim Nahman Bialik's "In the City of Slaughter," Rokhl Auerbach's recourse to the memorial Yizkor prayer in "Yizkor, 1943," written in hiding on the Aryan side, and, indeed, Perle's play on Sholem Aleichem's Motl's famous phrase "I'm alright, I'm an orphan!"—Mintz comments: "Taken together, these are not the sort of recondite intertextual allusions intended for the learned; they are signals meant to be picked up by any literate person. They are simply indicators of what it means to be part of a culture" (Mintz, "Two Models," 69). While Mintz is of course right that such references would have been broadly legible, the broad audience for such allusions had already been murdered when Perle and Auerbach wrote these texts in late 1942 (Perle) and early 1943 (Auerbach). And while Auerbach wrote in hiding and with a plausible (and ultimately realized) chance at survival, it is hard to discern in the Perle of "4580" any real expectation of surviving. Perle's many allusions and invocations of cultural practices evoke a culture, to be sure. He surveys "normal" cultural reference points as someone who has seen the eradication of the society and culture of which such markers signaled "simply" being a part—but there is nothing simple about that now. The Perle of "4580" is so utterly orphaned that even the modern Jewish cultural topos of orphanhood can only fail him.

And yet, he chooses to write as though his murdered culture were still intact and operative, even though there is nothing self-evident or straightforward in this choice. Emphatically, Perle never strips down his cultural repertoire to a generic idiom that would correspond to his identity-less status as a number. He is not at a loss for words or for culturally rich modes of expression. On the contrary, and despite his rage, Perle lovingly sifts through the ample cultural resources of his Yiddish and wider Jewish culture. "4580" is a text of extreme rage, grief, guilt, and despair. It is also a love letter from a number to the language, people, and culture that gave his name meaning.

IV. SHORT PROSE: TWO

REVISITING POPULAR LITERARY GENRES IN THE LODZ AND VILNA GHETTOS

CHAPTER 7

SHERLOCK HOLMES IN THE WARSAW AND VILNA GHETTOS

GUSTAWA JARECKA AND HERMAN KRUK

I am not the law, but I represent justice so far as my feeble powers go.[1]
—Sherlock Holmes in "The Three Gables"

DETECTIVE LITERATURE AND THE HOLOCAUST

Much of the literature that I am centrally concerned with in this book enters into complex dialogues with literary models and traditions well beyond the limits of a distinctly Jewish textual tradition. This chapter attends to the ways texts written in different ghettos explicitly evoked the genre of the popular detective story. For an array of writers including Oskar Rosenfeld (whom I explore in the next chapter, chapter 8) and Josef Zelkowicz (to whom I here merely allude), Gustawa Jarecka, and Herman Kruk, the detective genre provided structures of interpretation and narrative—and conceptions of crime, justice, and individual and collective agency—by which they took stock of ghetto life, even as the Nazis engineered the destruction of their individual and collective worlds. Rosenfeld and Zelkowicz wrote in the Lodz ghetto, while Jarecka and Kruk wrote in the Warsaw and Vilna ghettos, respectively. Both Jarecka and Kruk expressly invoke the figure of Sherlock Holmes (while Zelkowicz can be read as evoking Holmes and Watson more faintly and implicitly).[2]

In this chapter I examine the different ways that Jarecka and Kruk approach questions of epistemology, justice, and ethical agency in the context of the Warsaw and Vilna ghettos via references to Arthur Conan Doyle's master detective. In the first part of the chapter I explore a report on the Great Deportation of the Warsaw ghetto that Jarecka wrote in fall 1942 ("The Last Stage of Resettlement Is Death" ["Ostatnim etapem przesiedlenia jest smierc"]). In the longer second part I turn to a text by Kruk that we could call a "true crime" story of murder and the rendering of justice in the Vilna ghetto: "Six Gallows in the Vilna Ghetto: A Criminal Literary Chronicle of the Vilna Ghetto" ("Zeks tlies"),[3] written in August 1942.

It is striking that Jarecka, Kruk, and Rosenfeld—writing, respectively, in Warsaw, Vilna, and Lodz and in Polish, Yiddish, and German—elaborated texts with and against figures and conventions of the detective genre in their efforts to grapple with questions of epistemology, evidence, agency, and justice. In doing so, these authors anticipated what would become a widespread recourse to the detective paradigm in postwar reckonings with the Holocaust and its legacy. Quasi-detective novels and short stories grappling with the Holocaust and its political and familial memory abound, many written by child Holocaust survivors or children of Holocaust survivors. The detective genre is a fundamental point of reference in texts dealing with the Holocaust and its memory by postwar authors including the French writers Didier Daeninckx, Philippe Grimbert, Patrick Modiano, Georges Perec, and Henri Raczymow; the Hungarian novelist Imré Kertesz (like Modiano, a Nobel Prize winner); the Dutch writer Harry Mulisch; Austrian and German writers Doron Rabinovici, Bernhard Schlink, and W. G. Sebald; and the British writer Robert Wilson, among others.[4] The trope of searching for traces (in German, *Spurensuche*) is also prominent in key works of Holocaust cinema like Alain Resnais's *Nuit et brouillard* (*Night and Fog*, 1955) and Claude Lanzmann's *Shoah* (1985). Broad questions about the status of Enlightenment narratives and the politics of memory and forgetting as well as local questions about family histories that are inevitably marked by gaps, trauma, and incomplete transmission, lend themselves equally to being approached through varying forms of what we could call detective literature and cinema of the Holocaust and its aftermath.

The pronounced convergence of the detective genre and literary and cinematic reckonings with the Holocaust makes a great deal of sense in view of the salience of detection in modern regimes of knowledge and justice. Although a peripheral figure from the vantage point of high culture, the figure of the detective must nonetheless be granted a place in any archetypology of Western modernity as the embodiment of the modern pursuit of truth and justice. Detection, after all, lies at the heart of a great many quintessentially modern discourses and pursuits, including investigative journalism, evidentiary jurisprudence, medical evaluation and diagnosis, Marxist analysis, Nietzschean genealogy, and psychoanalysis (the last three constituting the modernist triumvirate that Paul Ricoeur famously characterized as enacting a hermeneutics of suspicion).[5] Against this backdrop it is perhaps unsurprising that detection has figured prominently as a schema for exploring the limits of what we can know about the Holocaust—an event widely seen as defying comprehension—as well as the moral imperatives such knowledge imposes on us. The industrial genocide of European Jewry was a crime so huge and unprecedented that it is often, rightly or wrongly, said to have thrown conventional juridical and epistemological categories into crisis and tested, in Saul Friedländer's phrase, "the limits of representation."[6] The detective and detective genre readily serve as nodal points suturing together an array of concerns about the Holocaust understood as a crisis in the major narratives of modernity's self-understanding.

While the detective's embodiment of crucial aspects of modern reason and understanding as well as the powers (and limits) of moral agency have made the detective genre attractive to a wide range of postwar writers and filmmakers attempting to reckon with the legacy of the Holocaust, I focus in this chapter on the less appreciated way that two writer-activists variously deployed the figure of Sherlock Holmes in their attempts to take the measure of the crises they were experiencing even as the events of the Holocaust were still unfolding. These texts exhibit the creative ways that victims of the Holocaust, during the Holocaust, drew on the detective genre to grapple with questions of evidence, genocidal crime, agency, and justice.

These works by Jarecka and Kruk mediate between the classical, hermeneutically and morally triumphant ratiocinative detective *à la* Holmes and Hercule Poirot, and the post-Holocaust career of the detective genre as a means of figuring an, at best, fragile and partial ability to comprehend the loss of, or do justice to, the murdered. The triumphant detective's decline was of course well advanced before the Holocaust, although the catastrophe certainly added to the strain on cultural confidence in the ultimate triumph of reason and justice. If the classic detective stories of Doyle[7] and Agatha Christie evoke modern anxieties about the increasingly inscrutable nature of what Luc Boltanksi has aptly called "the reality of reality," they do so only to domesticate and assuage such anxieties.[8] While a mystery may shake confidence in the solidity and coherence of a hegemonic sense of reality, the masterful detective in the mold of Holmes or Poirot is seldom if ever at a loss to restore the logical, moral, and social order briefly and uncannily exposed as fragile. The subsequent trajectory of the literary detective genre, however, tends toward increasing moral and epistemological equivocality. In contrast to their heroic precursors, the hard-boiled anti-heroes of, for example, Dashiell Hammett and Raymond Chandler in the 1920s and 1930s are marginal and corruptible: far from affirming what Koenraad Geldof nicely terms the "moral Manichaeism" (*manichéisme moral*) of the classic detective genre, the sleuths of *roman noir* are intricately implicated—financially, morally, and often sexually—in the violence, lies, double-crossing, and death that define their milieu (Geldof, "Modernité, excès, littérature," 138). As such, they lack both the epistemological vantage and the agential sovereignty to illuminate all enigmas and to set the world aright. As we will see, Jarecka and Kruk each variously put enormous strain on the figure of Sherlock Holmes as a sort of superhero of epistemology and justice to perform difficult if not impossible tasks of salvaging agency and justice.

Both the Polish novelist Jarecka, in the Warsaw ghetto, and the Bundist librarian Kruk, in the Vilna ghetto, expressly invoke the figure of Sherlock Holmes in nonfiction texts that grapple with challenges to and possibilities for compiling and transmitting evidence and rendering justice in the catastrophic circumstances of the ghettos. As we will see in the next section, Jarecka leans on Sherlock Holmes in a meta-reflection about what it meant to be writing while facing individual and collective death, a reflection that occurs within her report on the Great Deportation of the Warsaw ghetto that she wrote for the Oyneg Shabes, "The Last Stage of Resettlement Is Death." In the second and longer section of this chapter, I turn to Kruk's narrative "Six Gallows," a highly literary, albeit nonfiction ("true crime") reportage of events in and beyond the Vilna ghetto. While the generic conventions of the detective story are far from irrelevant for how Jarecka and, especially, Kruk —who traffics in suspense and the frisson of tales of murder—render their narratives, I argue that it is finally the model of justice that Sherlock Holmes embodies that is most attractive, and elusive, for both writers.

GUSTAWA JARECKA: MISREMEMBERING SHERLOCK HOLMES UNDER DURESS

Before the war Gustawa Jarecka (born 1908) was a teacher and well-known writer. She taught Polish, translated literary works into Polish, and authored four novels in Polish, set in whole or in part in proletarian milieux and concerned chiefly with the struggles of the poor.[9] It is not entirely clear how Jarecka came by her position as a telephone receptionist, typist, and translator in the chancellery of the Warsaw ghetto Judenrat. At the Judenrat chancellery, she worked closely with Marcel Reich-Ranicki, who would survive the war and go on to become an influential literary critic in West Germany, and later something of a television celebrity as the dominant figure in the German television program *Das Literarische Quartett* from 1988 through 2001.[10] According to Reich-Ranicki, it was due to her German skills and proficiency as a typist that she was assigned a position in the four-person unit, called the Office for Translation and Correspondence (Reich-Ranicki, *Mein Leben*, 203).

Reich-Ranicki does not give a precise date when he was hired to lead this unit, but in context (202–3) it seems that it was months before the German authorities ordered the ghetto sealed on November 15, 1940. Presumably Jarecka worked at the Judenrat from fall 1940 as well. Jarecka was raising two sons as a single mother: Marek and Karol were twelve and four, respectively, when they, with Jarecka, were deported to Treblinka in January 18, 1943, the first day of the January deportations.[11]

The politically left Jarecka had not been involved in Jewish cultural life before the war. According to Ringelblum, she had been "far afield of Jewish life" (*Ksovim fun geto II*, 187) and according to Reich-Ranicki, prior to the war Jarecka "had little in common with the Jewish world. She belonged to the sort of Polish Jews for whom religion was utterly and completely foreign" (*Mein Leben*, 239). However, as Ringelblum put it, "the ghetto pulled her ineluctably into the Jewish milieu. Being engaged in the offices [*sekretariat*] of the Jewish Council [*yidisher kehile*], she was at the center of Jewish distress [*tsores*] and suffering" (*Ksovim fun geto II*, 187–88). According to the Warsaw ghetto diary that Hillel Seidman published shortly after the war, at the end of her life Jarecka had come to regret having written in Polish, and vowed that, if she survived, she would learn and write in Hebrew and Yiddish.[12]

Jarecka used her position at the Judenrat to provide the Oyneg Shabes archive with many Judenrat documents. The most consequential of these was surely a transcript of the meeting on July 22, 1942, during which the SS Stürmbannführer Hermann Höfle, who oversaw the Great Deportation of the Warsaw ghetto, dictated the German orders for the deportations that were to begin that day. Reich-Ranicki gives an account of how he was called upon to transcribe this meeting and how, shortly after its conclusion, he dictated his transcript to Jarecka, who directly typed up her Polish translation (Reich-Ranicki, *Mein Leben*, 239–41). Ringelblum notes that Jarecka also wrote other works for the Oyneg Shabes, but the sole text by her preserved in the archive is the incomplete report about the Great Deportation of the Warsaw ghetto of summer 1942 that Ringelblum asked her to write in fall 1942.[13] Jarecka was only able to write the introduction to her Polish-language report before she and her sons were deported to Treblinka. Thanks to her position at the Judenrat, she had been spared deportation prior to then; however, Judenrat employees were among the first to be targeted for deportation in January 1943.

Jarecka begins "The Last Stage of Resettlement Is Death," in Kassow's apt words, by "trying to describe what it meant to write in the face of death."[14] She ponders what the legacy will be of the words that she and her colleagues were devoting the remaining bit of their lives to writing and preserving. It is in this context that Jarecka evokes a Sherlock Holmes novella by Doyle to convey her understanding of—and hopes for—the posterity of the work she and her Oyneg Shabes colleagues undertook. "We want to believe," she writes,

> that there is a point to carrying on in the empty battlefield among the human hyenas and jackals who survive by stripping down cadavers. These documents and notes are all that remains, which reminds me of traces in crime novels. I remember a novella [*nowelka*] by Conan Doyle from my childhood, where the dying victim writes upon the wall with a dying hand a single word that contains the evidence which incriminates the perpetrator. That word scrawled by the dying man had a powerful impact on my imagination. The traces we leave—we, whose survival is so uncertain—remind me of that clichéd image that once moved me. We note the evidence of the crime, evidence that can no longer help us in any way. The trace has to be pushed like a rock under the wheel of history, to arrest its movement. That rock weighs heavy: its weight is our knowledge, which probed the depths of human cruelty. (Trans. Anna Klosowska)[15]

Readers of Doyle will recognize that Jarecka is alluding to his first Sherlock Holmes novel (or novella), *A Study in Scarlet* (1887).[16] They might also observe that she is misremembering key aspects of the story. A murder victim is found in this narrative lying on the floor beneath the word *Rache* written on the wall in blood. While the characteristically obtuse Scotland Yard detectives entertain the possibility that this could be the name *Rachel* missing the final *l*, Sherlock Holmes points out that it is the German word for revenge. Ultimately, however, the word turns out not to have been scribbled by the dying victim, nor does it contain proof of the criminal's guilt. In fact, the word was written by the killer—in blood from his own nosebleed—as a dissembling maneuver intended to create the false impression that this had been a political murder carried out by a secret society of expatriate German revolutionaries rather than the personal vendetta that it was. The word *Rache,* that is, was not intended as a clue to help its interpreter discover the perpetrator but was rather a blood-red herring by which the murderer hoped to obfuscate his identity and motives.[17]

Questions of guilt and justice, moreover, remain ambiguous in this novella. The murderer, the American Jefferson Hope, was pursuing vengeance for egregious and unpunished wrongs done to him in a Mormon milieu in the American West. The marriage plans of Hope and his love, Lucy Ferrier, were dashed when Brigham Young himself, having learned that Lucy was engaged to a Gentile, presents Lucy's adoptive father John Ferrier with an ultimatum: Lucy must choose between marrying Drebber or Stangerson, both sons of elders of the Church of Latter-Day Saints, who already have seven and four wives, respectively. When Lucy and her father John refuse and flee with Hope, Drebber and Stangerson pursue them. Stangerson kills John Ferrier, and they abduct Lucy and force her to marry Drebber, whereupon she dies of a broken heart. Seeking revenge, Hope eventually pursues Drebber and Stangerson across the United States and Europe—to Cleveland, St. Petersburg, Paris, and Copenhagen—before finally catching up with and murdering them in London. Although Hope committed murders, Doyle's narrative couches them, in Stephen Knight's phrase, as "a largely justified punishment for past immorality" (Knight, *Form and Ideology*, 69). Hope shows no regret and never wavers regarding the justness of his acts. "After the lapse of time that has passed since their crime," he states, "it was impossible for me to secure a conviction against them in any court. I knew of their guilt though, and I determined that I should be judge, jury, and executioner all rolled into one. You'd have done the same, if you have any manhood in you, if you had been in my place" (*Complete Sherlock Holmes*, 78). Upon finishing his testimony to Watson, Holmes, and detectives of the Scotland Yard, he remains similarly steadfast: "That's the whole of my story, gentlemen. You may consider me to be a murderer; but I hold that I am just as much an officer of justice as you are" (*Complete Sherlock Holmes*, 82). While Holmes solves the case and apprehends Hope, Hope ultimately dies in police custody, obviating the thorny question of what sentence the narrative would pronounce on his guilt.

Jarecka's recollection of a scene in Doyle exemplifies the vagaries of memory. Selective or inaccurate memories of a book one read in childhood are common; sometimes a scene or character remains indelible, while the work's intricacies, or even its main thrust, recede. The triumphant work of deciphering clues en route to meting out justice that Jarecka retrojects into her memory of *A Study in Scarlet* thus seems to be filtered through familiarity with subsequent, tighter, and more formulaic Sherlock Holmes tales rather than the generically messy *Study in Scarlet* itself, which postpones the denouement of the English detective story with the sprawling Western melodrama (narrated by an omniscient narrator who contrasts jarringly with Watson's account of the London side of the story).[18] Of course the salient issue is not whether

Jarecka got the details of Doyle's novella right but rather the hopes that this (mis)remembered text helps her articulate and sustain. The very looseness of her grasp of this cultural reference point may even have facilitated her ability to invest it with such meanings in desperate times. Her appeal to Sherlock Holmes, that is, may have been informed as much by what Knight calls "the Holmes myth" (Knight, *Form and Ideology*, 104) as by the features of any particular Holmes story. As Knight argues, "Holmes was a hero shaped for a particular class in a particular time and place, but like many other heroes he has survived out of context as a figure of heroism" (*Form and Ideology*, 103) and come to "epitomiz[e] the rational hero who resolves urban disorder" (Knight, *Form and Ideology*, 104). Jarecka is not so much recalling a specific Sherlock Holmes text as her own private detective tale, a novella misremembered in ways that respond to the crisis in which she is caught. In the modern literary archetype of Sherlock Holmes, Jarecka finds a means to crystalize her desperate desire for justice and for posthumous agency in effecting that justice. To effectuate justice, the fragile, radically contingent signs—traces, clues—that she and her colleagues are trying to pass on require a Holmesian reader-hero who can, from them, reconstruct and comprehend the crime that has been committed and, what is more, deploy this evidence to effectively stop history in its tracks, to paraphrase Jarecka.

Such an analytic superhero who can not only detect and reconstruct the truth from clues but can also infallibly translate the revelation of such knowledge into justice is, needless to say, a mythic figure, a literary fantasy. Yet it would be erroneous to view the relationship between this literary fantasy and the genocidal reality of the Warsaw ghetto in terms of a neat opposition of fantasy versus reality. When in late 1942 Jarecka attempts to articulate what it means to write in the Warsaw ghetto, in hopeless circumstances, she appeals to a mythic hero of modern literature rather than a historical, or "real" person. Reich-Ranicki recalls that the main content of his many conversations with Jarecka in the ghetto was literature. He had a poor grasp of Polish literature, as did she of German literature, so they discussed the classics of the French and Russian traditions, which they both knew well: Flaubert, Proust, Tolstoy (Reich-Ranicki, *Mein Leben*, 240). Even in the direst of times, literature continued to play a vital role for Jarecka: the genre of modern detective fiction was an available cultural resource that she found apt for thinking through the aims and potential impact of the project of the Oyneg Shabes, and for envisioning justice. Jarecka's words powerfully exemplify how literature accompanied victims of the Holocaust in the most desperate circumstances and helped them frame their experience and mediate their desires for justice and posthumous agency.

One possible interpretation of the sort of desires to which Jarecka gives voice through distinctly literary means is that they were deluded and remained unfulfilled. While against long odds, the first two of the three buried caches of the Oyneg Shabes archive were indeed recovered (Jarecka is here referring to writings that went into the second cache, buried in February 1943 and unearthed in December 1950), the documents contained therein were not met with intense and ethically charged scrutiny but rather with neglect. Mainstream historiography of the Holocaust has been elaborated, until very recently, in almost complete disregard of this archive;[19] and Oyneg Shabes texts played little role in shaping the mainstream memory cultures of the Holocaust in Europe, North America, or Israel.

Although the fate of the Oyneg Shabes documents was to be almost systematically neglected for decades (even as the milk cans containing the second cache of these documents became something of a minor Holocaust icon), another interpretation of the hopes that Jarecka invested in her literary fantasy of justice *à la* Sherlock Holmes is nevertheless possible and (I find) compelling. We can take seriously the reality of Jarecka's literary fantasy (or of her fantasy mediated through literature) of posthumous readers and try to devote ourselves to reading the words that she and other victims wrote from within the unfolding events of the Holocaust. We can appreciate—even beyond the specific historical impact that the authors of these words sought, and alas failed, to achieve—the human depths that their words embody. The hopes that Jarecka and others communicated via detours into literature can be partially realized in an equally literary way in the attention we pay to their words. As readers today, we of course cannot help these writers in their quest to bring the perpetrators of the Holocaust to justice, nor can we do anything so grand as to halt the wheel of history; but we can extend these authors' posthumous agency by trying to read their words. As Kassow notes, "Jarecka believed that the written word was a link to a 'before' and an 'after'" (*Who Will Write Our History?*, 183). We inhabit the "after" to which Jarecka and many others who wrote in the ghettos were trying to build a bridge of words. Many of the texts they left can be likened to messages in bottles: their authors desperately wanted them to be read. Whether or not Jarecka and other ghetto writers have any of the posthumous agency they hoped to achieve depends, then, in some limited but significant measure, on us, on how we receive their words—on, we might say, our literary response to their literary hopes. In this extra-positivistic sense, the question of whether Jarecka's "literary" hopes were deluded cannot be answered with a simple yes or with a self-congratulatory no! The question, rather, remains an open-ended call to read.

HERMAN KRUK AND THE FATE OF HIS DIARY

Kruk fled Warsaw on September 5, 1939, four days after the Germans invaded Poland. He reached Vilna—also known as Wilno (Polish) and Vilnius (Lithuanian)—on October 10, just before the Soviets, who briefly occupied the city (September–October 1939), turned it over to independent Lithuania.[20] Vilna, which had been part of Poland since the 1920s, remained under control of Lithuania for almost a year, until June 1940 when the Soviet Union occupied Lithuania. The Germans took Vilna on June 24, 1941, only two days into their invasion of the USSR. With the aid of Lithuanian auxiliary units, they immediately set about killing some forty thousand Jews in the nearby Ponar woods. The remaining approximately forty thousand Jews in Vilna were confined to two ghettos in early September 1941. Mass killings of ghetto inmates continued in October: some four thousand people were rounded up on Yom Kippur (October 1) and killed in Ponar. On October 24, the German authorities ordered the Judenrat to institute a system of work permits: 3,500 yellow work permits (*Gelbscheine*) for valued workers and pink permits for up to three family members of each worker (a spouse and up to two children). The remaining inhabitants received white permits, and German troops swiftly rounded up five thousand holders of white permits and killed them in Ponar. On October 28–30, 1941, the Germans liquidated the smaller of the two ghettos (Ghetto no. 2), established only two months previously, in which people deemed incapable of "productive" work had been confined. Nearly all of its eleven thousand inhabitants were murdered in Ponar. From January 1942 there was an extended lull in the mass killings, and relative stability in the Vilna ghetto, until March 1943, when the final liquidation of the ghetto began. Its remaining inhabitants were shot in Ponar, deported to Sobibor, or sent to labor camps in Latvia (the women) and Estonia (the men). Kruk was among those deported.

Kruk's diary was edited and published in the original Yiddish by YIVO in 1961 under the title *Togbukh fun vilner geto* (Diary of the Vilna ghetto), and a significantly expanded English edition, incorporating material that had come to light since the publication of the Yiddish edition, was published in 2002 by Yale University Press under the title *The Last Days of the Jerusalem of*

Lithuania: Chronicles from the Vilna Ghetto and the Camps, 1939–1944. As with so many writings from ghettos, the story of the survival of Kruk's diaries is extraordinary in its own right, involving being buried in different caches, excavated, deposited in various archives and with private persons in several countries, and, eventually, painstakingly reassembled.[21]

A Bundist involved chiefly in library work, during the 1930s Kruk built up the Grosser Library into the largest and most popular Jewish workers' library in Warsaw. In historian David Fishman's estimation Kruk was "the most highly regarded Jewish librarian in all of Poland" (Fishman, *Book Smugglers*, 33). As a Yiddish socialist librarian, Kruk sought to combat Jewish cultural assimilation and to direct working-class readers away from lowbrow fare toward more serious reading.[22] In the Vilna ghetto, he headed up the ghetto library, an institution that the Germans largely left alone.[23] Thus Kruk had the "luxury" of access to a typewriter and even a secretary, to whom he dictated daily diary entries. Kruk was also a major figure in the so-called Paper Brigade in Vilna, the team of Jewish intellectuals tasked with aiding the Einsatzstab des Reichsleiter Alfred Rosenberg (Special Detail of Reich Administrator Alfred Rosenberg) in selecting the most important Judaica collections from Vilna for shipment to the Institut zur Erforschung der Judenfrage (Institute for the Study of the Jewish Question) in Germany.[24] Vilna had for centuries been a center of Jewish culture and learning and consequently was home to many important Jewish cultural treasures. The city's rich Jewish cultural heritage was why it was widely referred to, reverently, as the Jerusalem of Lithuania.

The Rosenberg detail aimed to loot the most significant Jewish books, manuscripts, and papers, and to destroy the rest. The Paper Brigade members including Kruk and Yiddish poets Abraham Sutzkever and Shmerke Kaczerginski, at great risk to themselves, subverted the Nazi agenda, slowing work wherever possible and secreting texts at various sites in the ghetto in the hopes of recovering them after the war. Since they worked in the YIVO building, located outside the ghetto, to save texts they regularly smuggled them *into* the ghetto when returning after their workday.[25] Some of these caches of books and documents were discovered and destroyed by the Germans, including the secret archive Kruk had hidden in the ghetto library, which was discovered only days before Vilna was liberated.[26] Some others, such as the large number of books and papers that Paper Brigade members had stashed in the attic of the YIVO building, were destroyed in bombings. Yet others survived. Sutzkever and Kaczerginski escaped the ghetto and joined partisan groups in the forests outside Vilna. In an unlikely rescue operation, Sutzkever and his wife Freydke were airlifted in March 1944 from their partisan unit in the Narocz forest to Moscow.[27] With Kaczerginski in a mixed partisan unit they eventually returned to what was left of Vilna, helping the Soviet army liberate the city (Fishman, *Book Smugglers*, 137). They recovered much of Kruk's diary from a ghetto bunker on Shavel Street, one of the key sites where the Paper Brigade had buried Jewish cultural materials.[28]

Sutzkever and Kaczerginski established a "Jewish Museum" on July 26, 1944, just thirteen days after Vilna was liberated. Their hope was that this would provide a safe and stable place to collect and catalogue what could be recovered of Vilna's past Jewish treasures. It quickly became evident, however, that the Lithuanian and Soviet authorities were hostile to the project.[29] Fishman notes how Kaczerginski later recalled, "'We, the group of museum activists, had a bizarre realization—we must save our treasures again, and get them out of there. Otherwise they will perish.'"[30]

It was to the imperiled Jewish Museum in Vilna that the final portions of Kruk's diaries, chronicling his time spent in two Estonian camps—first Klooga, then Lagedi—were taken. In these camps, Kruk continued to write on scraps of paper, often almost illegibly and after twelve to fourteen hours of labor. Kruk buried these manuscripts in Lagedi on September 17, 1944, in the presence of six witnesses. The next day he and most of the other remaining Jews in Klooga and Lagedi were shot and burned on a pyre. One day later the Red Army liberated those camps. Five of the witnesses perished along with Kruk. The sixth man, Nisan Anolik, dug up Kruk's manuscripts and brought them to Vilna.[31] Reading the writing on the wall that postwar Vilna would not be a safe place for the rescued Jewish cultural artifacts, Sutzkever eventually sent material, including pages recovered from Kruk's diaries, to the YIVO in New York. Other recovered pages were taken by Vilna partisan Ruzhka Korczak and others to Israel and deposited at Yad Vashem and in the Kibbutz Givat Haviva. Some of Kruk's manuscripts remained in Vilna and were not accessed until after the fall of the Soviet Union.[32]

Among Kruk's recovered wartime writings is his narrative of the execution of six men in the Vilna ghetto carried out by the Judenrat, the ghetto court, and the Jewish police on June 4, 1942. Historian Samuel Kassow and the editor of the English edition of Kruk's wartime diaries, Hebrew and Yiddish literary scholar Benjamin Harshav, have both remarked on Kruk's lack of literary talent.[33] My aim here is not to evaluate the literary merits of Kruk's narrative but rather to analyze how and why it draws on the paradigm of detective fiction to explore social and psychological aspects of life in the ghetto and, especially, to grapple with questions of ethical agency and possibilities for rendering justice within the ghetto's confines, under the eye of the Nazi authorities. Kruk recorded details of the crimes, sentencing, and public executions, and the reactions of the ghetto populace, in diary entries of June 4 and 5, 1942. Two months later, separate from his diary, he wrote a twenty-odd-page chronicle with literary ambitions, intercutting between the points of view of victims, criminals, Jewish authorities, Nazis, and the wider ghetto public as his text reconstructs the far-flung drama of two robbery-murders committed by a criminal gang of five, plus the assault of an on-duty Jewish police officer by a sixth man, Yankl Avidon.

SHERLOCK HOLMES IN YIDDISH CULTURE

Kruk gave his diary entry the heading, "The Murder in the Ghetto—A Sherlock Holmes Story,"[34] and in the subsequent literary version, titled "Six Gallows in the Vilna Ghetto: A Criminal Literary Chronicle of the Vilna Ghetto," he again invokes Sherlock Holmes as a reference point. Kruk begins with an account of the executions, then unfolds his narrative in ten numbered flashback vignettes. At the end of his introductory presentation of the executions, he writes: "The story we chronicle here is reminiscent of a Sherlock Holmes story. Everything that occurs in this narrative is no more than a criminal literary chronicle based on the events of June 1942 in the Vilna Ghetto. Vilna Ghetto, August 1942" (*Last Days*, 603 / "Zeks tlies," 3). Later in the narrative, commenting on how the ghetto police's criminal investigation of a robbery-murder by five of the six condemned men led, in turn, to the discovery of a previous robbery-murder by the same group, Kruk yet again invokes his generic frame of reference: "The whole police force was assigned to the criminal department. A series of searches began, complete with digging up melinas, interrogations, and confrontations; and every time a new discovery. Every time the mud became deeper. One murder led to another. The second one showed preparations for a third. One murder more horrible than the last. The third murder was still in process of being planned. . . . A Sherlock Holmes story, a labyrinth where you don't see the beginning and don't find the end" (*Last Days*, 612). What did Kruk hope to convey with his repeated evocation of narratives and scenarios *à la* Sherlock Holmes? It is impossible to answer this question definitively, but I would argue that Kruk uses Sherlock Holmes both in rather loose ways, which have little to do with actual Sherlock Holmes stories by Doyle, and also in ways that indeed have to do with specific features of Doyle's narratives, above all the way they pose questions about appearance and reality in social life and about the ultimate triumph of justice.

Considering Sherlock Holmes's place in the wider context of popular crime and adventure narratives in early twentieth-century Jewish culture can help us appreciate the looser associations Kruk evokes with his frequent references to "a Sherlock Holmes story." As Nathan Cohen has shown, Yiddish, like other European and American literatures, featured a wide range of popular crime stories from the second half of the nineteenth century on, including the 1865–1866 Yiddish translation of Eugène Sue's blockbuster *Les Mystères de Paris* (1842–1843); translations of Emile Gaboriau's classic detective narratives *L'Affaire Lerouge* (1866) and *La Corde au cou* (1873; translated 1893 and 1901, respectively, by Philip Krants); multiple narratives by the popular authors Nokhem Meyer Shaykevitch (pseudonym Shomer, 1846–1905) and Sholem Lederer (1860–1952), both of whom were decried as purveyors of *shund* (trash); and the dozens of Yiddish adaptations of the 1853–1871 German series *Die schwarze Bibliothek*, published in Warsaw by Yehude Leyb Morgenshtern in the first years of the twentieth century.[35] The booklets published by Morgenshtern were a miscellany of popular genres including stories of kidnappings, murder, robbery, romance, and more.

Crime fiction in nineteenth- and early twentieth-century Yiddish literature intermingled with other popular genres of adventure and romance, and as Sherlock Holmes emerged as the most famous (and most lucrative) literary detective, his name became attached to generically promiscuous popular works. In 1907–1908, the Warsaw weekly *Roman-tsaytung* published Yiddish translations of three Edgar Allan Poe stories and four of Doyle's Sherlock Holmes stories ("A Scandal in Bohemia," "The Reigate Puzzle," "The 'Gloria Scott,'" and "The Adventure of Charles Augustus Milverton"). Doyle's Sherlock Holmes story "The Resident Patient" was likewise published in Yiddish translation in booklet form in 1907.[36] In an attempt to stave off the competition of the new Warsaw Yiddish daily *Haynt*, the established daily *Yidishes Tageblat* announced a series of detective stories, "Di greste velt-geheymnisn" (The greatest world mysteries), which was to include Sherlock Holmes and Nat Pinkerton stories, among others. (The only story ultimately published in this planned series, however, was a further translation of Doyle's "A Scandal in Bohemia.") At the same time as these first Sherlock Holmes stories appeared in Yiddish in 1907–1908, anonymous booklets appeared in Yiddish, Russian, and Polish bearing the name Sherlock Holmes but with Harry Taxon as an assistant instead of Watson. According to Cohen, "Into these booklets were inserted stories of various bizarre murders lacking any connection to the original hero and his surroundings" (Cohen, "Sherlock Holmes," 272).[37]

A further noteworthy series of booklets traded similarly in Sherlock Holmes's literary celebrity. The prolific author, journalist, editor, and civil servant in the Austrian foreign ministry Yoyne (Jonas) Kreppel anonymously penned and published fifteen booklets in the Max Spitzkopf series, beginning in 1908.[38] Kreppel's Yiddish detective series featured "Max Spitzkopf: The King of Detectives, the Viennese Sherlock Holmes" and his assistant, Fuchs. Spitzkopf and Fuchs work out of an office in Vienna and frequently come to the aid of imperiled Jews in Galicia and beyond. In his memoir, *In My Father's Court,* Isaac Bashevis Singer recalls how fondly he read the Max Spitzkopf stories as a youth in Warsaw: "The detective stories seemed like masterpieces to me. A sentence from one of them remains in my memory, a caption under a drawing showing Max Spitzkopf and his assistant, Fuchs, guns in hand, surprising a robber. Spitzkopf is crying out, 'Hands up, you rogue. We've got you covered.' For years, these naive words ran like music through my mind."[39]

Bashevis Singer was born in 1903 and refers to reading "detective stories about Sherlock Holmes and Max Spitzkopf" alongside the newspaper in which his brother Israel Joshua Singer in 1916 began publishing his first stories and translations (Cohen, "Sherlock Holmes," 276).[40] Nearly seven years older than Bashevis Singer, Kruk was born 1897 and was between the ages of ten and thirteen between 1907 and 1910, the peak years in the publishing history of Yiddish crime and adventure stories in Yiddish booklets and newspaper serials, many of which, as we have seen, were closely or distantly associated with Sherlock Holmes. One can readily understand how Kruk could use "a Sherlock Holmes story" loosely to signify any number of sensational events involving crime and intrigue.

And yet, as I will argue in a moment, features of Sherlock Holmes stories in particular, and not merely of lowbrow criminal adventure stories in general, resonated with Kruk as he grappled with these cases of murder, trial, and execution and how to narrativize them. Before turning to the complex relationship between Kruk's narrative and classic detective stories, however, some background is in order regarding the legal systems internal to the Nazi ghettos and the specific historical context of the Vilna ghetto surrounding the trial and executions of June 4, 1942, that inspired Kruk's narrative.

LEGAL INSTITUTIONS IN THE VILNA GHETTO

In a monograph devoted to the fraught subject of the institutions of the police and courts internal to the Warsaw, Lodz, and Vilna ghettos, historian Svenja Bethke examines the different ways the Jewish Councils sought to implement legal norms—systems of laws and punishments—within their ambiguous (overwhelmingly but not entirely specious) sphere of autonomy. The ambiguous nature of the legal-moral agency and autonomy of the internal institutions of the Vilna ghetto lie at the heart of Kruk's crime narrative. Whence this ambiguity? Why did the Nazis allow the Jewish Councils as much autonomy —even as much pseudo-autonomy—as they did? Why did they grant them any legal authority at all? Following the pioneering research on the Jewish Councils by Isaiah Trunk, Bethke answers these questions by surmising that "the German occupiers must have believed that the Jewish Councils knew best how to ensure 'peace and order' within the ghetto community" (Bethke, *Dance on the Razor's Edge*, 27). If the maintenance of a certain "normality" in the ghettos was obviously advantageous to the German authorities, it is not difficult to see how the maintenance of order in the ghettos likewise seemed crucial to the Jewish Councils for the survival of at least some part of the community. As Bethke shows, the legal efforts of the councils were directed above all at internally regulating criminal activity that could otherwise lead to the intervention of the Germans, with devastating results. The internal legal institutions in the ghettos of Warsaw, Lodz, and Vilna, their differences notwithstanding, were part of the "Councils' quest to 'keep the ghetto calm' and their desperate attempt to prevent German intervention that could endanger the whole ghetto community" (Bethke, *Dance on the Razor's Edge*, 50).

The Jewish Councils' strategies for survival—especially the strategy of "rescue through labor" pursued in Lodz and Vilna—were predicated upon attempts on the part of the Jewish authorities to anticipate "the Germans' actions and interpret them as being governed by rational criteria" (Bethke, *Dance on the Razor's Edge*, 15). As Dan Diner has argued, however, the Nazis' genocidal project ultimately defied this sort of rational calculus. While the Nazis' murder of even productive Jewish laborers beneficial to their military aims can be described as "irrational" from a German vantage point, Diner argues, from the vantage point of the Jewish Councils attempting to orient their survival strategies on the basis of the most basic rational principle possible, namely their enemies', the Germans', own naked self-interest, the German's actions were not irrational but counter-rational.[41]

As Bethke notes repeatedly, the ideology of "rescue through labor" was strongest in the Lodz ghetto under the leadership of Jewish Council head Chaim Rumkowski. The idea never became a guiding strategy in the Warsaw ghetto. While the idea was central to the ideology of the Jewish Council under council head Jacob Gens in Vilna, the ghetto population there remained more suspicious of it, according to Bethke, because the Vilna ghetto was exceptional in that it was established after most of the Jews in Vilna had already been systematically murdered in Ponar in the second half of 1941.[42] The inhabitants of the Vilna ghetto thus had fewer illusions about the Nazis' ultimate genocidal aims.

The legal system internal to the Vilna ghetto was established with German approval in February 1942. It comprised a court, judges, prosecutors, and defenders. Even after the creation of the court, many offences remained within the purview of the Jewish police, for example "leaving the ghetto without permission, misconduct at the ghetto gate, escapes from ghetto jail, and injury to policemen." The new legal system, by contrast, dealt with "criminal acts, disputes between tenants, and non-compliance with Judenrat instructions." During the first half of 1942 the ghetto court processed 115 criminal cases involving 172 people. Sentences were diverse and included acquittals, cash fines, imprisonment, and, in the murder case that Kruk takes up in "Six Gallows," the death penalty (Arad, *Ghetto in Flames*, 291).

Kruk emphatically inscribes the time and locus of the narration of "Six Gallows" as "Vilna Ghetto, August 1942." As always when reading wartime writings, the moment of articulation is crucial.[43] I have already mentioned the timeline of the Vilna ghetto and the relative stability of the period between January 1942 and March 1943. During the period of the events that Kruk recounts (as well as the slightly but, as we will see, significantly later moment when he wrote his account) the mass deportations seemed to be over. Under Jacob Gens, there was an emphasis on law and order and the hope that, by contributing productively as a "working ghetto" to the German war effort, the surviving Jews in Vilna could remain alive.[44]

Kruk's narrative generally highlights the ethical legitimacy of the ghetto court and police, and sees them as carrying out the collective will of the ghetto's population. In this, Kruk's interpretation of this extraordinary event that held the attention of the entire ghetto populace seems to accord with Gens's own—largely successful—attempt to use the trials and executions to shore up his authority within the internal ghetto administration. Gens was the head of the Vilna ghetto Jewish Police at the time of the trial and executions of early June 1942. While the Jewish Police were officially subordinate to the Jewish Council, at that time still headed by Anatol Fried, Gens had in fact already managed to encroach on many of the council's functions, and had eclipsed Fried's authority. According to Yitzhak Arad, "The German administration, in resolving to continue the existence of the Vilna ghetto and control and exploit its Jewish manpower, had concluded that Gens was more suitable than Fried to implement its policy. During the period of the Aktionen, July–December 1941, Gens stood out in German eyes as a man of ability, ready to discharge instructions. The German authorities permitted Fried and the Judenrat to retain their official functions temporarily, but greatly restricted their executive powers" (Arad, *Ghetto in Flames*, 290). An important moment in this power shift occurred on April 29, 1942, when Franz Murer, the Nazi officer (Gebietskommissar) responsible for Jewish affairs (among other things, for provisioning the Vilna ghetto and supervising the ghetto's border; Bethke, *Dance on a Razor's Edge*, 36), published a document expanding the functions of the Jewish police. Effectively expressing a preference for Gens over Fried, the document stated that the Jewish police was answerable to Gens and that Gens, in turn, would henceforth be directly responsible to Murer. "All orders of the Gebietskommissar of the City of Vilna will be implemented with the help of the Jewish police," the document stated, making no mention of Fried or the Judenrat (quoted in Arad, *Ghetto in Flames*, 287).

Such was the balance of power between Gens and Fried when Yosef Gerstein was discovered murdered on June 3, 1942, and his murderers, under interrogation, confessed to their earlier murder of Hershl Lides. At this time, the five members of the Vilna Judenrat constituted the appellate authority for court judgments (a Court of Appeal would be established in August 1942). The full Jewish Council also had to approve capital sentences. Thus the ghetto court sentenced the five confessed murderers and Yankl Avidon for his unrelated assault of a Jewish police officer on June 4, 1942; the full five-member council, still with Fried at its head, unanimously ratified the sentences the same day; and the Jewish police carried out the executions at 3:00 pm that afternoon.[45] Gens and Fried posted an announcement the following day, June 5, 1942, declaring that "all crimes in the ghetto will be punished with the utmost severity, and the death penalty will be imposed for heinous crimes" (quoted in Arad, *Ghetto in Flames*, 293–94).[46]

Gens's hold on power within the internal ghetto administration was augmented when Murer officially installed him as head of the Judenrat on July 15, 1942. Thenceforth Gens controlled both the Jewish police and Jewish

Council. The timeline of Gens's consolidation of power is important to bear in mind when reading Kruk's "Six Gallows," which recounts events that occurred some six weeks before this final step in Gens's accrual of control, but which Kruk penned at least two weeks thereafter, in August 1942. Kruk's retrospective account in the form of a Sherlock Holmes story is inflected by Gens's consolidation of power and the strategy and ideology of labor and order that would guide his leadership of the ghetto moving forward. Gens announced the principles of "work, discipline, and order" and his expectation of absolute adherence to them in a speech on July 15, the day he was named head of the Vilna Judenrat. He was adamant that there was no place in the ghetto for people who shirked work or engaged in crime:

> The basis of existence in the ghetto is work, discipline and order. Every resident of the ghetto who is capable of work is a pillar on which our existence rests.
>
> There is no room among us for those who hate work and in devious ways engage in crime. In the belief that all the inmates of the ghetto will understand me, I have given orders to free all persons now under arrest in the ghetto. I hereby proclaim a general amnesty, in this way permitting the criminals of yesterday to return to better ways, in the understanding that this is in their own interest. But let no one doubt that in time of need I will not hesitate to use stringent methods in the struggle against criminal elements wherever they may appear.
>
> I believe that all inmates of the ghetto without exception will support this declaration. ("Address," 438)

Gens's orders granted amnesty for past crimes and freed prisoners from the ghetto jail. He ended his speech by stating that the amnesty he was granting could be rescinded for anyone who committed further crimes, or even showed "lack of discipline at his place of work" ("Address," 439–40).[47]

With this context in mind we can better appreciate Kruk's account of the murder trial and executions of early June 1942 (before Gens's being installed as Judenrat head) from the perspective of August 1942 (at least two weeks thereafter) as a reflection on the nature and extent of the power and autonomy that Gens could now wield vis-à-vis the Nazis. Would the "work, discipline and order," which Gens, in Bethke's words, "declared . . . the pillars of his survival strategy for the ghetto community" (Bethke, *Dance on a Razor's Edge*, 38), prove viable for weathering the storm? Viable for whom? Did it in fact signal a return to some sort of stability, autonomy, and agency in survival, or was it specious? Could the ghetto inhabitants be unified, as Gens claimed, in support of his survival through work strategy? At its most basic level, Kruk's "Sherlock Holmes story" is a reflection on the reality of this new reality.

KRUK AND THE IDEOLOGY OF SHERLOCK HOLMES

It is precisely at this most basic level that Kruk's account resonates most profoundly with Doyle's iconic stories. In *Mysteries & Conspiracies: Detective Stories, Spy Novels and the Making of Modern Societies,* sociologist Luc Boltanski traces the evolution in modernity of the sense—ranging from suspicion to paranoia—that we face two realities, the mundane and accessible one that we observe and inhabit in our daily lives, and a deeper, "truer" reality behind this reality, where hidden actors exercise profound powers that threaten to give the lie to the surface stability of our social and political world. Boltanski's reading of modern society through the lens of detective stories and spy novels hinges on the relationship between these two registers of reality. As manifest reality comes variously under suspicion of being illusory, a hidden, elusive reality menacingly emerges as more consequential. As Boltanksi puts it (here speaking of Doyle's Sherlock Holmes stories and Georges Simenon's Maigret novels), "Beneath reality there is something else that has to be identified because it threatens the very continuation and orderliness of reality" (*Mysteries & Conspiracies,* 107).

If an interplay between a surface reality and a threatening second reality behind it is characteristic of the world of detective stories, spy novels, and paranoid conspiracy theories alike, the threat posed by the ominous "something" plays out very differently across these different paradigms. The nature of the threats that Sherlock Holmes contends with are serious but, thanks to his extraordinary powers, they do not disrupt the order of reality permanently. The conservative and reassuring thrust of Sherlock Holmes tales, I would argue, is its greatest source of appeal to Kruk in his construction of his own "Sherlock Holmes story" of the Vilna ghetto. Kruk tends to interpret the power and autonomy of the ghetto's internal institutions in maximal terms, even as his narrative likewise signals anxiety and ambivalence in numerous ways. Kruk, that is, is at pains to minimize the rift between the stability and order that Gens has proclaimed and promised to maintain through the strict rule of the ghetto's internal institutions, and the ambient threat of the German authorities, who could at any time disrupt this order and the relative safety it seems to promise. Boltanski notes that disturbances affecting reality are only "local and temporary" in Sherlock Holmes stories. Reality possesses solidity and generally speaking is not belied by but rather corresponds to appearances. "There is no a priori reason to be skeptical about the reality of reality. In normal situations, actors can thus treat their environment as if it exists on a single plane, without positing another world underneath, which reality would be concealing. The tendency to suspicion is not a prerequisite, then, for grasping the social world (and thus for deploying strategies that have some chance of success)" (Boltanski, *Mysteries & Conspiracies*, 107).[48] A Sherlock Holmes story typically involves a rupture in the orderliness of social reality as supported by institutions of law, followed by its repair. As Boltanski continues, "In fact, the reality depicted in the Holmes stories is based on a legal order, liberal in inspiration, whose solidity is guaranteed by the competence of a large number of law enforcers exercising their vigilance over networks of contracts that everyone is presumed to respect" (Boltanski, *Mysteries & Conspiracies*, 107). While the legal apparatus guaranteeing the solidity of social reality in the extreme situation of the ghetto can hardly be said to be liberal, Gens's claim was indeed that it was possible to return to some semblance of legally reinforced normalcy, even after the mass murders of 1941. Kruk's Sherlock Holmes story ambivalently embraces Gens's vision.

In Boltanski's sociological reading, the anxiety that detective stories traffic in is at bottom an anxiety over whether what passes for reality will in fact hold, whether reality is as it appears to be, or is imperiled by a second order of reality that only suspicious interpretation can expose. The ideological work that Sherlock Holmes stories perform is to reassure readers that reality as commonly understood is under no radical threat. Rather than inviting a hermeneutics of suspicion, Sherlock Holmes narratives assuage readers' fears that reality might be suspect. As I will try to show, Kruk's narrative strains to apply the conservative and optimistic message of Sherlock Holmes tales to the situation in the Vilna ghetto as it crystalized around the murder cases of early June 1942 by willfully believing in the solidity and efficacy of the new order that Gens was proclaiming and the legal apparatus by which Gens promised to maintain it. In other words, Kruk strains to reconcile Gens's ideology of order and stability in the Vilna ghetto with the sort of social, legal, and moral order that Sherlock Holmes ingeniously works to safeguard.

Kruk's text opens with an introductory section titled "Interpretation" (*interpretatsye*) in which he lays out the basic facts regarding the sentencing and execution of six Jews in the Vilna ghetto on June 4, 1942. The six were "condemned by the Jewish ghetto court," and the executions were carried out by "dozens of Jewish policemen, under the leadership of the Jewish police chief in the ghetto" (*Last Days*, 602). As the section's title indicates, however, the focus here is not on the facts but on the cultural meaning of this extraordinary event, more specifically on how the ghetto population understood and felt about the sentences handed down and the executions carried out by the ghetto's internal institutions. As we will see, Kruk characterizes this response in terms of universal relief, social unity, and moral catharsis.

In a passage already quoted above from his introductory "interpretation," Kruk alludes explicitly to Sherlock Holmes stories as a paradigm for dramatizing the workings of crime and justice. "The author, with his journalistic sensibility, could not rest until he had registered this event for posterity. The story we chronicle here is reminiscent of a Sherlock Holmes story. Everything that occurs in this narrative is no more than a criminal literary chronicle based on the events of June 1942 in the Vilna Ghetto" (*Last Days*, 603 / "Zeks tlies," 2). Kruk's likening of his narrative to a Sherlock Holmes story in his opening interpretation suggests that he is thinking of the Holmesian paradigm not only on the level of plot elements, including suspense, crime, and murder, but also, and perhaps primarily, on the level of the ideological—or interpretive—work that Doyle's stories perform. It is with this literary paradigm, and the views of law, order, moral agency, and social cohesion that it sustains, that Kruk elaborates (*baarbet*) his "criminal literary chronicle" on the basis of the dramatic events of early June 1942. Like Doyle's narratives, Kruk's narrative—above all, his distilled "interpretation" of his own narrative—works to overcome the challenges of ominous powers that lurk behind immediate social reality and threaten to reveal it as fragile and illusory. Like Sherlock Holmes stories, too, Kruk's "Six Gallows" dramatizes crime as tearing at the ethos that binds a community but ultimately delivers an optimistic message regarding the resiliency and harmony of the community bound by moral and legal codes, and the agency of the powers of justice to repair the moral damage the community has suffered.

Kruk repeatedly stresses the unity of the entire ghetto population in support of this unprecedented act of justice on the part of the ghetto court and the Jewish police. "No one in the ghetto resented this act of justice. No one doubted the just verdict or the guilt of the accused. Everyone was relieved at the announcement that the accused would not be turned over to the 'outside world,' that their sentence would be carried out by the ghetto, and that . . ." (*Last Days*, 602 / "Zeks tlies," 2). Kruk's ellipsis signals the likely catastrophic consequences of what would have happened had the ghetto's internal apparatus of justice not been permitted to operate with autonomy and had the accused, as Kruk puts it, been "turned over to the 'outside world,'" i.e., to the German authorities. There was ample reason for such anxiety. In a case tried on February 9, 1942, three persons were found guilty of robbery by the Vilna ghetto court and sentenced to prison terms. The German Security Police, however, removed them from the ghetto jail and murdered them at Ponar.[49] This tragedy underscores how grounded fears of German intervention in the workings of the ghetto court were. One can assume that this brutal intervention exacerbated suspicions regarding the court's actual authority and the ultimate, if not the intended, effects of its rulings. With the trial, sentencing, and executions of June 4, 1942, Gens was at pains to reassert the autonomy of the ghetto institutions and their efficacy in protecting the ghetto's inhabitants.

In his "interpretation" of the case preceding his narrative proper, Kruk by and large accords with Gens's vision of the role and power of the ghetto court and police. Kruk goes well beyond merely registering relief that a brutal intervention by the Nazi authorities had been evaded. He frames as the most salient issue—one could indeed say the central mystery—how to understand the pragmatic capability of the ghetto's judicial apparatus to render justice and the nature of the justice they render. Kruk alludes to the announcements that the Judenrat and Gens, in his capacity of police chief, posted on June 5, 1942, the day after the executions, informing the ghetto inhabitants of the events of the previous day.[50] Kruk writes that of the "thousands" who read them, "no one felt any 'maybe,' any doubt, and spark of sympathy" (*Last Days*, 602 / "Zeks tlies," 2). On the contrary, Kruk depicts the sentences and executions as acts of justice carried out by autonomous ghetto institutions that were universally supported by the ghetto populace:

> The ghetto sentenced [*hot farmishpet*]. The ghetto carried out the sentence, and with complete equanimity the ghetto turns to its daily business regarding the six hanged men [*di geto geyt mit fuler ruikeyt ariber tsum tog-ordenung iber di 6 gehangene*].
>
> Why such truculence? [*Halmay aza farbisnkeyt?*]
>
> Why such calm? (*Last Days*, 602 / "Zeks tlies," 2; translation modified).

In answer to his own rhetorical questions as to the ghetto inhabitants' attitude to the justice rendered by the ghetto's internal authorities, Kruk stresses the universal moral catharsis that the sentences and executions afforded the broader populace. The ghetto's inhabitants, that is, were united not only in relief but, more profoundly, in their sense of being released from a collective shame.

In stressing this interpretation of the ghetto inmates' moral sentiments, Kruk rejects other possible answers to his questions regarding the calm with which the executions were received: "Is it only because, of 75,000 Jews in Vilna, barely 16,000 remain? // Or perhaps because the inhabitants of the Vilna Ghetto have gotten so used to murder and are calm and indifferent?" (*Last Days*, 602 / "Zeks tlies," 2). Kruk's rhetorical questions are self-negating, and against the image they propose of a defeated ghetto population morally indifferent in the face of so much murder, Kruk interprets the broad reaction to the June 4 executions as evidence of moral sensibility and agency.

> June 4 in the ghetto is, thus far, the day of the strongest emotions. Thousands fell here in Aktions. Thousands were caught by "Snatchers," and thousands remained orphaned, homeless, and without families; widows, broken and crushed people. For them, today has been one of the hardest days: the ghetto has to be purified. The Vilna Ghetto felt ashamed of that double bestial and wanton murder; debased and offended by the ten-time murderer Avidon.
>
> Everything that happened here had one great purpose: in view of the great events, face to face with the horrible historical situation of the local Jews, the shame [*kharpe*] has to be wiped out.
>
> The whole ghetto wanted to wash its hands! Therefore the "bloodthirstiness" of the Vilna Ghetto residents. (*Last Days*, 602–3 / "Zeks tlies," 2)

The ghetto inhabitants—this is the moral of Kruk's story—felt collectively ashamed of Jewish acts of murder in the face of the Nazis' mass murder of Jews. In executing the perpetrators of such dastardly deeds, the ghetto community felt that they removed this moral stain from their midst.

Kruk postulates perfect alignment of the ethos of the ghetto community with that of the leaders of the ghetto's internal legal-moral institutions who pronounce and carry out the six death sentences. The Judenrat and especially the Jewish police led by Gens execute the people's collective will. Kruk dramatizes this purported unity not only in his interpretive preface but also in the narrative itself. He portrays the judges' decision to sentence the five gang members and Avidon to death as a heroic act of rising to the momentous, "historic" demands confronting them. As Kruk emphasizes, capital punishment carried out by Jewish authorities was historically unprecedented.

For many years, a judge could work at his desk and live his whole life without pronouncing a death sentence.

These simple Jews, the Jewish ghetto judges, were cast by destiny in the role of pronouncing six death sentences.

They are all hunched over: the condemned certainly deserved it [*hobn es kosher fardint*]. The sentence must be carried out unhesitatingly [*on rikzikht*], as soon as possible. But they signed it, and they are the ones who send six people to the other world.

Deep in their hearts, worms burrow, and somewhere deep, a pain gnaws.

The chief of police, the linchpin of the action, is in complete control:

It must happen and we must be courageous [*Di zakh muz geshen un mir darfn zikh nemen dem mut*].

"It is our historical task!" (*Last Days*, 618–19 / "Zeks tlies," 19)

Kruk underscores that even for non-Jewish judges (Jews were generally not in a position to serve as judges in Eastern Europe), pronouncing a death sentence would be extraordinary. While Jewish courts historically did at times issue death sentences, for example in sixteenth-century Poland, this was extremely rare.[51] Now the weight of this momentous decision falls on the shoulders of six "simple Jews—one lawyer, one student, one engineer, one clerk, and just a decent man—these are the ghetto judges" (*Last Days*, 618). Their difficult decision is a show of Jewish bravery, strength, and integrity—indeed a form of redemption—not just for themselves but for the entire remaining Jewish community of the Vilna ghetto. The entire ghetto population steadfastly shares Gens's view, as quoted by Kruk above, that carrying out these death sentences was "our historical task!"[52]

The titular gallows are erected in a butchers' yard on Jatkowa Street. In fact, meat hooks from which calves formerly hung now serve as the gallows.

Instead of calves, ghetto Jews will hang here. Jews will hang them, and no one's hand will tremble. No one in the ghetto will moan!

Twenty thousand Jews against six, and twenty thousand are waiting for the moment of the end.

The sooner the better! (*Last Days*, 618 / "Zeks tlies," 19)

In Kruk's rendering, these public executions are effectively executions by the public; the ghetto's twenty thousand Jews are unified against the six

Jewish murderers, and the six average—representative—Jews who will carry out the executions with brave and steady hands act on the entire community's behalf. Kruk drives this point home by quoting a sample of remarks one could purportedly overhear coming from groups of Jews gathered in the streets after the sentences had been ratified and preparations for the executions were being made.

> Everyone feels ashamed. The ghetto is ashamed. Among the clusters of people gathering and commenting, you often hear:
> "It's the greatest disgrace of the ghetto!"
> "It's a shame for our enemies. . . ." [*Es iz a shande far unzere sonim. . . .*]
> The death sentence—six gallows in the ghetto—was a relief:
> "The ghetto must wipe off the disgrace."
> "It's a historic day."
> "The ghetto must clean itself for history."
> Six gallows in the Vilna Ghetto.
> A Jewish investigation, a Jewish court and sentence, written in the Yiddish mother tongue—six gallows.
> The ghetto is shaken by the events. No one is sorry. Everyone waits impatiently:
> "The ghetto must wipe off the disgrace!"
> "It is a historic day." (*Last Days*, 617 / "Zeks tlies," 17–18)

With the sensational sentences and executions, the internal ghetto administrative and legal institutions demonstrate their autonomy and efficacy. They carry out a "historic" act of justice with the universal support of the ghetto inhabitants and without the interference of the German authorities. Indeed, German authorities figure only peripherally in Kruk's dramatization (and prefatory "interpretation"). It is "the ghetto" itself—a term that seamlessly elides the ghetto population and the ghetto legal and administrative institutions—that unflinchingly exercises its collective agency ("The ghetto sentenced. The ghetto carried out the sentence" [*Last Days*, 602 / "Zeks tlies," 2]).

We discern Kruk's Bundist ideology, or at any rate remnants thereof, when he underscores the significance of "a Jewish investigation, a Jewish court and sentence, written in the Yiddish mother tongue" (*Last Days*, 617) and carried out by Jewish policemen with the approval of the entire ghetto community. As Harshav notes, even in the drastically reduced ghetto, the Bundist Kruk "still lived with the ideals and culture of a politically autonomous, secular Jewish nation . . . as formulated by . . . the . . . Bund" (xxii–xxiii). Kruk's "perennial optimis[m]," as he himself put it, and his devotion to the Bundist project of promoting political and cultural autonomy illuminate his appreciation of the Jewish institutions of justice in the ghetto as valid and authentic, even after, in his words, "of 75,000 Jews in Vilna, barely 16,000 remain[ed]" (*Last Days*, 602). Kruk's commitment to the key Bundist concept of *doikeyt* (promoting Jewish autonomy in the local here and now) remained at least partially intact even in the Vilna ghetto in August 1942.[53]

Although I am arguing that we can discern crucial if strained affinities between Sherlock Holmes stories and Kruk's "Six Gallows" on the level of the ideological work these narratives perform, it should be noted that on the level of its narrative construction, Kruk's literary elaboration strays from the Holmesian paradigm. Albeit in a variety of ways, actual Holmes stories, as Stephen Knight and others have observed, universally unfold according to a tripartite structure of "relation, investigation, and resolution of mysterious events" (Knight, *Form and Ideology*, 75). One of the most striking features of Kruk's narrative is that it essentially reverses this classic narrative sequence by beginning on a note of resolution and ending with the evocation of mystery. In the final lines of his narrative, Kruk returns to the conundrum of what the acts of justice that the ghetto court, Judenrat, and Jewish police have rendered ultimately mean to the inhabitants of the Vilna ghetto. As we have seen, Kruk frontloaded his literary account of these events with an interpretation stressing unity and catharsis. "Six Gallows" concludes ambiguously, however, on an unresolved note:

> The street waited impatiently. Thousands of people blocked the roads, and thousands lined up to watch the six gallows. No one came to mourn. No one could believe it, and they wanted to see it with their own eyes.
>
> They didn't believe their own eyes! (*Last Days*, 621 / "Zeks tlies," 21)

Whereas Holmes restores justice in unequivocal terms even as he reveals —makes visible—the underpinnings of mysterious crimes to the clients who employ him, to Watson, and to the readers of Sherlock Holmes stories, Kruk ends his narrative on a striking note of ocular disbelief. On the most straightforward level, Kruk uses the phrase "They didn't believe their own eyes! [*Men hot di oygn nit gegleybt!*]" to underscore the extraordinary nature of the sight of a Jewish judicial process at work in the ghetto: a court and police force and, almost unimaginably, the capacity to hand down and carry out death sentences. Yet Kruk's phrase equally betrays his own disbelief and that of the assembled crowd. The reason they could not believe that Jews really wield such authority was because their authority was indeed so precarious. Their ocular suspicion is well founded—a point to which I will return in a moment by way of conclusion.

Between the introductory "interpretation" stressing catharsis, unity, and resolution, and the concluding note of collective incredulity, Kruk elaborates the many-faceted story of intersecting crimes in and near the Vilna ghetto that culminates in the June 4 trial and executions.

Since the outcome is already laid out in the opening "interpretation" there is little mystery to uncover.[54] The only detective work that occurs is carried out by the Jewish police in their one-day (all-night) investigation of the murder of Gerstein. One might argue that readers are initially confronted with a hermeneutic puzzle of sorts regarding how the various vignettes introducing different figures and milieus will ultimately converge, yet the relations among the various actors and actions in this far-flung crime tale become clear quickly enough; and there is no systematic building of suspense followed by the sort of dramatic revelation so characteristic of Doyle's tales. To be sure, Kruk weaves in a certain amount of suspense at various moments, especially with allusions to the risk of German intervention ("An uneasy feeling burrowed its way into everyone's hearts: / 'And perhaps 'they' will feel like investigating the case?") and the possibility that Avidon could still denounce Jews to the Germans ("Who knows what such a character may try?" (*Last Days*, 618)). Kruk also follows conventions of crime fiction by depicting certain criminal milieus (especially part 4, "The School of the Gejwuszes!," which introduces readers to the prewar lives of the members of the gang who rob and murder Gerstein in the ghetto). Again, though, the affinity of Kruk's narrative to actual Sherlock Holmes tales, beyond such suspenseful moments and the sensational acts of murder themselves, typical of "Sherlock Holmes stories" in the wider sense discussed above, lies on an ideological or meta-interpretive level.

The narration is omniscient but frequently slides into free indirect discourse to convey the inner thoughts of key figures including Yosef Gerstein, Avidon, and the personified "ghetto" at large. Kruk opens his narrative proper —following his introductory "interpretation"—with the protagonist victim Gerstein, squeezed between the Bolsheviks and the Nazis, as he is fleeing Soviet-occupied Bialystok for still-independent Vilna, with the hope of being able to nurture his love of *yidishkayt* by continuing to study in yeshivas there. The exigencies of mere survival eventually pull Gerstein from yeshiva study to black market activity. Five Jewish gangsters lure him into what Gerstein thinks will be a lucrative transaction, only to rob and murder him. As later comes to light, the same gangsters had already followed this grisly script in robbing and murdering a different man, Hershl Lides, months earlier.

In a parallel narrative having nothing to do with the five gangsters, a hardened and wily criminal, Yankl Avidon, attacks Yankl Greenfeld, a Jewish policeman (and erstwhile fellow criminal) in Vilna, angering the Nazi officer Murer, who views the Jewish police as an extension of his own authority.[55] After escaping from Vilna to nearby Lida, Avidon is apprehended there on suspicion of involvement in the murder-robbery of a local Russian Orthodox priest—a righteous man who aided Jews. One of the priest's attackers dropped a garment bearing a star, tipping off the German authorities that the murderers were Jews. The Germans gave the Lida Judenrat ten hours to turn over the priest's murderers; if they failed or refused to do so, the Germans would kill one thousand Jews. The Jewish authorities resorted to apprehending six Jews known to be active in the underworld, Avidon among them. To save himself, Avidon makes a deal with the Nazi authorities.[56] He informs them that the Lida Judenrat had issued false passports to Jews who had fled from Vilna to escape the mass killings there, and identifies seventy-five alleged refugees, whereupon all seventy-five are shot, along with every member of the Lida Judenrat (*Last Days*, 610). For his cooperation with the German authorities, Avidon is allowed to go free. He returns to the Vilna ghetto, where he is arrested for his earlier attack against the Jewish policeman Greenfeld. Detained in the Vilna ghetto prison since March 1942, Avidon's undoing proves to be the sentencing in early June by the Jewish authorities of the five robber-murderers.[57] When sentencing these five men for double murder, the Jewish authorities seize the opportunity to get rid of this very dangerous man by also sentencing him to death for his earlier attack on the Vilna policeman. While what made Avidon particularly dangerous was of course his willingness to denounce Jews to the Nazis, understandably no mention was made during Avidon's trial in Vilna of his involvement in the Nazis' reprisal mass killings in Lida.

The reversed trajectory of Kruk's Sherlock Holmes story—from resolution to mystery—is the most striking of the many ways "Six Gallows" dramatizes, even as it also tries to minimize, the ambiguity and ambivalence of this complicated moment in the history of the Vilna ghetto. Needless to say the "fit" between the two planes of social order that the narrative tries to reconcile is intensely strained in multiple ways. I would argue that the task of reconciling them is largely what prompted Kruk to resort to a distinctly literary discourse; his reconciliation is largely the effect of shoehorning the situation of the Vilna ghetto in 1942 into the (fictional) safety of the world of Sherlock Holmes. By recounting the dramatic events of early June 1942 in the mode of popular "Sherlock Holmes" crime fiction, Kruk is better able to sustain the hope that the not-so-hidden reality behind the order and stability Gens was proclaiming—that of Nazi power—ultimately would not entirely subvert the autonomy of "the ghetto" and its institutions.

With the clarity of hindsight, we know that Jewish autonomy in the ghettos was illusory and belief in it a fantasy. But, writing in August 1942, in the middle of the slightly more than a year of relative stability that the Vilna ghetto experienced, Kruk of course had no omniscient perch from which to evaluate how far the autonomy and power of the ghetto institutions might reach or how efficacious they might prove in saving the drastically reduced ghetto community. Nonetheless, there was no shortage of reasons to suspect the efficacy of the internal ghetto administration. As already noted, the Vilna ghetto was established only after the vast majority of Jews in Vilna had already been systematically murdered. Unlike Lodz and Warsaw, for example, ghetto inhabitants were aware from the ghetto's inception of the Germans' genocidal actions. As also already noted, the German authorities had previously intervened in the workings of the ghetto court with catastrophic consequences. Mendl Balberyszski's 1967 memoir of the Vilna ghetto paints a more complicated picture of the emotions that the executions engendered in the ghetto population and even in the Jewish policemen who carried them out.[58] Whereas in Kruk's account the ghetto populace is steadfast and devoid of remorse in its support of the executions, Balberyszski remembers feelings of profound ambivalence in the community: "On the one hand, people were appalled that there had been, among Jews, murderous bandits who killed two innocent people for money. On the other hand people were shaken and broken by the sad, tragic fact of six Jews being hung by Jewish hands [*iz men geven dershitert un tsebrokhn af dem troyerikn, tragishn fakt fun hengen 6 yidn mit yidishe hent*]." (Balberyszski, *Shtarker fun ayzn*, 299). Balberyszski relates how, after the executions, he met with his old friend Khayim Moltshadski, a Jewish policeman in the Vilna ghetto whom Gens had forced to take part in the executions.

> Before the execution Gens turned to the policemen and said, "The small remnant of Jews in the ghetto is working hard and doing everything in order to survive this tragic time. Murderers and informants kill Jewish lives. That may not and will not be permitted. Murderers will receive their

> deserved punishment! Carrying out the court sentence is an obligation and a necessity for the ghetto [*a khoyv un a noytvendikeyt farn geto*]." So that no one would know who had hung whom, he ordered all the policemen to pull the rope together. In that way they hung all 6 murderers.
>
> "Yes, Mendl," my friend Maltshadski said with bitter tears. "I've become a hangman, a hangman in my elder years. A hangman. . . . That's what they've led us to [*Talyen, a talyen bin ikh gevorn af mayne alte yorn! A talyen. . . . ot tsu vos men hot undz derfirt*]." (Balberyszski, *Shtarker fun ayzn*, 299)[59]

In Balberyszski's account, not only are the residents of the Vilna ghetto inwardly deeply divided about the executions but even those who carry them out are despondent at having become hangmen.[60]

It should be noted that, compared to Warsaw or Lodz, the Judenrat and Jewish police in Vilna had greater trust among the ghetto's residents. So much so that in June 1943 the public sided with Gens rather than supporting FPO (Fareynikte Partizaner Oganizatsye / United Partisan Organization) leader Itzik Vitenberg's attempt to engage in armed resistance when the Germans demanded Vitenberg be handed over.[61] Nonetheless, Balberyszski's account alerts us to a degree of ambivalence among the Vilna ghetto community that Kruk's narrative goes out of its way to deny.[62] The coming to light of the murder of Jews by Jews for base venal ends was surely vexing to the ghetto population. The fact that the crime involved was murder is also key to Kruk's literary construction of the unifying effect it had on the ghetto community. As Bethke discusses, the broader ghetto communities generally regarded many of the acts designated as criminal by the internal ghetto legal institutions—including smuggling, gathering wood, and certain forms of manipulation of the system of rations—as simply necessary for survival.[63] The amnesty that Gens announced upon being installed as Judenrat head pertained to such offenses, but not, it is worth noting, to murder or the crime of "insulting or physically attacking a policeman carrying out his official duties, or in connection with these duties," the crimes for which the six men had been hanged on June 4, 1942 (Gens, "Address," 439). The "classic" crime of murder was one—and perhaps the only one—around which a collective ethos (even a semi-fictionalized one) among the various segments of the ghetto population could be consolidated. It was not only the heinousness of the crimes but also their individual nature that made them effective in unifying the ghetto community. Despite their awfulness, the murders could be, one could say, privatized, understood within a conventional legal-moral logic over against the genocidal killings that had been paused. The relief and redemption collectively experienced by the ghetto residents that figures so prominently in Kruk's account must be understood in part as relief at a return to a form of conventional crime—however heinous—committed by individuals for conventional base motives and addressable through sentencing and punishment. Despite the moral shock of these murders, the ghetto community—perhaps in reality and certainly in Kruk's fictionalized version of that reality—felt a good deal of relief at a return to a scale of crime that something approaching normal justice could contend with.

There is good reason to suspect that Kruk personally shared the ambivalence that his narrative strains to play down. Kruk's assessment of Gens shifted remarkably quickly after the latter's installment as Judenrat head, prior to which point Kruk on numerous occasions had expressed extreme suspicion of Gens and his motives.[64] To the socialist Kruk, the Revisionist Zionist Gens was a fascist to whom Kruk referred as "Il Duce of the ghetto."[65] Into July 1942, only weeks before writing "Six Gallows," Kruk continued to see Gens as a brutal, power-hungry "dictator."[66] It seems warranted to detect, behind the overall highly positive portrayal of Gens in "Six Gallows," a lingering ambivalence vis-à-vis this now-even-more powerful figure, one that Kruk tries to mitigate with recourse to the literary-ideological form of the Sherlock Holmes story. As Kruk strains mightily to depict a ghetto population united in a common ethos, he also seems to be trying to convince himself.[67]

If Kruk's "Sherlock Holmes story" strains rather dramatically at times to fit within the optimistic and socially reassuring paradigm of a tale of Holmesian agency and justice, it is because there is so much to strain against. I would argue that it was the unbearable ambiguity of the situation of the ghetto community that moved Kruk to avail himself of the literary tools—and, above all, of the literary ideology—of Sherlock Holmes narratives. The ambiguity, that is, could be resolved perhaps only by fictional means, and Sherlock Holmes offered Kruk the most promising model for organizing the realities of the Vilna ghetto in summer 1942 into a narrative arc culminating in a meaningful degree of autonomy and agency, communal harmony, and justice. Like detective fiction as analyzed by Boltanksi, Kruk's tale had to negotiate two realities. There was relative stability in the Vilna ghetto after the initial mass murders during the second half of 1941. Behind that relatively ordered reality, however, lurked the ever-present threat that, Gens's self-proclaimed agency as the head of the ghetto's internal institutions notwithstanding, the Germans could complete the genocidal project they had merely paused. It was this specific predicament that made the harmonizing and reassuring thrust of the Sherlock Holmes genre attractive to Kruk. Kruk was not someone who readily wrote fiction or fictionalized prose. Moreover, he bemoaned the escapist or "narcotic" relationship that the majority of the ghetto's inhabitants maintained to literature—such as the detective novels of Edgar Wallace, which were widely translated into Polish in the 1920s and 1930s and, to Kruk's chagrin, were among the most frequently borrowed books at the Vilna ghetto library. (Kruk's preference would have been for ghetto readers to borrow Yiddish translations of classics by Flaubert, Dostoevsky, or Romain Rolland.)[68] Thus Kruk's turn to the detective genre was far from a foregone conclusion —yet he clearly found it compelling in crucial ways. As Harshav notes, Kruk deployed multiple genres and modes of discourse and "was alert to the problems of genre and discourse in representing the Holocaust" (Harshav, preface in *Last Days*, xviii–xviv).

The Sherlock Holmes paradigm, as I have been arguing, offered Kruk a literary means for negotiating the terrible ambiguity of the two levels of agency and reality involved in the ghetto as spectacularly crystalized in the murder cases of June 4, 1942. While Kruk's "Sherlock Holmes story" plays up Gens's and the ghetto community's moral agency, it of course does not wholly elide the extreme precarity of the Jews and the fragile nature of the autonomy and agency they command. Even as it accords with Gens's assertion of authority in the Vilna ghetto, Kruk's Holmesian tale of crimes revealed and justice rendered is a story within a larger story, one that haunts and threatens to subvert it at every turn. The very institutions of justice through which the (frequently personified) ghetto can "wash its hands" (*Last Days*, 603) of the shocking crimes perpetrated by Jews against Jews—ghetto court, Judenrat, and Jewish police—are also cynically-deployed instruments of the Nazis.[69] The clarity with which we, in retrospect, know this to be the case, however, was not available to Kruk in summer 1942. He and the wider ghetto community were caught in a realm of ambiguity, with much reason to fear the worst and also some basis for hoping that Gens's strategy of exchanging Jewish labor for Jewish life could in fact save much of the remaining community. Writing the story of the situation of the Vilna ghetto in summer 1942 according to the ideological coordinates of Holmesian narratives aided Kruk in understanding the predicament of the ghetto in the most optimistic terms possible, but the terrible contradictions of ghetto existence could not be resolved altogether, not even within Kruk's narrative.

Many of these contradictions come to bear on the incredible—literally unbelievable—image of the six men hanging from the makeshift gallows. When the Jewish authorities ultimately manage to have Avidon executed, ostensibly for his role in the attack on the Jewish policeman, which Murer viewed as an injury to Nazi authority, but in reality more for his collaboration with the Nazis resulting in the death of so many Jews in Lida, they can be said to achieve a certain subversion of their own grotesque manipulation by the Germans. Despite this partial outwitting of the Nazi authorities, however, the question remains as to who the sovereign agents ultimately are who enact this brutal public spectacle. Is it the Jewish ghetto authorities, as Gens proclaims and Kruk's strained narrative generally echoes? Or is it the Nazis who have orchestrated this display of would-be Jewish juridical autonomy? "Six Gallows" leaves open the latter possibility. Kruk depicts how a sizable group of prominent Nazis arrive on the scene in limousines and presumably enjoy taking in the spectacle of Jews executing Jews. As Kruk describes it, "Three limousines slice into the ghetto: Gebietskommissar Hingst; his adviser for Jewish affairs, Murer; Hingst's chief-of-staff, Lakner, representatives of the Schutzpolizei, Gestapo, SS, Sonderkomando, and others" (*Last Days*, 619). An anonymous Jewish onlooker remarks, "Jews take Jews to the gallows, and [Gebietskommissar] Hingst and Murer are the witnesses . . ." (*Last Days*, 619).

Even as Gens is using the occasion of these executions to bolster his authority as head of the Vilna ghetto Jewish police, and even as the main thrust of Kruk's text is to accord with Gens's would-be demonstration of his authority and agency, it is clear to readers, as on some level it must have been evident to members of the ghetto populace assembled to view the unprecedented spectacle of Jewish criminals executed by Jewish authorities, that the German officers are playing with Gens et al. The Jewish authorities' judicial powers are at once extraordinary and a sham. Although the Jewish authorities manage to carry out an act of community self-protection that the Nazis would not have approved had they grasped what was really at stake, the sight of the six executed bodies may serve less as a sign of justice triumphant than as so many haunting question marks about the very possibility of rendering justice in the Vilna ghetto. Kruk draws our attention to how the five gangsters were tortured while being interrogated,[70] and he adds a gruesome detail to the execution scene in the literary version that is not mentioned in his earlier diary entries: Avidon's hanging fails on the first attempt. Following an ancient tradition of justice, he should therefore be let go. But as Kruk puts it, "Jews see it differently: his dozens of innocent victims begrudge him [their] death [*farginen im nit dem toyt*]. The German 'guests' suggest that the Jewish 'chief' decide [*Di daytshe 'gest' leygn for: zol der yidisher 'shef' detsidirn*]. And he decides: // 'We don't need him! . . .' // The beaten Avidon lies in a pool of blood on the ground, and the execution continues" (*Last Days*, 620 / "Zeks tlies," 21; translation modified). The publicly executed bodies signify the workings of Jewish institutions of justice, but also torture and the circumvention of ethical and legal standards, in the attempt to avenge innocent deaths.[71] Given the multiple and self-contradictory meanings that the executed bodies manifested and the way Jewish ethical agency and the pursuit of justice simultaneously subverted and served the spectating Nazis' will, it is understandable that the ghetto inhabitants experienced cognitive dissonance and "could not believe their eyes."

Readings of detective stories by Marxist scholars such as Franco Moretti and Ernest Mandel may, mutatis mutandis, offer insight into the ambivalent and somewhat contradictory aims of Kruk's Sherlock Holmes story from the Vilna ghetto. Moretti and Mandel critique the ways that detective fiction, and Sherlock Holmes stories in particular, render crime in ways that keep deeper structural crimes from coming to light. By defining crime as acts committed only by aberrant individual actors, such narratives (and mass cultural commodities) keep deeper causes of social misery from being detected. Thus for example Moretti notes that while theft is ubiquitous in the detective genre, this preoccupation with theft never extends to the systematic theft that is baked into the wage labor system. While "thefts, con-jobs, frauds, false pretenses, and so on" serve as the objects of moral indignation, "as for the factory—it is innocent, and thus free to carry on" (Moretti, "Clues," 139). Moretti notes further the way that the genre affirms a social totality predicated upon the disregard of the deeper causes of social injustice. The genre, that is, affirms a pseudo social unity in opposition to the aberrant individual criminal. Detective fiction creates a problem—the crime—"and declares a sole cause relevant: the criminal. It slights other causes" ("Clues," 144). For Moretti, detective fiction retreats from reality, against which it never has to check itself, and in this way it becomes "a hyper-literary phenomenon" characterized by "perfect self-referentiality" ("Clues," 149). As such it is a particularly effective ideological vector since the truth it purveys remains impervious to contradiction by external reality, based as it is on adherence to generic conventions governing its "non-referential world" ("Clues," 150). In short, Moretti (and Mandel's analysis reaches broadly similar conclusions) sees mass cultural detective fiction as a "full-fledged example of cultural fetishism" in the way that it displaces critical attention from the root causes that produce the surface phenomena it depicts, and thus renders those phenomena absolute ("Clues," 152).

It should be obvious that the applicability of Moretti's critique of the ideological function of detective literature to Kruk's literary grappling with the situation of the Vilna ghetto in summer 1942 is limited. Moretti theorizes how a highly commodified cultural product forecloses on detecting the deep violence that underpins capitalist society in its normal functioning; he is not attempting to account for the function of cultural narratives in moments of extreme (mass, genocidal) violence such as Vilna after the murder of more than three-fourths of its Jewish inhabitants. I in no way wish to elide these extremely different situations. There is, however, an important continuity between the way the detective genre as theorized by Moretti and as appropriated in extremis by Kruk works to block out systematic violence even as it reveals (and indeed by revealing) sensational individual acts of crime. Perhaps the best way to appreciate both the continuity and the break between the work that Doyle's and Kruk's Sherlock Holmes narratives perform is to see Kruk trying to deploy, as a project and from a place of extreme ambivalence, the cultural fetishism that is so effective in Doyle's narratives. I am suggesting that Kruk sought recourse to a feature of mass-cultural detective stories—their ability to frame out structural violence with narratives of sensational individual crimes—in an extreme situation that no longer operated according to the givens of the "normal" capitalist world. Kruk's story looks in a sense nostalgically to the work that cultural fetishism so effectively performed, from a vantage point beyond its effective operation. Whereas the soothing simulacra of individual agency, social unity, and ultimate triumph over danger, disorder, and injustice proffered by Doyle's texts work so effectively because they mask the ideological work they perform, Kruk's attempt to downplay the ambient threat of the Germans engaged in genocide cannot ultimately dissemble its status as the desperate project that it is. In Kruk's repeated references to Sherlock Holmes we can see not only an attempt to map the intractable and terrifying circumstances of the Vilna ghetto onto the reassuring ideological coordinates of this literary paradigm but also an acknowledgment (perhaps against Kruk's own intention) that both the Jewish ghetto authorities' restoration of Jewish honor and relative normalcy and his, Kruk's, literary account of it remain illusory conceits, staged fictions.

CHAPTER 8

OSKAR ROSENFELD'S HAUNTING LITERARY DREAM IN THE LODZ GHETTO

While Jews imprisoned in Nazi ghettos pursued various clandestine archival projects, only the Lodz ghetto had an official Department of Archives, authorized by Chaim Rumkowski, the head of the Lodz ghetto Jewish Council.[1] The most comprehensive product of the archives was the official Lodz ghetto *Chronicle*, to which Oskar Rosenfeld was a major contributor.[2] While the staff of the *Chronicle* were permitted to collect and record a remarkable range of information, there were limits to what could be said in the official record. Rosenfeld also wrote private diaries and notebooks. In these non-official writings, he records observations of ghetto realities alongside far-ranging reflections. He also regularly makes notes and sketches for literary stories and a novel he is writing (or planning to write) and a film he hopes to make about the ghetto should he survive. He furthermore reflects on the extensive and varied (mostly but far from only literary) reading he engaged in during his years in the Lodz ghetto. "Meine zwei Nachbarn" ("My Two Neighbors"), the fictional short story that is the focus of this chapter, belongs to the literary works Rosenfeld composed in the ghetto alongside his copious diaries and regular contributions to the *Chronicle*. It is the most complete work of fiction by Rosenfeld to have come down to us. At least one other story, "Das Geheimnis des Ghettos" (The secret of the ghetto) that Rosenfeld repeatedly alludes to in his notebooks and read to friends in the ghetto was lost.[3]

Rosenfeld was a cosmopolitan Central European Jew with a deep and abiding interest in Eastern European secular and religious culture. Born in 1884 in Moravia, he moved to Vienna in 1902 to study art history and philology and earned a doctorate in 1908 with a dissertation on "Philipp Otto Runge and Romanticism." He was introduced to the Zionist press by Theodor Herzl in 1903 and remained active in Zionist organizations as a writer, editor, and propagandist throughout his life, eventually supporting the revisionist Zionism of Ze'ev Jabotinsky. From his student days on he wrote art, literature, and theater criticism for Jewish newspapers as well as fiction with central Jewish characters. Rosenfeld's most ambitious literary work was *Die vierte Gallerie* (The fourth gallery, 1910), a novel populated with self-absorbed and art-obsessed Viennese posers with comical delusions of musical and literary grandeur. The main protagonist, a conflicted Jewish Wagner enthusiast, has the symbolic name Michael Irrgang (*Irrgang* means a disorienting path with many twists and turns, like a path in a maze). Also worthy of mention are Rosenfeld's 1914 short story "Mendl Ruhig: Eine Erzählung aus dem mährischen Ghettoleben" (Mendl Ruhig: A tale from Moravian ghetto life) and *Tage und Nächte* (Days and nights), a volume of six short stories published in 1920.[4] The stories in *Tage und Nächte* juxtapose and interweave scenes of, in Rosenfeld's own words, "das Alltägliche und das Wunderbare" (the everyday and the marvelous).[5] Rosenfeld also translated Yiddish literature—by Sholem Abramovitsh (Mendele Moykher Sforim), Sholem Aleichem, I. L. Peretz, and Israel Joshua Singer—into German and founded or co-founded two Jewish theaters in Vienna (1909 and 1927). After the Anschluss of Austria in March 1938, Rosenfeld and his wife Henriette fled to Prague. Henriette departed for London in 1939, but the outbreak of World War II prevented him from following her. Two years later, in November 1941, Rosenfeld was deported along with five thousand other Jews from Prague to Lodz.[6]

The transport that conveyed Rosenfeld to Lodz was part of a wider deportation of German Jews into the Lodz ghetto, not only from Prague but also from Berlin, Vienna, Frankfurt, Cologne, Hamburg, Düsseldorf, and Luxemburg. The influx of German Jews into the Lodz ghetto in autumn 1941 led to social and cultural tensions between the Western and the East European Jews. Rosenfeld was singularly poised to appreciate a breathtakingly broad range of the sociocultural and religious sensibilities that collided in the space of the most hermetically sealed of all Nazi ghettos. As David Roskies aptly writes of Rosenfeld's notebooks, "West and East, European and Jewish culture, the personal and reportorial, and sight and sound meet in these notebooks as nowhere else in wartime writing."[7] Rosenfeld's official position under the auspices of the Jewish Council allowed him to elude deportation until the ghetto's final liquidation. But in August 1944 he was deported to Auschwitz and murdered.

Like that of so many extant wartime writings by victims, the story of the survival, rescue, and (re)discovery of Rosenfeld's private notebooks is remarkable in its own right. Researchers looking in the late 1980s for materials for a planned exhibit on the Lodz ghetto at the Frankfurt Jewish Museum discovered Rosenfeld's ghetto diary, handwritten between February 17, 1942, and July 28, 1944, in twenty-one Polish school notebooks, in the archives of Yad Vashem, the Holocaust museum and research center in Jerusalem.[8] The notebooks had been sent in 1973 to Joseph Kermish, then the director of Yad

Vashem, by Abraham Cykiert (Zikert), a writer and journalist living in Australia, but with no documentation regarding how the notebooks had been salvaged and preserved. It would come to light only between the German publication of Rosenfeld's notebooks in 1994 and the English translation in 2002 that Moishe Lewkowicz, a friend of Rosenfeld's in the ghetto, had buried the notebooks for Rosenfeld in early August 1944 and recovered them in the summer of 1945. Rosenfeld's notebooks were among the papers left to Cykiert by Lewkowicz in 1970. They were in Cykiert's possession from 1970 to 1973, when he donated them to Yad Vashem.[9]

Written in German and dated August 4, 1943, "Meine zwei Nachbarn" works both with and against the conventions of popular genres like the murder mystery and the fantastic horror tale.[10] Beyond these genres, as we will see, Rosenfeld also pastiches narratives of suspense and romance. Throughout this book I have endeavored to show how confinement in ghettos engendered in many writers a painful self-consciousness about their now equivocal relationships to literary traditions, which they looked back on from positions of radical destitution and exclusion. Modern Yiddish literature was often a late arrival to major currents of European literature to which it looked with both desire and ambivalence. Being radically ostracized and persecuted in ghettos intensified the fraught self-positioning of Yiddish authors vis-à-vis European cultural ideologies and belletristic conventions.[11] But the radical estrangement from the society one had been part of was no less extreme for a German-language writer like Rosenfeld. In my reading, "Meine zwei Nachbarn" revisits and sifts through conventions of genre fiction from a perspective of anguished irony. The text effectively puts such conventions to the test, measuring against each other, on the one hand, unspoken assumptions (or conditions of possibility) of such genres and, on the other, the circumstances of the ghetto, which included squalor, starvation, and mass murder. Rosenfeld highlights the singularity of the experience of the ghetto by mapping ghetto existence onto the contours of popular literary genres; his narrative is arguably most illuminating in the incongruous fit it stages between generic assumptions about the nature of subjectivity, privacy, curiosity, desire, and epistemology—and the mutations all of these undergo in the ghetto.

ROSENFELD'S CINEMATIC AND LITERARY MODELS

Even beyond his stories and literary sketches, Rosenfeld's wider ghetto writings are profoundly marked by literary and esthetic sensibilities. While one can meaningfully distinguish between Rosenfeld's diary entries and his more properly literary works, it is important to appreciate how central various esthetic and representational modes were to how he framed the conditions and the experience of the ghetto in general. Rosenfeld's remarks—often on the ever-present scourge of hunger, for example—range from short notes to longer reflections to quasi-photographic "snapshots" taken with words in lieu of a camera.[12] Intending to use them for an eventual film project, Rosenfeld also recorded vividly significant scenes under the recurrent English heading "talkie," many dealing, again, centrally with hunger. In "Oskar Rosenfeld and Historiographic Realism," the philosopher Berel Lang argues that Holocaust writings necessarily rely on extra-literary historical referentiality. Lang leans on Rosenfeld's diaries to support his thesis but examines only aspects of Rosenfeld's writings in which "the representation intended is to be history lived as documentary."[13] He gives no serious thought to the significance of Rosenfeld's exploration of esthetic forms and figurative language or to his abiding commitment to writing fiction in the ghetto. By contrast, I see Rosenfeld's writings as singular precisely for the way they inextricably fuse the documentary and the esthetic. Whether he is recording scenes for his planned film project or for various literary projects, Rosenfeld weighs and sifts the brute realities he confronts through the genres and media he imagines could best do them justice.[14] As I elaborate below, Rosenfeld's "Meine zwei Nachbarn" engages in highly self-conscious play with and against generic conventions to illuminate aspects of the experience of the ghetto.

Such estheticized optics, I argue, enhance Rosenfeld's observational intelligence, his ability to see certain details in the first place. With his film project in mind, Rosenfeld on May 28, 1943, recorded the following "scene": "Talkie. Have you [*ihr*] ever seen a human being shortly before dying of hunger? His legs hardly support him, stomach caved in, sunken temples right and left, yellowish white coloring. Dizziness: collapses on the stairs despite cane. He's quickly administered some ressort soup.[15] Another ten hours! Too late. Dies, slowly fading away . . . with a sigh on his lips. Every day a dozen. To be seen [*zu Schau*] in the street, through open windows. They lie completely clothed because they are freezing cold" (Rosenfeld, *In the Beginning*, 192 / *Wozu noch Welt*, 212; translation modified). The anticipated cinematic medium may enhance Rosenfeld's ability to "see" the event vividly. It is also plausible, however, that Rosenfeld is here not referring to a particular scene he has witnessed but is rather constructing a representative or composite scene for maximum effectiveness in an eventual film about the ghetto. As literary scholar Sascha

Feuchert astutely notes, this passage could be intended as a direct address to the reader or as an eventual voice-over.[16] Do the open windows through which the freezing people lying in their clothes are "on display" (*zu Schau*) describe the sight lines of ghetto inhabitants, suggest film camera angles, or both? The fact that we at times cannot be sure where to locate the distinction in Rosenfeld's ghetto diaries between the recording of brute events and esthetic construction hardly throws the facticity of the Holocaust into question, but it does underscore the crucial role that considerations of esthetic, medial, and generic potentialities and conventions play in how Rosenfeld looks at, understands, and shapes the unprecedented events he grapples with.

That Rosenfeld was pondering literary form in the Lodz ghetto is clear from his diary entry of July 11, 1943. Here Rosenfeld holds up the stories by the Soviet Jewish writer Isaac Babel as a possible model for a radically new form of writing adequate to the realities of life in the ghetto: "Finally again desire to work. I'll be starting soon one of my projected stories. Wrestling with a concise style, structure. Perhaps the material requires a totally new form. Thinking of I. Babel in Malik-Verlag" (Rosenfeld, *In the Beginning*, 195 / *Wozu noch Welt*, 216). Rosenfeld considers whether the subject matter (*Stoff*) of the story he is about to embark upon might require a "totally new form" (*einer durchaus neuen Formung*), and whether Babel's stylistically innovative story cycles *Odessa Tales* and *Red Cavalry*, published in German translation by the leftist Malik-Verlag (beginning in 1926, virtually simultaneously with their original publication in Russian) might be able to serve as a model of sorts.[17] One can understand why in particular *Red Cavalry*, based on Babel's experiences as a military journalist riding with a Red Army cavalry unit in its ultimately unsuccessful 1920 campaign against Poland, could have interested Rosenfeld. In Babel's story cycle, brutality and graphic violence famously converge with wanton beauty. Babel was widely viewed as having invented an unprecedented literary style to render the realities and psychological experience of modern warfare and the clash of worlds and ideologies that it both issued from and entailed. That Babel paid considerable attention to the terrible fate of East European Jewish communities already devastated by World War I and again caught in the theater of the 1920 campaign likely also contributed to his attractiveness as a possible model for Rosenfeld.[18]

While we of course cannot know what Rosenfeld saw in (his memory of) Babel, one prominent aspect of Babel's *Red Cavalry* particularly illuminates literary strategies that Rosenfeld ultimately adopted. Babel memorably juxtaposes incongruent historical, cultural, and ideological elements violently forced into the same contested space. Babel highlights such catastrophic miscellany prominently in two closely related stories, "Gedali," which relates the narrator of *Red Cavalry* Lyutov's encounter with a Jewish junk dealer, and "The Rabbi's Son," the cycle's concluding story, which recalls scenes of some months earlier, when Lyutov accompanied Gedali to a Friday evening at the home of Rabbi Motale, the last rabbi (in Babel's fictionalized universe) of the Hassidic Chernobyl dynasty. Lyutov meets Gedali on a Friday evening when he is feeling homesick for things Jewish.[19] The congeries of objects that Gedali lovingly curates—"Everything from buttons to dead butterflies. . . . He roams through his labyrinth of gloves, skulls, and dead flowers, waving his cockerel-feather duster, swishing away the dust from the dead flowers" (Babel, *Complete Works*, 228)—in the face of so much ambient violence is mocked by the tragic mishmash of cultural, historical, and ideological elements jostled together by the clashing forces that Gedali experiences as parts of the same relentless catastrophe. From Gedali's perspective the Russian Revolution is scarcely distinguishable from the counter-revolution in its violence. It harbors no room for the Jewish Sabbath or Jewish culture more broadly (Babel, *Complete Works*, 228).

The violent encounter between Jewish spaces and time and the forces of modern ideology and war returns in a famous passage from the concluding story of *Red Cavalry*, "The Rabbi's Son."[20] Fleeing the failed Polish campaign in the train of the Polit-otdel (the political organ of the Soviet government, here charged with the political education of the military), and able to offer the "typhoid-ridden muzhik horde" only Trotsky leaflets in lieu of potatoes, Lyutov recognizes Ilya, the son of the Zhitomir rabbi to whom Gedali introduced Lyutov the same Friday evening Lyutov visited Gedali's shop. Ilya is pulled onto the train, but he is already wrecked and dying. Lyutov remarks on the incongruent things that Ilya carried: "I threw everything together in a jumble, the mandates of the political agitator and the mementos of a Jewish poet. Portraits of Lenin and Maimonides lay side by side—the gnarled steel of Lenin's skull and the listless silk of the Maimonides portrait. A lock of a woman's hair lay in the book of the resolutions of the Sixth Party Congress, and crooked lines of Ancient Hebrew verse huddled in the margins of Communist pamphlets. Pages of the Song of Songs and revolver cartridges drizzled on me in a sad, sparse rain" (Babel, *Complete Works*, 332). The dying Ilya embodies shards of traditional Jewish culture after their violent collision with Soviet ideology and propaganda and martial violence. This juxtaposition of traditional Jewish and Bolshevik elements is ephemeral and tragic, the frame fleetingly containing them the wrecked body of a dying man, a victim of incommensurate forces that he could not reconcile.

Babel's story provides a snapshot of an asymmetrical, impossible aggregation of texts, ideas, times, practices, histories, sensibilities, and identities in a moment of extreme (Jewish) crisis. The last lines of the story, and with it of *Red Cavalry*, further highlight the unresolvable incongruities between Jewish time, Jewish history, and the Soviet project. With Ilya, a Hasidic dynasty comes to an end, and Lyutov is left in a state of extreme ambivalence regarding the incompatible claims that his devotion to the revolution and his own "ancient" Jewish body make on him: "He died before we reached Rovno. He died, the last prince, amid poems, phylacteries, and foot bindings. We buried him at a desolate train station. And I, who can barely harness the storms of fantasy raging through my ancient body, I received my brother's last breath" (Babel, *Complete Works*, 333).

Babel's literary approach to the asynchronies of Jewish and revolutionary time and the way modern violence (World War I and the Soviet-Polish War) assembles fragments of these discordant cultures and histories into a single, impossible frame illuminates—both by analogy and by contrast—the "totally new form" of literature that Rosenfeld was seeking in his reading of Babel. Like Babel, Rosenfeld uses literature to gather incommensurable elements and (pre-ghetto and ghetto) temporalities within the same impossible frame. Rosenfeld did not ultimately emulate Babel, however, in trying to develop a radically new style. What constitutes the "entirely new form" in Rosenfeld's literary approach to the realities of the ghetto, I argue, is rather his way of deploying from the cruelly ironic perspective of the Lodz ghetto, a miscellany of well-worn generic conventions. Rosenfeld, that is, developed a strategy of generic pastiche from his (unwilled) position of heightened self-consciousness vis-à-vis the underlying assumptions or preconditions of typical literary genres that, in normal times, are taken for granted. From his perspective in the ghetto, Rosenfeld self-consciously jostled together a miscellany of generic topoi in a way that ultimately underscores their incompatibility with ghetto conditions. The formal novelty of Rosenfeld's approach lies in his meta-literary rifling through of stock genres to tell a story about the ghetto; the story told is largely about the incompatibility of ghetto existence with the very narrative genres by which the tale proceeds.

Elsewhere I have analyzed a different, undated literary text written by Rosenfeld in the Lodz ghetto, a philosophical dialogue titled "Golem und Hunger." In this text the central issue is the specific nature of hunger in the ghetto, which to the protagonist seems incomparable to phenomena such as famine in India or China, which he understands as having natural not human causes.[21] By contrast, while starvation is so generalized in the ghetto that it seems like a natural, indeed even like a cosmic condition, it is produced by human calculation. It is inescapable; the connection between the ghetto and any outside has been totally severed. The ghetto exists as that which has been abjected from the world, as that which has been de-worlded, and so cannot be contextualized by comparison to phenomena in the world beyond it.[22] I should be clear that I believe that the Nazi ghettos—and the Holocaust more generally—certainly can be illuminated through contextualization vis-à-vis other historical atrocities and genocides. But what interests me here is the subjective experience that Rosenfeld articulates of being placed beyond the human community in an unprecedented way that does not allow one to find any point of comparison that provides a feeling of human connection or communion. "Golem und Hunger" grapples not only with the experience of individual and collective starvation but also with the lived reality of its radical resistance to any sort of mitigating contextualization.

Like so many works of ghetto literature, "Meine zwei Nachbarn" is likewise ineluctably about starvation. It also takes up the crisis of comparison so central to "Golem und Hunger," albeit in a less thematically direct manner. The story dramatizes this problem in a highly literary, or indeed in a meta-literary, way insofar as the text rifles through a wide variety of literary tropes and genres, none of which can gain purchase on the story or serve as a viable organizing principle. That is, the play with and against literary conventions in "Meine zwei Nachbarn" suggests that Rosenfeld could not write the experience of the ghetto in an established genre or literary mode. Rather, literary writing from and about the ghetto could only grasp at, deploy, and denaturalize literary conventions that had their proper place elsewhere, in a time before and a world beyond, from which the ghetto had been radically excluded.

GENRE PASTICHE IN EXTREMIS: "MEINE ZWEI NACHBARN"

"Meine zwei Nachbarn" is narrated by a first-person narrator and comprises nine numbered sections. It opens with a vivid description of the setting, a mostly empty apartment building in the Lodz ghetto, a description to which I will return. When the narrator is assigned an apartment in this building, only the flat adjacent to his is still occupied. The other inhabitants have been deported. The central drama involves only three characters: the unnamed narrator; his male neighbor, whom he calls "Cymbalist," and a figure who seems to be Cymbalist's female companion, at least as far as the narrator can gather from the enigmatic fragments of speech he overhears his neighbor address to her.

The apparently erotic nature of the relationship between Cymbalist and his female roommate greatly contributes to the narrator's curiosity about what is happening in their apartment. The narrator relates an instance when his neighbor's voice "becomes audible" at "a surprising hour." Through the wall he hears Cymbalist speaking to his companion:

> "You're surprised that I'm home at noon? What? Why don't you say something? Strange creature! Or do you take me to be a fool, like most around here? In the ressort they say: 'Our boss'—they really say 'our boss'—'seems to have a lover at home. At work's end he gets nervous and makes sure he's first out the door. However, only for the last few days . . .' That's funny, isn't it. The people don't even know how right they are. Ha, ha, ha." (*In the Beginning*, 217 / *Wozu noch Welt*, 235)

Cymbalist's titillating monologue to his silent roommate intensifies the narrator's eavesdropping, or *écouterism*:

> "You must agree, I'm pampering you!"
>
> After a longish pause, he continued: "Instead of answering, she nods with her eyebrows and taps with her legs. Nice behavior, that! I'd better not tell anybody what a bad roommate I have . . ."
>
> I moved closer to the wall so I wouldn't miss a single word, a single breath. I had already become so used to being neighbors with Cymbalist that his chatter and his roommate's silence seemed quite natural to me. Nonetheless, my curiosity did not diminish. For a while I surmised that Cymbalist's companion was ill, gravely ill, and perhaps therefore bedridden and silent. His care and tenderness bespoke a good heart and touched me. I even resolved to express to him my willingness to help.
>
> "We," he began again, "make the most beautiful clothes . . . charming blouses, night robes, aprons. Luckily you don't need any of that. Your garment was designed by the greatest of all artists. Noble in cut, elegant in color . . . ash gray I love best, especially with a black dice-patterned waistline and back . . . Not to forget the yellowish brown of the skirt . . . Really a harmonious assemblage . . . Topped off with little black ankle

> boots, shoes that make a statement [*Panierschuhe*], or—what do they call them now—pumps. . . ." (*In the Beginning,* 218–19 / *Wozu noch Welt,* 236–37; translation modified)

We can see how Rosenfeld proliferates tropes of popular literature—here titillating descriptions of women and sentimental scenes of goodhearted caregiving. Wedged between the two portraits that the neighbor elaborates of his female companion, which allow the protagonist (and perhaps readers) to picture her in erotically charged ways, Rosenfeld gives us a sentimental miniature in which the protagonist is interpellated by the scene he projects of his good-hearted neighbor attending tenderly to his gravely ill, bedridden companion. The protagonist feels his heartstrings being pulled by his own *mise-en-scène* of a sentimental trope.

The narrator's sentimental identification with his nurturing neighbor is soon disrupted when Cymbalist's always erotically tinged words betray a violent streak. The narrator listens to his increasingly furious neighbor and is "seized by a desire to knock on the wall and call out to Cymbalist that he should cease his lamenting and reproaching. But I did nothing of the sort. On the contrary. I tensed my nerves so that nothing that was going on would escape me" (*In the Beginning,* 219 / *Wozu noch Welt,* 237). The closely followed happenings next door now take a most disturbing turn, leaving the narrator with the impression that his neighbor has murdered his companion:

> A few seconds passed in indescribable anticipation. Not a sound from the other side—only a soft scratching with the feet, a rustling of the upholstery, a choking scream.
>
> I walked to the side of the door. Next door, heavy breathing, almost rattling. "Now you have enough, beast, contemptible, faithless . . . why aren't you screaming when I strangle you, when I squash your legs . . . despicable tramp . . . Go to the devil!"
>
> These were Cymbalist's last words before he left the room, slammed the door, and went down the stairs. (*In the Beginning,* 219–20 / *Wozu noch Welt,* 237)

The curiosity and desire of Rosenfeld's *écouteur* narrator continue to propel him in the role he now assumes of an amateur sleuth investigating a murder mystery. Although overcome by physical weakness and fatigue, he is seized by an implacable wish to discover what has happened, and so ventures into the apartment next door when his neighbor is out. But instead of following clues to an ultimate discovery and a tidy denouement, the story subverts the conventions of the murder mystery in at least two ways. First, the female companion whom Cymbalist has "murdered, strangled," and "finished off" (*ermordet, erdrosselt, den Garaus gemacht* [*Wozu noch Welt*, 240]) turns out to be not a woman but a fly. Second, the narrator ultimately awakens in his bed, and we realize that much of the forgoing action has been a hunger-induced fever dream. Although Rosenfeld's text in general and these moments in particular are not without an element of humor, I would argue that they do not provide the sort of relief that generally accompanies ironic deflation. That the two male neighbors project their romantic energies onto an insect tends rather to underscore the poverty of erotic life in the ghetto, and the denouement revealing that much of the nightmarish action has in fact been a literal nightmare, as I argue in the conclusion of this chapter, show up the protagonist's (literary) fantasies of agency as cruelly illusory. I see the humor of these moments as part of the story's broader self-awareness that the very categories by which literature operates, its assumptions regarding individual integrity, agency, desire, and private space have been transformed and largely undermined by the conditions of the ghetto. A work of literature that proceeds in the awareness that its most basic elements have become inoperative is indeed darkly funny, but sadly and poignantly so.

The dream conceit of "Meine zwei Nachbarn" is itself a well-worn literary topos, and the dream space the protagonist inhabits allows him to wander through an oneiric catalogue of literary roles and conventions. As Feuchert notes, it is not possible to pinpoint exactly when the protagonist's dream starts (Feuchert, *Oskar Rosenfeld*, 386). As I will argue in a moment, there are clues at various points throughout the text that suggest mental states governed by a sort of dream logic. The question as to when "the" dream begins may thus be somewhat ill-posed, as we may not be dealing (only) with one discreet dream but (also) with a consciousness prone to swerving in and out of, or to hovering at the threshold of, dreamlike states. That said, Rosenfeld gives readers ample clues to mark the onset of the dream from which the protagonist awakens in the story's final lines as occurring in section 7, when weakness overcomes the narrator and he seems to faint.

The depiction in this section of the narrator's crossing of the threshold from reality to dream world is marked, notably, by a proliferation of literary topoi that will take on ever greater density in—one could even say, will essentially make up—the dream world that the protagonist enters. This dream world will also coincide with the space of Cymbalist's apartment. The relatively brief section 7, mediating between wakefulness and dream, is thus worth quoting in full:

> I was overcome with weakness, which I had lately noticed more and more. It started with flickering, bright-colored rings dancing before my eyes and a languid feeling in the cavity of my heart. My feet were cold; only with great effort was I able to clench my hands into fists. I stood by the window facing the yard. All sorts of people crossed the yard with hasty steps and disappeared behind rotten doors.
>
> It was after five. The ressorts were spitting their workers out into the streets. Children carried pots wrapped in pieces of cloth, old people carried heavy burdens on their skeletal backs. "What is all this about? Why the haste? You'll get to your *kolazia* on time![23] Nice and slow! Patience, my dears . . ." I thought to myself.
>
> I groped for the window frame to keep from falling. The weakness that had come over me forced me to cancel my plans for the day. Wishes and intimations were blending into one another in my head. Inadvertently I reached for my temples with both hands. All around, darkness descended. A rushing in my ears. My tongue searched for a wet spot on the palate. Suddenly I felt as if I had bitten into a lemon.
>
> But in the midst of this condition, I was seized by the desire to find out what had been going on in Cymbalist's room. I didn't hesitate long. A few steps and I was in front of Cymbalist's door. I rattled it. It was not locked. Cymbalist had forgotten . . . I was happy. (*In the Beginning*, 220 / *Wozu noch Welt*, 237–38; translation modified)[24]

Toward the end of this passage, the protagonist clearly seems to be losing consciousness: "I reached for my temples with both hands. All around, darkness descended. A rushing in my ears." Moreover, the dryness of and bitter taste in the mouth that accompany this loss of consciousness—"My tongue searched for a wet spot on the palate. Suddenly I felt as if I had bitten into a lemon"—reappear just before the narrator wakes up at the end of the story: "My tongue was bitter and dry." (*In the Beginning*, 223 / *Wozu noch Welt*, 241). The fact that when the narrator awakens "the potatoes were done, the evening meal was ready" (*In the Beginning*, 223 / *Wozu noch Welt*, 241) likewise rhymes with the moment that he lost consciousness and entered his dream, which was "after five" in the evening, when everyone was rushing home for their evening meal.

What this means is that the narrator does not enter Cymbalist's room but rather a dreamscape of his own projected desires. Again, Rosenfeld signals quite clearly (at least upon a second reading of the text) the dreamlike nature of his protagonist's entry into Cymbalist's flat. "But in the midst of this condition, I was seized by the desire to find out what had been going on in Cymbalist's room. I didn't hesitate long. A few steps and I was in front of Cymbalist's door. I rattled it. It was not locked. Cymbalist had forgotten . . . I was happy" (*In the Beginning*, 220 / *Wozu noch Welt*, 238). Propelled by his desire, the protagonist is suddenly able to move with new energy and ease, needing only "a few steps" to transport himself to Cymbalist's door, which just happens to be unlocked. If we have unmistakably entered a projected dream world by this point, the earlier portions of section 7 are more ambiguous. The narrator tells us that lately he has "more and more" found himself overcome with weakness. He appears to be on the verge of losing consciousness: his eyes flicker, his heart feels weak, and he loses motor function. Moreover, the narrator signals that "wishes and intimations were swirling together in my head" (*Wünsche und Ahnungen quirlten in meinem Hirn durcheinander* [*Wozu noch Welt*, 238, my translation]).[25] In his twilight state between lucidity and dream, the narrator cannot distinguish between intimations of reality (*Ahnungen*) and fantasy (*Wünsche*).

The narrator's episode raises the question of how far back—he has been experiencing such moments "more and more" of late—his hovering at the threshold between reality and dream extends. A dream logic seems to govern a number of occurrences from earlier in the story, and the repeated mentions of fatigue or sleeping, beginning on the story's first page, likewise support an interpretation of at least some of the action as occurring in, or at the threshold of, dreams. Section 1 of the narrative ends, "Lying in bed, I hear him come in. My dear, good neighbor. He doesn't disturb me as I am dozing. I am happy" (*In the Beginning*, 215 / *Wozu noch Welt*, 233). Section 2 ends similarly: "I am tired and I fall quickly and easily asleep. The arm under my cheek, rushing in my ears—I am happy" (*In the Beginning*, 216 / *Wozu noch Welt*, 234). Other moments in the narrative preceding what we could call the narrator's dream proper likewise suggest a hovering at the threshold between dream and lucidity. For example, a stranger comes looking for a Dr. Cymbalist at the door of the narrator's neighbor. He asks the narrator if it is a Doctor Cymbalist who lives in that apartment: "'Cymbalist,' he repeats. 'Doctor Cymbalist?' I nod in agreement. My neighbor, I think to myself, is Dr. Cymbalist. He couldn't be anybody else. That I hadn't known this all along! None other than Dr. Cymbalist" (*In the Beginning*, 216 / *Wozu noch Welt*, 234). The stranger who came looking for Doctor Cymbalist quickly realizes, however, that Cymbalist could not be living at this address any longer because he had left for Warsaw when the war broke out. To this information the narrator responds, "Thank God, my neighbor is not Dr. Cymbalist. I am happy" (*In the Beginning*, 216–17 / *Wozu noch Welt*, 234). The narrator "learns" that his neighbor is named Cymbalist, then that he cannot possibly be Cymbalist, within the span of a few seconds. Upon "learning" his neighbor's name, the fit between name and neighbor strikes the narrator as so self-evident that he wonders how it could not have been obvious to him all along. A mere ten lines after marveling at the naturalness of Cymbalist's name, he is relieved and thankful to learn that his neighbor is in fact not Dr. Cymbalist. His two reactions apparently engender no cognitive dissonance. The narrator seems to be operating according to a principle of non-contradiction that frequently governs dreams whereby something and its opposite can coincide in apparent harmony. While this may not suggest a discreet dream of the sort the narrator has at the end of the narrative, it does suggest that the narrator's mind is functioning, even in waking states, according to a dream logic.

Dream states and reality mingle intermittently throughout "Meine zwei Nachbarn." In section 7, to which I now return, they begin to do so in ways that nod, in a self-reflexive, metafictional manner, to stock literary scenarios and topoi. As we will see, the narrative's self-conscious recourse to literary commonplaces will only pick up steam as the protagonist's dream progresses. The narrator has already signaled himself to be alienated from the wider ghetto community. In section 2, he describes overhearing, on his way home between six and eight o'clock, people talking of "potatoes, vegetables . . . of wood, of cooking . . . These are the daily concerns of the ghetto. I too hurry home. But I don't care much about the daily concerns of the ghetto" (*In the Beginning*, 216 / *Wozu noch Welt*, 233). The narrator claims to have become accustomed to eating anything and thus to have become essentially immune to the diseases that plague the ghetto inhabitants. The posture of the isolated individual standing at his apartment window observing and commenting on the people below extends into the ghetto this topos of the estranged (and esthetic) modern individual familiar from texts by, for example, E. T. A. Hoffmann or Arthur Schnitzler: "I stood by the window facing the yard. All sorts of people crossed the yard with hasty steps and disappeared behind rotten doors. . . . The ressorts were spitting their workers out into the streets. . . . 'What is all this about? Why the haste? You'll get to your *kolazia* on time! Nice and slow! Patience, my dears . . .' I thought to myself" (*In the Beginning*,

220 / *Wozu noch Welt*, 238).[26] The questionable status of what he is seeing bolsters the possibility that the protagonist might be using his literary imagination when he observes the rushing people below. His window gives onto the courtyard, and thus it seems questionable whether it could also provide a view onto the streets into which the ressorts are "spitting their workers." Moreover, the narrator and his neighbor, if we are to believe the admittedly unreliable narrator, are the only occupants in the building. Why, then, would "all sorts of people" be crossing the courtyard? We do not get many clues regarding the configuration of buildings around this yard (*Hof*), and it is possible that other, occupied buildings abut it or that its location makes it convenient for people to traverse. But it is also possible that the narrator is daydreaming. Even if he is in fact looking at people scurrying home, his disdainful attitude toward them seems contrived, almost studied. Would anyone starving in the ghetto really remark on the unnecessary haste with which people are hurrying home in anticipation of their evening meal? It would seem that the narrator is putting on literary airs.

The narrator's self-projection into clichéd literary characters and scenarios accumulates density as he enters and inhabits the dream-space of his neighbor's apartment as a would-be sleuth investigating the mysteries next door that he has long been following aurally. For example, the narrator's surveying of "Cymbalist's" room is interrupted by approaching steps.

> I was slowly retreating to the door when I heard steps. Somebody from below was approaching the attic floor. The steps were heavy and measured, ceasing from time to time as if the visitor was resting periodically. Did Cymbalist have friends or relatives who would visit him? What if somebody came in now and found me in the room? Was I a thief who sneaked in to rob Cymbalist of his meager possessions? Or did I even have an eye on the female on whom in the last hours Cymbalist had bestowed flattery and threats? Be that as it may [*Wie dem auch gewesen sein mag*]—the steps were approaching Cymbalist's room, where I was an intruder [*in der ich mich als Fremder befand*].
>
> To leave the room and return to my own lodging seemed inappropriate. Counting the time that had passed since the stranger had begun his ascent, I figured he must have reached the attic floor already. I heard heavy breathing, rattling in the chest of a strong man, snorting from mouth and nostrils. Escape was impossible.

> I therefore decided to risk an encounter with the intruder and even to defend myself . . .
>
> As I thus deliberated, it occurred to me that a witness could betray me and prevent me from defending myself—my neighbor's female companion. Or could I perhaps find in her a friend? She was no doubt somewhere in the room, as Cymbalist had gone out alone. (*In the Beginning*, 221 / *Wozu noch Welt*, 239; translation modified)

If already in the moment the narrator begins to lose consciousness, and likely for an extended period prior to that point, his perceptions and intimations are overdetermined by *Wünsche*, in the dreamscape of "Cymbalist's" apartment, desires are given freer reign. The protagonist's fantasies tend conspicuously to align with stock situations from genre fiction. In a melodramatic pastiche, we are given tropes of suspense (approaching footsteps of "a strong man," escape is impossible!); masculine heroism (the protagonist's resolve, if necessary, to fight); and more than a hint of romance (whose side will the woman who has so fascinated the protagonist take in this dream of a fight? Will she betray him or show herself to be his loyal friend?). In a manner of speaking, the protagonist's dream is a dream of literature: in the dreamed space of Cymbalist's apartment, he can entertain his fantasies of embodying various stock roles of genre fiction: the sleuth, the masculine hero willing to fight and, perhaps, win the girl.

Rosenfeld accentuates the narrator's sifting of available literary characters that he might embody and scenarios he might act out when he has the narrator pose not-quite-rhetorical questions regarding his own status in the evolving action: "What if somebody came in now and found me in the room? Was I a thief who sneaked in to rob Cymbalist of his meager possessions? Or did I even have an eye on the female on whom Cymbalist had bestowed in the last hours flattery and threats?" On one level the narrator is merely imagining what impression he would make on someone who caught him in the middle of his exploration of Cymbalist's apartment. But Rosenfeld raises the ontological stakes of the narrator's questions by having him ask himself, literally, what he is (*War ich ein Dieb*) and what his actual intentions are (*Oder hatte ich es gar auf das weibliche Wesen abgesehen*) rather than how he might appear to an observer. One gets the distinct sense that in wondering what sort of impression he might make, the narrator is wondering what kind of story this is and what role he is playing in it; in a word, who he *is*.

As we saw, in his dreamlike state when learning and unlearning "Cymbalist's" name, the protagonist grapples not only with the name of the other main figure in his story but also with the character that this name might signify (of course he's Cymbalist!; thank God he's not Cymbalist!). There is an intimate connection between the narrator's dream-thoughts and the narrative's construction of literary character, plot, and genre. Even as the narrator dreams himself into stories, he is trying to figure out what sort of story he finds himself in. He projects himself into a dreamscape of readymade generic scenarios, all the while seeking to discover what sort of characters he and his neighbor(s) might be.

The protagonist's dream is indeed in no small part a dream of being able to inhabit literary roles. There are several instances when dream logic facilitates his perpetuation of such a role, when, that is, the protagonist deploys a logic that would not hold up under normal circumstances but that he can, in his dream, nonetheless use to sustain his embodiment of literary roles like the detective and the romantic hero. After the protagonist searches for Cymbalist's female companion (and even as the approaching steps draw ever nearer), he abruptly becomes distracted. He simply disregards the approaching danger and starts investigating every corner of the apartment: "After that—without any regard for the looming danger from outside—I poked through every corner and what was heaped up there: shreds, scarves, sacks, tar paper, coal pieces, and sundry unidentifiable stuff. I did this without thinking, without a plan, so I had afterward no idea why I did it" (*In the Beginning*, 221–22 / *Wozu noch Welt*, 239). After the approaching man, whom the narrator identifies by his voice as "Cymbalist" himself, arrives at the door only to leave again without entering, muttering about how he did not need his backpack after all, the protagonist continues his search for clues: "Cymbalist had hardly left the house—I saw him cross the yard—when I set out to look around some more. I pushed bucket, broom, rucksack aside with my foot, without uncovering anything suspicious. Every object stood in a natural relationship to Cymbalist. Even the smell of ripened fruit and cognac seemed to me self-evident" (*In the Beginning*, 222 / *Wozu noch Welt*, 240; translation modified). The protagonist's dream logic allows him to embody the role of the detective, albeit weirdly: he uncovers a great deal of objects, but they all seem self-evident (*selbstverständlich*) to him, as do even the aromas of extreme ghetto rarities like ripe fruit and cognac. Perhaps he cannot discover anything suspicious precisely because all that he uncovers appears to him according to the unassailable logic of dreams. If the classic ratiocinative literary detective as typified paradigmatically by Sherlock Holmes and as theorized by Siegfried Kracauer is all head and no emotion, Rosenfeld's character, sustained by *Wünsche*, is an oneiric variation on this type for whom any possible discovery is self-evident a priori. Even when the narrator-protagonist notices a plate whose edges are covered with white flour and sugar, he takes it in as a "sight that didn't surprise me despite its rarity" (*In the Beginning*, 222 / *Wozu noch Welt*, 240).

The protagonist is not really out, however, to accomplish effective detective work or to get the girl as a romantic hero, either. His desire seems to be much more aligned with continuing to inhabit these literary subjectivities—and virtually any contextual support or "evidence," it seems, can aid him in sustaining them. Even when the circumstances—or the evidence he gathers—become incompatible with such fantasies, the narrator continues to dream a dream of literary roles and desires. He uses the language of a literary detective describing a murder even after he knows that the woman who has been strangled was in fact a fly, and he seems to yearn for her companionship only more intensely. The realization that the female companion he has been searching for was an insect "should" spell the end of the murder mystery and the romantic plot but augments them instead. Despite having learned that the victim was a fly, the narrator proceeds to describe "her" as "murdered, strangled" and to limn "her" physical features in language that recalls the description he had earlier heard his neighbor give (which had excited his erotic curiosity and which now, in retrospect, readers recognize as having been consistent with a fly's appearance): "The fly was dead. Murdered, strangled [*Ermordet, erdrosselt*]. Waistline and back in a black dice pattern, belly and legs yellowish brown, the balls of the toes black." (*In the Beginning*, 222–23 / *Wozu noch Welt*, 240). Continuing to use the language of homicide, the narrator concludes, "Cymbalist, so much was clear, had bumped the fly off [*hat der Fliege den Garaus gemacht*] and was now alone again" (*In the Beginning*, 223 / *Wozu noch Welt*, 240), and he subsequently refers to Cymbalist's victim as "the strangled fly [*die erdrosselte Fliege*]" (*In the Beginning*, 223 / *Wozu noch Welt*, 241).

The narrator's continuing use of such anthropomorphizing terms for the dead insect point up his desire for "her." In the concluding lines of the story's penultimate section (8), directly following his conclusion that "Cymbalist, so much was clear, had bumped the fly off and was now alone again," the narrator muses that Cymbalist "doesn't need a female companion. The death of the fly does not bother him. He was humming, singing, and chirping. He had been venerating the beauty that governs the world outside. Happy Cymbalist!" (*In the Beginning*, 222–23 / *Wozu noch Welt*, 240–41). This train of thought continues in the opening lines of the final section (9), where he contrasts Cymbalist's callousness with his own apparent emotional investment in the murdered creature: "I, however, couldn't suppress a whistle of horror. The strangled fly [*die erdrosselte Fliege*] stirred in me all kinds of thoughts. I repeated as far as possible the words Cymbalist had dispensed to his roommate a few hours earlier" (*In the Beginning*, 223 / *Wozu noch Welt*, 241). The narrator recalls the words he had earlier followed with such fervent interest while believing his neighbor's companion to be a young woman. If, in contrast to Cymbalist's insouciance and rapprochement with the beauty of the external world, the narrator's melancholy desire seems only to deepen, I would argue that this is because it had never been a desire for a woman so much as a desire for desire—a desire to embody a (literary role of) the pining romantic hero.

Rosenfeld's denaturalization of eroticism in "Meine zwei Nachbarn"—his staging of it as literary fantasy and decidedly not as bodily impulse—is part of a wider meditation on the loss of eroticism in the ghetto. In a diary entry of February 23, 1943, Rosenfeld notes how eroticism (*Erotik*) has become a function of power. Only so-called "dignitaries" such as Jewish policemen who wield power (and can dole out work positions, coupons, clothing, and the like) are in the position to lead—one could say to wield—erotic lives. Trembling with excitement, these men leave their wives and demonstratively, publicly "strut with their cats" in the street (*In the Beginning*, 159 / *Wozu noch Welt*, 181).[27]

In contrast to ghetto "dignitaries," non-privileged inhabitants of the ghetto, as Rosenfeld reflects in two different entries in a notebook of thoughts and literary sketches begun in mid 1942, have essentially lost the erotic as a sphere of their existence. In a study for a planned story Rosenfeld notes various social and pragmatic reasons people might want to wed in the ghetto (pooling rations, for example), then goes on to contemplate the status of erotic love beyond such strategic social considerations. "That's the social condition. But, say the philosophers, why shouldn't a man and a woman find each other *an sich*? Why should the longing of the sexes for each other die out? Marriage in itself without social conditions? Without social causes? It is to be considered that eroticism has died completely. That this category of human life has been totally lost, and indeed must be regarded as something extraordinary! Just as the more delicate aspects of life were lost to us, just as music, literature [*Buch*], spring, flowers, and the like, so also love" (*In the Beginning*, 165–66 / *Wozu noch Welt*, 185; translation modified). It is noteworthy that Rosenfeld likens the loss of erotic life to the loss of literature and culture more generally given how entwined the categories of the literary and the erotic become in "Meine zwei Nachbarn." In a further entry from the same literary notebook, Rosenfeld associates eroticism with another key element of "Meine zwei Nachbarn"—dreams.[28] It is difficult to tell from this note whether Rosenfeld is recording something that actually occurred in the ghetto or sketching a scene for a literary story, or both:

> On the way to the post office, Koscielny Square, scraps of movie posters. . . . German text. We try to reconstruct. Names of well-known actors, then completely hidden "Broadway 1939!"
>
> We hear jazz, singers, revues, girl dancers, etc. A dream, an absurd dream. Will there ever be anything like this again? We talk about it, no lascivious word is uttered. We sense: Eroticism has been lost. (*In the Beginning*, 172–73 / *Wozu noch Welt*, 192; translation modified)

Rosenfeld's meditations on the loss of eroticism in the Lodz ghetto, and his likening of its lost status to both literature and "an absurd dream" help us appreciate the self-consciousness of his treatment in "Meine zwei Nachbarn" of the literary and the erotic through the guise of dreams and dreamlike states. Neither the erotic nor literature itself are givens in this constantly self-questioning erotic literary tale. Both are enacted at a remove from their former "natural" selves; both take the form of dreams of themselves, a point to which I will return in a moment.

From this point until the protagonist awakens from his dream a short while later, illogical, typically and stereotypically dreamlike incidents proliferate: he finds an egg and eats it raw, slurping it with delight; finds and drinks a bottle of cognac, and then, "done with the bottle, I bit into an apple that had somehow gotten into my hands" (*In the Beginning*, 223). He has discovered that "Cymbalist" has a completely unhidden radio (possessing a radio was both extraordinary and extraordinarily dangerous for a ghetto inhabitant, punishable by death)[29] and—ostensibly unphased—is about to turn it on when he notices that his neighbor has returned and is standing in the middle of the room, with blood stains on his clothing where a Jewish star would normally have been affixed. The narrator experiences bliss: "A feeling of being swept up by a blast of wind came over me. I felt as if some invisible being was pulling a silken cover over my ears. A profound sense of bliss permeated my whole being down to the tip of my toes" (*In the Beginning*, 223). He wants to go to "Cymbalist" but slips and awakens. In the story's final lines, the narrator states that his hunger has allowed him to enjoy the "most beautiful things":

"I groped for my pillow. Nothing had changed in my room. The water was steaming. The potatoes are done, the evening meal ready. For a second, my hunger made me savor the most beautiful things. Didn't I have reason to be happy [*Durfte ich nicht glücklich sein*]?" (*In the Beginning*, 223 / *Wozu noch Welt*, 241; translation modified).

Although the narrator is explicit that it was his hunger that allowed him to enjoy "the most beautiful things," it is significant that it is in fact the culinary elements of his dream that, at its conclusion, constitute the bridge back to waking life. "Slowly, ever so slowly, the pleasure of the apple and the taste of the cognac slipped away from me. My tongue was dry and bitter" (*In the Beginning*, 223 / *Wozu noch Welt*, 241). The tastes the narrator enjoys ultimately return full circle to the bitter acid taste (akin to lemon) he experienced just before the onset of his dream. His hunger, then, lets him experience beautiful things not only, and seemingly not primarily, by driving him to seek out foods and tastes in his dream that are lacking in his life. Rather, the hunger to which his waking life is so tightly tethered cuts him, so to speak, oneiric slack to try on roles and entertain desires in dreams that are not directly reducible to the desire for food. The narrator's two forms of hunger—his literal hunger for food and a more metaphorical hunger to play out the roles of (literary) subjectivities—are inversely correlated: it is ostensibly only when the protagonist is dreaming that he is free enough from his visceral hunger to be able to cast himself in various roles and live out literary fantasies. The bliss he experiences is not the result only of the cognac, apple, and egg he consumed in his dream but also of the literary roles of detective and romance hero that he was able to dream himself into.

WRITING LITERATURE BEYOND THE COLLAPSE OF ITS CONDITIONS OF POSSIBILITY

Rosenfeld, I am arguing, is thinking with literature about the mutations human status undergoes in the Lodz ghetto's conditions of extreme destitution. He explores, in a literary short story, subjectivity deprived of conditions and qualities so constitutive of literary characters that they are normally taken for granted. Such conditions and qualities include agency and integrity, recourse to private space, ambition, erotic desire, and social curiosity directed at other similarly individuated persons. "Meine zwei Nachbarn," that is, is both a short story and a meta-reflection in extremis on literature's fragile human conditions of possibility. In self-consciously pushing stock literary scenarios, characters, and plots beyond the realm of the social givens they presuppose, Rosenfeld draws attention to the grotesque incongruency between conventional literary worlds and the world of the ghetto. His ironic deployment of genre fiction thus takes the measure by literary means of the dehumanizing conditions of the Lodz ghetto. In this sense, "Meine zwei Nachbarn" is an experiment in continuing to write literature beyond the collapse of its social conditions of possibility.

But if literature for Rosenfeld is capacious enough to stage and yet survive its own demise, it can do so only by countenancing an ineluctable irony, which ranges from wry if poignant humor to moments of abysmal incommensurability between literary topoi and the circumstances in which they are activated. The melodrama and rifling through of stock literary tropes in the dream scene in Cymbalist's apartment provide ample instances of the former, as we have seen. The devastating opening paragraphs of the story are the most striking example of the latter:

> At that time, I lived close to the wire, there, where the ghetto ends and the city begins. The room I had been assigned was on the fourth floor of one of the many wooden buildings that everywhere lurk in the streets like barracks ornamented with scrollwork. They are grayish brown, dirty, dilapidated. They bear carved gables. They peer out of shattered windowpanes. The front sides have no lodgers. One stumbles over foul-smelling gutters and trudges up rotting wooden stairs. On the doors, a Star of David made of yellow cloth, affixed with thumbtacks. The names of the inhabitants are unknown. On the landing, hole-ridden, greasy buckets containing sand, refuse, rags.
>
> On the second floor, decaying weeds, potato peels, stinking, broken dishes. Above that, beneath the attic, dirty laundry hung on lines to dry. And everywhere, at the entrance to the building, on the stairs, in corners, opposite the apartment doors, human excrement of yesterday and today. . . .
>
> The building is uninhabited. No one lives there anymore. Just before I moved in, all the inhabitants were "resettled," that is, loaded onto horse-drawn carts and taken away—except for my neighbor. I hear sounds next door; the man himself I've never encountered. When I leave my room, he is asleep. When I come back, he is at work. Lying in bed, I hear him coming. My dear, good neighbor. He doesn't disturb me in my dozing. I am happy (*In the Beginning*, 215 / *Wozu noch Welt*, 233; translation modified).

Rosenfeld begins with something akin to a cinematic establishing shot, not, however, without some jarring shifts in focus. He begins in the first person and the past tense ("At that time, I lived close to the wire"), then quickly shifts from speaking about the particular building he lived in to describing such buildings in general, in the present tense (and in highly personified ways: they stand around or lurk [*herumstehen*]; they peer out of broken windows). The description then zooms in and zooms out simultaneously as the focus returns to the particular apartment house in which the narrator lives (*Die Vorderfront beherbergt niemand*), even as the specific first-person pronoun *ich* yields to the general third-person *man* (*Man stolpert über übelriechende Ausguß-Rinnen und schleppt sich über morsche Holzstiegen aufwärts*). Although the narrator can only be describing his own impressions upon first entering the building, he eschews the pronoun *ich* while inventorying what he found, and speaks in the first person again only in the sentence informing us that all of the building's inhabitants save for the narrator's neighbor have been *ausgesiedelt*—"resettled," the dissembling Nazi euphemism for deported to their deaths. By then, the narrator is ensconced in his room, listening to the sounds from the adjacent apartment. The psychological mystery involving these two (and eventually three) neighbors can begin.

The notebook (Heft 16) in which Rosenfeld wrote "Meine zwei Nachbarn" is dated August 4, 1943. As I have had occasion to note repeatedly in the pages of this book, chronology is crucial. While presumably written in August 1943, the story is likely set more than a year earlier. The first mass deportations from the Lodz ghetto began in early 1942, when between January 16 and January 29, 10,003 people were deported to Chelmno and gassed.[30] A month later, on February 22, a new wave of deportations began, and by April 2, 34,073 more people had been killed in Chelmno. Then between May 4 and May 15 a further 10,914 souls were deported to Chelmno and murdered, bringing the total number of those deported in early 1942 to 54,990, over a third of the Jewish population of the ghetto on January 1, 1942 (162, 681). West European Jews, and in particular West European Jewish women, who had been deported into the Lodz ghetto in autumn 1941, constituted the majority of those killed in the May 1942 deportations (among the 10,914 people deported in May, 10,161 were Western Jews; 7,039 women and 3,408 men).[31] Thus by May 15, 1942, about 61 percent of the Western European Jews in the ghetto before the deportations began in January had been murdered or driven to suicide. As historian Andrea Löw notes, many of the Western Jews who remained in the ghetto after the May 1942 deportations, and who had been living in collective houses since their arrival, were assigned apartments that had belonged to deportees. "At this time [after the May 1942 deportations], the Western Jews to whom no private apartment had yet been assigned moved out of the collective lodgings [*Sammelunterkünften*] into new homes, or more precisely: into the apartments of those who had been deported to the extermination camp" (Löw, *Juden im Getto*, 281–82). At the end of May 1942, Rosenfeld himself described this phenomenon: "May 30 [1942]. From the collective into private apartments. Nobody knows where he will be housed. Suddenly he gets an assignment from the housing office, hurries to get there with his belongings —some hole without furniture, without a stove, without a bed frame, filth everywhere. . . . Has to sleep on the bare floor. . . . If permitted to take a small chair or table, it's immediately used up as heating fuel" (*In the Beginning*, 63 / *Wozu noch Welt*, 92).

The apartments being assigned to these German Jews—filthy holes that they may have been—were made available only by the mass evacuation and murder of their erstwhile inhabitants. But did Rosenfeld know this? The question of when specific people in specific locations came to know of the Nazi mass killings of Jews is often a very complex one. Frequently diarists inside and outside ghettos record fairly accurate information about Nazi killing operations; but this information, albeit accurate, may appear to them to be just one rumor among many. Given how sealed the Lodz ghetto was, its inmates were generally less informed than their counterparts in Warsaw or Vilna. News of the killings at Chelmno reached the Warsaw ghetto in late January 1942, when "Szlamek," a religious Jew from Izbica who had been forced to work in the Sonderkommando in Chelmno, arrived in Warsaw after having managed to escape.[32] However, conveying that knowledge to anyone in the Lodz ghetto proved difficult. In interviews with Yechiel Szeintuch conducted in 1973, Shaye Shpigl, whose Lodz ghetto short stories are the topic of the following chapter, chapter 9, maintains that he was unaware of the fate of the deported, and even of his destination when he was taken to Auschwitz in August 1944![33] Yet evidence of mass murders did reach the inhabitants of the Lodz ghetto. In May 1942, large loads of clothing with bloodstains and Jewish stars reached the ghetto, along with personal items recalling those recently deported—fairly plain evidence that they had not been relocated somewhere but killed.

The mass killings of Lodz ghetto inhabitants continued in September 1942, when sixteen thousand people including the sick and hospitalized, the elderly, and children under ten were forcibly deported.[34] This deportation was the occasion of Chaim Rumkowski's infamous and shattering appeal on September 4, 1942, to parents to "give me your children" in the hopes of saving the rest of the ghetto. Parents hid their children, and the Jewish police were unable to round up the numbers demanded by the Nazis. Ultimately, the Gestapo took over and brutally carried out the deportations. It was in response to the absolute terror of the September 1942 roundups that Josef Zelkowicz wrote his harrowing text *In Those Nightmarish Days*.[35] Although the Lodz ghetto was not liquidated entirely in fall 1942 and was preserved as a site of slave labor until August 1944, the terrible mass deportations of September 1942 made clear to many that the deportees from Lodz were not being relocated, but murdered.[36] While seemingly set in spring of 1942, Rosenfeld's story was thus almost certainly written (or at the very least rewritten) after such knowledge.

As we have seen, Rosenfeld's *mise-en-scène* draws heavily on the detective genre. The protagonist takes up lodging in a vast crime scene, amidst the debris of the murdered. We are presented with evidence and objects. The description is heavy with clues that testify to recent life, however abject. We see dirty laundry, rotting weeds and potato peels, refuse and rags. And the human excrement from as recently as earlier the same day that the narrator moves in. The apartment doors bear only Jewish stars but no names.[37] The name of even the building's sole other living person, the narrator's neighbor, has to be fabricated and misassigned to the neighbor; as we have seen, "Cymbalist" is a ghostly echo, the name of a prior, prewar inhabitant of the neighbor's apartment. We know almost nothing about these people, not even their names. Our only clues as to their identities are the indices they have left behind in the form of laundry, rotting food, garbage, and excrement.

Even as Rosenfeld's narrative clearly echoes the murder mystery, he begins by presenting traces of murder on a scale too immense for this genre. The scale of this erasure of an entire building of anonymous inhabitants (along with, surely, those of many other buildings) simply exceeds the parameters of the detective genre, driven as it is by the motives of and intrigue among bourgeois individuals. Search as we might among the tattered and abject indices they have left behind, we will never be able to reconstruct who these people were. The sheer scale of the "evidence" to be taken in indeed seems temporarily to displace the narrator's recourse to the first-person pronoun: he cannot confront this scene as an *ich* but only as *man*.

Yet the mass murder to which these crime scenes attest is the ironic precondition for the scaled-down, individualized murder mystery to follow: It is only in the empty space the deported have left behind that private bourgeois interiors can even be approximated in Rosenfeld's pastiche. Only the mass deportation that has preceded this tale provides a version of the social space in which a detective story involving mysterious and curious neighbors can unfold. This is the brilliant and terrible irony that structures Rosenfeld's text: the iteration of the detective story that unfolds in "Meine zwei Nachbarn" confronts at the outset the impossibility of this very genre. Paradoxically, it is the collapse of the conditions of possibility of the detective-driven murder mystery that serves as the condition of possibility for Rosenfeld's iteration —or dismantling—of the genre. The extended dream scene in "Cymbalist's" room reiterates a related paradox in a sort of *mise en abyme*: the protagonist can embody literary roles (the detective, the romantic hero) only in his dream world but not his real world. Within the self-consciously literary text of "Meine zwei Nachbarn," such literary roles can only be dreamt of; they constitute a literary dream of literature aware of itself as a dream.

While Rosenfeld in "Meine zwei Nachbarn" does not engage in formal or stylistic innovation comparable to Babel in *Red Cavalry*, his use of the detective genre and his quotation of other popular genres in the dream scene do, like Babel, insert these miscellaneous generic elements into an anachronistic and impossible frame. The pursuit of grotesquely scaled-down and domesticated questions like, "Who is my neighbor?" "What is going on next door?" or "What has he done to his (sexy) female companion?" can only be undertaken because of the deportation of the building's inhabitants, whose experiences remain beyond the story's generic reach. Rosenfeld's strategy, rather than literary innovation per se, might thus be best described as self-conscious deployment of ready-made generic elements in circumstances that subvert them.

There is, however, one distinctly experimental motif running through Rosenfeld's text, namely variations on the statement, "Ich bin glücklich" (I am happy, I am lucky, I am fortunate), which conclude each of the text's nine numbered sections. Several instances of this refrain have featured in passages already quoted. The first four sections of the story end with the narrator's assessment, "Ich war glücklich" (I was happy, I was lucky), with the sections thereafter generally concluding with more equivocal variations. In the final sentence of section 5, the verb tense switches (or reverts, since, as we have seen, "Meine zwei Nachbarn" begins in the past tense) from the present to the past tense. After eavesdropping on Cymbalist's monologue to his female companion when Cymbalist, breaking with his normal routine, returns to his apartment at lunchtime (prompting gossip in his ressort of his having a "Geliebte" at home), the narrator listens with pleasure to him slurping the soup he has prepared: "A few seconds later I heard slurping and gurgling, all the noises that accompany the eating of a hungry man. Cymbalist filled his stomach and I was happy" (*In the Beginning*, 218; translation modified).[38] Why the narration switches (back) to the past tense at exactly this point (or at all) can be variously interpreted, but the story remains in the past tense from this point to the end.[39] The narrative's shifts from the past to the present and back to the past highlight an instability in the first-person narrator.

The subsequent four iterations of the "ich bin glücklich" motif further accentuate instability in the narrating persona. Section 6, in which the ostensible murder takes place, concludes on a supremely inconclusive note: "Those were Cymbalist's last words before he left the room, slammed the door, and went down the wooden stairs. I asked myself if I was happy now but got no answer" (*In the Beginning*, 219–20; translation modified).[40] The equivocal nature of what has just happened next door renders the narrator incapable of answering the question he poses to himself. In a manner of speaking, he simply does not know what kind of story he is in at that moment. The narrator is once again happy (or lucky) at the end of section 7 when—in his dream, as readers realize later—he discovers that his neighbor has forgotten to lock his door and that he will thus be able to enter the intriguing apartment: "I rattled it [Cymbalist's apartment door]. It was not locked. Cymbalist had forgotten . . . I was happy" (*In the Beginning*, 220 / *Wozu noch Welt*, 238).[41] We have seen that at the end of section 8, from within the romantic subplot that has been playing out in his dream, the narrator contrasts his own torment with what he views—with a seeming mixture of envy and contempt—as his neighbor's insouciant indifference to the demise of his female companion. "The death of the fly does not bother him. He was humming, singing, and chirping. He had been venerating the beauty that governs the world outside. Happy Cymbalist!" (*In the Beginning*, 223).[42] The last lines of the story (section 9), finally, depict the narrator awakening from his dream and leave us with a haunting question: "I groped for my pillow. Nothing had changed in my room. The water was steaming. The potatoes were done, the evening meal was ready. For a few seconds, my hunger had let me savor the most beautiful things. Wasn't I allowed to be happy?" (*In the Beginning*, 223; translation modified).[43]

One would have to strain mightily to read the narrator's recurrent commentary on his state of happiness or good fortune through a realist psychological lens. Even though the range of meanings of *glücklich* (happy, lucky, fortunate) lends a degree of plausibility to the narrator's use of the phrase in changing circumstances, the sheer repetition of the motif renders it a decidedly anti-naturalistic element; it tends to detach itself from the plane of the action and assert itself ever more insistently as a self-conscious literary device. In its persistent reiteration this motif functions less to assess the nameless protagonist's happiness than to denaturalize the speaking *ich* altogether. As the narrator attempts to live out impossible literary roles, to find his place in generic paradigms that seem radically incompatible with his circumstances, his recurrent assessment of his happiness may be read as a comment more on the characters and roles he is trying to inhabit than on the happiness of any stable psychological entity behind or beyond them. It is thus fitting that the narrator's various statements about the state of his happiness converge not on a definitive statement but on a question, "Durfte ich nicht glücklich sein?" (Wasn't I allowed to be happy?). The question is whether the conditions are given for the narrating *ich* to be happy. Do they permit him to inhabit any of the roles he has dreamed forth? What refuge can literature offer?

Although "Meine zwei Nachbarn" is narrated from beginning to end by this first-person narrator, we ascertain virtually no details about him. Whereas we learn that the narrator's neighbor has a position of some privilege in his ressort—the workers there refer to him as their "boss"—we find out nothing about where the narrator works. The opening section mentions that when the narrator leaves his room his neighbor is asleep and that when he returns home the neighbor is at work, but the rest of the text suggests few if any regular daily rhythms. Despite narrating in the first person, the narrator remains a cipher. The status of the narrating *ich* is thus always in question, less an integral psychological subject than a literary figure manqué. He is a figure who at the close of each section checks in on his (literary) status: Am I in a happy story? Is the scenario I have fabricated out of—or contra—my circumstances a happy one? Am I even—can I be—a literary figure? Or am "I" and the scenarios I am involved in just the dream of a dream, the literary dream of being a viable literary figure?

The pronounced literary self-consciousness—and self-reflexive skepticism—of "Meine zwei Nachbarn" distinguishes it fundamentally from the sorts of narratives and scenarios it pastiches, including earlier stories of alienated urban individuals by Rosenfeld himself. I thus disagree with Feuchert, who has written extensively on Rosenfeld, when he stresses an essential continuity between Rosenfeld's most elaborated extant ghetto story and the concerns with modern isolation and alienation in his 1920 story collection *Tage und Nächte* in general and the story from that collection "Das Mietzimmer" (The rental room) in particular. Feuchert sees Rosenfeld in "Meine zwei Nachbarn" as transposing motifs from his earlier novella into the ghetto: the protagonists of both stories are isolated and alienated; both look down at people in the streets from their apartment windows, and listen to neighbors through walls; and both texts prominently feature flies. Feuchert reads these intertextual similarities as adding up to an extreme intensification in the ghetto story of themes, and of the basic plight of the alienated modern individual, that were already at the heart of the 1920 story set in Vienna: "The first-person narrator of 'Meine zwei Nachbarn' is—like the narrator of 'Das Mietzimmer'—one of the lonely people of the modern world: the fact that he is incarcerated in the ghetto makes the issue much worse, but it changes little in the fundamental problematic [*aber an der Grunddisposition ändert das wenig*]" (Feuchert, *Oskar Rosenfeld*, 382).[44] Such a reading of "Meine zwei Nachbarn" as an extreme version of what Rosenfeld was doing all along in his stories—ghetto existence as a cruelly intensified iteration of modern loneliness and alienation—fails to appreciate adequately how genocide in "Meine zwei Nachbarn"—the deportation of the entire building's inhabitants—is what creates both the architectural and the literary space for the action and for Rosenfeld's quotations of literary commonplaces—including his own.

My reading of Rosenfeld as self-consciously mobilizing fragments—or shards—of generic tropes (of detective fiction, the thriller, romance, and the fantasy/horror tale) makes the relationship between "Nachbarn" and "Mietzimmer" appear in a crucially different light. The very categories and building blocks of the 1920 story of modern alienation (private subject, living space, relationship between the alienated individual and wider society, etc.) can only be (grotesquely) approached in the ghetto tale because of the deportation of the inhabitants of the recently overcrowded house, which created the (negative) space for the narrator and his literary scenarios to inhabit. Rather than merely intensifying modern literary commonplaces, Rosenfeld's ghetto story revisits and profoundly reevaluates them. "Nachbarn" confronts the constitutive components of genre fiction and the conditions of possibility of modern subjectivity they presuppose from the radically altered vantage point of the ghetto.

Rosenfeld's self-conscious deployment of generic conventions to take the measure of what has become of human subjectivity in the Lodz ghetto comes to a head in the story's denouement when the protagonist awakens and much of the preceding action is revealed to have been a fever dream. In this way, Rosenfeld's story presents, finally, a meta-generic puzzle, a contest of sorts, in which two genres vie to frame what has occurred: the murder mystery, and the macabre fantasy/horror tale that equivocates between dream and reality—such as Gustav Meyrink's popular 1914 novel *Der Golem* and Robert Wiene's seminal 1920 film *Das Cabinet des Dr. Caligari.*[45] At stake, I would suggest, is the question of what sort of narrative, or what structure of meaning, can accommodate this tale set in the Lodz ghetto. At the heart of the issue of generic framing lies the problem of to what extent the scale of the ambient violence is compatible with the individual experience that is the traditional focus of narrative literature, a question that haunts "Meine zwei Nachbarn" from beginning to end.

Caligari ends with a similar twist, but the distinction between the revelation at the conclusion of Wiene's film and Rosenfeld's story is all-important. In Caligari, the protagonist, Franzis, who has narrated the terrifying tale of his pursuit of the serial murderer Caligari, turns out to be a paranoid patient in Dr. Caligari's mental asylum. In a famous critique of the film's ideological thrust, Siegfried Kracauer maintains that the frame story reduces the protagonist's anti-conformist horror at a mad authoritarian to the mere symptomatology of a paranoid mind.[46] Rosenfeld's narrative ostensibly follows this script but turns it inside out. In Caligari, a private individual dreams forth an authoritarian world gone mad, but with the concluding shift of frame viewers are liberated from the protagonist's private nightmare. In Rosenfeld's story what the narrator dreams is that he is the protagonist in a human-scale mystery involving apartment neighbors, replete with thriller and romantic subplots. He awakens to realize that his ability to relate to the ghetto and its violence as a sleuth gathering clues en route to resolving a mysterious murder has been a private hallucination. The scale of the violence cannot be contained within the generic parameters of the bourgeois detective story, and the structural violence of the ghetto undermines the very integrity of the would-be sovereign sleuth. Indeed, the protagonist's self-image in the role of a mystery-solving detective (as well as fighting hero and lover) has been engendered by his wasting, hungering body. If in Caligari, the systematic madness is ultimately contained within the private individual and thereby rendered harmless, in Rosenfeld's narrative the very possibility of being a conventional protagonist is ultimately overwhelmed both by the context of mass murder and by the extreme deprivation that allows him to play literary roles only in fevered hallucinations.

CHAPTER 9
GHETTO GOTHIC
SHAYE SHPIGL'S UMHEYMLEKHE TALES FROM THE LODZ GHETTO

I want to speak to my child, the last words [reyd] for her last, lonely road. Not to bid farewell, not to take leave, for the dead do not leave us; they are among us and we breathe in their non-being. Their non-being hovers over our thoughts like silken mists hanging over a quietly babbling stream on the cusp of dawn before the sun's golden birth.
—Shaye Shpigl, "Mayn tekhterl" (Szeintuch and Solomon, *Yesha'yahu Shpigel,* 220)

I'm not a chronicler; I don't record annals.
—Shaye Shpigl, interview with Yechiel Szeintuch
(Szeintuch and Solomon, *Yesha'yahu Shpigel,* 375)

Born in 1906, Shaye Shpigl (also known and published as Yeshaye Shpigl, Yeshayahu Shpigel, and Isaiah Spiegel) was a native of Balut, the impoverished, predominantly Jewish suburb where the ghetto was eventually established in Lodz (or Lodzsh [Yiddish], Łódź [Polish], or Litzmannstadt, as the occupying German regime renamed the city).[1] In fact, he had married Rebeka Ungier and moved with her into an apartment near the center of the city only a few months before the outbreak of World War II. The establishment of the ghetto forced them to "return" to his old neighborhood, where his parents still lived. Shpigl spent over four years in the Lodz ghetto, from its inception in May 1940 until its end. He had various jobs under the auspices of the ghetto administration including a position in the statistics department, which helped him and his family evade deportation until the very last transport from the ghetto in August 1944, to Auschwitz.[2] Shpigl's infant daughter died of starvation in the ghetto only months after it was sealed.[3] His parents and three of his sisters were murdered in Auschwitz, and his wife died in Stutthof. Shpigl, however, survived and returned to Poland, initially to his native Lodz. Before the war he had earned his livelihood by teaching Yiddish and Yiddish literature in the Bund's secular Yiddish school system, TSYSHO (Tsentrale Yidishe Shul Organizatsye / Central Yiddish School Organization), and from 1945 to 1948 he taught in the I. L. Peretz School in Lodz. He lived in Warsaw from

1948 to 1950 before moving to Israel in 1951. In Israel, he continued to write prolifically in Yiddish until his death in 1990.[4]

Shpigl had published a book of poems, *Mitn ponem tsu der zun* (Facing the sun), in 1930 and continued to publish poems as well as his first prose pieces in Yiddish newspapers throughout the 1930s. He had completed a Yiddish translation of Byron's *Cain* and had two further books of his own ready for publication when the Second World War broke out—a second book of poems and a collection of stories about Jewish weavers in Balut, a milieu he knew well as his father had been a Balut weaver. All of these manuscripts were lost (Szeintuch, "Ghetto Literature," xiii).

Shpigl was one of the most prolific writers in the Lodz ghetto. While interned there he continued to write both poetry and, especially, short stories about ghetto life. Indeed, no other writer in any ghetto wrote as many literary stories as Shpigl. Many of these manuscripts were destroyed in various ways. Shpigl took a number of his ghetto manuscripts with him when he was deported to Auschwitz, where they were taken from him and destroyed (Szeintuch, "Ghetto Literature," xiii). However, as I mention in this book's introduction, he was able to recover some of his ghetto manuscripts after the war. Shortly before being deported, Shpigl and his father buried many of his manuscripts in the basement of his parents' building.[5] Upon his return to Lodz he managed to recover sixteen of them. Recovering them was not as simple as returning to the cellar of his parents' old parterre flat and digging them up, however. When Shpigl returned to Lodz in mid-June 1945, a Pole was already living in the apartment. Shpigl asked for permission to go into the cellar, and the Pole replied, "We've already looked; we thought you had hidden gold or money, but we found only some papers with writing we couldn't read."[6] Shpigl and a brother who had also survived spent "a few days" combing through the trash heap in the courtyard, where the new occupants of his parents' apartment had discarded his manuscripts, recovering as many pages as they could.[7]

All of the manuscripts that Shpigl was able to recover are set in the early period of the Lodz ghetto, before the first mass deportations to Chelmno between January and May 1942. They do not refer to any events that occurred after the summer of 1941. Since numerous other manuscripts Shpigl wrote in the ghetto were destroyed, we cannot be certain whether he wrote stories while still in the ghetto that were set after summer 1941.[8] Only two of these wartime texts, however, were written in something like immediate proximity to the events they depict: the story "Avrashe geyt tsum nieman" (Avrashe goes to the Nieman River) and (parts of) Shpigl's address to his recently dead daughter, "Mayn tekhterl" (My little daughter).[9] The sixteen extant ghetto manuscripts bear no date, so we cannot be certain of precisely when Shpigl wrote them; but according to Shpigl the other fourteen stories were written at a certain temporal remove from the events they depict, most of them in 1943 or early 1944, a period of relative calm after the deportations of 1942 and before the final liquidation of the ghetto in August 1944.[10] Although according to Shpigl virtually every story he wrote has some basis in a scene or event he witnessed personally in the Lodz ghetto, such an event would take on "quite different dimensions" in the context of the literary text he would build around it (Szeintuch and Solomon, *Yesha'yahu Shpigel*, 353). Indeed, Shpigl often observed the events that provided the real kernel of his stories from a certain esthetic distance even initially. Shpigl recounted to the scholar of Yiddish literature Yechiel Szeintuch his practice of strolling in the ghetto after work hours, looking for interesting material to write about.

> I derived great, great writerly delight from wandering in the ghetto after work, in the afternoon hours, in the evening hours, and observing—observing everywhere: in the little alleys, in the little houses, and talking with people, listening. From all these experiences, encounters, and sights certain realistic seeds, as it were, were here and there planted with me [*hobn zikh bay mir opgeshtelt*], which I later wrote down; and from that seed the pale plants of my story sprouted [*un arum dem zoymen zenen oyfgegangen di blase flantsn fun mayn novele*]. (Szeintuch and Solomon, *Yesha'yahu Shpigel*, 353)

As Szeintuch has argued, the esthetic distance that Shpigl maintained to events allowed him to treat harrowing topics and situations for which people who were immediately caught up in them may not have been able to muster words. While viewing the awful realities of ghetto existence through an esthetic prism may have distorted the actual events that served as the impetus for Shpigl's stories, it surely helped him depict them at all rather than succumbing to silence.[11]

In this chapter I read Shaye Shpigl not only as a recorder of ghetto life but as the literary writer he tenaciously remained throughout more than four years interned in the Lodz ghetto. Shpigl's project was not to record scenes of ghetto life in an immediate way but rather to draw on a wide range of literary models to write well-crafted prose fiction that illuminates aspects of the human experience of the ghetto. His stories make pronounced use of symbolism and various genre conventions including, as I examine in detail, those of gothic literature. As Shpigl described himself in his extensive 1973 interview(s) with Szeintuch—a statement that serves as one of this chapter's two epigraphs—"I'm not a chronicler; I don't record annals" (*Ikh bin nisht keyn khroniker, ikh fir nisht keyn pinkes*; Szeintuch and Solomon, *Yesha'yahu Shpigel*, 375).[12] Both from his esthetic and from statements regarding his understanding of himself as an author, moreover, it is clear that Shpigl subscribed to a humanistic conception of the institution of literature, and that by continuing not merely to write but to write *literature* in the ghetto and after, he saw himself resisting the sort of dehumanization that the Germans were systematically imposing on the Jews.[13]

Shpigl published most of the sixteen recovered manuscripts, usually after significant revision, in the years after the war, beginning with the story collection *Malkhes geto: noveln* (*Ghetto Kingdom*, Lodz, 1947) and continuing with *Shtern ibern geto* (Stars over the ghetto, Paris, 1948), *Mentshn in thom: geto-noveln* (People in the abyss: Ghetto stories, Buenos Aires, 1949), *Likht funem opgrunt: geto-noveln* (Light from the abyss: Ghetto stories, New York, 1952), and *Vint un vortslen* (Wind and roots, New York, 1955). Shpigl reconstructed other stories from memory, but surely also revised and rewrote them in the process.[14] For the purposes of this study, where I am centrally concerned with literature written in (and not only about) ghettos, I focus on those manuscripts that Shpigl recovered from the trash heap. These were published in unrevised form in a critical edition by Yechiel Szeintuch and Vera Solomon in 1995, five years after Shpigl's death.[15]

In the above-mentioned volumes of ghetto stories published in the late 1940s and 1950s, Shpigl was not forthcoming about what he had written in the ghetto and what he had written or rewritten after the war. Beginning with his second volume of stories, *Shtern ibern geto,* he also adopted the practice of assigning a date between 1940 and 1944 to virtually all the ghetto stories he published, including those for which no manuscript was preserved and that he thus not only revised but completely reconstructed (or possibly composed *tout court*) after the war.[16] Shpigl's postwar books gave the erroneous impression that the stories as published were the texts he was able to recover, which contributed to the amazement that prominent Yiddish literary critics including Shmuel Charney, Jacob Glatshtein, and Alexander Mukdoni (pen-name of Alexander Kappel) expressed at the literary elegance and artfulness of Shpigl's stories (ostensibly) written in the Lodz ghetto.[17]

SHPIGL AND ENGLISH LITERATURE

While postwar literary critics at times singled out as most noteworthy and as possessing the greatest literary—and memorial—value works and passages that Shpigl wrote after the war, the texts that Shpigl wrote in the Lodz ghetto were emphatically and self-consciously literary in their own right. Shpigl's wartime stories form an extensive and varied corpus, and doing anything like justice to each text would far exceed the scope of this chapter. I wish to focus instead on just one literary tradition or modality, albeit a prominent one, that Shpigl draws on in his literary engagement with the extreme circumstances of the Lodz ghetto, namely gothic literature.

Shpigl's recourse to gothic has gone virtually unremarked. While neglect of this aspect of Shpigl's wartime writings is part and parcel of the relative neglect of Shpigl's work in general, the less prominent role that anglophone literature tended to play for Yiddish writers in Eastern Europe (for whom Polish, Russian, German, and even French literary traditions generally provided more immediate reference points) may have hindered due appreciation of Shpigl's far-ranging deployment of gothic tropes. Although gothic literature has had "legs" and has achieved a truly global reach, it originated in the British context with Horace Walpole's 1764 *The Castle of Otranto*; and even as several European literatures feature numerous and significant gothic works, the most widely recognized classics plotting the evolution of the genre, including the multi-volume novels Ann Radcliffe published in the 1790s, Mary Shelly's *Frankenstein* (1818), Charlotte Brontë's *Jane Eyre* (1847), Robert Louis Stevenson's *The Strange Case of Dr. Jekyll and Mr. Hyde* (1886), Oscar Wilde's *The Picture of Dorian Gray* (1890), Bram Stoker's *Dracula* (1897), and the ghost stories of M. R. James (originally published between 1904 and 1925), also come out of the British tradition. The likewise anglophone tradition of American gothic, including Edgar Allan Poe's "The Fall of the House of Usher" (1839) and other stories, and Henry James's *The Turn of the Screw* (1898), also contributed importantly to the genre. Whereas it was relatively rare for East European Jewish writers to be immersed in English literature, Shpigl not only read English but the English language and anglophone literature were for many years his passion.

Shpigl's intensive engagement with anglophone literature began when he wrote to an aunt who had emigrated to America before World War I, asking her to send him a book to help him learn English. She sent him a dictionary by

Alexander Harkavy. Using the dictionary along with a Langensheidt German-English primer and a great deal of perseverance, he advanced to the point of being able to read literary texts.[18] Shpigl began with Oscar Wilde's early stories, and eventually tackled his novels, including *The Picture of Dorian Gray*.[19] As I have already alluded to, Shpigl eventually prepared a translation of Byron's *Cain*. His translation was scheduled to be published in the publishing house of the prestigious Yiddish literary journal *Literarishe bleter* (the coming publication was even noted in one of the last prewar issues of *Literarishe bleter*), but Germany's invasion of Poland interrupted those plans, and, to his great disappointment, Shpigl lost the manuscript of his translation during the war.[20]

In addition to Yiddish, Polish, and English, Shpigl read German fluently (Szeintuch and Solomon, *Yesha'yahu Shpigel*, 290) and read (but could not write) Hebrew. His formal education was limited. He attended a secular Yiddish *folkshul*, six years of *gymnasium*, and beyond that had pedagogical training to become a teacher. Yet what he considered his "university" study were the long years he spent reading at the Lodz city library, which had tens of thousands of books in a great many languages (Szeintuch and Solomon, 274).[21] Shpigl generally spent whole days in the library ("where you could sit from eight in the morning until nine at night"; Szeintuch and Solomon, 274); he would arrive in the morning and leave when the library was closing (Szeintuch and Solomon, 275). Shpigl followed this routine for a good decade, beginning in 1922 and continuing until 1932 (Szeintuch and Solomon, 276). He had a sympathetic interlocutor in the Polish socialist library director, Jan Augustyniak, who granted Shpigl access to all the books in the library's collection, including rare editions and other volumes not regularly lent out (Szeintuch and Solomon, 277).

The Lodz city library was also a place where Shpigl acquired years of practice reading and writing while hungry. Having negligible income in those years, he would spend whole days at the library with only a roll for sustenance. When the library's other patrons—mostly university students—left for lunch at one o'clock, Shpigl, who could not afford to eat anywhere, would stay behind and eat his roll. Although he does not comment on this expressly, it seems likely that this long familiarity with engaging in intellectual and literary pursuits while hungry prepared Shpigl to some extent for the years he would remain active as a writer in the far direr circumstances of the Lodz ghetto.

WHY GOTHIC IN THE GHETTO?

Given the fact that he characterized English literature as his passion during his hungry decade spent reading in the Lodz city library and that his gateway into English literature was Wilde's *Picture of Dorian Gray*, it seems virtually inconceivable that Shpigl's reading would not have extended to other anglophone works of gothic literature. However, my argument is not that Shpigl's use of gothic devices and topoi can positively be traced back to any specific set of works. By the 1920s and 1930s, when Shpigl was engaged in intensive reading in many languages—English, Yiddish, Polish, German, and, to a lesser extent, Hebrew—the vocabulary of gothic literature had become sufficiently widespread that its portable toolbox of literary techniques would certainly have been available to a litterateur like Shpigl, even if his enthusiasm for British literature had not (as, again, it very likely had) attuned him more acutely to the genre's possibilities. As Jerrold Hogle has argued, gothic themes, tropes, and representational strategies have proliferated globally in large part because gothic literature, from Walpole's *The Castle of Otranto* on, pastiches different historical eras and styles; gothic was in this sense proto postmodern from its inception.[22] It is, among other things, a highly conventionalized form of citation and is thus highly citable in turn in different contexts. As Hogle notes, the gothic has been able to migrate from its "Anglo-Western beginnings into other ethnicities within the Western world" and to "vaul[t] over international boundaries" in part because it was "never solidly rooted anyway" ("Introduction," 16).

Beyond the general critical neglect of Shpigl's writings compounded by the seeming distance between East European Yiddish writing and the (British) gothic tradition, the inescapable aura of trashiness that attaches to the genre may have further worked against critical attention to Shpigl's deployment of gothic tropes. To guardians of high culture, gothic literature is, in a word, embarrassing. It is popular, recycles well-worn topoi, and feeds the consumerist literary market with danger, thrills, and exotic enticements.[23] Gothic is not only literary but ostentatiously literary, to the point of often bordering on kitsch. The taint of such associations may have steered Shpigl's readers away from dwelling on gothic elements in his ghetto stories, however pronounced they are in both the manuscript versions and the postwar texts. Shpigl's early critics understandably preferred to stress his lofty literariness, the "aristocratic" (Glatstein) and "lyrical" (Charney) quality of his stories, their undeniable moments of remarkable beauty and the experience of transcendence they seem to offer, both to characters in the stories and to readers.[24]

Definitions of literary value are, of course, historically contingent, and virtually all the significant developments in literary and cultural inquiry since the 1970s have, to the relief of some and the chagrin of others, eroded, redistributed, and pluralized standards of literary value and redefined what sort of literary and wider cultural dynamics are worthy of serious attention.[25] When we consider what literary tools the gothic genre makes available, it makes perfect sense why Shpigl would avail himself of them to confront, in literature, the extreme, terrifying, and bewildering circumstances of the Lodz ghetto. A number of celebrated authors have turned to gothic elements in general, and to ghosts and haunting in particular, to grapple with the experience and legacies of modernity's most harrowing and traumatizing forms of violence, including Elizabeth Bowen in her wartime ghost stories portraying London during the Blitz, collected in *The Demon Lover* (1945); Toni Morrison in her treatment of American slavery and its aftermath in *Beloved* (1987); and Isaac Bashevis Singer in a number of texts about the Holocaust and its haunting, ghostly afterlives, such as the stories "A Wedding at Brownsville" (English 1964), "The Lecture" (English 1967), and the novel *Enemies: A Love Story* (Yiddish 1966; English 1972).[26] More recently, Jesmyn Ward has used the ghost story to explore the ravages of the systematic incarceration of African American men in her novel *Sing, Unburied, Sing* (2017). Gothic has also been one of the key literary means for negotiating postcolonial histories, identities, and entanglements, as novels from Tayeb Salih's *Season of Migration to the North* (1966) to Viet Thanh Nguyen's *The Sympathizer* (2015) and *The Committed* (2021), and the emergence in recent decades of the critical concept of "postcolonial gothic," attest.[27]

A number of features of gothic literature make it particularly apt for adaptation to the circumstances of the ghetto. Gothic is, arguably, most fundamentally about death and dying.[28] It is also centrally about boundaries, (failed) projects of containment, and uncanny proximities between different realms and worlds. The gothic tradition frequently dramatizes the mutual interpenetration of the everyday and the extreme; of the familiar and the irrational and unfathomable. All these basic gothic ingredients readily served a writer like Shpigl in his literary treatment of the Lodz ghetto. The Nazi system of ghettoization was obviously about violently imposing spatial boundaries between populations. Non-Jews residing in areas marked off to become the ghetto were forced out, and Jews living outside those small areas were forced into them, whether from a few blocks away in the same city, from near or distant East European towns, or from different countries. The boundary between the ghetto and the city was spatial but entailed existential distinctions regarding access to housing, schooling, employment and income, medical care, and the most basic nourishment. The boundary between the ghetto and the rest of the world could also take on metaphysical significance, as discernible in the title story of Shpigl's first postwar volume of ghetto stories, "Ghetto Kingdom" ("Malkhes geto"), or in fellow Lodz ghetto inmate Oskar Rosenfeld's musing that "In the beginning was the ghetto" (*Am Anfang war das Ghetto*).[29] As ghetto inmates succumbed en masse to epidemics and starvation and were ultimately deported to killing centers, the ghetto boundary became one between life and death.

Freud's concept of the uncanny has played a prominent role in discussions of gothic literature, and with good reason.[30] Freud's famous essay "The Uncanny" ("Das Unheimliche," 1919) explores the anxiety that occurs when what was meant to be contained through processes of repression manages to return to consciousness, paradigmatically in the form of the dead returning to life and the living being reduced to a corpse-like state. It is a meditation on borders that demark the rational from the irrational and on the anxiety engendered by the mutual contamination of these domains. Freud's essay is also a work of literary criticism of a gothic (or, as the German and French variants of the genre are more commonly referred to, fantastic) story, E. T. A. Hoffmann's "Der Sandmann" ("The Sandman"; 1816) in which Freud finds the psychological dynamics of the uncanny paradigmatically at work. Freud opens his reflection on the uncanny, however, with an analysis of the shifting boundaries demarcated by the word *unheimlich* itself. He notes that the meanings of *heimlich* (of the home, homely, and, by extension, that which is associated with the security of the domestic space) and *unheimlich* (the non-domestic, or that which belongs or comes from outside the home) are mutually constitutive in their opposition. Yet the clear semantic boundary between these two opposing terms does not hold, as the word *heimlich* harbors within itself unheimlich connotations: *heimlich* also means "secret" (what is kept within the home rather than shared publicly) and so frequently coincides with its ostensible opposite: instead of connoting what is familiar and safe within the domestic sphere, it refers to something hidden, secret, unknown, beyond view—and threatening.[31] The very semantic field of the heimlich has an unheimlich tendency to flip into its opposite.

The bulk of Freud's analysis of Hoffmann's tale is grounded in his theory of the Oedipus complex and the role of castration anxiety within it. Yet while Freud's reflection on *das Unheimliche* tends to move away from its initial parsing of the literal meanings of the word *unheimlich*, Shpigl's literary meditations on the Lodz ghetto return us to the literal register of Freud's starting point. Shpigl's Yiddish term *umheymlekh* resonates like no other word throughout his ghetto texts. Even when he at times uses *umheymlekh* in highly metaphorical ways, the term remains tethered to a literal loss of home. In a paper given at the September 1945 conference of the Central Jewish Historical Commission, Nachman Blumental identified the loss of home as among the most recurrent motifs in Yiddish literature written under the German occupation.[32] The historically specific existential reality of the suddenly and violently imposed condition of homelessness undergirds other, less tangible forms of unfathomable strangeness in Shpigl's wartime stories.

As Carol Margaret Davison argues, what secular modernity tries by various means to contain and deny, and what inevitably returns in haunting ways, is death itself. "Death serves as the quintessential emblem of the Freudian uncanny in the Gothic; while being 'of the home' and familiar, it also remains secret, concealed, and unfamiliar" (Davison, "Introduction," 2). Death becomes uncanny in modernity—and accordingly in gothic literature—precisely because "the advent of secular modernity, the putative triumph of Reason, and the unsettling of religious certainties during the Enlightenment about the existence of God, the soul, and the afterlife, constituted a type of cultural trauma that alienated us from an earlier familiarity with death while giving rise to greater anxieties and uncertainties about mortality, loss, and remembrance" ("Introduction," 2–3). Death becomes qualitatively more terrifying as Enlightenment reason displaces the religious practices and belief systems that guaranteed continuity of the soul across the barrier of death and thus, in both a literal and a figurative sense had domesticated death, rendered it heimlich—intimate and experienced in the home. The secular transformation of death into an imminent and no longer a transcendent phenomenon, the absolutizing of death as an ultimate, awful terminus, causes death to become banished from the home, medicalized, sanitized, professionalized, compartmentalized; in a word, repressed. Encounters with death henceforth take uncanny forms; death returns to haunt us. As Davison argues, gothic literature has served in modernity as a site for different forms of mourning in the wake of historical traumas such as the French Revolution, which prominently displayed the corpses it prodigiously produced.[33] Gothic literature, that is, mourns not only death but the loss of frameworks for relating to death; it mourns the loss of the ability to mourn. For Jerrold E. Hogle gothic literature is irreducibly ambivalent and contentious; it is "Janus-faced," looking both forward as a decidedly modern literary form, and backward to the belief systems and transcendent causalities of the past, whose loss it mourns. "The ever-extending tentacles of modern enterprise are always haunted by the doubts, conflicts, and blurring of normative boundaries that the Gothic articulates in every form it assumes because, at its best, it is really about the profoundly conflicted core of modernity itself."[34]

In the strange and terrifying new realm of the ghetto, prewar certainties collapsed, social semantics were abruptly and radically rewritten; and cultural codes, meanings, and practices, not least as they pertained to death on an unprecedented and unmanageable scale, became radically unstable. Shpigl's various depictions of the ever-present eeriness of the ghetto; his preoccupation with boundaries and with what can and cannot traverse them; and his grappling with death and dying in gothic literary keys show us that the gothic genre's longstanding obsession with modern death and the equivocation or collapse of normative categories and structures of meaning resonated deeply with him as he confronted the culturally chaotic, socially upended, and deadly circumstances of the ghetto.

The ghetto in Lodz was the most hermetically sealed of all Nazi ghettos. Unlike in Warsaw, there was virtually no smuggling of food into the ghetto and no (slave) laborers who left the ghetto regularly for work assignments. The boundary between the ghetto located in the Balut suburb and the city of Lodz was nearly absolute. And yet the city of Lodz was so near.[35] Many people, including Shpigl himself, had been driven out of their apartments in Lodz into the ghetto. Their former homes and lives seemed both tantalizingly close and a world apart. In several of his stories, Shpigl dwells on the interplay of intimacy and estrangement that resulted from the radical removal from a still-proximate place and time. In doing so, he develops a historically specific iteration of the literary uncanny: ghetto gothic.[36]

JEWISH HOMES AND UMHEYMLEKHKEYT: SHPIGL'S HISTORICAL UNCANNY

As I have already signaled, a significant number of Shpigl's manuscript stories use a literalized version of the quintessential gothic trope of the uncanny to explore the multidimensional experience of dislocation from one's home. The literalization of umheymlekhkeyt in these stories is itself uncanny, for it reverses a typically escapist trajectory of gothic literature, which tends to move from depictions of everyday reality into eerie and fantastic realms. Shpigl's stories, conversely, bring the literary unsettlement of the gothic genre, its evocation of otherworldly strangeness, to bear on a very specific historical experience: interment in the Lodz ghetto. The strange and otherworldly realm conjured in gothic texts becomes uncannily grounded in a reality that literalizes the frisson-inducing tropes central to the gothic mode—death, corpses, the sudden transformation of domestic safety into existential danger. Shpigl's stories engender all the potent associations of unsettlement for which the literary trope of the uncanny or das Unheimliche does shorthand, yet they make this realm of literary associations confront the historical experience of extreme dislocation and danger that the Nazi ghetto system entailed. Shpigl's stories, that is, signal that what finally is umheymlekh is the historical experience of Jews being severed from their homes, and indeed from the existential ground of home per se. Shpigl performs an uncanny operation on the literary uncanny by bringing the otherworldly fantastic literary realm face to face with its terrifying historical double. In Shpigl's stories, gothic topoi do not haunt reality; rather, the reality of the Lodz ghetto haunts the gothic. The six Lodz ghetto short stories by Shpigl that I analyze in this section powerfully exemplify his uncanny operation of historicizing uncanny gothic literary tropes.

A literalized umheymlekhkeyt figures prominently in Shpigl's story "Der yid yosi-ber fun dolne yari," which is set earliest chronologically among Shpigl's ghetto manuscript stories—at the beginning, in fact, of the German invasion of Poland. Yosi-Ber is a rarity: a son of a tenant farmer (*an arendar*) in the western Polish village of Dolny-Yary, he and his wife Dobbe have become Jewish peasants living among Polish peasants. Aside from occasional brief visits to the nearest shtetl for holidays or to recite kaddish for his parents among a quorum of Jews, Yosi-Ber has few ties left to Jews or Jewishness, even as his connection to the local landscape and the rhythms of rural life—the soil, farm animals, the poplars, and the waters of the Varta river—has become profound. Yosi-Ber and Dobbe have no children, and while they had intermittently entertained the idea of moving to a city "so as not to become coarsened [*fargrebt*] here with the handful of peasants, and to be among Jews" (Szeintuch and Solomon, *Yesha'yahu Shpigel*, 134), each time Yosi's father would well up in his memory and ask him, "Where will you settle in the world? Your father was also here and your grandfather was here. You have no son to recite kaddish for you [*Keyn kadish iz bay dir nishto*]. Stay here and love the earth and the earth will love you" (Szeintuch and Solomon, *Yesha'yahu Shpigel*, 134).

As the local peasants join the caravan of Poles passing through Dolny-Yary from points west in flight from the invading German army, Dobbe admonishes Yosi-Ber to flee with them to Warsaw before the Germans arrive and kill them both; but he refuses. "I won't run away from here, Dobbe. (A man can't run away from his fate)" (Szeintuch and Solomon, *Yesha'yahu Shpigel*, 135).[37] Ahead of the advancing German soldiers, Polish ethnic Germans arrive at Yosi-Ber and Dobbe's home and torture and kill him, forcing him to dance by stabbing at his bare feet with bayonets. Dobbe hides with their dogs in the cellar for two days, and when she emerges Yosi-Ber is nowhere to be found. The dogs lead her to a mound of earth where Yosi-Ber lies buried.

Shpigl's repeated use of the word *umheymlekh*—three times within the story's first two pages, twice in the first paragraph—helps to establish the atmosphere of profound unsettlement. The inhabitants of Dolny-Yary feel the very ground beneath their feet shifting, but the Polish peasants and "the Jew Yosi-Ber" from Dolny-Yary experience this loss of home differently. The opening sentence reads: "From the middle of the night on uncanny hoofbeats [*umheymlekhe klep*] began clopping on the road between Oshini and Topoguvke, which runs alongside the water of the Varta" (Szeintuch and Solomon, *Yesha'yahu Shpigel*, 131). The sounds of horse hooves on the road are umheymlekh and signal that the peasants are being uprooted from their quasi-natural place in the local geography. The road is not a generic road but the road running next to the Varta River between Oshini and Topoguvke, part of a lived world that is being dismantled. In the villages, the terrified Polish peasants pack up their worldly belongings, wake their sleeping wives and children, and lead the cows out of their stalls and hitch them to loaded wagons. "In the darkness, the cows bellowed uncannily and plaintively [*umheymlekh un veymutful*], and let themselves be tied with sunken heads" (Szeintuch and Solomon, *Yesha'yahu Shpigel*, 131). Even the cows, occupying a space between the natural and the human world, sense the disruption of the order of things and bellow umheymlekh. The void left behind by the fleeing families constitutes a generalized umheymlekhkeyt, a negation of place felt even by the animal realm. "From all the villages around the waters of the Varta, the peasant wagons departed that night with people, cows, chickens, dogs. In the abandoned villages a nocturnal uncanniness [*nakhtishe umheymlekhkeyt*] settled, [ ] emptiness and only abandoned geese, roused from their sleep, screeched into the desolate void [*geshrign in der vister leydikeyt arayn*]" (Szeintuch and Solomon, *Yesha'yahu Shpigel*, 132).[38]

As the people flee who inhabited—and constituted—the rural world, or home, in which Yosi-Ber and Dobbe have settled, Yosi-Ber must decide whether to flee with them. He does not, for he seems to identify radically with the locality his Polish neighbors are abandoning. One could interpret "earth" in his father's advice to "love the earth and it will love you" as metonymically signifying the wider rural world into which Yosi-Ber and Dobbe have integrated. Yet as this world or home collapses into a generalized umheymlekhkeyt so prominently evoked in the story's opening paragraphs, "earth" becomes increasingly literal. Yosi-Ber is left not with a home but with an absolute identification with a location—indeed with the very soil, the earth that will soon cover his murdered corpse. The Jew Yosi-Ber of Dolny-Yary, to invoke the story's title, is both less and—therefore—more local than his peasant neighbors. His neighbors fleeing with the vestiges of their lives exert little pull on Yosi-Ber, for, despite being regularly invited to local weddings and funerals, he is not really of that world. He has also effectively severed ties with the Jewish community and at this critical moment can fall back only on something approaching an absolute identification with the earth; his very being has become inextricably tied to that specific locus. In Shpigl's complex and arresting meditation on the—or at any rate a—Jewish relationship to the Polish earth, Dolny-Yary, the place that the Jew Yosi-Ber is of or from (*fun*), becomes literally umheymlekh and receives Yosi-Ber's corpse.[39]

Written in the Lodz ghetto, "Der yid yosi-ber fun dolne yari" is set in the first days of the German invasion of Poland, well before the ghetto's establishment in early 1940. Several of Shpigl's wartime stories are set during the establishment and first months of the ghetto and depict the disorientation people experienced upon violently being forced out of their Lodz homes and into the ghetto. As I explore elsewhere, "Der toyt fun anna yakovlevna temkin" ("The Death of Anna Yakovlevna Temkin") deals largely with this experience, as do the stories "Di drite partye" (The third party), "M'hot gekokht barilkes" (They were boiling beets), "Shtivl" (Boots), and "Fir vos zenen gegangen" (Four who went).[40] Each of these stories meditates on the literally and figuratively umheymlekh displacement their characters suffer in the process of ghettoization.

A group of Jews already in the ghetto await, in the freezing cold, the arrival of that night's third party of Jews—thus the title, "Di drite partye" —whom German soldiers are to deliver. Shpigl describes the scene of the waiting men with gothic tropes. "The night lay in the streets like a bird of black magic [*shvartser kishef-foygl*] spreading out long uncanny wings [*umheymlekhe fligl*]. The electrical light dripped through the darkness. The Jews stood huddled together like so many chickens being herded into a pit[41] for slaughter. With their bare heads and with Reb Bunem's grey head in the lead, it looked as if a chapter [*kapele*] of monks had gone somewhere with bare heads in a medieval night. If anything moved, it was the wind, which strew over them wisps [*reshtlekh*] of falling snow" (Szeintuch and Solomon, *Yesha'yahu Shpigel*, 185). Replete with a bird of dark magic with umheymlekh wings and the image of medieval monks, this passage mobilizes gothic images to convey the eeriness—and seeming historical regression—of the creation of the ghetto. When the long-awaited third party finally arrives, the German soldier leading them is struck by the King George VI beard worn by Bunem Faytlovitsh, the leader of the receiving party. He laughs at, then punches, Bunem Faytlovitsh in the face (Szeintuch and Solomon, *Yesha'yahu Shpigel*, 185). After the party has made its way to their temporary shelter in a movie theater, they fall on their bundles and begin to process the violence and trauma they have just suffered.[42] The majority of them have wounds, including torn off ears and fingers, broken elbows, split noses, shattered jaws, smashed feet, punctured heads, split open foreheads, and oozing eyes. With their eyes closed, these brutalized people lie on the floor and remember their lost homes.

> And behind their closed eyes what they had experienced a couple of hours earlier floated by for the last time. In their weakened, enfeebled hearts returned for the last time the luster of their abandoned Jewish apartments [*shtubn*], of their abandoned homes [*heymen*]. The apartments returned to the Jews with their floors and ceilings, with their walls and windowpanes, with the hanging lamps and landscape paintings, with their abandoned wardrobes, tables, beds, chairs, and glassware. The forsaken home weighed, weighed upon the barely breathing Jews who lay there curled up in a ball on the floors, where scores of feet had dragged in the sticky black snow from the courtyard. Over their heads stirred sharp wicked wings, like knives. Their heads were dizzy with the apartments, houses, gloomy stairways, cellars, streets, din, and darkness. In the Jews lying there [*In di ligndike yidn*] cried the emptiness of all the voided Jewish homes [*di leydikeyt fun ale yidishe pust gevorene heymen*]. (Szeintuch and Solomon, *Yesha'yahu Shpigel*, 187)

The sharp, wicked wings moving above the battered Jews' heads recall the umheymlekh wings of the bird of black magic that defined the darkness in the streets earlier in the text, and also evoke the angel of death. Under the sign of these stirring wings, the battered people return one final time to the Jewish homes they still inhabited that morning but that are now an uncannily proximate entire world away. What they remember are not only the furnishings that were the hallmark of a more comfortable life but also the structures that supported, literally and figuratively, their most basic and intimate senses of everyday reality: floors, ceilings, and walls.

"M'hot gekokht barilkes" dramatizes the abrupt forced evacuation of Jewish families, and in particular the Lipshitz family, from their homes in Lodz. Like hundreds of other families, the Lipshitzes—parents Isaak and Nekhame and their children, the teenaged Stefan and his younger siblings Simele and Mirele—must abruptly leave their comfortable Lodz apartment for the "north side" (*tsofn-zayt*), i.e., the Balut neighborhood that is in the midst of becoming the ghetto. They frantically rifle through their belongings and hastily decide what to take with them. The Lipshitzes carry and pull on sleighs what they can, and they are able to hire one of the Polish peasants with wagons "who wanted in the chaos to bring in money one final time from Jews" (*vos hobn in der behole gevolt fardinen dos letste mol bay yidn*; Szeintuch and Solomon, *Yesha'yahu Shpigel*, 172). Arrived in Balut, the wagon driver refuses to go any farther and threatens to throw their belongings into the street.

At that moment, as if by a miracle, "Feter Yankl" (Uncle Yankl) appears and recognizes his distant relative "Dreyzl" (Madame Lipshitz) and invites the family to his home (Szeintuch and Solomon, *Yesha'yahu Shpigel*, 179). Shpigl's story is largely about changed family relationships between the weavers, tailors, cobblers, and other working-class Jews of Balut, and their bourgeois relatives who had been living comfortably in central Lodz. Many erstwhile middle-class Jewish families now frantically try to recall the addresses—or even the names—of Balut relatives whom they had previously shunned (Szeintuch and Solomon, *Yesha'yahu Shpigel*, 179). The Lipshitz family, too, had largely lived as a nuclear unit apart from their Balut relatives. Yankl would occasionally appear at their apartment, smelling of wool, to ask for help with buying a crib or a couple of beds. When invited to the weddings of Yankl's children, the Lipshitz family would arrive in a fancy droshky to make a merely perfunctory appearance. Madame Lipshitz is astonished at the kindness she and her family are shown by Yankl, a widower, and his two remaining unwed daughters. She has never met these daughters and cannot fathom that they are calling her "Aunt Dreyzl" (Szeintuch and Solomon, *Yesha'yahu Shpigel*, 179). Yet the girls and Yankl insist that they are all family, indeed that "all Jews are today a single family . . . a calamity has befallen us"

(Szeintuch and Solomon, *Yesha'yahu Shpigel,* 181). The story ends by cutting back to the Lipshitzes' former apartment as it is being occupied by a Polish family. This family laughs when they see the beets still cooking on the stove.

Crucially, "M'hot gekokht barilkes" is focalized through a non-Jewish character, the devout Polish Catholic Marianne Shivek, who works as domestic help to the Lipshitz family and especially as a nanny to the two youngest Lipshitz children, Simele and Mirele. The story's non-Jewish characters consist primarily of Polish wagon drivers exploiting desperate Jewish families and Polish families quickly taking over evacuated Jewish homes. Among the Jewish characters we see branches of families that have been estranged by socioeconomic divisions suddenly renegotiating the terms of their kinship under the traumatic circumstances. Marianne Shivek occupies a complex and liminal position between these Polish and Jewish groups. She came to the city from her village already approaching forty and has no children of her own. She is very close to Simele and Mirele. Much of the story is devoted to Marianne's attempt to wrap her head around what is happening. As a devout Catholic, she heard priests before the war preaching that Jews were flush with gold and wanted to take over all of Poland and bring down the religion of the holy Christians; that it was the Jews' fault that Polish workers did not have enough to eat; and that it is the Jews who were pulling Poland's enemies into Poland in the war and in this way destroying the fatherland (Szeintuch and Solomon, *Yesha'yahu Shpigel,* 174). Marianne struggles to reconcile the priest's words with her experience with the Lipshitz family with whom she lives, none of whom seem like plausible embodiments of such pernicious enemies of the fatherland, its economy, or Christianity.

When the war broke out, Marianne Shivek was once again confused. The Jews were running around distraught, the women crying, and waving off (Jewish) soldiers heading to the front. The Germans arrive in a matter of only days. One day Marianne looks out the window and sees all the Jews wearing yellow armbands, which they later are forced to replace with yellow stars. It is Marianne who affixes the yellow star to their apartment door. The paper star would not stick, so she got up on a chair and nailed it in with her veiny peasant hands. And now she finds herself pushing a wagon through the snow with a crowd of Jews being evacuated. Marianne looks back over her shoulder: "As far and wide as the street stretched beneath her she saw the fleeing Jews moving. How frightful and uncanny [*moyredik un umheymlekh*] the stampede [*dos geloyf*] of that black mass of people appeared, with their wide-open, wild eyes, with their clenched mouths and gloomy, black garments beneath the snow and wind" (Szeintuch and Solomon, *Yesha'yahu Shpigel*, 177)

Shpigl's deceptively simple stories contain considerable subtlety and complexity. As usually in Shpigl's wartime stories, the literal register of umheymlekhkeyt is close to the surface: what Marianne Shivek sees as umheymlekh is in fact a mass of desperate Jews who have just been driven out of their homes. On another level, the uncanny aspect of what she sees issues from her subjective experience of the strangeness of Jews. While she can fully relate to the Lipshitzes as individuals and as an individual family, what she is seeing is perhaps something more akin to "the Jews" that priests have long warned her about. They are foreign and frightening to her in their strange and gloomy garb, and in their sheer numbers. But what one experiences as merely foreign to oneself is not necessarily uncanny per se; what renders what Marianne sees truly uncanny is that she finds herself more profoundly among these (strange) people than the wagon drivers merely out to make a final profit from Jews, or the Poles quickly occupying evacuated Jewish homes. As a Polish woman intimately entwined with a Jewish family and a Jewish milieu, Marianne Shivek both belongs and does not belong in this terrified crowd. It is thus apt that it is she who has the vision of the umheymlekhkeyt of it all since it is she who resides in a liminal social space between Jews and non-Jews, a space fast being foreclosed on as all Jews are being removed from the erstwhile multiethnic city.

After the Lipshitz family and their Balut relatives have reunited in the wake of the day's terrible events, it is Marianne who unpacks the food and cuts the bread—the food and bread she managed to grab as they were forced to leave their apartment in haste—for the meal the estranged relatives share as "one (Jewish) family." She mediates the familial breaking of communal bread, but her place in the rapidly shifting ground of wartime Lodz remains elusive. Just as it is she who has the umheymlekh vision of the panicked Jewish multitude stripped of their homes, she herself becomes an uncanny figure, devoid of any obvious place or home in the newly and violently redrawn topography of Lodz.

The story "Shtivl" (Boots) likewise exemplifies Shpigl's intermingling of literal and figurative registers of the umheymlekh, whereby the historical uncannily haunts the literary. The text begins by highlighting the disorientation entailed by forcible relocation into the ghetto. Ayzikl and his wife Motl Hoyker have settled into their ghetto room and start discussing how they will provide for themselves. A shoemaker by trade, Ayzikl believes that even though the erstwhile wealthy businessmen, brokers, and industrialists have had to leave their fortunes behind, they still will not allow themselves to go barefoot. (Like so many plans for securing one's livelihood in the ghetto, his idea of continuing to work as a shoemaker seems not to have panned out, and we later see him working as a plasterer.)

The army boots highlighted in the story's title, dating from his service in the Russian army (thus at the latest during World War I), embody for Ayzikl a status to which he continues to cling in the ghetto. He maintains these boots in tip-top shape. Ayzikl also eventually gains a measure of social status in the ghetto. Even as the ghetto quickly erodes many people's professional and social station, others move into positions of augmented power. Ayzikl becomes something of an important person (*a yakhsn*) by assuming a leadership role in weighing, dividing, and delivering the rationed food for his courtyard. Such brief reversals in social position, however, are overshadowed by the even more profound changes in human status ultimately wrought by hunger. "Hunger meanwhile slipped into the ghetto rooms [*shtubn*] like hidden mice and crept out of the holes at night, while everything dozed. People lay in their beds, unable to sleep and a dream arose [*un s'hot zikh gekhoylmt*]: (fields of [ ]) bread. Hunger lay down with the people in the beds and sang in their ears the uncanny howling of wolves [*dos umheymlikhe voyen fun velf*] that lurk—in winter—in the fields" (Szeintuch and Solomon, *Yesha'yahu Shpigel*, 111–12). Hunger slips into the domestic space like mice and begins to turn it inside out by troubling the human-animal distinction. The hungry wolves who howl menacingly from the fields surrounding human homes have now infiltrated the very being of the people in what should be the safest domestic space: their beds at night.

This invasion and perversion of the home by hunger plays out tragically for Ayzikl. "In Ayzikl's home there is an uncanny silence [*Bay Ayzikl in shtub iz an umheymlekhe shtilkeyt*]" (Szeintuch and Solomon, *Yesha'yahu Shpigel*, 112). As Ayzikl lies on his cot unable to sleep in the umheymlekh stillness, his thoughts roam to the "other side," when you did not have to go to bed hungry. He thinks of what he used to eat regularly just for breakfast! Ultimately, Ayzikl goes to the cabinet and looks at the bread divided into seven portions, one for each family member (two parents and five children). He cuts off a slice from each portion, returns to bed, and, with the blanket drawn over his head, devours the bread. Hunger has transformed Ayzikl into a quasi-animal who takes food from his own wife and children, the very people he would want to keep alive and safe in their home.

Wracked by guilt and shame, Ayzikl henceforth denies himself his portion of bread, dividing it to augment his wife and children's diets under the false pretense that he is being fed at work. As he starves he hallucinates that the plaster he works with is food, and his coworkers eventually find him up to his neck in plaster (*kalk*). They pull him out barely alive and take him home. Initially, his wife and children set his bread portion aside for him to eat when he recovers, but after seven days with no improvement, they share it—and go to bed full for the first time in a very long time. They begin to worry that Ayzikl might in fact recover and start claiming his bread again, though they cannot bring themselves to say this.

One night a deranged Ayzikl tells Motl to bring him his boots and belt. She is filled with fear, but his eyes cast "uncanny lightning flashes [*umheymlekhe blitsn*]," so she does as he demands. Ayzikl insists on donning his military belt and boots in order to go "parade, as before" (*af parad, vi amol*; 111). When Motl and the children try to dissuade him, Ayzikl threatens to kill them all. With their help he manages to get dressed, shouts military orders, and expires.

Ayzikl's first thoughts upon entering the ghetto were given to strategies of how to provide for his family. The workings of hunger, however, turn the domestic space, the *shtub*, into its umheymlekh opposite. The husband and father Ayzikl is transformed into a quasi-animal, and Ayzikl's attempt to repent and aid his family leads to insanity and death amid desperate and distorted memories of a status he once could claim.

The story "Ite bensht iber di kandelyabres" (Ite makes a blessing over the candelabras) is likewise dense with uncanny juxtapositions of past and present, life and death, the integral and the abject. As in several wartime stories, Shpigl uses the word *umheymlekh* in the opening paragraph to convey the nature of the experience of the ghetto in general and of Ite's experience in particular. Traumatized by the loss of her home and family, Ite has lost the ability to distinguish between reality and fantasy. "If you will, Ite has by now lost the sense of where reality [*di vor*] ends and where the web of uncanny [*umheymlekhe*], blurred thoughts [*nit-klore rayones*] begins, bordering on madness [*shigonen*]. In the course of a year, Ite's household has been eradicated, like other Jewish families that had in fact managed to bring some remnants [*etlekhe shpliters*] of their households when entering the ghetto." So great is the transformation that "If one were even to show her a reflection [*opsheyn*] of her lost (life), Ite might no longer recognize it now" (Szeintuch and Solomon, *Yesha'yahu Shpigel*, 188). The story's plot is sparse. Ite is standing in line with others, holding a pot for receiving soup. Everyone in line has been transformed by hunger, and they emit a smell of starving bodies. "Some strange odor emanates from the people, from their garments, from their hands, and from their movements. Those who catch a whiff of that smell try to keep themselves at a distance, moving away from the people; but the smell moves with them out of the line, surrounds them even a few steps farther, and they can't free themselves of it. Maybe it is the smell of the human body succumbing to hunger. When you look at those people from the side, it is hard to believe how fast the human body collapses and how unnatural [*meshunedik*] the color of the starving body is: grey-yellow" (Szeintuch and Solomon, *Yesha'yahu Shpigel*, 189). This smell of human bodies consuming themselves is haunting but inescapable—because not only others' bodies emit it but also one's own. The abject, which should remain external to one, has moved within. If, as Julia Kristeva has postulated, the corpse is the "utmost of abjection," the smell that cannot be evaded in this scene is the smell of becoming corpses, of others' bodies—and one's own—consuming themselves.[43]

A creaking noise becomes audible from behind the soup line and a wagon for collecting corpses (*agole*) abruptly enters the courtyard, stopping near the soup kitchen window. The grotesque banter between the kitchen director, Shloyme-Zalmen, and the driver (*bal-agole*), Moyshe-Khayim, intensifies this uneasy juxtaposition between kitchen and hearse. Shloyme-Zalmen yells out the kitchen window to Moyshe-Khayim and his coworkers, who are readying themselves with the corpse plank, "You didn't have anywhere else to drive up with your wagon but right there, in front of the cauldron, eh?" To Moyshe Khayim's question as to what Shloyme-Zalmen is cooking today, he again calls out from inside the kitchen, "I'm cooking water . . .What should I be cooking?" before whispering in the driver's ear, "I'm lining up business for you [*kh'greyt dir tsu skhoyre*], eh, Moyshe-Khayim?" (Szeintuch and Solomon, *Yesha'yahu Shpigel*, 189–90). The crassness of this dialogue notwithstanding, it acknowledges a grim truth. The proximity of corpse wagon and kitchen—of life-sustaining nourishment and a vehicle for collecting dead bodies—is only superficially inappropriate but on a more profound level entirely apt. The watery soup from the kitchen is not enough to sustain human life, and Shloyme-Zalmen is indeed effectively producing the merchandise (*skhoyre*)—corpses—in which Moyshe-Khayim trades.

Shpigl depicts a collective reverie in the minds of the people gathered in line amid such overwhelming presence of death. They look at Moyshe-Khayim's wagon and wonder if death might be better than continuing to live in this way, and they anticipate that they too will be gathered eventually by Moyshe-Khayim, maybe in that very wagon, that very box.

> The people in the line hold their pots closer to their bellies and look at the hearse, at the open crate on top. The wagon that so suddenly came to a stop there before their eyes killed off their hunger at once. The people forgot what they came there for and what they were standing in line for. [. . .] The people's heads sat on their idle, desiccated necks as if halfway severed [*vi halb untergeshnitene*]. As the youth took the rough plank under his arm and was making his way into the foyer [*ofitsine*]—only then did the women begin to talk amongst themselves. They talked of death, (of a nasty [*beyzn*], difficult, Jewish death,) and of the dead being better off. Of how in a week, in a day, each and every one of them standing there will fall into Moyshe-Khayim's hands. And maybe in that very wagon, in the same crate they're looking at now. (Szeintuch and Solomon, *Yesha'yahu Shpigel*, 190)

Moyshe-Khayim's name—*Khayim* means *life* in Hebrew—is darkly ironic, for he is both a person and an allegorical figure akin to Death itself. Just as the starving people collectively see themselves ending as corpses in Moyshe-Khayim's hearse, it is the sight of Moyshe-Khayim that causes Ite's repressed traumatic memories to well up in her mind. She looks Moyshe-Khayim directly in the eyes and drops her pot. In her mind she sees her husband Mendele in a corner of a home of strangers, her son Zanvele as he implores her, "Mama, I can't go on" (Szeintuch and Solomon, *Yesha'yahu Shpigel*, 191), and her oldest child, Brokhe, and she thinks: "The same Jew. The same wagon. The same hands" (Szeintuch and Solomon, *Yesha'yahu Shpigel*, 191). Whether or not actually the same person who carried away the corpses of her husband and children, Moyshe-Khayim embodies death in the form it has assumed in the ghetto. He is the supernatural figure of the collector of all the corpses of those who have died ghetto deaths and of the future corpses—the becoming corpses—of those still alive.

Someone behind Ite picks up the pot she dropped and presses it back into her hands. Profoundly disoriented, she takes a seat on the pump near the kitchen after receiving her soup. She does not notice as a group of children circle ever nearer until one takes her pot of soup and in his haste spills it on the sandy ground. The children scream, then immediately sink to the ground —like "angry chickens" when they are thrown feed—and scoop the soup-drenched sand into their mouths. Eventually, as Ite continues to take no notice of them, the children begin to fear her, and make themselves scarce.

At the end of the story two men arrive, pulling a cart with a round tin wagon for sewage removal. They are observant Jews with long beards and fringed garments (*taleskotns*) peeking out from beneath their tattered gaberdines. Taking a break, they sit down on the pump next to Ite and ask her for help tying pieces of canvas around their dirty hands before they touch their bread. The scraps of canvas have an unsettling provenance: burial shrouds. "The canvas reeked of shrouds [*takhrikhim*], of a white cold death" (Szeintuch and Solomon, *Yesha'yahu Shpigel*, 192). Once again, the abject, in the form of excrement and death, contaminates the sphere of nourishment (bread) and the sacred (the blessing). The association with death becomes all the stronger when we consider that the job of excrement removal was tantamount to a death sentence due to the high rate of infection.[44] It is thus apt that the scraps of canvas with which the two men attempt to divide the profane from the sacred come from funeral shrouds. They are the walking dead.

As the men recite the blessing over their bread, Ite, too, recites a blessing. In her confused mind she is lighting Sabbath candles, the quintessential ritual act of the Jewish home, and a principal act of boundary demarcation between the profane and the sacred. "While the Jews make their blessing over their wrapped [*farbundene*] hands, it seems to them that they hear how the lady next to them moves her sunken, dry lips, like a babble of a gentle stream over stones. And maybe this was not a mere impression, for Ite was in fact no longer with them: she was at that moment, bent over the Jews' hands, already lighting large sabbath candles in the four shining branches of her tall silver candelabrum. And leaning over the flickering, white candelabrum, she blessed the Jews' dead, outstretched hands" (Szeintuch and Solomon, *Yesha'yahu Shpigel*, 192–93). The many forms of contamination of categories and uncanny proximities of opposites evident throughout the story, the intermingling of nourishment and life with decay, excrement, and death; of what is integral to oneself with what is abjectly other; and of the sacred with the profane create an ambiance of generalized uncanniness. The story's ending (and title) return these uncanny dynamics to the level of historicized umheymlekhkeyt, as Ite makes her blessing not over Sabbath candles in the four branches of her silver candelabrum in the bosom of her home and family (now ghosts) but over the four already-dead hands of two barely living men.

Shpigl's story "Fir vos zaynen gegangen" (Four who went) can serve as a final example of his redoubling of uncanny effects by reinserting a register of literal umheymlekhkeyt into the workings of the uncanny. Shpigl does not use the word umheymlekh in this text, but it draws heavily on gothic tropes —above all a seemingly supernatural encounter with a corpse—and aptly exemplifies how Shpigl uses the literary uncanny as a means to explore a wide and subtle array of ways that Lodz ghetto inmates experienced existential unsettlement and terror. Like several other of Shpigl's wartime tales, this story is centrally about the traumatic experience of expulsion from one's home and entering a new, hardly imaginable reality. "Fir vos zenen gegangen" is set in late March 1940, as Jews are being forced out of their Lodz apartments and driven into the ghetto, which was officially sealed May 1, 1940. It tells the story of the violent removal of Iser and his family and their neighbors from their apartment building in the city. Iser stands alone (his wife and their children having gone off somewhere), dazed, in the Balut apartment where he and his family have wound up. It had belonged to a Polish worker, but Poles and ethnic Germans had been abruptly forced to leave to make room for the Jews being evacuated from the city into the ghetto (Szeintuch and Solomon, *Yesha'yahu Shpigel*, 104). The traumatized Jews did not choose apartments but stayed wherever they were dumped, often with ten strangers crammed into apartments meant to house four. Iser looks around the room and tries to fathom that, only yesterday, he and his wife were in their comfortable apartment in the city with three rooms and a kitchen. He wonders if it has not all been a dream (Szeintuch and Solomon, *Yesha'yahu Shpigel*, 105).

The narrative then flashes back to the roundup in the city the previous day. The residents of the hoyf (apartment buildings around a courtyard) were given just three minutes to report to the courtyard, and many thus stand there half naked. A dull thud is heard, a body hitting the ground. As often in Shpigl's ghetto stories, moonlight provides gothic ambiance.[45] "The fallen body, lying near, convulses again on the paving stones and lies still. The final convulsion. The pale light of the moon will soon flood into that street and illuminate the courtyard. The people hide their faces and wish not to see. If they could have held back the moon, they would have. No one wants to recognize the reality. . . . Pitilessly cold [light] from the moon falls on the courtyard and slithers its way [*glitsht zikh*] to where the body lies" (Szeintuch and Solomon, *Yesha'yahu Shpigel*, 106). The moonlight reveals a woman's mangled body in her blood-splattered white nightgown lying in the mud. The stormtrooper overseeing the evacuation orders the "drek" to be removed, and Iser is among the four men who carry the dead woman to the street (hence the story's title, "Four that went"). Iser does not know the woman's name, but he recognizes her as the teacher who lived alone on the third (and top) floor. Her head is smashed in, but one eye is open and looks at him. The four bearers, two in front and two in back, trudge barefoot and half naked through the cold mud of the courtyard and through the corridor of the front house (*forderhoys*) on their way to the street. In the corridor, however, they are ambushed and shot at. The dead woman and the other three bearers are loaded onto a waiting truck. Only Iser remains on the floor, wounded. The narrative then returns to Iser and his wife in the Balut room.

What is remarkable about the story, however, is less its plot than the reveries Iser and his fellow bearers have about the anonymous teacher and the interactions they have with her corpse as they carry her before they are shot. She was a secretive woman who intrigued and erotically captivated the men in the hoyf. "Yes, that is her. Her long slender fingers, which were always hidden beneath gloves. The teacher was withdrawn [. . .], never went to neighbors. It was known that she was getting ready to leave Poland. Her closest kin [*ire nonte*] were somewhere very far away. She had about her [. . .] the mysterious silence of a person who carries a sorrow. Her clothes were always grey, refined, and pining [*farbenkte*]. She possessed a warm, alluring mystery of womanhood, and to the men in the house her tread on the stairs in the late evening hours was like some sort of soft song from a beautiful lost world" (Szeintuch and Solomon, *Yesha'yahu Shpigel*, 107). Mysterious and full of longing, the woman served as a repository for the yearnings of the men in the hoyf, and even after her death her male bearers continue to experience her corpse as erotically charged. Her dead body is not only erotic, however, but also sacred to these men; it is at once a repository for their desires and the remains of a martyred saint. "They are carrying the enigmatic [*soydesfuln*] shadow of a life that they did not know. The fear for their own lives has disappeared somewhere. Onto their shoulders drips the blood of a holy, yearning martyr [*a heylikn, farbenktn korbn*]. They don't know where they are going, but they feel that the way is a holy one. They could have carried the dead body on their shoulders until dawn" (Szeintuch and Solomon, *Yesha'yahu Shpigel*, 107). As they proceed, the dead woman's hand falls down, and the "first" bearer in front—Iser—holds it for a long moment, then in an arresting gesture inserts her cold dead fingers into his mouth. Independently of each other the other three carriers join Iser in symbolically ingesting the woman's sacred and eroticized corpse.

> The hand [of the dead person] slid down, so he raised it up and held it for a long while in his hand. Then he brought her fingers to his mouth and for a moment closed his mouth around the cold dead skin of her fingers.
>
> The other bearer did the same.
>
> The two in back, not able to see each other, pressed their lips against the cool, dead skin of her legs. (Szeintuch and Solomon, *Yesha'yahu Shpigel*, 107–8)

The story ends with Iser closing his eyes, remembering the powerful experience with the corpse, and reenacting the gesture of sucking the corpse's fingers by placing his mouth to his wife's hand. "When his wife sits down, he takes her hand. They look at each other for a while. He closes his eyes. And like that, with shut eyes, like little children lost in a forest, he moves his mouth to her fingers and remains a long while with bated breath on the cold flesh of her hand" (Szeintuch and Solomon, *Yesha'yahu Shpigel*, 108). But Iser remembers more than the sacred corpse of the teacher when he performs this charged and ambiguous gesture with his wife's hand. Since the ghetto was not yet sealed, Iser and his wife had been able to return to the courtyard of their old apartment earlier that morning, the day after they were forced out. They recovered a bundle of laundry and bedclothes, which now, at the story's end later that day, sits in front of the door. Their old Jewish courtyard to which they returned this final time had already been completely transformed. "In front of the door lies a bundle of salvaged laundry and bedclothes. Someone threw that to them from their [*zeyer*] apartment when they went there that morning. Strangers were already living there. Germans from Volynia. The courtyard, that Jewish courtyard in the city, already looked like a foreign courtyard somewhere in a foreign city. From all the windows there peered out strange red faces of newly arrived [*tsugeforene*] Germans" (Szeintuch and Solomon, *Yesha'yahu Shpigel*, 108).

Iser remembers his home in tandem with the mystical corpse under whose spell he remains as he brings his mouth to his wife's fingers. His gesture seems exceedingly ambiguous. It is one of both helplessness (he is like a child lost in the forest) and of erotic longing. Is he trying to displace the memory of the corpse's dead fingers with his wife's living hand? Is he measuring his wife against his recent experience with the transcendently affecting corpse? Does his gesture intimate that his wife, too, is effectively already a corpse? Is it a gesture of abiding love? Of resilience? Of helpless resignation? A repetition compulsion? The interpretive possibilities could be multiplied, but what underlies the overdetermined gesture is the radical disruption of the coordinates that had defined Iser's and his wife's most basic understanding of everyday reality, their basic ontological moorings. It is in the midst of the experience of radical, literal umheymlekhkeyt that Iser experiences sacred-erotic transcendence in the act of ingesting the teacher's corpse, and it is still in the midst of that disorienting loss of home that he repeats the gesture with his wife's hand. All that had until only days ago seemed stable and inviolate has been shattered, and this eruption of the unfathomable into the everyday has left everything, down to the meaning of the loving touch of Iser and his wife, equivocal.

Together, the stories "Di drite partye," "Fir vos zenen gegangen," "Ite bentsht iber di kandelyabres," "M'hot gekokht barilkes," and "Shtivl" aptly show Shpigl's double operation of both drawing on gothic tropes to convey the overwhelming peril and unsettling strangeness of the experience of ghettoization, and of confronting those exotic tropes with radical historicization. Iser's sacred, mystical, erotic experience is predicated on "that Jewish courtyard in the city" suddenly becoming "a foreign courtyard somewhere in a foreign city" with "strange red faces of newly arrived Germans" peering out the windows. In "Shtivl" the threshold between the human domestic and wild realms is marked by the wild beast of relentless hunger. Stories such as "Di drite partye" and "Ite bentsht iber di kandelyabres" reverse the trajectory of gothic texts, which typically begin on the plane of everyday reality before propelling characters and readers into uneasy encounters with the otherworldly. The visions of the traumatized characters in these stories are not otherworldly but rather visions of what—until unfathomably recently—constituted the ordinary, safe, and habitual: apartments, furniture, walls, and floors, or the act of lighting Sabbath candles. What used to pass for everyday reality had become the stuff of haunting visions and nightmares.

"SHTROY" (STRAW): SHPIGL'S META-LITERARY GOTHIC TALE

Although Shpigl draws on—while also uncannily literalizing and historically inscribing—gothic literary conventions in all the stories I have analyzed in this chapter, and in further texts to which I can here only allude (notably "Malkhes geto" ["Ghetto Kingdom"] and an untitled story that Shpigl significantly revised after the war and published under the title "Vedibarta bam"), his most fully realized gothic story from the Lodz ghetto is "Shtroy" (Straw).[46] Shpigl's commitment to literariness in the Lodz ghetto—and to elements of the ostentatiously literary gothic genre—can only be described as self-conscious. Even so, "Shtroy" stands out by the degree of literary self-consciousness it exhibits. As his English co-translator David Hirsch notes, Shpigl had little affinity for literary modernism or experimentalism.[47] "Shtroy" is by no means a highly experimental text, either, yet in its sheer accumulation of gothic tropes, verging on pastiche, it exhibits a greater degree of literary self-reflexivity and self-questioning than perhaps any of his other ghetto writings. I indeed read "Shtroy" as a meta-literary reflection on relationships between literary devices and conventions, on the one hand, and the very real conditions of destitution, disease, and death in the Lodz ghetto, on the other.

Shpigl's gambit in this story is to approach extreme ghetto conditions in the form of a gothic horror tale: the main action in "Shtroy" takes place literally on a dark and stormy night. In this self-conscious recourse to an established genre, Shpigl takes up the tools of literature to grapple with the direst of circumstances, and likewise confronts literature with those circumstances. That is, Shpigl uses the popular genre of the uncanny horror tale to grapple with the continuities and ruptures between European cultural traditions and Jews caught in the unfolding horror.

In classic gothic fashion, "Shtroy" is a frame narrative. Shpigl used frame narratives in a number of his ghetto stories, including in "Der toyt fun anna yakovlevna temkin." That story, as I discuss elsewhere, opens with a narrator relating the perturbing oddness of the androgynous figure he has recently encountered wandering barefoot in a ghetto alley, and then fills in the backstory of how Anna Yakovlevna Temkin met with this fate and how she ultimately met her outlandish and exceedingly symbolic death, falling from the ghetto's footbridge and being impaled on a German soldier's bayonet, which he extracts from her body "the way you would pull a knife out of a loaf of bread." (*Ghetto Kingdom*, 23).[48] The story "Avrashe geyt tsum nieman" (Avrashe goes to the Nemen river) likewise exhibits something akin to a frame narrative around a strange internal tale.[49] The narrative frame in "Shtroy," however, is presented even more conspicuously as a generic device. The text begins:

> The young man sitting across from me tells me [*dertseylt*]:
>
> It's very possible, if not for the letter that arrived for a relative of mine, that the whole affair wouldn't have occurred and the incident involving me that I'm going to relate to you now wouldn't have come to pass [*volt*

> *inem vint fun teg nisht geboyrn gevorn*]. But as you know everything has to have a beginning. And the beginning of this story, as it happened, was the letter. (Szeintuch and Solomon, *Yesha'yahu Shpigel*, 164)[50]

"Shtroy" unfolds as a story narrated orally to the narrator of the frame narrative. The device of the frame is ostentatious because it is so slight. It could hardly be less elaborated: stripped to its almost self-referential functional minimum, it establishes a frame and little more. Yet the establishment of this narrative structure is exceedingly important for the kinds of questions the text poses about relationships between ghetto and "normal" realities; about literary conventions in the face of extreme crisis; and about the implication of readers in such considerations. In a pioneering study of gothic and sentimental fiction, Elizabeth MacAndrew articulates the function of the sort of first-person frame narratives Shpigl opts for in "Shtroy": "The first-person narrator may be the central character, a major, or a minor one, or one who appears only in the slenderest frame to start the story rolling and sometimes to round it off at the end. Which he is will, of course, determine his effect, but the narrative method is always used to make the world of the novel strange."[51] Frame narratives have indeed been a prominent feature of the gothic genre from its inaugural work, Walpole's *The Castle of Otranto* (1764), through such classics of the genre as Samuel Taylor Coleridge, "The Rime of the Ancient Mariner" (1798); Mary Shelley, *Frankenstein* (1818); and Edgar Allen Poe, "The Fall of the House of Usher" (1839), to name only a few.[52] Beyond the way frame narratives serve as entry points into a strange reality within the everyday world, MacAndrew underscores how they situate readers virtually among the listeners hearing the strange tale. "When . . . a narrator returns to tell his hearers about people and events they know nothing of, this narrative method places the reader in the same relation to the world described as the listeners to the tale."[53] I would argue that precisely because he is wholly un-fleshed out, the first-person narrator of Shpigl's frame story serves as an effective stand-in for the reader of the text. There is precious little about him that would personalize or singularize him in any way and thus distinguish him meaningfully from us, the story's readers. Virtually devoid of biography, he is all ear. Readers and the frame narrator listen to the same tale.

A narratological device running through "Shtroy" enhances the slippage between the rather generic addressee within the text and the text's readers outside it in ways that heighten and complicate the story's ethical and epistemological stakes. The narrator of the main, internal narrative—the entire text save for the slight framing narrative at the very beginning and end—repeatedly (some fifteen times over the course of the story's seven pages) says to his interlocutor, "Ir vayst dokh." "Ir vayst" means "You know" and *dokh* is an intensifying particle, so that "Ir vayst dokh" could be rendered as "You well know," "You know of course," "You know as well as I do," and so forth. Shpigl attenuates the already slight gap between the narrator's address of the narratee within the text (the frame narrator), on the one hand, and the text's address (or Shpigl's authorial address) of the reader outside the text, on the other, by having the internal narrator address his interlocutor with the formal pronoun *ir* rather than the informal *du*. *Ir* is the second-person formal nominal pronoun in Yiddish for both the singular and the plural. (And like the French *vous*, *ir* is the informal second-person plural nominal pronoun as well.)[54] Given how emphatically the internal narrator of the main tale insists that his interlocutor has known him for a long time, it might seem more natural for him to use the informal pronoun. Yet while readers might be wont to receive address in the familiar singular (du) as the overheard speech between two confidants, *ir* interpellates not only the textual narratee (the narrator of the frame story) but also, uneasily, readers—"us."

By letting the phrase resound throughout "Shtroy," Shpigl deploys "Ir vayst dokh" as a kind of epistemological pivot, ever and again implicating readers in the elusive knowledge that the phrase signals. Just as the internal narrator insists that his interlocutor knows what he is talking about and can recognize as true the uncanny tale he is telling him, the text also insists that we, the text's readers, know something or are coming to know something. "Ir vayst dokh" hails us as well, appealing to a knowledge that we can neither easily disavow nor straightforwardly lay claim to. The story insists that we know something, or must know something, or that it is making us know something. It is the strangeness of what we are being told coupled with the insistence that we know it that makes for much of the uneasy experience of reading Shpigl's tale. Shpigl deploys what Jerrold E. Hogle has aptly called "an extreme form of fiction"—and one frequently associated with escapism and a rejection of realism—to insist that literature can have epistemological force, can inspire and convey modes of knowledge.[55]

The bulk of "Shtroy" consists of the protagonist's account of his experience in the street that he visits in his—ultimately unsuccessful—attempt to deliver the letter to his relative. The setting of this street is rendered as gothic landscape par excellence:

> It was a narrow, unpaved street. The street twisted and turned like most alleys in the ghetto, you know. A house shoved in, a house pulled out, one roof on, one roof off, open spaces near [*bay*] the houses because the fences had been taken during the winter. All the freestanding fences, all the wooden fences, gates, and shudders from windows and stores —everything got burnt, you know. The whole alley lies open, picked clean [*an ofns, an opgetsukts*], like a person who has cast off their outer garments [*oybermalbushem*] and stands naked. And because the fences and gates had been taken, few people walk in the street itself. It's easy to get from one street to the next, from one courtyard to another because of the missing fences, you know. The fear of the foremost streets nearest the wires also contributed to this. People avoid the foremost streets. They stand empty and abandoned. Therefore, beginning at dawn feet shuffle [*a geshar fun fis*] through the courtyards, through the chopped-out openings in the wall that connect one end of one street with the next. There, from the countless courtyards two youths carry away wrapped human bodies without pause. The wagon is parked somewhere on the other side of the alley. It waits; it can't maneuver into the alley. They carry the black body, like a wrapped-up roll of fabric [*vi eyn ayngeviklt balk skhoyre*], through all the open courtyards to the wagon. When there, they toss it high into the crate [*kastn*], the way they used to pile pieces of fabric [*skhoyre*] high onto the wagon before taking them to be treated [*far der apretur*], you know [*ir vayst dokh*]. (Szeintuch and Solomon, *Yesha'yahu Shpigel*, 164–65)

Twisting, desolate, decaying, denuded of wood fences and shutters after the long cold winter and thus naked and exposed, the street is also strewn with corpses.[56] In keeping with the basic dualism, the ontological grammar, of gothic horror, readers are introduced to another realm. They are forced to be in (at least) two worlds at once, one that seems to operate according to recognizable, "realistic" principles, the other according to weird, obscure, and terrifying ones.

It is worth noting that Shpigl did not deem his wartime experiments in approaching the conditions of the Lodz ghetto through the conventions of the gothic horror tale inapt in retrospect. The version of "Shtroy" that Shpigl revised for publication in 1948 under the title "In a toytn gesl" ("In a Death Alley") adds a great deal of eerie, morbid, and recognizably gothic detail, in addition to certain elements that render the published text more of a memorial for the murdered than is the case in the wartime version.[57] The post-Holocaust perspective of the revised version is evident, for example, in the way the houses that the protagonist sees in the desolate alley now tell "the secrets of past generations of Jews and their Jewish practice" (*dem sod fun fargangene doyres yidn un yidishkayt*). That is, they have become memorials of sorts. Some of the recognizably gothic details added in revision could also plausibly be seen as serving a similar commemorative purpose: here and there an isolated remaining fence board protrudes "like an old, forgotten grave marker" (*vi an alte fargesene matseyve*), and the protagonist experiences an "eerie feeling that the abandoned narrow alley merged with a dead-end street that led to an ancient cemetery; I don't know how to explain it, but that alley eventually did lead to a forsaken burial ground." The narrator further compares the alley's emptiness to that of "a street on the outskirts of town leading to an old cemetery. Though I can't say why, that alley indeed struck me as leading to a desolate burial ground."[58] Likening fence boards to grave markers and the bleak alley to an ancient cemetery or forsaken burial ground bespeaks a post-*khurbn* memorial perspective, even as it accentuates the gothic tropes of the original version. Several other morbid details in the revised text inscribe it more deeply in the gothic horror genre without necessarily serving such memorial ends. "A putrid wind" now blows a "moldy stench" into the protagonist's face, "a stale stench of decaying Jewish bodies" (*a tukhlekeyt fun tsefalenem yidishn guf*) that no one has come to collect.[59] The most haunting and uncanny detail added to the revised text is undoubtedly the semi-animation of the body parts of the corpses being collected, a detail that recalls the nature and "behavior" of the teacher's corpse in "Fir vos zenen gegangen." The hapless youths carrying off the dead now do so with the greatest haste because the hands and legs of the corpses seem imbued with a will of their own, a will to remain in the alley of death. These limbs serially dangle from the stretcher, inclining to the ground to which they seem to have a natural affinity.[60] Shpigl clearly found in the gothic horror genre a fecund set of literary resources for exploring the "otherworldly" nature of death in the Lodz ghetto, both throughout the more than four years of his imprisonment there as well as in the postwar years, in full knowledge of the devastating dimensions of the Nazi genocide.

When a storm suddenly breaks, the protagonist of "Shtroy" takes cover in what turns out to be a corpse-strewn house of horrors. Virtually everyone is dead, dying, or bereaved by the recent loss of a loved one to dysentery or starvation.[61] With each frightening flash of lightning and crash of thunder, the protagonist progresses further into the house and witnesses further scenes of death, destitution, and bereavement. The story also contains a strong element of erotic compulsion; the protagonist is led upstairs by an apparition-like prostitute. At first, she is all enticing breath and voice from the darkness, but on the way up the half-missing stairs (every other step having been burnt for heating the previous winter), the protagonist catches his balance by grasping the "thick flesh of her legs" (Szeintuch and Solomon, *Yesha'yahu Shpigel*, 169). Quoting another literary topos, the prostitutes upstairs turn out to have something like hearts of gold: it is only they—who earn a certain income in the ghetto—who have the luxury of a straw mattress and can thus spare a bit of straw on which to lay out, according to the traditional practice, each new corpse in the house below. The narrative's seemingly ineluctable progression toward a sexual encounter is interrupted when a neighbor from downstairs comes up to ask for some straw and for the protagonist's help in carrying out the husband whom the narrator had just seen in his death throes in the first apartment. The protagonist grabs his jacket and flees for his life.

Dorothea von Mücke's analysis of the fantastic tale sheds light on what is at stake in Shpigl's recourse to the gothic horror genre. Von Mücke theorizes that "the aesthetics of the fantastic transcends a representational model of literature," i.e., the fantastic breaks with the communicative model whereby literature represents the world, instead offering an exhilarating, absorptive, and escapist reading experience, driven by shock and seduction.[62] While it is undeniably true, as I have discussed, that highly renowned authors from various traditions of world literature have used the gothic mode to explore the most serious imaginable forms of historical trauma, it is equally true that gothic literature—or more narrowly the fantastic as von Mücke defines it —departs from realistic representation in order to engender a strong emotional effect in readers, to involve them in an erotics of reading, aptly figured in Shpigl's tale by the sexual energy propelling the protagonist. Von Mücke's distillation of the workings of the fantastical esthetic and in particular the way it breaks with Enlightenment ideals of transparent communicative language in favor of a literature of experience uncoupled from communicative or even moral aims elucidates a central tension in Shpigl's story. He opts for an esthetic widely associated with thrill, sensual titillation, and entertainment —and decidedly not with a morally committed project of transparently conveying reality—to portray a reality concerning the fictionalization of which there have been, and to some extent continue to be, strong taboos. Shpigl's stories thus frame the question of the role and the ethics of fictionalization of the Holocaust in ways that complicate the often simplistically conceived binary between the literary and the real. As a conspicuous iteration of a highly conventionalized and, once again to quote Hogle, "extreme form of fiction," replete as it is with a virtual checklist of gothic tropes, "Shtroy" highlights Shpigl's challenge to would-be prohibitions on fictionalization. Shpigl's story is not, moreover, the product of a post-Holocaust author seeking to imagine their way into the events of the Holocaust via fiction but rather the work of someone who lived through the catastrophe yet chose to confront it, even as it was still unfolding, via distinctly fictional means, including carefully deployed conventions of a lowbrow popular genre. His uncanny stories from the Lodz ghetto are not subsequent, artificial stylizations of the brute historical events of the years of genocide but rather cultural artifacts of those very years. Fictionalized short stories were Shpigl's primary means of thinking through and responding to the events of the Holocaust as they were happening.

The relationships in Shpigl's story between the real horrors of the Lodz ghetto, on the one hand, and stock literary conventions, on the other, cut in several directions. Shpigl deploys the tropes of the gothic horror tale—a deserted, desolate, decaying setting; a thunderstorm on a dark night; morbidity, death, and corpses; danger and suspense; a highly emotional, terrifying confrontation with a sublimely otherworldly realm; and even an erotic encounter with a seductive, ghost-like woman—to underscore a reality that has caught up with or surpassed the pleasurably frightening scenarios of our imagination. Conversely, the story also ponders how and whether literature can truly approach such conditions as those of the Lodz ghetto. Is literature doomed to trivialize such horrors, to offer them up in ways that ultimately elicit only pleasure, titillation, and frisson? In short, does literature have the resources to tell such a tale without it devolving into prurient escapism, quasi-pornographic horror?

While many readers consume exotic gothic tales in order to flee the mundane reality they "know" and temporarily enter a seductive world of suspense, danger, eroticism, and romance, Shpigl mobilizes the well-worn tropes of this genre to bring readers closer to the lived horror of conditions in the ghetto. Shpigl thus turns the gothic genre's esthetic inside out, something that becomes condensed in the internal narrator's adamant truth claims. He avers repeatedly that he is not making anything up, that he is telling only the truth, as when he states: "You maybe think I'm inventing things out of thin air? God forbid! [*Oser!*] You didn't meet me yesterday. I'm not going to tell you any lies. You know this [*Ir vayst dokh*]" (Szeintuch and Solomon, *Yesha'yahu Shpigel*, 166). Such literary disavowals of fictionality are of course a fictional topos par excellence and normally serve only to sustain the *effet de réel* necessary for readers to remain within their escapist fantasy, the hesitation that is, according to Tzvetan Todorov's classic definition, a constitutive component of the fantastic.[63] Here, however, the trope of disavowing fictionality is both the quintessentially literary trope that it is, and an uncanny literalization of the strange, otherworldly horrors at the heart of the genre.

Shpigl's text comments strikingly on the tension between historical representation or witness, and gothic literary seduction, when the protagonist recounts how the prostitute's voice made all he had seen in the first two apartments momentarily seem like nothing. "It's bizarre, but I've undertaken to tell you the truth (even if you should take me for a scoundrel). I'm not just making up some story. I'm not inclined to that sort of thing, as you well know. Yet everything I'd just seen: in one door a dying man, in another an old woman sitting shiva, and who knows behind how many doors in that moment people were breathing their last—all of that suddenly washed away from me like water, as if it had never been. And I'm standing beneath the staircase and a warm feminine hand leads me by the arm up the steps in a mysterious darkness" (Szeintuch and Solomon, *Yesha'yahu Shpigel*, 169). The protagonist's erotically determined forgetting of what he had just witnessed in the apartments rehearses by way of virtual parody the antirepresentational thrust of the fantastic. The erotic story line competes with and seems momentarily to overpower and displace the story's historical content. But unlike in more typical fantastic literature, only momentarily: Shpigl's tale finally rescinds the invitation to absorption and escape. "Shtroy" engages the erotic, absorptive, anti-representational, anti-communicative tendencies and techniques of the fantastic genre but also short-circuits them. It blocks off the escape route into the virtual world of otherworldly danger by making us confront the fact that this grisly haunting realm is not only a textual effect, a literary seduction, but also a historical reality. In Shpigl's uncanny reversal of the literary uncanny, the dangers the text evokes via gothic tropes of otherworldliness and horror are shown to coincide with a specific historical crisis. In this way, Shpigl uses gothic conventions to convey knowledge of a reality that can neither be reduced to the seductive effects of literary devices nor conceived in simple opposition to literature.

COMMUNICATION BY LITERARY INDIRECTION: THE FUNCTION OF THE LETTER

By way of conclusion let us revisit the letter that, as we have seen, "Shtroy's" internal narrator highlights at the very beginning of the story as the impetus for his foray into the death-saturated world of the alley. Later he again calls attention to the letter's role in leading him into that otherworldly, quasi-fantastic realm: "that letter for my relative led me into an entirely different world" (*hot arayngefirt mikh gor in an ander velt*; Szeintuch and Solomon, *Yesha'yahu Shpigel*, 165). While the letter initiates the plot, its communicative function remains unfulfilled. The return to the frame narrative at the story's end, while more extensive than the frame narrator's single opening sentence, nonetheless remains minimal. We do, however, learn the fate of the letter.

> "But what happened with the letter for your relative? Did you deliver the letter?" I ask the young man sitting across from me. Sweat appears on his white brow.
>
> "The letter, you ask? Here it is!" The young man pulls a crumpled sheet of paper [*beygele*] from the inside pocket of his jacket. "I've been carrying it in my pocket for three months now, and who knows if I'll ever deliver it. I'm afraid to enter into that death alley." (Szeintuch and Solomon, *Yesha'yahu Shpigel*, 170)

The boundary into the "other world" of the death alley—the strange world within the strange world of the ghetto—is not the first threshold the letter has crossed, for before that it of course had to enter the ghetto itself. The letter's sender remains as mysterious to us as its contents.

During the early months and years of ghettos like Warsaw and Lodz, while there were still Jews living in provincial towns in Poland, communication was possible between the shtetls and the ghettos via the postal service. Until the United States' entry into the war in December 1941 and Germany's invasion of the Soviet Union in June 1941, moreover, inmates of ghettos could receive letters—and life-sustaining packages—from friends and relatives in the United States and, especially, the Soviet Union.[64] Correspondence between the ghettos and Western Europe was also initially possible.[65]

I would like to suggest that Shpigl's decision to leave the provenance of the letter unspecified needs to be understood in connection with the narrative strategies in "Shtroy" for implicating readers in the ambiguous but nonetheless emphatically transitive mode of communication that it enacts, its desperate and anguished insistence that a form of knowledge is being imparted in the dialogue between the text's two narrators, and by extension between the story and its readers. By not specifying a particular sender or even a specific geographical location from which the letter hailed, the possibility remains that it could have been dispatched from any of the far-flung places to which various forces of dispersal, from prewar emigration to more recent desperate flight, had scattered the members of the story's implied readership. Any member of whatever implied audience Shpigl's text in its sheer precarity can be said to project (who could know, we might paraphrase the story's internal narrator, if it would ever be "delivered" to any audience?) could potentially be the author of the letter. The letter takes us into the ghetto, just as it takes the internal narrator (and us with him) into the terrifying death alley. In this way Shpigl's ghetto gothic horror tale meditates on what communication is (im)possible across the uncanny boundary separating the normal world and the extreme and dehumanizing realm of the ghetto. If, as I am suggesting, "Shtroy" inscribes its readers as potential senders of the letter, our missive to this realm neither reaches its destination, nor do we receive a straightforward reply. Instead, the story "Shtroy" is the reply we receive by literary indirection.

That abiding questions about the ethics, epistemology, and possibilities and limits of literary approaches to the Holocaust, which we might be quick to assume are problems that arose only "after Auschwitz," already animated many authors writing from within the unfolding catastrophe is a vastly underappreciated fact. It bears underscoring that Shpigl meditated on such questions in and through literature. While Shpigl's ghetto gothic stories in general, and "Shtroy" in particular, raise questions concerning the limits of literature in confronting the Holocaust, his body of work from the Lodz ghetto also powerfully models the capaciousness and epistemological force of literature to grapple with such concerns.

EPILOGUE

I began this book about literary writing in the Warsaw, Lodz, and Vilna ghettos with the story of Shaye Shpigl's efforts, upon returning to his native city of Lodz after deportation to Auschwitz and other camps, to recover his wartime literary manuscripts that he and his father had buried in the Lodz ghetto. Shpigl's abiding commitment to writing short fiction and poetry throughout his more than four years in the Lodz ghetto and his efforts to recover his manuscripts powerfully exemplify the importance of literature for people imprisoned within Nazi ghettos. If Shpigl's connection to ghetto literature as one of its most important authors was deeply personal, a footnote to this story illustrates the importance cultural activity likewise had for the first—Yiddish—Holocaust historians.

In the same extensive 1973 series of interviews with the scholar of Yiddish literature Yechiel Szeintuch that I have cited repeatedly in the pages of this book, Shpigl relates an anecdote in which the personal and the general historical importance of artifacts recovered after the war come to a head. Shpigl had left a note in the Lodz ghetto archives indicating where his manuscripts were buried. Shortly after he had finished recovering what he could of his papers from the trash heap where they had been discarded, Shpigl ran into his friend Nachman Blumental, a member of the Central Jewish Historical Commission (CJHC), then based in Lodz. Blumental had just found Shpigl's note in the archives and was on his way to Lagiewnicka 9, the address of the Shpigls' erstwhile apartment. Shpigl implored Blumental to let him have the note, but Blumental refused, insisting on its historical importance (Szeintuch and Solomon, *Yesha'yahu Shpigel*, 385). A passionate *zamler*, Blumental dedicated himself to recovering as many documents and artifacts pertaining to Jewish life under the German occupation as possible.

Like Philip Friedman (1901–1960), Isaiah Trunk (1905–1981), Joseph Kermish (1907–2005), and Mark Dworzecki (1908–1975), Blumental was a Holocaust survivor who pursued historical research on the Holocaust, predominantly in Yiddish, starting in its immediate aftermath. All but Dworzecki were members of the Jewish historical commissions in Poland that collected documentation and recorded survivor testimony during the final months of World War II and the first postwar years.[1] Friedman was the founder and first director of the CJHC in Lublin, but he left Poland in May 1946, eventually emigrating to New York. Having earned a PhD from the University of Vienna in 1925 in Central and East European History, Friedman, with Salo Baron's help, was able to secure the marginal position of adjunct professor at Columbia University and was also affiliated with the YIVO. Blumental succeeded Friedman as director of the CJHC (from fall 1947, the Jewish Historical Institute, Warsaw) with Kermish the assistant director. In the face of ideological constraints on their research agendas in the context of Stalinizing Poland as well as antisemitic violence, Blumental, Kermish, and Trunk as well as Rokhl Auerbach all left Poland in the course of 1948, eventually making their way to Israel. "Sooner or later," Laura Jockusch observes poignantly, "the [CJHC] activists came to the painful realization that the now monoethnic Polish state had no room for the Jewish minority, nor did the political climate allow for independent historical scholarship on its tragedy."[2] Blumental, Kermish, and Trunk founded the research center at the Ghetto Fighters' House (Bet Lohame ha-Geta'ot). Auerbach, Blumental, and Kermish would become affiliated with Yad Vashem, whereas Trunk left Israel in 1953 for Canada and, a year later, New York, where he worked as chief archivist at the YIVO. Dworzecki was a survivor of the Vilna ghetto and several slave labor camps. Like his Yiddish historian colleagues, he began writing Holocaust research immediately after the war, first based in Paris and thereafter in Israel, to which he emigrated in 1949.

As Mark L. Smith shows in his exquisitely researched monograph *The Yiddish Historians and the Struggle for a Jewish History of the Holocaust*, what distinguished the orientation of these first Holocaust historians was precisely their approach to the Holocaust as a period in Jewish history.[3] Their focus was on how Holocaust victims struggled to stay alive individually and collectively under Nazi occupation. Jews were the subjects of this history, subjects embedded within a culture and society. The specific foci of each historian naturally varied, but they all tended to focus on the day-to-day lives of Jews in these devastating years.

The cultural activity of Jews during the Holocaust had a secure place among the topics the Yiddish historians pursued. In a 1949 proposal (which was rejected) for establishing a research institute for the period of Jewish history between 1933 and 1945 at the Hebrew University, Dworzecki indicated six areas of Jewish struggle worthy of research, the second of which was "spiritual struggle," in which he included, alongside religious life, family life, and Jewish legal institutions in the ghettos, "cultural creativity in the Holocaust period (schools, diaries, and testimonies, literary activities, arts)."[4] And in his more than five-hundred-page history of the Vilna ghetto published in Yiddish in 1948, Dworzecki includes, in addition to chapters on schools in the ghetto; important cultural activists who perished; songs, humor, and folklore; and religious life in the ghetto, a discrete chapter on "literature and art in the ghetto."[5] Trunk's history of the Lodz ghetto, originally published in Yiddish in 1962 and in English translation only in 2006, contains (albeit relatively brief) subchapters on cultural life and on religious life, and his groundbreaking monograph *Judenrat* includes a substantial chapter on "Religion, Education, and Other Cultural Activities."[6] Kermish's anthology of documents from the Oyneg Shabes archive includes groups of documents on religious life, clandestine cultural activities, and clandestine schooling in the Warsaw ghetto. Blumental, who had earned a master's degree from the University of Warsaw in Polish literature before the war, was the most attuned among the early Yiddish historians to specifically literary production, literary culture, and language more generally. The seriousness that he attributed to literature written during the *khurbn* is evident in his choice of topics to present on at the second academic conference of the CJHC in Lodz in September 1945. He gave a paper on literature written in Yiddish under the German occupation, versions of which he published and republished in various venues in the early postwar years along with numerous other essays on literature in the Lodz ghetto, especially on songs, poems, and poets.[7] The examples from each of the above historians are but a few among many more publications they devoted to cultural topics.

I do not mean to exaggerate the importance of cultural production for the early Yiddish Holocaust historians, only to register that the culture of Holocaust victims had a self-evident place among other topics in this historiography that focused, in Smith's words, "on how Jews lived and not how they died" (Smith, *Yiddish Historians*, 316). One can easily imagine an alternative field of Holocaust studies in which a reading knowledge of Yiddish was a basic professional requirement. Yiddish was spoken by five million or roughly 85 percent of Holocaust victims.[8] While Yiddish speakers were generally not monolingual, Yiddish language and culture were at least a small and frequently a large part of the cultural life of most Holocaust victims, who left thousands upon thousands of pages of wartime writing that have come down to us (and surely many multiples thereof that were destroyed). It indeed begs the imagination to think that if a comparable number of victims of the Nazi genocide had spoken a West European language—French, German, or Spanish, say—and had left behind comparably rich archives, that linguistic competence and conversance with some aspect of these archives would not be a basic requirement for anyone working in the field. (Let me quickly add that my point is about the structure of the field of Holocaust studies as it developed, not about the shortcomings of any given scholar. I am in no position to wag fingers at anyone. My Yiddish remains a work in progress, and I cannot read Polish or any other Slavic language.)

Needless to say, this is not how the field developed. The initiatives of survivor historians and *zamler* on the CJHC in Poland who "urgently collected every scrap of paper and material object relating to the Jewish catastrophe that they could get their hands on," "fell into oblivion long before the wider public even began to recognize their potential."[9] They lacked the institutional, political, and financial power and, in most cases, the academic credentials to set the parameters for Holocaust research. As already mentioned, with the Stalinization of Poland they left for the United States and Israel, where they pursued important work but remained on the margins of the academy. Victims of genocide and cultures that fall victim to cultural genocide are, precisely because of their genocidal devastation, generally not able to marshal the resources to dictate the framework for how they will be remembered or historicized. The past is remembered in the present and responds to the needs of the present; destroyed cultures are remembered not on their own terms but through the prism of the cultures and ideologies of the societies that have the institutional, financial, and political means to remember.

Although important Israeli historiography of the Holocaust, especially the work of Yehuda Bauer and Israel Gutman and their students, took Jewish society as its central focus, not even this strain built meaningfully on the work of the CJHC or the early Yiddish Holocaust historians but rather grew out of intellectual and historiographical trends in the Israeli academy.[10]

The most dominant currents in Holocaust historiography in the Anglo-American and German contexts, influenced not least by Raul Hilberg's seminal 1961 *The Destruction of European Jews*, were decidedly focused on perpetrators and German, not Jewish, documents.[11] Dan Michman observes that "'Perpetrator History,' especially in Germany . . . tended to canonize the written official German documents and records, but dismissed oral testimony as suspect, and Jewish testimony in particular as unreliable, because of its 'lack of objectivity.'"[12] Indeed German Holocaust researchers sweepingly dismissed Jewish documents and testimony as too subjective, emotional, and biased, even as they had no trouble squaring their own pasts in the Hitler Youth with rigorous standards of objectivity, as Nicolas Berg has shown.[13]

Whereas Jews are the subjects of the early historical work on the Holocaust by the survivor historians, Nazis and their accomplices are the subjects of perpetrator history. Noting a pronounced "parochialism" (writing in 2003) in German research on the Holocaust, Michman notes that "Jews and their fate are viewed as mere objects of official policies, public opinion, the attitudes of various population groups, etc. . . . Owing to this focus on the perpetrators . . . the research agenda in [the German] sphere is overwhelmingly focused inwardly, towards Germany."[14]

Recent polemics about German Holocaust historiography and (the politics of) Holocaust memory culture in Germany have highlighted the parochialism of German memory culture of the Shoah. This culture has always been centrally concerned with German self-understanding given the legacy of the Third Reich's crimes. As significant as the issues—including the discourse of Vergangenheitsbewältigung and the cultural politics of Reunification—animating the dynamics of German memory culture have been, as Fabian Wolff starkly puts it, Germany's "memory culture is designed to just serve the country, not memory or culture. . . . It was never truly about the Jews, never truly about the victims."[15]

In his contribution to what is sometimes called the second German "Historians' Debate," Mischa Gabowitsch argues that the provincialism of German Holocaust memory culture continues to characterize German academic discourse as well.[16] He notes that "it is still acceptable in German speaking Europe to undertake studies of, say, the system of German occupation or annihilation Aktionen in East Europe without knowledge of the relevant local languages," and further that "even among historians the debate in Germany over the uniqueness of the Holocaust was—and is—largely carried out by people who cannot read, much less speak, the native languages of most of the people murdered in the Holocaust. Not to mention the victims of other genocides."[17] Gabowitsch's essay calls for a wider understanding of the cultures and contexts of the victims of Nazi atrocities in East Europe, both Jewish victims of the Holocaust and non-Jewish victims of Nazi mass violence in East Europe.

As merely the objects of perpetrator history, the only historical significance the victims possess is that they were persecuted and murdered by Nazis and their accomplices. Their societies, languages, culture, customs—in a word, their lives—are of no real historical consequence. From the vantage point of histories of the Holocaust understood as the history of the acts of its perpetrators and the forces that made them possible, what is paramount about the six million Jewish victims is their death. And the language of the dead is silence —which, conveniently, does not require years of study to learn.[18]

But if the massive foreclosing on victims' voices in the most prominent strains of Holocaust historiography can be characterized as a kind of parochialism, a lack of curiosity about the culture—or the situated humanity—of the victims of the Nazi genocide, this is not the primary parochialism that has been criticized in the recent debates in the field of Holocaust studies. The by all means important—but as I will argue, insufficient—critique has been of the isolated and calcified nature of Holocaust memory and history, especially given the significant political stakes of whether we view the Holocaust as unique or as one cataclysmic genocide that should be approached within a comparative framework that includes other genocides and other forms of systematic mass violence. I concur with Yehuda Bauer (and needless to say many others who make similar arguments) that "the very claim that a historical event is unprecedented can be made only when that event is compared with other events of a presumably similar nature. . . . Unless one finds a measure of comparability, unprecedentedness can mean only that the event is not human—in other words is not historical—in which case it is useless to talk about it except in putative theological or mystical contexts."[19] Recent calls for comparative frameworks for approaching discourses of both Holocaust memory and Holocaust historiography have advocated moving outward from perspectives that look at the Holocaust in isolation to engage with wider comparable but distinct examples of devastating mass violence, in particular colonialist violence.

Michael Rothberg's concept of multidirectional memory, articulated in his 2009 study of cultural texts that dramatize dialogic relationships between the memory of the Holocaust and colonial violence, is highly useful for approaching how memory cultures of different traumatic histories intersect and inflect each other in changing sociocultural and political landscapes.[20] In an editorial published in *Die Zeit* calling for an end to the German taboo on comparing the Holocaust to other historical phenomena, Rothberg and Jürgen Zimmerer posit that the tendency in German memory culture to remove the Holocaust from history and treat it as a wholly incomparable set of events amounts to a kind of self-involved "provincialism" and that multidirectionality is "exactly the opposite of the orientation of 'provincialism'" (*Diese Multidirektionalität ist genau das Gegenteil zum Leitbild "Provinzialität"*).[21] To be sure, this is in important ways true. Multidirectional frameworks may indeed be an antidote to the typically but not uniquely German provincialism that for political rather than scholarly reasons eschews even historically informed comparison. But multidirectional perspectives can themselves easily leave intact or even consolidate a fundamental provincialism that has been a negatively constitutive part of mainstream Holocaust memory and historiography, namely the vast neglect of the extensive archives left by East European victims of the Holocaust.

As helpful as Rothberg's concept of multidirectional memory is for exploring how the memory of the Holocaust relates to the experience and memory of other phenomena like decolonization, it is also important to question, at a fundamental level, what about the Holocaust and its victims has been remembered and what has been systematically excluded from memory. At issue is not only the politics of Holocaust memory in changing cultural and political constellations but also the politics of whose individual and collective voices have been deemed worthy or unworthy of being remembered in the first place. I hope this book, in attempting to engage seriously with but a few of the literary texts written in ghettos and preserved, against great odds, might inspire readers to read and reread them, their authors, and many other authors as fundamental thinkers of the Holocaust in real time and as critical voices for comparative studies of the lived experience of the Nazi genocide and other atrocities.

Gabowitsch notes how the presence in contemporary German society of descendants of victims of Nazi crimes can sometimes expand the visibility of victims of Nazi persecution and advocate for their memorialization.[22] I would argue that the case is significantly different for East European Holocaust victims. While in today's increasingly heterogeneous German society, there are citizens with backgrounds in Poland, the former Soviet Union, and former Yugoslavia who carry the memories—and who often still embody the language and cultures—of the victims of Nazi violence, as a result of the biological and cultural genocide the Nazis wrought on East European Jewry, that specific culture has few representatives in contemporary Germany. Decimated in the Holocaust, that culture is not alive and well among Jews living in Germany today. Rothberg's concept of multidirectional memory is excellent for thinking through the dynamic that Gabowitsch highlights, an example of the increasing complexity of the relations among the multiple memory cultures within contemporary German society (and most open societies today).

Yet predicated as it is on the co-presence of different collective memories that increasingly characterizes societies in an era of mass migration and displacement, multidirectional memory as an analytical model may not be equally helpful for appreciating the voices and cultures that due to genocidal violence are absent from the social landscape. With its emphasis on the "inevitable," whether conflictual or empathetic, solidarity-fostering, "dialogical exchange between memory traditions" at different synchronic moments, Rothberg's model of multidirectionality tends not to concern itself with the terms and power structures that dictated these memory traditions in the first place.[23] For Rothberg, the "comparative critic must first constitute the archive by forging links between dispersed documents" (*Multidirectional Memory,* 18). The archive that Rothberg assembles in his book is one of fascinating multicultural and transnational dialogic encounters, staged in postwar texts in French and English, between memory traditions of the Holocaust and of colonial violence. Let me be clear that my point is not to polemicize against Rothberg's important model, which has found considerable resonance, but only to note that multidirectional memory's anti-provincial thrust can very well leave in place a constitutive provincialism of Holocaust memory, the massive disregard of the vast majority of (East European) victims' voices. Precious little in the model would send anyone back to the neglected archives to discover voices that could and should change what Holocaust memory thinks it is remembering. Calls to move on from what are perceived to be exhausted paradigms tends to presume that those paradigms were in fact exhaustive; they were not, and they should not be assumed to be settled. New departures in Holocaust studies should go hand in hand with new approaches to the study of the overlooked lives, thoughts, and speech of Holocaust victims. If not, so many Jewish voices long neglected by the most influential treatments of the Holocaust will once again be effectively silenced, ostensibly moved on *from* without in fact ever having been attended to in the first place.

To state the obvious, perpetrator history is crucial; the problem is not that there is a robust corpus of perpetrator historiography but rather that it has been pursued to the exclusion of historiography that recognizes Jews as the subjects of their history and the Holocaust as something that they endured, struggled against, thought deeply about, and wrote about at virtually every phase of the tragedy. As Jockusch aptly puts it, "From today's perspective it is surprising that for so long subsequent generations of academic historians who laid out in detail the Nazi regime's policies toward the Jews and the actions, motivations, and ideological backgrounds of the perpetrators did so almost entirely *at the expense* of the voices of the Nazis' victims" (Jockusch, *Collect and Record!,* 200; original emphasis). The inattention to Yiddish sources by generations of Holocaust researchers has left a hole at the center of the field.

I by no means want to minimize the extraordinary and inspiring Holocaust studies scholarship that has focused on Yiddish, much of which I have noted and drawn on throughout this book. Nonetheless, work based on Yiddish sources remains something of a niche within the wider field of Holocaust studies and has played little part in shaping the memory of Holocaust victims. This book has been an attempt to contribute to the shared project of listening to these underheard voices, one that will require the work of numerous scholars bringing their particular cultural competences, academic specializations, and intellectual temperaments to the task. Listening to Jewish voices in Yiddish and, although it exceeds my own competence, Polish and other East European languages, opens unique doors onto how victims thought through and tried to negotiate the events of the Holocaust as they were unfolding, and how survivors thought about and memorialized them after the fact with the limited financial and institutional resources they could marshal.

As a historically minded literary scholar, I have focused on literary writing in the Warsaw, Lodz, and Vilna ghettos—and in what has become a lengthy book, I have barely been able to scratch the surface of even the Yiddish (and in the case of Rosenfeld, the German) literary component of the underread multilingual archives of East European Holocaust victims. Few things would be more satisfying than to see this book eventually on a library shelf crowded with other monographs engaging with the rich materials in these archives. How readers will receive this book is of course ultimately up to the readers themselves. But I hope to have gone some way in conveying the importance and intellectual rewards of attending to this extraordinary corpus.

I have intentionally steered clear of two concepts widely invoked when cultural pursuits of Holocaust victims are at issue: testimony and resistance. Smith shows that the concepts of spiritual or cultural resistance that have come to be enfolded into the broad signifier *amidah* were first articulated by Dworzecki as early as June 1946.[24] I do not reject the idea of cultural resistance, but it seems to me too blunt a concept for the sort of readings I have attempted in this book. With its origins in a wish to rescue the honor of Jewish victims from the charge of meekness and passivity, or having gone "like lambs to the slaughter," Dworzecki's expansion of the concept of resistance from narrowly defined armed resistance to include all nonviolent forms of struggle to sustain Jewish life retains an apologetic strain. I take as self-evident that the honor of Holocaust victims is not in question, and, starting from this position, I prefer to remove the literary corpus I have engaged with from the terms of the misguided charge and the apologetic response. Similarly, while I do not disagree with the contention that all writings by victims during World War II have a testimonial value, I find the concepts of witness and testimony both too inflated and too limiting for the sort of open-ended readings that the literary works that I have focused on inspired me to pursue. Without denying that wartime cultural production by victims evinces resistance and constitutes testimony, we should remain open to following texts and other cultural artifacts wherever they seem to invite us. If we read for resistance and testimony, we will find them, but we may miss much else that may be only partially or awkwardly subsumable beneath these concepts.

I would therefore propose that we view the wartime texts that victims of the Holocaust produced as embodying thinking, and that we strive to think with them. The proposition that these texts embody dynamic thought is admittedly general, but that is also the point. To start, we do not know how a given text thinks, only that it does. We can engage with its thought from various vantage points and via different approaches. The thinking in question is always situational, so we must try to reconstruct the most salient context(s) in which it moves. These texts also think within and against cultural traditions, practices, and expectations, so we must strive to become conversant with the culture(s) of the authors. Approaching the authors and their works as engaged in thought that we can benefit from thinking with acknowledges the authors' subjectivity, agency, and creativity and, equally importantly, situates us, their readers, as having a cognitive deficit that might inspire humility and patient listening. Such an approach to these texts does not minimize the various ways they can offer documentary evidence, but it does not allow them to be reduced to mere objects of our positive knowledge. Thinking with—or what humanists of a certain vintage still call *reading*—these authors and texts opens unique, fierce, poignant, and frequently brilliant perspectives on culture and the human status under threat in times of extreme crisis.

NOTES

INTRODUCTION

1. In his introduction to his postwar book of poetry *Un gevorn iz likht*, Shpigl pays tribute to his murdered father, Moyshe Beer Shmuel Shpigl, for burying his manuscripts for him (Shpigl, "Araynfir-vort," in *Un gevorn iz likht*, 4).

2. See Szeintuch-Shpigl interview in Szeintuch and Solomon, eds., *Yesha'yahu Shpigel—prozah sipurit mi-geto Lodz': shishah-'asar sipurim mefu'naḥim 'al pi kitve-yad she-nitslu be-tseruf mavo ve-re'ayon 'im ha-meḥaber* (Isaiah Spiegel: Yiddish narrative prose from the Łódź Ghetto; 16 stories edited from rescued manuscripts with introductions and a series of oral interviews with their author), 384; see also Julian Levinson, "Translator's Introduction," in Isaiah Spiegel, *Flames from the Earth: A Novel from the Łódź Ghetto*, xxi–xxii.

3. At the end of a series of extensive 1973 interviews with Yechiel Szeintuch, Shpigl describes his situation after returning to Lodz: "There on the ruins of the erstwhile ghetto with its entire atmosphere I walked around once more. I'd returned naked, empty, virtually slaughtered, with some wretched scraps of 'sheymes' that I had dug up and collected. After that I began the task of once again reconstructing the entire life that I had put into those 'sheymes.' And a great miracle happened: all these 'sheymes' came out in print, in books, across the entire Yiddish world" (Szeintuch and Solomon, *Yesha'yahu Shpigel*, 385). See also Levinson, "Translator's Introduction," xxi–xxii.

4. Shpigl's recovered Lodz ghetto manuscripts have been published in Szeintuch and Solomon, *Yesha'yahu Shpigel*.

5. The first cache of the Oyneg Shabes archive was unearthed on September 18, 1946. A second cache was found in December 1950 by a construction team digging to lay a foundation for a new building. On Emanuel Ringelblum and the Oyneg Shabes project, see Samuel David Kassow, *Who Will Write Our History? Emanuel Ringelblum, the Warsaw Ghetto, and the Oyneg Shabes Archive*. Readers of Polish can access the complete archive in the Jewish Historical Institute, Warsaw's thirty-eight-volume complete edition, *Archiwum Ringelbluma: Konspiracyjne Archiwum Getta Warszawy*. An English translation of the entire archive is ongoing.

6. Auerbach is a key figure in Roberta Grossman's 2019 film *Who Will Write Our History?* about the Oyneg Shabes project, based on the book by the same title by Samuel Kassow.

7. This is true for classics of the field of Holocaust literature such as Sidra DeKoven Ezrahi, *By Words Alone: The Holocaust in Literature* (1980), and Lawrence Langer, *The Holocaust and the Literary Imagination* (1975). In *A Double Dying: Reflections on Holocaust Literature* (1980), Alvin H. Rosenfeld devotes part of one chapter to wartime victim diaries but emphasizes above all their testimonial and documentary function; see Rosenfeld, chapter 2, "Holocaust and History." More recent examples

of works on Holocaust literature that take no account of literature written by victims during the Holocaust include Sue Vice, *Holocaust Fiction* (2000) and Susan Gubar, *Poetry after Auschwitz: Remembering What One Never Knew* (2003). (In her 2004 article "The Long and Short of Holocaust Verse," however, Gubar treats Miklós Radnóti's "Picture Postcards" and Katzenelson's "Song of the Murdered Jewish People.") Although in *Holocaust Poetry: Awkward Poetics in the Work of Sylvia Plath, Geoffrey Hill, Tony Harrison and Ted Hughes* (2006), Antony Rowland does treat some wartime poems by victims, including Radnóti, to my mind he does not distinguish adequately between wartime and postwar—or victim and bystander—poetry, instead treating these various strains as part of "Holocaust poetry" in general.

8. Mintz, Roskies, and Kassow all stress the crucial importance of how wartime writings capture experiences in a phenomenological rather than anamnestic mode. As Mintz argues: "The enormous claim this [ghetto] literature makes on us is that it opens a window onto the experience of Jewry in real time rather than in recollected time. . . . The contribution made by the growing profusion of survivor memoirs and videotaped testimony is invaluable, but it is necessarily subject to the selective and retrospective understanding of parallel developments and final outcomes. This was precisely the kind of knowledge that actors in the drama could not have; the inhabitants of an individual ghetto could know with only very imperfect certainty what was happening at the same time to Jews elsewhere, not to mention what would be the next moves of the German administration" (Alan Mintz, *Popular Culture and the Shaping of Holocaust Memory in America*, 65). Kassow emphasizes how the need to capture the lived experience of the ghettos in its temporal unfolding was acutely felt already by Ringelblum: "Ringelblum realized that Oyneg Shabes had to perform a task that might well elude retrospective reconstruction, recording the facts in all their simultaneity. Only thus could a record of Jewish society under stress be maintained. To wait was dangerous, not only because the recorders might be killed but also because human memory, under the stress of events, would choose to forget too much. Ringelblum's concern can be framed in another way, one that certainly makes sense today: that the sheer weight of the horror would retroactively erase the victims' previous identity" (Kassow, *Who Will Write Our History?*, 206). And Roskies aptly notes: "Wartime writings show us (almost uniquely) how the time of terror took on flesh and blood" (David G. Roskies, *The Jewish Search for a Usable Past*, 32). On the function of time in the writings of the Oyneg Shabes, see Roskies, *Usable Past*, 30–33. See also Roskies' important call for attending to a "historical poetics" when reading wartime writing by Holocaust victims, an "ethics of reading" that requires a micro-chronological practice of contextualization or "reading in time" (David G. Roskies, "Did the Shoah Engender a New Poetics?," 350).

9. See Hélène Berr, *The Journal of Hélène Berr*; Dawid Sierakowiak, *The Diary of Dawid Sierakowiak: Five Notebooks from the Łódź Ghetto*; and Yitskhok Rudashevski, *The Diary of the Vilna Ghetto*.

10. Primo Levi, "The Canto of Ulysses" (109–15), in *Survival in Auschwitz*.

11. Although she composed two poems about Auschwitz, "Auschwitz" and "Der Kamin" ("The Chimney"), while interned in Christianstadt (the latter of which she

recited to fellow camp inmates), Klüger was not able to write them down until after the war ended in 1945, when she regained access to pen and paper; see Ruth Klüger, *Weiterleben*, 124–25, 164. On her strategy of reciting Schiller ballades during roll call at Auschwitz, see 124; on sabotaging the aims of the work she was forced to do at Christianstadt with the aid of reciting poems, 151; on the importance for her of being able to read "Osterspaziergang" ("Easter Walk") from Goethe's *Faust* while in Christianstadt, 161. For Klüger's incisive remarks on the importance of literature for understanding the Holocaust and her skepticism about the widespread insistence that literature should be passed over in favor of documents, 123–28. On the importance of poetry to concentration camp inmates, see also Andrés José Nader, *Traumatic Verses: On Poetry in German from the Concentration Camps, 1933–1945*, which includes an illuminating discussion of Klüger's two Auschwitz poems and their intricate and in cultural-political terms highly significant publishing history (51–70).

12. Chava Rosenfarb, *Confessions of a Yiddish Writer and Other Essays*, 6–7.

13. "The Great War occurred at a special historical moment when two 'liberal' forces were powerfully coinciding in England. On the one hand, the belief in the educative powers of classical and English literature was still extremely strong. On the other, the appeal of popular education and 'self-improvement' was at its peak, and such education was still conceived largely in humanistic terms. It was imagined that the study of literature at Workmen's Institutes and through such schemes as the National Home Reading Union would actively assist those of modest origins to rise in the class system. The volumes of the World's Classics and Everyman's Library were to be the 'texts'" (Paul Fussell, *The Great War and Modern Memory*, 157).

14. On Jewish youth movements in interwar Poland, see Ido Bassok, "Jewish Youth Movements in Poland between the Wars as Heirs of the *Kehilah*." More specifically on the centrality of books, libraries, and reading for these movements, see Ido Bassok, "Mapping Reading Culture in Interwar Poland—Secular Literature as a New Marker of Ethnic Belonging among Jewish Youth." In the introduction to *Hunger for the Written Word: Books and Libraries in the Jewish Ghettos of Nazi-Occupied Europe*, David Shavit addresses the role of literature and reading in the new post–World War I Jewish youth movements, and he refers to the continuing role of these movements and their literary dimension in the ghettos throughout. See also "Di yidishe yugent-bavegung in Poyln tsvishn beyde velt-milkhomes (a sotsyologishe shtudye)," where Moyshe Kligsberg notes how books and literary heroes were also frequent topics of discussion during intimate group walks undertaken outside the framework of the official activities of the youth organizations (Kligsberg, "Di yidishe yugent-bavegung," 174–75).

15. See Chone Shmeruk, "Hebrew-Yiddish-Polish: A Trilingual Jewish Culture," 293–94.

16. Shavit, *Hunger for the Written Word*, 4–7.

17. Shavit, *Hunger for the Written Word*, 7, 12. Kligsberg notes that even in a small town (*shtetl*) each youth movement strove to have its own library, in part to maintain prestige, and, more pragmatically, because "it kept members from having

to go borrow books from a competing organization, and it was also a charm [*sgule*] for attracting unaffiliated youths" (Kligsberg, "Di yidishe yugent-bavegung," 166).

18. According to Shavit, "literature and theater played almost as large a role in the Jewish youth movements as ideology" (Shavit, *Hunger for the Written Word*, 5). On the emphasis the various youth movements placed on far-ranging reading of literature (and not only of works that promoted the movement's particular ideology), see Kligsberg, "Di yidishe yugent-bavegung," 161. Kligsberg notes that there were also many unaffiliated libraries in Polish small towns (*shtetlekh*), some truly unaffiliated and organized by people devoted to pursuing education without committing to a political program, and others unaffiliated in name only but in fact places for young Jewish communists to meet clandestinely. Since the Communist Party was illegal in interwar Poland, communists frequently used officially unaffiliated cultural and sport organizations as covers (Kligsberg, "Di yidische yugent-bavegung," 166).

19. Shavit, *Hunger for the Written Word*, 31.

20. See Kligsberg, "Di yidishe yugent-bavegung," 166–67.

21. Shavit, *Hunger for the Written Word*, 23. Herman Kruk is the author of the "true crime" account from the Vilna ghetto, "Six Gallows," which is the main focus of chapter 7.

22. This statistic as well as the 425 libraries with 290,000 volumes operated by Tarbut comes from Shavit, *Hunger for the Written Word*, 11. Gennady Estraikh puts the number of libraries coordinated by the Kultur-lige throughout Poland at around 400 ("The Kultur-Lige in Warsaw: A Stopover in the Yiddishists' Journey between Kiev and Paris," 339). The vast majority of Warsaw's more than 50 Jewish libraries were established during or after World War I; see Shavit, *Hunger for the Written Word*, 20–21.

23. Shavit, *Hunger for the Written Word*, 11; Kligsberg, "Di yidishe yugent-bavegung," 167.

24. Shavit gives some striking examples, including that 75 percent of the books borrowed from the Hazamir Library in Warsaw were fiction, and that in Białystok's Sholem Aleichem library, 82 percent of readers read fiction and only 18 percent nonfiction (Shavit, *Hunger for the Written Word*, 32).

25. See Bassok, "Jewish Youth Movements," and "Mapping Reading Culture," 16–17.

26. On the basis of the same YIVO autobiographies that serve as Bassok's archive, Marcus Moseley argues that reading "opened up a path to communion with the self but also conduced to sundering of communion with family and community" (Moseley, "Life, Literature: Autobiographies of Jewish Youth in Interwar Poland," 9).

27. Bassok, "Mapping Reading Culture," 17. Moseley makes a related point in "Life, Literature," 6.

28. On the role of European literature and the normative codes of gender, sexuality, and romantic love they embody as models that nineteenth- and twentieth-century Jewish authors both adopted and subverted, see Naomi Seidman, *The Marriage Plot: Or, How Jews Fell in Love with Love, and with Literature*; on the role of Mapu's *The Love of Zion* in the lives of Haskalah authors, see 21–25. Based

on a study of the YIVO youth autobiographies of the 1930s, Moseley sees the emergence of modern forms of (autobiographical) Jewish selfhood as intimately tied to literary models of modern subjectivity encountered through private reading and the wider literary youth culture centered around the *lokal* and the library: "Empathetic identification with literary 'heroes' enabled the individual to give voice to aspects of the inner life that, without the mediation of literature, would not and could not have come to light. In other words, the library and the local played no small role in teaching Jewish youth to think, speak, write—autobiographically. They were 'autobiographical workshops'" (Moseley, "Life, Literature," 26–27). While affirming the central importance of reading for interwar Jewish youth, Bassok sees Moseley's interpretation of the importance of European models of literary selfhood as exaggerated and his support for it somewhat cherry-picked; see Ido Bassok, "The Historical Value of Young People's Autobiographies from the YIVO Collection" (Hebrew), 148–52. I thank Yael Teff-Seker for translating these pages of Bassok's Hebrew article for me.

29. In an entry of January 22, 1942, Ringelblum himself noted and reflected on how books, after all Jewish bookstores had been closed, were now being sold in the streets. See Emanuel Ringelblum, *Notes from the Warsaw Ghetto*, 244–45.

30. See Shavit, *Hunger for the Written Word*, 63–75, and Philip Friedman, "The Fate of the Jewish Book."

31. Shavit, *Hunger for the Written Word*, 46. On the libraries maintained in the Warsaw ghetto by the Zionist youth movements Ha-Shomer ha-Tsa'ir and Dror, see Shavit, *Hunger for the Written Word*, 75–76, and on those maintained by Ha-Shomer ha-Tsa'ir in Lodz as well as by the communists and the Left Poale Tsiyon in Lodz, see 85–86.

32. Emanuel Ringelblum, "Oyneg Shabes," 388; Shavit, *Hunger*, 76–77. On this aspect of the Oyneg Shabes's envisioned "Two-and-a-Half Year" report, see also Aaron Ayzenbakh, "Visenshaftlekhe forshungen in varshever geto," 72–73.

33. On the Vilna ghetto library and Kruk, see Shavit, *Hunger for the Written Word*, 99–112.

34. Herman Kruk, *The Last Days of the Jerusalem of Lithuania: Chronicles from the Vilna Ghetto and the Camps*, 283; see also Herman Kruk, *Togbukh fun vilner geto*, 257–58.

35. See Herman Kruk, "Library and Reading Room in the Vilna Ghetto, Strashun Street 6," and anon [Kruk et al.], "Vilna Ghetto Library Annual Report, 1941–1942," in *The Holocaust and the Book: Destruction and Preservation*, ed. Jonathan Rose, 171–76, 177–200. Appointed as director of the library center of the Kultur-lige and the Grosser Library in Warsaw in 1930, which that year consolidated the collections of eight smaller workers' libraries to become the largest and most popular worker's library in Poland, the Bundist activist Kruk was the most prominent Jewish socialist librarian in Poland. Under the umbrella of the Kultur-lige, he and his colleagues used the practices of modern librarianship to coordinate "some 400 (i.e., about half of all) Jewish libraries in towns around the country" (Estraikh, "The Kultur-Lige in Warsaw," 339). The practice of keeping detailed statistics about who used libraries and how, which Kruk and his staff continued in the Vilna ghetto, is highlighted in a

1929 handbook for workers' libraries as crucial for their mission. See Y. Rauchfleisch and L. Weiss, *Hantbukh far biblyotekn,* especially chapter 11, "Statistik fun der biblyotek," 37–46. For an English translation of selections from this handbook, see Jordan Finkin, "Workers' Libraries in Interwar Poland: Selections Translated from a Yiddish Handbook." On Kruk's far-reaching efforts to improve workers' libraries and to aid and educate non-professional librarians, see Ellen Kellman, "*Dos yidishe bukh alarmirt!* Towards the History of Yiddish Reading in Inter-War Poland," 234–40.

36. "Vilna Ghetto Library Annual Report," 192–93. In this passage, Kruk refers to a number of the most salient moments in the mass murder of Vilna Jews in fall 1941: the Germans rounded up nearly four thousand Jews from Ghettos 1 and 2 on Yom Kippur (October 1) 1941 and killed them in the Ponar woods. On October 24, the German authorities ordered the Judenrat to institute a system of work permits: yellow certificates (*Gelbscheine*) for valued workers and pink permits for up to three family members. The remaining inhabitants received white permits, and German troops swiftly rounded up five thousand holders of white permits and killed them in Ponar. On October 28–30, 1941, the Germans liquidated the smaller of the two ghettos (Ghetto No. 2).

37. Even in the library's reading room, which drew more "sophisticated" readers than the broader library (and more male readers: 86.2 percent male vs. 13.8 percent female visitors as compared to the 59 percent female vs. 41 percent male borrowers from the library at large), fiction accounted for 60 percent of what was read (Kruk, "Library and Reading Room," 196).

38. Kruk lamented that in the Vilna ghetto, where Yiddish was the language of the street, "Polish accounts for over 70 percent of the average book circulation . . . ; Yiddish, barely 20 percent; Hebrew, not even 2 percent" (Kruk, "Library and Reading Room," 195).

39. Ringelblum, "Oyneg Shabbes," 386.

40. Rosenfarb, *Confessions of a Yiddish Writer,* 4–5. In a paper dating from September 1945 Nachman Blumental likewise refers to an "epidemic of writing [*epidemye af shraybn*]" among Jews during the German occupation, from highly educated to simple people and even virtual analphabets, who improvised as best they could. See Blumental, "Di kharakteristik fun der yidisher literatur unter der daytshisher okupatsye," 28–29.

41. See Mintz, *Popular Culture,* chapter 2, "Two Models in the Study of Holocaust Representation." The "exceptionalist" paradigm in scholarship on the literature of the Holocaust, most influentially exemplified by Lawrence Langer, discourages the kind of reading I pursue in this book insofar as this approach, in Mintz's apt characterization, "discovers in the Holocaust a dark truth that inheres in the event" (Mintz, *Popular Culture,* 40–41), and, consequently, tends to reduce the active and culturally situated creativity and insight of Holocaust victims' interpretations of their experience to a depersonalized and predictable symptamotology of trauma. For a trenchant critique of Langer, see Gary Weissman, *Fantasies of Witnessing: Postwar Efforts to Experience the Holocaust,* chapter 2, "The Holocaust Experience." Among other problems in Langer's approach, Weissman highlights how, instead of attend-

ing to what Holocaust literature as such has to tell us, Langer strives to "remove the stain of the literary" from what he understands to be the fundamental Truth revealed by the Holocaust (Weissman, *Fantasies of Witnessing*, 132).

42. In *Holocaust and Memory*, Barbara Engelking draws on interviews with survivors of the Warsaw ghetto to reconstruct the ghetto as lived experience. In *Numbered Days: Diaries and the Holocaust*, Alexandra Garbarini "explores the strategies Jews employed in their search for meaning," including how Holocaust diarists frequently anticipated contemporary historiographical debates by expressly grappling with the question of the representability of the events they were witnessing (Garbarini, *Numbered Days*, 21). Amos Goldberg, in an important programmatic essay, "The History of the Jews in the Ghettos: A Cultural Perspective," calls for greater attention to how Jewish sources record the experience of radical transformation and disintegration of social and cultural systems of meaning. See also Goldberg's study of the hermeneutics of rumor in the Warsaw ghetto: "Rumor Culture among Warsaw Jews under Nazi Occupation: A World of Catastrophe Reenchanted." Kassow's *Who Will Write Our History?* richly contextualizes the massive documentary and literary project Ringelblum led and much of the cultural life of the ghetto. In *Text in the Face of Destruction: Accounts from the Warsaw Ghetto Reconsidered*, Jacek Leociak subtly analyzes diverse forms of written testimony from the Warsaw ghetto, paying particular attention to the subjective meanings, voicing, and what we could call the subjective phenomenology of this witnessing. Amy Simon's *Emotions in Yiddish Ghetto Diaries: Encountering Persecutors and Questioning Humanity* attends to the emotional experience of Yiddish diarists in the ghettos—how these writers felt about their persecution and those they understood to be responsible for it.

43. For a helpful taxonomy of the most common poetic themes and genres among an extensive corpus of unpublished poems written primarily by non-professional writers in ghettos and camps, see Miryam Trinh, "L'écriture poétique Durant la Shoah."

44. In *Trauma in First Person: Diary Writing During the Holocaust*, Amos Goldberg analyzes the experience of shattering symbolic structures in the diaries of Viktor Klemperer and Chaim Kaplan.

45. All the literary works from the Oyneg Shabes archive, original versions of works written in Polish and Polish translation of works written in Yiddish and other languages, have been collected in Agnieszka Żółkiewska and Marek Tuszewicki, eds., *Utwory literackie z getta warszawskiego* (Literary works from the Warsaw ghetto), vol. 26 of the complete edition of *Archiwum Ringelbluma* (The Ringelblum Archive), 29.

46. On the emergence of modern Jewish literature alongside and in ambivalent interaction with European models, see Seidman, *Marriage Plot*. As Seidman argues, "secular Jewish culture developed as distinctively Jewish even in its (always partial and ambivalent) embrace of European cultural models" (*Marriage Plot*, 301).

47. Conceiving of East European Jewry in minoritarian terms, according to Seidman, "hardly registers the 'thickness' of the Jewish worlds in which Hebrew and Yiddish literature emerged. It is within this rich cultural context that the stigmatization

of Jewish difference shows its other face as the *wielding* of Jewish distinctiveness" (*Marriage Plot*, 300–301).

48. Ringelblum writes, "Because most of our coworkers were suffering great hunger in Warsaw, that city of pitiless Jews, *O[neg] S[habes]* had to provide for them. We lobbied the social institutions to supply them with food parcels" (Ringelblum, "Oyneg Shabbes," 390). Nearly all the writers I analyze in this book received some measure of support. The director of the American Jewish Joint Distribution Committee (JDC, also commonly referred to as "the Joint") in Poland from 1921 until World War II, Yitzhak Giterman co-led the Joint in occupied Poland and played an important role in Aleynhilf efforts in the Warsaw ghetto and was a major supporter of the Oyneg Shabes. It was Giterman to whom Yoysef Kirman sent a desperate note from the Umschlagplatz at some point during the Great Deportation of summer 1942, from where he was about to be deported to Treblinka, and who was able to extricate Kirman (Kassow, *Who Will Write our History?*, 307). In a letter to Giterman, Shmuel Marvil expresses how honored he had felt to have received a stipend arranged by Giterman, not just as a person but as a *writer*. The single day depicted in the life of Arke, the protagonist of Leyb Goldin's "Chronicle of a Single Day," is organized around the one bowl of soup he gets daily at a soup kitchen. Goldin's autobiographical scenario is based on the nourishment he received at the soup kitchen for writers run by Rokhl Auerbach, one of the key members of the Oyneg Shabes team. Upon his return to Warsaw from Lviv (Lwów/Lemberg) after the German invasion of the Soviet Union, Yehoshue Perle was given a job by Shmuel Winter in the Judenrat's clothing department, which was run by Winter (who also maintained close ties with and provided aid to the Aleynhilf and the Oyneg Shabes). Jarecka worked as a telephone receptionist, typist, and translator in the chancellery of the Warsaw ghetto Judenrat. In the Lodz ghetto, Shaye Shpigl, Oskar Rosenfeld, and other writers, including Oskar Singer, were aided by the influential lawyer Henryk Naftalin, who headed the ghetto administration's Statistical Department, under whose auspices the ghetto archive and ghetto *Chronicle* were housed. Naftalin secured many writers relatively light and protected administrative positions, and more than once removed the name of a writer from lists of people to be deported. Herman Kruk was the director of the Vilna Ghetto Library.

49. That I do not engage in a more sustained way with the Vilna ghetto poems of Avrom Sutzkever will likely strike some readers as odd, since Sutzkever is by far the most renowned victim poet who wrote during the Holocaust. The published versions of his poems, however, seem to be overwhelmingly *revisions* of the texts he wrote in the Vilna ghetto and in the forests as a partisan. Unfortunately, due to the impossibility of traveling during my Covid-era sabbatical, I had to abandon plans to visit archives in Israel to discover whether there exist any unrevised ghetto manuscripts.

50. See Roskies, "Did the Shoah Engender a New Poetics?," 347–63.

51. The copy I have of the Yiddish text of "Zeks tlies," which Samuel Kassow generously shared with me, is missing the title page, and I have not been able to find this document in the YIVO Archives.

CHAPTER 1: NOVELISTIC TIME, HISTORICAL TIME, AND THE END OF OMNISCIENCE

1. We know that others wrote novels or parts of novels in Nazi ghettos, but none of them have been preserved. Israel Dimentman was awarded a literary prize by a jury nominated directly by Judenrat head Jakob Gens for his Hebrew novel *Ad ha-sha'ar* (Up to the gate), about the liquidation of the "little ghetto" in Vilna, submitted by the competition deadline of August 25, 1942; see Solon Beinfeld, "The Cultural Life of the Vilna Ghetto," 104. In an entry of March 28, 1943, Dawid Sierakowiak writes of his friend Wolman: "In the afternoon I went to Wolman's. He let me read the introduction to a novel he had begun writing" (Sierakowiak, *The Diary of Dawid Sierakowiak: Five Notebooks from the Łódź Ghetto*, 263). Likewise in the Lodz ghetto, among the many notes and sketches Oskar Rosenfeld made for literary works, he labels some of them as being explicitly for a novel; see Oskar Rosenfeld, *Wozu noch Welt: Aufzeichnungen aus dem Getto Lodz*, 252–53 / *In the Beginning Was the Ghetto: Notebooks from Łódź*, 235. According to Ber Mark, while in the Warsaw ghetto, Yehoshue Perle wrote a satirical novel, titled "Stivln" (Boots), about the Jewish police, which was lost. See Ber Mark, *Di umgekumene shrayber fun di getos un lagern un zeyere verk*, 139n7, and Ber Mark, ed., *Tsvishn lebn un toyt*, 13. In his 1948 *Azoy iz geven (khurbn varshe)* (The way it was [The destruction of Warsaw]), Jonas Turkow, however, makes no mention of the Jewish police being Perle's chief object of satire, describing this lost work merely as a "comedic satire [*komedye-satire*] based on local life in the Warsaw ghetto" (*Azoy iz geven*, 92) and later mentioning that Perle had depicted the Warsaw ghetto comedian Rubinshteyn in the work (*Azoy iz geven*, 124). In stating that "Turkow is our only source on the specific content of Perle's ghetto satire," David Roskies appears to leave Mark's (accurate or inaccurate) account out of consideration; see David G. Roskies, ed., *Everyday Jews: Scenes from a Vanished Life*, xxviii. Shortly before the war, Perle had completed a sequel to *Yidn fun a gants yor*, but the outbreak of World War II interrupted publication plans. Perle deposited a typescript of the novel with a friend when he left for Lemberg, and he was able to recover it when he returned to Warsaw. However, this copy was also eventually lost in the Warsaw ghetto. On this, see Rokhl Auerbach, *Varshever tsvoes: bagegenishn, aktivitetn, goyroles 1933–1943*, 331–33. Another example of longer works that have come down to us are the biblical dramas that Itzhak Katzenelson wrote in the Warsaw ghetto; for these (*Al neharot bavel* [By the rivers of Babylon] and *Iev* [Job]), see Itzhak Katzenelson, *Yidishe geto-ksovim, Varshe 1940–1943*.

2. The slightly discrepant handwritten titles of part 1 exemplify how the handwritten edits to the two copies of both parts 1 and 2 generally correspond closely but are not identical.

3. Page references to "Part 1" (RA I/605 CZ I) and "Part 2" (RA I/605 CZ III) in this chapter are to these typescripts. Four typescript copies (which sustained various degrees of damage) of a further, significantly abridged version of Skalov's novel were likewise preserved in the Oyneg Shabes (RA I/605 CZ II). This version comprises forty-seven pages in total (part 1, 1–20, and part 2, 21–47). Who made this condensed

version and why is unclear. Part 2 of the version is titled "Der kraytsshpin" (The cross spider). Skalov uses the symbolically resonant image of a cross spider and its web as a metaphor in the second part of his novel. Copy 1 of part 2 of the longer version is subtitled "Quo Vadis," but above this typed title someone has handwritten: "2ter teyl der kraytsshpin / kapitl I" (2nd part the cross spider / chapter 1). (Copy 2 of part 2 sustained significant damage and the title is missing.) Skalov's original manuscript may also have been included in the Oyneg Shabes archive, but it is presumed to be lost; see Żółkiewska and Tuszewicki, eds., *Utwory literackie z getta warszawskiego*, 29n52.

4. The Communist Yidish-bukh publishing house published over three hundred books, both new and classical works, in the 1950s and 1960s; see Zachary M. Baker, "Yiddish Publishing after 1945: A Brief Overview," 63. On the Warsaw Yidish-bukh publishing house and its publications, see Joanna Nalewajko-Kulkov, "The Last Yiddish Books Printed in Poland: Outline of the Activities of Yidish Bukh Publishing House." To what extent Mark was a willing agent of ideological revision and to what extent he may have responded reluctantly to ideological pressures when he subtracted from—and occasionally added to—Skalov's text is a complex issue. This is not the place to analyze the myriad discrepancies between Skalov's manuscript and Mark's edition. It is worth noting, however, that Mark's interventions were not always obviously ideologically driven. A great many of the passages in Skalov's novel that Mark suppressed have to do with sexuality and with sexual violence. For an analysis of the editorial interventions that resulted in significant discrepancies between the original versions of three literary works preserved in the Oyneg Shabes archive, including Skalov's novel, and the versions published in the 1950s by Yidish-bukh, see Katarzyna Person and Agnieszka Żółkiewska, "Edition of Documents from the Ringelblum Archive (the Underground Archive of the Warsaw Ghetto) in Stalinist Poland." Person and Żółkiewska note that the editorial censorship of these Yiddish literary texts from the Warsaw ghetto not only responded to political pressures within the context of Stalinist Poland but also strove to manipulate the image of life in the Warsaw ghetto for a postwar Yiddish reading audience by removing numerous passages that would have been acceptable to state authorities but that the editors (above all Ber Mark) deemed "'controversial,' 'shameful,' or ideologically unsound" (Person and Żółkiewska, "Edition of Documents," 37). On Mark's difficult situation in postwar Poland, see Audrey Kichelewski, "Être un historien juif en Pologne communiste: Bernard Mark (1908–1966), directeur de l'Institut d'histoire juive de Varsovie." On the Warsaw Jewish Historical Institute's Holocaust research agenda under Mark's leadership in Stalinist 1950s Poland, see Stephan Stach, "'The Spirit of the Time Left Its Mark on These Works': Writing the History of the Shoah at the Jewish Historical Institute in Stalinist Poland."

5. This anthology was published by the East German CDU's Union-Verlag with an introduction by Rudolf Hirsch. The edition indicates that the "literary adaptation" of Skalov's novel, titled *Unter dem Hakenkreuz: Fragment eines Romans* (Under the swastika: Novel fragment), was made by Hirsch on the basis of a translation into German by M. Weinryb. For this highly inaccurate version, see J. Bernstein et al., eds., *Ghetto: Berichte aus dem Warschauer Ghetto 1939–1945*, 17–114.

6. See Żółkiewska and Tuszewicki, eds., *Utwory literackie z getta warszawskiego.* For Agnieszka Żółkiewska's Polish translation of "Di hak on krayts," see 282–390.

7. Skalov had also published one further story, "Griln" (Crickets), in a Warsaw monthly literary journal in 1937.

8. For the twenty-nine-page handwritten manuscript of Skalov's reportage "A Shpatsir iber di punktn" see RA I/1146. For the published Yiddish text, see Ber Mark, ed., *Tsvishn lebn un toyt,* 73–96; a problematic German translation can be found in Bernstein et al., eds., *Ghetto,* 147–67. The punktn Skalov explores in this essay are: the Ogrodowa Street centers, 3 Dzika Street (with approximately two thousand residents, the largest refugee center in the Warsaw ghetto), 24 Cesia Street, 61 Dzika Street, 9 Stawki Street, 5 Elektoralna Street, and 11 Cesia Street.

9. In the sparse secondary literature on Skalov, one encounters references also to other essays by him in the Oyneg Shabes collection. In his introduction to *Di hak on krayts,* Mark writes: "He [Skalov] was also active as a close collaborator of the underground ghetto archive (Ringelblum archive). At the behest of the archive's leadership he wrote a series of reportages about expulsions, street life, and punktn for the homeless" (7). According to Mark, these reportages were at the time all in the JHI's collection. Presumably following Mark, the Yiddish poet Melech Ravitch notes: "In the underground archive of the Warsaw ghetto a few other things by him [Skalov] were preserved: "a stroll around the punktn," "in no one's land," "work of many," reportages on life in the centers for the homeless" (Melech Ravitch, entry on Skalov in vol. 6 of the *Leksikon fun der nayer yidisher literatur,* column 531). I have, however, been able to find only Skalov's reportage on the punktn, which is also published in Mark, ed., *Tsvishn lebn un toyt,* 73–96. JHI archivists have confirmed to me that some of the texts Mark refers to as existing in the JHI collection seem no longer to be there.

10. "Zelman Skalov displayed extraordinary perseverance during the blockades. He used to circulate in the streets during times of greatest danger. . . . I helped him and several other valuable people get themselves into the brush shop, and from there, it seems, he was seized. Skalov wrote a long time, particularly about current issues" (Ringelblum on Skalov, quoted in Ber Mark's introduction to his edition of *Di hak on krayts,* 8).

11. Two Yiddish writers, the militant polemicist Yashe Bronshteyn and Khatskel Dunets, addressed what Gennady Estraikh has called "the quasi spectacle" of the 1934 Congress, not as Yiddish writers per se but rather "as . . . general theoretician[s] of socialist realism." See Gennady Estraikh, "A Touchstone of Socialist Realism: The 1934 *Almanac* of Soviet Yiddish Writers," 24–25.

12. The key texts of the "Expressionism Debate," carried out chiefly in the German-language exile journal *Das Wort* published in Moscow, are available in Hans-Jürgen Schmitt, ed., *Die Expressionismusdebatte: Materialien zu einer marxistischen Realismuskonzeption.*

13. In his entry on Skalov in the *Leksikon fun der nayer yidisher literatur,* vol. 6, Melech Ravitch rightly calls Skalov's text a "sotsyal" novel.

14. In his 1987 book *To Live with Hope, to Die with Dignity,* Joseph Rudavsky claims that "Der Hakenkreitz [*sic*]" was written in its entirety in the Warsaw ghetto,

yet he does not indicate how he arrived at this conclusion; see Rudavsky, *To Live with Hope*, 27. Ber Mark speculates that Skalov prepared to write subsequent parts of the book and that he may indeed have done so, but he admits that whether Skalov actually continued to write remains unknown; see Mark, introduction to Skalov, *Di hak on krayts*, 8, and *Di umgekumene shrayber*, 80–81.

15. In one of the two typescript copies, the dating of the work is crossed out by hand (and rendered illegible); in the other, the dating reads: "Varshe, nay-yor, 1940."

16. Part 1 (57) refers, for example, to the detonation of the monument to Tadeusz Kosciuszko (the Polish national hero who in 1794 led an uprising against the partitioning of Poland) on Plac Wolnosci in Lodz, in which the Germans forced Jews to take part. This historical event took place on November 10–11, 1939. Five pages later the text describes a Jewish children's game of playing the part of Germans voicing anti-Jewish orders and insults in German and describes it as a "sadly monotonous [*monotone*] game on the cusp of a new year" (Skalov, part 1, 62). A page and a half before the end of part 1, Skalov's text makes reference to the character Bernard's psychological reaction to the regulation requiring Jews to wear special identifying signs, a practice that, an authorial footnote informs us, was instituted on December 1, 1939. Thus, the manuscript of part 1 (again, dated "New Year's, 1940") refers to events that had occurred as late as December 1939.

17. On page 49 of the 104-page manuscript of part 2.

18. These three pages of Skalov's manuscript, from the mention of the first (and quickly delayed) announcement of the ghetto through Ede's experience of rape and humiliation at the hands of Nazis in Lodz, is omitted in Mark's edition.

19. See for example Chaim Kaplan's diary entries for November 5 and 8, 1939, in Chaim A. Kaplan, *A Scroll of Agony*, 64–65 and 66–67. See also the diary entry by Ludwik Landau for November 5, 1939, quoted in Barbara Engelking and Jacek Leociak, *The Warsaw Ghetto: A Guide to the Perished City*, 54. The Germans took Jewish hostages and threatened that they would release them only after the plan had been realized; but after several negotiations with the Jewish Council, led by its chairman, Adam Czerniakow, the Germans gave up on the plan and freed the hostages. On this first German plan to establish a ghetto in Warsaw and the negotiations that forestalled it, see Engelking and Leociak, *Warsaw Ghetto*, 53–55.

20. Ber Mark is mistaken when he interprets the "New year's, 1940" date of part 1 as the date when Skalov began writing his manuscript rather than when he completed it. Mark writes: "That is surely the date when the author began writing the novel because the first part, which begins with the mobilization in September 1939, ends at the time when the ghetto in Warsaw was sealed, i.e. October 1940" (Mark, *Di umgekumene shrayber*, 80). Mark assumes that mention of the ghetto toward the end of part 1 refers to the creation of the ghetto in fall 1940 when it in fact refers to the initial plans for a ghetto, which the Nazi authorities announced in November 1939. It is customary to sign a manuscript with the date of its completion. And while it is not uncommon for an author to give the dates when a text was begun *and* completed, it is hard to imagine an author intending a single date they add at the conclusion of a manuscript to be understood as the date they began writing it.

21. This would have been just a few blocks north, where Graniczna flows into Plac Żelaznej Bramy.

22. That Skalov made this plot choice early on in fall 1939 finds support in Skalov's authorial footnote added to the end of part 1, in which he corrects aspects of his depiction of the massacre of Jews at Vishkov on the basis of information that had clearly reached him between the time he wrote that scene and "New Year's, 1940," when he completed part 1. See Skalov's long footnote, part 1, 66.

23. The subtitle is in part an allusion to the Polish novelist Henryk Sienkiewicz's 1896 historical novel by the same title that depicts the persecution of early Christians in the time of Nero (and by analogy, the persecution of Poles at various historical junctures).

24. The earlier discussion of systematic clearing of Jews from certain neighborhoods follows a scene in which characters discuss recent events that had occurred in August 1940 (for example, France's capitulation on August 16 and a speech by Hans Frank, also of August 16, 1940). Thus the news of the forced evacuation of Jews from certain areas was likely an allusion to the intensification of evacuations that ensued after Leist's decree of August 7, 1940, requiring Jews to move out of the proposed German district; see Engelking and Leociak, *Warsaw Ghetto*, 39. The Fayfer family learns in this scene that they are being evicted from their home in the vicinity of (*in der gegent fun*) Zshuravye (Żurawia) Street (part 2, 19). Jewish diarists in Warsaw understood Leist's August 1940 decree as a step toward creating a ghetto. See the entry for August 9, 1940, by Ludwik Landau (quoted in Engelking and Leociak, *Warsaw Ghetto*, 62) and Chaim Kaplan's entry for August 10, 1940, where he writes, "The first step has just been taken for the establishment of a ghetto. In connection with this, the matter of the walls dividing the streets, which the Judenrat erected at its own expense, is now clarified" (Kaplan, *Scroll of Agony*, 178).

25. See Engelking and Leociak, *Warsaw Ghetto*, 63. The *Gazeta Żydowska* was the (only) official newspaper for all of the ghettos in the Generalgouvernement, the first number of which appeared on July 23, 1940.

26. For the historical background of Jewish refugees in the Soviet Union who chose to return to Nazi-occupied Poland after April–May 1940, see Ben-Cion Pinchuk, "Jewish Refugees in Soviet Poland, 1939–1941," 151–53.

27. Moreover, the narrative signals the real need for Jewish police to bring order into the chaotic ghetto, especially in the foot traffic in the dangerously crowded streets (Skalov, part 2, 76). On the attitudes toward the Jewish police among the ghetto population see Katarzyna Person, *Warsaw Ghetto Police: The Jewish Order Service during the Nazi Occupation*, chapter 9, "Police in the Eyes of the Ghetto Population."

28. Marszałkowska, like Żurawia, where (or near where) the Fayfer family had lived, was "cleansed" of Jews in September 1940. See Engelking and Leociak, *Warsaw Ghetto*, 64.

29. Belzec began in April 1940 as a labor camp. Construction on the extermination camp began in November 1941. Thus when Albert was draining swamps in the Belzec camp in fall 1940, it was still in its first iteration as a work camp.

30. Such a dreaded *reynikungaktsye*—*paruvke*, from the Polish *parówka* (steam-

ing)—figures importantly in Peretz Opoczynski's literary reportage "Building No. 21," 22–30.

31. For his part, Mazur finds himself fairly ruined and abandoned as well. Usually drunk before, he is now drunk constantly. The company "Irene" has ceased to exist, and his mistress Irene for whom it was named leaves the room she had been renting from him. His wife, Marisha, turns away from him. He continues to be plagued by his uncontrollable sexual fantasies, and he drifts into insanity and is institutionalized. See part 2, 43–44, 48.

32. See Agnieszka Żółkiewska and Marek Tuszewicki's introduction to vol. 26 of the complete edition of Oyneg Shabes texts published by the Jewish Historical Institute, Warsaw; here 29. This volume collects the literary texts preserved in the archive, including Skalov's novel; I thank Anna Klosowska for translating Żółkiewska and Tuszewicki's introduction to this volume for me. The Polish introduction can be found at https://cbj.jhi.pl/documents/1019524/0/.

33. See Engelking and Leociak, *Warsaw Ghetto*, 311.

34. Engelking and Leociak, *Warsaw Ghetto*, 314.

35. Between April and November 1941, the mortality rate among deportees into the Warsaw ghetto rose 300 percent, and in August 1941 it was three times higher per thousand inhabitants compared to the ghetto population at large. See Engelking and Leociak, *Warsaw Ghetto*, 314.

36. Quoted in Christopher R. Browning, *The Origins of the Final Solution: The Evolution of Nazi Jewish Policy, September 1939–March 1942*, 158. The skyrocketing death rate in the Warsaw ghetto would peak in July 1941 (5,550) and August 1941 (5,560) before beginning to decline and stabilize (Browning, *Origins of the Final Solution*, 159).

37. Reyzl's father has, however, been killed in the German bombing of Warsaw and his carpentry shop destroyed. She and her mother now live in the apartment that Moyshe will eventually use for smuggling.

38. This is one of Skalov's many evocations of a spider or its web; part 2 of the abridged version of Skalov's novel bears the title "the cross spider."

39. More recently, the Lodz ghetto has been the subject of a further ambitious novel, Steve Sem-Sandberg's *De fattiga i Łódź* (*The Emperor of Lies*, 2010).

40. Melech Ravitch, "Vegn a nay khurbn-bukh, vos iz dershinen in varshe" (Regarding a new Holocaust book published in Warsaw), 6.

41. "A book such as Skalov's is more of a chronicle. It is an attempt to depict the life of Jews at the very threshold of their disappearance. This bundle of descriptions and depictions threaded together into a novel was merely a means to open up the abyss. For such a novel in the ghetto had no possibility to grow and encompass a normal course of a more or less settled way of life" (Shtern, "An interesante khronik," 45).

42. Anita Norich, *The Homeless Imagination in the Fiction of Israel Joshua Singer*, 50.

43. On Némirovsky's recourse to musical models of esthetic unity, see Marta Laura Cenedese, "The Rhythm of Unity: Irène Némirovsky's *Suite française* and

Leo Tolstoy's *War and Peace*"; Dominique Délas and Marie-Madeleine Castellani, "Une symphonie inachevée: Structure de *Suite française* d'Irène Némirovsky"; and Olivier Philipponnat, "'Un ordre différent, plus puissant et plus beau': Irène Némirovsky et le modèle symphonique." While Némirovsky indeed makes repeated mention of musical models in her working notes included in appendix 1 to *Suite française*, she also repeatedly conceives of esthetic rhythm and unity in cinematic terms; see Némirovsky, *Suite française*, appendix 1, 376, 283–84.

44. For a measured and thoughtful consideration of the lack of Jews in *Suite française*, see Susan Rubin Suleiman, "Irène Némirovsky and the 'Jewish Question' in Interwar France."

45. For a careful analysis of Némirovsky's portrait of the French nation in *Suite française*, see Nathan Bracher, *After the Fall: War and Occupation in Irène Némirovsky's* Suite française, 32–44.

46. See Némirovsky's rich working notes included in appendix 1 of *Suite française*, 373–89; here 383. The need to subordinate historical events to esthetic harmony is something of a leitmotif throughout Némirovsky's working notes, for example: "As many meetings as possible but not historical, rather the masses, social events or battles in the streets or something like that!" (385); and, in the final lines included in this appendix to *Suite française*, "The most important and most interesting thing here is the following: the historical, revolutionary facts etc. must be only lightly touched upon, while daily life, the emotional life and especially the comedy it provides must be described in detail" (389). As Marta Laura Cenedese aptly summarizes, "It emerges that with *Suite française* Némirovsky was writing a historical narrative in which, against the backdrop of historical crisis, fictionalized reactions and actions on the part of individuals and communities were to take predominance for their 'universal' quality" (Cenedese, "The Rhythm of Unity," 73).

47. At least one further wartime novel deserves mention here, David Vogel's first-person autobiographical Yiddish novel based on his experience of internment in various concentration camps for foreigners in France. Vogel's novel has never been published in the original Yiddish. Menachem Peri's Hebrew translation appeared under the title *Kulamyazu lakrav* (They all went out to battle) in the anthology of Vogel's prose works *Takhanot kavot* (Stations that have lost their light). Since I am unable to read Hebrew, my only access to the novel has been Rosie Pinhas-Delpeuch's French translation of Peri's Hebrew translation, *Et ils partirent pour la guerre*. Given my multiple removes from the Yiddish text and the fact that, according to Pinhas-Delpeuch, without Peri's "work of selection and quasi adaptation" the manuscript "could never have been published," I can here only allude to this clearly fascinating work; see Rosie Pinhas-Delpeuch and Menahem Peri, "Postface" to David Vogel, *Et ils partierent pour la guerre*, 242–45; here, 244–45.

48. On the absence, indeed the impossibility, of foreshadowing in processual novels, see Gary Saul Morson, *Prosaics and other Provocations: Empathy, Open Time, and the Novel*, 109, 111, 120.

49. In a paper he originally presented on September 19, 1945, in Lodz at the second scientific (*visnshaftlekh*) meeting of the Central Jewish Historical Commission,

Nachman Blumental identified the sentiment that "justice will prevail!" as one of the recurrent motifs of literature written in Yiddish during the war years. See Blumental, "Di kharakteristik fun der yidisher literatur unter der daytshisher okupatsye," 35. Miryam Trinh confirms Blumental's findings on the basis of a study of 651 unpublished poems in multiple languages by non-professional authors held in multiple archives. Trinh concludes that "from the Yiddish part of [this] corpus emanates the attachment to justice as a supreme moral value and the persistent confidence in the future of the [Jewish] people despite the awareness of the annihilation" (Trinh, "L'écriture poétique durant la Shoah," 9).

50. Frank Kermode, *The Sense of an Ending: Studies in the Theory of Fiction.*

51. One of several words that mark Nickel's speech as German, although rendered in Yiddish.

52. The word *velt* in "velt-progres" is stricken through in typescript copy 1, and it is omitted in Mark's edition (see p. 97).

53. The reference is to Adolf Hitler and Hans Frank, the Nazi Governor-General of Poland during World War II.

54. I borrow the term and concept of backshadowing from Michael André Bernstein, *Foregone Conclusions: Against Apocalyptic History.*

55. See Opoczynski, "Building No. 21."

PREFACE TO CHAPTERS 2–4

1. Scholars of the recent cultural turn in Holocaust studies have dealt extensively with diaries (e.g., Garbarini, *Numbered Days,* and Goldberg, *Trauma in First Person*), personal narratives (e.g., Barbara Engelking, *Holocaust and Memory: The Experience of the Holocaust and its Consequences; An Investigation Based on Personal Narratives*), and testimonial prose (e.g., Leociak, *Text in the Face of Destruction* and Nicholas Chare and Dominic Williams, *Matters of Testimony: Interpreting the Scrolls of Auschwitz*). Eric Sundquist's 2018 anthology *Writing in Witness: A Holocaust Reader* likewise participates in this turn by focusing primarily on wartime writing. David Roskies's source reader of texts from the Oyneg Shabes archive, *Voices from the Warsaw Ghetto: Writing Our History,* has likewise made many key wartime texts easily available in English translation. Wartime victim poetry has, however, received comparatively little attention, aside from the poems of Paul Celan (the earliest of which were written during the war years) and, to a lesser extent, the Hungarian poet Mikós Radnóti, whose stunning, ironically titled "Picture Postcards" have received significant attention, including readings by prominent scholars of Holocaust literature such as Susan Gubar and Sue Vice. Among the Yiddish poets, Avrom Sutzkever has received the most attention, including work on his wartime and early postwar poems by, for example, Hannah Pollin-Galay ("The Epic Demands of Postwar Yiddish" and "Avrom Sutzkever's Art of Testimony") and Jan Schwarz ("After the Destruction of Jewish Vilna" and *Survivors and Exiles,* chapter 1, "Vilna: Avrom Sutzkever"). Roskies reconstructs a turning point in the consciousness of the Holocaust in 1943 in a number of writers, including Sutzkever and Katzenelson (see Roskies, "Did the Shoah Engender a New Poetics?"). Frieda Aaron's earlier

(1990) study, *Bearing the Unbearable: Yiddish and Polish Poetry in the Ghettos and Concentration Camps*, presents a selection of wartime poems in Polish and Yiddish, including rather extensive treatment of Sutzkever and the Polish language poet Władysław Szlengel, but does so rather uncritically. Daniel Feldman and Efraim Sicher's worthwhile study *Poesis in Extremis: Literature Witnessing the Holocaust* appeared with Bloomsbury Academic (2024) after I had already submitted the manuscript of this book, so I was not able to engage it here.

2. Theodor W. Adorno, "Kulturkritik und Gesellschaft," 49. My translation.

3. As Adorno's defenders would be right to point out, his original pronouncement on the barbarity of writing poetry after Auschwitz points up important dangers not only in continuing, without serious critical examination, to affirm the role that cultural forms play within totalizing systems that have engendered unprecedented genocidal violence but also, self-reflexively, the dangers that any attempt on the part of cultural critics like himself to underscore these dangers could be flattened, tamed, and absorbed into the terrifying workings of reified capitalist society. In the passage in which Adorno's dictum appears, he is indeed warning that even statements underscoring how culture is inextricably implicated in barbarity—including his own—remain vulnerable to becoming reduced to commodified clichés. The reduction of Adorno's complex thought to a single soundbite widely circulated as a commodified cliché aptly, if bleakly, demonstrates his point. As is well known, throughout the 1960s Adorno qualified his original statement about writing poetry after Auschwitz in a number of subtle and intellectually fascinating texts (to which I can here only allude). For an overview of the key texts in the Adorno-inspired poetry-after-Auschwitz debate, see Theodor W. Adorno, *Lyrik nach Auschwitz? Adorno und die Dichter*.

4. In Petra Kiedaisch's view, Adorno intended his original thesis as a "provocative incitement to think (*Denkanregung*) and not as a prohibition" (Kiedaisch, "Einleitung," in *Lyrik nach Auschwitz?*, 15). Günther Bonheim sees Kiedaisch's interpretation as an example of a widespread dismissal of the seriousness of Adorno's diagnosis that poetry had become impossible, a diagnosis Bonheim endorses (Günther Bonheim, *Versuch zu zeigen, daß Adorno mit seiner Behauptung, nach Auschwitz lasse sich kein Gedicht mehr schreiben, recht hatte*, 12). For Dieter Lamping, as I read him, Adorno shows the way beyond his own proscription, toward the possibility of writing poems after Auschwitz, but also sets the esthetic limits within which such poems may be articulated; see Dieter Lamping, "Gedichte nach Auschwitz, über Auschwitz." In equating indirect allusions to abstract suffering with writing from "the perspective of the victims," Otto Lorenz continues Adorno's foreclosure on speech by victims, poetic or otherwise, that conveys anything more than raw inarticulate suffering; see Otto Lorenz, "Gedichte nach Auschwitz oder: Die Perspektive der Opfer."

5. This can be seen, for example, in how in their introduction to a journal issue dedicated to "Holocaust Poetry," Antony Rowland and Robert Eaglestone muse about how different the writing and reception of poems about the Holocaust might have been had Adorno not delimited the parameters for thinking about "poetry after

Auschwitz." Departing from French political deportee Robert Antelme's important remarks about the status of poetry by deportees as perhaps the truest account of the camps, Rowland and Eaglestone write: "The development of Holocaust poetry and criticism could have been very different if Antelme's comments had become [*sic*] to be regarded as maxims instead of Adorno's polemics. There might not, for example, have been such an emphasis on the resistant, modernist aesthetics of writers such as Celan and Adorno. The testimonial poetics of authors such as Borowski might not have been ignored" (Antony Rowland and Robert Eaglestone, "Introduction: Holocaust Poetry," in *Holocaust Poetry*, 4). Although Rowland and Eaglestone productively unsettle ways in which critical focus on Adorno's dictum has narrowly delimited discourse about poetry and the Holocaust, their suggestion to focus, instead, on Antelme's question in turn frames out any mention of East European Jewish wartime poets or songwriters. These include (but are by no means limited to) Hirsh Glik, Shmerke Kaczerginski, Leyb Rozental, Leah Rudnitsky, and Avrom Sutzkever, who wrote poetry and songs in Yiddish in the Vilna ghetto; the Warsaw ghetto poets Yoysef Kirman and Shmuel Marvil (who wrote in Yiddish), Katzenelson (Yiddish and Hebrew), and Władysław Szlengel (Polish); the Lodz Yiddish poets Yankele Herszkowicz, Chava Rosenfarb, Simkhe Bunem Shayevitsh, Shaye Shpigl, and Miriam Ulinover; Avrom Akselrod, who wrote Yiddish poetry in the Kovno ghetto; and Mordechai Gebirtig, who wrote Yiddish poems in the Krakow ghetto. Rose Ausländer and Rokhl Korn also wrote wartime poems in German and Yiddish, respectively.

6. On the importance of poetry in the increasingly oral literary culture of the ghettos—as opportunities to circulate written literature became scarcer—see Nachman Blumental, "Di kharakteristik fun der yidisher literatur unter der daytshisher okupatsye," 32–34. Although he published this essay in 1966 in the postwar Polish Jewry series published in Buenos Aires, Blumental indicates in a footnote (26n4) that he originally presented it as a paper (*referat*) in September 1945, at the second academic conference of the Central Jewish Historical Commission, then based in Lodz. On the role of songs in the Lodz ghetto, see Gila Flam, *Singing for Survival: Songs of the Lodz Ghetto.*

CHAPTER 2: SHMUEL MARVIL'S TORN WORDS

1. The Oyneg Shabes documents are housed in the archives of the Jewish Historical Institute in Warsaw. Yad Vashem and the United States Holocaust Memorial Museum in Washington, DC, each have a complete set of copies. For Ber Mark's summary of and remarks on Marvil's "Di gas" and on Marvil more generally, see Mark, *Di umgekumene shrayber*, 128–29. Writing in Stalinist Poland, Mark's idiom is typically ideological. For a nuanced attempt to understand Mark's position and that of the Jewish Historical Institute that Mark led within and against this Stalinist context, see Stach, "Spirit of the Time."

2. See the largely verbatim entries on Marvil in Zalmen Zylbercweig, *Leksikon fun yidishn teater*, vol. 5, 4558–59, and Shmuel Charney [Niger] and Jacob Shatzky, *Leḳsiḳon fun der nayer yidisher liṭeraṭur*, vol. 5, 498–99.

3. For background on Yitzhak Giterman, see note 48 to this book's introduction.

Giterman was shot to death by the Germans on January 18, 1943, the day on which the first shots were fired at Nazis by the Jewish resistance in the Warsaw ghetto. He "was running to warn his neighbors on Mila 69 that the SS had entered the ghetto" (Kassow, *Who Will Write Our History?*, 356).

4. On the Warsaw ghetto Aleynhilf, see, for example, Engelking and Leociak, *Warsaw Ghetto*, 292–316, and Kassow, *Who Will Write Our History?*, 112–19.

5. In this letter Marvil mentions reading his poems to "friends Sh. Stefinski, Hillel Zeitlin and Yitzkhok Katzenelson" (Marvil, letter to Giterman).

6. See Sarah Traister Moskovitz's biographical blurb on Marvil: https://poetryinhell.org/appendix-b-brief-biographies-of-authors/shmuel-marvil-1906-1943/. Zalmen Zylbercweig states only that Marvil was born in 1906 and "killed by the Nazis" (Zylbercweig, *Leksikon fun yidishn teater*, vol. 5, 4558).

7. The poem features extended apostrophes: stanzas 1–3, 9–10, 17–18, 34–36, and possibly also 37. It is impossible to know with certainty in the case of the last stanza (37) because the final page of the manuscript decomposed while it was buried in the Oyneg Shabes archive.

8. Sarah Traister Moskovitz has published her translations of the Yiddish-language poetry preserved in the Oyneg Shabes in a bilingual edition on her website Poetry in Hell (most of these poems were written before World War II, but a number, like Marvil's, were written in the Warsaw ghetto). Moskovitz includes the original Yiddish of each poem, using published versions when possible, and otherwise using an image of the manuscript. These are sometimes typescripts but frequently, as in the case of Marvil's poem, handwritten manuscripts. Thus, for many Yiddish-language poems preserved in the Oyneg Shabes, including Marvil's "The Street," what is currently available are only the handwritten manuscripts and Moskovitz's English translations. It should be noted that it is usually impossible to tell whether a given manuscript is in the author's hand or in that of an Oyneg Shabes copyist. In this chapter, I frequently modify (and, much less frequently, correct errors in) Moskovitz's rhyming and more poetic translation of "The Street." The translation of these first two stanzas is modified.

9. In its final paradoxical twist, however, Ashbery's poem reduces the poem and the *you* who has been addressed throughout, ostensibly as a reader, to a point of indistinction, so that it is possible, in retrospect, to understand the addresses to that *you* as having been the poem's apostrophes to itself all along:

I think you exist only
To tease me into doing it, on your level, and then you aren't there
Or have adopted a different attitude. And the poem
Has set me softly down beside you. The poem is you.

10. I accessed the more literal bridge translation of Gaarriye's "Mandheela" by Martin Orwin and Maxamed Xasan "Alto" on the Poetry Translation Center website (https://www.poetrytranslation.org/poems/mandela/literal); however, it seems to be no longer available. The Somali original was also available there. For a concise overview of Somali poetics that includes explanations of *hees* songs and *jiifto* metrics, see Martin Orwin's entry on "Somali Poetry" in Roland Greene et al., eds., *The*

Princeton Encyclopedia of Poetry and Poetics, 4th ed., 1313–14, which includes a bibliography of secondary literature.

11. For Rosenfarb's "Mimaamakim," see Chava Rosenfarb, *Di balade fun nekhtikn vald un ander lider*, 45–53; for Hannah Pollin-Galay's English translation, from which I quote, see Rosenfarb, "From the Depths."

12. See the first paragraph of Hannah Pollin-Galay, introduction to Rosenfarb, "From the Depths."

13. Culler sees justification in "identifying" apostrophe and "lyric itself" (Jonathan D. Culler, *The Pursuit of Signs: Semiotics, Literature, Deconstruction*, 137).

14. This is in fact how Culler accounts for the "embarrassment" with which apostrophe has often been met: those who care most deeply about lyric poetry and its timeless, transcendent quality are loath to acknowledge the extent to which this eternity effect is dependent on the awkward apostrophic device (*O!*).

15. Chaim Kaplan's comments on individual burial (for the privileged few) vs. mass burial (for the majority who have died of hunger or disease, etc.) provides illuminating context on the breakdown of burial rites to which Marvil is also responding. Dated March 7, 1942, Kaplan's entry stems from roughly the same time as Marvil's poem. After remarking on two classes who get buried individually, Kaplan moves on to the larger "third class":

> The third class is the dead, victims of hunger and epidemic—the majority—gathered up in the streets of the ghetto, who went to their deaths outdoors in the ghetto, who perished in the hospitals, who died of hunger in some attic, in general the children of indigence and poverty, who have no one to labor in their behalf and bring each one to burial in his own individual grave. Dead of that sort are brought to burial in a huge, deep mass grave, just as they are: naked, without purification, without planks. For that "elite" no individual funerals are held for each one. Their burial is, after all, a wholesale business. What were formerly the stables of the cemetery have become chambers for the dead. They're thrown there like the carcasses of animals. Body after body of the departed, laid one on top of the other. In such positions, insulting the humane feelings within you, half breaking your body. The impression crushes your breath from you like a vise. Is that man and his end? A living man is unlike a dead one in his ugliness. Ugliness that has some movement is relative ugliness; still ugliness, with no movement, is absolute ugliness. Then man is revealed in all his nothingness and weakness.
>
> Dead of that sort accumulate during the day by the dozens and dozens. Like dung they pile up in the stables waiting for burial till they reach the grave digger's quota. The dawn is still spread over the new cemetery annexed to the left side of the old one, behind the stables. That is an enormous, square grave, nearly fifty meters by fifty meters in length and breadth; and in depth—ten meters. There they are brought down a wooden ladder leaning on the lip of one end of the pit. Down that ladder they are brought to their eternal rest one by one. A thin layer of dust is spread over them, which does not cover them,

so that limbs reach out and protrude. But not for long. The next morning new corpses are lowered, laid down, and "buried" in the same fashion. Row after row; layer upon layer. One need fear no strife among the brethren buried together, perish the thought. They lived in darkness, they went to death in darkness and in darkness they were buried [editorial note: paraphrase of "Bontshe shvayg" by I. L. Peretz]. No one knows of their grave.

But the day will come when the Jewish people will raise a permanent memorial upon that very mass grave. (Kaplan, *Scroll of Agony*, 301–2)

16. The speaker of Katzenelson's first of two "Songs of the Cold," dated January 10, 1942 (roughly the same time as Marvil's "Di gas"), depicts a similar scene:

I went out into the empty streets.
I stepped over people who were frozen
Lying like felled trees.
Their arms flung out in a dumb terror,
Like a vain, empty cry.
Stiff ones,
Is it me you greet?"
(trans. Elinor Robinson, in Roskies, ed., *Voices from the Warsaw Ghetto*, 179)

For the Yiddish text of this poem, see Katzenelson, *Yidishe geto-ksovim*, 620.

17. Yoysef Kirman's reportage "Fun pleytim-shtetl—Dzshike un Niske" (Of the refugee-shtetl at Dzshike and Niske Streets) ends poignantly with the depiction of pious Jews who come at dawn to the refugee centers and try to approximate traditional Jewish rituals by paying final respect to—and asking forgiveness (*betn mekhile*) of—those who have died on the street overnight: "Kumen mentshn, frume mentshn, got-forkhtike un tsiterdike—dekn in kaltn baginen-sheyn di toyt-farshteyfte meysim-gufim mit vayse papir-boygn ayn; leygn royte tsigl-shtiker di bar-minanes tsukopens un arum di zaytn, vi neshome-likht—lehavdil . . . sheptshen derbay a tfile shtil, betn mekhile far zikh, far eygn vayb un kind, far vayte un noente un far gants varshe vegn . . ." (People, pious people, come, God-fearing and trembling. By the cold light of dawn they cover the corpses in the throes of rigor mortis with sheets of white paper, lay shards of red brick at the head and around the sides of the dead [*bar-minanes*], like—excuse the comparison—memorial candles [*neshome-likht*]. They whisper a quiet prayer while doing so, ask forgiveness [*betn mekhile*] for themselves, for their own wife and child, for those far and near and for all of Warsaw for . . .) Yoysef Kirman, "Fun pleytim-shtetl—Dzshike un Niske," 43; the ellipses are in the original and conclude Kirman's text.

18. When Kaplan (in the passage quoted in n. 15 in this chapter) bemoans the many dead who are buried "naked, without purification, without planks," he is likewise referring to the ritual of *taharah* (during which bodies being purified rest on planks).

19. In his letter to Yitzhak Giterman of April 13, 1942, Marvil writes: "I have lately written a lot, I've finished several books. I send you one thing from the (last one?), a poem 'The Street and Life Today.' Take your time and read it through. Lately I often

read to friends Sh. Stefinski, Hillel Zeitlin and Yitzkhok Katzenelson. They say that someday I will be able to say that the zlotys that were given to me were not for nothing."

20. Sarah Moskovitz comments on how painful it was for her to encounter Marvil's damaged manuscript during her translation work:

> Shmuel Marvil's poem . . . "Di gas" [The Street] was very painful to look at because as he is describing the destruction he sees of people and houses in the Warsaw Ghetto streets, the last stanzas on the last page of the poem are also disappearing, torn away, destroyed as was its author. The illegibility of words written by a person who was murdered is a particularly disturbing frustration for me. I feel a great responsibility to preserve the words of a person who did not survive. But this was not always possible. To guess mistakenly would be unforgivable. And to face missing blanks without resolution is a kind of mourning. (Sarah Moskovitz, Introduction to Miriam Ulinover, "'Rich with this Tradition': Ghetto Poetry," 81)

21. For Marek Tuszewicki's Polish translation, see Żółkiewska and Tuszewicki, eds., *Utwory literackie z getta warszawskiego*, 246–50.

22. The *lamed* in the two lines *Azoy iz shoyn l*[. . .] could plausibly be the first letter of *levone* (moon) or *likht* (light).

23. While the latter construction is more common in German, it would be plausible in a Yiddish poem.

24. Or to paraphrase the 1934 lyrics to the now-standard American ballad "Blue Moon" by Lorenz Hart, a great-grandnephew of Heinrich Heine: The moon sees us standing alone, hears us when we say a prayer.

25. Percy Bysshe Shelley, "To the Moon," in *The Complete Works of Percy Bysshe Shelley*, 621.

26. See John Keats, *Complete Poems*, 247.

27. I have read Rupert Moreton's English translation of Pushkin's "The Moon" published on the *Lingua Fennica* website: https://linguafennica.wordpress.com/2017/05/20/the-moon-месяц-alexander-pushkin/. The Russian original is also available there. For a more standard edition see A. S. Pushkin, *Sobranie sochinenii*, vol. 1.

28. See Heinrich Heine, *Die Heimkehr*, XXVI ("Mir träumte: traurig schaute der Mond") in *Heinrich Heine, Historisch-kritische Gesamtausgabe der Werke*, Band 1, *Buch der Lieder*, 237.

29. I have described the later version of this poem. For the earlier and the later versions, see Johann Wolfgang von Goethe, *Werke*, vol. 1: *Gedichte und Epen I*, 128–30.

30. See Joseph von Eichendorff, "Mondnacht," *Werke in sechs Bänden*, Band 1, 322–23. I quote from the translation by Richard Stokes, *The Book of Lieder*, 447. Eichendorff's "Mondnacht" was set to music by Robert Schumann in 1840 (op. 39, 5) and by Johannes Brahms in 1853–1854; see Eichendorff, *Werke in sechs Bänden*, Band 1, 1036.

31. The original Polish of these lines read: "Moją lirę tymczasem zajmie przypomnienie / Chwil, na które ty patrząc z nieba wysokości, / Widziałaś mnie w rozko-

szy, smutku lub radości." I thank Anna Klosowska for generously providing me with a literal translation of Słowacki's "Księżyc."

32. See Dovid Einhorn, *Shtile gezangen*, 20. In Moyshe Kulbak's similarly titled "A levone nakht" (A moonlit night), moonlight contributes to the beauty, enchantment, and sublimity of the cold Cheshvan (October–November) landscape and sky, but the poem does not feature a central lyric subject. See Moyshe Kulbak, *Shirim*, 8.

33. This poem is included in Elinor Robinson's translation in David G. Roskies's anthologies *The Literature of Destruction: Jewish Responses to Catastrophe* and *Voices from the Warsaw Ghetto*. In each, the date is erroneously given as January 10, 1942. Szeintuch states that February 10 was the date of all four poems in Katzenelson's "Lider fun kelt" ("Songs of the Cold") cycle; see Yechiel Szeintuch, "Araynfir" to "Lider fun kelt," in Katzenelson, *Yidishe geto-ksovim*, 619.

34. For the Yiddish text of this poem, see Katzenelson, *Yidishe geto-ksovim*, 620–21.

35. See Sutzkever, "Glust zikh mir tsu ton a tfile . . . ," in *Lider fun geto*, 13. For an English translation by C. K. Williams see David Roskies, ed., *Literature of Destruction*, 492–93 (translations of this poem here, however, are my own). It should be noted that Sutzkever generally revised his wartime writings before publishing them. I have not visited the Sutzkever archives to see if there is an extant ghetto manuscript of this poem.

36. As David E. Fishman succinctly puts it, "Abrasha Sutzkever harbored the mystical faith that poetry was the animating force behind all of life. As long as he remained devoted to poetry—writing it, reading it, and rescuing it—he would survive." See David E. Fishman, *The Book Smugglers: Partisans, Poets, and the Race to Save Jewish Treasures from the Nazis*, 87.

37. For Ber Mark's remarks on Marvil in general, and his critique of Marvil's "An di hern" in particular, see Mark, *Di umgekumene shrayber*, 128–29.

38. On the function of negative art in Adorno's œuvre, see Koenraad Geldof, "Modernité, excès, littérature: une lecture contrastive de Michel Foucault et de Stephen Greenblatt," 92–94.

CHAPTER 3: THE JEWISH DEAD CONFRONT THEIR GERMAN MURDERERS

1. For other details of Katzenelson's life, see the engaging biography of Katzenelson by his sister: Cypora Katzenelson-Nachumov, *Yitshak Katzenelson: zayn lebn un shafn*.

2. On the significance of Katzenelson's, and other Jewish writers', choice of language, see David Roskies, *Against the Apocalypse: Responses to Catastrophe in Modern Jewish Culture*, 200–201.

3. Katzenelson's name appears as one of the poets, for example, on the invitation for a concert entitled "Hour of Yiddish Writers and Artists" that took place on February 15, 1941, at the locale of the TOZ (Society for the protection of health) at 43 Gęsia Street (RA I/601). He also participated in an evening dedicated to the novelist Shlomo Gilbert on February 15, 1942. Even after the Great Deportation, in fall 1942,

Katzenelson read his poem "Treblinka" near the brushmakers' "shop." See Engelking and Leociak, *Warsaw Ghetto*, 545, 602.

4. See Katzenelson, *Yidishe geto-ksovim*. For an early, highly tendentious but historically significant treatment of Katzenelson's Warsaw ghetto writings, see Mark, *Di umgekumene shrayber*, 90–108. For an overview of Katzenelson's Warsaw ghetto works, see Yechiel Szeintuch, "The Works of Yitzhak Katzenelson in the Warsaw Ghetto."

5. See Szeintuch, "Araynfir" to "Vey dir," 632.

6. Roskies, "Did the Shoah Engender a New Poetics?," 358.

7. On the Polski Hotel trap, see Engelking and Leociak, *Warsaw Ghetto*, 745–48.

8. See Serge Klarsfeld's note to Convoy 72, April 29, 1944 (Serge Klarsfeld, *Memorial to the Jews Deported from France 1942–1944: Documentation of the Deportation of the Victims of the Final Solution in France*, 544).

9. Itzhak Katzenelson, "Dos lid funem oysgehargetn yidishn folk," 26.

10. Quotations in English from Katzenelson's "Song" are from the translation by Noah H. Rosenbloom, Y. Tobin, and Jacob Sonntag included in Roskies, *The Literature of Destruction*.

11. Biermann gives virtually no weight to the substantial number of texts Katzenelson wrote in the Warsaw ghetto when contrasting Katzenelson's prewar nature poetry with his "Song," written in Vittel, as though there wasn't an entire corpus of work by Katzenelson—his ghetto writings—mediating between these two moments; see Wolf Biermann, trans., *Dos lied vunem ojsgehargetn jidischn volk / Großer Gesang vom ausgerotteten jüdischen Volk*, 189. Biermann does acknowledge that Katzenelson wrote a great deal in Yiddish after his wife and two youngest sons were deported but doesn't discuss any of these texts (181). For Biermann's appreciation of Katzenelson's treatment of the Warsaw Ghetto Uprising in "Song" as offering a counternarrative to the "like lambs to the slaughter" narrative of Jewish passivity, see Biermann, *Großer Gesang*, 10–11, 15.

12. For an account of the Warsaw Ghetto Uprising in early Holocaust memory, see Avinoam Patt, "The Jewish Heroes of Warsaw: The Meaning of the Revolt in the First Years after the Uprising." Władysław Szlengel's poem "Counterattack," written after the first acts of Jewish armed resistance in the Warsaw ghetto, which occurred on January 18, 1943, is a brilliant example of how much psychological—and poetic—difference armed resistance immediately made. For the English translation of "Counterattack" by John and Bogdana Carpenter, see Roskies, ed., *Voices from the Warsaw Ghetto*, 218–22.

13. These scenes all occur in the final canto (XV) of Katzenelson's "Song," entitled "Nokh alemen" (It's all over).

14. The English renderings of "Vey dir" that I cite throughout this chapter are based on Whitman and Rothstein's translation. I have, however, generally modified their translation to emphasize particular aspects of the original or simply to offer a more literal rendering of Katzenelson's words.

15. Here Katzenelson echoes Leviticus 20:22: "And you shall keep all My statutes and all My laws and do them, lest the land to which I bring you to dwell here spew

you out" (Robert Alter translation). See also Leviticus 18:25, which Leviticus 20:22 largely repeats.

16. See Naomi Seidman, *Faithful Renderings: Jewish-Christian Difference and the Politics of Translation,* chapter 5. As Roskies remarks of Katzenelson's poems during this period, "Katzenelson discovered the cathartic, transformative power of rage" (Roskies, "Did the Shoah Engender a New Poetics?," 352).

17. The one notable exception occurs in stanzas 21–22, where the German men, returning to their ruined homes, are met by the curses not only of the Jewish dead but also those of their dead wives and children. Here, the Jewish dead and the dead German women and children work in tandem to curse the German men. In his *Vittel Diary* Katzenelson continued to blame the entire German nation for murdering the Jewish people, insisting repeatedly that all Germans knew, all supported the genocide, and that claims of ignorance are bald lies. See Itzhak Katzenelson, *Vittel Diary,* 109, 112, 141, 170, 189, 194, 220, 222.

18. Most of the Jews of Lublin and the vicinity were deported to Belzec. Of Lublin's 1939 population of 122,000, approximately 43,000 were Jews.

19. For Chaim Kaplan's reaction to the shattering news of the destruction of the Lublin Jewish community, see his diary entries of March 22 and April 7, 1942 (Kaplan, *Scroll of Agony,* 304–5, 312–14).

20. On the circumstances regarding how and when Katzenelson wrote "Vey dir," see Yechiel Szeintuch's introduction to the poem. See also Szeintuch's introduction to Katzenelson's poem "Der yid hot gelakht" (The Jew laughed), where he indicates that "Vey dir" was to be published in an edition of Katzenelson's "tsorn-lider" (poems of wrath)—to have included also "Der yid hot gelakht" and "Shloyme Zshelikhovski."

21. Roskies, "Did the Shoah Engender a New Poetics?," 350, 352. Dated May 31 (1942), the original handwritten manuscript—torn and often illegible—as well as a typed copy made in the Warsaw ghetto are held in the archive of the Ghetto Fighters' House in Israel. See Yechiel Szeintuch, introduction to "Vey dir," 633. A typescript copy was also preserved in the Oyneg Shabes archive and can be accessed at Sarah Traister Moskovitz's website Poetry in Hell: https://poetryinhell.org/index-by-authors/katzenelson-itkhok/katsenelson-yitzkhok-woe-to-you/.

22. As Katzenelson recalled in an entry to his *Vittel Diary* of September 9, 1943:

> I drew out of my coat pocket the scroll on which I had written the curse when Chanah and my two sons were as yet alive. It was written on thin paper, in small letters crowded together. They were the curses that I invoked against this vilest of nations, after they had annihilated the great and holy Jewish community of Lublin. There was not a single survivor. Hillel Zeitlin, of blessed memory, heard these curses some time before the commencement of the massacre of the Jews of Warsaw. About two years ago [i.e., two years earlier], when I still had a family, we shared the same house. Now my family is no more . . . just I and one son. On one occasion, early one morning, I happened to pass through the dining room and I found Reb Hillel at prayer. I could not see his face because he was facing the window, but I heard him cursing violently in

Yiddish both Hitler and his nation. He finished up with the words: "Oh Lord of the Universe. It is Terrible!" . . . I trembled with emotion on that occasion. Two years later, on the eve of the complete annihilation of the Jewish people, I read out my curse to the old man. Two years ago [i.e., two years earlier], Rabbi Hillel had begun the curse but did not express all of it; he could not find the words: "Oh! Lord of the Universe. It is terrible!" Two years later, this curse had matured within me, and I wrote it down and read it out to Kadushin. Gitterman, Guzshik and the charming but sad Aubfall, [*sic*] heard it then on the eve of the Mila tragedy. (Katzenelson, *Vittel Diary*, 246–47)

23. In memoirs and diaries, no one makes mention of "Vey dir," but several people, Katzenelson included, refer to this poem as "di klole." See Szeintuch, introduction to "Vey dir," 632.

24. The main section of the morning, afternoon, and evening prayers, the *amidah* consists of nineteen benedictions: three blessings of praise, thirteen petitionary benedictions that are omitted on the Sabbath, and three of thanksgiving. The *amidah* is often referred to by the name *shemoneh esrei* (Hebrew for eighteen) because it originally comprised only eighteen blessings. I thank Jeremy Brown for bringing to my attention the likelihood that Zeitlin's curses were an improvisation on the birkat haminim.

25. Ruth Langer, *Cursing the Christians? A History of the Birkat HaMinim*, 5.

26. Israel Jacob Yuval, *Two Nations in Your Womb: Perceptions of Jews and Christians in Late Antiquity and the Middle Ages*, 94.

27. Yuval, *Two Nations*, 94–95. Yuval analyzes Ashkenazic *piyyutim* that draw on, but also radically transform, the Palestinian Haggadic tradition. Analyzing the Porphyrion motif in these two contexts, he finds that in Ashkenazic culture "vengeance is transformed from a legal event to a universal occurrence, one at the very heart of the messianic process. . . . The vision of vengeance against the Gentiles takes center stage, because that vengeance alone will facilitate the upheaval of the messianic period, when the kingdom of Edom will be wiped off the face of the earth" (Yuval, *Two Nations*, 99).

28. Yuval, *Two Nations*, 115.

29. See Primo Levi, *The Drowned and the Saved*, 83–84. For Giorgio Agamben's problematic but influential interpretation of the predicament in which Levi felt himself caught, see Giorgio Agamben, *Remnants of Auschwitz: The Witness and the Archive*.

30. Like the French *vous*, *ir* in Yiddish is both the formal (singular and plural) and the informal plural pronoun.

31. The way the lyric present frames and dominates other verb tenses and temporalities is one of the lyric structures that Jonathan Culler explores at length in *Theory of the Lyric*; see especially 275–95.

32. The silence of the dead is similarly violent in stanzas 16–18, for example: "Run, every German with a murdered Jew around your neck! / We dead squeeze your throat silently—/ we'll choke you, choke you but not to death" (stanza 16).

33. See for example Irene Kacandes, "Are You in the Text? The 'Literary Perfor-

mative' in Postmodernist Fiction." My understanding of this aspect of second-person narration as well as of second-person narration more generally has also been aided by Monika Fludernik, "Second Person Fiction: Narrative 'You' as Addressee and/or Protagonist" and James Phelan, *Narrative as Rhetoric: Technique, Audiences, Ethics, Ideology*, chapter 2, "Narratee, Narrative Audience, and Second-Person Narration: How I—and You?—Read Lorrie Moore's 'How.'"

34. See Brian Richardson, "The Poetics and Politics of Second Person Narrative," 319.

35. See Dianna Fuss, *Dying Modern: A Meditation on Elegy*, 4–7, 107–9.

36. For Culler, "the lyric time of enunciation . . . is both that of a speaker/poet and that of the reader, who may speak these words also"—i.e., an "iterable *now*," a "moment of time that is repeated every time the poem is read" (Culler, *Theory of the Lyric*, 294–95).

37. My argument here falls between a historicist argument like Virginia Jackson's (here critiquing Paul DeMan's 1979 essay "Anthropomorphism and Trope in the Lyric") that we must not lose sight of how specific verse (Jackson is here referring to verse by Emily Dickinson) was "exchanged by people with varying degrees of access to one another who may have read according to their own historical referents," and Culler's countervailing argument, against such reconstruction of would-be historically determinative modes of interpretation and paths of circulation, that it is paramount to appreciate "lyric as iterable discourse, open to being reperformed in a variety of contexts (Jackson, *Dickinson's Misery: A Theory of Lyric Reading*, 100; Culler, *Theory of the Lyric*, 85). Both Jackson's and Culler's approaches are illuminating, and which one is methodologically more useful will vary situationally—I see it as unnecessary and counterproductive to construe their different emphases as locked in a zero-sum contest. Significantly, however, my reading here cannot be reconciled to either approach. Importantly, Katzenelson read "Vey dir" to certain real people, carried the poem on his person, and so forth. This micro-material context is indeed crucial. But my broader point is that "Vey dir" structurally *implies* a specific readership, one that is both more general than the empirical audience the poem had in the Warsaw ghetto and more restricted than Culler's conception of infinite reperformability is well equipped to get at.

38. Although, generally speaking, Katzenelson's poem would have been completely illegible to Germans in the 1940s due to the Yiddish alphabet, when voiced it is partially comprehensible to German speakers. As far as I can tell, Katzenelson did not strive to make his poem either more or less comprehensible to German speakers (for example, by either making greater or lesser use of the Germanic component in Yiddish) because, while written *at* them, it wasn't written *for* them. Nonetheless, it is an interesting fact that "Vey dir" would be partially intelligible to German speakers, but only when the poem is voiced (or romanized, which is a phonetic rendering, a kind of voicing in its own right). In order for German speakers to understand Yiddish in general and "Vey dir" in particular, they have to hear it speaking, as it were.

39. Peter J. Rabinowitz introduced the term "authorial audience" in his classic article "Truth in Fiction: A Reexamination of Audiences." James Phelan notes the

largely interchangeable nature of the concepts of implied reader and authorial audience; see Phelan, *Narrative as Rhetoric*, 209n6.

40. Attending to the complex ways that lyrics can inscribe particular listeners might open up productive points of intersection between historicist approaches and Culler's formal poetics of the lyric.

41. Peter J. Rabinowitz, *Before Reading: Narrative Conventions and the Politics of Interpretation*, 22.

CHAPTER 4: YOYSEF KIRMAN'S POETICS OF DURATION

1. See Auerbach, *Varshever tsvoes*, 299, and "Yoysef Kirman (Bagegnishn 1933–1943)," 149.

2. Written in pencil, the note was preserved in the Oyneg Shabes archive (RA II/219/1), and reads:

> J. Giterman
> Lubeckiego 6/15
> Dear, dear Giterman, I implore you to save me. It's still possible. I was grabbed on the street and taken away to the Umschlagplatz. I want to see my wife and two children again, whom I've installed in a safe place. Rescue me as fast as possible. Yours, Y. Kirman (quoted in Kassow, *Who Will Write Our History?*, 307)

3. See Auerbach, *Varshever tsvoes*, 287–307. For an English translation by Samuel D. Kassow see Rokhl Auerbach, *Warsaw Testament*, 238–55. See also the slightly modified version of these pages in Auerbach, "Yoysef Kirman." For Ber Mark's remarks on Kirman and his two poems "Nokh der blokade" and "Di oygn blaybn ofn," see Mark, *Di umgekumene shrayber*, 134–36.

4. For a similar but not identical quote, see Auerbach, *Varshever tsvoes*, where Auerbach describes the content of the poems Kirman would read to her in doorways and courtyard entrances on Leszno Street as follows: "Dos iz alemol geven a lid vegn dem vos hot undz arumgeringlt" (literally, "It was always a poem about what was surrounding us"; 294). Given the similarity between this quote and Auerbach's description in "Yoysef Kirman" of Kirman's poems "always being about what they were seeing before their eyes" (*dos iz alemol geven a lid vegn dem vos mir hobn gezen far undzere oygn*), I think Samuel Kassow abstracts rather too much when he renders "vegn dem vos hot undz arumgeringlt" as "about our common plight." Auerbach seems to be talking about (at least also talking about) what was concretely surrounding them: scenes before their eyes. See Kassow's translation of Auerbach, *Warsaw Testament*, 244.

5. This is not to say that he did not also read his poems on more formal occasions; Kirman is among the poets listed on the invitation for a concert entitled "Hour of Yiddish Writers and Artists" that took place on February 15, 1941, at the locale of the TOZ (Society for the protection of health) at 43 Gęsia Street (RA I/601). As mentioned later in this chapter, Kirman also published in the (Bundist) underground press.

6. See Auerbach, *Varshever tsvoes*, 300; in Kassow's translation, 249.

7. All of Kirman's texts from the Warsaw ghetto that have come down to us were

preserved in the Oyneg Shabes archive. Handwritten manuscripts of his two poems "Di oygn blaybn ofn" and "Nokh der blokade (a khronik)" can both be found in RA II/351.

8. These two reportages by Kirman, "Fun pleytim shtetl—Dzhike un Niske" (On the refugee-shtetl—Dzhike and Niske [Streets]) and "Froy Krashevitshes toyt" (The death of Mrs. Krashevitsh), can be found in RA I/426. These two texts were published in Ber Mark's anthology of literary texts from the Warsaw ghetto, *Tsvishn lebn un toyt*, 39–45.

9. See Engelking and Leociak, *Warsaw Ghetto*, 282–85.

10. Kirman, "Fun pleytim-shtetl" in Mark, ed., *Tsvishn lebn un toyt*, 41.

11. The idiom "iber shtok un shteyn" could also be rendered as "over hill and dale" or "in headlong flight."

12. See Auerbach, *Varshever tsvoes*, 287; in Kassow's translation, 238–39. Born in 1895, the year before Kirman, Perets Markish was among the most prolific, and most provocative, modernist Yiddish poets of his day. He lived primarily in Warsaw from 1921 until he moved to the Soviet Union in 1926. Along with fellow Yiddish modernist poets Uri Zvi Grinberg and Melech Ravitch, Markish established Warsaw as the center of Yiddish modernism, among other ways with the publication of several (mostly short-lived) journals, such as the almanac *Khalyastre* (Gang), which Markish co-edited, and the weekly *Literarishe bleter*, which Markish co-founded in 1924.

13. Auerbach, *Varshever tsvoes*, 291; in Kassow's translation, 241–42.

14. The biographical entry for Kirman in Shmuel Charney and Jacob Shansky's *Leksikon* does not elaborate on the details, stating only "geven arestirt tsulib politishe taymim" (was arrested because of political views; Shmuel Charney and Jacob Shansky, *Leksikon fun der nayer yidisher literatur*, vol. 8, 202).

15. Auerbach, *Varshever tsvoes*, 300–303; in Kassow's translation, 249–51.

16. See Kassow, *Who Will Write Our History?*, 459n61; see also Auerbach, *Varshever tsvoes*, 287 and 304–6, and "Yoysef Kirman," 152–54.

17. Auerbach, *Varshever tsvoes*, 292–93; in Kassow's translation, 242–43.

18. Kirman, "Der khesed fun a shtiln toyt," in Mark, ed., *Tsvishn lebn un toyt*, 31.

19. See Kirman, "Der khesed fun a shtiln toyt (dos kind der umshuldiker korbn mont zayn kheshbn)" (The blessing of a quiet death [the innocent child victim demands his due]), *Biuletin* (Bulletin, the underground periodical of the Bund) no. 14 (December 20, 1941): 10–15, RA I/682 (all significantly damaged); published in Mark, ed., *Tsvishn lebn un toyt*, 30–35. Kirman's prose poems "Kh'red tsu dir ofn, mayn kind: kurtsinke poemes in geveyntlekher proze (shtimungen, bilder, troymen in geto)" (I speak to you openly my child: short poems in ordinary prose [moods, images, dreams in the ghetto]) was published in the underground Bundist journal *Yugnt shtime* 2/3 (February–March 1942): 11–13, RA I/685. This work was also published in Mark's *Tsvishn lebn un toyt*, 35–39. An English translation of three of this text's four vignettes can be found under the title "I Speak to You Openly, Child (Short Poems in Prose)" in Roskies, ed., *Literature of Destruction*, 474–76. This translation silently omits the vignette "Brikn, vos tsesheydn" (Bridges that divide).

20. Moskovitz's translation and a scan of the handwritten manuscript of Kirman's

poem preserved in the Oyneg Shabes can be found here: https://poetryinhell.org/index-by-authors/kirman-yosep/the-eyes-remain-open/. Accessed July 25, 2023.

21. One of the more famous twentieth-century variations on this medieval Jewish text is Leonard Cohen's 1974 song "Who by Fire."

22. As noted in chapter 3, Katzenelson recounted in his *Vittel Diary* how he read his poem "Vey dir" to friends "on the eve" of the tragic days of the Cauldron, or what Katzenelson calls "the Mila tragedy" because so many thousands of people were confined to a section of Mila Street. See Katzenelson, *Vittel Diary*, 246–47.

23. The time of year on the Jewish calendar may also have contributed to evocation of the Unetanneh Tokef and Yom Kippur practices by the Lodz ghetto Yiddish diarist and chronicler Josef Zelkowicz in an entry dated "The Sabbath, September 5, 1942," almost exactly when Kirman presumably wrote "After the Blockade" and "The Eyes Remain Open." Zelkowicz describes people preparing for an approaching *Sperre*, during which a portion of the ghetto population will be deported:

> At five o'clock the curfew begins. From five o'clock on people will no longer be allowed on the streets. Now it's only three p.m., with two hours left until the locking of the gates. Another two hours and your fate will be sealed. Those fates will be varied. "Who will live, and who will die?"—it will be decided who will be snatched and thrown on the wagons and who will simply walk right by, and even who will be tossed on the wagon and then, by some miracle are able to survive and escape it . . . even cases like these have been known to occur. "Who will starve, and who will eat his fill?"—the difference between those who've already gotten their eight kilos of potatoes home and thus been able to salt them away "at the first call," and those who haven't yet been able to get their potatoes and so will probably never obtain their ration at all. (Peretz Opoczynski and Josef Zelkowicz, *In Those Nightmarish Days: The Ghetto Reportage of Peretz Opoczynski and Josef Zelkowicz*, 257–58)

Further on in the text, Zelkowicz likens those scurrying to get home before curfew to Jews running to synagogue when they are late for Yom Kippur eve services, and to pious Jews waiting to learn if God's judgment for them will be life or death:

> Those who haven't managed to make it home from the streets—though their backs carry no life-saving sacks since the potato yard has closed, since its employees and guards have to get home as well—they push themselves along as well. They hurry. They run. No one walks in the ghetto today. Everyone runs, propelled by sheer nerves. Tired, stumbling feet expend a last burst of energy, kicking like people who are drowning and struggling to reach the shore. Swollen feet pinch against their clumsy cloth shoes, but look at their quickness and speed today: people will do anything to keep from being on the street, where the air is aflame and dust sizzles with hatred that falls like the dew, with destruction, as the pavement burns under their feet. And so in dribs and drabs the streets begin to clear. Here and there a straggler can still be seen, running with terror in his eyes. As he runs he often becomes confused, unable to recognize the entrance to his own building. This is the way Jews run into the synagogue the eve of Yom Kippur when they are late or the way

> pious Jews tremble on the day when their fates will be determined, when they throw themselves at the mercy of their severe judge and wait for him to deliver judgment: "life" or "death." (Opoczynski and Zelkowicz, *In Those Nightmarish Days*, 260–61)

For an argument that Zelkowicz in this passage uses the analogy to Yom Kippur and divine judgment in a distinctly secular mode that denies God any agency in the life-and-death decisions to be made, see Amy Simon, "The Modern Haman: Ghetto Diary Writers' Understanding of Holocaust Perpetrators," 133.

24. This supremely vexing issue is reflected in myriad ghetto texts, including Abraham Lewin, *A Cup of Tears: A Diary of the Warsaw Ghetto*; Rokhl Auerbach, "Yizkor 1943"; Yehoshue Perle, "4580," the focus of chapter 7 of this book; Emmanuel Ringelblum, *Notes from the Warsaw Ghetto*; and the diary of Shmuel Winter; see Ber Mark, "Shmuel Winters togbukh." In keeping with a postwar communist interpretation that tended to conflate the Jewish police with both the Nazis and the capitalist Western democracies, Mark especially highlights Kirman's contempt for the Jewish policemen who participated in rounding up Jews for deportation to their deaths. See Mark, *Di umgekumene shrayber*, 134–35.

25. "Zumer-tog" (summer day) in quotation marks presumably refers to the song "S'iz geven a zumer-tog" (It was a summer day). Written in the Vilna ghetto by the eighteen-year-old Rikle Glezer and based on the popular prewar Yiddish theater song "Papirosn" (Cigarettes), composed by Herman Yablakoff, the song was sung widely in various versions in different ghettos. It describes Jews being driven into the Vilna ghetto and then taken to the Ponar woods and executed on a "lovely summer day." See Flam, *Singing for Survival*, 95.

26. In the JPS *Tanakh* translation the lines read: "My God, my God, / why have You abandoned me; / why so far from delivering me / and from my anguished roaring?" (1434).

27. There is an extensive tradition in modern Jewish literature and art of figuring Jewish suffering through Jesus's passion, for example Marc Chagall's 1938 "White Crucifixion" (and the ensuing series of Jesus as a figure of Jewish suffering, including "Yellow Crucifixion"); short stories written in the Lodz ghetto by Shaye Shpigl including "Malkhes geto" and "Vedibarta bam"; and Itzhak Katzenelson's *Vittel Diary* to name only a few. On the figure of Jesus in Jewish literature, see Matthew Hoffman, *From Rebel to Rabbi: Reclaiming Jesus and the Making of Modern Jewish Culture*, and Neta Stahl, *Other and Brother: Jesus in the 20th Century Jewish Literary Landscape*.

28. The only other verses that could be considered rhymes would be verse 4, with "hent" (hands) continuing the rhyme of the opening couplet, and verses 8 and 9, which create a near rhyme with *oysgezetst-kets* (broken-cats).

CHAPTER 5: WRITING THE HUNGERING SELF IN A MODERNIST KEY

1. For a thorough study of the phenomenon of hunger in Nazi ghettos and how Jews imprisoned in ghettos tried to mitigate its dire effects with the limited means

at their disposal, see Helene J. Sinnreich, *The Atrocity of Hunger: Starvation in the Warsaw, Łódź and Kraków Ghettos during World War II.*

2. For Opoczynski and Zelkowicz, see Opoczynski and Zelkowicz, *In Those Nightmarish Days.* For Oskar Singer's reportages, see Oskar Singer, *"Im Eilschritt durch den Gettotag . . .": Reportagen und Essays aus dem Getto Lodz.* For Sierakowiak's diary, see Dawid Sierakowiak, *The Diary of Dawid Sierakowiak: Five Notebooks from the Łódź Ghetto.* Marian Turski focuses on the treatment of hunger in Lodz ghetto diaries in "Individual Experience in Diaries from the Lodz Ghetto," 117–24.

3. Poems by Shmuel Marvil, Itzhak Katzenelson, and Yoysef Kirman are the focus of chapters 1, 2, and 3 of this book, respectively.

4. Sutzkever treats hunger explicitly in poems such as "The Manikin of Bread" (Vilna ghetto, August 1943) and "For My Child" (Vilna ghetto, January 18, 1943), and direct and metaphorical references to hunger characterize his ghetto poems in general. As Ruth Wisse aptly notes of Sutzkever's ghetto poetry, "No doubt piercing hunger was . . . responsible for the many references to eating, biting and swallowing that endow these poems with a more harrowing private 'subtext' than literature has known." Ruth Wisse, "Introduction: The Ghetto Poems of Abraham Sutzkever," in *Burnt Pearls: Ghetto Poems of Abraham Sutzkever*, 15.

Several poems preserved in the Oyneg Shabes archive deal centrally with hunger, including Hershele (Hersh Danielovitch), "My wife and children are hungry"; Yitzkhok Viner, "My Childhood"; Peretz Opoczynski, "Poverty"; Pesakh Vayland, "Very Honored Director"; and Itzhak Katzenelson, "The Ball" and "The Chronicle of Hershele's Death." For English translations by Sarah Traister Moskovitz of all the poems from the Oyneg Shabes archive, see the website Poetry from Hell (http://poetryinhell.org). Katzenelson encouraged Hershele to ask for assistance, but he was too hungry and weak to manage to do so, and eventually starved to death; see the headnotes to "Theme Three: Ghetto, Hunger, Struggle" on Poetry from Hell. See also Katzenelson's "Lid fun hunger," which was preserved along with the bulk of his ghetto writings in the Dror Hechalutz archive; For an English translation ("Song of Hunger"), see Roskies, ed., *Literature of Destruction*, 472–73. For the Yiddish texts of poems by Katzenelson (and all of Katzenelson's extant ghetto writings), see Katzenelson, *Yidishe geto-ksovim.*

Shaye Shpigl's poem "Hunger" is also worth mentioning, although no manuscripts of the poetry Shpigl wrote in the Lodz ghetto survived, and the poem was thus reconstructed (and likely somewhat revised or rewritten) after the war. Shpigl published a volume of poetry, *Un gevorn iz likht (lider)* (And there was light [poems]), in 1949. The middle section (of three), titled "Gezang in der fintster" (Song in darkness), however, is subtitled "lider geshribn in geto" (poems written in the ghetto) and each poem is dated by year. Whether accurately or inaccurately, "Hunger" (77) is dated 1943.

5. Jacob Glatstein describes "Malkhes geto" as a story that is "in fact not a story but rather a depiction of death by starvation" (*faktish nisht keyn dertseylung, nor a shilderung fun dem hunger-toyt*; Jacob Glatstein, "Yeshayohu Shpigl," 454).

6. Rosenfeld's undated philosophical dialogue, "Golem und Hunger" (and related

diary passages) explore the phenomenon of ghetto starvation in its (non-)relation to instances of famine across the globe, and to the world beyond the ghetto writ large. I analyze this text in Sven-Erik Rose, "Oskar Rosenfeld, the Lodz Ghetto, and the Chronotope of Hunger."

7. Bernshteyn's writings from the Warsaw ghetto are now available in the Polish edition of the Oyneg Shabes archive (*Archiwum Ringelbluma: Konspiracyjne Archiwum Getta Warszawy*, vol. 26: *Utwory literackie z getta warszawskiego*), but the only one of his many writings so far published in the original Yiddish that I am aware of is "Varshe 5701," which Ber Mark included under the title "Hunger in Varshe" in his anthology *Tsvishn lebn un toyt*, 66–69.

8. Yehuda Feld's stories were preserved in the Oyneg Shabes archive and were published in 1954 in *In di tsaytn fun Homen dem tsveytn* (In the times of Haman the Second). It should be noted that Ber Mark lightly edited Feld's texts so that the published versions are not identical to the texts in the Oyneg Shabes archive.

9. See Sierakowiak, *Diary*, 189, 190, 194, 209, 252.

10. For more on Kruk, see chapter 7, and later in this chapter.

11. I follow the practice of referring to "Khronik fun a mes-les" ("Chronicle of a Single Day") as the title of Goldin's text; however, this in fact seems to be its subtitle. "Khronik fun a mes-les" appears in parentheses beneath what was presumably a short title now missing due to damage to the manuscript. See figure 4.

12. Engelking and Leociak quote a passage from Goldin's story as documentation of abuses connected with soup cards (Engelking and Leociak, *Warsaw Ghetto*, 310–11). Perhaps because of Leociak's emphasis on first-person testimony, he consistently refers to events narrated in "Chronicle of a Single Day" as so many scenes and objects described by Goldin rather than the fictionalized Arke (Leociak, *Text in the Face of Destruction*, 181, 184). Kassow presents Goldin's text as "an extraordinary account of how a soup kitchen looked . . . through the eyes of a 'customer'" that provides an illuminating contrast to Rokhl Auerbach's account of running a soup kitchen in the ghetto (Kassow, *Who Will Write Our History?*, 139–40). Kassow certainly, however, recognizes the literary qualities of what he describes as "Goldin's masterful literary monologue," and is careful not to conflate Goldin with his fictionalized character Arke; see Kassow's reading of Goldin's "Chronicle" in *Who Will Write Our History?*, 140–42. In *Voicing the Void: Muteness and Memory in Holocaust Fiction*, Sara R. Horowitz refers to Goldin's "Chronicle of a Single Day" alongside non-literary chronicles such as the Lodz *Chronicle* and diaries such as Ringelblum's, and she characterizes statements that Goldin's character Arke makes as statements that Goldin makes about himself (Horowitz, *Voicing the Void*, 58). This lack of precision is not egregious in light of how autobiographical Goldin's text certainly is. It nonetheless exemplifies the tendency, even among literary scholars like Horowitz, to sidestep the sort of literary reading that Goldin's text demands.

13. While Joyce's *Ulysses* and Woolf's *Mrs. Dalloway* are the most celebrated examples of the twenty-four-hour narrative, the phenomenon was widespread before World War II, and has continued to flourish since. Works within Goldin's cultural orbit include the one-day interior monologue novellas by Arthur Schnit-

zler, *Leutnant Gustl* (1892) and *Fräulein Else* (1924), as well as Leo Perutz's 1918 novel *Zwischen neun und neun*. For a partial survey of one-day novels in several languages, see David Leon Higdon, "A First Census of the Circadian or One-Day Novel." Scholars have noted the tendency of the one-day literary text to concern itself with and celebrate the riches of the everyday rather than, say, great historical events. In this, too, Goldin's text occupies a position, albeit a peripheral one, within this corpus. While Goldin does occupy himself with an "everyday" experience in the Warsaw ghetto (and does not treat at length the wider historical context of the German occupation or the war, for example), this "quotidian" register is extreme, denuded, and full of existential (and not merely psychological or mythologized) peril. For a theoretical meditation on the everyday in the one-day novel, see Byrony Randall, "A Day's Time: The One-Day Novel and the Temporality of the Everyday." For an analysis of the treatment of the everyday in one-day novels by Virginia Woolf, Margaret Storm Jameson, and Mollie Panter-Downes, see Ciara Briganti, "Giving the Mundane Its Due: One (Fine) Day in the Life of the Everyday."

14. Garbarini finds Roskies's interpretations of Holocaust diaries—as participating in a long and specifically Jewish literary tradition of bearing witness to catastrophe—illuminating but also limiting. She argues that "the fact that so many Europeans took up diary writing during this period attests to how widespread an endeavor it had become, reaching beyond its Jewish roots. Thus, Jewish diary writing during the Holocaust reflected Jews' particular wartime circumstances and also connected to broader European cultural practices of the nineteenth and twentieth centuries" (Garbarini, *Numbered Days*, 3).

15. For Roskies's readings of Goldin's story, see Roskies, *Usable Past*, 31–32, and *Against the Apocalypse*, 212–14; and David G. Roskies and Naomi Diamant, *Holocaust Literature: A History and Guide*, 57.

16. Kassow gives the date when Goldin wrote "Chronicle of a Single Day" as November 1941, but the original manuscript is dated August 1941, and Mark and Roskies each follow this dating; see Mark, ed., *Tsvishn lebn un toyt*, 65; and Roskies, ed., *Literature of Destruction*, 434. Engelking and Leociak refer to Goldin's literary monologue as an "essay" (Engelking and Leociak, *Warsaw Ghetto*, 310). Leociak motivates his generic classification of Goldin's story as an "essay" and a "terrifying essay" in *Text in the Face of Destruction* (17, 37), where he describes the essay as "a mixture of the element of the personal document and of literature, of referentiality and fictionality, and an emphasis on giving a factual account as well as on creativity" (Leociak, *Text in the Face of Destruction*, 16–17). While this expansive definition of the essay indeed captures many of the dynamics of Goldin's story, it does not adequately respect Goldin's decision to compose his text not in his own voice but rather as an extended interior monologue of his literary figure Arke. While I appreciate that genre study is "not the purpose" of Leociak's research, and while I agree that "highly advanced precision" regarding genre classification of the testimonial literature from the Warsaw ghetto is "neither possible nor useful" for his analysis (Leociak, *Text in the Face of Destruction*, 12), it nonetheless seems misleading to refer to Goldin's "Chronicle" as an essay. In calling Goldin's story an essay, Leociak and

Engelking may, however, be alluding to the way it, in its self-reflexive meditation on the status of literature, verges on experimental literary criticism.

17. On mail service and food packages to the Warsaw, Krakow, and Lodz ghettos, see Sinnreich, *Atrocity of Hunger*, 69.

18. Jonas Turkow, *Azoy iz geven (khurbn varshe)*, 124.

19. Robinson's translation of "Chronicle of a Single Day" is also included in Roskies, ed., *Voices from the Warsaw Ghetto*, 115–35, as well as in Sharon Leder and Milton Teichman, eds., *Truth and Lamentation: Stories and Poems of the Holocaust.*

20. For this biographical information on Goldin, see Kassow, *Who Will Write Our History?*, 140.

21. The contention, in the brief biography of Goldin at the end of Roskies's *Literature of Destruction*, that Goldin "died of starvation in the [Warsaw] ghetto in 1942" (625), repeated in Leder and Teichman, eds., *Truth and Lamentation* (498), is superseded by Engelking and Leociak, according to whom Goldin "died during the liquidation Aktion in the summer of 1942" (Engelking and Leociak, *Warsaw Ghetto*, 310). Leociak refers to documentary evidence placing Goldin in the ghetto on August 3, 1942; see Leociak, *Text in the Face of Destruction*, 37.

22. Of this opening onto European literary genres and currents, Roskies writes: "As for Yiddish, the lowly vernacular, it was a kind of Third World culture that had at least 150 years of European art and literature to catch up with—which it did, with a vengeance" (David G. Roskies, *A Bridge of Longing: The Lost Art of Yiddish Storytelling*, 5). Seth Wolin makes a similar point: "Modernism for Yiddish literature meant not only the incorporation of the advanced sectors of contemporary European art and thought but catching-up, the inclusion of all the newly embraced accomplishments of Western culture. The discovery of the sentient individual, the romantic vision of self and nature, and even neo-classicism all tumbled pell-mell into the Yiddish notion of modernism" (Seth Wolin, "The Kiev-Grupe (1918–20) Debate: The Function of Literature," 359).

23. "Responding to the challenges of this new [post-1905] reality, Yiddish literature more often than not followed the models of European realism and modernism. This change of orientation created a chasm between the classical tradition of Mendele, Sholem Aleichem, and Peretz, and the aspirations of young Yiddish writers in Russia, Poland, and the United States. The young generation abandoned the search for authentic Yiddish forms, such as the *yiddisher roman* (Yiddish/Jewish novel), which figured so prominently in the creativity of Mendele and Sholem Aleichem, and accepted the norms of contemporary European realism and modernism" (Mikhail Krutikov, *Yiddish Fiction and the Crisis of Modernity, 1905–1914*, 211). For an in-depth local analysis of key moments in Yiddish modernism's engagement with Russian and European models, see Wolin, "Kiev-Grupe" and "Between Folk and Freedom: The Failure of the Yiddish Modernist Movement in Poland."

24. See, for example, Dan Miron, *A Traveler Disguised: The Rise of Modern Yiddish Fiction in the Nineteenth Century*, 60–63. Ruth Wisse, too, sees Peretz as "ridicul[ing] his own attempt to write a love story in a language 'smelling of goose fat'" (Ruth Wisse, *I. L. Peretz and the Making of Modern Jewish Culture*, 14). Peretz

cut the section of "Monish" on the poverty of Yiddish altogether from the final, 1908 version. Naomi Seidman, in contrast, highlights the "double-edged" nature of Peretz's irony that "provides an opportunity for comic reflection on both Jewish sexual inadequacies and the flimsy fantasies of the European romance"; see Seidman's excellent discussion of this passage of Peretz's "Monish" in Seidman, *Marriage Plot,* 45–48 and 56; here, 56.

25. As several scholars have noted (for example, David G. Roskies, "The Small Talk of I. L. Peretz," 5), Sholem Aleichem rather freely edited the 1888 text Peretz sent him. It seems plausible that he might have substituted "goose fat" for Peretz's "pig fat."

26. For a rich account of how "secular Jewish culture developed as distinctively Jewish even in its (always partial and ambivalent) embrace of European cultural models," see Seidman, *Marriage Plot,* 301. For Seidman's treatment of Peretz's "Monish" (in which, however, she does not take up the distinction between goose versus pig fat), see 45–48, 55–57, and 305.

27. On how the ambivalence of "Monish" vis-à-vis the Gentile world reflects Peretz's own knowledge and experience of "how fickle the Gentile could be," see Wisse, *I. L. Peretz,* 15–16.

28. Roskies sees Goldin's text as effecting a reversal vis-à-vis the dilemma dramatized in Peretz's "Monish": "The weight of experiences had shifted, for now the question was no longer whether Jewish sensibilities were adequate to world events, but precisely the opposite" (*Apocalypse,* 213). This is an illuminating reading (although what the precise opposite of "whether Jewish sensibilities were adequate to world events" remains, for me at least, elusive.) Since I am inclined to read Peretz's "Monish," however, as not simply pointing up the shortcomings of Yiddish as compared to European literary culture, but also undercutting European literature from the position of Yiddish's poverty, I see Goldin's project less as a reversal or the opposite of Peretz's project and more as a continuation of Peretz's complex and ambivalent weighing of European and Yiddish culture against each other, albeit now under the most extreme of circumstances.

29. William Franklin "Frank" Knox (1874–1944), secretary of the US Navy from July 1940 to April 1944.

30. Roskies identifies the news agency as "probably the *Gazeta Zydowska,* published in Cracow" (Roskies, *Usable Past,* 32). "Chronicle" ends with these lines: "Tokyo. Hong Kong. Vichy. Berlin. General number of enemy losses: six thousand eight hundred and forty-nine. Stockholm. Washington. Bankok. The world's turning upside down. A planet melts in tears. And I—I am hungry, hungry. I am hungry" (Goldin, "Chronicle," 434).

31. See Goldberg, "Rumor Culture."

32. On how the *Gazeta Zydowska* was widely despised, see Goldberg, "Rumor Culture," 95. On the importance of newspaper reading for modern Europeans in general and Jews in particular, see Garbarini, *Numbered Days,* 61–62.

33. That starvation imposed this temporal structure on the days of ghetto inhabitants can be seen in Dawid Sierakowiak's diary entry of June 23, 1942: "I'm deterio-

rating more rapidly. Even reading is difficult for me. I can't concentrate on anything for long. Time runs from one meal to another. The shop, work, eating, sleeping, then the same all over again" (Sierakowiak, *Diary*, 189).

34. The actual soup kitchen on which Goldin's story is based was most likely Rokhl Auerbach's kitchen at 40 Leszno Street; see Engelking and Leociak, *Warsaw Ghetto*, 310. Arke mentions being in Leszno Street shortly after leaving the soup kitchen (Goldin, "Chronicle," 433). Roskies and Diamant describe Auerbach's soup kitchen as one "where writers and intellectuals like Goldin received their daily ration" (Roskies and Diamant, *Holocaust Literature*, 65–66). One of Ringelblum's closest associates, Auerbach began a report on her kitchen for the Oyneg Shabes archive, which was cut short by the Great Deportation of the Warsaw ghetto in the summer of 1942. She survived and published a (rewritten) account in *Varshever tsvoes*, 63–130. On Auerbach and Goldin as offering different perspectives—that of a director and that of a "customer," see Kassow, *Who Will Write Our History?*, 136–43.

35. This, like Arke's fantasy of writing to Czerniakow to request a daily ration of bread, has to be understood against the background of the soup kitchens organized by the Aleynhilf, the unofficial, grassroots social aid network established by activists in the Warsaw ghetto, beyond the auspices of the Judenrat. Kassow writes that "the entire Aleynhilf was imbued with a sense of moral superiority to the Judenrat" (Kassow, *Who Will Write Our History?*, 142); it is the betrayal of the Aleynhilf's ethical code that weighs so heavily on Arke.

36. Arke's abandonment of communism and his—or his stomach's—dismissal of communist slogans remembered from his political past as mere "phrases!" (Goldin, "Chronicle," 425), and what Roskies has aptly called the "extreme and reportorial individualism" of "Chronicle of a Single Day" (Roskies, *Against the Apocalypse*, 214) may have added to the harshness of Ber Mark's critique of Goldin:

> Goldin's victim of hunger is an isolated individual, a ruminating intellectual, a victim who has isolated himself from his surroundings, a sufferer who is ruled by one bestial thought: to satisfy the hunger, which, however, one cannot tame, cannot control and—cannot satisfy. . . . It is a study, in literary garb, of how the hunger hydra encompasses the total person, all his senses, and kills him off, deadens his will.
>
> But Goldin does not see the social; he doesn't situate the starving person vis-à-vis the satiated and over-satiated upper ten thousand. He doesn't meditate on the causes. He doesn't rally himself to protest and rebellion. (Mark, *Di umgekumene shrayber*, 111; my translation)

Mark's understanding of the "causes" of hunger in the Warsaw ghetto according to vulgar Marxist class categories may seem astonishing from our remove; however, we should not underestimate the constraints under which he worked as a Yiddish intellectual in Stalinist Poland. Mark's critique of Goldin's individualism and lack of understanding of the (class-based) "causes" of hunger in the ghetto may have been a price he had to pay for publishing Goldin's text at all. On the precarious position of Mark and the Jewish Historical Institute in Stalinist Poland, see Stach, "'Spirit of the Time.'"

37. Faust voices his famous lament to Wagner in the "Vor dem Tor" scene in *Faust I*: "Zwei Seelen wohnen, ach! in meiner Brust" (Two souls dwell, ach! in my breast; *Faust I*, line 1112).

38. Jean-Christophe, Annette, and Breugnon are characters in eponymous novels by Romain Rolland: the ten-volume *Jean-Christophe* (1904–1912), *Annette et Sylvie* (1922), and *Colas Breugnon* (1919). Rolland was admired by Bundist intellectuals. As Samuel Kassow notes, in 1937, the Grosser Library in Warsaw, run by Herman Kruk, "encouraged its clientele to read not only Jewish books but non-Jewish 'progressive' authors like Romain Rolland and Upton Sinclair" (Samuel D. Kassow, "Vilna and Warsaw, Two Ghetto Diaries: Herman Kruk and Emanuel Ringelblum," 195). All three works by Rolland mentioned in Goldin's text, and many others, were translated into Yiddish. In their introduction to Jeffrey Shandler's translation of selected autobiographies written by Jewish youth in Poland and submitted to YIVO prize competitions in the 1930s, Barbara Kirshenblatt-Gimblett, Marcus Moseley, and Michael Stanislawski note the extent to which the young autobiographers internalized literary models in rendering their own life experiences, and they note: "If one book spoke more directly than any other to the minds and hearts of the YIVO autobiographers it was *Jean Christophe*, French novelist Romain Rolland's monumental *Bildungsroman*, published between 1904 and 1912 (a book, it should be noted, that teems with Jewish motifs and characters, from Biblical figures to Dreyfusards). No other literary work is mentioned with greater frequency in these autobiographies. For many of these young men and women, reading *Jean Christophe* constituted a revelation" (Kirshenblatt-Gimblett, Moseley, and Stanislawski, introduction to Shandler, ed., *Awakening Lives: Autobiographies of Jewish Youth in Poland before the Holocaust*, xxxiv). See also Moseley's "Life, Literature," where he discusses the resonance of Rolland's *Jean-Christophe* on pages 3–5, 11, 20, and 23–24.

39. Arke's position—like that of so many victims in the ghettos—at a threshold to naked biological existence poses a challenge to Giorgio Agamben's interpretation of the "Muselmann," a figure Agamben theorizes as the quintessential embodiment of his category of the *homo sacer*, a person placed by sovereign authority in a state (and geography, paradigmatically the concentration camp) of exception, beyond any claim to human rights, and reduced to pure biological existence. Agamben's provocative theory of the constitutive relationships between sovereignty, the state of exception, and the *homo sacer* has had an enormous influence across numerous disciplines in the humanities and social sciences. His philosophical manipulation of the figure of the Muselmann, and tendency to reduce the significance of the Holocaust to this figure, however, have the effect of disregarding, trivializing, or both, the words that victims, like Goldin, managed to produce as they negotiated the chaotic space between collapsing social, political, and cultural norms and meanings, on the one hand, and abject naked existence, on the other. Agamben radicalizes the silence of Holocaust witnesses when he defines the "Muselmann" as the witness who "has much to say but cannot speak," in contrast to those who could or can speak but (thus) have "nothing interesting to say" (Agamben, *Remnants of Auschwitz*, 120). Goldin's and many other ghetto texts powerfully belie Agamben's ahistorical

removal of "true" witnessing from the possibility of speech. Agamben's philosophical meditation on ethics after Auschwitz has been widely criticized by scholars including J. M. Bernstein, Dominick LaCapra, Neil Levi and Michael Rothberg, and Debarati Sanyal. For a critique of the decontextualizing thrust of Agamben's conceptualization of the Holocaust, see Philippe Mesnard and Claudine Kahan, *Giorgio Agamben à l'épreuve d'Auschwitz*. For a trenchant critique of Agamben's theory of Holocaust witnessing in *Remnants of Auschwitz*, see Thomas Trezise, *Witnessing Witnessing: On the Reception of Holocaust Survivor Testimony*, chapter 4, "Theory and Testimony."

40. Metaphors of hunger both as an animal and as something that reduces people to animals are common in writings from the ghettos. One particularly haunting example occurs in Josef Zelkowicz's notes from the Lodz ghetto:

> Shadows that used to be people move about in the ghetto streets. All that remains of these people are sunken faces, black or gray, their eyes giving off a strange glint. One finds sizzling eyes such as these only among starving wolves on harsh winter nights in dense forests.
>
> Such a man moves about with sizzling eyes, a feverish soul, and a heart so heavily burdened that even a vise cannot free it. He feels as though an animal is sitting inside him, ceaselessly sucking at his innards with its toothless mouth. (Opoczynski and Zelkowicz, *In Those Nightmarish Days*, 194)

41. Isaac Bashevis Singer also translated two works by Hamsun, *Victoria* and *Pan*. Having no knowledge of Norwegian, however, he translated *Victoria* from available German and Polish translations, and translated *Pan* from a Hebrew translation. See Isaac Bashevis Singer, *Pan: fun Leytenant Tomas Glans ksovim* and *Viktorya*. Bashevis Singer likewise translated works by two of the authors he here characterizes as Hamsun's disciples: Thomas Mann's great 1924 novel *Der Zauberberg* (*Der Tsoyberbarg*) and Stefan Zweig's 1920 biography of Romain Rolland, *Romain Rolland, der Mann und das Werk* (*Romain Rolland, der mentsh un dos verk*). On Bashevis Singer's translations into Yiddish, see Stephen H. Garrin, "Isaac Bashevis Singer as Translator: 'Apprenticing in the Kitchen of Literature.'"

42. The first page references are to *In the Beginning Was the Ghetto* and the second, after the slash, to *Wozu noch Welt*. Rosenfeld's Lodz ghetto writings are the focus of chapter 8.

43. On book peddling in the streets of Warsaw after the Nazis closed all of the Jewish bookstores, see Ringelblum's entry of January 22, 1940, in *Notes from the Warsaw Ghetto*, 244–45; on books bought and sold in the Warsaw ghetto streets see also Shavit, *Hunger for the Written Word*, 58–62.

44. See Sverre Lyngstad, introduction to Shavit, *Hunger for the Written Word*, xix.

45. See Chone Shmeruk, "Yisroel Rabon and his Book *Di Gas* ('The Street')," xxv.

46. As Wolf points out, however, unlike the protagonist of Hamsun's novel, whose journey is into his own damaged interiority, Rabon's narrator "has his eyes almost entirely on people and events outside himself" (Leonard Wolf, "Afterword" to Israel Rabon, *The Street*, 190). Goldin remains closer to Hamsun in this regard.

47. Kruk's extensive diary from the Vilna ghetto includes the literary-journalistic account of a murder tale "à la Sherlock Holmes," "Six Gallows in the Vilna Ghetto: A Criminal Literary Chronicle of the Vilna Ghetto," which I explore in chapter 7.

48. Zachary Baker's translation of Kruk's essay reads "[Emile] Zola's *War*" (Kruk, "Library and Reading Room," 194); I am presuming that the Zola novel Kruk had in mind was *La Débâcle*.

49. Franz Werfel's *Forty Days of Musa Dagh* clearly had profound resonance for Jews during the Holocaust. Drawing on Kruk's account of book borrowing and reading practices in the Vilna ghetto, David E. Fishman notes "by far the most popular European novel among the socially mature readers was Werfel's *Forty Days*, based on the events in a town in Turkey at the outset of the Armenian genocide. Readers sensed that they were facing the same fate as had befallen the Armenians" (Fishman, *Book Smugglers*, 46). In addition to Kruk's reference to the novel, Hillel Seidman, in his Warsaw ghetto diaries, describes a conversation amongst various sorts of intellectuals in the Warsaw ghetto after the Great Deportation of July–September 1942, which they were trying unsuccessfully to wrap their heads around. The discussion turned to precedents. Ultimately, they felt there were none, but among those Seidman lists as not offering adequate points of comparison are the Armenian genocide and Werfel's *Forty Days*: "Not in the massacres [*skhites*] of the Armenians, not in the '40 days of Musa Dagh' (which Franz Werfel captured so masterfully)" (Hillel Seidman, *Togbukh fun varshever geto*, 172). Dina Abramowicz, a colleague of Kruk's in the Vilna ghetto library who would survive the war and have a long career working at the YIVO in New York, recalled the popularity of Werfel's novel among certain reading constituencies: "Among the works of the German-Jewish writers, Feuchtwanger's *The Wars of the Jews* and especially Werfel's remarkable *Forty Days* were the most popular. Werfel described an infamous episode of World War I, the annihilation by the Turks of an entire Armenian population living in their country. The idea of a total annihilation of a racial group, the method of destruction, the helplessness of the victims, and the futility of diplomatic rescue efforts—this presented such an astonishing similarity to our situation that we read the book with a shudder, perceiving it almost as a prophetic vision, revealing for us our inevitable fate" (Dina Abramowicz, "The Library in the Vilna Ghetto," 168). In a paper on literature during the German occupation originally presented in September 1945, Nachman Blumental refers to Werfel's *Forty Days* as among the most significant examples of prewar works that were "actualized" (*aktualizirt*—read with intensity for the new significance they yielded) during the war years. See Blumental, "Di kharakteristik fun der yidisher literatur unter der daytshisher okupatsye," 19–20.

50. Jürgen Zimmerer and Michael Rothberg observe that "comparisons and analogies accompanied the memory of the Holocaust from the beginning" and should indeed be extended backward into the experience of the Holocaust itself, prior to its memory. See Zimmerer and Rothberg, "Entabuisiert den Vergleich!"

51. Recent Holocaust scholarship has also shown an interest in the meanings Holocaust victims sought in different sorts of reading. Alexandra Garbarini highlights the healing function that reading literature had for many of the Holocaust diarists

she examines, including Adam Czerniakow, who read, among other works, Proust's *Within a Budding Grove* during sleepless nights in the Warsaw ghetto to gain a modicum of relief; as well as two German-speaking diarists who each found a line from Rilke's 1899 short story "Die Weise von Liebe und Tod des Cornets Christoph Rilke" ("Und der Mut ist so müde geworden und die Sehnsucht so gross" [quoted 134]) particularly resonant. Garbarini finds that reading for the Holocaust diarists she studies offered both "insight into and escape from their present circumstances" (Garbarini, *Numbered Days*, 133) and that, indeed, "reading became the primary vehicle for Jews to forget the present and connect with their past" (135). Whereas *writing* frequently tormented diary authors, "Reading brought [Holocaust diarists] a measure of relief. Their encounters with literature offered a means of mental escape from inhumane conditions and thereby allowed them to reestablish contact, however fleeting, with the world outside. In this way reading connected people to a sense of self that stretched beyond the confines of German occupation" (136). Barbara Engelking touches on reading during the Holocaust when she quotes from an interview with a Holocaust survivor who recalled the pleasure he derived from the intensive and diverse reading he undertook in the Warsaw ghetto. However, Engelking also notes the difficulty, which Goldin so memorably dramatizes, of reading under ghetto conditions: "Not everyone was, however, able to read in the living conditions imposed by the ghetto. Housing conditions, the psychological pressure caused by the overcrowding in the ghetto, hunger, illness and exhaustion, all influenced this. Living under stress, and constant oppression by the Other, made concentration impossible" (Engelking, *Holocaust and Memory*, 185). In an essay published in 2001, the year after she died at age ninety, Dina Abramowicz recalls her work as a librarian in the Vilna Ghetto Library, and how books provided young people in the ghetto with a means of imaginative escape and a connection to the outside world from which they were cut off: "The need of the youthful imagination to transport itself to the world of fantasy was not suppressed in the ghetto. On the contrary, the need grew even more intense in an environment that was so confined and deprived of play and joy. Books were possibly the only vehicle for reaching out to the world from which the Jewish children were cut off, possibly forever" (Abramowicz, "Library," 168).

52. Among major theorists of intertextuality including Mikhail Bakhtin, Roland Barthes, Harold Bloom, Gérard Genette, Julia Kristeva, and Michael Riffaterre, I have found Bakhtin and Genette most helpful, for different reasons, for thinking through the specific work of intertextuality in Goldin's "Chronicle"—Bakhtin because of his attention to social and cultural situatedness, and Genette because of his more restricted conception of intertextuality in terms of allusion and quotation over against poststructuralists like Barthes and Kristeva, who theorize intertextuality in terms of the play of signification and semiotic plurality, or anonymous social and cultural codes that always already precede the production of discourse.

CHAPTER 6: THE AUTOBIOGRAPHY OF A NUMBER

1. "Der Eigenname eines Menschen ist nicht etwa wie ein Mantel, der bloß um ihn her hängt und an dem man allenfalls noch zupfen und zerren kann, sondern

wie ein vollkommen passendes Kleid, ja wie die Haut selbst ihm über und über angewachsen, an der man nicht schaben und schinden darf, ohne ihn selbst zu verletzen" (Johann Wolfgang von Goethe, *Aus meinem Leben: Dichtung und Wahrheit*, part 2, book 10, 407). Goethe made this remark apropos of an unkind joke that Johann von Gottfried Herder had made about Goethe's name.

2. "Der Gefangene hat eine Nummer als Namen. Von ihr würde niemand sagen, was Goethe von Personennamen sagt" (Ludwig Wittgenstein, *Bemerkungen über die Philosophie der Psychologie*, §326, 71).

3. Ber Mark dates the composition of "4580" to between October and December 1942. See Mark, *Di umgekumene shrayber*, 137.

4. For Kassow's fuller discussion of Perle's "4580," see Kassow, *Who Will Write Our History?*, 195–97. In March 1943, Perle would in fact manage to escape with his son Lolek to the Aryan side of Warsaw, supplied with Aryan papers by one of Lolek's Polish friends. Father and son were drawn out of hiding in the so-called Hotel Polski Affair in which the Germans sold South and Central American passports that would purportedly secure their owners' ultimate freedom. They were sent to Bergen-Belsen under the pretense that they would be exchanged eventually for German POWs. For three months in Bergen-Belsen, they were treated relatively well and not forced to work. Along with 1,800 others who had been caught up in the Hotel Polski trap, they were sent off on a train heading for, they thought, Switzerland. Instead, they were taken to Auschwitz-Birkenau and murdered upon arrival. On Perle's end, see Auerbach, *Varshever tsvoes*, 333–35, and for Auerbach's moving account of her efforts to track down survivors who might have seen Perle during his months at Bergen-Belsen, an undertaking she describes poignantly as "zukhn shpurn in di berg mit ash" (searching for clues in the mountains of ashes), see *Varshever tsvoes*, 336–37; here, 336. For Kassow's translation, see *Warsaw Testament*, 282–92.

5. Thus, in his 2002 monograph *Analytik und Ethik der Namen* Ian Kaplow underscores that the numbers to which prisoners' names have been reduced function only in a particular concrete context—in prison—but not within "a universal frame of reference" (Kaplow, *Analytik und Ethik*, 224).

6. "Weisen der Bezugnahme sind die Infrastruktur der Ontologie" (Modalities of reference are the infrastructure of ontology). See David Lauer, "Wittgenstein—Die Gewalt des Namens," here 139.

7. I am thinking here of Giorgio Agamben's influential construction of the figure of the Muselmann in Nazi concentration camps. The construction of the traumatic experience such as that of the Holocaust as axiomatically unspeakable in prominent strains of trauma theory including the seminal work of Dori Laub and Cathy Caruth also provides an alibi for ignoring the speech that Holocaust victims produced.

8. See Mintz, *Popular Culture*, chapter 2, "Two Models in the Study of Holocaust Representation," hereafter cited parenthetically in the text as Mintz, "Two Models."

9. The Perle family were able to return to their apartment on Nowolipie Street upon their return to Warsaw. See Roskies, introduction to Perle, *Everyday Jews*, xv.

10. Yehoshue Perle, "Tsifern," *Varshever almanakh*: 52 pages (each work in the

Varshever almanakh has its own pagination, beginning with page 1; Perle's story is the third work in the anthology), and Yehoshue Perle, *Nayn a zeyger inderfri.*

11. Roskies, introduction to Perle, *Everyday Jews*, xvii.

12. Unless otherwise indicated, quotations from "4580" in English are from the translation by Elinor Robinson in Roskies, ed., *Literature of Destruction*, 450–54; here, 450. Hereafter cited parenthetically in the text.

13. Arabic literary criticism frequently describes a poem as a "string of pearls," and this metaphor likening each of a poem's verses to a pearl gets picked up by medieval Hebrew authors as well. It is probably impossible to know whether Perle might be using the image of a woman adorned by pearls to evoke not only himself but also specifically literary writing. But if so, he would not be the only ghetto writer to do so: Avrom Sutzkever uses pearls—or rather "burnt pearls"—to figure poetic words struggling to respond to the Holocaust in his famous poem by that title, which he published with the notation "Vilna ghetto 1943." I thank Jonathan Druker for bringing to my attention the widespread use of "a string of pearls" to describe poems in Arabic and medieval Hebrew literary criticism.

14. Unless otherwise indicated, citations of the text of "4580" in Yiddish are from Mark, ed., *Tsvishn lebn un toyt*, 142–49; here, 143. Hereafter cited parenthetically in the text.

15. See Kassow, *Who Will Write Our History?*, 218–19. The initial uncertainty over—and thus anonymous publication of—Perle's own account of the Great Deportation of the Warsaw ghetto, "Khurbn varshe," in the Warsaw journal *Bleter far geshikhte* in fall 1951 was largely responsible for the controversy that arose around the authenticity of that text. It was in fact only in tandem with "4580" that the curators of the Oyneg Shabes documents were able to identify Perle as the author of both "Khurbn varshe" and "4580." "4580" was first published in *Bleter far geshikhte* 5, no. 3 (1952), the same issue that contained Ber Mark's blistering reply to H. Leyvik, who had erroneously accused the editors of *Bleter far geshikhte* of having published a forgery when they printed, anonymously, "Khurbn varshe." The author of "4580" and "Khurbn varshe" were thus revealed at the same time. The headnote to "4580" in *Bleter far geshikhte* reads:

> The manuscript "4580" was found in the second part of the underground ghetto archive (Ringelblum archive), devoid of the author's signature. After a thorough analysis the archivists of JHI and the editors of "Bleter far geshikhte" have come to the conclusion that the manuscript is Yehoshue Perle's. It has also been determined that Yehoshue Perle is the author of the chronicle "Khurbn varshe," which was printed in "Bleter far geshikhte" B' IV H' 3.
>
> On that, see also the article by Mark in the present issue of "Bleter."
>
> (Headnote "fun redaktsye" to "4580," 53).

16. E.g., Roskies: "'Number 4580'—also the title of Perle's last-known work—was Yehoshue Perle himself, a once proud Polish Jew transformed into a faceless, historyless set of digits" (Roskies, introduction to Perle, *Everyday Jews*, xvii). Or Kassow, in a passage already quoted above: "The Germans handed out 30,000 numbers in all, and Perle wrote another essay about his new name, '4580'" (Kassow, *Who Will*

Write Our History?, 195–96); "In this essay . . . Perle discussed the new status that gave him a temporary right to life—the tin tag that hung around his neck with the number 4580" (196).

17. On page 1 of the manuscript, Perle crosses out 1580 (spelled out as *fuftsenhundert un akhtsik*) and replaces it with 4580 (spelled out as *firtoyzent finfhundert un akhtsik*), and on page 3 he twice crosses out *fuftsenhundert akhtsik*, replacing one of them with *firtoyzent finfhundert akhtsik*. By page 10 of the manuscript Perle simply writes *firtoyzent finfhundert un akhtsik* without writing the other number first.

18. See Philippe Lejeune, "The Autobiographical Pact." Page references to this work are given parenthetically in the text.

19. Martin Löschnigg has argued that the narratological distinction, so often used in the analysis of autobiographical writing, between the protagonist *I* and the narrator *I* (or the experiencer and the narrator), is frequently less pronounced than generally presumed, and that the "autobiographical act" might productively be thought of as itself "an experiential site" and "an act of identity-construction" rather than a "detached subject['s]" interpretation of "itself as object." Such a view "allows one to emphasize the continuity of narration and experience" (Martin Löshnigg, "Postclassical Narratology and the Theory of Autobiography," 271). Löshnigg's revision of the classical narratological approach to autobiography is helpful to be sure. We should not be quick to dismiss out of hand ways that, even in moments of extreme crisis, autobiographical acts may construct bridges over the very subjective discontinuities they seem to introduce. Holocaust-era autobiographies, however, provide dramatic examples of radical discontinuities between protagonist and narrator. As Amos Goldberg underscores, in circumstances of extreme trauma, the disjunction between the experiencing and the writing subjects becomes acute since the writing *I* must try to make sense of subjective experience even as the hermeneutic frames that had previously lent meaning to the world and the *I*'s place in it have largely collapsed. Rather than as an act of continuous identity construction, Goldberg views autobiography in extremis in terms of symbolic death and resurrection: "Autobiographical writing is, in its most extreme moments, an attempt to recount symbolic death and thereby overcome it, if only very partially. In such situations, writing is a kind of 'resurrection'" (Goldberg, *Trauma in First Person*, 79). In "4580," the gulf between the protagonist and the narrator is vast: the protagonist had a name and a world; the narrator has neither. Goldberg's conception of writing as partial resurrection is, moreover, particularly apt in view of Perle's own use of the metaphor of resurrection in exploring the bleak prospects the narrator faces of ever regaining his name and the human status it once signaled; see Perle, "4580," in Roskies, ed., *Literature of Destruction*, 453.

20. The note to the death bed confessional prayer in the *ArtScroll Siddur* (2nd edition), for example, states: "If a sick person is near death, Heaven forbid, someone should recite the following confession with him. However, it is required that this be done in such a way that his morale not be broken because this may even hasten death. . . . If the patient cannot speak, he should confess in his heart. One who is unsophisticated should not be asked to confess because it may break his spirit

and cause him to weep" (Nosson Scherman and Meir Zlotowitz, eds., *The Complete ArtScroll Siddur: Weekday/Sabbath/Festival*, 796).

21. Perle, "4580," RA II/245.

22. For examples of textual interpretation in the Warsaw ghetto (often involving gematria, or numerology) in an attempt to determine the (imminent) advent of the Messiah, see Shimon Huberband, *Kiddush Hashem: Jewish Religious and Cultural Life During the Holocaust*, 121–25. Lucy S. Dawidowicz notes that in the ghettos, "Religious people turned to superstition and fantasy to buttress their hopes. They searched for concealed meanings in words and texts, looking for indications of the war's end and the Messiah's coming" (Dawidowicz, *The War against the Jews, 1933–1945*, 218).

23. I thank Jonathan Decter for pointing out "to attack" or "to attack violently" as Hebrew meanings of 580 (תקף, *tekaf*), and for generally encouraging me to take seriously the way Perle invites readers to pursue a version of the gematria that he eschews.

24. Although one cannot know for certain, it seems entirely plausible that Kirman and Perle would have shared with each other these texts written in such close temporal proximity. Both were working in the artificial honey factory on Franciszkanska 30. Kirman's two poems about the Great Deportation as well as Perle's texts "Khurbn Varshe" and "4580" were preserved in the second cache of the Oyneg Shabes, buried in February 1943 and unearthed in December 1950.

25. Perle's interest in highlighting specifically Jewish cultural and hermeneutic practices (ways of making meaning) may be at the bottom of why he struck a substantial passage from the first page of the manuscript of "4580." Perle struck and replaced certain lines in the below passage, notably changing the number 1580 to 4580, before striking the whole passage. (I indicate the doubly struck words with a strike-though.)

> A hungry person might be struck by the thought of ~~fifteen hundred eighty~~ four thousand five hundred and eighty dollars in gold. He will imagine how many loaves of rye bread he could buy for that sum. How many living carps he could treat himself to on the Sabbath. And in general, how prosperous he'd become if God sent him the treasure of ~~fifteen hundred eighty~~ four thousand five hundred and eighty ~~dollars in gold~~ golden dollars.

> (A hungerikn veln efsher kumen afn rayon ~~fuftsen hundert un akhttsik~~
> fir toyznt finfhundert un akhtsik dolar in gold. Er vet zikh for-
> shteln vifl gebeytelte broyt er volt gekont koyfn far
> ot di sume. Vifl lebedike karpn er volt zikh
> gekont farginen af shabes. Un bkhlal, vi azoy er volt
> dos oyfgerikht gevorn ven got shikt im tsu dem
> oyster fun ~~fuftsen hundert un akhttsik~~ firtoyzent funfhundert un akhtsik ~~dolar in gold~~ goldene dolar.)

This hungry person is clearly situated outside the context of the ghetto and within an altogether Jewish social world (even if in late 1942 a person in the ghetto had

4580 golden dollars—an absurdity—they still would not have been able to procure unlimited loaves of rye bread or carps for the Sabbath). While I can only speculate as to why Perle struck this passage, perhaps this hypothetical hungry person nonetheless struck Perle as too adjacent to the conditions of the ghetto, which he conspicuously avoids focusing on in this text. Perle's emphasis throughout is on the Jewish society and cultural world that have been lost rather than on the details of the impoverished existence of the "chosen" few remaining in the ghetto.

26. Roskies glosses this reference: "Based on rabbinic legend about King Solomon trying to reclaim his throne from Ashmedai, king of the devils" (Roskies, ed., *Literature of Destruction*, 451).

27. The published English translation of "4580" renders "malekh-doyme" as "The Angel of Death," but Perle does not use *malakhamoves* but rather *malekh-doyme*. In his memoir *Of a World That Is No More*, I. J. Singer evokes the same custom that is at stake here when he describes how a particular Gehenna-obsessed melamed of his youth, Reb Moshe, would endeavor to strike fear into the hearts of his card-playing kheder pupils by evoking "the Angel Dumah, who stands with a fiery rod over the graves of newly buried corpses and shouts, 'Sinner, what is thy name?'" (I. J. Singer, *Of a World*, 61).

28. Roskies has explored the widespread use of Jewish archetypes by authors writing during the years of the Holocaust in numerous articles and book chapters as well as, notably, in his magisterial study of Yiddish and Hebrew literary responses to anti-Jewish persecution including—but not limited to—the Holocaust, *Against the Apocalypse*.

29. See Sven-Erik Rose, "The Oyneg Shabes Archive and the Cold War: The Case of Yehoshue Perle's *Khurbn Varshe*."

30. Perle served on a national committee chaired by A. Pdeyev, the secretary of the Soviet Writers' Association, to organize celebrations throughout the USSR of the ninetieth anniversary of I. L. Peretz's birth. In early 1941 Perle also visited Kiev with fellow writers I. Ashendorf and Nachum Bomze, where they each read works at the Writers House, which held a feast in their honor; see Dov Levin, *The Lesser of Two Evils: Eastern European Jewry under Soviet Rule, 1939–1941*, 136, 233. On Perle's time in Soviet-occupied Lwów/Lemberg and his contact there with Soviet Yiddish writers, see also Auerbach, *Varshever tsvoes*, 326–31; in Kassow's translation, 284–87.

31. Kassow relates that Shmuel Winter "provided money and food for Ringelblum and his staff—and a priceless telephone to communicate with the Aryan side. He could also procure jobs for people whom the Oyneg Shabes wanted to save—such as Rokhl Auerbach and Shie Perle. It was through Winter's telephone, with its link to Adolf Berman (who had left for the other side in September [1942]) that Ringelblum, Auerbach, and others were able to prepare their eventual escape from the ghetto." (Kassow, *Who Will Write Our History?*, 157). And: "In September 1942, as Perle was writing 'Khurbn Varshe,' Shmuel Winter secured him a job in the artificial honey factory on Franciszkanska 30—the same factory that would also employ Rachel Auerbach" (Kassow, *Who Will Write Our History?*, 195).

32. Marcus Moseley glosses the basic disavowing move in this way:

> Time and again in these preambles [to late nineteenth- and early twentieth-century Eastern European Jewish autobiographies], there is a specific disavowal of autobiographical intent. The author is persuaded by importunate editors, literary associates—frequently better-known than himself—to write his autobiography. He eventually succumbs, but with extreme reluctance. Having capitulated, however, he is at pains to stress that in writing of his own life-story, it is not of the inner, hidden self that he would speak, but of the wider tapestry of the history of the Jewish collective of which his own self forms a slender thread. (Moseley, *Being for Myself Alone: Origins of Jewish Autobiography*, 438)

See also Alan Mintz, *"Banished from Their Father's Table": Loss of Faith and Hebrew Autobiography*, 14–15. As Mintz explains: "Hebrew and Yiddish intellectuals worked within literary cultures that promoted the collective and denigrated the prerogatives of interiority and 'affective individualism' so crucial to autobiography. The reticulated inner workings of the 'I' were not encouraged" (Alan Mintz, "Writing about Ourselves: Jewish Autobiography, Modern and Premodern," 283).

33. Rousseau's epochal *Confessions* famously begin with the sentence: "Je forme une entreprise qui n'eut jamais d'exemple et dont l'exécution n'aura point d'imitateur" (I'm undertaking a project without precedent, the result of which will have no imitator).

34. Perhaps the most famous example of the disavowal of any unique interest on the part of the Jewish would-be autobiographer is voiced by Shloyme in Abramovitsh's *Shloyme reb khayims / Ba-yamim ha-hem*, who tries to parry the demands of his Odessa writer friends that he should at long last write his autobiography with this comically exaggerated statement:

> What has ever happened to me, that makes my life deserve the distinction of being recorded? What has happened to me has happened to thousands of our people; it's a familiar story. Is there any other people in the world among whom the life of every individual, from the moment he comes into the world until his last breath, goes on and on according to a single pattern as it does among us? The way they are reared and educated, the words of their prayers, the tunes of their hymns and liturgical poems are all identical; even their food and drink are the same. Who has ever heard of a people who at a given hour, say, Friday night, all over the globe are all eating fish, noodle pudding, and vegetable stew; and on Saturday morning, radishes, jellied cow's foot, liver with onions and eggs, and dried out *kasha* with a marrow bone in it; on a certain day, *kreplakh*, on another day *hamantashen*, on another day twisted yellow *khala* with saffron. At the very moment when someone in Berdichev is singing "He who sanctifies" on the Sabbath Eve, or shouting "He lives forever" on Rosh Hashana, the same tune and the same voice reverberate in Argentina at the other end of the world. We are an ant-hill, in which the individual has no existence apart from the community. In books on natural history, scientists devote a separate chapter to the genus of ants as a whole, but not to the individual ant. (Sholem Abramovitsh, "Of Bygone Days," 273–74)

Of course, this and many other statements by Jewish authors disavowing autobiography are anything but straightforward. They tend instead to be part of complex performances of authorial self-construction. For an analysis of how Abramovitsh reinvents himself as a modern urban Jewish (especially Hebrew) novelist in "Of Bygone Days," see Allison Schachter, "The Shtetl and the City: The Origins of Nostalgia in *Ba-yamim ha-hem* and *Shloyme reb khayims*."

35. Both of these texts were published shortly before their authors' deaths by suicide.

36. See Mintz, "*Banished from Their Father's Table*."

37. As Moseley argues, "No account of the historical/cultural moment of Eastern European Jewish autobiography would . . . be complete without mention of an extra-literary factor that would appear to be inexplicable by reference to any larger configuration of social, literary or intellectual relations: orphanhood—or, more accurately, bereavement of one parent at a young age" (Moseley, *Being for Myself Alone*, 458). While there are well-known orphans in non-Jewish autobiographical writing (Rousseau, Edmund Gosse, Stendhal, Gide, Gorky), "the ratio between those deprived of one parent in childhood and those who left autobiographical testament in Jewish Eastern Europe is quite phenomenal. And the sheer frequency with which the experience of orphanhood is depicted, the centrality that the theme assumes in this literature, makes of Jewish autobiography, in this respect, a law unto itself" (458).

38. "The parentless child, as he emerges from Jewish Eastern European autobiographical writings, presents . . . an enigmatic figure in whom the literary and extraliterary intersect in an exceedingly complex manner. . . . To end a discussion that attempts to provide a heuristic framework for the autobiographical phenomenon in Jewish Eastern Europe with an enigma is, perhaps, fitting and serves as salutary reminder of what the greatest autobiographers have always known: *Individuum ineffabile est*" (Moseley, *Being for Myself Alone*, 461).

39. Singer, *Of a World*; Abramovitsh, "Of Bygone Days"; Perle, *Yidn fun a gants yor: a bukh fun a fargangen lebn*, to name only a few.

40. The subtitle appears only once in Kumove's translation. See Perle, *Ordinary Jews*, 25.

41. "Vanished" seems slightly too emphatic for *fargangen*, especially given the inevitable post-Holocaust associations that attach to *vanished*, forged not least by the uses and abuses of Roman Vishniac's photographs of the 1930s, collected in *A Vanished World*. Perle is nonetheless very much part of the wider literary phenomenon of writing the modern Jewish self against the backdrop of the disintegration of traditional ways of life.

42. Sholem Aleichem wrote the first part of *Motl* during and shortly after his visit to the United States in 1906–1907 and published it serially in the New York Yiddish newspaper *Der amerikaner*. He began working on part two of *Motl*, set in New York, in 1915. Unfinished at the time of Sholem Aleichem's death in 1916, part two was serialized in the Yiddish newspaper *Di varhayt*. An English translation was serialized simultaneously in an array of newspapers.

43. Shmuel Charney published under the (obviously problematic) pseudonym

Shmuel Niger. For an argument for why we should refer to him by his family name, see Eli Bromberg, "We Need to Talk about Shmuel Charney," *In geveb* (October 2019): accessed April 8, 2023. Charney begins his review by remarking on what a heavy, ugly, and depressing impression the opening of Perle's novel makes on the reader. But then he comes to realize that this is only a ruse, as Mendl is in fact a version of Sholem Aleichem's Motl: "I realize that Mendl, the boy telling the story, has tricked me. He is not at all a gloomy soul; on the contrary, he is a jovial lad. He has something of Motl, Peyse the Cantor's son. So why did he just make our hearts so heavy? He did it on purpose so that we should feel all the more relieved by the thin smile on his lips" (Shmuel Charney, "A shrayber, vos shmeykhlt: Yehoshue Perle, *Yidn fun a gants yor*," 504). Later in the review, Charney will put Perle's Mendl in a triangulated constellation of child narrators including not only Sholem Aleichem's Motl but also Penek, the child narrator of the first volume (1932) of Dovid Bergelson's autobiographical novel *At the Dnieper* (*Baym Dnyepr*); see e.g., 504–5.

44. See David Roskies, "Sholem Aleichem and Others: Laughing Off the Trauma of History." Roskies does not discuss *Motl* in this article, but it nonetheless exemplifies the phenomenon he analyzes. Elsewhere Roskies aptly characterizes Motl as "the living embodiment of adaptability and freedom" (Roskies, *Against the Apocalypse*, 176).

45. See book 2 of Sholem Aleichem's *Motl peysi dem khazns*.

46. In fact, Perle used similar refrains two further times for a total of six times. On page 17 of the manuscript of "4580," he wrote, "Mir iz dokh gut—ikh bin a numer," and on page 18 he wrote, "Iz dokh mir gut—ikh bin a numer." However, he struck both of those phrases and they don't appear in the published version.

CHAPTER 7: SHERLOCK HOLMES IN THE WARSAW AND VILNA GHETTOS

1. Arthur Conan Doyle, *The Complete Sherlock Holmes*, 1032.

2. One of the directors of the Lodz ghetto archives (where he was a colleague of Oskar Rosenfeld, whom I focus on in chapter 8), Zelkowicz was a major contributor to the Lodz ghetto *Chronicle* and *Encyclopedia* and the author of numerous reports for the archives about various aspects of life in the ghetto. Zelkowicz, like Shaye Shpigl, who is the focus of chapter 9, also participated in the literary circle in the Lodz ghetto that met in the poet Miriam Ulinover's apartment. Zelkowicz's "Twenty-Five Chickens and One Dead Document" uses detective work to uncover the tragic story behind the murder of twenty-four Jews by a ghetto guard. In "In the Bałuty Apartments, Łódź Ghetto," based on his work as a welfare inspector surveying the living conditions in apartments of the ghetto's poorest inhabitants to determine who qualified for assistance from the ghetto administration, Zelkowicz stylizes himself, I would argue, as something of a Sherlock Holmes making clues legible to his fellow welfare inspector Riva Bramson. As, in Kassow's description, "an educated woman who knew little Yiddish and had scant rapport with ordinary Jews," Bramson suffers from a Watson-like interpretive deficit (Kassow, introduction to *In Those Nightmarish Days*, xxxvi).

3. I have not been able to find this document in the YIVO Archives.

4. Didier Daeninckx, *Murder in Memorium*; Philippe Grimbert, *A Secret*; Patrick Modiano, *Dora Bruder* (and many of his novels); Georges Perec, *W, or the Memory of Childhood*; Henri Raczymow, *Writing the Book of Esther*; Imré Kertesz, *Liquidation* and *Detective Story*; Harry Mulisch, *The Assault*; Doron Rabinovici, *The Search for —M*; Bernhard Schlink, *The Reader*; W. G. Sebald, *Austerlitz*; Robert Wilson, *The Hiding Room*. On the detective paradigm in novels by Bernard Schlink, see William Collins Donahue, "The Popular Culture Alibi: Bernhard Schlink's Detective Novels and the Culture of Politically Correct Holocaust Literature" and *Holocaust as Fiction: Bernhard Schlink's "Nazi" Novels and Their Films*. On the Holocaust in five early twenty-first-century German crime novels see Magdalena Waligórska, "'Darkness at the Beginning': The Holocaust in Contemporary German Crime Fiction." Both Donahue and Waligórska stress the exculpatory thrust that German crime fiction about the Holocaust has for its German reading audience.

5. Paul Ricoeur, *Freud and Philosophy: An Essay on Interpretation*, 32–36.

6. Friedländer reflects on the nature of the (un)representability of the Shoah in his introduction to this landmark volume; see Saul Friedländer, ed., *Probing the Limits of Representation: Nazism and the "Final Solution,"* 1–21.

7. I follow the current scholarly practice of referring to Arthur Conan Doyle's last name simply as Doyle rather than Conan Doyle.

8. See Luc Boltanski, *Mysteries & Conspiracies: Detective Stories, Spy Novels and the Making of Modern Societies*, 15; original emphasis. There is widespread agreement in the secondary literature regarding Sherlock Holmes's function as restoring reason and order. See for example Jeremy Tambling, "Holmes, Law, and Order" (e.g., 112, 117). Peter Brooks argues that in Sherlock Holmes stories "crime is an aberrancy in the world, the introduction of the menace of chaos. But discovery through reason shows that the chaos is only apparent. Holmes's discovery sounds as a victory of law over chance, reason over aberrancy, and it restores a world of perfect order" (Brooks, "Clues, Evidence, Detection: Law Stories," 11). Boltanksi stresses the imbrication of rational and moral order in the world of Sherlock Holmes: "The common sense of normality on which the detective's imagination relies . . . is also a *moral sense*. Ultimately, this moral sense is what grounds the detective's intervention in the conclusive narrative sequences where we see him pass from thought to action, from the (strictly intellectual) resolution of the mystery to the reparation of the disordered reality of which certain singularities were the first signs" (Boltanski, *Mysteries & Conspiracies*, 52; original emphasis).

9. Marcel Reich-Ranicki, *Mein Leben*, 239. Jarecka's four novels were: *Inni ludzie* (Other people, 1931), *Stare grzechy* (Old sins, 1934), *Przed jutrem* (Before tomorrow, 1936), and *Ludzie i sztandary* (vol. 1 *Ojcowie*, 1938; vol. 2 *Zwycięskie pokolenie*, 1939 [People and banners, vol. 1, Fathers, 1938; vol. 2, The victorious generation, 1939]). Jarecka's novels do not appear to have been translated into any language that I can read, so my characterization of them is secondhand. Ringelblum refers to Jarecka as a translator of literary classics (*iberzetserin fun der velt-literatur*); see Ringelblum, *Ksovim fun geto*, vol. 2, 187. Reich-Ranicki recalls that Jarecka, having asked him if

he knew Saint-Exupery's *Vol de nuit* and learned that he did not, translated it into Polish for him as a birthday gift. For other details of Jarecka's biography and work for the Oyneg Shabes archive, I have relied on Kassow, *Who Will Write Our History?*, 5–7 and 182–84; and an online article by Anna Majchrowska dated August 17, 2019: https://onegszabat.org/en/a-stone-thrown-under-the-wheel-of-history/.

10. Among other activities, Reich-Ranicki was a staff literary critic for the influential weekly *Die Zeit* from 1960 to 1973, and from 1973 to 1988 the literary editor for the *Frankfurter Allgemeine Zeitung*, the German newspaper with arguably the most highly regarded cultural pages (*Feuilleton*).

11. For Reich-Ranicki's account of how he and his wife Tosia fled from the Umschlagplatz after signaling to Jarecka to follow, see Reich-Ranicki, *Mein Leben*, 270. Ultimately, Jarecka and her sons did not make a run for it, likely because the attempt would have been futile with Jarecka's four-year-old, Karol. Kassow speculates that Jarecka may have run out of time, or broken off her report because it was unbearable to write; see Kassow, *Who Will Write Our History?*, 184.

12. According to Samuel Kassow, "Seidman's diary, however, is not entirely reliable" (Kassow, *Who Will Write Our History?*, 439n36). The context of the Jarecka remark Seidman recounts is a conversation among intellectuals in the Warsaw ghetto after the Great Deportation, including Rabbi J. L. Orlean, who before the war had led the Bais Yaakov school for Orthodox girls, Ringelblum, Isaac Schiper, Katzenelson, and Perle, among many others. At one point, Schiper moves the discussion in the direction of the question of the Jewish influence on Polish culture, and Orlean answers

> that he can't stand to hear the word Polish or European culture. The Germans, he says, were the cultural avatars with a capital A! . . . [*zenen geven di kutur-treger behey hayedie! . . .*]
>
> A discussion develops about the "Jewishness" of the Christianizing Jakob Wassermann, of Stefan Zweig and the like. Adam Hershaft speaks of the painter [Max] Liebermann. Ms. Jarecka, the famous Polish writer, agrees with Orlean. She regrets that she has written in Polish. Should she survive, she will learn Hebrew and Yiddish and write in these languages. (Seidman, *Togbukh fun varshever geto*, 173)

13. Ringelblum writes that, in addition to her report on the Great Deportation, "Froy Jarecka hot oykh ongeshribn andere arbetn fun dem yidishn lebn in geto" (Ms. Jarecka also wrote other works on Jewish life in the ghetto). Ringelblum also praises the beautiful style, thoroughness, and objectivity (*zakhlekhkeyt*) of Jarecka's report. See Emanuel Ringelblum, *Ksovim fun geto II*, 188.

14. Kassow, *Who Will Write Our History?*, 6. See also Kassow's introduction to *The Warsaw Ghetto Oyneg Shabes-Ringelblum Archive: Catalog and Guide*, xxiii.

15. I thank Anna Klosowska for providing this translation from page 1 of Jarecka's original text, *Ostatnim Etapem Przesiedlenia Jest Smierc* (AR II/197). The text is also included in vol. 33 of the complete edition of the Oyneg Shabes archive in Polish (*Archiwum Ringelbluma: Konspiracyjne Archiwum Getta Warszawy*, vol. 33). The published English translation of Jarecka's text, "The Last Stage of Resettlement Is Death," renders this passage as follows:

That there is some sense in still being alive among the shambles, among human hyenas and jackals who live by stripping the dead. These documents and notes are a remnant resembling a clue in a detective story. I remember from childhood such a novel by Conan Doyle, in which the dying victim writes with a faint hand one word on the wall containing the proof of the criminal's guilt. That word, scrawled by the dying man, influenced my imagination in the past. The records left by us, whose survival is so uncertain, remind me of that stereotype image that once so moved me. We are noting the evidence of the crime. This will no longer be of any help to us. The record must be hurled like a stone under . . . history's wheel in order to stop it. That stone has the weight of our knowledge that reached the bottom of human cruelty. (Gustawa Jarecka, "The Last Stage of Resettlement Is Death," 704)

16. Jarecka would presumably have read the 1903 (republished 1906) Polish translation of *A Study in Scarlet* by the prolific journalist and translator Bronisława Neufeldówna (1857–1931), *Czerwonym szlakiem* (The red trail).

17. In connection with how Jarecka's flawed or creative memory made this Holmes story harmonize with the widespread longing among ghetto prisoners for revenge on their captors and murderers, it is noteworthy that Nachman Blumental, in a piece originally written in 1945, reports that "a Kovner Jew, with his last bit of strength, wrote on the wall of the house where he was slaughtered, in his own blood, the word 'revenge' [*nekome*]" (Blumental, "Di kharakteristik fun der yidisher literatur," 29).

18. As Caroline Reitz remarks, *A Study in Scarlet* has "the odd organization of a story casting about for its generic footing" (Reitz, "The Empires of *A Study in Scarlet* and *The Sign of Four*," 135).

19. Early Yiddish historians, especially Blumental and Kermish, worked closely with Oyneg Shabes documents. Joseph Wulf's use of documents from the Oyneg Shabes archive played a significant role in a dispute between him and German historians at the Institut für Zeitgeschichte (IfZ). Wulf drew on these documents to expose Dr. Wilhelm Hagen as an accomplice in his role as head of the medical authorities in the Warsaw ghetto. Martin Broszat and his IfZ colleagues, however, disputed the credibility of statements by Ringelblum about Hagen and defended Hagen. On the so-called Hagen-Affair, see Nicolas Berg, *The Holocaust and the West German Historians: Historical Interpretation and Autobiographical Memory*, 214–28; on the role of Oyneg Shabes documents, 214–15. In addition to Kassow's groundbreaking account of Emanuel Ringelblum and the Oyneg Shabes project, *Who Will Write our History?*, works by the prolific Polish historian Katarzyna Person are noteworthy for their extensive use of the Oyneg Shabes (or Ringelblum) archive. See for example Katarzyna Person, *Assimilated Jews in the Warsaw Ghetto, 1940–1943*, and *Warsaw Ghetto Police*.

20. For Kruk's account of his arduous trek from Warsaw to Vilna, see *Last Days*, 1–23. Kruk explains that he set out on his own because he anticipated being conscripted into military service and didn't want his wife to be alone in an unfamiliar place (Kruk, *Last Days*, 1). Kruk and his brother Pinkhas received American visas in

spring 1940, but Herman remained and continued to try to track down his wife and child. See Fishman, *Book Smugglers*, 33–34.

21. On Kruk, his diary and notebooks, and the postwar recovery of his wartime writings, see Benjamin Harshav's "Preface" to Kruk, *Last Days*, xv–xx, and Fishman, *Book Smugglers*, 33–37; 113; 125–28; 159–60; 172; 183; 218–20.

22. See Samuel Kassow, "Vilna and Warsaw," 194–95, and Kruk, "Library and Reading Room," 193.

23. On Kruk's tireless work to make the ghetto library the major cultural institution that it was, see Fishman, *Book Smugglers*, 36–38, 42–51.

24. On the Paper Brigade in Vilna, see Fishman, *Book Smugglers*. For an earlier, concise account, see Fishman, *The Rise of Modern Yiddish Culture*, chapter 10, "Embers Plucked from the Fire: The Rescue of Jewish Cultural Treasures in Vilna."

25. YIVO, an acronym for Yidisher visnshaftlekher institut (Yiddish Scientific Institute) was (and is) a Yiddish research institute for the humanistic sciences. Founded in Vilna in 1925, it moved to New York after World War II. Max Weinreich, the YIVO's founder and driving force, was in Denmark for a linguistics conference when World War II broke out and eventually made his way to New York.

26. See Fishman, *Book Smugglers*, 140.

27. Sutzkever and the poet Justas Paleckis had become friends in early 1940 at a meeting of Lithuanian and Yiddish writers. Paleckis joined the Communist Party when the Soviet Union incorporated Lithuania in June 1940, and, a few months later, he was appointed to the (largely symbolic) position of president of the Lithuanian Soviet government. After the Germans invaded, Paleckis was evacuated to Moscow, where he remained the Lithuanian Soviet president in exile. When news reached him that Sutzkever was alive and writing poems in a partisan unit, he arranged for the Sutzkevers' private evacuation. See Fishman, *Book Smugglers*, 129.

28. Gershon Abramovitsh's bunker on 6 Shavel Street, also used by the Vilna ghetto resistance organization (FPO) for stockpiling weapons. Sutzkever found some dozens of pages of Kruk's diary and took them with him when he left for Moscow on September 10, 1944. In October 1944, Kaczerginski found several hundred pages. Of the three copies of his diary that Kruk deposited in three different locations, only the copy in the bunker on Shavel Street was spared being destroyed. See Fishman, *Book Smugglers*, 158–60.

29. No material support was extended to the Jewish Museum, and Jewish books continued to be destroyed, now by the Lithuanian authorities. A communist from before the war, Kaczerginski traveled to Moscow to complain about the Lithuanian authorities' treatment of the Jewish Museum. On his return, he discovered that thirty tons of YIVO materials that had been discovered in the Trash Administration's courtyard had been delivered to the train depot for shipment to a paper mill rather than delivered to the Jewish Museum as the museum staff had requested. Kaczerginski pulled what he could off the train by hand but was unable to stop the shipment. Moreover, the NKVD frequently visited the museum and obstructed its

activities. No books were allowed to be made accessible to the public without first being reviewed by NKVD censors, but volumes submitted to the censors were never returned. See Fishman, *Book Smugglers*, 145–52; 160–63; 171–77, and *Modern Yiddish Culture*, 139–53.

30. Quoted in Fishman, *Modern Yiddish Culture*, 150, and *Book Smugglers*, 177.

31. Also incredibly, the day before Kruk and his fellow inmates of Lagedi were murdered on Rosh Hashanah (September 18, 1944), a courier brought him the notebooks he had kept while in the Klooga camp. The transfer from Klooga to Lagedi occurred so abruptly on August 22, 1944, that he hadn't been able to take the notebooks with him. By receiving them the day before his murder, he was able to bury them. See Fishman, *Book Smugglers*, 125–28.

32. The Jewish Museum was closed by the NKVD in 1949, its holdings ransacked. They dumped everything into trucks and took it to an archive in the Church of St. Yiri, which was repurposed as a state archive. There they remained, inaccessible, until after the end of the Soviet Union. How they avoided being destroyed during the Stalinist years through the courageous protection of the sympathetic Lithuanian archivist Dr. Antanas Ulpis is a remarkable story in its own right. See Fishman, *Modern Yiddish Culture*, 151–52, and *Book Smugglers*, 233–36 and 244–48.

33. See Kassow, "Vilna and Warsaw," 201, and Harshav, introduction to Kruk, *Last Days*, xxviii–xxix.

34. *Last Days*, 300 / *Togbukh fun vilner geto*, 276.

35. My overview of crime fiction in Yiddish is thoroughly indebted to Nathan Cohen's richly researched article "Sherlock Holmes in the Pale of Settlement: Yiddish Crime Stories 1860–1914."

36. Although "Sherlock Holmes" stories peaked in Yiddish culture 1907–1910, they by no means vanished from the scene thereafter. For example, in 1928 the Hebrew Publishing Company in New York published a translation of the collection of Sherlock Holmes stories *Sherlock Holmes: The World's Greatest Detective* under the title *Der grester detektiv*. Earlier, in 1919, the New York publisher Idish published a two-volume edition of works by Edgar Allan Poe that included the classic detective story "Di mordn af der morg-gas" ("The Murders of Rue Morgue"; Edgar Allan Poe, *Di Verk*, vol. 1, 78–131).

37. These Yiddish stories were translated from two Polish series, one published in Warsaw (1907–1909, 52 booklets), the other in Cracow (1908–1909, 86 booklets). The Polish series published in Cracow was translated from the German series *Aus den Geheimakten des Weltdetektivs*, which launched in 1907 and eventually encompassed 230 booklets. The hero of this series was Sherlock Holmes, and his assistant was Harry Dickson. According to Cohen, it is unclear whether the Yiddish stories from this series were translated from the original German or from the Polish translations.

38. Kreppel wrote in German, Hebrew, Polish, and Yiddish. He edited and/or published several Yiddish-language Galician newspapers and was active in the Orthodox Zionist Agudas Israel movement. In addition to his Max Spitzkopf booklets, he authored four series of popular booklets in Yiddish between 1924 and 1930. His most significant work in German is *Juden und Judentum von Heute* (Jews and Juda-

ism today), a nearly-nine-hundred-page encyclopedic handbook and bibliography of contemporary Jewry. Kreppel was murdered in the Buchenwald concentration camp on July 21, 1940. See the online English translation of the *Yiddish Leksikon* entry on Kreppel by Yekhezkl Lifshits: http://yleksikon.blogspot.com/2019/04/yoyne-krepel-jonas-kreppel.html (accessed September 3, 2023) and David Mazower, Elissa Sperling, and Michael Yashinsky, "Max Spitzkopf, the Viennese Sherlock Holmes: The Jewish Detective Hero Who Inspired the Young Bashevis Singer," https://www.yiddishbookcenter.org/max-spitzkopf-viennese-sherlock-holmes (accessed September 3, 2023). For a fuller account of Kreppel's life and career, see Klaus Kreppel, *Jonas Kreppel—Glaubenstreu und vaterländisch: Biografische Skizze über einen österreichisch-jüdischen Schriftsteller.* Most relevant for the context of Kreppel's Spitzkopf detective stories are chapters 6, "Ein Jiddisher Verleger" (51–58), and 23, "Jiddischer Schriftsteller" (204–14).

39. See Isaac Bashevis Singer, *In My Father's Court,* 252–53 (for the Yiddish original, see Bashevis Singer, *Mayn tatns beys-din shtub,* 301). Klaus Kreppel identifies the quote that stuck in Bashevis Singer's memory in *Jonas Kreppel,* 208. According to Cohen, the Spitzkopf stories were "inspired by popular stories about the Viennese detectives Josef Müller (created by the writer August Groner, 1850–1929) or Dagobert Trosler (by Balduin Groller, 1848–1916)" (Cohen, "Sherlock Holmes," 273). For a story by Groner ("The Golden Bullet") and one by Groller ("The Vault Break-In") in English, see Mary W. Tannert and Henry Kratz, eds., *Early German and Austrian Detective Fiction: An Anthology,* 190–216 and 227–42, respectively.

40. Bashevis Singer refers to this as an Orthodox newspaper started by Nahum Leib Weingut in which Israel Joshua Singer published his first stories as well as his translation from the German of the historical novel *Rabbi Joselmann von Rosheim* by Marcus Lehmann. In a later memoir published in English as *More Stories from My Father's Court,* Bashevis Singer describes rushing to a newsstand to buy detective and adventure stories after finding himself, due to unexpected circumstances, with enough money in his pocket for six booklets. "I run to Tvarda Street. The news vendor stands there wearing a little red cap. His small book rack is packed with books: Sherlock Holmes, Max Spitzkopf, and titles like *Terrible Secrets, The Secret of the Kaiser's Court, The Captive Princess, The Enchanted Orphan Girl, The 1,200 Thieves.* Each title pulls me like a magnet. Each booklet has its own mystery, cleverness, and bizarre intrigues. But I can't buy them all. I have to choose" (Isaac Bashevis Singer, *More Stories from My Father's Court,* 84).

41. See chapters 6 and 7 of Dan Diner, *Beyond the Conceivable: Studies on Germany, Nazism, and the Holocaust.*

42. See Svenja Bethke, *Dance on the Razor's Edge: Crime and Punishment in the Nazi Ghettos,* 56, 157.

43. See Ringelblum, "Oyneg Shabes," 391. See also Roskies's argument for the importance of "reading in time" in "Did the Shoah Engender a New Poetics?"

44. See Harshav, introduction to Kruk, *Last Days,* xlv, and Fishman, *Book Smugglers,* 43.

45. Yitzhak Arad, *Ghetto in Flames: The Struggle and Destruction of the Jews in*

Vilna in the Holocaust, 292. For Arad's account of the trial and executions on June 4, 1942, see 292–94.

46. An image of this announcement, in Yiddish, is reproduced in Mendl Balberyszski, *Shtarker fun ayzn: iberlebungen in der Hitler-tekufe*, 298.

47. On Gens's amnesty of July 1942 and how "the commitment to an 'honest life'" that Gens promoted was "based on the hope that the survival of the ghetto community could be secured through labour until the arrival of the Red Army," see Bethke, *Dance on the Razor's Edge*, 119.

48. A bit further along, the passage continues: "This reality thus relies on a postulate of *trust*, that is, on a common adherence to the social order as it is, so that to manifest a propensity to distrust the reality of reality, or even to voice simple doubts about it, is the best way to lose all credibility, and thereby to be marginalized or excluded from society" (Boltanski, *Mysteries & Conspiracies*, 107–8).

49. On this case, see Arad, *Ghetto in Flames*, 291, and Bethke, *Dance on the Razor's Edge*, 94.

50. For a reproduction of this announcement in the original Yiddish, see n46 in this chapter.

51. Michael Ausubel and Michael J. Broyde note that at the height of Jewish communal autonomy in fifteenth- and sixteenth-century Poland, Jewish courts could hand down punishments of imprisonment and sometimes even execution:

> In some instances, the authority of the autonomous Jewish courts knew no bounds: a number of East European communities were empowered to punish criminals by execution. Although this power was used selectively and with little fanfare, it is indicative of the degree of independence and power that communal bodies possessed. No formalized procedures were developed for adjudicating capital offenses; indeed, the process remained somewhat secretive. In most cases, the manner and method of implementation were left to the discretion of individual tribunals or to agents acting on their behalf (see Isserles' responsa 11 and 17). Jewish leaders would also occasionally decide to hand over egregious violators to secular authorities for execution. As Jewish communal autonomy waned and judicial independence was curtailed, the leadership increasingly resorted to this option, although dealing with the non-Jewish authorities could be fraught with complications.

See Michael Ausubel and Michael J. Broyde, "Legal Institutions," *YIVO Encyclopedia of Jews in Eastern Europe*, https://yivoencyclopedia.org/article.aspx/Legal_Institutions (accessed September 11, 2023).

52. In context, "It is our historical task" ("Es iz unzer historishe oyfgabe!" ["Zeks tlies," 19]) appears to be quoted from the speech Gens gave at the gallows in which he promised that he and the Jewish police would be able to protect the remaining ghetto population. Kruk quotes a longer portion of this speech on the following page (*Last Days*, 620). Bethke quotes and contextualizes Gens's speech (as recorded by Kruk) in *Dance on the Razor's Edge*, 114–15.

53. Kassow notes Kruk's "fierce loyalty to the Bund" and that in the Vilna ghetto he "clung to [the Bundist vision of the world] to the very end" and "remained a

firm believer in the principle of party supremacy" (Kassow, "Vilna and Warsaw," 203, 204).

54. Nor does Kruk's narrative follow the paradigm of the reversed or inverted detective story, the "howcatchem" as opposed to the classic "whodunit."

55. According to Arad, the attempted murder of Greenfeld occurred at the end of October 1941. See Arad, *Ghetto in Flames*, 292.

56. Kruk's initial diary entry (*Last Days*, 235–36) on the murder of the priest and reprisal mass killings of Jews in Lida makes no mention of Avidon. His account of the "Lida tragedy" in "Zeks tlies" (609–11) states that Avidon was one of the six Jews known to be active in the underworld and thus chosen to be handed over to the German authorities but does not say whether or not he actually was involved in the murder of the priest. Arad states that Avidon was responsible for the death of the Lida priest (Arad, *Ghetto in Flames*, 202–3).

57. See Kruk, *Last Days*, 301, and Bethke (referring to Kruk), *Dance on the Razor's Edge*, 114.

58. For Balberyszski's account of the trial and executions of June 4, 1942, in the Vilna ghetto, see Balberyszki, *Shtarker fun ayzn*, 297–99.

59. The corresponding passages in the bowdlerized English translation *Stronger Than Iron* bear little relationship to the original Yiddish text; see Mendel Balberyszski, *Stronger Than Iron: The Destruction of Vilna Jewry, 1941–1945; An Eyewitness Account*, 201–2.

60. Reacting to claims by Kruk such as that "no one in the ghetto resented this act of justice," Bethke judiciously writes, "Whether the majority of residents really did agree with the verdicts remains open to question. What is certain, however, is that death sentences could be imposed in Vilna—unlike in Lodz—without any appreciable resistance from Jewish functionaries or the ghetto community. The attitude of residents is likely to have been ambivalent: on one hand, the verdicts must have provoked fears of suffering a similar fate one day, particularly among those who had joined the armed resistance movement despite Jewish Council opposition. On the other hand, people in Vilna had already seen at first hand how criminal behavior on the part of individuals could pose an existential threat to the community" (Bethke, *Dance on the Razor's Edge*, 148).

61. On the Vittenberg Affair, see for example Arad, *Ghetto in Flames*, 387–98; Balberyszski, *Stronger Than Iron*, 238–44; Daniel Feierstein, "The Jewish Resistance Movements in the Ghettos of Eastern Europe," 224–25; and Isaiah Trunk, *Judenrat: The Jewish Councils in Eastern Europe under Nazi Occupation*, 470.

62. Although the Vilna teenager Yitskhok Rudashevski began writing contemporary (as opposed to retrospective) entries in his diary only in September 1942 and so does not remark on the June executions, in an entry of October 18 he writes:

> Suddenly one bright day Jewish policemen donned official hats. I walk across the street and here go some of them wearing leather jackets, boots, and green round hats with glossy peaks and Stars of David. Here goes Smilgovski (an "officer") in a dark blue hat and a golden Star of David. They march smartly by in unison. (Jackets are being "loaned" by force in the streets.) They impress

you as Lithuanians, as kidnappers. An unpleasant feeling comes over me. I hate them from the bottom of my heart, ghetto Jews in uniforms, and how arrogantly they stride in the boots they have plundered! The entire ghetto is stunned. Everyone feels the same way about them and they have somehow become such strangers to the ghetto. In me they arouse a feeling compounded of ridicule, disgust and fear. (Rudashevski, *Diary of the Vilna Ghetto*, 69–70)

63. Bethke notes that while the Jewish Councils defined many acts as criminal in an attempt to avoid intervention by the Germans, "For the public they were addressing . . .—the ordinary ghetto inhabitants, who did not play a part in the Jewish self-administration—it was a very different story. For them, the newly defined criminal acts were in many cases the only means of individual survival, and their values were therefore often diametrically opposed to the Councils' definitions" (Bethke, *Dance on the Razor's Edge*, 7, 164–65).

64. As Arad notes, Gens opened a "Club" in his home for lectures and discussions and invited people from the full political spectrum within the ghetto: from the Revisionists to the Bundists and communists (Arad, *Ghetto in Flames*, 290). Gens's Club became a meeting place for members of the liberal professions and intelligentsia and gave Gens the image of an "enlightened intellectual" (*Ghetto in Flames*, 291), not just a police chief. Kruk attended the first meeting on May 15, 1942, which featured a lecture on "A Nation and a People" followed by discussion until 3:00 am; but he declined to attend the second meeting, which featured a lecture and debate on "Jews and Jewry," and on May 29 he noted two reasons for not doing so: "First, the gathering of dubious elements, and second, you cannot speak what you think, and just speaking makes no sense. I considered it more suitable to stay home" (Kruk, *Last Days*, 297). Bethke observes that "even members of the Jewish self-administration who were otherwise extremely critical of Gens's actions, such as Kruk and Balberyszski, seem to have supported the imposition of the death penalty. Advocates argued that it was a necessary measure for the protection of the community, given the 'exceptional circumstances.' And . . . there was even a measure of pride surrounding the fact that it was a *ghetto-internal* measure" (Bethke, *Dance on the Razor's Edge*, 131, emphasis in original).

65. See Kruk's entry of January 1, 1942 (Kruk, *Last Days*, 148–49), in which he describes a New Year's Eve party held by Gens, and fiercely criticizes Gens's self-praise for the "hard work" he had done in the past year. As Benjamin Harshav glosses Kruk's reference to Gens as "Il Duce": "Kruk, the Socialist, resents the 'Fascist' Revisionists. In fact, the Revisionist Party did have contacts with the Italian Fascists in the 1930s" (Harshav, note 75 in Kruk, *Last Days*, 148).

66. For example, on July 2, 1942, Kruk records criticism of Gens's cynical motivations for trying to establish a literary competition and notes that to his (Kruk's own) credit, he refused Gens's invitation to read works to him (*Last Days*, 316). In an entry of July 5, 1942, Kruk notes that Gens personally beat a Dr. Steinman for disobeying his order to report to the forest for medical work, noting with bitter sarcasm, "Beaten bloody and flogged until he fainted—this is a step forward for our ghetto dictator. / Just so we're moving forward and not backward!" (*Last Days*, 320). On July 11, Kruk

referred to Murer's appointment of Gens as head of the ghetto as "The Putsch in the Ghetto" (*Last Days*, 326–27).

67. On Kruk's changing but always strained relationship to Gens, see Kassow, "Vilna and Warsaw," 201–2; Kassow here draws on Kruk's wider diary and on "Six Gallows."

68. See Kruk, "Library and Reading Room," 193. Kruk's lament about the ghetto residents' love of lowbrow fiction, including Edgar Wallace, in Polish would seem to confirm Nathan Cohen's hypothesis that the increased use of Polish among Jews in interbellum Poland contributed substantially to the decline in crime literature in Yiddish after its peak years of 1907–1910. See Cohen, "Sherlock Holmes," 276.

69. "Everything that happened here had one great purpose: in view of the great events, face to face with the horrible [*eymediker*] historical situation of the local Jews, the shame [*di kharpe*] has to be wiped out.

"The whole ghetto wanted to wash its hands [*zikh reyntsuvashn*]! Therefore the 'bloodthirstiness' of the Vilna Ghetto residents" (*Last Days*, 603 / "Zeks tlies," 2).

70. "Six persons now lie stretched out on the floor of the Jewish police headquarters. Most half naked, beaten, and bleeding. The large room is steeped in tension, sweat, and bloodstains. Around the murderers are the entire police leadership, the Judenrat, the ghetto court, and the criminal police. The prosecutor demands a sentence of death by hanging for the six accused" (Kruk, *Last Days*, 616).

71. A further ambiguity has to do with the historical mode of these "historic" executions. Public execution belongs to an older judicial paradigm of spectacular display of sovereign power over subjects, gradually replaced in modernity by the rehabilitative paradigm. Are these public executions marking this Jewish (juridical) return to history the result of an exercise of moral autonomy on the part of modern Jewish institutions of justice (police, secular courts), or do they demonstrate a regression to the brute display of a premodern sovereign violence? Bethke illuminates the public nature of the death penalties in the Vilna ghetto: "As for the function of ghetto-internal punishments, it can be described as essentially preventive, the aim being to contain the feared dangers to the community posed by the Germans. The penalties were partly directed at the 'offenders' themselves but were also designed to have a deterrent effect on the rest of the ghetto population. Their primary purpose, therefore, was one of 'general prevention'—hence the fact that sentences were publicly announced in newspapers or proclamations, and that the few death penalties imposed by the Jewish Council in Vilna were executed in public" (Bethke, *Dance on the Razor's Edge*, 140–41).

CHAPTER 8: OSKAR ROSENFELD'S HAUNTING LITERARY DREAM IN THE LODZ GHETTO

1. The official term for the internal ghetto administration in territories annexed by the Third Reich was *Ältestenrat* (Council of elders), not *Judenrat* (Jewish Council), which was used in ghettos in the Generalgouvernement. I use the term Jewish Council to refer to the Lodz ghetto administration, however, since this term is widely understood.

2. For a sizable if still abbreviated edition of the official *Chronicle*, see *The Chronicle of the Łódź Ghetto, 1941–1944*, ed. Lucjan Dobroszycki.

3. Rosenfeld refers to his story (*Novelle*) by different titles. In an entry of June 1, 1942, he sketches, for his story "Er sucht das Geheimnis der Gettos," the gaunt, wasted appearance of Jewish men in the ghetto, reduced to the image of the "Wandering Jew," a term Rosenfeld uses in English (see *Wozu noch Welt*, 93). In an entry of Friday, September 25, 1942, Rosenfeld records his plans to give a reading of his story "Das Geheimnis des Gettos" the following day ("Morgen Samstag lese ich Novelle 'Das Geheimnis des Gettos' beziehungsweise Prag-Lodz vor. Freu mich darauf." See *Wozu noch Welt*, 160). On May 30, 1943, Rosenfeld was still pondering this text (which he here again refers to by the title "Das Geheimnis des Gettos" but now calls an *Erzählung*) and sketches out an ostensible revision involving a scene in a "Beth Midrasch" that has possibly been improvised in a ghetto courtyard, but this is not entirely clear; see *Wozu noch Welt*, 212–13.

4. The subtitle "aus dem mährischen Ghettoleben" was added when the story was reprinted in *Menorah: Illustrierte Monatsschrift für die jüdische Famile* (Illustrated monthly for the Jewish home).

5. *Tage und Nächte*, 9. For a thorough overview of Rosenfeld's writings—journalistic and literary—before and during his years in the Lodz ghetto (as well as of the oeuvre of fellow German-language Lodz ghetto inmate Oskar Singer), see Sascha Feuchert, *Oskar Rosenfeld und Oskar Singer: Zwei Autoren des Lodzer Gettos*.

6. For biographical background on Rosenfeld, see Hanno Loewy, "Editor's Introduction" to *In the Beginning Was the Ghetto: Notebooks from Łódź*, xiii–xxii.

7. David Roskies and Naomi Diamant, *Holocaust Literature: A History and Guide* 215. The authors and titles that Rosenfeld reads or reflects on in the Lodz ghetto include the classic Yiddish writer Sholem Aleichem (Rosenfeld, 69/99, 128/154, 147/170); the modernist Yiddish prose writer Dovid Bergelson (147/170); the poet of the Hebrew revival Hayim Nahman Bialik (186/207); Knut Hamsun, *Hunger*, which Rosenfeld read in Yiddish translation (76/106, 109/138, 147/170); the proto-Zionist treatise by Moses Hess, *Rome and Jerusalem* (147/170); novellas by Ivan Turgenyev and Maxim Gorki (147/170); Baruch Spinoza (138/163, 173/193), especially his *Theological-Political Treatise* (143/167, 147/170); the Hebrew Bible (64/94, 87/116, 127/153); the mishnaic *Pirkei Avot* (*Sayings of the Fathers*, 134/159); Gemara (87/116); Jean-Jacques Rousseau's *Confessions* (147/170); Thomas Mann's *The Magic Mountain* (157/179); Erich Maria Remarque's *All Quiet on the Western Front* (157/179); Heinrich Heine (147/170, 169/188, 181/201); Friedrich Schiller (141/165, 143/167); Johann Wolfgang von Goethe (136/161, 138/163, 176/197, 181/201, 246/263); Friedrich Nietzsche (155/177); William Shakespeare (181/201, 186/207); Dante Alighieri (197/217, 198/218, 199/219); Miguel de Cervantes' *Don Quixote* (265/282); Edgar Allan Poe (186/207); Fyodor Dostoevsky (190/210, 250/266, 251/269); Alfred Kubin's *The Other Side* (21/54, 109/138); Émile Zola's *The Belly of Paris* (109/138); Otto Weininger's *Sex and Character* (195/215, 265/282); and the Russian-Jewish modernist Isaac Babel (195/216). These examples are far from exhaustive. (Page numbers indicate Rosen-

feld, *In the Beginning*, on the left side of the slash and Rosenfeld, *Wozu noch Welt*, on the right side of the slash.)

8. The catalogue of this exhibit was published under the title *Unser einziger Weg ist Arbeit*, ed. Hanno Loewy and Gerhard Schoenberner. Of Rosenfeld's twenty-one notebooks, notebooks eighteen and nineteen are missing.

9. See Hanno Loewy's "Editor's Introduction" to Oskar Rosenfeld, *In the Beginning Was the Ghetto*, esp. xxvii–xxix. Rosenfeld's notebooks were published in German under the title *Wozu noch Welt* and in English as *In the Beginning Was the Ghetto*. The English title is not a translation of the German title. Rather, each title is derived from a different sentence in the notebooks. Referring to the deportation of the children from the Lodz ghetto in September 1942, a devastated Rosenfeld wrote: "If something like this was possible, what's left? What point does war still have? What point hunger? What point a world? [*Wozu noch Welt?*]." Oskar Rosenfeld, *Wozu Noch Welt: Aufzeichnungen aus dem Getto Lodz*, 195 (my translation). The English title stems from a reflection closely related to Rosenfeld's experience of the ghetto as a world unto itself, incommensurable with human experience and agency beyond it, akin to an alternate world created by God. Rosenfeld writes that the tragedy of the ghetto lacks heroes because the pain experienced is beyond all human scale. It "is something incomprehensible that coincides with the cosmos; a natural phenomenon like the creation of the world. One would have to begin again from the creation, with 'Berajschitt' [Rosenfeld's transliteration of the Hebrew for 'in the beginning,' the first word of the Hebrew Bible and thus also the Hebrew title of the book of Genesis]. In the beginning God created the Ghetto." Rosenfeld, *Wozu noch Welt*, 133 (my translation).

10. While it is impossible to know precisely what horror tales Rosenfeld had read, it may be worth noting that he uses "Poe" as a code name for the United States (and "Shakespeare" for England) in an entry of April 22, 1943, in which he, characteristically, filters recent news—here the news of the only days-old Warsaw Ghetto Uprising—through a cinematic esthetic.

> Talkie and realities [in English in the original] . . .
>
> Die schwarze Hand geht los auf Judenviertel Varsovie und will sie verjagen. Sie wehren sich. Hände gegen Waffen, Gewehre und Panzer—Schießerei, Belagerung. Kommt Hilfe? Alles schreit: Rettet unsere Seelen . . . Die Stadt brennt!—Wie soll das enden? (Bild des zionistischen Rußland). Die Menschen verbergen sich in Kellern, auf Dachböden, Closetts, Friedhöfen, etc. Von oben Brandbomben. Ein Geschrei und Gewimmer—Schma Israel! Will es die Welt nicht hören? Sie hört nicht. Shakespeare und Poe schweigen. (*Wozu noch Welt*, 207)

> Talkie and realities . . .
>
> The black hand is storming the Jewish quarter of Varsovie, seeking to drive them out. They resist. Hands against weapons, rifles, and tanks—exchange of fire, siege. Will help arrive? All call out: Save our souls . . . The city is in flames!

—How will it all end? (Image of Zionist Russia.) People hide in cellars, attics, toilets, cemeteries, etc. From above, firebombs. Wild screaming and whimpering —*Shma Israel!* Does the world not want to hear? It doesn't hear. Shakespeare and Poe are silent. (*In the Beginning*, 186; translation modified)

11. On the emergence of modern Jewish literature alongside and in ambivalent interaction with European models, see Naomi Seidman, *The Marriage Plot: Or, How Jews Fell in Love with Love, and with Literature.*

12. In Rosenfeld's complex lament, "If only a camera could memorialize this curiosity, this devil's spawn of a city, this Ghetto Litzmannstadt, which, like a ruler over the medieval ghettos, has the right and obligation to look down on it in its ghetto backwardness" (Rosenfeld, *In the Beginning*, 53 / *Wozu noch Welt*, 85), we see both how the desire for a camera is a wish for an objective image, a means of recording (*festhalten*) a reality, and how this desire is also freighted with extra-documentary meanings. The highly figurative language is both in lieu of a camera, and a necessary supplement to what a camera, even if one were available to Rosenfeld, would be able to memorialize.

13. Berel Lang, "Oskar Rosenfeld and Historiographic Realism (In Sex, Shit, and Status)," 119.

14. On February 12, 1944, for example, in the face of unfolding catastrophic events, Rosenfeld pondered how the "extreme despair" and "hunger—cold—fear of outsettlement" accompanied by "no hope for a good ending" could, and could not, be accommodated within different modes of representation, including Dostoevsky, Dickens, Walter Scott, Cervantes, and the Russian novelists (Rosenfeld, *In the Beginning*, 251 / *Wozu noch Welt*, 269). I take up Rosenfeld's consideration of Isaac Babel as a model later in this chapter. For a partly overlapping discussion of esthetic and medial mediations of Rosenfeld's gaze, see Sven-Erik Rose, "Oskar Rosenfeld, the Lodz Ghetto, and the Chronotope of Hunger."

15. The slave-labor factories in the Lodz ghetto were referred to as *ressorts*.

16. Feuchert, *Oskar Rosenfeld und Oskar Singer*, 392n1109.

17. The Malik-Verlag published the following works by Babel in German translation: *Budjonnys Reiterarmee*, trans. Dmitrij Umanskij (1926); *Geschichten aus Odessa*, trans. Dmitri Umanski (authorized translation, 1926); *Drei Welten: Gesammelte Erzählungen*, trans. Dmitri Umanski (1931); and "Nach dem Kampf," trans. E. Honig, in *30 neue Erzähler des neuen Russlands* (1931), 149–56. On the selection, re-sequencing, and translation of Babel's *Red Cavalry* cycle for German publication, see Ulrike Yekutsch, "Isaak Babel's 'Konarmija' in Germany of the 1920s."

18. On Babel as a Jewish writer see for example Efraim Sicher, "The Jewishness of Babel" (on *Red Cavalry* in particular, 172–73) and Ruth R. Wisse, *The Modern Jewish Canon*, 99–119 (on *Red Cavalry*, 104–19).

19. Isaac Babel, *The Complete Works of Isaac Babel*, 227. Hereafter, page references to this work are given parenthetically in the text.

20. I should note, however, that the German edition of Babel's *Budjonnys Reiterarmee* had only thirty stories (as compared to thirty-four in the Soviet edition), ar-

ranged somewhat differently. In the German edition, "Der Sohn des Rabbi" was the penultimate story, and "Der Verrat" (Treason) closed the cycle. In the 1933 seventh edition of the Soviet edition, Babel, under political pressure, added an additional concluding story, "Argamak." This text tended to resolve the antinomies of "The Rabbi's Son" by depicting Lyutov as far more seamlessly integrated into the Red Army. See U. Yekutsch, 261–62.

21. In *Late Victorian Holocausts: El Niño Famines and the Making of the Third World*, Mike Davis contests the "natural" nature of the devastating late nineteenth-century famines in Brazil, China, and India, arguing that these tragedies were at least as much political as natural.

22. See Sven-Erik Rose, "Oskar Rosenfeld, the Lodz Ghetto, and the Chronotope of Hunger."

23. *Kolacja* is Polish for dinner; *kolazia* is Rosenfeld's transliteration.

24. Mich befiel eine Schwäche, die ich in der letzten Zeit mit immer größerer Deutlichkeit wahrnehmen konnte. Sie kündigte sich mit einem Flimmern, mit einem Tanzen buntfarbiger Ringe vor den Augen und einer Mattigkeit in der Herzgrube an. Die Füße wurden kalt, die Hände ließen sich nur schwer zu Fäusten ballen. Ich stand beim Fenster, das in den Hof hineinsah. Menschen aller Art gingen raschen Schritts über den Hof und verschwanden in verfaulten Türen.

> Es war nach fünf Uhr. Die Ressorts spien ihre Arbeiter in die Gassen. Kinder trugen Töpfe, in Tücher gewickelt, alte Menschen schleppten Lasten auf ihren hageren Rücken. „Wozu das alles? Wozu das Eilen? Ihr werdet noch rechtzeitig zu eurer Kolazia kommen! Nur langsam! Geduld, meine Lieben . . . ,„ dachte ich bei mir.
>
> Ich tastete nach dem Fensterrahmen, um nicht umzufallen. Die Schwäche, die mich befallen hatte, zwang mich, die Pläne des Tages aufzugeben. Wünsche und Ahnungen quirlten in meinem Hirn durcheinander. Unwillkürlich fuhr ich mit beiden Händen über die Schläfen. Dunkel wurde es ringsum. Es sauste in den Ohren. Die Zunge suchte eine feuchte Stelle auf dem Gaumen. Mir kam plötzlich vor, ich hätte in eine saure Zitrone gebissen.
>
> Aber inmitten dieses Zustandes packte mich die Gier, zu erfahren, was in Cymbalists Stube vorgegangen war. Ich überlegte nicht lange. Ein paar Schritte und ich stand vor Cymbalists Wohnungstür. Ich rüttelte an ihr. Sie war nicht versperrt. Cymbalist hatte vergessen. . . . Ich war glücklich. (Rosenfeld, *Wozu noch Welt*, 237–38)

25. The translation of Rosenfeld's Lodz ghetto notebooks by Brigitte M. Goldstein is admirably readable but also plagued by errors. Her translation of "Wünsche und Ahnungen quirlten in meinem Hirn durcheinander" as "Sentiments of longing and foreboding quarreled together in my head" (*In the Beginning*, 220) is a case in point.

26. Modern texts from the German tradition alone that prominently feature (writer or artist) protagonists looking out through windows include E. T. A. Hoffmann's "Des Vetters Eckfenster" (1822) and the novel by Rosenfeld's fellow Viennese Jewish writer Arthur Schnitzler, *Der Weg ins Freie* (*Road into the Open*; 1908).

27. "Eroticism: So-called dignitaries are now seen quite publicly with their lovers in the street; trembling, [they] left their wives and now strut with their cats. . . . They're quite shameless and public, especially young policemen. In connection with that also corruption: allocations, positions in ressorts, coupons, vacation home, clothing" (*In the Beginning*, 159 / *Wozu noch Welt*, 181; translation modified).

28. Rosenfeld had an abiding interest in using dreams in his ghetto writings. In an undated entry presumably from spring or summer 1942 (entries around it bear dates of May or July 1942), Rosenfeld notes his plan to incorporate dream scenes into "Hunger," and adds that "das Golemartige" (the golem-like quality) must always be stressed. He is thus referring to his philosophical dialogue "Golem und Hunger." See Rosenfeld, *In the Beginning*, 108 / *Wozu noch Welt*, 136.

29. The premise of Jurek Becker's celebrated 1969 novel *Jakob der Lügner* (*Jacob the Liar*) is that the inhabitants in a Nazi ghetto come to believe that Jacob is in possession of a radio and thus able to listen to reports from the Allied Forces. This is not the case, but the desire among the ghetto population for news is so great—and the thought that someone could have a radio in the ghetto so marvelous—that Jacob feels obliged to make up fictive reports. Although in his adult life he was unable to recall them, Becker spent years of his childhood in the Lodz ghetto. On clandestine radio listening in the Lodz ghetto, see Isaiah Trunk, *The Łódź Ghetto: A History*, 397–99. Shaye Shpigl discusses radio listeners in the Lodz ghetto including among the circle led by Chaim Widawski in his interview with Yechiel Szeintuch (see Szeintuch and Solomon, *Yesha'yahu Shpigel*, 314–15).

30. Simkhe Bunem Shayevitsh wrote his long poem "Lekh-lekho" (dated February 13, 1942) in the Lodz ghetto in response to the January 1942 deportations. For an English translation of the Yiddish poem, see Roskies, *Literature of Destruction*, 520–30.

31. For these statistics, see Trunk, *Łódź Ghetto*, 236–37, and 267.

32. Bluma and Hersh Wasser, the secretary of the Oyneg Shabes, interviewed Szlamek personally and recorded his chilling testimony. For an account of this, see Kassow, *Who Will Write Our History?*, 287–93.

33. See interview with Shpigl in Szeintuch and Solomon, *Yesha'yahu Shpigel*, 313.

34. Of course, it is hypothetically possible that Rosenfeld began writing "Meine zwei Nachbarn" earlier and copied/rewrote it in notebook 16, dated August 4, 1943. There is no particular reason to think this, but exactly when he began writing the text is strictly speaking likely unknowable. However, even if he might have begun the story before the September 1942 deportations, he finished it well after.

35. See Peretz Opoczynski and Josef Zelkowicz, *In Those Nightmarish Days: The Ghetto Reportage of Peretz Opoczynski and Josef Zelkowicz*, 188–309.

36. The longevity of the Lodz ghetto had much to do with power struggles between competing German bureaucracies in Berlin and the Warthegau. While the SS wished to deport all the Jews from Lodz, ghetto supervisor Hans Biebow and the local Nazi administration opportunistically wished to exploit Jewish slave labor for financial gain. This led to what Samuel Kassow has called a "bizarre partnership" of sorts between Biebow and Chaim Rumkowski, who sought to make the ghetto pro-

ductive for the German cause as a strategy for buying time. See Kassow, introduction to *In those Nightmarish Days*, xxvii–xxviii.

37. Goldstein's rendering of "Den Namen der Insassen kennt man nicht" as "The names of the inhabitants are unfamiliar" gives the erroneous impression that the doors bear names but that these names are unfamiliar to the narrator. The point, however, is that the doors are devoid of names.

38. "Ein paar Sekunden später vernahm ich ein Schlürfen und Glucksen, all die Geräusche, die das Essen eines Hungrigen begleiten. Cymbalist füllte seinen Magen und ich war glücklich" (Rosenfeld, *Wozu noch Welt*, 236).

39. Feuchert's reading of this shift—"The ostensible family idyll next door makes the narrator try to distance himself from his own story—and from his self-accentuating interest [in his neighbors]. Henceforth he *is* no longer happy, he *was* happy" (Feuchert, *Oskar Rosenfeld*, 383)—does not strike me as compelling in the full context of the story, and may betray an attempt to interpret an essentially cipher-like subjectivity according to the standards of a more conventionally conceived character.

40. "Das waren Cymbalists letzte Worte, bevor er die Stube verließ, die Tür zuschlug und die Holztreppe hinabstieg. Ich fragte mich selbst, ob ich jetzt glücklich sei, bekam aber keine Antwort" (Rosenfeld, *Wozu noch Welt*, 237).

41. "Ich rüttelte an ihr [Cymbalists Wohnungstür]. Sie war nicht versperrt. Cymbalist hatte vergessen . . . Ich war glücklich" (Rosenfeld, *Wozu noch Welt*, 238).

42. "Der Tode der Fliege geht ihm nicht nahe. Er hat gesummt, gesungen, geträllert. Er hat der Schönheit gehuldigt, die draußen in der Welt regiert. Glücklicher Cymbalist!" (Rosenfeld, *Wozu noch Welt*, 240–41).

43. "Ich tastete nach dem Bettpolster. In meiner Stube hatte sich nichts verändert. Das Wasser dampfte. Die Kartoffeln sind gar, die Abendmahlzeit war fertig. Einige Sekunden lang hat der Hunger mich die schönsten Dinge genießen lassen. Durfte ich nicht glücklich sein?" (Rosenfeld, *Wozu noch Welt*, 241).

44. In a similar vein, Feuchert concludes that "the nameless first-person narrator is thus primarily a victim, one lost to the national socialist ghetto—whose narrative, however, in its intertextual dynamics, functions *also* [*dessen Ergebnisse aber wirken in einem intertextuellen Zugriff auch als*] as a continuation, intensified to the extreme, of what Rosenfeld had always perceived as essential characteristics of modernity, and combated on many levels" (Feuchert, *Oskar Rosenfeld*, 387).

45. Directed by Robert Wiene, *Caligari* was written by Hans Janowitz and Carl Mayer. The highly influential works *Caligari* and *Der Golem* by Meyerink partially overlapped chronologically with Rosenfeld's own literary career, which comprised the novel *Die vierte Galerie: Ein Wiener Roman* (1910), the novella *Mendl Ruhig* (1914), and the story collection *Tage und Nächte* (1920). In Meyrink's novel, it is ultimately unclear whether events are actually taking place in the real world or only in the protagonist's dreams or hallucinations, or perhaps in a different metaphysical realm altogether. At the end of the narrative readers are left in complete confusion as to what, if anything, has actually occurred.

46. For Kracauer's critique, see *From Caligari to Hitler*, 61–76. As Leonardo Quare-

sima shows, however, Kracauer was mistaken in some of his assumptions about the origins of the frame story, and, arguably, overly blunt in the contrast he draws between the "revolutionary" nature of the original screenplay by Hans Janowitz and Karl Mayer, and the "conformist" frame Wiene adopted. The recovered screenplay by Janowitz and Mayer already has a frame story, albeit a different one that, crucially, does not reduce the main story to the ravings of a mad Franzis but rather recalls the horrific events from a temporal remove of twenty years. To my mind, the fuller and more complicated picture that has come to light about the origins of the frame story thus does not seriously vitiate the main thrust of Kracauer's critique of how the frame story undercuts the film's anti-authoritarian ethos by reducing the horror story to the projection of an individual lunatic mind. See Quaresima, "Introduction to the 2004 Edition," to Sigfried Kracauer, *From Caligari to Hitler*, xliii–xlvii.

CHAPTER 9: GHETTO GOTHIC

1. General Karl Litzmann (1850–1936) led the German forces in the World War I Battle of Lodz (November 11–December 6, 1914) and later became a member of the Nazi Party.

2. As was often the case with writers in other ghettos, many writers in the Lodz ghetto had a certain, if inherently fragile, level of protection. In a rich and extensive series of interviews that Yechiel Szeintuch conducted with Shpigl, Shpigl speaks of how the lawyer Henryk Naftalin used his considerable influence as head of the Statistical Department, under whose auspices the Lodz ghetto archive and *Chronicle* were housed, to provide writers in the Lodz ghetto with relatively favorable jobs, and more than once managed to remove writers' names from lists of people marked for deportation. For these interviews with Shpigl, see Yechiel Szeintuch and Vera Solomon, *Yesha'yahu Shpigel—prozah sipurit mi-geṭo Lodz'* (Isaiah Spiegel —Yiddish narrative prose from the Lodz ghetto), 244–386; on Naftalin's support for writers, see 301, 311–12. On Naftalin's efforts to protect writers in the Lodz ghetto, see also Trunk, *Łódź Ghetto*, 256–57.

3. See Szeintuch and Solomon, *Yesha'yahu Shpigel*, 316–17. See also Shpigl's text "Mayn tekhterl" (My little daughter) in Szeintuch and Solomon, *Yesha'yahu Shpigel*, 213–40. Shpigl wrote this text in the Lodz ghetto and dedicated it "to the memory of my only child, Evele, who lived and died in the Litzmannstadt ghetto—and to the memory of all those who followed her with their sacred death" (213). Shpigl published a significantly revised version of this text in 1955; see "Epistol far meyn toyt tekhterl" in *Vint un vortslen: Noveln*, 48–60. Shpigl also dedicated his 1948 story collection *Shtern ibern geto* to his daughter Eva's memory: "Hallowed be the memory of my little daughter Eva, who died in the ghetto" (Shpigl, *Shtern ibern geto*, n.p.).

4. For information on Shpigl's biography, in addition to the Szeintuch-Shpigl interviews mentioned above, see for example, Noah Gris, *Fun finsternish tsu likht: Yeshaye Shpigl un zayn verk*, 9–12; David H. Hirsch, "Introduction to the Ghetto Stories of Isaiah Spiegel" in Isaiah Spiegel, *Ghetto Kingdom: Tales of the Łódź Ghetto*, vii–ix; and Julian Levinson, "Translator's Introduction" to Isaiah Spiegel, *Flames from the Earth: A Novel from the Łódź Ghetto*, ix–xxx.

5. In his introduction to his postwar book of poetry *Un gevorn iz likht*, Shpigl pays tribute to his murdered father, Moyshe Beer Shmuel Shpigl, for burying his manuscripts—both poems and stories—for him in a ghetto cellar. (He does not say, however, that his poems were not in fact recoverable.) It was his father who "with half-dead hands, during the liquidation of the ghetto, buried my manuscripts, the poems and stories, in a tin box [*pushke*] in the dark ghetto cellar. He lay them in the darkness of the earth the way one plants a seed [*fargrobt a zoymen*] that must sprout sometime under good, bright skies" ("Araynfir-vort" to *Un gevorn*, 4).

6. Szeintuch-Shpigl interview, in Szeintuch and Solomon, *Yesha'yahu Shpigel*, 384. On non-Jews in Eastern Europe searching, both during and after the war, for gold and other valuables they believed Jews had buried, see "Der Goldroysh," the concluding chapter of Mordkhe Tsanin's *Iber shteyn un shtok*, 306–13; Jan Gross and Irena Grudzinska Gross, *Golden Harvest: Events at the Periphery of the Holocaust*; and Jan Grabowski, *Hunt for the Jews: Betrayal and Murder in German-Occupied Poland*, 74, 109. Grabowski attributes the "absolute conviction and deep belief about the universality of 'Jewish gold'" among Poles to "the influence of prewar nationalist-led antisemitic propaganda and the German efforts in the same direction" (Grabowski, *Hunt for the Jews*, 109).

7. Some pages were not found or were too damaged to salvage (Szeintuch and Solomon, *Yesha'yahu Shpigel*, 384).

8. Several ghetto stories that Shpigl published after the war depict the period of 1942–1944, but it is unclear whether these are rewritings of stories he originally wrote in the ghetto or new creations dating from after the war.

9. On the circumstances of writing "Avrashe geyt tsum nieman," within months after Germany invaded the Soviet Union in summer 1941, see Szeintuch and Solomon, *Yesha'yahu Shpigel*, 358–59 and 367–68; on the time and circumstances of writing "Mayn tekhterl," see Szeintuch and Solomon, 368.

10. See 29n19 in Szeintuch's Hebrew introduction to Szeintuch and Solomon, *Yesha'yahu Shpigel* (hereafter Szeintuch, "Introduction").

11. Szeintuch, "Introduction," 90.

12. In a similar vein, Shpigl distinguishes his specifically literary project from documentary writing in the following exchange with Szeintuch:

> Shpigl: "I don't think that literature needs to represent evil [*darf gebn dos shlekhts*]; I don't think that literature needs to depict ugliness [*dos miese*].
>
> Szeintuch: "Did you think that then as well?"
>
> Shpigl: "A proof [*a raye*]: I only noted down those current and true facts which could serve as a springboard, so to speak, for my dreams and for my writerly intentions [*shrayberishe intentsn*]. But I didn't want to depict [*gebn*] bitter naturalism and evil [*rishes*]. That is a subject matter more apt for documentary [*dokumentatsye*]. (Szeintuch and Solomon, *Yesha'yahu Shpigel*, 358)

13. For example: "Things happened in the ghetto, which . . . I also think that art, literature musn't depict everything [*darf nisht alts ibergebn*]. Literature was not made to represent everything. For depicting everything there are chronicles, registers, testimonies [*khronikes, pinkeysim, gviyes-eydes*]. Literature, however, that

is, the culled, the isolated, indeed pure material [*der opgeshtelter, der opgeshtanener, shoyn reyner khoymer*] that must become a symbol—an artistic symbol—for a great esthetic consciousness with all the ethical values that Jewish writing [*dos yidishe shriftum*] must have" (Szeintuch and Solomon, *Yesha'yahu Shpigel*, 369).

14. Shpigl also published a book of poems in 1949, *Un gevorn iz likht* (And there was light), some of which, he indicates in his introduction, he wrote in the Lodz ghetto (Shpigl, "Araynfir-vort" to *Un gevorn iz likht*, n.p.). Although Shpigl dates a section of poems in this book 1940–1944, he was not in fact able to recover manuscripts of any poems he wrote in the ghetto (see Szeintuch, "Introduction," 24n3). These are thus postwar reconstructions from memory—and likely also revisions—of the poems he wrote in the ghetto.

15. See Szeintuch and Solomon, *Yesha'yahu Shpigel*.

16. Shpigl continued to antedate even later stories such as those in the 1976 two-volume collection *Shtern laykhtn in thom: Gezamelte dertseylungen (1940–1944)* (Tel Aviv: Yisroel-bukh, 1976).

17. I analyze Shpigl's early postwar reception by these critics and aspects of Shpigl's revisions of his wartime texts for postwar publication in "Holocaust Literature and Autorevision: Shaye Shpigl's Ghetto Stories Written in, and Rewritten after, the Lodz Ghetto." Nachman Blumental highlighted the distinction between Shpigl's wartime manuscripts and postwar revisions to them—and the question of whether revised works by Shpigl and other surviving authors should be classified as wartime or postwar writing—already in September 1945 at a conference of the Central Jewish Historical Commission in Lodz. See Blumental, "Di kharakteristik fun der yidisher literatur unter der daytshisher okupatsye," 24–25.

18. Shpigl describes the dictionary by Harkavy as already "an old dictionary" when he received it as a teenager (*a dervaksener bokher*; Szeintuch and Solomon, *Yesha'yahu Shpigel*, 289), so it was presumably Harkavy's 1910 Yiddish-English/English-Yiddish dictionary, not his 1925 Yiddish-English-Hebrew dictionary.

19. Szeintuch and Solomon, *Yesha'yahu Shpigel*, 289–90, 277, 290. Shpigl goes so far as to compare his relationship to reading—and especially to reading English literature—in these years to a poor and hungry yeshiva student's relationship to learning Gemara. "Later I perfected [my English] and studied and read until I began reading Oscar Wilde's short stories—the first stories, which are very accessibly written. I had a great deal of diligence [*hasmode*]—that I can say. I was very alone; I was very hungry; and there exists nothing that better satiates a hungry youth [*bokher*] like learning Torah. We know this of course from yeshiva students [*yeshive-bokhrem*], who actually ate Gemara, which is to say that they 'ate days'—ate at different homes on different days [*hobn gegesn teg—teg bay andere*]. I advanced so far that I began reading books and novels" (Szeintuch and Solomon, *Yesha'yahu Shpigel*, 290).

20. Shpigl also taught English privately to individuals and groups, often to people planning to emigrate to America. Szeintuch and Solomon, *Yesha'yahu Shpigel*, 290.

21. On how libraries served as the de facto universities for many Polish Jews born

in the early twentieth century, see Barbara Kirshenblatt-Gimblett, Marcus Moseley, and Michael Stanislawski, introduction to *Awakening Lives: Autobiographies of Jewish Youth in Poland before the Holocaust*, xxx–xxxi.

22. See Jerrold E. Hogle, introduction to the *Cambridge Companion to Modern Gothic*, 9–11.

23. Fred Botting remarks on how a grand conception of sublime nature developed in early gothic literature is "appropriated by romantic poets, while Gothic finds itself relegated to the popular and trashy realm of cheap, formulaic fiction" and "expelled from the new-forged heights of proper culture" (Botting, "In Gothic Darkly," 22).

24. Jacob Glatstein, "Yeshayahu Shpigl," review of *Malkhes geto* and *Mentshn in thom*, 453–65; here, 457. Glatstein's review of Shpigl's *Malkhes geto* and *Mentshn in thom* was originally published in *Yidisher kemfer* on July 7, 1950; and Shmuel Charney, "Shtern ibern geto: vegn Yeshayahu Shpigls 'Malkhes geto' (Lodzsh, 1947) un 'Shtern ibern geto' (Pariz, 1948)," 7–14; here 13.

25. For a pioneering argument that esthetic value is radically contingent, see Barbara Herstein Smith, *Contingencies of Value: Alternative Perspectives for Critical Theory* (1991).

26. "Wedding in Brownsville" appeared in Bashevis Singer's 1964 *Short Friday and Other Stores*; "The Lecture" was first published in *Playboy* in 1967 and included in Bashevis Singer's 1968 *The Séance and Other Stories*.

27. For introductions to the postcolonial gothic, see Ken Gelder, "The Postcolonial Gothic" and Alison Rudd, "Postcolonial Gothic in and as Theory."

28. On gothic death, see for example Carol Margaret Davison, ed., *The Gothic and Death*, and Andrew Smith, *Gothic Death, 1740–1914: A Literary History*.

29. Rosenfeld's statement that "In the beginning was the ghetto," which serves as the title of the English translation of his Lodz ghetto notebooks, occurs in the context of a reflection on how ghetto existence is *sui generis* and incommensurable with all other human experience, as though derived from a separate creation, whether cosmic or divine. See *Wozu noch Welt*, 133. See also note 9 in chapter 8 of this book.

30. As Andrew Smith remarks, Burke's theorization of the sublime in *A Philosophical Enquiry* (1757) and Freud's "The Uncanny" are "two theoretical accounts of anxiety which have played an important role in shaping Gothic criticism on Romantic and post-Romantic Gothic" (Smith, *Gothic Literature*, 10).

31. See Freud, "The Uncanny." For Freud's discussion of the uncanny philological dynamics of the terms *heimlich* and *unheimlich* themselves, see especially 220–26.

32. See Blumental, "Vos zenen di hoypt-strikhn fun der literatur?," 35–36.

33. See Davison, "Introduction," 5. Davison notes how mourning and memorialization become transformed—and how mourning is indeed extended to now-lost ways of relating to death: "In the face of Enlightenment-generated anxieties about the afterlife and the loss of subjectivity, ideas, sites and practices around mourning and memorialization were radically altered. Mourning became a more fraught process that could lend itself, as readers readily recognize in the cases of both Heathcliff and Victor Frankenstein, to melancholic excess, an emotional extreme

that characterizes most Gothic hero-villains. Notably, mourning was extended in this industrializing era of rapid change, to the past more generally—to former, lost belief systems and certainties rendered obsolete due to historical shifts" (Davison, "Introduction," 6).

34. Jerrold E. Hogle invokes Diane Long Hoeveler's concept of "ambivalent secularization" to characterize gothic literature as emblematic of how modern individuals and groups are "pulled between retrograde or regressive and emergent or progressive" currents in their "quests for workable configurations of human psychology, class, sex and gender, race, nationality, power, law, culture 'superiority' or 'inferiority, and even aesthetic form" ("Introduction," 7). In other words, gothic is a distinctly modern literary mode, but one that displays deep longing for premodern beliefs and practices as these appear to us moderns in retrospect, i.e., for a premodern dispensation as seen from a postmodern vantage point. See Hogle, introduction to *The Cambridge Companion to the Modern Gothic*, 7.

35. A good example of Shpigl's treatment of the world beyond the ghetto as tantalizingly proximate yet inaccessible is the story "Durkh a shpare," in which a brother and sister, whenever their parents are out, look through cracks in their apartment wall at the bread and cheese in the display window of a bakery on the other side of the barbed wire enclosing the ghetto. They can eat only with their eyes, food for them having become phantasmatic.

36. It is probably impossible to know definitively whether Shpigl had read Freud's essay "Das Unheimliche," but it is worth noting that when asked by Szeintuch in their 1973 series of interviews what subjects he read during his decade of intensive reading at the Lodz city library, Shpigl included psychology among them. See Szeintuch and Solomon, *Yesha'yahu Shpigel*, 275.

37. The parenthetical phrase was added in green ink; see Szeintuch and Solomon, *Yesha'yahu Shpigel*, 135n14. Szeintuch dates this and various other edits and additions made in green ink to 1944, before Shpigl buried his manuscripts prior to being deported to Auschwitz in August 1944. See Szeintuch, "Introduction," 102. I thank Yael Teff-Seker for reading Szeintuch's Hebrew introduction for me.

38. Empty brackets—[ ]—indicate gaps in the recovered manuscripts. I reproduce these gaps according to the texts of Shpigl's ghetto manuscripts as published in Szeintuch and Solomon, *Yesha'yahu Shpigel.*

39. When he revised and published the story after the war, Shpigl gave it the title "Erd" (Earth). For the published version of the Yiddish story, see Shpigl, *Malkhes geto* (1947); for an English translation, see *Ghetto Kingdom: Tales of the Łódź Ghetto*, 3–10.

40. See Sven-Erik Rose, "Holocaust Literature and Autorevision: Shaye Shpigl's Ghetto Stories Written in, and Rewritten after, the Lodz Ghetto."

41. The published text prints the word here as *lamed-yud-langer khof*, which appears to be a typo, possibly for *lokh*, meaning *hole* or *pit*.

42. In the significantly changed, published version of this story, the party takes refuge not in a movie theater but in a synagogue. For the published version, see Shpigl, *Shtern ibern geto*, 24–30. For an English translation of the published version, see "In the Dark" in *Ghetto Kingdom: Tales of the Łódź Ghetto*, 11–15.

43. Julia Kristeva, *Powers of Horror*, 4.

44. An entry in the official *Chronicle of the Łódź Ghetto* of July 26 describes the crisis in excrement removal. Due to a shortage of horses, people must pull the wagons themselves. "To replace a draft horse is beyond human power, which has caused, and continues to cause, a mortality rate that is record high, even under ghetto conditions. Last year there were 250 cesspool cleaners, while now there are less than 120, or 130 at most. And none of them has quit his job. Some of them have died, and some, bedridden, have been placed in hospitals. Thus, for example, last week alone six cesspool cleaners died of complete exhaustion while 12 were sent to the hospital" (*Chronicle*, 229–30). It is also worth noting that sewage removal was assigned as a punishment within the internal Lodz ghetto penal system. As Svenja Bethke writes, "'Sewage duty' was a sanction imposed increasingly by Rumkowski following the establishment of the summary court in spring 1941, and from summer 1941 onwards" (Bethke, *Dance*, 126). Excrement removal is a key theme in Shpigl's wartime story "Af der gas fun heylikn Frantsiskus" [On Saint Francis Street].

45. Other notable scenes of what we might call gothic weather in Shpigl's ghetto writings include the striking descriptions of night and dawn at the beginning of "Malkhes geto." See Shpigl, "Malkhes geto," in Szeintuch and Solomon, *Yesha'yahu Shpigel*, 125–26. For an English translation of the corresponding revised passage, see Isaiah Spiegel, *Ghetto Kingdom*, 95.

46. Shpigl retitled "Shtroy" "In a toytn gesl" ("In a Death Alley") in the revised version that he published in *Shtern ibern geto* (Stars over the ghetto) in 1948. For the English translation of the revised, published text, see *Ghetto Kingdom: Tales of the Łódź Ghetto*, 24–31. The revised version of "Malkhes geto" served as the title story for Shpigl's first book published after the war, *Malkhes geto (noveln)* (Ghetto kingdom [stories]; 1947). For the English translation of the published text, see *Ghetto Kingdom: Tales of the Łódź Ghetto*, 95–99. "Vedibarta bam" is Hebrew for "and you shall speak of them" and derives from Deuteronomy 6:5–9, a passage that is recited in every Jewish prayer service as the Sh'ema and Veahafta prayers. For the revised, published text of "Vedibarta bam," see Shpigl, *Mentshn in thom* (1949), 39–47.

47. See Hirsch, "Introduction" to Spiegel, *Ghetto Kingdom*, x.

48. For an analysis of what I call Anna Yakovlevna Temkin's "reverse transubstantiation," see Sven-Erik Rose, "Holocaust Literature and Autorevision" (n.p.).

49. An elderly woman accosts the narrator of this story in the street, and aside from the very beginning, the narrator's function is only to serve as the woman's addressee. Thus, as in "Shtroy," the narrator's position as narratee shades into the position occupied by the reader. Obviously traumatized and confused, the woman asks, "Where can one bury oneself?" (*Vu kon men zikh bagrobn?*). In her extended monologue the story of her son Avrashe emerges by and by: years ago, the family lived in Lithuania (Lite), and she remembers idyllic family scenes on the Neman River at sundown when Avrashe was a child. A year ago, Avrashe, like so many others, left Lodz ahead of the approaching Germans. He told his *mamele* that he was going to the Neman, to Uncle Yenkl. After many people who fled east to evade the Germans begin returning, Sorele makes inquiries about Avrashe. Following leads,

she eventually arrives in a town where she is brought to a rabbi's (rav) house. There packages are being sorted, the orphaned belongings of fleeing refugees who did not make it. Sorele is brought the bag she had packed for Avrashe when he fled. He lies buried in that town with "10 other Avrashes." Sorele is left to wander, asking strangers like the narrator if it is far to the Neman, and whether they know where one can be buried. The manuscript and published versions of this story are very similar. A few details and some of the opening dynamics of narrational address differ, but this is one of the texts that Shpigl revised least for publication. For the published Yiddish text, see "Avrashe geyt tsum nieman," in Shpigl, *Mentshn in thom* (1949), 57–62.

50. This passage in the version Shpigl published in 1948 under the title "In a toytn gesl" is only lightly revised; see *Shtern ibern geto*, 24.

51. Elizabeth MacAndrew, *The Gothic Tradition in Fiction*, 11.

52. On frame narratives in gothic literature, see Clayton Carlyle Tarr, *Gothic Stories within Stories: Frame Narratives and Realism.*

53. MacAndrew, *Gothic Tradition*, 10.

54. *Ir* is recognizably cognate with the German *Ihr*, formerly used as a formal singular second-person pronoun but in modern German used exclusively as the informal second-person plural pronoun, the formal second-person pronoun, singular and plural, having been replaced by *Sie*.

55. Jerrold E. Hogle, introduction to *Cambridge Companion to the Modern Gothic*, 7.

56. Any available wood was apt to be seized not only by desperate individuals. On April 25, 1941, the Lodz Jewish Council chairman Mordechai Chaim Rumkowsi announced in the *Geto-tsaytung* (Ghetto newspaper) that the dismantling of "wooden and brick latrines and refuse pits" that had been occurring over the last few months "in order to sell the stolen wood at extortionate prices" would henceforth be classified as criminal vandalism. See Bethke, *Dance*, 3. For Rumkowski's article, see *Geto-tsaytung* no. 8, April 25, 1941, 2. On Rumkowski's measures against theft of wood, see also Dawid Sierakowiak, *The Diary of Dawid Sierakowiak*, 82.

57. See in particular "In a toytn gesl" (in *Shtern ibern geto*, 24–30), 24–25, and "In a Death Alley" (in *Ghetto Kingdom: Tales of the Łódź Ghetto*, 24–31), 24–25.

58. "In a toytn gesl," 24 (my translation).

59. "In a Death Alley," 24, 25 / "In a toytn gesl," 24, 25.

60. See "In a toytn gesl," 25 / "In a Death Alley," 25. One could point to many other examples of the workings of a gothic esthetic among the stories Shpigl revised (or simply wrote) after the war. I will mention only the story (for which no manuscript from the ghetto exists) "Heinz Freidrich Levi." The titular character arrived in the Lodz ghetto on the third transport from Berlin and remains a mystery (*retenish*) to the Jews in his courtyard. He is quasi-vampiric, never coming out during daylight, and never opening the crooked gothic window in his garret apartment, which resembles a monastic cell. To his neighbors, he is like a sorcerer (*mekhashef*), among other gothic elements. For the Yiddish version of this story, see Shpigl, *Malkhes geto* (1949), 60–66; and for the English translation see *Ghetto Kingdom: Tales of the Łódź Ghetto*, 63-67.

61. The story is set in spring or summer 1941. The dysentery epidemic in the Lodz ghetto from May 1940–December 1941 had two peaks, June–August 1940 and August 1941. For August 1941, the ghetto administration officially registered 924 cases of dysentery, which accounted for 77 percent of the total number of cases of infectious disease recorded (1200). On the Lodz ghetto dysentery epidemic, see Trunk, *Łódź Ghetto*, 199–202.

62. See Dorothea von Mücke, "The Occult, the Fantastic, and the Limits of Rationality," 521–26; here 524. Von Mücke underscores a pragmatic thrust of fantastic esthetics, which Shpigl is able to exploit in his generic meditation on the boundaries between historical and literary horror: "The fantastic tale's aesthetics of shock and seduction is cast with a view toward its pragmatic dimension in terms of the overpowering impact on the reader/observer, and as a reflection on the nature and power of art, substituting art's representational model of reality with a model of art's ability to simulate life" (von Mücke, *The Seduction of the Occult*, 248).

63. "The fantastic requires the fulfillment of three conditions. First, the text must oblige the reader to consider the world of the characters as a world of living persons and to hesitate between a natural or supernatural explanation of the events described. Second, this hesitation may also be experienced by a character; thus, the reader's role is so to speak entrusted to a character, and at the same time the hesitation is represented, it becomes one of the themes of the work—in the case of naive reading, the actual reader identifies himself with the character. Third, the reader must adopt a certain attitude with regard to the text: he will reject allegorical as well as 'poetic' interpretations." Tzvetan Todorov, *The Fantastic: A Structural Approach to a Literary Genre*, 33.

64. For a fascinating reportage about delivering mail in the Warsaw ghetto, see Peretz Opoczynski, "The Jewish Letter Carrier." On mail service and food packages to the Warsaw, Krakow, and Lodz ghettos, see Sinnreich, *The Atrocity of Hunger*, 69.

65. The *Chronicle of the Łódź Ghetto* notes on July 22, 1941, that "the Post Office has not been accepting letters addressed to Holland, Belgium, France, and Sweden since Tuesday the 22nd. Letters to America have recently been returned to the senders and stamped: *Zurück. Kein Postverkehr* [Send back, There is no postal service]" (*Chronicle of the Łódź Ghetto*, 66). Further information about the postal service in the Lodz ghetto can be found in Dobroszycki, ed., *The Chronicle of the Łódź Ghetto, 1941–1944*, 25, 35, 63, 64, 72, 75, and 229. On the establishment, scope, restrictions, and periodic suspensions of the Lodz ghetto postal service, see Trunk, *Łódź Ghetto*, 45–46.

EPILOGUE

1. On the efforts of the Jewish historical commissions to gather documentation and testimony, see Laura Jockusch, *Collect and Record! Jewish Holocaust Documentation in Early Postwar Europe*.

2. Jockusch, *Collect and Record!*, 120.

3. See Mark L. Smith, *The Yiddish Historians and the Struggle for a Jewish History of the Holocaust*.

4. See "Meir (Mark) Dworzecki's research plan presented to the Hebrew University in 1949," in Boaz Cohen, *Israeli Holocaust Research: Birth and Evolution*, 279–81; here 280.

5. See Trunk, *Łódź Ghetto*, "Cultural Life" (334–40) and "Religious Life" (342–49).

6. See Trunk, *Judenrat*, 186–229.

7. Blumental's presentation at the September 1945 conference was eventually published as chapters 1 and 2 of his 1966 *Shmuesn vegn der yidisher literatur unter der daytsher okupatsye*. See Smith's complete bibliography of Blumental in Smith, *Yiddish Historians*.

8. Linguist Neil Jacobs estimates that roughly five million Yiddish speakers perished in the Holocaust, out of eleven million living worldwide before the war. See Neil G. Jacobs, *Yiddish: A Linguistic Introduction*, 3. Of the approximately six million Jews who died in the Holocaust, nearly 85 percent were Yiddish speakers. See Ghil'ad Zuckermann, *Revivalistics: From the Genesis of Israeli to Language Reclamation in Australia and Beyond*, 202.

9. Jockusch, *Collect and Record!*, 203, 193.

10. Tensions between the survivor historians at Yad Vashem (Rokhl Auerbach, Blumental, Kermish) and the first Yad Vashem director, Zionist historian Ben-Zion Dinur, led to Dinur's resignation in 1959. But this "victory" for the survivor historians had the effect of cutting them off from academic Holocaust research. Yad Vashem turned away from research to focus on commemoration of the Holocaust, and "the historians still at Yad Vashem had no influence on the young scholars being educated" at Israeli universities (Dan Michman, "Is There an 'Israeli School' of Holocaust Research?," 43). Even Dworzecki, who, after earning a PhD at the Sorbonne, became the first person to hold a chair in Holocaust studies at an Israeli university (Bar-Ilan) "as a scholar . . . had little influence on the development of Holocaust research" in Israel (or elsewhere) (Michman, "Is There an 'Israeli School,'" 43), and "his name and work were all but forgotten" (Boaz Cohen, "Dr Meir (Mark) Dworzecki: the Historical Mission of a Survivor Historian," 35). For an in-depth account of the evolution of Holocaust research in Israel, see Cohen, *Israeli Holocaust Research*.

11. "Until recently, this focus on perpetrators, the use of German documents, and the categorizing of the Holocaust as part of German or European rather than as Jewish history remained the dominant trends in German and Anglo-American historiography on the Third Reich and the Holocaust" (Jockusch, *Collect and Record!*, 200).

12. Michman, "Is There an 'Israeli School,'" 58.

13. See Berg, *Holocaust and the West German Historians*, chapter 5 (on the travails in West Germany of the Polish Jewish historian and erstwhile Jewish Historical Commission worker in his native Krakow Joseph Wulf), and Berg, "Joseph Wulf, a Forgotten Outsider among Holocaust Scholars," 167–206.

14. Dan Michman, *Holocaust Historiography: A Jewish Perspective; Conceptualizations, Terminology, Approaches and Fundamental Issues*, 301, 303.

15. Fabian Wolff, "Refusing the Extended Hand," 74. On the parochialism of Ger-

man memory culture, Wolff notes Germans' lack of interest in the victims' own cultures and their cultural Germanification: Germans around Wolff "knew about Nazis . . . but not about the lives of Jews in Lyon, Brody, Thessaloniki, Czernowitz who were murdered. In fact most of the six million Jews magically became German in their mind: the sort of educated and friendly, even patriotic, Jewish neighbour they so longed for" (Wolff, "Refusing the Extended Hand," 73).

16. The first historian's debate over the uniqueness or comparability of the Holocaust and the political implications of those questions played out in West Germany in the mid to late 1980s. It elicited contributions from a wide range of historians and intellectuals, broadly speaking in two camps: a conservative camp led by historian Ernst Nolte arguing against the singularity of the Holocaust and for its moral equivalence to other, in particular Soviet, atrocities, and a left-leaning camp led by philosopher Jürgen Habermas, whose counter arguments that the Holocaust was unprecedented and should not be compared to other genocides were generally seen as having prevailed. The more recent debate was engendered by a polemical piece that genocide historian A. Dirk Moses published in May 2021 in the online journal *Geschichte der Gegenwart*, in which he attacked taboos in German culture around comparing the Holocaust to other, especially colonial, genocides and the political ends such taboos in his view serve; see A. Dirk Moses, "The German Catechism." For two rich collections of contributions to this debate, see the blog entries of May 25–June 2, 2021, collected on the New Fascism Syllabus website as "The Catechism Debate," edited by Jennifer Evans and Brian J. Griffiths, as well as *Historiker Streiten: Gewalt und Holocaust—Die Debatte*, edited by Susan Neiman and Michael Wildt.

17. Mischa Gabowitsch, "Zuhören statt belehren: Für eine Osterweiterung der deutschen Erinnerung an Krieg und Holocaust," 300, 303.

18. This is not the place to expound this point or to engage with the intricate arguments of specific thinkers or works, but I would argue that the historiographical neglect of the extensive victim's archives finds its counterpart in the philosophical, literary critical, and psychoanalytic paradigms that constructed the Holocaust (generally reduced to "Auschwitz") as unspeakable, unfathomable, incommunicable—a traumatic event and civilizational rupture so great that it was virtually impossible to coax into language. The various discursive investments in constructing the Holocaust as unspeakable share an anarchivic thrust. The thesis that the Holocaust was unspeakable was not arrived at on the basis of engagement with the extant archive of victims' speech but rather posited a priori. The general, and by no means necessarily intended, consequence of this orientation was to belittle and authorize the neglect of the thousands of preserved pages of what victims in fact said. If "Auschwitz" in its negative sublimity was the profound essence of the Holocaust, how important could anything that Holocaust victims said be if they were in fact able to say it?

19. Yehuda Bauer, *Rethinking the Holocaust*, 39.

20. See Michael Rothberg, *Multidirectional Memory: Remembering the Holocaust in the Age of Decolonization.*

21. See Jürgen Zimmerer and Michael Rothberg, "Enttabuisiert den Vergleich!"

22. See Gabowitsch, "Zuhören statt belehren," 304–5.

23. Rothberg, *Multidirectional Memory*, 21.

24. For Smith's extensive account of the origins and evolution of Dworzecki's conceptual innovation of a wide array of nonviolent forms of resistance (including spiritual or cultural resistance), see Smith, *Yiddish Historians*, 246–78.

BIBLIOGRAPHY

DOCUMENTS FROM THE RINGELBLUM ARCHIVE (OYNEG SHABES ARCHIVE), UNITED STATES HOLOCAUST MEMORIAL MUSEUM ARCHIVES, WASHINGTON, DC

Goldin, Leyb. "Khronik fun a mes-les." RA I/1167.

Katzenelson, Itzhak. "Vey dir." RA II/348.

Kirman, Yoysef. Note to Yitzhak Giterman, written from the Umschlagplatz. RA II/219/1.

Marvil, Shmuel. "Di gas." RA II/352.

Perle, Yehoshue. "4580." RA II/245.

Skalov, Zelmen. "A shpatsir iber di punktn." RA I/1146.

———. *Di hak on krayts*. Part 1: RA I/605 CZ I. Part 2 ("Kvo vadis" / "Quo vadis"): RA I/605 CZ III.

PRIMARY SOURCES

Abramovitsh, Sholem [Mendele Moykher Sforim]. "Of Bygone Days." In *A Shtetl and Other Yiddish Novellas*, edited by Ruth R. Wisse, 254–358. Detroit: Wayne State University Press, 1986.

Abramowicz, Dina. "The Library in the Vilna Ghetto." In *The Holocaust and the Book: Destruction and Preservation*, edited by Jonathan Rose, 165–70. Amherst: University of Massachusetts Press, 2001.

Babel, Isaac. *The Complete Works of Isaac Babel*. Edited by Nathalie Babel. Translated by Peter Constantine. New York: W. W. Norton, 2001.

Balberyszski, Mendl. *Shtarker fun ayzn: iberlebungen in der Hitler-tekufe*. Tel Aviv: Ha-Menorah, 1967.

———. *Stronger Than Iron: The Destruction of Vilna Jewry, 1941–1945: An Eyewitness Account*. Edited by Theodore Balberyszski. Translated by Abraham Cykiert and Theodore Balberyszski. Jerusalem: Gefen, 2010.

Bashevis, Yitskhok. *Mayn tatns beys-din shtub*. New York: Der Kval, 1956.

———. *See also* Singer, Isaac Bashevis.

Bernstein, J., et al. *Ghetto: Berichte aus dem Warschauer Ghetto 1939–1945*. East Berlin: Union Verlag Berlin, 1966.

Berr, Hélène. *The Journal of Hélène Berr*. Translated by David Bellos. New York: Weinstein Books, 2008.

[Danielovitch], Hershele. "Vayb un kinder nebekh hungern." In *Lider fun khurbn*, edited by Kadia Molodovsky, 27. Tel-Aviv: Farlag I. L. Peretz, 1962.

Dobroszycki, Lucjan, ed. *The Chronicle of the Łódź Ghetto, 1941–1944*. Translated by Richard Lourie et al. New Haven, CT: Yale University Press, 1984.

Doyle, Arthur Conan. *Der grester detektiv*. New York: Idish, 1919.

Eichendorff, Joseph von. "Mondnacht." In *Werke in sechs Bänden.* Band 1: *Gedichte/Versepen,* 322–23. Frankfurt am Main: Suhrkamp Verlag, 1987.

———. "Moonlit Night." In *The Book of Lieder: The Original Texts of Over 1000 Songs,* chosen, translated and introduced by Richard Stokes, 447. New York: Faber, 2005.

Eynhorn, Dovid. *Shtile gezangen.* Warsaw: Farlag progres, 1910.

Feld, Jehuda. *In di tsaytn fun Homen dem tsveytn.* Warsaw: Farlag yidish bukh, 1954.

Freud, Sigmund. "The Uncanny." In *The Standard Edition of the Complete Psychological Works of Sigmund Freud,* vol. 27 (1917–1919), 218–53. London: Hogarth, 1953.

Gens, Jakub. "Address by Gens after His Appointment as Ghetto Leader, July 1942." In *Documents on the Holocaust: Selected Sources on the Destruction of the Jews of Germany, Austria, Poland, and the Soviet Union,* edited by Yitzhak Arad, Israel Gutman, and Margaliot Abraham, 438–40. Jerusalem: Yad Vashem, 1981.

Goethe, Johann Wolfgang von. *Werke* (Hamburger Ausgabe). Vol. 1: *Gedichte und Epen I,* edited by Erich Trunz. Munich: Deutscher Taschenbuch Verlag, 1998.

———. *Werke* (Hamburger Ausgabe). Vol. 9: *Autobiographische Schriften I,* edited by Erich Trunz. Munich: Verlag C. H. Beck, 1994.

Goldin, Leyb. "Chronicle of a Single Day." In *The Literature of Destruction: Jewish Responses to Catastrophe,* edited by David G. Roskies, 424–34. Philadelphia: Jewish Publication Society, 1988.

———. "Khronik fun a mes-les." In *Tsvishn lebn un toyt,* edited by Ber Mark, 49–65. Warsaw: Farlag yidish bukh, 1955.

Hamsun, Knut. *Hunger.* Translated by Sverre Lyngstad. New York: Penguin, 1998.

———. *Pan: Fun leytenant Tomas Glans ksovim.* Translated by Y. Bashevis. Vilna: Vilner Farlag fun B. Kletskin, 1928.

———. *Viktorya.* Translated by Y. Bashevis. Vilna: Vilner Farlag fun B. Kletskin, 1929.

Headnote "fun redaktsye" to "4580." *Bleter far geshikhte* 5, no. 3 (1953): 53.

Heine, Heinrich. *Die Heimkehr* XXVI ["Mir träumte: traurig schaute der Mond"]. In *Heinrich Heine, Historisch-kritische Gesamtausgabe der Werke,* Band 1, *Buch der Lieder,* edited by Manfred Windfuhr, 237. Hamburg: Hoffmann und Campe, 1975.

Huberband, Shimon. *Kiddush Hashem: Jewish Religious and Cultural Life During the Holocaust.* Edited by Jeffrey S. Gurock and Robert S. Hirt. Translated by David E. Fishman. Hoboken, NJ: KTAV Publishing House, 1987.

Jarecka, Gustawa. "The Last Stage of Resettlement is Death." In *To Live with Honor and Die with Honor! Selected Documents from the Warsaw Ghetto Underground Archives "O.S." ("Oneg Shabbath"),* edited by Joseph Kermish, 703–8. Jerusalem: Yad Vashem, 1986.

Jewish Publication Society. *JPS Hebrew-English Tanakh: The Traditional Hebrew Text and the New JPS Translation.* 2nd ed. Philadelphia: Jewish Publication Society, 1999.

Kaplan, Chaim A. *Scroll of Agony*. Translated by Abraham I. Katsh. Bloomington: Indiana University Press, 1999.

Katzenelson, Itzhak. *Dos lid funem oysgehargetn yidishn folk*. New York: YKUF, n.d.

———. "Lid fun hunger." In *Lider fun khurbn*, edited by Kadia Molodovsky, 37–38. Tel-Aviv: Farlag I. L. Peretz, 1962.

———. "The Song of the Murdered Jewish People." Translated by Noah H. Rosenbloom, Y. Tobin, and Jacob Sonntag. In *The Literature of Destruction: Jewish Responses to Catastrophe*, edited by David G. Roskies, 531–47. Philadelphia: Jewish Publication Society, 1988.

———. *Vittel Diary*. Translated by Myer Cohen. Tel Aviv: Ghetto Fighters House, 1972.

———. *Yidishe geto-ksovim: Varshe 1940–1943. Aroysgegebn loyt opgeratevete ksav-yadn mit araynfirn un derklerungen fun Yechiel Szeintuch*. [Yiddish ghetto writings: Warsaw, 1940–1943. Published according to the recovered manuscripts, with introductions and notes by Yechiel Szeintuch.] Tel Aviv: Ghetto Fighters House and Hakibbutz Hameuchad, 1984.

———. *See also* Katzenelson, Jizchak; Katzenelson, Yitzhak.

Katzenelson, Jizchak. *Dos lied vunem ojsgehargetn jidischn volk / Großer Gesang vom ausgerotteten jüdischen Volk*. Translated by Wolf Biermann. Cologne: Kiepenheuer & Witsch, 1994.

———. *See also* Katzenelson, Itzhak; Katzenelson, Yitzhak.

Katzenelson, Yitzhak. "Woe to You." Translated by Ruth Whitman and Menachem Rothstein. *Jerusalem Quarterly* 83, no. 26 (Winter 1982): 67–70.

———. *See also* Katzenelson, Itzhak; Katzenelson, Jizchak.

Keats, John. *Complete Poems*. Edited by Jack Stillinger. Cambridge, MA: Belknap Press, 1982.

Kirman, Yosef. "After the Blockade (A Chronicle)." Translated by Sarah Traister Moskovitz. Available on Poetry in Hell: Yiddish Holocaust Poetry with Translations from the Warsaw Ghetto Ringelblum Archives. https://poetryinhell.org/index-by-authors/kirman-yosep/after-the-blockade/.

———. "The Eyes Remain Open." Translated by Sarah Traister Moskovitz. Available on Poetry in Hell: Yiddish Holocaust Poetry with Translations from the Warsaw Ghetto Ringelblum Archives. https://poetryinhell.org/index-by-authors/kirman-yosep/the-eyes-remain-open/.

———. *See also* Kirman, Yoysef.

Kirman, Yoysef. "Fun pleytim-shtetl—Dzshike un Niske." In *Tsvishn lebn un toyt*, edited by Ber Mark, 39–43. Warsaw: Farlag Yidish Bukh, 1955.

———. *Iber shtok un shteyn*. Warsaw: Kletskin, 1930.

———. *See also* Kirman, Yosef.

Kirshenblatt, Mayer, and Barbara Kirshenblatt-Gimblett. *They Called Me Mayer July: Painted Memories of a Jewish Childhood in Poland Before the Holocaust*. Berkeley: University of California Press, 2007.

Klüger, Ruth. *Weiter leben: Eine Jugend*. Munich: Deutscher Taschenbuch Verlag, 2012.

Kulbak, Moyshe. *Shirim.* Vilnius: Farayn fun di Yidish Literatorn un Zhurnalistn in Vilne, 1920.

Kruk, Herman. *The Last Days of the Jerusalem of Lithuania: Chronicles from the Vilna Ghetto and the Camps, 1939–1944.* Edited by Benjamin Harshav. Translated by Barbara Harshav. New Haven, CT: Yale University Press, 2002.

———. "Library and Reading Room in the Vilna Ghetto, Strashun Street 6." Translated by Zachary M. Baker. In *The Holocaust and the Book: Destruction and Preservation,* edited by Jonathan Rose, 171–200. Amherst: University of Massachusetts Press, 2001.

———. *Togbukh fun vilner geto.* New York: YIVO, 1961.

Levi, Primo. *The Drowned and the Saved.* Translated by Raymond Rosenthal. New York: Vintage, 1989.

———. *Survival in Auschwitz.* New York: Touchstone, 1996.

Lewin, Abraham. *A Cup of Tears: A Diary of the Warsaw Ghetto.* Translated by Christopher Hutton. London: Fontana, 1990.

Mann, Thomas. *Der tsoyberbarg.* Translated by Y. Bashevis. Vilna: Vilner Farlag fun B. Kletskin, 1930.

———. *Der Zauberberg.* Berlin: S. Fischer Verlag, 1952.

Marvil, Shmuel. Letter to Yitzhak Giterman (April 13, 1942). Translated by Sarah Traister Moskovitz. Available on Poetry in Hell: Yiddish Holocaust Poetry with Translations from the Warsaw Ghetto Ringelblum Archives. https://poetryinhell.org/index-by-authors/marvil-shmuel/letter-to-gitterman/.

———. "The Street." Translated by Sarah Traister Moskovitz. Available on Poetry in Hell: Yiddish Holocaust Poetry with Translations from the Warsaw Ghetto Ringelblum Archives. https://poetryinhell.org/index-by-authors/marvil-shmuel/the-street/.

Némirovsky, Irène. *Suite française.* Translated by Sandra Smith. New York: Knopf, 2006.

Opoczynski, Peretz. "Building No. 21." In Opoczynski and Zelkowicz, *In Those Nightmarish Days,* 3–30.

———. "The Jewish Letter Carrier." In Opoczynski and Zelkowicz, *In Those Nightmarish Days,* 31–53.

Opoczynski, Peretz, and Josef Zelowicz. *In Those Nightmarish Days: The Ghetto Reportage of Peretz Opoczynski and Josef Zelkowicz.* Edited by Samuel D Kassow and David Suchoff. Translated by David Suchoff. New Haven, CT: Yale University Press, 2015.

Perle, Yehoshue. "4580." *Bleter far geshikhte* 5, no. 3 (1952): 53–62.

———. "4580." In *Tsvishn lebn un toyt,* edited by Ber Mark, 142–49. Warsaw: Farlag Yidish Bukh, 1955.

———. "4580." Translated by Elinor Robinson. In *The Literature of Destruction: Jewish Responses to Catastrophe,* edited by David G. Roskies, 450–54. Philadelphia: Jewish Publication Society, 1989.

———. *Everyday Jews: Scenes from a Vanished Life.* Edited by David G. Roskies.

Translated by Maier Deshell and Margaret Birstein. New Haven, CT: Yale University Press, 2007.
———. *Nayn a zeyger inderfri.* Vilna: Farlag fun B. Kletskin, 1930.
———. *Ordinary Jews.* Translated by Shirley Kumove. Albany: Excelsior Editions, 2011.
———. "Tsifern." *Varshever almanakh.* Warsaw: Beletristn-fareynikung, 1923.
———. *Yidn fun a gants yor: a bukh fun a fargangen lebn.* Warsaw: Farlag Ch. Brzoza, 1936.
Poe, Egar Allan. "Di mordn af der morg-gas." *Di Verk,* vol. 1., 78–131. New York: Idish, 1919.
Pushkin, A. S. *Sobranie sochinenii.* Vol. 1. Moscow: Gosudarstvennoe izdanie khudozhestvennoi literatury, 1959.
Ringelblum, Emanuel. *Ksovim fun geto.* Vol. 2: *notitsn un ophandlungen (1942–1943).* Tel Aviv: Farlag I. L. Perets, 1985.
———. *Notes from the Warsaw Ghetto.* Translated by Jacob Sloan. New York: ibooks, 2006.
———. "Oyneg Shabbes." In *The Literature of Destruction: Jewish Responses to Catastrophe,* edited by David G. Roskies, 386–98. Philadelphia: Jewish Publication Society, 1988.
Rosenfarb, Chava. *Confessions of a Yiddish Writer and Other Essays.* Edited by Goldie Morgentaler. Montreal: McGill-Queen's University Press, 2019.
———. *Di balade fun nekhtikn vald (un andere lider).* London: Narod Press, 1947.
———. "From the Depths." Translated by Hannah Pollin-Galay. *In geveb,* June 2022. https://ingeveb.org/texts-and-translations/from-the-depths/.
Rosenfeld, Oskar. *Die vierte Galerie: Ein Wiener Roman.* Vienna: Hugo Heller, 1910.
———. *In the Beginning Was the Ghetto: Notebooks from Łódź.* Edited by Hanno Loewy. Translated by Brigitte M. Goldstein. Evanston, IL: Northwestern University Press, 2002.
———. "Mendl Ruhig: Eine Erzählung aus dem mährischen Ghettoleben." *Menorah: Illustrierte Monatsschrift für die jüdische Familie* [Illustrated monthly for the Jewish home] 1, vol. 2/3 (1923): 16–22.
———. *Tage und Nächte: Novellen.* Leipzig: Ilf-Verlag, 1920.
———. *Wozu noch Welt: Aufzeichnungen aus dem Getto Lodz.* Edited by Hanno Loewy. Frankfurt am Main: Verlag Neue Kritik, 1994.
Rudashevski, Yitskhok. *The Diary of the Vilna Ghetto.* Translated and redacted by Percy Matenko. Tel Aviv: Beit Lohamei Haghetaot, 1973.
Rumkowski, Chaim. "Announcement." *Lodzsh geto-tsaytung* 8, vol. 25, no. 4 (1941), 2.
Scherman, Nosson, and Meir Zlotowitz, eds. *The Complete ArtScroll Siddur: Weekday/Sabbath/Festival.* Translated by Nosson Scherman. Brooklyn: Me'sorah, 1999.
Seidman, Hillel. *Togbukh fun varshever geto.* Buenos Aires: Tsentral-farband fun poylishe yidn in argentine, 1947.

Shelley, Percy Bysshe. "To the Moon." In *The Complete Works of Percy Bysshe Shelley*, edited by Thomas Hutchinson, 621. London: Oxford University Press, 1961.

Sheynkinder, Sh. "Oyf di gasn." In *Tsvishn lebn un toyt*, edited by Ber Mark, 97–99. Warsaw: Farlag Yidish Bukh, 1955.

Sholem Aleichem. *The Letters of Menakhem-Mendl & Sheyne Sheyndl and Motl, Peysi the Cantor's Son*. Translated by Hillel Halkin. New Haven, CT: Yale University Press, 2002.

Shpigl, Shaye. *Mentshn in thom: Geto noveln*. Buenos Aires: IKUF, 1949.

———. *See also* Shpigl, Yeshayahu; Shpigl, Yeshaye; Spiegel, Isaiah.

Shpigl, Yeshayahu. *Shtern ibern geto*. Paris: Yidishe folks biblyotek, 1948.

———. *Un gevorn iz likht (lider)*. Warsaw: Farlag Yidish Bukh, 1949.

———. *Likht funem opgrunt: Geto-noveln* [Light from the abyss]. New York: Tsiko, 1952.

———. *Vint un vortslen* [Wind and roots]. New York: Alveltlekhn Yidishn Kultur-Kongres, 1955.

———. *See also* Shpigl, Shaye; Shpigl, Yeshaye; Spiegel, Isaiah.

Shpigl, Yeshaye. "Araynfir-vort" [Introduction] to *Un gevorn iz likht*. Warsaw: Farlag Yidish Bukh, 1949. 3–4.

———. *Malkhes geto (noveln)*. Lodzsh: Farlag "Dos naye leben," 1947.

———. *Mitn ponem tsu der zun: lider*. Lodzsh: Farlag "Alfa," 1930.

———. *See also* Shpigl, Shaye; Shpigl, Yeshayahu; Spiegel, Isaiah.

Shtern, Israel. "Mentshn, vos hungern." In *Dos lid iz geblibn: Lider fun yidishe dikhter in poyln, umgekumene beys der hitlerisher okupatsye; Antologye*, edited by Binem Heller, 246–47. Warsaw: Farlag Yidish Bukh, 1951.

Sierakowiak, Dawid. *The Diary of Dawid Sierakowiak: Five Notebooks from the Łódź Ghetto*. Edited by Alan Adelson. Translated by Kamil Turowski. Oxford: Oxford University Press, 1996.

Singer, Isaac Bashevis. *In My Father's Court*. Translated by Channa Kleinerman Goldstein, Elaine Gottlieb, and Joseph Singer. New York: Farrar, Straus, and Giroux, 1967.

———. *More Stories from My Father's Court*. Translated by Curt Leviant. New York: Farrar, Strauss, and Giroux, 2001.

———. *See also* Bashevis, Yitskhok.

Singer, Israel Joshua. *Of a World That Is No More*. Translated by Joseph Singer. New York: Vanguard Press, 1970.

Singer, Oskar. *"Im Eilschritt durch den Gettotag . . .": Reportagen und Essays aus dem Getto Lodz*. Edited by Sascha Feuchert. Berlin: Philo, 2002.

Skalov, Zelmen. "A Shpatsir iber di punktn." In *Tsvishn lebn un toyt*, edited by Ber Mark, 73–96. Warsaw: Farlag Yidish Bukh, 1955.

———. *Di hak on krayts*. Warsaw: Farlag Yidish Bukh, 1954.

———. "Griln." *Shriftn: Literarisher khoydesh-zhshurnal* no. 4 (June 1937): 3–7.

———. *Tsaytn baytn zikh: Dertseylungen*. Warsaw: Literarishe bleter, 1938.

———. *Vayse hent: Palestine dertseylungen*. Warsaw: Azil, 1936.

Spiegel, Isaiah. "A Ghetto Dog." In *A Treasury of Yiddish Stories*, edited by Irving Howe and Eliezer Greenberg, 614–24. Revised ed. New York: Penguin, 1990.

———. *Ghetto Kingdom: Tales of the Łódź Ghetto*. Translated by David H. Hirsch and Roslyn Hirsch. Evanston, IL: Northwestern University Press, 1998.

———. *See also* Shpigl, Shaye; Shpigl, Yeshayahu; Shpigl, Yeshaye.

Sutzkever, Abraham. *Burnt Pearls: Ghetto Poems of Abraham Sutzkever*. Translated by Seymour Mayne. Oakville, Ontario: Mosaic Press, 1981.

———. "Glust zikh mir tsu ton a tfile . . ." In *Lider fun geto*, 13. New York: Yikuf Farlag, 1946.

———. "Pray." Translated by C. K. Williams. In *Literature of Destruction: Jewish Responses to Catastrophe*, edited by David G. Roskies, 492–93. Philadelphia: Jewish Publication Society, 1988.

———. *See also* Sutzkever, Avrom.

Sutzkever, Avrom. *Di festung: Lider un poemes geshribn in vilner geto un in vald 1941–1944*. New York: Ikuf, 1945.

———. *See also* Sutzkever, Abraham.

Tannert, Mary W., and Henry Kratz, eds. *Early German and Austrian Detective Fiction: An Anthology*, translated by Mary W. Tannert and Henry Kratz. Jefferson, NC: McFarland, 1999.

Vishniac, Roman. *A Vanished World*. New York: Farrar, Strauss, and Giroux, 1983.

Winter, Shmuel. "Shmuel Winters togbukh." [Shmuel Winter's diary]. *Bleter far geshikhte* 3, nos. 1–2 (1950): 29–50.

Żółkiewska, Agnieszka, and Marek Tuszewicki, eds. *Utwory literackie z getta warszawskiego*. [Literary works from the Warsaw ghetto]. Vol. 26 of the *Archiwum Ringelbluma*. [The Ringelblum archive]. Warsaw: Żydowski Instytut Historyczny, 2017.

Zweig, Stefan. *Romain Rolland, der mentsh un dos verk*. Translated by Y. Bashevis. Warsaw: Kooperativ "Bikher," 1929.

SECONDARY SOURCES

Aaron, Frieda. *Bearing the Unbearable: Yiddish and Polish Poetry in the Ghettos and Concentration Camps*. Albany: State University of New York Press, 1990.

Adorno, Theodor W. "Kulturkritik und Gesellschaft." In *Lyrik nach Auschwitz? Adorno und die Dichter*, 27–49. Stuttgart: Reclam, 1995.

Agamben, Giorgio. *Remnants of Auschwitz: The Witness and the Archive*. New York: Zone Books, 2002.

Alter, Robert, trans. *The Hebrew Bible*. Vol. 1: *The Five Books of Moses: A Translation with Commentary by Robert Alter*. New York: W. W. Norton, 2019.

———. *The Hebrew Bible*. Vol. 3: *The Writings: A Translation with Commentary by Robert Alter*. New York: W. W. Norton, 2019.

Arad, Yitzhak. *Ghetto in Flames. The Struggle and Destruction of the Jews in Vilna in the Holocaust*. Jerusalem: Yad Vashem, 1980.

Auerbach, Rokhl. *Varshever tsvoes: Bagegenishn, aktivitetn, goyroles 1933–1943*. Tel-Aviv: Farlag Yidish Bukh, 1974.

———. *Warsaw Testament.* Translated by Samuel Kassow. Amherst, MA: White Goat Press, 2024.

———. "Yoysef Kirman (bagegnishn 1933–1943)." *Di goldene keyt* 75 (1972): 142–54.

Ausubel, Michael, and Michael J. Broyde. "Legal Institutions." *YIVO Encyclopedia of Jews in Eastern Europe.* https://yivoencyclopedia.org/article.aspx/Legal_Institutions.

Ayzenbakh, Aaron. "Visenshaftlekhe forshungen in varshever geto." Warsaw: Yidisher historisher institut, 1948.

Baker, Zachary M. "Yiddish Publishing after 1945: A Brief Overview." In *Yiddish after the Holocaust*, edited by Joseph Sherman, 60–73. Oxford: Boulevard Books, 2004.

Bassok, Ido. "Mapping Reading Culture in Interwar Poland—Secular Literature as a New Marker of Ethnic Belonging among Jewish Youth." *Simon Dubnow Institute Yearbook* 9 (2010): 15–36.

———. "Jewish Youth Movements in Poland between the Wars as Heirs of the *Kehilah*." *Polin: Studies in Polish Jewry* 30 (2018): 299–320.

———. "The Historical Value of Young People's Autobiographies from the YIVO Collection" [Hebrew]. *Mada'ei Hayahadut* [Jewish studies] 44 (5767/2006–2007): 137–64.

Bauer, Yehuda. *Rethinking the Holocaust.* New Haven, CT: Yale University Press, 2001.

Beinfeld, Salon. "The Cultural Life of the Vilna Ghetto." In *The Nazi Holocaust: Historical Articles on the Destruction of European Jews* 6, vol. 1: *The Victims of the Holocaust*, edited by Michael R. Marrus, 94–115. Westport, CT: Meckler, 1989.

Berg, Nicolas. *The Holocaust and the West German Historians: Historical Interpretation and Autobiographical Memory.* Translated and edited by Joel Golb. Madison: University of Wisconsin Press, 2015.

———. "Joseph Wulf, a Forgotten Outsider among Holocaust Scholars." In *Holocaust Historiography in Context: Emergence, Challenges, Polemics, and Achievements*, edited by David Bankier and Dan Milchman, 167–206. Jerusalem: Yad Vashem, 2008.

Bernstein, Michael André. *Foregone Conclusions: Against Apocalyptic History.* Berkeley: University of California Press, 1996.

Bethke, Svenja. "Crime and Punishment in Emergency Situations: The Jewish Ghetto Courts in Lodz, Warsaw and Vilna in World War II—A Comparative Study." *Dapim: Studies on the Holocaust* 28 (2014): 173–89.

———. *Dance on the Razor's Edge: Crime and Punishment in the Nazi Ghettos.* Translated by Sharon Howe. Toronto: University of Toronto Press, 2021.

———. *Tanz auf Messers Schneide: Kriminalität und Recht in den Ghettos Warschau, Litzmannstadt und Wilna.* Hamburg: Hamburger Edition, 2015.

Bethke, Svenja, and Hanna Schmidt Holländer. "Lebenswelt Ghetto: Raumtheorie und interpretatives Paradigma als Bereicherung für die Erforschung jüdischer Ghettos im Nationalsozialismus." *Ghetto: Räume und Grenzen im Judentum. PaRDeS: Zeitschrift der Vereinigung für Jüdische Studien e.V.* 17 (2011): 35–52.

Blumental, Nachman. "Di kharakteristik fun der yidisher literatur unter der daytshisher okupatsye." In *Shmuesn vegn der yidisher literatur unter der daytsher okupatsye*, 19–34. Tsentral-farband fun poylishe yidn in argentine (Central Union of Polish Jews in Argentina): Buenos Aires, 1966.

———. "Vos zenen di hoypt-shtrikhn fun der literatur?" In *Shmuesn vegn der yidisher literatur unter der daytsher okupatsye*, 34–38. Tsentral-farband fun poylishe yidn in argentine (Central Union of Polish Jews in Argentina): Buenos Aires, 1966.

Boltanski, Luc. *Mysteries and Conspiracies: Detective Stories, Spy Novels and the Making of Modern Societies*. Translated by Catherine Porter. Malden, MA: Polity, 2014.

Bonheim, Günther. *Versuch zu zeigen, daß Adorno mit seiner Behauptung, nach Auschwitz lasse sich kein Gedicht mehr schreiben, recht hatte*. Würzburg: Königshausen & Neumann, 2002.

Botting, Fred. "In Gothic Darkly: Heterotopia, History, Culture." In *A New Companion to the Gothic*, edited by David Punter, 13–24. Malden, MA: Blackwell, 2012.

Bracher, Nathan. *After the Fall: War and Occupation in Irène Némirovsky's* Suite française. Washington, DC: The Catholic University of America Press, 2010.

Bromberg, Eli. "We Need to Talk about Shmuel Charney." *In geveb*, October 2019. https://ingeveb.org/articles/we-need-to-talk-about-shmuel-charney.

Brooks, Peter. "Clues, Evidence, Detection: Law Stories." *Narrative* 25, no. 1 (2017): 1–28.

Browning, Christopher R. *The Origins of the Final Solution: The Evolution of Nazi Jewish Policy, September 1939–March 1942*. Lincoln: University of Nebraska Press, 2004.

Bruner, Jerome. "The Narrative Construction of Reality." *Critical Inquiry* 18, no. 1 (1991): 1–21.

Cenedese, Marta Laura. "The Rhythm of Unity: Irène Némirovsky's *Suite française* and Leo Tolstoy's *War and Peace*." *Comparative Literature* 71, no. 1 (2019): 64–85.

Chare, Nicholas, and Dominic Williams. *Matters of Testimony: Interpreting the Scrolls of Auschwitz*. New York: Berghahn, 2016.

Charney, Shmuel [Shmuel Niger]. "A shrayber, vos shmeykhlt: Yehoshue Perle, *Yidn fun a gants yor*." *Di tsukunft* (July 1936): 504–7.

———. "Shtern ibern geto: vegn Yeshayahu Shpigls 'Malkhes geto' (Lodzsh, 1947) un 'Shtern ibern geto' (Pariz, 1948)." In *Yeshayahu Shpigl in likht fun der farloshener pen*, vol. 2, 7–14. Tel Aviv: Yisroel Bukh, 1986.

Cohen, Boaz. "Dr Meir (Mark) Dworzecki: The Historical Mission of a Survivor Historian." *Holocaust Studies* 21, nos. 1–2 (2015): 24–37.

———. *Israeli Holocaust Research: Birth and Evolution*. New York: Routledge, 2013.

Cohen, Nathan. "Sherlock Holmes in the Pale of Settlement: Yiddish Crime Stories 1860–1914." In *Yiddish Studies Today*, vol. 1, edited by Marion Aptroot, Efrat

Gal-Ed, Roland Gruschka, and Simon Neuberg, 253–78. Düsseldorf: Düsseldorf University Press, 2012.

Culler, Jonathan D. "Omniscience." *Narrative* 12, no. 1 (January 2004): 22–34.

———. *The Pursuit of Signs: Semiotics, Literature, Deconstruction.* Second ed. Ithaca, NY: Cornell University Press, 2002.

———. *Theory of the Lyric.* Cambridge, MA: Harvard University Press, 2015.

Daube, David. *Collaboration with Tyranny in Rabbinic Law.* Oxford: Oxford University Press, 1965.

Davis, Mike. *Late Victorian Holocausts: El Niño Famines and the Making of the Third World.* New York: Verso, 2001.

Davison, Carol Margaret, ed. *The Gothic and Death.* Manchester: Manchester University Press, 2017.

———. "Introduction—The Corpse in the Closet: The Gothic, Death, and Modernity." In *The Gothic and Death,* edited by Carol Margaret Davison, 1–17. Manchester: Manchester University Press, 2017.

Dawidowicz, Lucy S. *The War against the Jews, 1933–1945.* New York: Bantam Books, 1986.

DeKoven Ezrahi, Sidra. *By Words Alone: The Holocaust in Literature.* Chicago: University of Chicago Press, 1980.

Délas, Dominique, and Marie-Madeleine Castellani. "Une symphonie inachevée: Structure de *Suite française* d'Irène Némirovsky." *Roman 20–50,* no. 54 (December 2012): 87–97.

Dhamac, Maxamed Xaashi ("Gaarriye"). *Biography and Poems.* Edited by Jama Musse Jama. Pisa: Ponte Invisible (redsea-online), 2012.

Diner, Dan. *Beyond the Conceivable: Studies on Germany, Nazism, and the Holocaust.* Berkeley: University of California Press, 2000.

Donahue, William Collins. *Holocaust as Fiction: Bernhard Schlink's "Nazi" Novels and their Films.* New York: Palgrave, 2010.

———. "The Popular Culture Alibi: Bernhard Schlink's Detective Novels and the Culture of Politically Correct Holocaust Literature." *German Quarterly* 77, no. 4 (2004): 462–81.

Doyle, Arthur Conan. *The Complete Sherlock Holmes.* Garden City, NY: Doubleday, 1930.

Engelking, Barbara. *Holocaust and Memory: The Experience of the Holocaust and Its Consequences: An Investigation Based on Personal Narratives.* Edited by Gunnar S. Paulson. Translated by Emma Harris. London: Leicester University Press, 2001.

Engelking, Barbara, and Jacek Leociak. *The Warsaw Ghetto: A Guide to the Perished City.* Translated by Emma Harris. New Haven, CT: Yale University Press, 2009.

Epsztein, Tadeusz. "Structure and Organization of the Ringelblum Archive and Its Catalog." In *The Warsaw Ghetto Oyneg Shabes-Ringelblum Archive: Catalog and Guide,* edited by Tadeusz Epsztein and Robert Moses Shapiro, translated by Robert Moses Shapiro, 1–22. Bloomington: Indiana University Press, 2009.

Estraikh, Gennady. "The Kultur-Lige in Warsaw: A Stopover in the Yiddishists'

Journey between Kiev and Paris." In *Warsaw, The Jewish Metropolis: Essays in Honor of the 75th Birthday of Professor Antony Polonsky*, edited by Glenn Dynner and François Guesnet, 323–46. Boston: Brill, 2015.

———. "A Touchstone of Socialist Realism: The 1934 *Almanac* of Soviet Yiddish Writers." *Jews in Eastern Europe* 37, no. 3 (Winter 1998): 24–37.

Evans, Jennifer, and Brian J. Griffiths, eds. "The Catechism Debate." *New Fascism Syllabus*, May 25–June 2, 2021. https://newfascismsyllabus.com/wp-content/uploads/2021/08/The-Catechism-Debate.pdf.

Feierstein, Daniel. "The Jewish Resistance Movements in the Ghettos of Eastern Europe." *In Life in the Ghettos during the Holocaust*, edited by Eric J. Sterling, 220–57. Syracuse, NY: Syracuse University Press, 2005.

Feldman, Daniel, and Efraim Sicher. *Poesis in Extremis: Literature Witnessing the Holocaust.* London: Bloomsbury Academic, 2024.

Feuchert, Sascha. *Oskar Rosenfeld und Oskar Singer: Zwei Autoren des Lodzer Gettos.* Frankfurt am Main: Peter Lang, 2004.

Finkin, Jordan. "Workers' Libraries in Interwar Poland: Selections Translated from a Yiddish Handbook." *Judaica Librarianship* 22 (2021): 84–102.

Fishman, David E. *The Book Smugglers: Partisans, Poets, and the Race to Save Jewish Treasures from the Nazis.* Lebanon, NH: ForeEdge, 2017.

———. *The Rise of Modern Yiddish Culture.* Pittsburgh: University of Pittsburgh Press, 2005.

Flam, Gila. *Singing for Survival: Songs of the Lodz Ghetto, 1940–1945.* Champaign: University of Illinois Press, 1992.

Fludernik, Monika. "Second Person Fiction: Narrative 'You' As Addressee And/Or Protagonist." *Arbeiten aus Anglistik und Amerikanistik* 18, no. 2 (January 1993): 217–47.

Friedländer, Saul, ed. *Probing the Limits of Representation: Nazism and the "Final Solution."* Cambridge, MA: Harvard University Press, 1992.

Friedman, Philip. "The Fate of the Jewish Book." In *Roads to Extinction: Essays on the Holocaust*, edited by Philip Friedman, 88–99. Philadelphia: Jewish Publication Society, 1980.

Fuss, Dianna. *Dying Modern: A Meditation on Elegy.* Durham, NC: Duke University Press, 2013.

Fussell, Paul. *The Great War and Modern Memory.* Oxford: Oxford University Press, 2000.

Gabowitsch, Mischa. "Zuhören statt belehren: Für eine Osterweiterung der deutschen Erinnerung an Krieg und Holocaust." In *Historiker Streiten: Gewalt und Holocaust—die Debatte*, edited by Susan Neiman and Michael Wildt, 291–307. Berlin: Propyläen, 2022.

Garbarini, Alexandra. *Numbered Days: Diaries and the Holocaust.* New Haven, CT: Yale University Press, 2006.

Garrin, Stephen H. "Isaac Bashevis Singer as Translator: Apprenticing in the Kitchen of Literature." In *Recovering the Canon: Essays on Isaac Bashevis Singer*, edited by David Neal Miller, 50–57. Leiden: E. J. Brill, 1986.

Gelder, Ken. "The Postcolonial Gothic." In *The Cambridge Companion to the Modern Gothic*, edited by Jerrold E. Hogle, 191–207. Cambridge: Cambridge University Press, 2014.

Geldof, Koenraad. "Modernité, excès, littérature: Une lecture contrastive de Michel Foucault et de Stephen Greenblatt." *Littérature*, no. 151 (September 2008): 90–110.

Gilman, Sander L. "Poetry and Naming in Ruth Klüger's Works and Life." *The Legacy of Ruth Klüger and the End of the Auschwitz Century*, edited by Mark H. Gelber, 1–29. Berlin: De Gruyter, 2022.

Glatstein, Jacob. "Yeshayahu Shpigl." In *In tokh genumen: Eseyen 1948–1956*, 453–65. New York: Farlag fun yidish natsyonaln arbeter farband, 1956.

———. "Yeshayahu Shpigls lider." In *In tokh genumen: Eseyen 1949–1959*, 279–86. Buenos Aires: Kiem, 1960.

Goldberg, Amos. "The History of the Jews in the Ghettos: A Cultural Perspective." In *The Holocaust & Historical Methodology*, edited by Dan Stone, 79–100. New York: Berghahn, 2012.

———. "Rumor Culture among Warsaw Jews under Nazi Occupation: A World of Catastrophe Reenchanted." *Jewish Social Studies: History, Culture, Society* 21, no. 3 (2016): 91–125.

———. *Trauma in First Person: Diary Writing During the Holocaust*. Translated by Shmuel Sermoneta-Gertel and Avner Greenberg. Bloomington: Indiana University Press, 2017.

Grabowski, Jan. *Hunt for the Jews: Betrayal and Murder in German-Occupied Poland*. Bloomington: Indiana University Press, 2013.

Gris, Noah. *Fun finsternish tsu likht: Shaye shpigl un zayn verk*. Tel Aviv: Yisroel Bukh, 1974.

Gross, Jan Tomasz, and Irena Grudzinska Gross. *Golden Harvest: Events at the Periphery of the Holocaust*. Oxford: Oxford University Press, 2012.

Gubar, Susan. "The Long and the Short of Holocaust Verse." *New Literary History* 35, no. 3 (2004): 443–68.

———. *Poetry after Auschwitz: Remembering What One Never Knew*. Bloomington: Indiana University Press, 2003.

Hájková, Anna. *The Last Ghetto: An Everyday History of Theresienstadt*. Oxford: Oxford University Press, 2020.

Higdon, David Leon. "A First Census of the Circadian or One-Day Novel." *The Journal of Narrative Technique* 22, no. 1 (Winter 1992): 57–64.

Hirsch, David H. "Introduction to the Ghetto Stories of Isaiah Spiegel." In *Ghetto Kingdom: Tales of the Łódź Ghetto*, by Isaiah Spiegel, translated by David H. Hirsch and Roslyn Hirsch, vii–xxiv. Evanston, IL: Northwestern University Press, 1998.

Hoffman, Matthew. *From Rebel to Rabbi: Reclaiming Jesus and the Making of Modern Jewish Culture*. Stanford: Stanford University Press, 2007.

Hogle, Jerrold E., ed. Introduction to *The Cambridge Companion to the Modern Gothic*, 3–19. Cambridge: Cambridge University Press, 2014.

Horowitz, Sara R. *Voicing the Void: Muteness and Memory in Holocaust Fiction.* Albany: State University of New York Press, 1997.

Jackson, Virginia. *Dickinson's Misery: A Theory of Lyric Reading.* Princeton: Princeton University Press, 2005.

Jacobs, Neil G. *Yiddish: A Linguistic Introduction.* Cambridge: Cambridge University Press, 2005.

Jockusch, Laura. *Collect and Record! Jewish Holocaust Documentation in Early Postwar Europe.* Oxford: Oxford University Press, 2012.

Kacandes, Irene. "Are You in the Text? The 'Literary Peformative' in Postmodernist Fiction." *Text and Performance Quarterly* 13, no. 2 (April 1993): 139–53.

Kaplow, Ian. *Analytik und Ethik der Namen.* Würzburg: Königshausen & Neumann, 2002.

Katzenelson-Nachumov, Cypora. *Yitshak Katsenelson: Zayn lebn un shafn.* Buenos Aires: Tsentral Farbund fun poylishe yidn in argentine, 1948.

Kassow, Samuel D. "Introduction." In Opoczynski and Zelkowicz, *In Those Nightmarish Days,* xii–lii.

———. Introduction to *The Warsaw Ghetto Oyneg Shabes-Ringelblum Archive: Catalog and Guide,* edited by Tadeusz Epsztein and Robert Moses Shapiro, translated by Robert Moses Shapiro, xv–xxiv. Bloomington: Indiana University Press, 2009.

———. "Vilna and Warsaw, Two Ghetto Diaries: Herman Kruk and Emanuel Ringelblum." In *Holocaust Chronicles: Individualizing the Holocaust through Diaries and Other Contemporaneous Personal Accounts,* edited by Robert Moses Shapiro, 171–215. Hoboken, NJ: KTAV, 1999.

———. *Who Will Write Our History? Emanuel Ringelblum, the Warsaw Ghetto, and the Oyneg Shabes Archive.* Bloomington: Indiana University Press, 2007.

Kellman, Ellen. "*Dos yidishe bukh alarmirt!* Towards the History of Yiddish Reading in Inter-War Poland." *Polin* 16 (2003): 213–41.

Kermode, Frank. *The Sense of an Ending: Studies in the Theory of Fiction.* New York: Oxford University Press, 1967.

Kichelewski, Audrey. "Être un historien juif en Pologne communiste: Bernard Mark (1908–1966), directeur de l'Institut d'histoire juive de Varsovie." In *Terres promises : Mélange offerts à André Kaspi,* edited by Hélène Harter, Antoine Marès, Pierre Mélandri, and Catherine Nicault, 527–37. Paris: Sorbonne, 2006.

Kiedaisch, Petra, ed. *Lyrik nach Auschwitz? Adorno und die Dichter.* Stuttgart: Reclam, 1995.

———. "Einleitung." In *Lyrik nach Auschwitz? Adorno und die Dichter,* edited by Petra Kiedaisch, 9–25 Stuttgart: Reclam, 1995.

Kirshenblatt-Gimblett, Barbara, Marcus Moseley, and Michael Stanislawski. Introduction to *Awakening Lives: Autobiographies of Jewish Youth in Poland before the Holocaust,* edited by Jeffrey Shandler, xi–xliii. New Haven, CT: Yale University Press, 2002.

Klarsfeld, Serge. *Memorial to the Jews Deported from France 1942–1944:*

Documentation of the Deportation of the Victims of the Final Solution in France. New York: Beate Klarsfeld Foundation, 1983.

Kligsberg, Moyshe. "Di yidishe yugnt-bavegung in poyln tsvishn beyde velt-milkhomes (a sotsyologishe shtudye)." In *Studies in Polish Jewry 1919–1939: The Interplay of Social, Economic, and Political Factors in the Struggle of a Minority for its Existence*, edited by Joshua A. Fishman, 137–228. New York: YIVO Institute for Jewish Research, 1974.

Knight, Stephen. *Form and Ideology in Crime Fiction*. Basingstoke, UK: Macmillan, 1980.

Kracauer, Sigfried. *From Caligari to Hitler: A Psychological History of the German Film*. Edited by Leonardo Quaresima. Princeton: Princeton University Press, 2019.

Kreppel, Klaus. *Jonas Kreppel—Glaubenstreu und vaterländisch: Biografische Skizze über einen österreichisch-jüdischen Schriftsteller*. With contributions by Evelyn Adunka und Thomas Soxberger. Vienna: Mandelbaum Verlag, 2017.

Kristeva, Julia. *Powers of Horror: An Essay on Abjection*. Translated by Leon S. Roudiez. New York: Columbia University Press, 1982.

Krutikov, Mikhail. *Yiddish Fiction and the Crisis of Modernity, 1905–1914*. Stanford: Stanford University Press, 2001.

Lamping, Dieter. "Gedichte nach Auschwitz, über Auschwitz." In *Poesie der Apokalypse*, edited by Gerhard R. Kaiser, 237–55. Würzburg: Königshausen & Neumann, 1991.

Lang, Berel. "Oskar Rosenfeld and Historiographic Realism (In Sex, Shit, and Status)." In *Post-Holocaust Interpretation, Misinterpretation, and the Claims of History*, 117–27. Bloomington: Indiana University Press, 2005.

Langer, Lawrence L. *The Holocaust and the Literary Imagination*. New Haven, CT: Yale University Press, 1975.

Langer, Ruth. *Cursing the Christians? A History of the* Birkat HaMinim. Oxford: Oxford University Press, 2012.

Lauer, David. "Wittgenstein—Die Gewalt des Namens." In *Philosophien sprachlicher Gewalt: 21 Grundpositionen von Platon bis Butler*, edited by Hannes Kuch and Steffen K. Herrmann, 134–53. Weilerswist: Velbrück, 2010.

Leder, Sharon, and Milton Teichman, eds. *Truth and Lamentation: Stories and Poems of the Holocaust*. Urbana: University of Illinois Press, 1994.

Lejeune, Philippe. "The Autobiographical Pact." In *On Autobiography*, edited by Paul John Eakin, 3–30. Minneapolis: University of Minnesota Press, 1989.

Leociak, Jacek. *Text in the Face of Destruction: Accounts from the Warsaw Ghetto Reconsidered*. Translated by Emma Harris. Warsaw: Zydowski Instytut Historyczny, 2004.

Levin, Dov. *The Lesser of Two Evils: Eastern European Jewry under Soviet Rule, 1939–1941*. Translated by Naftali Greenwood. Philadelphia: Jewish Publication Society, 1995.

Levinson, Julian. "Translator's Introduction." In *Flames from the Earth: A Novel from the Łódź Ghetto*, by Isaiah Spiegel, translated by Julian Levinson, ix–xxx. Evanston, IL: Northwestern University Press, 2022.

———. "Translator's Afterword." In *Flames from the Earth: A Novel from the Łódź Ghetto*, by Isaiah Spiegel, translated by Julian Levinson, 133–45. Evanston, IL: Northwestern University Press, 2022.

Lifshits, Yekhezkl. "Yoyne Krepel (Jonas Kreppel)." Yiddish Leksikon. http://yleksikon.blogspot.com/2019/04/yoyne-krepel-jonas-kreppel.html.

Loewy, Hanno. "Editor's Introduction." In *In the Beginning Was the Ghetto: Notebooks from Łódź*, by Oskar Rosenfeld, edited by Hanno Loewy, translated by Brigitte M. Goldstein, vii–xxxv. Evanston, IL: Northwestern University Press, 2002.

Lorenz, Otto. "Gedichte nach Auschwitz oder: Die Perspektive der Opfer." In *Bestandaufnahme Gegenwartsliteratur*, 35–54. Munich: text + kritik, 1988.

Löshnigg, Martin. "Postclassical Narratology and the Theory of Autobiography." In *Postclassical Narratology: Approaches and Analyses*, edited by Jan Alber and Monika Fludernik, 255–74. Columbus: Ohio State University Press, 2010.

Löw, Andrea. *Juden im Getto Litzmannstadt: Lebensbedingungen, Selbstwahrnehmung, Verhalten*. Göttingen: Wallstein, 2006.

Löwy, Hanno, and Gerhard Schoenberner, eds. *"Unser einziger Weg ist Arbeit"* [Unzer eyntsiger ṿeg iz arbeyṭ]: *Das Getto in Łódź, 1940–1944*. Wien: Löcker, 1990.

Lyngstad, Sverre. Introduction to *Hunger*, by Knut Hamsun, translated by Sverre Lyngstad, vii–xxv. New York: Penguin, 1998.

MacAndrew, Elizabeth. *The Gothic Tradition in Fiction*. New York: Columbia University Press, 1979.

Mandel, Ernest. *Delightful Murder: A Social History of the Crime Story*. London: Pluto Press, 1984.

Mark, Ber. *Di umgekumene shrayber fun di getos un lagern un zeyere verk*. Warsaw: Farlag Yidish Bukh, 1954.

———. "Forvort." [Introduction]. In *Tsvishn lebn un toyt*, edited by Ber Mark, 5–15. Warsaw: Farlag Yidish Bukh, 1955.

———. "Zelmen Skalov (Pluskalovski)." In *Der haknkrayts (Di hak on krayts)*, by Zelmen Skalov, edited by Ber Mark, 5–8. Warsaw: Farlag Yidish Bukh, 1954.

Mazower, David, Elissa Sperling, and Michael Yashinsky. "Max Spitzkopf, the Viennese Sherlock Holmes: The Jewish Detective Hero Who Inspired the Young Bashevis Singer." *Pakntreger: Magazine of the Yiddish Book Center* 77 (Fall 2018). https://wwwyiddishbookcenter.org/max-spitzkopf-viennese-sherlock-holmes.

Mesnard, Philippe, and Claudine Kahan. *Giorgio Agamben à l'épreuve d'Auschwitz: Témoignages, interpretations*. Paris: Kimé, 2001.

Michman, Dan. *The Emergence of Jewish Ghettos during the Holocaust*. Cambridge: Cambridge University Press, 2011.

———. *Holocaust Historiography: A Jewish Perspective: Conceptualizations,*

Terminology, Approaches and Fundamental Issues. Portland: Vallentine Mitchell, 2003.

———. "Is There an 'Israeli School' of Holocaust Research?" In *Holocaust Historiography in Context*, edited by David Bankier and Dan Michman, 37–65. Jerusalem: Yad Vashem, 2008.

Mintz, Alan. "Banished from their Father's Table": Loss of Faith and Hebrew Autobiography. Bloomington: Indiana University Press, 1989.

———. *Popular Culture and the Shaping of Holocaust Memory in America*. Seattle: University of Washington Press, 2001.

———. "Writing about Ourselves: Jewish Autobiography, Modern and Premodern." Review of *Being for Myself Alone: Origins of Jewish Autobiography*, by Marcus Mosley. *Jewish Quarterly Review* 98, no. 2 (Spring 2008): 272–85.

Miron, Dan. *A Traveler Disguised: The Rise of Modern Yiddish Fiction in the Nineteenth Century*. New York: Schocken Books, 1973.

Moretti, Franco. "Clues." In *Signs Taken for Wonders: On the Sociology of Literary Forms*, translated by Susan Fischer, David Forgacs, and David Miller, 130–56. New York: Verso, 1983.

Morson, Gary Saul. *Prosaics and Other Provocations: Empathy, Open Time, and the Novel*. Boston: Academic Studies Press, 2013.

Morson, Gary Saul, and Caryl Emerson. *Mikhail Bakhtin: The Creation of a Prosaics*. Stanford: Stanford University Press, 1990.

Moseley, Marcus. *Being for Myself Alone: Origins of Jewish Autobiography*. Stanford: Stanford University Press, 2006.

———. "Life, Literature: Autobiographies of Jewish Youth in Interwar Poland." *Jewish Social Studies* 7, no. 3 (Spring/Summer 2001): 1–51.

Moses, A. Dirk. "The German Catechism." *Geschichte der Gegenwart*, May 23, 2021. https://geschichtedergegenwart.ch/the-german-catechism/.

Moskovitz, Sarah. Introduction to "'Rich with This Tradition': Ghetto Poetry," by Miriam Ulinover. *Bridges* 14, no 2 (2009): 78–83.

———. "Theme 3: Ghetto, Hunger, Struggle." Poetry in Hell: Yiddish Holocaust Poetry with Translations from the Warsaw Ghetto Ringelblum Archives. Accessed March 7, 2025. https://poetryinhell.org/ghetto-hunger-struggle-2/.

Mücke, Dorothea von. "The Occult, the Fantastic, and the Limits of Rationality." In *A New History of German Literature*, edited by David E. Wellbery, 521–26. Cambridge, MA: Belknap Press, 2004.

———. *The Seduction of the Occult and the Rise of the Fantastic Tale*. Stanford: Stanford University Press, 2003.

Mukdoni, Alexander. "Y. Shpigls noveln." Review of *Likht funem opgrunt* (1952) by Y. Shpigl, in *Yeshayahu Shpigl in likht fun der farloshener pen* (yoyvl-bukh), vol. 2, 19–23. Tel Aviv: Yisroel Bukh, 1986.

Nader, Andrés José. *Traumatic Verses: On Poetry in German from the Concentration Camps, 1933–1945*. Rochester: Camden House, 2007.

Nalewajko-Kulkov, Joanna. "The Last Yiddish Books Printed in Poland: Outline of the Activities of Farlag Yidish Bukh Publishing House." In *Under the Red*

Banner: Yiddish Culture in the Communist Countries in the Postwar Era, Jüdische Kultur 20, edited by Elvira Grözinger and Magadalena Ruta, 111–45. Wiesbaden: Harrassowitz Verlag, 2008.

Neiman, Susan, and Michael Wildt, eds. *Historiker Streiten: Gewalt und Holocaust —Die Debatte.* Berlin: Propyläen, 2022.

Niger, Shmuel, and Jacob Shatzky. *Leḳsiḳon fun der nayer yidisher liṭeraṭur.* 8 vols. New York: Alveltekhn yidishn kultur-kongres (Congress for Jewish Culture), 1956.

Norich, Anita. *The Homeless Imagination in the Fiction of Israel Joshua Singer.* Bloomington: Indiana University Press, 1991.

Orwin, Martin. "Somali Poetry." In *The Princeton Encyclopedia of Poetry and Poetics,* 4th ed., edited by Roland Greene, Stephen Cushman, Clare Cavanagh, Jahan Ramazani, and Paul Rouzer, 1313–14. Princeton: Princeton University Press, 2012.

Patt, Avinoam. "The Jewish Heroes of Warsaw: The Meaning of the Revolt in the First Years after the Uprising." *American Jewish History* 103, no. 2 (April 2019): 147–75.

Person, Katarzyna. *Assimilated Jews in the Warsaw Ghetto, 1940–1943.* Syracuse, NY: Syracuse University Press, 2014.

———. *Warsaw Ghetto Police: The Jewish Order Service during the Nazi Occupation.* Translated by Zygmunt Nowak-Solinski. Ithaca, NY: Cornell University Press, 2021.

Person, Katarzyna, and Agnieszka Żółkiewska. "Edition of Documents from the Ringelblum Archive (the Underground Archive of the Warsaw Ghetto) in Stalinist Poland." In *Growing in the Shadow of Antifascism,* edited by Stephan Stach, Peter Hallama, and Kata Bohus, 21–38. Vienna: Central European University Press, 2021.

Phelan, James. *Narrative as Rhetoric: Technique, Audiences, Ethics, Ideology.* Columbus: Ohio State University Press, 1996.

Philipponnat, Olivier. "'Un ordre différent, plus puissant et plus beau': Irène Némirovsky et le modèle symphonique." *Roman 20–50,* no. 54 (December 2012): 75–86.

Pinchuk, Ben-Cion. "Jewish Refugees in Soviet Poland, 1939–1941." *Jewish Social Studies* 40, no. 2 (Spring 1978): 141–58.

Pinhas-Delpeuch, Rosie, and Menahem Peri. "Postface." In *Et ils partierent pour la guerre,* by David Vogel, 242–45. Paris: Denoël, 1993.

Pohl, Dieter. "Ghettos im Holocaust: Zum Stand der Historischen Forschung." In *Ghettorenten: Entschädigungspolitik, Rechtsprechung und historische Forschung,* edited by Jürgen Larusky, 39–50. Munich: Oldenbourg Verlag, 2010.

———. "Historiography: Ghettos during the Holocaust." Translated by Kerry Jago. Ehri Online Course in Holocaust Studies. https://training.ehri-project.eu /historiography-ghettos-during-holocaust.

Pollin-Galay, Hannah. "Avrom Sutzkever's Art of Testimony: Witnessing with the

Poet in the Wartime Soviet Union." *Jewish Social Studies: History, Culture, Society* 21, no. 2 (2016): 1–34.

———. "The Epic Demands of Postwar Yiddish: Avrom Sutzkever's *Geheymshtot* (1948)." *East European Jewish Affairs* 48, no. 3 (2018): 331–53.

———. Introduction to "From the Depths," by Chava Rosenfarb, translated by Hannah Pollin-Galay. *In geveb*, June 2022. https://ingeveb.org/texts-and-translations/from-the-depths.

Porat, Dina. "The Justice System and Courts of Law in the Ghettos of Lithuania." *Holocaust and Genocide Studies* 12, no. 1 (1998): 49–65.

Quaresima, Leonardo. "Introduction to the 2004 Edition: Rereading Kracauer." In *From Caligari to Hitler: A Psychological History of The German Film*, by Sigfried Kracauer, edited by Leonardo Quaresima, translated by Michael F. Moore, xv–xlix. Princeton: Princeton University Press, 2019.

Rabinowitz, Peter J. *Before Reading: Narrative Conventions and the Politics of Interpretation*. Ithaca, NY: Cornell University Press, 1987.

———. "Truth in Fiction: A Reexamination of Audiences." *Critical Inquiry* 4 (1976): 121–41.

Randall, Byrony. "A Day's Time: The One-Day Novel and the Temporality of the Everyday." *New Literary History* 47, No. 4 (Autumn 2016): 591–610.

Rauchfleisch, Y., and L. Weiss. *Hantbukh far biblyotekn*. Warsaw: Farlag A. Sklar, 1929.

Ravitch, Melech. "Skalov, Zelmen (Y. Sluskolovski [*sic*])." In *Leksikon fun der nayer yidisher literatur* [Biographical dictionary of modern Yiddish literature], edited by Shmuel Charney [Niger] et al., vol. 6, columns 531–32. New York: Alveltlekhn Yidishn Kultur-Kongres [Congress for Jewish culture], 1956–1981.

———. "Vegn a nay khurbn-bukh, vos iz dershinen in varshe." [Review of *Der Haknkrayts* (Di hak on krayts) by Zelmen Skalov, edited by Ber Mark. Warsaw: Farlag Yidish Bukh, 1954]. *Der keneder odler*, April 4, 1955, 6.

Reich-Ranicki, Marcel. *Mein Leben*. Stuttgart: Deutsche Verlags-Anstalt, 1999.

Reitz, Caroline. "The Empires of *A Study in Scarlet* and *The Sign of Four*." In *The Cambridge Companion to Sherlock Holmes*, edited by Janice M. Allan and Christopher Pittard, 127–39. Cambridge: Cambridge University Press, 2019.

Richardson, Brian. "The Poetics and Politics of Second Person Narrative." *Genre: A Quarterly Devoted to Generic Criticism* 24, no. 3 (1991): 309–30.

Ricoeur, Paul. *Freud and Philosophy: An Essay on Interpretation*. New Haven, CT: Yale University Press, 1977.

Rose, Sven-Erik. "Holocaust Literature and Autorevision: Shaye Shpigl's Ghetto Stories Written in, and Rewritten after, the Lodz Ghetto." *In geveb*, March 2023. https://ingeveb.org/articles/holocaust-literature-and-autorevision.

———. "Oskar Rosenfeld, the Lodz Ghetto, and the Chronotope of Hunger." In *The Aesthetics and Politics of Global Hunger*, edited by Manisha Basu and Anastasia Ulanowicz, 27–56. New York: Palgrave Macmillan, 2017.

———. "The Oyneg Shabes Archive and the Cold War: The Case of Yehoshue

Perle's *Khurbn Varshe." New German Critique* 112, no. 38:1 (Winter 2011): 181–215.

———. "A Poetics of Genocide: The Jewish Dead Confront their German Murderers in Itzhak Katzenelson's Warsaw Ghetto Poem 'Vey dir.'" *Nexus: Essays in German-Jewish Studies* 5, *Moments of Enlightenment: In Memory of Jonathan M. Hess*, edited by Eric Downing and Ruth von Bernuth (2021): 135–63.

———. "A poetik fun skhite: Yitskhok katzenelson un yoysef kirman in varshever geto." [A Poetics of Genocide: Yitshak Katzenelson and Joseph Kirman in the Warsaw Ghetto]. *Afn shvel*, no. 380–18 (Summer/Fall 2018): 16–22.

———. "Writing Hunger in a Modernist Key in the Warsaw Ghetto: Leyb Goldin's 'Chronicle of a Single Day.'" *Jewish Social Studies: History, Culture, Society* 23, no. 1 (Fall 2017): 29–63.

Rosenfeld, Alvin H. *A Double Dying: Reflections on Holocaust Literature*. Bloomington: Indiana University Press, 1980.

Roskies, David G. *Against the Apocalypse: Responses to Catastrophe in Modern Jewish Culture*. Syracuse: Syracuse University Press, 1984.

———. *A Bridge of Longing: The Lost Art of Yiddish Storytelling*. Cambridge, MA: Cambridge University Press, 1995.

———. "Did the Shoah Engender a New Poetics?" In *Eastern European Jewish Literature of the 20th and 21st Centuries: Identity and Poetics*, edited by Klavdia Smola, 347–63. Washington, DC: Otto Sagner, 2013.

———. "The Holocaust According to Its Anthologists." In *The Anthology in Jewish Literature*, edited by David Stern. New York: Oxford University Press, 2004.

———. Introduction to *Everyday Jews: Scenes from a Vanished Life*, by Yehoshue Perle, edited by David G. Roskies, translated by Maier Deshell and Margaret Birstein, vii–xxx. New Haven, CT: Yale University Press, 2007.

———. *The Jewish Search for a Usable Past*. Bloomington: Indiana University Press, 1999.

———, ed. *The Literature of Destruction: Jewish Responses to Catastrophe*. Philadelphia: Jewish Publication Society, 1988.

———. "Sholem Aleichem and Others: Laughing Off the Trauma of History." *Prooftexts* 2 (1982): 53–77.

———. "The Small Talk of I. L. Peretz." *In geveb: A Journal of Yiddish Studies* (May 2016): 1–28.

Roskies, David G., and Naomi Diamant. *Holocaust Literature: A History and Guide*. Waltham, MA: Brandeis University Press, 2012.

Rothberg, Michael. *Multidirectional Memory: Remembering the Holocaust in the Age of Decolonization*. Stanford: Stanford University Press, 2009.

Rowland, Antony. *Holocaust Poetry: Awkward Poetics in the Work of Sylvia Plath, Geoffrey Hill, Tony Harrison and Ted Hughes*. Edinburgh: Edinburgh University Press, 2006.

Rudavsky, Joseph. "Chapter 9: Poetry and Song." In *To Live with Hope, to Die with Dignity*, 107–25. New York: University Press of America, 1987.

Rudd, Alison. "Postcolonial Gothic in and as Theory." In *The Gothic and Theory: An Edinburgh Companion*, edited by Jerrold E. Hogle and Robert Miles, 71–88. Edinburgh: Edinburgh University Press, 2019.

Schachter, Allison. "The Shtetl and the City: The Origins of Nostalgia in *Ba-yamim ha-hem* and *Shloyme reb khayims*." *Jewish Social Studies* 12, no. 3 (2006): 73–94.

Schmitt, Hans-Jürgen, ed. *Die Expressionismusdebatte: Materialen zu einer marxistischen Realismuskonzeption*. Franfkurt am Main: Suhrkamp-Verlag, 1973.

Schwarz, Jan. "After the Destruction of Jewish Vilna: Avrom Sutzkever's Poetry, Testimony and Cultural Rescue Work, 1944–1946." *East European Jewish Affairs* 35, no. 2 (2005): 209–25.

———. *Survivors and Exiles: Yiddish Culture after the Holocaust*. Detroit: Wayne State University Press, 2015.

Seidman, Naomi. *Faithful Renderings: Jewish-Christian Difference and the Politics of Translation*. Chicago: University of Chicago Press, 2006.

———. *The Marriage Plot: Or, How Jews Fell in Love with Love, and with Literature*. Stanford: Stanford University Press, 2016.

Shavit, David. *Hunger for the Printed Word. Books and Libraries in the Jewish Ghettos of Nazi-Occupied Europe*. Jefferson, NC: McFarland, 1997.

Shmeruk, Chone. "Hebrew-Yiddish-Polish: A Trilingual Jewish Culture." In *The Jews of Poland between Two World Wars*, edited by Yisrael Gutman, Ezra Mendelsohn, Jehuda Reinharz, and Chone Shmeruk, 285–311. Hanover, NH: Brandeis University Press, 1989.

———. "Yisroel Rabon and His Book *Di gas* ('The Street')." In *Di gas*, by Yisroel Rabon, v–l. Jerusalem: Magnes Press, Hebrew University, 1986.

Shtern, Sholem. "An interesante khronik fun khurbn yidishn-poyln." [Review of *Haknkrayts* by Zelmen Skalov]. *Yidishe kultur* (November 1954): 43–45.

Sicher, Efraim. "The Jewishness of Babel." In *Jews in Soviet Culture*, edited by Jack Miller, 167–82. New Brunswick, NJ: Transaction Books, 1984.

Siebert, Hilary, and Begoña Sío-Castiñeira. "Invention or Proclamation: Jewish Identity in the Stories of Bernard Malamud and Isaiah Spiegel." *Journal of the Short Story in English* 32 (Spring 1999): 1–15.

Simon, Amy. *Emotions in Yiddish Ghetto Diaries: Encountering Persecutors and Questioning Humanity*. New York: Routledge, 2023.

———. "The Modern Haman: Ghetto Diary Writers' Understanding of Holocaust Perpetrators." *Holocaust Studies: A Journal of Culture and History* 17, no. 2–3 (2011): 123–44.

Singer, Isaac Bashevis. "Knut Hamsun, Artist of Skepticism." In *Hunger*, by Knut Hamsun, translated by Robert Bly, v–xii. New York: Farrar, Strauss and Giroux, 1967.

Sinnreich, Helene J. *The Atrocity of Hunger: Starvation in the Warsaw, Łódź, and Kraków Ghettos during World War II*. Cambridge: Cambridge University Press, 2023.

Smith, Andrew. *Gothic Death: 1740–1914; A Literary History*. Manchester: Manchester University Press, 2016.

———. *Gothic Literature*. Edinburgh: Edinburgh University Press, 2013.

Smith, Barbara Herstein. *Contingencies of Value: Alternative Perspectives for Critical Theory*. Cambridge, MA: Harvard University Press, 1991.

Smith, Mark L. "Joseph Wulf and the Path Not Taken: The Turn from Writing Jewish History in Yiddish to Writing Nazi History in German." *Holocaust and Genocide Studies* 37, no. 1 (Spring 2023): 125–39.

———. *The Yiddish Historians and the Struggle for a Jewish History of the Holocaust*. Detroit: Wayne State University Press, 2019.

Sneh, Perle. "*Khurbn Yiddish*: An Absent Absence." *Lessons and Legacies XII: New Directions in Holocaust Research and Education*, edited by Wendy Lower and Lauren Faulkner Rossi, 215–31. Evanston, IL: Northwestern University Press, 2017.

Stach, Stephan. "'The Spirit of the Time Left Its Mark on These Works': Writing the History of the Shoah at the Jewish Historical Institute in Stalinist Poland." *Remembrance and Solidarity: Studies in 20th Century European History*, no. 5 (December 2016): 185–212.

Stahl, Neta. *Other and Brother: Jesus in the 20th Century Jewish Literary Landscape*. Oxford: Oxford University Press, 2013.

Stanislawski, Michael. *Autobiographical Jews: Essays in Jewish Self-Fashioning*. Seattle: University of Washington Press, 2004.

Suleiman, Susan Rubin. "Irène Némirovsky and the 'Jewish Question' in Interwar France." *Yale French Studies* 121 (2012): 8–33.

Sundquist, Eric. *Writing in Witness: A Holocaust Reader*. Albany: State University of New York Press, 2018.

Szeintuch, Yechiel. "Araynfir" [Introduction] to "Lider fun kelt." In *Yidishe geto-ksovim: Varshe 1940–1943*, by Itzhak Katzenelson, 619–20. Tel-Aviv: Bet Lohamei Hageta'ot, 1984.

———. "Araynfir" [Introduction] to "Der yid hot gelakht." In *Yidishe geto-ksovim: Varshe 1940–1943*, by Itzhak Katzenelson, 650–51. Tel-Aviv: Bet Lohamei Hageta'ot, 1984.

———. "Araynfir" [Introduction] to "Vey dir." In *Yidishe geto-ksovim: Varshe 1940–1943*, by Itzhak Katzenelson, 632–33. Tel-Aviv: Bet Lohamei Hageta'ot, 1984.

———. "The Corpus of Yiddish and Hebrew Literature from Ghettos and Concentration Camps and Its Relevance for Holocaust Studies." *Studies in Yiddish Literature and Folklore*, 186–207. Jerusalem: Institute for Jewish Studies, The Hebrew University, 1986

———. "Ghetto Literature and I. Spiegel's Ghetto Manuscripts." In *Yesha'yahu Shpigel—prozah sipurit mi-geṭo Lodz': Shishah-'asar sipurim mefu'naḥim 'al pi kitve-yad she-nitslu be-tseruf mavo ṿe-re'ayon 'im ha-meḥaber* [Isaiah Spiegel: Yiddish narrative prose from the Lodz ghetto; 16 stories edited from rescued manuscripts with introductions and a series of oral interviews with their author], edited by Yechiel Szeintuch and Vera Solomon, iii–xiv. Jerusalem: Magnes Press, Hebrew University, 1995.

———. "Fun Yeshaye Shpigls umbakante ksav-yadn fun lodzsher geto." *Di goldene keyt* 130 (1990): 37–39.
———. "The Work of Yitzhak Katzenelson in the Warsaw Ghetto." *The Jerusalem Quarterly*, no. 26 (Winter 1983): 46–61.
Szeintuch, Yechiel, and Vera Solomon, eds. *Yeshaʻyahu Shpigel—prozah sipurit mi-geṭo Lodzʹ: Shishah-ʻasar sipurim mefuʻnaḥim ʻal pi kitve-yad she-nitslu be-tseruf mavo ve-reʼayon ʻim ha-meḥaber*. [Isaiah Spiegel: Yiddish narrative prose from the Lodz ghetto; 16 stories edited from rescued manuscripts with introductions and a series of oral interviews with their author]. Jerusalem: Magnes Press, Hebrew University, 1995.
Tambling, Jeremy. "Holmes, Law, and Order." In *The Cambridge Companion to Sherlock Holmes*, edited by Janice M. Allan and Christopher Pittard, 111–24. Cambridge: Cambridge University Press, 2019.
Tarr, Clayton Carlyle. *Gothic Stories within Stories: Frame Narratives and Realism in the Genre, 1790–1900*. Jefferson, NC: McFarland, 2017.
Todorov, Tzvetan. *The Fantastic: A Structural Approach to a Literary Genre*. Translated by Richard Howard. Cleveland, OH: Case Western Reserve University Press, 1973.
———. "The Typology of Detective Fiction." In *The Poetics of Prose*, translated by Richard Howard, 42–52. Ithaca, NY: Cornell University Press, 1977.
Trezise, Thomas. *Witnessing Witnessing: On the Reception of Holocaust Survivor Testimony*. New York: Fordham University Press, 2013.
Trinh, Miryam. "L'écriture poétique Durant la Shoah." *Yod: Revueu des études hébraïques et juives* 16 (2011): 1–12.
Trunk, Isaiah. *Judenrat: The Jewish Councils in Eastern Europe under Nazi Occupation*. Lincoln: University of Nebraska Press, 1996.
———. *The Łódź Ghetto: A History*. Edited and translated by Robert Moses Shapiro. Bloomington: Indiana University Press, 2006.
Tsanin, Mordkhe. *Iber shteyn un shtok: A rayze iber hundert khorev-gevorene kehiles in poyln*. Tel Aviv: Farlag "letste nayes," 1952.
Turkow, Jonas. *Azoy iz geven (khurbn varshe)*. Buenos Aires: Tsentral-faband fun poylishe yidn in argentine, 1948.
Turniansky, Chava. "Di gilgulim fun Y. L. Peretzes 'Monish.'" *Di goldene keyt* 52 (1965): 205–24.
Turski, Marian. "Individual Experience in Diaries from the Lodz Ghetto." In *Holocaust Chronicles: Individualizing the Holocaust through Diaries and Other Contemporaneous Accounts*, edited by Moses Shapiro, 117–24. Hoboken, NJ: KTAV, 1999.
Tych, Feliks, and Ruta Sakowska, eds. *The Ringelblum Archive, Complete Edition*. 36 vols. Warsaw: Jewish Historical Institute, 1997–2020.
Vice, Sue. *Holocaust Fiction*. New York: Routledge, 2000.
———. "Holocaust Poetry and Testimony." *Critical Survey* 20, no. 2 (2008): 7–17.
Waligórska, Magdalena. "'Darkness at the Beginning': The Holocaust in Contemporary German Crime Fiction." *Tatort Germany: The Curious Case of*

German-Language Crime Fiction, edited by Lynn M. Kutch and Todd Herzog, 101–19. Rochester: Camden House, 2014.

Weissman, Gary. *Fantasies of Witnessing: Postwar Efforts to Experience the Holocaust.* Ithaca, NY: Cornell University Press, 2004.

Wisse, Ruth R. "Introduction: The Ghetto Poems of Abraham Sutzkever." In *Burnt Pearls: Ghetto Poems of Abraham Sutzkever*, translated by Seymour Mayne, 9–18. Oakville, Ontario: Mosaic Press/Valley Editions, 1981.

———. *I. L. Peretz and the Making of Modern Jewish Culture.* Seattle: University of Washington Press, 1991.

———. *The Modern Jewish Canon: A Journey through Language and Culture.* New York: Free Press, 2000.

Wittgenstein, Ludwig. *Bemerkungen über die Philosophie der Psychologie: Schriften 8.* Frankfurt am Main: Suhrkamp, 1982.

Wolf, Leonard. "Afterword" to *The Street*, by Israel Rabon, translated by Leonard Wolf, 185–92. New York: Schocken Books, 1985.

Wolff, Fabian. "Refusing the Extended Hand." In "The Catechism Debate," edited by Jennifer Evans and Brian J. Griffiths, 71–74. *New Fascism Syllabus*, May 25–June 2, 2021. https://newfascismsyllabus.com/wp-content/uploads/2021/08/The-Catechism-Debate.pdf.

Wolitz, Seth L. "Between Folk and Freedom: The Failure of the Yiddish Modernist Movement in Poland." In *Yiddish Modernism: Studies in Twentieth-Century Eastern European Jewish Culture*, 365–80. Bloomington, IN: Slavica Publishers, 2014.

———. "The Kiev-Grupe (1918–20) Debate: The Function of Literature." In *Yiddish Modernism: Studies in Twentieth-Century Eastern European Jewish Culture*, 355–63. Bloomington, IN: Slavica Publishers, 2014.

Yekutsch, Ulrike. "Isaak Babel's 'Konarmija' in Germany of the 1920s." *Zeitschrift für Slawistik* 50, no. 3 (January 2005): 255–69.

Young, James E. *Writing and Rewriting the Holocaust: Narrative and the Consequences of Interpretation.* Bloomington: Indiana University Press, 1988.

Yuval, Israel Jacob. *Two Nations in Your Womb: Perceptions of Jews and Christians in Late Antiquity and the Middle Ages.* Translated by Barbara Harshav and Jonathan Chipman. Berkeley: University of California Press, 2006.

Zimmerer, Jürgen, and Michael Rothberg. "Enttabuisiert den Vergleich!" *Die Zeit*, April 4, 2021. https://www.zeit.de/2021/14/erinnerungskultur-gedenken-pluralisieren-holocaust-vergleich-globalisierung-geschichte.

Żółkiewska, Agnieszka, and Marek Tuszewicki. "Wstęp" [Introduction] to *Archiwum Ringelbluma: Konspiracyjne Archiwum Getta Warszawy*, vol. 26: *Utwory literackie z getta warszawskiego*, xix–xl. Warsaw: Jewish Historical Institute (Żydowski Instytut Historyczny), 2017.

Zuckermann, Ghil'ad. *Revivalistics: From the Genesis of Israeli to Language Reclamation in Australia and Beyond.* New York: Oxford University Press, 2020.

Zylbercweig, Zalmen. *Leksikon fun yidishn teater.* Vol. 5. Elisheva Farlag: Mexico, 1967.

INDEX